Italian Film

Italian Film examines the extraordinary cinematic tradition of Italy, from the silent era to the present. Analyzing film within the framework of Italy's historical, social, political, and cultural evolution during the twentieth century, Marcia Landy traces the construction of a coherent national cinema and its changes over time. Examining the cinematic uses of landscape, architecture, regional, rural, and metropolitan locales, and representations of social customs and rituals, Landy also discusses genres, stars, and narrative and anti-narrative forms. This study traces how social institutions – school, family, the church – as well as Italian notions of masculinity and femininity are dealt with in cinema and how they are central to the conceptions (and misconceptions) of national identity. It also demonstrates the vital links between Italian film and other art forms, including opera, popular music, literature, and painting. A comprehensive survey of this subject, *Italian Film* also offers fresh readings of key films from each period surveyed.

Marcia Landy is Distinguished Service Professor of English and Film Studies at the University of Pittsburgh. She is the author of *Fascism in Film: The Italian Commercial Cinema, 1930-1943; Film, Politics, and Gramsci;* and *The Folklore of Consensus: Theatricality in the Italian Cinema, 1930-1943.*

National Film Traditions

General Editor
David Desser, University of Illinois, Urbana–Champaign

National Film Traditions examines the cinematic heritages of Great Britain, France, Italy, Russia, India, China, Japan, and Australia, from their origins in the silent film era to the present. Relating film production in these countries to the changing social, political, and cultural contexts in which they were created, volumes in this series will also analyze the problematic concepts of nation and nationalism, and their impact on cinema. Designed for use in undergraduate and graduate courses, volumes in this series will include in-depth readings of paradigmatic films, as well as filmographies, videographies, and selected bibliographies.

ITALIAN FILM

Marcia Landy

University of Pittsburgh

CAMBRIDGE
UNIVERSITY PRESS

PUBLISHED BY THE PRESS SYNDICATE OF THE UNIVERSITY OF CAMBRIDGE
The Pitt Building, Trumpington Street, Cambridge, United Kingdom

CAMBRIDGE UNIVERSITY PRESS
The Edinburgh Building, Cambridge CB2 2RU, UK   http://www.cup.cam.ac.uk
40 West 20th Street, New York, NY 10011-4211, USA   http://www.cup.org
10 Stamford Road, Oakleigh, Melbourne 3166, Australia
Ruiz de Alarcón 13, 28014 Madrid, Spain

First published 2000

Printed in the United States of America
Typeface ITC Garamond Book 10.25/13 pt.   *System* QuarkXpress®   [MG]

A catalog record for this book is available from the British Library

Library of Congress Cataloging in Publication Data
Landy, Marcia, 1931–
Italian film / Marcia Landy
p.   cm. – (National film traditions)
Includes bibliographical references
ISBN 0 521 64009 1 (hardbound)   ISBN 0 521 64977 3 (paperback)
1. Motion pictures – Italy – History.   I. Title.   II. Series.
PN1993.5.I88L38   2000
791.43´0945-dc21   99-35247
CIP

ISBN   0 521 64009 1   hardback
ISBN   0 521 64977 3   paperback

Contents

Illustrations

Preface

Histories of national cinemas are a staple of film studies. What has changed over the course of time is the theoretical and methodological scope of these studies as well as the range of the national cinemas under examination, now extending beyond Hollywood and Europe. In the case of Italian cinema, scholarly research probes, rather than takes for granted, the national form as expressed through writings on modernity, urbanity, geography, regionalism, ethnicity, and sexuality. Instead of automatically assuming the essential character and integrity of a nation, these studies recognize that "cinematography has always been a worldwide craft. Its history ought to be told from two different vantage-points, an international as well as a national one."[1] It is necessary to "distinguish the ways Italians conceive of themselves and the reasons why we bestow on a given film the label 'typically Italian.'"[2] Building on these statements by Sorlin, I would suggest that Italian films (and scholarly writings on the Italian cinema) have played a prominent role until recently in producing a collective narrative of the Italian people. My study identifies strands interwoven into this collective narrative, indicating where ostensibly unified elements are only fragments, thus opening the way to understanding fictions of the Italian nation.

In her unraveling of the national narrative, Giuliana Bruno in *Streetwalking on a Ruined Map*, writes that her study

> offers a theoretical meditation on the problems of historiography and addresses the challenge posed by feminist theory to both film history and theory. Such a meditation is conveyed through, and grounded in, a microhistorical case: the lost or forgotten work of Italy's first and foremost prolific woman filmmaker, Elvira Notari, the driving force of Dora Film (Naples, 1909–1930).[3]

Regional production and, even more particularly, considerations of gender regarding the participation or nonparticipation of certain groups reveal how collective narratives are formed, disseminated, and reiterated. Bruno's examination of Notari's work becomes an opportunity to explore "a territory of subjugated popular knowledge"[4] that is not merely additive but opens up different ways of conceptualizing Italian cultural history, affecting conceptions of history, geography, the enigmatic role of woman, and spectatorship.

My examination is primarily concerned with exploring the narratives, images, and sounds and their relation to other cultural forms through which this "fictive" entity known as Italian cinema has been disseminated and recognized as national. The book explores the persistence of various styles and motifs and the differing ways these have been expressed in Italy from the silent cinema to the present. I examine attempts to challenge prevailing cinematic models and film language. However, I do not measure the films' various treatments of history against factual history: I regard the films as historical documents in the sense that their modes of staging history are an index to the folklore of the culture. This "history" is evident not merely in the reiteration of myths of origin and of a common destiny but in the specific ways the narratives invoke "the people" through language, landscape, architecture, customs, superstitions, and through images that conjure up a sense of common cultural fears and aspirations.

My discussion is predicated on ways in which images of femininity, masculinity, the family, childhood, juridical practices, the city, the school, the church, art forms (e.g., literature, opera, and painting), and other media (e.g., popular music and television) are intrinsic to the narratives, not as sociological data but as an indication of the eclectic, fragmentary, and contradictory nature of national consensus. I explore how regional, metropolitan, and rural locales are important indices of the formation of a national cinema and its conceptions (and misconceptions) of "the people." I discuss the ways in which the country and the city are variously represented, and the tenacious cultural, political, and social divisions between North and South Italy and between changing (and contentious) notions of "tradition" and "modernity." The forms and motifs of Italian national cinema are not necessarily unique but are shaped by other cultures and by other film traditions derived from Hollywood (or more broadly Americanism) as well as from other European cinemas.

The book is structured around case studies involving the various cinematic traditions identified with Italian cinema, and is attentive to the uses of history, especially those moments within Italian history and cinema to which filmmakers return obsessively: the Risorgimento, Fascism, neorealism, and the Resistance. I regard these retrospective uses of history as central to ways "in which the imaginary singularity of national formation is constructed daily, by moving back from the present to the past."[5] The invocation of these different moments is tied closely to different conceptions of the desired direction for an Italian national culture. Debates over cinematic style are not mere squabbles about aesthetic form but signs of conflict concerning the uses of memory, treatments of the past, and their relation to the formation and deformation of cultural identity.

My book does not gloss over or underestimate films from the years of Fascism. I explore the motives that led postwar critics to underestimate the role of these films within the broader landscape of Italian cinema. By examining certain films from that era, I identify how, through their narratives, reliance on stardom, uses of genre (especially melodrama and comedy), and their contradictory relation to the ideology of the time and, particularly, to the nature and travails of modernity, the films are pivotal to any consideration of the formation of a national culture. The labors of neorealism to expunge the presumably deleterious effects of theatricality and to create a new politics of style are built on the desired extinction of the politics of style identified with the cinema of the Fascist era.

The genre system is not confined to the cinema of the Ventennio, the twenty years of Fascist rule, any more than neorealism as a movement and style is restricted to the films of the late 1940s and early 1950s. Both forms of cinematic production, the genre system and neorealism, function as reiterative concerns, instrumental in highlighting connections between cinema and the narratives of nationhood. From the 1960s to the 1990s, in the return of genre films, in the auteurist cinema, in modernist experimentation, and in the latter-day concern with the "end of cinema" and with film's relation to television, a variety of cinematic forms have emerged that further complicate conceptions of a national cinema.

My study is concerned with the nature of reception, but not restrictively in quantitative terms. I regard the films' reception within the context of their incorporation of the issue of spectatorship, implying a putative audience and anticipated responses. I do not regard reception as monolithic: One of the characteristics of the commercial cinema is its eclecticism, its attempts to cast as wide a net as possible to capture its audiences; thus, a study of reception has to address different constituencies. In the case of texts that regard themselves in opposition to the national narrative, their refusal to conform is also telling of the films' intended and actual reception. Box-office receipts are an indication of the size of the cinemagoing audiences; profits and losses affect what is produced and consumed. Always a factor to be considered is the presence and impact of non-Italian films, particularly (but not exclusively) Hollywood cinema. Although the analysis of economic factors in the commercial cinema is an index to certain trends in popular taste, their narrow consideration cannot penetrate the differing and heterogeneous character of audiences; nor can they reveal the specific contractual nature of strategies for capturing audiences. A discussion of the industrial, technological, and historical conditions must be integrated with appropriate textual analysis. Toward these ends, the notion of the cinematic text has to be expanded beyond the framework of individual genres or texts. Thus, allusions to the text identify an ensemble of all the conditions of its production, and sources (political, social, and stylistic) of address and circulation.

In the chapters that follow, I outline what I consider the dominant motifs, the prevailing (and countervailing) styles, and describe what I term a *politics of style,* the ways in which the texts selected exemplify connections between culture and social life, cinema and society, production and reception. Chapters 1–3 examine the silent era and the early sound cinema in terms of how these films draw on the folklore of nation formation and how, through their uses of narrative, genre conventions, choreography, and stars, the films seek to establish the singularity of Italian history and the role of cinema as a popular medium for the dissemination of common cultural values. The discussion highlights how these films constitute a major contribution to an Italian film tradition that persistently returns to the uses of the past throughout the course of cinema production, even to the present, albeit with significant aesthetic and political difference. Chapter 1, "Early Italian Cinema Attractions," covers the evolution of the early cinema and the appearance of such films as *Quo Vadis?* (1913) and *Cabiria* (1914) as exemplary of the collusion among cinema, spectacle, and folklore. The chapter discusses the importance of the star system (*divismo*) during the silent era, and also the role of melodrama, as exemplified by the Neapolitan-produced *Assunta Spina* (1915).

Chapter 2, "National History as Retrospective Illusion," focuses on the historical spectacle *Scipione l'Africano* (1937), a film identified with Fascism but that problematizes representations of Fascism in cinema through its intertextuality and its reliance on prior historical films (Italian, American, and European) and on a now-established grammar and set of codes for the presentation of history on film – its choreography of large casts, use of male and female stars, emphasis on landscape, evocation of the architecture of ancient Rome, and attention to action. Even more than classical subjects, the Risorgimento was a popular topic during the years of Fascism, and the focus of the second part of the chapter is Blasetti's *1860* (1934). This film, seen by some critics as prefiguring neorealism because of its use of nonprofessional actors and location shooting, draws on painting and on landscape to reanimate the national imaginary but avoids the monumentalism and theatricality associated with *Scipione.* The final section of the chapter examines *Cavalleria* (1936), a costume film set during World War I, which draws on the tropes of the nation aligned to melodrama in order to dramatize heroic images of war and provide images of masculine duty and sacrifice.

Chapter 3, "Challenging the Folklore of Romance," continues the discussion of the uses of the past but centers on those texts that reveal rents in the national imaginary. Beginning with a fantasy film produced in the last years of the regime, *La corona di ferro* (1941), and with a satiric film, *Sorelle Materassi* (1943), the chapter explores images of a world of dissimulation, obsession, illegitimate power, and violence. Of the films identified with neorealism, *Paisà* (1946), although set in a contemporary context (the Allied invasion of Italy), dramatizes a confrontation between different cultures and among various elements in Italian culture, laying bare the romance of a unified nation.

In films of the postwar era, such as *Senso* (1954) and *Il generale Della Rovere* (1959), there is a similar preoccupation with betrayal and, even more, with the complexity of historical judgment. (The writings of Antonio Gramsci are touched upon in the discussion of *Senso;* they are discussed in more detail in Chapter 6.) The films produced in the final years of the regime and those identified under the rubric of neorealism introduced forms of filmmaking that were not only critical of the cinema of Fascism but laid the groundwork for a different relationship to the cinematic image and to storytelling.

Chapter 4, "Comedy and the Cinematic Machine," explores the various uses of comedy in the Italian cinema, from the much-vilified "white telephone" films (e.g., *Gli uomini che mascalzoni . . .*, 1932), to contemporary comedies. A profitable and prominent genre, Italian comedy relies on established conventions derived from the *commedia dell'arte,* opera, literature, folklore, and comics. This genre has deep roots in the cultural imaginary and in Italian politics and ideology. Reliant on cultural stereotypes concerning physical appearance, national and regional landscapes, rituals, and customs, Italian comedy has served to provide a window on prevailing values as well as immediate and long-standing discontents. The chapter examines narrative strategies, iconography, traditional comic modes and styles, and relations to other cultural forms in such films of the Fascist era as *La segretaria privata* (1931), *Darò un milione* (1935), and *Batticuore* (1939). In the postwar era and beyond, as an analytic response to cinematic culture under Fascism, comedy assumes a more critical and satiric mode in such films as *La macchina ammazzacattivi* (1948–52) and *Amarcord* (1974).

Chapter 5, "The Landscape and Neorealism, Before and After," examines the cinema's use of the metropolitan locale. More than backdrop, the city has served as a synecdoche for the nation and its "people." In films of the 1930s and early 1940s, Naples was a major site for comedies and melodramas in such films as *Napoli d'altri tempi* (1938) and *Napoli che non muore* (1939), and the chapter explores how these films connect landscape to tropes of the nation. The city of Naples serves as a place of iniquity and threat, but also as a site of pleasure and creativity, identified with music and dance. In the films of neorealism, a new face of the city is presented, and the actor-director Vittorio De Sica and the actress Sophia Loren become identified with the "spirit" of Naples in such films as *L'oro di Napoli* (1954). The spectator is engaged in a journey through cinematic space where place no longer has a familiar appearance and where things are no longer predictable or comprehensible but indeterminate and unsettling. The chapter also examines filmic treatments of the city of Rome in *Roma, città aperta* (1945), *Ladri di biciclette* (1948), and *Fellini's Roma* (1972), Finally, another consistent landscape in Italian cinema, that of the Italian South, is discussed in the context of the film *Il mafioso* (1962).

Chapter 6, "Gramsci and Italian Cinema," assesses the impact of Antonio Gramsci's ideas on the politics and style of several generations of filmmakers, A victim of Fascism, Gramsci dedicated his years in prison to an understanding of Italian history, of the nature and role of intellectuals, of strategies, means, and ends in the attainment of power, and, especially important for filmmakers, of the role of culture in political and social transformation. These motifs are evident in such films as *Accattone* (1961), *Il gattopardo* (1963), *Il Vangelo secondo Matteo* (1964), *I compagni* (1963), *Padre padrone* (1977), and *L'albero degli zoccoli* (1978), all of which are discussed.

Chapter 7, "History, Genre, and the Italian Western," examines the form and style of the Italian ("spaghetti") western within the context of changing conceptions of genre in the Italian cinema, its resurgence, and the ways it establishes links between Italian and American cinematic culture. Though considered by many critics as specializing in gratuitous violence, the Italian western is, in fact, is a prime example of the complex character of popular cinema. This chapter, in developing the complexity of the spaghetti western, its relation to politics, and its eccentric treatments of nation, discusses the following films (listed by their better-known American-release titles): *Once Upon a Time in the West* (1968), *A Fistful of Dollars* (1964), *For a Few Dollars More* (1965), *Duck, You Sucker* (a.k.a. *A Fistful of Dynamite*, 1971), and *My Name Is Nobody* (1973). The films' portraits of homosocial bonding provide an intervention, if only through parody, into codes of masculinity so central to the narrative of nation. Situating Italian westerns within the context of the historical and costume "epics" of the 1960s (e.g., such films as *Il colosso di Rodi*, 1961), the chapter traces the style and eclecticism of these films, their intensified internationalization, and the internationalization of Italian culture in the name of Americanism.

Chapters 8–11 explore how conceptions of the family, childhood, femininity, and masculinity have circulated through narratives, the star system, and film genres. Chapter 8, "*La famiglia:* The Cinematic Family and the Nation," discusses a group of films specifically for the ways in which the narratives dramatize and critically undermine traditional conceptions of heterosexual romance and of the family. The cinema under Fascism contains a number of narratives that focus on the family, such as Mario Camerini's *T'amerò sempre* (1933) and Blasetti's *Terra madre* (1930) and *Quattro passi fra le nuvole*, made midway through World War II (1942). De Sica addressed the family in *I bambini ci guardano* (1942) and *Ladri di biciclette* (1948). In Visconti's *Ossessione* (1942), family is identified with the world of violence, predation, and surveillance, and his *La terra trema* (1948) shows it subjected to new economic pressures. Portraying family life from a comic and satiric perspective, Pietro Germi's *Divorzio all'italiana* (1961) treats the intersections of family with political, juridical, and sexual power. Spectatorship is central to its dissection of family life in the Sicilian milieu, and the film situates the paternalism within the community's controlling surveillance, key in enforcing the code of honor. Pasolini's documentary *Comizi d'amore* (1964) links familial practices to regionalism, conceptions of sexuality, the law, and gender. Bertolucci's *La tragedia di un uomo ridicolo* (1981) provides a critical analysis of family life in the 1980s, linking generational and familial conflict to political struggle. In *La famiglia* (1987), directed by Ettore Scola, the family, critically linked to different moments in Italian life, is central to a rethinking of the national imaginary.

Chapter 9, "A Cinema of Childhood," explores the ways in which the figure of the child looms large in Italian cinema, serving either as a focal point for a reconstructed national unity or as a measure of its failure. In the silent era, a child might require heroic rescue, as in *Cabiria* (1914); the Fascist era's *Vecchio guardia* (1934) portrayed a child as heroic martyr. The greater focus on children in the early sound cinema can be accounted for in part by the powerful sway exerted by Hollywood cinema, with its emphasis on youth through the influence of such musical stars as Shirley Temple and Deanna Durbin (the latter reflected in Matarazzo's 1943 *Il birichino di papà*). In De Sica's *I bambini ci guardano* (1942), *Sciuscià* (1946), and *Ladri di biciclette* (1948), as well as in the more recent films *Nuovo Cinema Paradiso* (Tornatore, 1988) and *Il ladro di bambini* (Amelio, 1992), the child functions as an index to new forms of spectatorship. Discussed in the context of these other films is the Tavianis' *La notte di San Lorenzo* (1982): Focusing on a child's perspective, the film returns to World War II and to Fascism but in ways that seek to interrogate that past by complicating the nature of storytelling and narration. In the 1990s, young people were featured prominently in such films as *Mery per sempre* (1989) and *Io speriamo che me la cavo* (1993).

Chapter 10, "The Folklore of Femininity and Stardom," peruses cinematic representations of femininity, starting with another look at *divismo* through a discussion of Francesca Bertini and her appearance in *L'ultima diva* (1982). In the transition to the sound cinema, the character of Isa Miranda, a popular star of the 1930s and 1940s, is explored through a film that captures the complex connections of femininity and cinema: Max Ophuls's *La signora di tutti* (1934), in which she plays a film star. Many films produced during the Fascist era were so-called woman's films, focusing on the plight of unwed mothers, women gone astray, and female entertainers, The chapter describes and analyzes two such films: *Il carnevale di Venezia* (1940) and *Zazà* (1942), both of which portray women performers. Though the star system was eclipsed during the brief heyday of neorealism, in the 1950s it reemerged, with great force on the international scene, with newer, more seductive feminine star images, integrally related to national recuperation. The star persona of Sophia Loren is examined as she plays a wartime mother in *La ciociara* (1960) and a range of characters in *Ieri, oggi, domani* (1963), a film that connects her various permutations and dimensions to "Italianness" but also to aspects of international stardom. Anna Magnani offers another, but related, image of femininity through her roles in such films as *Roma, città aperta* (1945), which brought her to international attention, and *Mamma Roma* (1962). A spectrum of other feminine figures can be seen in *La strada* (1954), *Riso amaro* (1949), and *L'avventura* (1960). The final section of the chapter focuses on two films directed by Lina Wertmüller that directly confront questions of femininity: *Film d'amore e d'anarchia* (1972) and *Sotto . . . sotto . . . strapazatto da un anomala passione* (1984).

Chapter 11, "Conversion, Impersonation, and Masculinity," focuses on exemplary representations of "masculinity," including the narratives of conversion both earnest (*Squadrone bianco*, 1936) and satiric (*Il fu Mattia Pascal*, 1937). Class notions of masculinity are probed in the "white telephone" film *Il signor Max* (1937). Poggioli's *Gelosia* (1953) offers a bleak, melodramatic portrait of the disintegration into madness of an ignoble nobleman. The potential for male wartime heroism, featured in *Squadrone bianco,* is portrayed also in *Roma, città aperta* and, somewhat more antiheroically, in *Il generale Della Rovere* (1959). The *commedia all'italiana,* largely identified with male stars, has traditionally centered on absurd figures who overly embody Italian masculinity (though caricatures of femininity are also evident): Such is the case in Germi's *Sedotta e abbandonata* (1963), a dissection of patriarchy that features men absurdly and self-destructively committed to maintaining the code of honor. The chapter also examines the explosion of "peplum epics" set in classical times, which resurrected such figures as Ulysses, Hercules, and Maciste, and connects their appearance to the preoccupation with the masculine body and with sexuality evident in such films as *Le fatiche di Ercole* (1957). Stardom and the male is explored in an examination of the star persona of Marcello Mastroianni (especially through the films of Fellini) and of Giancarlo Giannini (especially through the films of Wertmüller). This is followed by a discussion of *1900* (1976), where masculinity plays a key role in the film's focus on Fascism and its effects. The chapter ends with a discussion of *Lo zio indegno* (1989) and its portrait of an aging male figure as played by Italian star Vittorio Gassman.

Chapter 12, "Cinema on Cinema and on Television," examines a group of films preoccupied with the nature and fate of the cinema. *Figaro e la sua gran'giornata* (1931) and *Dora Nelson* (1939), two films of the Fascist era – the latter involving a film actress – demonstrate the theatricality of the medium. Antonioni's *Deserto rosso* (1964), on the other hand, is an exercise in style, probing, as the title suggests, color and barrenness, suggesting zero meaning: Through its female protagonist and the many perspectives of the geometry of landscape, the spectator is invited to visualize and consider alternative forms of perception generated through the cinematic image. Pasolini is another filmmaker whose theorization of the cinematic image is explored, via his *Teorema* (1968). *Profondo rosso* (1975), a horror picture, is discussed in the context of the intertextuality of film and the psychosexual basis of cinematic pleasure. The changing character of cinema and politics in Italian life is the focus of Scola's *C'eravamo tanto amati* (1974), which dramatizes changes in social life from the Resistance to the film's present and ties them to the dissolution of certain cultural and political hopes: These were the hopes exemplified in the postwar neorealist cinema (especially *Ladri di biciclette*), which saw itself as engaged in a massive enterprise of rebuilding Italian culture. The persistent romance of cinema is revealed by Tornatore, whether it be genuine as in *Nuovo Cinema Paradiso* (1988) or fraudulent as in *L'uomo delle stelle* (1994). The chapter also focuses on connections and antagonisms between cinema and television, discussing Fellini's *Ginger e Fred* and Maurizio Nichetti's *Ladri di saponette* (1989), a film that vies with many complex critical texts in its exposure of television's capacities for distractions, discontinuities, "channel surfing," and muting of sound. In terms consonant with writings on postmodernism, Nichetti's film may be considered an excursus on the end of history, of the nation form, and of meaning, as well as on the international triumph of "Americanism." Conversely, the film can be regarded as part of crucial enterprise to rethink the culture of postmodernity and the Italian cinema of the late 1980s and the 1990s. Finally, Nanni Moretti's *Caro diario* (1993) takes its own cinematic trip through the contemporary cultural landscape of Italy, including cinema and television. This film addresses a question posed by the philosopher Gilles Deleuze in relation to the modern cinema: "What are the forces at work in the image and the new signs invading the screen?"[6]

Acknowledgments

I am grateful to David Desser, editor for the Cambridge University Press series "National Film Traditions," for inviting me to contribute this volume, for his helpful comments on the manuscript, and for his sustained support of the project. Similarly, I appreciate the critical remarks and sustaining encouragement of Beatrice Rehl, Fine Arts and Media Studies Editor for the Press. The research on this book has been made immeasurably easier by the staff at the Motion Picture Division of the Library of Congress. In particular, I want to thank Madeline Matz for her energetic searches for the many texts I requested, her promptness in responding to my inquiries, and for making my visits to the library productive. I am also indebted to Patricia Colbert and Patricia Duff at the Interlibrary Loan section of the Hillman Library at the University of Pittsburgh: They never failed in finding, with grace and in timely fashion, the hard-to-get books that I requested. As always, I am grateful to Mary Corliss and Terry Geesken at the New York Museum of Modern Art Stills Archive for making available scores of stills at short notice and for granting permission to reproduce the images. I am fortunate in having colleagues, such as Lucy Fisher, Jane Feuer, Moya Luckett, Sabine Hake, and Colin MacCabe in the Film Studies Program at the University of Pittsburgh, who are supportive of my work. Similarly, I want to thank Dennis Looney, Chair of the French and Italian Department at the University of Pittsburgh, for encouraging me over the years to teach courses on Italian cinema and for his intellectual support. I wish also to express my appreciation to Giuseppina Mecchia of the French and Italian Department, who took precious time out of her busy schedule to read the manuscript and provide me with invaluable suggestions for revision, and to Henry Veggian of the University of Pittsburgh for his indefatigable efforts in tracking down information for the Filmography. Carol Mysliwiec and Sara Morriss were indispensable in the final preparation of the manuscript. I am deeply indebted to Michael Gnat, free-lance production editor and typesetter for Cambridge University Press, for his meticulous editing of the manuscript, his boundless knowledge, his critical acumen, and his humor. Above all, I owe a deep debt of gratitude to my friend Stanley Shostak, who generously devoted time to reading and commenting critically on the various shapes and contents of the manuscript. I hope the finished product is a worthy compensation for his efforts.

Introduction

From its inception, the Italian cinema has never been a purely national enterprise. In its technological, commercial, and political concerns, this cinema has been attentive and responsive to international developments, and the intersecting strands of the national and international are part of the nation's cinematic form. The Italian cinema reveals itself as engaged in a social fiction but a necessary one, relying on a narrative that perpetuates itself in terms of the "people." The national community is forged through the assumed common bonds of unitary language, the nation as a family, conceptions of gender and ethnicity that rely on an identity of "origins, culture, and interests," and geographical (and sacrosanct) borders. However, the cinema does not reside solely in familiar narratives or in political polemic but also in the images, sounds, and motifs that animate the imaginary community.

Christopher Wagstaff describes how:

> The social history of the development of the popular mass-cultural medium, and of the way it integrated itself into the general growth of other forms of popular culture throughout the 1930s and 1940s, requires attention to a multitude of manifestations that are not strictly cinematic: the way people spent their leisure time, the publishing of fan periodicals, the cult of pin-ups, the star system, the relations between cinema and theatre, radio and sport . . . the building and location of cinemas, forms of transport, the penetration of foreign cultural forms into Italian society (from 1916 to 1965 Italians saw mostly American films).[1]

Even in the cases where the films focus on derived landscapes and rural, regional, and foreign milieux, these images can be identified with photography, with stereopticon shots of place, and with literary forms.

Of the many strata that are inherent to the cultural development and impact of the cinema, the question of the milieu of the spectator is primary – both the milieu presented on the screen and that of the movie theater. The interior and exterior landscape relating to the experience of moviegoing is an index to images central to the formation of cinema and to Italian cinema in particular: "It tantalizes with its vision of urban life, its architecture, its street life with bodies in motion, automobiles, street cars, train stations, and consumer locales, especially the department store."[2] From the inception of the movies, audiences were confronted with an extension of the world outside the home. As they traveled through the film they were further initiated into the world of crowds, the nervous energy of jostling crowds, the perpetual motion of buses, cars, and trains. The derived imaginary worlds were not divorced from the "real milieux of geographical and social actualisation"[3] but appear as affective intensification of the viewers' experiences within the urban landscape, including those involving their alienated encounters with others who also maneuver their way through the actual space of the city.

The production of images from the silent cinema to the present time is closely tied to yet another landscape, to the "spectatorial embodiments," in particular of the female and male "bodyscape," that entails all forms of making visible the physiognomy and anatomy of the body. To the present, the cinema has relied on the affective potential of the face and of the body that inheres also in a long tradition of painting and photography, a tradition that is inseparable from considerations of gender, sexuality, and power, which are in turn subject to historical change as well as continuity. The cinema, identified as it is with mechanical and mass production, introduced new sets of relations to the body, relations that could be more closely identified with modernity and with an expanded field of vision. As Walter Benjamin wrote:

> By close-ups of the things around us, by focusing on hidden details of familiar objects, by exploring commonplace milieus under the ingenious guidance of the camera, the film, on the one hand extends our comprehension of the necessities which rule our lives; on the other hand, it manages to assure of us an immense and unexpected field of action. . . . The camera introduces us to unconscious optics as does psychoanalysis to unconscious impulses.[4]

In his analysis, Benjamin focuses on differences among painting, photography, and filming, stressing the relations between cinema and the commonplace and everyday but also the ways in which cinema penetrates into the psycho-social life of the spectator. In its century-long history, the cinema as an agent of modernity has played a major role in the transformation of social life, loosening moorings to a stable reality. If cinema has not fulfilled dreams of a revolutionary social transformation of society, it has created a dynamic, ever-changing, and apprehensive relation to the world where, in Benjamin's terms, the spectator is confronted with "an immense and unexpected field of action." This "field of action" has served more largely to destabilize than to produce voluntary adherence and consensus. The films are not unaware of this disorientation, adopting a number of strategies to enhance or mitigate its effects.

Since cinema has always been largely a cosmopolitan phenomenon, it is not surprising that the first movements toward utilization of the moving image took place within an international framework, involving the sharing of information about the nature and potential of the new medium, its technological character, and its possible directions. The emergence of the Italian cinema can be traced, like that of so many other national cinemas, to the last decades of the nineteenth century and to the exploration of photographic machines for scientific and commercial purposes that could record movement. By 1895, thanks to the inventions of such men as the Lumière brothers and of Thomas Edison, among others, the moving picture was circulated on a worldwide basis, capitalizing on a range of events from major political and aristocratic figures of the day to images of everyday life. In Italy, the Lumières' representative was Vittorio Calcina, a photographer. What is important about early images on film is that they were geared to the transmission of information on a worldwide scale, creating a sense of immediacy and reality for the masses, gratifying curiosity about people and events hitherto accessible only in the medium of print.

The pioneers of the new technology were uncertain about the directions for this new machine – as scientific instrument, as industrial handmaiden, as recorder of events, as source of entertainment relying on earlier narrative modes. In one sense, the cinema has been all of these things, but the narrative of commercial cinema has received the largest share of critical attention. With the turn toward large-scale narrative production from the midteens, the cinema became identified with the profit and power associated with the telling of stories derived from the theater, novels, short stories, and news of the day (especially those involving highly melodramatic material) and culled from national and international literary and popular archives.

In recent years, the critical examination of early cinema has taken a more complex and less linear analysis of the first films and the character of the silent cinema, regarding it as eclectic, and drawing on production history, ethnography, and cultural studies. Cinema theory and criticism has focused less on the evolution of narrative and paid due regard to the many-stranded elements of its evolution. For example, in the creation of an Italian cinema, the first films prior to the creation of movie theaters were seen in photography studios and "were used as interludes in musicals, reviews, vaudeville or variety shows."[5] While primarily identified with urban life, there were traveling shows that went from the cities to the countryside presenting their wares at fairs and in regular theaters. The subject matter of these films featured such events as the film *Umberto e Margherita di Savoia a passeggio per il parco* (Umberto and Margherita of Savoy Walk in the Park, 1896) shot by the studio of Filoteo Alberini. Among the other films shot in the 1890s were those by Leopoldo Fregoli, which were highly dependent on the work and assistance of Louis Lumière. A music-hall impersonator, Fregoli introduced these short films into his acts. He went on to make his own films, which involved various locales – restaurants, the army, the hair salon, and so on.[6]

The first decades of the twentieth century saw a proliferation of film companies, for example, Cines, Ambrosio, Itala, and Dora, the latter managed by one of Italy's rare producer-directors, Elvira Notari (see Chapter 1). A particularly influential film of this decade was *La presa di Roma* (*The Taking of Rome*, 1905), known for its highlighting historical and national subject matter. Moreover, the films of this decade testify to a variety of cinema attractions yet to be studied in detail.

World film histories have neglected modes and genres of film production other than the costume drama and historical film, due partially to the paucity of silent film documents and partly to the spectacular financial successes of such films as *La caduta di Troia* (The Fall of Troy, 1911), *Quo Vadis?* (1912), and *Cabiria* (1914) and the critical attention they have received. Thanks to the continuing discovery of silent film texts, we now know that the early Italian output of films went beyond the monumental epics to encompass regional comedies as well as melodramas. The comedies, made in imitation of French models and often starring French actors, were based on gags, chase scenes, cops and robbers, and trick photography (an homage to Méliès). The melodramas too have been commented upon often enough, particularly two of them – *Sperduti nel buio* (Lost in the Dark, 1914) and *Assunta Spina* (1915) – that in histories of cinema are legendary for their vaunted "realism," their location shooting, use of nonprofessional actors, and focus on working-class figures.[7] In the recounting of Italian cinema history, two movements are identified, one traced to the work of Gabriele D'Annunzio, to illusionism, and to the costume drama, the other to Giovanni Verga and *verismo,* and to the valorization of the realist tradition. The tendency to create strict boundaries between realism and theatricality has not only crowded out important considerations of important regional filmmakers but has often served to appreciate one form at the expense of the other.

D'Annunzio's work in literature, film, and as a public figure was characterized by flamboyance and by theatricality as in such films as *Cabiria.* His ornate language, his preoccupation with decadence, history, virility, and nationalist rhetoric have been linked to Fascism and hence derided and denigrated. However, his work and his life were melodramatic masterpieces devoted to adventure and excess.[8] In particular, his name is coupled to that of Eleonora Duse, one of the major divas of the Italian theater and cinema. However, as Bruno has pointed out, the attention to *dannunzianesimo* has erased other works of early Italian cinema, especially certain works of Neapolitan regional cinema. It has definitely effaced the contributions of female directors such as the aforementioned Elvira Notari, though the work of the censor is also responsible for silence in regard to her work.

Although other films could address eroticism and violence, "the representations of deviant and manifest sexuality and the culture of the plebeian metropolis made Notari's films unwelcome to the censorship system, which also disapproved of [their] popular ideology, iconography, and linguistics."[9] Treating such subjects as madness, suicide, maternity, seduction, sexuality, marginality, and self-immolation, Notari's films touch chords of femininity and its discontents. Even the forms of the films were considered problematic by the censors: "The mythology of the 1920s preferred that Italy be pictured as a country where order, work, and morals reigned or were in the process of being affirmed."[10] In Notari's films, shot often on location, neither the social world nor the nation were exalted.

In the mainstream of the commercial silent Italian cinema, stardom played a major role even before the Hollywood star system and in the dissemination and transgression of sexual and gendered values. Identified with *divismo,* the Italian star system was vastly profitable and popular in the first two decades of the twentieth century. The system was ultimately identified with such figures as Eleonora Duse, Francesca Bertini, Lyda Borelli, Pina Menichelli, and Itala Almirante Manzini. The phenomenon of the femme fatale was concomitant with the huge influx of Italian immigration to the United States and to South America during the war in Libya. Brunetta regards *divismo* as an ideological phenomenon inherent to mass culture and to its penchant for spectacle. *Divismo* has its roots in the theater and in operatic melodrama. although the cinema brought new dimension to its presentation, particularly involving the visualization of the feminine figure as the incarnation of fascination and desire – like the cinema itself.

In the cinema, the spectator was brought closer not only to the spectacle of femininity in the face (through close-up), the body, and the slightest gesture but also in the "hidden details of familiar objects through the 'unconscious optics' made possible by the camera."[11] The diva emerges from a narrative of pain and suffering: "thanks to her fascination, to her sexual power, she dominates and destroys a world that controls economic and political power."[12] Furthermore, Brunetta sees her as compensating for a prevailing sense of cultural and national inferiority on the part of the bourgeois public. Whether this assessment can be ascertained, there is no doubt that *divismo,* like the star system later, is inextricable from the cinematic apparatus. Its capacity, as Benjamin had so aptly described and Deleuze augments, is its ability to penetrate into the psychic life of the spectator to evoke desire and to generate a range of affects – "power becomes action or passion, affect becomes sensation, sentiment, emotion or even impulse."[13]

Though *divismo* included masculine figures, it is the feminine figure that is identified with sensation, sentiment, and impulse. She emerges as a divine form of power, a goddess. The divas (or *dive* in Italian), described by Brunetta and identified with melodramas and costume films produced by male directors to great acclaim and profit, were largely upper-class figures driven mad by passion. They were forced finally to subjugate heterosexual desire to nationalist aspirations, but not without a struggle. The intensity of this struggle and the power of the diva's passion removed them from the world of the everyday, making them a perfect analogue for the cinemagoing experience, where boundaries between fiction and reality are slippery and increasingly indeterminate.

The divas demanded and received huge sums of money for their performances, a situation that would in the next decade lead to the near-demise of the Italian cinema. While for certain major studios the financial picture looked rosy, there were in the teens a growing number of studios that competed with one another, hoping to cash in on the profits to be made. Many of them went bankrupt, but others such as Cines, Ambrosio, and Itala-Film were successful at home and abroad, particularly on the American continent. The success of the Italian historical films and costume dramas has been attributed to a combination of cultural and technical factors: "skill in creating luminous compositions"; skill in creating a depth of field that linked background to foreground; the fortuitous nature of the Italian climate, with its steady and abundant sunlight; the equally fortuitous existence of the ruins of antiquity for the historical epics; on-location shooting, which was conducive to the production of historical films.[14] These same features are relevant to the production and successful reception of films set in contemporary settings, such as *Assunta Spina* and the films of Elvira Notari and Francesca Bertini. Filmmakers drew on a variety of sources from canonical, popular literary, and theatrical sources, as well as creating (often improvising) their own comic and melodramatic scenarios. The grandiose choreography of crowd scenes and the system of *divismo* contributed to the appeal of the texts.

The spectator's relation to movement on the screen is based on relational qualities, including perception, affection, and action, which give rise to forms of thought. In the prewar cinema, it is not merely the narratives that are the vital source of the cinematic experience, but also the power of the images as they express movement and through movement generate a set of powerful responses to the filmed images: "Because the cinematographic image itself 'makes' movement, because it makes what the other arts are restricted to demanding (or to saying), it brings together what is essential to the other arts . . . it converts into potential what was only possibility."[15] The power of cinema is its arousing of shock: a shock that can give rise to new ways of thinking. In the early cinema, this shock was communicated through an organic regime of narration that relied on various affective strategies, "emotional fullness" or "passion," and produced a sense of the spectator's relation to the whole through a sense of "organic totality."

The movement-image in "classical cinema participated in its own way in representing the teleological becoming of the people as identical with the ineluctable unfolding of history."[16] In the early cinema, the capacity to express collectivity and a sense of totality was articulated through the ways images were distinguished, then "grouped conceptually, into ever-growing ensembles or sets through a process of differentiation and integration."[17] Parts were continuously reassembled into a whole, "grouping actions, gestures, bodies, and decors in a motivated ensemble . . . projecting a model of truth in relation to totality."[18] The Italian silent cinema in its pre–World War I manifestation participates in this creation of a world, which creates the illusion of wholeness and suggests a mastery over environments and opponents through its affective power and its focus on the efficacy of action. Whether drawing on images from the past or focusing on the modern world, the power of the silent cinema of the early teens was instrumental, for better and for worse, in creating the first three generations of Italian filmgoers.

The financial and cultural situation of the cinema was to change in the period after World War I for a number of reasons: companies that produced too many haphazard, improvisational, and unprofitable films; the disorganized and decentralized character of film production companies; the mounting costs of production, particularly attributable to the extravagant costs of the system of *divismo,* which could not be sustained given the falling rates of film profits, the loss of foreign markets, and the steep competition from foreign film producers, from Hollywood and also from Germany; the increasing lack of technical equipment and expertise; and, of course, the resistance on the part of film producers, who "had neither the means or the ability to adjust to the new reality of the post war era."[19] The postwar years of the Great War were characterized by intense political strife, which took the form of direct political struggle in the factories, on the streets, and in the parliament. The crisis of the Italian film industry would finally be addressed, but not until another political and cultural crisis was confronted – namely, through the emergence of Fascism as regime.

Although the advent of Fascism did not immediately effect film production in a dramatic fashion, it did begin to set in place measures to address the ailing film industry. However, neither new narratives nor forthcoming financial support were evident to bolster the sickly cinema. The most notable attempts at rejuvenating production involved the creation of ENAC (Ente Nazionale per la Cinematografia) to create ties with foreign film companies in 1926, but this effort failed in 1930. More successful, though still fragile, were the efforts of Stefano Pittaluga, who not only bought up many theaters but attempted to find a balance between foreign imports and indigenous production. The Società Anonima Pittaluga was a joint state and private entity designed to regularize production, but it too faltered after Pittaluga's death in 1931. The transition to sound in 1929–30 brought further financial and technical problems, though it also introduced and mandated innovation. The early

1930s witnessed the entry of new directors, technicians, and actors into the cinema as well as experimentation with both traditional and new forms of narratives.

Among the directors associated with this movement were Raffaello Matarazzo, Guido Brignone, Mario Serandrei, Alessandro Blasetti, and Mario Camerini. New faces became more apparent in the appearance of such actors and actresses as Amedeo Nazzari, Vittorio De Sica, Sergio Tofano, Isa Miranda, Elsa Merlini, Assia Noris, and Maria Denis. The theater helped supply new talent. Apparent too were gradual changes in physiognomy, bodily contour, costume, makeup, and acting. Music, popular and operatic, became an important factor in rejuvenating Italian popular cinema, as it did in other nations. Hollywood's influence was to remain preeminent – as economic threat and as source of emulation.

The sound cinema, from 1929 to 1943 to the advent of "neorealism," continued to be a drama of crisis and of strategies to confront that crisis successfully. There were gradual changes in personnel, types of narrative, technical expertise, and modes of organization of production. Although the coming of sound on film posed problems for the Italian cinema, as it did for other European cinemas, it also contributed to changes in production modes. According to Elaine Mancini:

> The existence of sound caused a host of thought and discussions; those who never before had been interested in cinema now became engrossed by it; those who had mastered silent film techniques questioned the artistic motives of this new element that drew cinema closer to the theater; those who did want to work with sound nonetheless questioned its validity in marketing terms. In short, the coming of sound gave, sometimes directly, occasionally indirectly, the strongest incentive the Italian cinema had known in years.[20]

The successful *Figaro e la sua gran'giornata* (1931), a milestone in the Italian sound cinema, revealed that "Italy had successfully found her own style of sound film that related to her own cultural tradition."[21] Working largely within the genre system, the early sound cinema increasingly specialized in comedies, melodramas, musicals, historical films, and star vehicles. The much-vilified but popular "white telephone" films – a name assigned to the comedies of the era because of their focus on the foibles of upper-class life symbolized by the white telephone in the boudoir – belonged to the emerging sound films of the 1930s.

The production of sound films increased during the mid-1930s, and by 1942, the Italian film industry ranked fifth in the world, having risen from "260 million seats in 1936 to 470 million in 1942."[22] Why did the number of spectators increase at a time of economic hardship? In response to this question, Sorlin points to the recruitment of new viewers, both suburban and rural. The inauguration of the Venice Film Festival in 1932 was an incentive, as was the inception of training and educational facilities at the newly founded Centro Sperimentale di Cinematografia and the building of new studios at Cinecittà. Thanks to the increased technical quality of the films, the diversification of the types of narratives offered, the adoption with modification of Hollywood and European models of narration and acting, and the creation and introduction of new stars, Italian cinema was on the road to renewal, a renewal that is only now evident as a result of research on this moment in Italian cinema.

The first priority of the Italian commercial cinema was profit rather than strict ideological conformity. The cinema of the Fascist era was instructive for the disjunctions as well as the collaborative relations that were evident between official Fascist culture and the economic opportunism of the commercial film industry. The collusion between profit and pleasure, not only in the Italian cinema of the era but in other national film production as well, often worked against a tidy and unified assumption of consonance between cinema and formal politics. To recognize differences between the regime and the industry is to arrive at a different and more complicated understanding of the relations between civil society and the state under Fascism. Official history often elides or overgeneralizes the effect of political events on a populace, thus making judgments about the character of an age that often tend to subsume contradictory elements. The formal, institutional aspects of the politics of the era need to be measured against the contradictions, evasions, and indifference that distinguish the cultural and social life.

The rise to power of Fascism in Italy was symptomatic of a crisis of liberalism and of capitalism that also existed in Germany. It was symptomatic of changing cultural conditions characteristic of the interwar era and of the growing pains attendant on modernity. In Italy the period between the wars was noted for class conflicts, opposition to the liberal state, inflation, strikes, land occupations in the south, struggles for higher wages and reduced working hours, reaction against the country's traditional leadership, and increasing and aggressive nationalism, leading to the occupation of Fiume under the aegis of D'Annunzio and his followers, the Arditi. The failure of the factory takeovers, the commitment to a Bolshevik-style revolution ill-adapted to the resolution of Italy's unique problems of economic growth and national integration, and the rise of the syndicalists with their emphasis on productivism only intensified political disarray and assisted the rise of Fascism in the 1920s. Initial congruence among socialists, futurists, and incipient Fascists was severed, signaling the failure of traditional political alliances and making a clearer path for Fascism.

Italy was not unique in the 1930s in its obsession with the power of media and their mass potential through the transmission of slogans, manifestoes, and the dissemination of images of collective aspirations. Although the media do play a crucial role in the ways in which this folklore is expressed and received, it is necessary to abandon notions of consensus that imply univalent acceptance and adherence on the part of a given populace and adopt more striated, mobile, and dispersed analysis of "real needs and desires." Thus, while there is some agreement about the ways the Fascist regime in Italy sought to create consensus through institutional structures and particularly through uses of the moving image, there is less unanimity about the regime's success in achieving its aims.

In consolidating power, the regime created state organizations after the March on Rome as a means of "Fascistizing" society, in both urban centers in the north of Italy as well as in the south and Sicily. In relation to economic policies, the regime expressed a

general commitment to private property[,] and any policy likely to favour economic efficiency and maximise production was translated into specific proposals for the privatisation of public utilities, cutbacks in and tight control over government spending, and tax and fiscal reform to stimulate private enterprise. This was a rolling back of the state, in other words, in the interests of taxpayers and entrepreneurs.[23]

Significantly, these policies, at odds with the statist predilection associated with Italian Fascism, would continue to create tensions between entrepreneurs and Fascist leaders. As in the commercial cinema, contradictions were evident in the pressure on the one hand toward productivity and profit and, on the other, the Fascist insistence on the power of the state and of the party.

The Catholic Church was brought into the Fascist orbit, subordinating or eliminating to a great degree opposition to Fascism from Catholic political parties. Most striking, of course, were the ways that the regime sought to organize the social and work life of Italians. The Balilla or ONB (Operazione Nazionale Balilla) was aimed at young people from eight to seventeen years of age in an effort to indoctrinate them in the values of Fascism. The Dopolavoro or OND (Operazione Nazionale Dopolavoro) was designed to organize people's leisure time. The OND was responsible for welfare disbursements as well as recreation, and by 1938 its membership had grown to 3.8 million.

Women were also organized through the OND and through the ONMI (Opera Nazionale per la Maternità ed Infanzia, i.e., National Organization for Maternal and Infant Welfare), which sought to establish "desirable" qualities that emblematized Fascist womanhood: "[M]aternity became tantamount to the physical act of making babies." Women were not only excluded from political life, but their "rights in the workplace, their contributions to culture, and their service as volunteers were called into question by the official message that their permanent duty was to bear the nation's children."[24] Edicts promulgated to ban "illegitimate sexuality" and prostitution resulted in the imprisonment, regulation, and surveillance of those involved in their practice. Legal restrictions were also instituted against those who performed or received abortions, and mass spectacles advocated maternity and reproduction in the interests of the state. A "Mother's Day" was instituted and held on December 24th to reward women for their fecundity – another public spectacle designed to highlight mothers' services to the state.

These attempts were not maintained unanimously and were productive of familiar contradictions:

> Propaganda insisted on the sexual puritanism, economic frugality, and austere leisure habits associated with early industrialism. Meanwhile burgeoning consumer industries often of foreign, especially American, provenance publicized ready-made clothing, synthetic fibers, cosmetics, household items, and processed foods, as well as the commodified sexuality typical of a modern consumer economy.[25]

The anastomosis of traditional and reiterated views of the sanctity and privacy of the family was in tension with modern life, its consumerist and its outward look, thus highlighting and putting strain on yet another area of Fascist eclecticism and potential conflict. The feature films of the era, rather than being a carbon copy of official propaganda, are revealing of this tension between modernity and tradition.

Women's position and representation under Fascism offers a corrective to the notion of the complete totalization of Italian life. Not only was subversion practiced through forms of birth control and family management, but the regime itself created the terms of conflict. Every aspect of woman's everyday life – her growing up, role in the family, child rearing, uses of leisure time, work, forms of organizing, role in the war effort, and later role in resisting Fascism – presents a checkered story of involvement in, and even conflict with, the regime, not a seamless and unified picture. Since the cinema draws liberally on prevailing and timely cultural images, even when it purports to restrict itself to the past, conflicting representations of femininity insinuate themselves into the film narratives. Films featuring women and the family open a window to the problematic construction of the national mission as it relates to women and the family.

In the commitment to and reaffirmation of the mission of the Italian nation, the cinema of the era offered its historical spectacles, empire films, war films, and melodramas that glamorized both imperialism and colonialism. These films too cannot be read merely as reflections of propaganda but were further indices of the tenuousness of consensus. Their often blatantly theatrical styles also tended to expose the grandiosity and artifice of imperialist adventure. The imperialist aspirations of the regime were not universally endorsed, became a source of its weakness in relation to the garnering of consensus, and were ultimately to account for its failure. Although not unique to Fascism, the emphasis on nationalism and imperialism was developed as another aspect of the regime's designs on the hearts and minds of the populace. Under Mussolini, Italy sought to expand into the Balkans, Greece, and the Danube, and plans were set in motion as early as 1927 for expansion into Libya and Ethiopia – plans realized in 1935. The Rome–Berlin accords, the Italian involvement in the Spanish Civil War between 1936 and 1939, the establishment of Nazi-style racism, and the entry into the global war along with Hitler are the fruits of the expansionist policy. These are also identified with the "crisis of consent" that characterized the latter years of the regime.[26]

These imperialistic and bellicose policies and the actions to which they gave rise had the effect of creating a series of critical problems in domestic affairs exemplified by inflation, shortages in foodstuffs and other consumer items, and the Allied bombings of Italy in 1942. The results were the disruption of production, creating homelessness and then mass evacuations to rural areas. These dislocations strained urban and rural populations, resulting in a further loss of confidence in Mussolini's leadership. In relation to women's situation, the war produced new contradictions. At the same time that it created new opportunities for women in leadership positions, militarism also accentuated the "polarization of gender relations, frustrating the efforts of women to identify with the Fascist hierarchy and national collectivity."[27]

Meanwhile, the new man so prized, advertised, and lauded by Fascism was also undermined, so that the former "homoerotic pride of comrades-in-arms gives way to the pathos of men abandoned," resulting in rebellion, desertion, and resistance.[28] An examination of actual behaviors derived from accounts of the time reveals that there was a variety of responses to Fascist practices, ranging from expediency and adaptation, to a withdrawal on the part of many to private life, and "other more abrasive forms" characterized by refusals to "take the Fascist Party card, to make the Fascist salute, or to wear the black shirt where public occasion demanded it."[29] These views of apparent nonconformity are not the same as resistance or opposition in a militant sense; they offer clues to specific expressions of discontent, ranging from Fascist attempts to control the body to matters of style, and to the disparity between the everyday and the ritualistic.

In the heart of the Centro Sperimentale di Cinematografia, created in the mid-1930s to promote film production and film education, was a group of critics and filmmakers who were themselves critical of Fascism and who sought new forms of cinematic expression, forms not aligned to prevailing modes of filmmaking. They turned, in part, to American literature rather than Hollywood cinema for their models. Not that forms of critical filmmaking were nonexistent: The films of Luigi Chiarini, Ferdinando Maria Poggioli, Mario Soldati, the early films of Roberto Rossellini, and Luchino Visconti's *Ossessione* offered oblique but trenchant images of the ravages of contemporary life, of power, and of belief. One axis of the filmmaking of the late 1930s and early 1940s was identified with *calligraphism,* a preoccupation with form through the creation of a highly patterned, claustrophobic, and destructive world where violence and aggression are commonplace. The central characters in the films were often somnambulists, depraved noblemen, avaricious priests, or mad and suicidal women, characters often derived from past literary works and set in the past, though not exclusively. Comedy and satire also offered complex images of contemporary life in such films as Camerini's *Il cappello a tre punte* (*The Three-Cornered Hat,* 1935) and *Batticuore* (*Heartbeat*), Blasetti's *Quattro passi fra le nuvole* (*Four Steps in the Clouds*), and Poggioli's *Sorelle Materassi* (*Materassi Sisters*). Rarer were the films that drew on foreign (particularly U.S.) popular literary works; an exception would be *Ossessione,* Visconti's reworking of James M. Cain's *The Postman Always Rings Twice.* As might be expected, there were contemporary war films, but Rossellini's *La nave bianca* (*The White Ship,* 1941) and Francesco De Robertis's *Uomini sul fondo* (*Men of the Deep,* 1941) in particular offered images of the hardships of combat rather than propagandistic celebration of war.

In the writings on cinema of the last years of the Fascist regime in such journals as *Bianco e nero, Il film,* and *Cinema,* one finds mounting disaffection with the "trashy histories, our rehashes of the 19th century, and our trifling comedies."[30] Armed with the battle cry of "realism," critics like Umberto Barbaro turned to the *verismo* of Giovanni Verga, to earlier Italian films such as *Assunta spina* and *Sperduti nel buio,* praising them for their "depiction of the ordinary, everyday life of typical Italians" as a desideratum for a renewed cinema and, even more, a renewed culture. The impetus for the cinema identified as *neorealism,* largely associated with the postwar years, has been accounted for in a number of ways: It was a movement that aimed to make connections with the Risorgimento, the unification of Italy as a nation, and its unfinished "revolution."[31] It was a cinema of anti-Fascism, expressing the aspirations of the Left, focusing on social injustice and the arrogance of power, critical of the clichés and formulas of genre and with the spectacle and rhetoric of the cinema under Fascism.

As most writers on film have indicated, "neorealism" means different things to film critics, writers, and filmmakers. There is no standard definition of neorealism any more than there is a fixed definition of realism. For some, "neorealism" has assumed the proportion of a hallowed mythology and a source of nostalgia for a world not realized. Neorealism has also been subject to the most formulaic of interpretations: for example, the reiterative description of the recourse to location shooting, the use of nonprofessional actors, the focus on contemporary events and not on the historical past, the loose construction of narration, the intermingling of fiction and nonfiction, and the privileging of marginalized and subaltern groups. However, too rigid an adherence to these criteria distorts the differing techniques and preoccupations of the neorealists. More disturbing yet, these criteria can also be identified with those films that are not part of the canonical texts of neorealism, in films of the Fascist era such as *Sole* (1929), *Rotaie* (1929), and *Acciaio* (1933). Millicent Marcus has insisted that neorealism has to be considered beyond "technical considerations," which leads her to valorize its "shared moral commitment" rather than strict stylistic characteristics.[32]

That certain films produced in the 1940s and the early 1950s are identified with neorealism and its impact on Italian cinema, and then more broadly with international filmmaking, is indisputable. Indisputable too is the fact that neorealism introduced new dimensions into the cinema that signaled a move away from classical modes of filmmaking and hence of ways of thinking about the world. It was clear that the movement-image had been exhausted, incapable of producing the necessary shock that would give rise to new modes of thinking.[33] Italian neorealism can be identified with the inauguration of the time-image, and with reintroducing thought into cinema. The Italian cinema

> had at its disposal a cinematographic institution which had escaped fascism relatively successfully, on the other hand it could point to a resistance and a popular life underlying oppression, although one without illusion. To grasp these, all that was necessary was a new type of tale [*récit*] capable of including the elliptical and the unorganised, as if the cinema had to begin again from zero, questioning afresh all the accepted facts from the American tradition. The Italians were therefore able to have an intuitive consciousness of the new image in the course of being born.[34]

The particular qualities of this "new image" are that it is open rather than closed, descriptive rather than prescriptive, philosophical rather than interpretive. The image "no longer refers to a situation which is globalising or synthetic, but rather to one that is dispersive."[35] The characters are multiple rather than singular. Space is no longer unified, but fragmented, and chance rather than purposive action becomes central: "Linkages, connections, or liaisons are deliberately weak."[36] Actions and situations are no longer governed by purposiveness but by aimlessness characterized by the stroll, the voyage that can occur anywhere. Also, the texts are governed by the consciousness of ubiquitous clichés that circulate not only "in the external world, but which also penetrate each one of us and constitute his internal world, so that everyone possesses only psychic clichés by which he thinks and feels."[37] Furthermore, the cinema exposes the means whereby a "plot" circulates and disperses these clichés through all the avenues of power.

The movement known as neorealism unleashed "the powers of the false," where conventional notions of truth, virtue, heroism, good and evil, and, above all, the real and the artifactual are put into crisis, and where the possibility of a more complex relation to the world is possible. In this case, it is not the truthful person who becomes the protagonist but the forger, the somnambulist, the neurotic. In effect, what this kind of filmmaking does, exemplified so powerfully in a film such as *Umberto D,* is to immerse the spectator in time that is open rather than closed, that does not order but creatively disorders, freeing the spectator from appearance as well as from truth,[38] simulating "the character's way of seeing."[39] The "realism" is conceptual – a fact that makes the post–World War II cinema from Michelangelo Antonioni to Nanni Moretti problematic in relation to the commercial cinema.

Rethinking neorealism from the vantage point of the time-image releases the film critic from the dreary round of having to first establish the precise moment of neorealism's beginning as well as marking its absolute limits and absolute distinctions among such films as *Roma, città aperta* (*Open City*), *Ladri di biciclette* (*The Bicycle Thief*), *Umberto D,* and the works of such auteurs as Fellini, Antonioni, and Pasolini. Rethinking neorealism from a mechanical formalism to changes in the cultural milieu involves a more flexible understanding of media effects that inhere in the cinematic medium from its inception to the present. Neorealism was not polemic, a conduit for "messages" concerning ethics, politics, and morality, though it invoked these concerns. It was, foremost, a harbinger of the attention that must be paid to the visual image in a world that had been set in motion by the powers of the visual and their relation to the dynamism of time, motion, and change.

Neorealism was a cinema of auteurs, particularly identified with the works of Vittorio De Sica, Roberto Rossellini, Giuseppe De Santis, and Pietro Germi, among others. Like the French New Wave in their films, as well as in their writing on film, the "neorealists" revealed their own conception of *le caméra stylo,* a personal, poetic, and therefore engaged sense of the director as "author" of the filmic text. The work of the neorealist critics and filmmakers was an extension of the intellectual and cultural concerns of earlier critics of the cinema of the 1920s. Ricciotto Canudo had sought to realize the potential of film not merely as a narrative medium but as a means for realizing its power to generate thought. Although the auteur theory in the post–World War II cinema could be reduced to a formulaic and singular notion of authorship, its initial inspiration was to transform the cinematic medium to make it a more flexible medium capable of opening onto serious questions concerning the capacity of the visual image to engage audiences in ways consonant with the complexity of postwar life.

According to some, neorealism is reputed to have died with the appearance of the "economic miracle" in Italy in the 1950s. In Leprohon's account:

> [A]s neorealism moved on from the Resistance film to the social film, its audience dwindled. In Italy it was equally unpopular with the upper classes and the Church, whose peace of mind it disturbed, and with the lower and middle classes, who had little desire to see their problems and sufferings displayed on the screen.[40]

Thus a narrative is often constructed in which one has to account for the success of neorealism in new terms within the films of such filmmakers as Visconti, Fellini, and Antonioni. If neorealism as a movement identified with the Resistance lost its impetus in the wake of the political defeats identified with the coming to power of the Christian Democrats in 1948, its mode of challenging the clichés of the genre cinema persisted. Its treatment of narrative, or rather its tendency to subordinate the action-image to the time-image, can be seen in its preoccupation with theatricality and with "the powers of the false." The neorealist concern with exploring the possibilities of the cinematic medium to challenge habituated forms of knowledge persisted and can be seen from the 1950s through the 1970s in the films of Pier Paolo Pasolini, Bernardo Bertolucci, Ettore Scola, the Taviani brothers, and in the "spaghetti westerns" of Sergio Leone and Tonino Valerii, among others. As Millicent Marcus has commented,

> Italian cinema may have lost its immediate postwar optimism about the attempt to shape political reality according to a moral idea, but it never lost its deep and abiding commitment to that attempt, nor has the movement ceased to examine the reasons for that failure.[41]

In short, neorealism altered to meet the changing cultural situation.

Italian cinema, much like other national cinemas, moved more intimately into the orbit of international cinema, a situation already in evidence in the aftermath of World War II. Although the neorealist films identified with the immediate postwar era directly addressed the Italian context and can be said to constitute a rejuvenation of the national form, these films had an enormous impact on the cinemas of Latin America, of Japan (especially such films as *Drunken Angel* [1948] and *Ikiru* [1952]), of India (in the works of Satyajit Ray), and on such African films as Sembène's *La Noire de . . .* (Black Girl,

1966). Since neorealism eschewed the monumental and epic dimensions of the historical film that often functioned in the interests of nationalist rhetoric, and since it seemed to offer new versions of the nation, it presented new forms of address and interrogation to filmmakers involved in postwar reconstruction, decolonization, and reconsiderations of the subaltern. Although neorealist texts initally focused on individuals and groups marginalized because of war, urban displacement, poverty, and unemployment, the films after the mid-1950s became more attentive to the immediacy and challenges of changing economic and cultural conditions.

David Forgacs describes how changes in Italian cultural consumption were already evident even before the 1960s, a period identified with increased incomes and cultural consumption:

> The decade after the Second World War needs to be revalued, then, as a distinctive period in which, despite the relatively low wages and consumer spending compared with the 1960s, changes in cultural consumption were visible all over the country. In addition to radio-listening and cinema-going, both of which had their golden age in 1945–55, there was an increase in the popularity of spectator sports – particularly tour cycling and football . . . and a rapid growth in magazine readership.[42]

Television also entered into the picture as a force to be reckoned with, altering cinematic production and cultural consumption. In the images of the films one sees the emphasis on youth, shifting patterns of gendered and sexual behavior, new configurations of the urban landscape, a greater emphasis on urban alienation and acts of violence. *The Bicycle Thief* and *Umberto D* both already reveal the changed urban landscape: the appeal of spectator sports, generational tensions, and the centrality of media.

It has been customary to trace two different lines of descent in Italian cinema: one identified with the struggle of realism to assert itself, of which neorealism is an important instance; the other identified with the cinema of genres, which from the very first was preeminent. In any examination of Italian film production, what is evident is the importance of certain genres: comedies (above all), adventure films, historical epics, and melodramas. However, histories of world cinema tend to favor, even create, canonical works, and the major share of attention has been accorded to the films of auteurs, what has been identified as "art cinema" (aside from discussions of the historical epics of the teens). This valorization of "serious" films against frivolous commercial films is characteristic not only of the critical assessment of the cinema under Fascism, but also of the evaluation of films from the mid-1950s, slighting the return of melodramas, comedies, and adventure and action films.

From the 1950s onward, one sees the emergence of new stars, a series of comic films identified as *commedia all'italiana*, and the rise of a number of historical films that were to prove quite profitable. Although Forgacs identifies the "golden age" of Italian cinema as 1945–55, Peter Bondanella writes that "[t]he decade between 1958 and 1968 may in retrospect be accurately described as the golden age of Italian cinema, for in no other period was its artistic quality, its international prestige, and its economic strength so consistently high."[43] The output was quite varied: It included works by Antonioni, Pietro Germi, Fellini, and Visconti; De Sica continued to direct films until his death in 1974. It also included the films of Raffaello Matarazzo, whose comedies and melodramas were popular during the era of Fascism and who, in the 1950s, made extremely popular melodramas such as *Catene* (Chains, 1950), *Tormento* (1950), and *I figli di nessuno* (*Nobody's Children,* 1951), films that have received scant critical attention. Similarly, costume dramas returned with a vengeance in such widely popular "peplum epics" as *Ulisse* (*Ulysses,* 1954), *Spartaco* (*Spartacus,* a.k.a. *Sins of Rome,* 1954), *Le fatiche de Ercole* ([*The Labors of*] *Hercules,* 1957), and a spate of others, including biblical epics, in the 1960s.

These popular films were not a mere resurrection of the earlier Italian cinema. Not only were they international productions utilizing international texts and stars; they also ran parallel to many of the political concerns that animated the art cinema of the period, addressing questions of authority, struggles by oppressed and marginalized figures to oppose the reigning powers. They were a response to the emphasis on beleaguered masculinity that inheres in many of the social realist films. They employed visual effects in ways that appear to respond to the overwhelming visualization of culture in relation to body building, sports, fashion, and the cultivation of personality.

The Italian ("spaghetti") western, crossing over between the art cinema and the genre cinema, enjoyed a success that has been amply documented and analyzed. The reasons for this financial success have been attributed to several factors, including Hollywood's inability to meet the popular demand for this genre during its years of financial crisis and its willingness to finance films by Italian directors and actors. (The success of the peplum epics had already created a precedent for this kind of cooperation.)

Even more than the economic possibilities and promises held out by the genre, the spaghetti western followed a tradition of film and politics exemplified by the Hollywood western. The spaghetti western drew on a long history of infatuation with and ambivalence toward the United States, relying for its inspiration on the reworking of the classic Hollywood film and on the popularity of the western on television. Such revisionist westerns as *The Wild Bunch* (1969) and *Yojimbo* (1961) had garnered international acclaim, becoming increasingly part of the cultural lexicon of the 1960s and early 1970s. Christopher Frayling also attributes its popularity to a phenomenon of the period 1963–73: the desire to escape from the confines of society.[44] The internationalist cast of the spaghetti western can be registered in several ways: the genre's appropriation of Americanism for its own ends, its critical stance toward authority and social order, its confusion and complication of the character of hero and villain, and its focus on violence – a violence often generated by the powers-that-be and often indirectly related to the Vietnam War. The films are a cornucopia of cultural knowledge about conceptions of masculinity, its relation to power, authority and violence. In a sense, they are counterparts to the concerns of Marxist filmmakers – early Pier Paolo Pasolini, Bernardo Bertolucci, and Francesco Rosi – addressing Gramscian common sense as folklore, struggles over hegemony, and the creation of a national-popular culture. They utilize clichés only to dissolve them and are intertextual in their dialogue with other films. Their engagement with genre is dependent on the personality of the director and of the stars.

In a cinema that has been conspicuous for its paucity of women directors, the 1970s also witnessed the appearance of the films of Liliana Cavani and Lina Wertmüller. However, thanks to the ways that histories of cinema have been organized, with their focus on only the most visible auteurs, the works of other female artists has been largely ignored; even then, films by these two prominent directors have gone largely uncommented upon in the critical literature. In the 1970s and 1980s, thanks largely to the feminist movement in Italy, a number of filmmakers have produced short and feature-length films for the screen and for television, some in collaboration with such directors as Marco Bellochio (e.g., Elda Tattoli); these films have highlighted the social and cultural position of women. (In their filmography in *Off Screen: Women's Film in Italy*, Giuliana Bruno and Maria Nadotti list films by women, from the first decade of this century through the 1980s, addressing feminism, history, fantasy, biography, and media theory, and documenting the increased involvement of women in the production of films.)

The film industry in the 1980s suffered a fate similar to other European national cinemas. It had to come to terms with television. It had again to confront the Hollywood competition. It suffered from financial crisis. It had to develop a new generational identity, a different sense of history, an awareness of the ubiquity of consumerism on a global scale, and a recognition of living in a world without cultural paternity, where tradition (even that of modernism) no longer served as guide. Though there are a number of directors whose names continued to be conspicuous in this decade – Lina Wertmüller, Federico Fellini, the Taviani brothers, Ettore Scola, Ermanno Olmi – only a few filmmakers gained a measure of international prominence (e.g., Nanni Moretti, Gianni Amelio, and Giuseppe Tornatore). There are a host of others, described in Gian Piero Brunetta's monumental *Storia del cinema italiano, 1895-1993,* who are known only within Italy and identified with film and television.

The cultural situation in Italy in the 1980s has been described by Robin Buss in relation to presentations of the family: "The children of the 1980s are growing up in a world of erotic television, liberal laws on divorce and abortion, the threat of AIDS and the exhaustion of the political hopes that drove their parents to 'historical compromise' or revolutionary anarchism or the search for an alternative society."[45] Manuela Gieri sees Scola's films as becoming "more than any other director . . . the forum for the free contamination of tragedy and comedy, as well as between the many codified genres."[46] His films confront questions of history, cinematic history, styles, and forms, the role of television, the family, the nation, and, above all, the inevitable signs of change – irrevocable change – that characterize contemporary Italian culture and politics. One of the major changes in relation to cinema and society has been the central role played by television. Not only did it bring Silvio Berlusconi, a media magnate, into the forefront of Italian politics, but it has altered cinema, spectatorship, and the face of politics.

The 1980s and the 1990s were marked, therefore, by the attempts to understand the role of information and the televisual – not merely the "world in the box" – but ways of seeing, thinking, and disseminating images and information that had marked differences in cultural and politics at the end of the century. Most especially, the world as transmitted and received through the medium of television intensified the boundaries between the real and the imaginary, the virtual and the actual, bifurcating two tendencies. In particular, one propensity moves backward into the realm of traditional and commonsensical formulations of the family, gender, sexuality; the other struggles with the aid of poststructuralist thinkers such as Lyotard, Baudrillard, De Certeau, and others to understand the "regime of the image," its construction, its dissemination, and its cultural impact.

Pier Paolo Pasolini had anticipated and explored these issues in his films and writings in the 1970s, dramatizing in his films the "new fascism" that was intimately bound to consumerism and media. Sexuality has become a major aspect of commodification, and the cinema has become a major conduit in cannibalizing all of reality. However, in my examination of recent Italian cinema (see Chapter 11), I explore how certain films and filmmakers are cognizant of this commodification and seek a pedagogy to dissect, disseminate, and share that knowledge with audiences.

The chapters that follow identify strands that constitute the collective enterprise known as Italian cinema. The properties of narration are identified with a national form, touching on history, language, regional identification, landscape, nation, and internationalism, and are part of a large context of popular and mass representation. Representations of gender, sexuality, race, class, and politics offer insight as to how the "nation" and its "people" are often conflated to suppress difference and foster the illusion of unity and unanimity.

CHAPTER ONE

Early Italian Cinema
Attractions

T
he Italian cinema of the silent era, like other national cinemas, has undergone a reconsideration in the light of additional film texts and new scholarly studies that are shedding light on the cultural milieu and conditions of production and reception of early cinema. This cinema is important not as a way station to the development of the longer feature film but as an index to the massive changes attendant on modernity that films helped to create, changes that affected the social behavior of the population and their views of the world. A study of the silent cinema offers an unprecedented opportunity for assessing the particular directions open to entrepreneurs and artists in this new medium, involving such issues as projection venues, subjects to be filmed, and its political and moral effects. It also allows an examination of the uses of narrative, both with regard to spectacle and in the context of early cinema's relationship to the other arts and especially to the popular culture of its time. Italian cinema does not suffer from being described as "primitive" in its early phases, having been successful and highly profitable in the pre-World War I years; but it does suffer, like other national cinemas, from being too rigidly assessed as a narrative medium. For instance, in relation to the initiating moments of cinema, Tom Gunning writes:

> The history of early cinema, like the history of cinema generally, has been written and theorized under the hegemony of narrative films. . . . A few observations will indicate that the sway of early cinema was not dominated by the narrative impulse that later asserted its narrative sway over the medium.[1]

In examining the early films that are travel films, documents of events of the day, records of the movements of prominent personalities, and vignettes that capture domestic life and scenes of work, too often critics have tied them to the emergence of a "narrative impulse," relegating them to a subordinate role in the history of cinema. Gunning has proposed the notion of a "cinema of attractions . . . a cinema that displays its visibility, willing to rupture a self-enclosed fictional world for a chance to solicit the attention of the spectator."[2]

This conception of cinema is a productive way of regarding the visual image and particularly the visual image minus sound on film. Although distinctions can be made between early trick films, newsreels, recordings of people and events produced in Italy before 1908, and the appearance of narrative films drawn from historical events, novels, and plays, these earliest forms have an integrity that can be recognized. Only recently has an alternative assessment of silent cinema come into focus that challenges the overzealous attachment to the inevitability of cinema as a storytelling form, an attachment that has impeded an understanding of the complexity of the media image. Closer attention to the unique properties of the silent cinema reveals the multifarious ways in which the pioneers in cinema envisioned the possibilities of the new invention, the different cultural sources on which it drew, and its impact on audiences of these images.

Restricting early cinema to a narrative tradition not only occludes the conditions of reception but implies that there were no alternatives to the directions taken by the cinema. The exclusive attention to narrative also misrepresents the unique conditions of production and reception, and their relations to an audience that saw these films under circumstances far different from the movie theater. Knowing that these short early films were produced and received in a different milieu – as parts of larger theatrical and music-hall programs, traveling shows, fairground exhibitions, vaudeville, arcades, and photography studios – suggests that one cannot make easy generalizations about narrative tradition.

The films of the silent era were more than simply innovative in exploiting the commercial and cultural possibilities of the new moving visual medium that was tied to a vast array of existing forms of popular culture. They also created an audience that, unfamiliar with the new medium, was actively engaged in the process of acclimatization. It is thus insufficient to attribute the interest of spectators in the new medium to mere curiosity, a simple fascination with motion, or the novelty of the cinematic apparatus per se:

> [T]he cinema succeeded because exhibitors cleverly exploited its potential, because in moving picture-shows spectators found something which appealed to them, and because the medium, while it offered escape into a world of fantasy where distances no longer existed and where illusions could become reality, also opened a window on current issues and helped [spectators] to understand the contemporary world.[3]

These early films were closely tied to the environment in which they were exhibited: the landscape of urban life with its crowding, places of commerce, and sense of constant movement. They were integrally tied to changes being wrought in relation to the process of industrialization under way in Italy, particularly in the north of Italy. According to Brunetta:

> The process of urbanization of the cinema, its transformation from a traveling cultural show and suddenly into a stable performance, is not only connected to the terrain of a still-virginal productive investment but needs to be analyzed in the context of a general transformation of Italy from an agrarian to an industrial country.[4]

It is the very character of this transformation that is exemplified both in and by the new medium – in its deployment of space in the images projected and by the spaces created for exhibition.

The first films, prior to the creation of movie theaters, were seen in photography studios or "were used as interludes in musicals, reviews, vaudeville or variety shows."[5] The films were shown as part of larger programs that took place in a number of venues. Cinema was primarily identified with urban life, but there were traveling shows that went from the cities to the countryside, presenting their wares at fairs and in regular theaters. The subject matter of these films varied but included newsreel footage of such events as the movements of the royal family in *Umberto e Margherita di Savoia a passeggio per il parco,* shot by the studio of Filoteo Alberini. Among other films shot in the 1890s were those of Leopoldo Fregoli, whose attractions were highly dependent on the work and assistance of Louis Lumière. Fregoli, a music-hall impersonator, began by projecting the films of Lumière, interspersing them with his own acts. He then went on to make his own films, which involved various locales – restaurants, the army, the hair salon. and so on.[6] Inventive in his exploration of cinematic movement, Fregoli experimented with trick films and eventually with a sound accompaniment. His work, like that of other early filmmakers, was closely allied to the tradition of popular entertainment, focusing on showmanship – not on the telling of stories.

Among the other individuals who contributed to the creation of cinematic entertainment were Luigi Topi and Ezio Cristofari, who founded a Franco-Italian moving picture company that produced *tableaux vivants*.[7] In Turin, which was, along with Milan, Naples, and Rome, an important source of film production during the early years of cinema, the work of Arturo Ambrosio in conjunction with the photographer Roberto Omegna was noteworthy, and Omegna went on to produce documentaries. *La presa di Roma (The Taking of Rome,* 1905), a feature film produced by Alberini and documenting the annexation of Rome to the Italian nation, signaled a direction for future production: the historical film. The links between the subject of this film and social institutions, such as the world of the military, attests to a connection between cinema and its images of the nation. Its uses of the past were tied to the folklore of the culture, but the cinema also drew on a mélange of images and events derived from the sights and sounds of modern life – shops, street life, fashion, sports events, and personalities – as well as on earlier art forms, such as painting and architecture.

Along with Ambrosio Films, founded in 1906 [Fig. 1], the Cines company was created by Alberini and Dante Sansoni with the financial aid of Ernesto Pacelli, a relation of Pius XII. Cines became one of the major studios in Italy and was to remain prominent in Italian film production, indicating that "the new industry was controlled by men who had nothing in common with the fairground showmen who launched the cinema in France, and this fact explains the tremendously rapid rise of the cinema in Italy."[8] From the standpoint of commerce and cultural commodities, companies such as Cines and Itala were evidence that filmmaking in Italy was no flash in the pan but was well on its way to establishing itself as a player on the national and, subsequently, international markets. In Naples, Dora Film, under the guidance of producer-director Elvira Notari, generated actualities, short films for national and foreign consumption, documentaries, and also feature films – testimony to a greater range and variety of film production than has often been claimed for Italian silent cinema.

The character of these early films can be located in their emphasis on the visual, on their ability to create for the spectator a sense of the sights and sounds of the everyday world, as well as on a glimpse into the magical properties of the medium through the uses of film "magic," that is, through editing and "theatricality."[9] In discussions of the Lumière films, it has been argued that one-shot texts like *Arrivée d'un train à La Ciotat* (*Train Arriving at a Station,* 1895) are, in fact, narrative films. However, the difference between this film and "classical" narratives resides in the character of the narration. The one-shot narrative is iconic: It tells its "story" via its visualization through mimesis but without benefit of the narrator, that is, the storyteller;[10] it is representative of a form of viewing that is less controlled, more spontaneous, and more concentrated on spectacle than motivation.[11] The spectator thus occupies a different space than she or he does within a stricter narrative form. The films prior to 1908, those cited above by Fregoli, Omegna, and Alberini among others, situate the spectator in a space parallel to the filmmaker, as tourists or, in Bruno's terms, as "streetwalkers." In these films, the audience performs a different, more active, role than in the narrative cinema.

Equally important in regard to audiences is that a new form of acculturation was coming into being, what Miriam Hansen describes in relation to American cinema as the creation of a new public sphere. She finds, moreover, that the "relative imperfections of 'primitive' cinema – tableau style that may require a lecturer, disregard for continuity editing – suggest that the experience in front of the screen was at least as significant as the actions depicted on the screen."[12] Furthermore, "early cinema also provided a social space, a

Figure 1. The Italo–French Connection and Ambrosio Films. (Courtesy New York Museum of Modern Art Stills Archive)

place apart from the domestic and work spheres, where people of similar background and status could find company (not necessarily of their own kin), where young working women would seek escape from the fate of their mothers."[13] The cinema was a major force in socializing the population to the sights and sounds of modern life, and the social dimensions of cinemagoing play as important a role as the subject matter of the films. These early images projected on the screen addressed familiar events, people, and places, providing loci for communal gathering. Spectators could also make contact with new and distant vistas (as earlier imaged in the popular stereopticons), further gratifying through the moving image their fascination with travel and making the cinema a passport to different and remote parts of the world. The kaleidoscopic images of modern life could be seen in panoramic terms. The short films offered views of royalty, different aspects of street life, military formations, sports (automobile races, etc.), folk dances, domestic scenes, and festivals, films made in different regions of Italy, and, of course, natural and man-made catastrophes. Increasingly, cinema programs catered to various social groups – men, women, professionals, working people, and the upper classes – through a wide array of films.

What accounts for the movement toward the feature film that gradually emerged toward the middle of the first decade of the twentieth century? One conventional explanation has it that as a consequence of audiences' waning interest in these "novelties," new, longer, fictional, and more elaborate cinematic forms were generated. Another explanation for the triumph of the feature film relies on the rapidly evolution of cinematic technology, allowing longer narratives to replace the short films that were often part of equally long but diversified mixed-media programs. Still another view relies on the cultural embeddedness of narrative, thus suggesting the inevitability of the cinema becoming a narrative form. Most critics agree that the silent cinema changed decidedly from what Tom Gunning has described as the "cinema of attractions" to the development of more and longer narrative forms. In Italy by 1910, the cinema of attractions had become allied to storytelling through comedies, historical films, and melodramas.

Competition for hegemony in early cinema production was not only fierce but decentralized and, above all, governed by the lure of profits. There were increasing numbers of production houses, intense competition among regions and companies, and attempts to gain a foothold in foreign markets. Historians of Italian cinema underscore the rapidly developing nature of the technology, the quest for profits based in cost reduction through forms of standardization, and, consequently, the creation of new types of spectatorship that would enlarge audiences. In accounting for changes in production and exhibition that have relevance for Italian cinema, Thomas Elsaesser writes, "The change from selling to renting, and the emergence of fixed sites other than vaudeville theaters are thus interdependent factors."[14] There is a symbiotic relation between the "fixed settings" and the kinds of films produced. Leprohon describes how "[t]he tremendous boom that began in 1908 was marked by a blooming, virtually unique to Italy, of the costume film."[15]

These historical epics relied increasingly on industrialization, with its centralization and division of labor; they also drew on the talents of the theater and of the phenomenon of *divismo*, the Italian version of the star system in the silent era.[16] By contrast, the works of a filmmaker like Elvira Notari and certain other regional filmmakers were of an artisanal character. This shift from the artisanal to the industrial, from the spectator as flâneur-participant to stationary and isolated viewer, and from the live event to the represented one becomes evident in the middle of the first decade of the twentieth century. It should be noted, though, that this trend toward narration does not abandon spectacle: It assimilates, cannibalizes, or accommodates it. Films – especially the silent films with which we are concerned in this chapter, the historical film and the melodrama – offer evidence of the anastomosis of profilmic events onto the filmic. A certain eclecticism is evident whereby, through the focus on landscape, the body, gesture, chases, comic events, and catastrophes (e.g., fires and earthquakes), narrative and spectacle are fused.

There is no clear set of markers to distinguish the conditions that can explain the transition from "primitive" to "classical" cinema, since it is not merely the form of editing, eye-line matches, camera movement, and so on. Though formal film analysis conjoined to production history has dislodged the organic and linear narrative of cinema as it moves from a "primitive" to "sophisticated" form of narrative, one must be wary of creating new and discrete stylistic categories that slight the importance of social and political conditions that are an ever-important index to changes in the medium. Economics is of major importance in a cultural form that relies on private enterprise for profitability through internal and foreign competition. In the rapidly mutating modern world, change in taste and in fashion, whether due to advertising or to overexposure to certain images, dictate changes in representation. The relation of the narrative cinema to other arts, particularly theater and literature (now, TV and video) are also determinants of change. Certainly, cataclysmic events, such as those brought on by drastic political changes and by war, have also been part of the cinematic landscape, affecting narrative forms.

In the history of Italian narrative cinema, the films that are most cited in the teens are *Gli ultimi giorni di Pompeii* (*The Last Days of Pompeii,* 1908, remade several times), *Quo Vadis?*, *La caduta di Troia* (The Fall of Troy), *Cabiria*, *Assunta Spina,* and the missing *Sperduti nel buio* (Lost in the Dark). These films are regarded as evidence of Italy's "golden age" in the cinema, not only because of their commercial success but because of their high level of technical expertise. In these longer films, there is now a fusion of spectacle and narrative, an attention to continuity and transitions in the multiple actions, a focus on acting, the eventual creation of the star as diva, and the use of landscape for purposes of orchestrating the many elements that contribute to the film's theatricality. At the time, there was a growing anxiety about the moral and political effects of films like these on audiences, expressed since the 1890s by various social groups, the Roman Catholic Church, and the state, that was by 1913 to result in specific prohibitions concerning the presentation of sexuality and the adverse criticism of the state and religion.

An examination of the films produced during the teens testifies to their varied social contexts and sources. Not all of the films were set in classical Rome and Greece; some were set in the Risorgimento. They were also based, if often loosely, on literary works by Tasso, Ariosto, Émile Zola, Alexandre Dumas, Grazia Deledda, Gabriele D'Annunzio, Henrik Ibsen, Paolo Giacommetti, and Matilde Serao, among many others. In addition, the role of operatic texts and style play a key role in the Italian cinema not only of this era but throughout its history. The sources for the films, and the treatment of those sources, are an index to how Italian silent cinema plundered aspects of Italian culture and social life.

Although it appears that the historical film was indeed a major genre, the Italian cinema was not bereft of comic films. The work of André Deed, a French entertainer renamed Cretinetti for Italian audiences, was popular for several years and appreciated for his surreal comedy, which relied on fast action, mimicry, and tricks.[17] Polidor (Guilliaume F.), another French comedian working in the tradition of burlesque, was popular with Italian audiences. More in the tradition of a circus performer, he focused on locomotory gags that relied on the disruption of social rituals. There is little sign of an early flowering of Italian film comedy as a genre and more evidence of its reliance on French performers and styles, although there are indications of comic episodes in the costume dramas and historical films (e.g., *Quo Vadis?*).

In the cultural history of the teens and twenties, futurism was a political and aesthetic movement identified with modernism and with such figures as Filippo Tomasso Marinetti, who argued for a total technological and cultural revolution in society based on the power of the machine. Worshipers of movement, futurists in their manifestos stressed the imperative of creating a new and more modern, albeit nationalistic, society thanks to the benefits of technology – industrialization, the machine, the airplane, the automobile, and instruments of war. The futurists played a modest role in the development of cinema as opposed to the other arts. Though there are few instances of futurist films, there are aspects of films from the 1920s and 1930s that celebrate technology (e.g., *Acciaio* [Steel], 1933). Futurist ideas made more of an impact on literature, painting, theater, furniture, cuisine, and even advertising than on the cinema.[18] The attitude of many Italian futurists toward cinema was critical, seeing this medium as allied to traditional aesthetics and inimical to the antinarrative and freer forms they saw realized in the other arts. Peter Bondanella credits them with articulating "one of the earliest considerations of cinema's right to an existence that is no longer dependent upon its sister art forms."[19]

While the futurists and such modernists as D'Annunzio celebrated freedom from traditional sexual and moral restraints, even libertinism, the guardians of morality associated with the Roman Catholic Church and with the government were identified with the integrity of the traditional family, reproduction, and national honor. Hence, it is not surprising that censorship, as in other national cinemas, plays a decisive role in the development of the early Italian cinema – a sign of the general tendency of the state and civil groups to "discipline and punish" infractions in acceptable social and moral codes. In regarding the role of censorship, it is important to consider both the formal apparatus of censorship and indirect modes for the surveillance and restriction of cultural material, particularly as they involve formal political issues and the portrayal of sexuality.[20] Although legal forms of censorship for the cinema were not in place until 1913, there were guidelines for safety in the places of projection as well as civil and religious expressions of concern for displays of immorality involving adultery, murder, perverted curiosity, lasciviousness, and so on.[21]

Increasingly, the expression of anxiety for safeguarding public morality led to the articulation of interdictions that could constitute the basis for action against specific texts:

1 offenses against decency in the clothing of the characters;
2 material contrary to national decorum and public order that could disrupt international relations, or that consistute offenses against public institutions and authority;
3 scenes that display cruelty to animals, or incite to crime or suicide;
4 scenes or facts that could compromise economic and political interests, or national decorum, prestige, and authority; and
5 scenes or facts that compromise the power and authority of the army and the navy, scenes that would not guarantee public dignity.[22]

These strictures were refined and augmented in 1917 in relation to scenes that portray depravity, present adultery sympathetically, incite to hatred, defame virtuous action, are disrespectful toward the dead, or lend credibility to hypnotism or other "supernatural" actions.

In 1920, a commission was created comprising a government official, a police officer, a magistrate, a "mother with family," and a publicist to oversee and apply the strict letter of the law. Despite considerable arbitrariness and latitude in enforcing the laws, there were titles changed, certain scenes removed, and offensive material altered. With regard to censorship under the Fascist regime, little new was added to the list by 1923: "since the number of films was decreasing rapidly, the producers and the censorship board were more concerned about production than censorship."[23] In the 1930s, in the area of political surveillance, censorship was to be somewhat more stringent (see Chapter 3).

In looking at a popular and influential film such as *Quo Vadis?*, it is evident that the film dramatizes a number of taboo topics involving drunken orgies, cruelty to animals (during the burning of Rome scenes), female wantonness, and suicide. However. since the film treats these scenes within the context of Nero's reign, and since Petronius' suicide was a historical fact, these were considered acceptable. Thus, though formal censorship and self-censorship may have played a role in the selection and handling of subject matter, they did not necessarily eliminate transgressive treatments of sexuality or morally and nationally suspect material: These may just have appeared in more veiled and circumspect fashion. A film that might have raised the suspicions of the censor but for its religious subject matter – the struggle of the Christians against the licentious and pagan Roman court – *Quo Vadis?*, based on Henry Sienkiewicz's novel, would be produced in 1913 and 1924 in Italy, and 1951 in Hollywood, after having been a successful play in the 1890s and early 1900s. The 1913 Italian version, directed by Enrico Guazzoni, was highly influential in the French cinema of that era.[24] The film is quintessentially theatrical and operatic. Loosely constructed from episodes in the novel, it highlights those visual moments that dramatize intense passion, jealousy, or vindictiveness: voluptuous orgiastic banqueting scenes in the court of Nero [Fig. 2], destruction in the burning of Rome, mutilation of the Christians in the gladiatorial arena, and the melodramatic suicide of Petronius and his favored slave, Eunice.

Lasting two hours, *Quo Vadis?* relies on the framework of a romantic love story tied to a parable about the sufferings of Christians during the rise of Christianity and the fall of the pagan world. The film's evocation of the classical world is derived from painting and from the uses of statuary. The spectacle includes images of chariot races over which Nero presides, the burning of Rome at his behest, gladiatorial scenes in the arena, massively choreographed scenes of Roman spectators intercut with Christians being mauled by the lions, and the dramatic killing of a bull to which Lygia is strapped by Ursus (a slave a counterpart to the figure of Maciste in *Cabiria*). According to Pierre Leprohon:

> Enrico Guazzoni, in his creations of ancient Rome, was the first to place great volumes of space between the camera and his sets, which were no longer erected in the studio but outdoors. He used more architecture and curves in his compositions and filled the intervening spaces with pompous chariots of triumph, potbellied amphorae, and cumbersome tricilinia.[25]

The landscape scenes, costuming, and architecture suggest further connections between Italian cinema and painting to produce images of the classical era. In the development of character, *Quo Vadis?* was less innovative, hewing to a theatrical (and static) mode of presentation of scenes between the lovers, Lygia and Vinicius, between Vinicius and the comic figure of Chilon (related to the "Monkey" in *Cabiria*), the mad Nero and his courtiers, and the saintly Peter and his Christian followers.

These scenes are presented as tableaux, emphasizing composition and setting much more than movement, which is reserved for the monumental scenes in the arena (where a moving camera is in evidence at times in the panning of the crowd). Eschewing close-up, relying on physical gesture, hand movements, and posture, the dramatic power of the film derives from these crowd scenes [Fig. 3]. The effect of the choreography, especially the composition and emplacement of the groups of people, is visually overwhelming and enhances the melodramatic plight of the major characters. In short, the film's theatricality resides in its visual power, its ability to call attention to the

Figure 2. A Roman banquet in Guazzoni's *Quo Vadis?* (Courtesy New York Museum of Modern Art Stills Archive)

Figure 3. The gladiatorial arena, *Quo Vadis?* (Courtesy New York Museum of Modern Art Stills Archive)

potential of the cinema to exploit spectacle and movement and to grapple with the conquest of space specifically in relation to the masses.

In Guazzoni's words, "the cinema could exploit on a large scale the movements of the masses."[26] This supports the idea that early cinema should not be considered exclusively from the vantage point of narrative continuity and unity but must also be examined with regard to its tackling spectacle in its choreography to organize space and movement. This is not to say that character interactions are negligible in the unraveling of the narrative, but rather that they are to be regarded as being integrally tied to the melodramatic and operatic in the way that passion and pathos can be understood as being closely tied to spectacle. In writing about the role of character in melodrama and its relation to spectacle, A. Nicholas Vardac asserts:

> Character on the screen tended to remain impersonal. . . . The concept of character in screen melodrama or spectacle gained its dramatic value either through large-scale, rapid, and vigorous action or through elaborate spectacle. In other words, character became dramatic on the screen through the visual presentation of external actions, paces or events rather than through the dynamics of deliberation resulting in action. Screen character had become a symbol of certain elements of action, melodrama, and spectacle.[27]

Vardac's emphasis on "action, melodrama, and spectacle" is also applicable to *Cabiria* (1914), a film that provides a monumental and theatrical vision of a mythical world through the properties of the costume drama. If, in revisionist histories of the Italian cinema dating from the 1940s, *Assunta Spina* came to stand in for the Italian penchant for realism fully realized later in neorealism, the costume drama was identified in world film histories with the penchant of the Italian cinema for spectacle. Directed by Giovanni Pastrone, *Cabiria* was produced by Itala-Film, one of the survivors among the many competing companies at that time. While not as large a producer of film as Cines, Itala-Film was identified with costume films and with comedies. Pastrone was himself involved in the early years of Itala-Film as company secretary, and, among its costume dramas, the company produced *Agnese Visconti* (1910), *La caduta di Troia* (1910), *Il fuoco* (1915), and several films featuring the character Maciste.

The company invested heavily in the film's production (not to mention advertising), a fact in evidence in its settings, costumes, crowd-scene choreography, dolly shots, multiple cameras, and painted intertitles. Certain scenes were shot on location in Tunisia and Sicily. Equally important was Pastrone's decision to invite Gabriele D'Annunzio to lend his prestigious name (and personality) to the production. The choice of Italia Almirante Manzini as Sofonis-

Figure 4. The eruption of Mount Etna, *Cabiria*. (Courtesy New York Museum of Modern Art Stills Archive)

ba was another potential drawing card for audiences during the heyday of the diva. A further aspect of *divismo* was also important in the development of the Italian adventure films: the masculine protagonist as embodied in the character of Maciste, the Roman's slave. Pastrone hired a dockworker, Barto-lomeo Pagano, to play the role of that strong man, a role he was to repeat in several sequels. His was a character type who recurs in the peplum epics of the 1950s. Sorlin also notes that Pagano resembled Mussolini.[28] The iconog-raphy of masculinity and femininity is inherent to the cinematic lexicon, and the figure of Maciste offered an outsized version of masculinity.

The film begins with a lengthy sequence that portrays the eruption of Mount Etna [Fig. 4] and its effects on the family of Cabiria. In many early si-lent films, the viewing of disasters, fires, floods, storms, and earthquakes is a perennial staple of the cinema's attractions. In *Cabiria,* the natural upheaval serves diegetic ends in foreshadowing the conflicts and disruptions to come. As a consequence of the earthquake, Cabiria is torn from her family and with her nurse, Cresa, is set on the path of a series of encounters, threatening her survival. Characteristic of melodrama, the endangered female figure is the fulcrum of the narrative, highlighting the role of woman as central to the social order of the nation, with her violation a sign of its dissolution.

Cabiria skillfully weaves the spectacular elements of war [Fig. 5], natural disaster, and human suffering into a loosely constructed narrative that draws on traditional melodramatic conventions, with their emphasis on the epic war of nations, cultures, and peoples. The disasters that befall her are markers along the film's path of dramatizing social conflict and its resolution. Cabiria is wrenched from her nurse by Carthaginian pirates and slated to be sacrificed at the pagan Temple of Moloch. In true melodramatic fashion, her troubles are only beginning. Despite her nurse's enlisting the efforts of a noble Roman and his slave, Maciste, to rescue her from a fiery death as a sacrificial victim to Moloch, she is again captured and brought to an aristocratic woman, who protects her until she is again kidnapped, only to be saved again by her protector. The Second Punic War wages between the Carthaginians and the Romans, finally decided in behalf of the Romans, thus peripheralizing and then expunging the pagan (and racist) elements and ensuring the triumph of Christianity, Roman civilization, and the family.

The film's melodrama relies heavily on the inevitable and cumulative struggles to preserve Cabiria's chastity and her life in the countless scenes of chase and rescue between her protectors and her potential despoilers. The melodrama is enhanced through pathetic fallacy, wherein nature expresses human conflicts, as in the volcanic eruption of Mount Etna. On the technological side, the images of the brutality of warfare dramatize threats to the social order, as evinced by the engine of war constructed by the Carthaginians to destroy the Roman navy. The "genius" of Archimedes in harnessing the rays of the sun for destructive purposes results in visually brilliant scenes of the conflagration of the ships and highlights the power of technology – its role within and its role *as* film. This underscores the power of cinema to visualize the ravages of nature and time in its ability to create images of disaster, destruction, and death. Connections between war technology and cinema are part of the cinematic lexicon. The image of fire as a dominant and integrative thread throughout the film further reinforces the threat of chaos identified with the non-Roman world and of the inhumane Africans. Their negative role suggests the need for the more civilized, purifying power of Rome to come to the aid of the future nation. The film constructs a cornucopia of historical images identified with a past that exalts the nation, conjuring images of founding myths of Italy.

In ways anticipatory of *Scipione l'Africano,* the 1937 sound-film version of the Second Punic War, *Cabiria* highlights the character of the Carthaginian Sofonisba even more than that of Cabiria. As a Sicilian Roman victimized at the hands of a barbaric culture, Cabiria (Lidia Quaranta) is the passive recipient of others' efforts to free her and return her to her rightful land; she

Figure 5. The engines of war, *Cabiria*. (Courtesy New York Museum of Modern Art Stills Archive)

does not act but is acted upon. By contrast, the noblewoman Sofonisba – histrionically played by Italia Almirante Manzini, a popular diva of the era – is distinguished by her active role as queen and transgressive female. Her acting, similar to that of operatic heroines, is characterized by an alteration between languidity and fiery passion, as well as by pronounced hand and body movements, especially evident in the death scene. Her costuming, like that of the diva generally, is flamboyant and contrasts directly with the subdued gowns of Cabiria as an adult. Sofonisba's headdress, her jewelry, and her floor-length, loosely shaped, and sequined gowns are in the spirit of art deco fashions identified with the teens.

In the spirit of *divismo,* the character of Sofonisba follows the pattern of the femme fatale, the self-willed powerful woman who defies the world for desire and honor. The operatic character of her suicide by poison is intercut with scenes of battle for the supremacy of Rome over a barbarian culture, thus combining the drama of political power – subordination to the will of the state, duty, and service – with that of personal desire. As characteristic of melodrama, the private and the public spheres are initially in conflict but ultimately conjoined through the figure of this female character: Sofonisba, who embodies wild passion more than sentimental love, cannot, however, be neatly classified as a villainess. Her loyalty to Cabiria – protecting her, contrary to the dictates of the priests of Moloch, and finally freeing her – removes Sofonisba from the stigma of being a one-dimensional evil character. She is the source of spectacle, the fulcrum for the film's creation of a sensual world that far exceeds the national narrative. Of the uses of classical history in the cinema, Maria Wyke writes, "The reconstructions of Roman history produced by the Italian and Hollywood industries have always exceeded in function any imperative to make proprietary claim on classical virtues and victories (or to question these claims)."[29] Wyke adds, in terms particularly appropriate to *Cabiria* and to the role of Sofonisba, "the projection of ancient Rome on the screen has often worked to place its spectators on the side of decadence and tyranny."[30]

In this context, the historical pleasures offered by the diva in her various incarnations in the Italian cinema of the teens can best be read as a characteristic of the new medium to exploit the possibilities of the moving image. The figure of woman becomes a trope par excellence to enhance the fascination not only with "decadence and tyranny" but with the erotic pleasures of sexual transgression. Her disruptive character is further aligned to the familiar world of racial difference and its associations with uncontrollable power and sensuality that can be found in the silent cinema and in the cinema of the Fascist years. Similarly, *Cabiria* is able to evoke through its spectacles of Carthage a luxurious world alien to the everyday world of its audiences, perhaps only glimpsed in paintings or through such operas as *Aïda.* By contrast, the role of Cabiria, for whom the film is named, further draws on the power of femininity in its other incarnation – as subjugated to the control of others, threatened bodily and subject to their scrutiny [Fig. 6]. Cabiria's character yokes sexuality to questions of difference concerning race and ethnicity. Chaste, submissive, and childlike (even after the film moves ahead ten years to her adulthood), Cabiria is identified by means of her iconography with the European world, whereas Sofonisba belongs to the dark continent of North Africa. In these two female characters the film becomes a metacommentary on cinema in its capacity to unsettle fixed categories of appearance and behavior and as sufficiently powerful to control the threat of disorder.

The portrait of half-clothed Maciste, slave to Fulvius and emblem of superhuman masculine power, is a counterpart to the restrained Romans (Fulvius and Scipio) whose actions are indicative of superior agility, determination, and astuteness. The antecedents for his character are described by Angela Dalle Vacche as follows: "Pastrone's Maciste was cast on the basis of type or physical appearance, according to a theatrical tradition that, in Italian culture, goes

Figure 6. An incarnation of service: Lidia Quaranta as the title character in *Cabiria*. (Courtesy New York Museum of Modern Art Stills Archive)

back to the *commedia dell'arte*. His muscles tell the story."[31] His gestures and appearance reinforce the melodramatic tenor of the film, though the pathos of melodrama always threatens to topple into comedy through the extreme stylization. His character is also a reminder of how the film pilfers various myths – for example, the Samson story when he is chained by his captors to the mill and becomes the subject of taunting [Fig. 7]. All of the portraits of masculinity and femininity in their various theatrical posturing are testimony to a tension between narrative and spectacle. The character of Sofonisba cannot be contained within narrative; rather, she erupts with an excess of gesture and spectacle that is characteristic of most historical extravaganzas and costume dramas. The film's theatricality and spectacle is eclectic rather than tightly tied to a particular ideological direction.

The film's excessiveness can also be found in the ornate and painted title cards of the film. These do more than provide a sense of location, dialogue, and continuity; they point to another aspect of early cinema in the ways that they insist on making themselves evident even when the visual images and action appear to be self-explanatory. Their abundance and ornateness go be-

Figure 7. Bartolomeo Pagano as Maciste in *Cabiria*. (Courtesy New York Museum of Modern Art Stills Archive)

yond their descriptive function and contribute to the excessive visual detail. The titles serve as another source of spectacle parallel to the monstrous Temple of Moloch, with its fiery pit for the child martyrs, the battlements of the North African city of Cirta, and the interior of Sofonisba's palace, crammed with statuary, bas reliefs, paintings, and draperies to highlight luxury, exoticism, and opulence [Fig. 8]. Sofonisba's diaphanous gowns, headdresses, and the ambience of her boudoir offer the spectacle of a cinema given over to sensual delights.

Accompanying the dizzying spectacle of palaces are the scenes of destruction. The initial idyllic scenes of the Sicilian residence of Batto, father of Cabiria, give way to lengthy scenes depicting the devastation of this harmonious setting: fire, smoke, falling pillars and stones [see Fig. 4]. In the insertion

Figure 8. Sofonisba's palace, *Cabiria*. (Courtesy New York Museum of Modern Art Stills Archive)

of Archimedes' invention, the emphasis is on its destructive effects as the images of the burning Roman ships linger on the screen [see Fig. 5]. The characters and action are highlighted through the emphasis on vertical and horizontal space. Throughout the film, the spectator is aware of heights, seen in the images of Mount Etna and of the mountains crossed by the Carthaginians. Fulvio, with the aid of his human ladder and the shields of the men, is able to scale the walls of Cirta; later, with the aid of Maciste, he descends these same walls. The contested Carthaginian battlements are often filmed in long shot to emphasize the raining of stones and boiling oil onto the heads of the Romans. The focus on verticality is related to the film's preoccupation with size, evident in the juxtaposition of the megamuscled Maciste with others, the tininess of humans in relation to the Temple of Moloch, and the ever-present contrast between hordes of people moving in the background and the characters in the foreground. Similarly, the choreography of the palatial tableaux, with carefully positioned groups surrounding the protagonists (especially in Sofonisba's palace) – contrasted with scenes of multitudes scurrying through the streets – also testify to the film's monumentalism.

Magic, which from the earliest short films (especially those of Georges Méliès and his imitators) has been a central feature of the cinema – both as a subject and as a way of describing the cinema's capacity to overcome spatial and temporal boundaries – makes its appearance in *Cabiria.* Here it is associated specifically with the character of Cresa, young Cabiria's nurse, who possesses a magic ring that she later offers to Fulvius when pleading with him to save Cabiria from a fiery death. Though the magic ring does not ostensibly play a prominent role in the ensuing events, the *promise* of magic is everywhere in evidence in the film's use of place and events: for example, in Cresa's chance meeting with Fulvius after her beating; in the delivery of the child Cabiria to Sofonisba, who accepts her; in the later appearance of Cabiria outside Fulvius' and Maciste's cell; in Sofonisba's dream and its realized prophecy; and, at film's end, in the circling female angels superimposed as Fulvius and Cabiria, with Maciste, head for Rome. The narrative thrives on numerous accidents and chance encounters, contingencies that are an indirect sign of the power of cinema to overwhelm, through the magic of technology and its power of illusionism, a sense of actuality and causality.

The importance of theatricality is complicit with the allusions to magic and chance. The film's choreography, uses of landscape, interior settings, and costuming are conjoined to the acting, highlighting not submerging the elements of spectacle and calling attention to the relations between cinema and the other arts. The spectacular character of the cinema transports the spectator into the world of the fantasmatic by way of calling attention to the constructed, not transparent, character of representation.

In contrast to *Cabiria* and *Quo Vadis?, Assunta Spina* (1915) has in histories of Italian cinema been singled out, along with the lost text of *Sperduti nel buio,* "as cinematic paradigms of the naturalist literary tradition of *verismo* and examples of the great national realistic tradition [and] as singular predecessors of neorealism."[32] In this recounting, *Assunta Spina* is distinguished for its "realism" and its ties to regional cinema. Like the films of Elvira Notari, *Assunta Spina* (directed by Gustavo Serena) was made in Naples and relies on the ambience of the city and of Neapolitan culture. This film, too, is an instance of the existence of a regional cinema before the consolidation of filmmaking in Rome. Moreover, *Assunta Spina* is distinguished by the presence of Francesca Bertini, one of the prominent divas and the leading actress of the silent cinema [Fig. 9]. The elevation of these films within these "paradigms" is, of course, another indication of the ways in which cinematic history must perforce function within the context of a "national" cinema. However, *Assunta Spina* poses a number of questions about the nature of realism, its relations to melodrama, and how women are represented in the idiom of melodrama. In several ways, *Assunta Spina* follows many of the thematics

Figure 9. Francesca Bertini in *Assunta Spina*. (Courtesy New York Museum of Modern Art Stills Archive)

and stylistic aspects of Notari's films: in its focus on street life, in the lower-class characters portrayed by members of the lower class, in the linking of their bodies to the city's geography, in the interpenetration of public with private space, and in the reliance on melodrama.

Assunta Spina is a melodrama, employing all the gestural devices of that theatrical genre within the framework of a narrative that focuses on the transgressiveness and disruptive nature of femininity. The film does not present a portrait of a virtuous woman gone astray. Far more interestingly, Assunta's past is portrayed as much less conventional. Her history involves relationships with other men even before her engagement to Michele, and it is this past that creates difficulties for Assunta in the unraveling of the narrative. Raffaele, for example, a jealous and vindictive former lover, seeks to break up the couple's relationship and sends a letter to Michele informing him of Assunta's infidelity. Michele's jealousy causes him to physically attack her and wound her in the face. Though the violence in the film is initiated by men, it is ultimately traced to the woman and to her departure from accepted standards of fidelity and monogamy – a pattern repeated more than once in the film.

When Michele goes to prison, Assunta is seduced by Don Federico's offer of arranging for the transfer of Michele to a Neapolitan prison in exchange for sexual favors. Initially Assunta agrees in order to aid Michele, but inevitably she becomes more deeply involved with Federico. In predictable melodramatic fashion, as she becomes more dependent on him, he tires of her and, also predictably, she becomes more distraught. In the final moments of the film, Assunta is confronted by Michele, released from prison two months early and eager now to resume his relationship with her. He enters her home, sees the table set for company, and questions her about the identity of the guest. She lies and says it is "Peppina," but after his persistent and failing attempts to regain her affection, she confesses her relationship to Don Federico. At the window, Federico sees and is seen by Michele, who grabs a knife from the table and runs out, unable to be restrained by Assunta. He struggles with Federico on the street and stabs him. Mortally wounded, Federico staggers into the room and, after an operatic encounter with Assunta, dies. She crouches on the floor as the police and neighbors arrive. When asked about the identity of the killer, she assumes responsibility for the death. She is led away as one policeman remains by the body, and the final shot of the film is the body of the murdered man.

Assunta Spina was filmed in Naples and, in most of the scenes, the spectator is confronted with images of the Neapolitan landscape. Most prominently featured is the Bay of Naples against which Bertini as Assunta and her lover, Michele (played by director Gustavo Serena) are filmed. In one of the romantic scenes, Assunta and Michele are filmed on a boat with the Bay as background as they exchange embraces. Also in prominence are the streets – not the major metropolitan centers, but the byways, the shops where the protagonists work, and where Raffaele (Alberto Albertini) follows them, planning his revenge on them for Assunta's affection shifting from him to Michele. The buildings are shabby, with graffiti in display; the passageways are narrow. The film is shot largely from stationary and middle-distance positions, eschewing close-ups and camera movement. The action occurs within the frame, and characters enter from offscreen as onto a stage. The intensity of affect among the characters is largely carried by the gestures and action and particularly by the viewer's prior knowledge of the familiar melodramatic scenario of transgression and violence.

The costuming is modest. Assunta is dressed in a plain skirt and blouse, the men in suits. The most notable change in her costume occurs when she dresses for her engagement party and drapes a shawl with long fringes over her. The acting, contrary to usual descriptions of it as highly exaggerated and excessive is, in fact, quite subtle. This subtlety is evident especially during scenes of high tension, as when Michele gets a note from "a well-wisher" informing him that Assunta, consistent with her history, has been cavorting with other men. Director Gustavo Serena, formerly an actor, underplays the melo-dramatic dimensions of the character, allowing for a greater focus on the role of Raffaele, the inevitable obstruction to romance, the initial source of narra-tive discord, and the melodramatic figure that, in familiar fashion, invokes the necessity of violence and the law. However, the socially transgressive charac-ter in the film is finally revealed to be Assunta. Not content to be a submissive partner to any of the men in her life, she, like a femme fatale, is unable to re-main faithful and brings misfortune to the men in her life. As a fatal woman, she incarnates all of the desirable attributes associated with woman as ob-ject to be viewed and possessed, but she is also a threat, since she is the in-carnation of a cultural fantasy and, therefore, illusory and unattainable.

This is a "woman's" film not only because of its focus on a female protag-onist but because, in the unfolding of the narrative, the film clearly reiterates the familiar tropes of woman's transgression and subsequent imprisonment. The law is not merely another vacuous convention but an integral dimension of woman's social containment that invokes legality. Its presence speaks to the melodramatic connection between women's sexuality and the necessity of the law. By confessing to a crime she does not directly commit, Assunta assents to a different infraction – namely, her violation of codes of feminine behavior, already enumerated by Michele's mother and foreseen by the for-tuneteller. These maternal roles link the literal aspects of justice portrayed in the courtroom scenes to the power of the state. Domestic transgressions involve the integrity of the family, and expectations of female monogamy, ser-vice, and loyalty are deemed the basis of civil order.

In its focus on femininity, on the woman's body, and on the problem of who lays claim to that body – the father, the men in her life, and the law – the film does not present her transgression as unattractive. In fact, Bertini's attractiveness as Assunta resides in her beauty, her indifference to others, and her self-absorption. She glides through the film like a somnambulist, the cam-era and her actions stressing her isolation and distinction from others. If she embodies the essence of the diva, it is less in her fiery passion and more in her seeming lack of awareness of her overwhelming effect on others until too late. The film focuses predominantly on her. All events are satellite to her actions. In Bertini's acting, one is aware that the shawl that she dons becomes the sign of her unstable femininity and her attempts to express it. During the sequence of the engagement party, her disfigurement by Michele, and the scenes in the courtroom, she uses the shawl as a bivalent expression of her seductiveness and also of her attempts to ward off threats.

In subsequent scenes, she no longer wears the shawl but is dressed in simple black, foreshadowing her demise, her remorse, and her attempts at restitution. Her gestures are carefully choreographed to convey her ambiva-lence toward the men in her life. In all of her encounters with them, she displays indifference. The men, on the other hand, are involved in scrutinizing her, dogging her footsteps, and punishing her. In her initial meeting with Michele at the train station, she seems reticent to participate wholly in the joy of union with him. In the following scene in her home with her father, her distance is revealed in understated but nonetheless obvious ways, as when she takes her food even before serving him, seeming more interested in it than in him. Even at the engagement party, she appears indifferent to the consequences of Raffaele's toying with her to create conflict with Michele.

The film plays with alternating scenes between the home and the outside world. In her discussion of the melodramas of Notari, Bruno comments on the importance of alternating shots of the home and the street, on the dual role of landscape, in terms that are applicable to *Assunta Spina:* "More than just a background or tableau, the architecture of the city blends into the architecture of the melodrama. Notari's melodrama is intricate, obscure, dark, tortuous, and at times suffocating, like the space of the old district of town used to be."[33] In *Assunta Spina* the landscape dramatizes the tension as well as the relationship between the domestic and the public, interiority and exteriority. It also preserves links with the cinema of attractions insofar as it highlights the urban landscape, calling attention to the tendency of early film to focus on the visual sights of the city, to capitalize on the fascination with the metropolis, and to create vignettes of a familiar urban world. Thus, the film provides the necessary conjunction between the domestic and the public so central to the drama of a beleaguered femininity that stands in the intersection between the public and the private, the home and the world, transgression and the law.

Beginning with the images of the Bay of Naples and of the urban landscape in the distance, focusing on the images of the water and of the boats in the bay, and moving to the streets as the site of movement through the images of pedestrians, crowds, and traffic [Fig. 10], the film increasingly narrows its sites to the legal, then domestic interiors. However, Assunta's dwelling (with its portrait of the Madonna) is a *basso,* a small, cramped basement room that, having been originally intended for a shop, opens directly onto the street. Thus the spectator is aware of movement between the street and the *basso* that links interior to exterior, the public and the domestic spheres. The struggle between Michele and Federico (and Michele's escape) takes place on the street, whereas the death of Federico and Assunta's arrest take place inside the *basso,* invaded by the law. The world has shrunk to the narrow dwelling that, in its use of closed space and noir lighting, appears like a prison to entrap Assunta.

The film, based on a play, has many of the elements associated with theatricality. The scenes are constructed on stage conventions. *Assunta Spina* does not use close-ups of the key characters; during the moments of tension

Figure 10. A Neapolitan street scene, *Assunta Spina*. (Courtesy New York Museum of Modern Art Stills Archive)

the camera remains stationary, confined to the space of the action and to the gestures and actions of the characters that convey their emotional dilemma. The film's theatricality transcends this form of staging, however, implicating the external audience in the narrative as observers to the events along with the internal audiences. Significantly, the conflicts between Assunta and others are underscored by the inclusion of an audience within the frame. There is much that about the film that stresses spectatorship as central to the melodrama, involving the interaction of the protagonist with the various crowds that observe her in critical moments of the action – at the engagement party, during her disfigurement by Michele and his arrest on the street, in the courtroom scenes, and the final, public act of violence observed by passersby. The presence of groups of people creates a sense of the vitality of Neapolitan life but also reinforces the sense of melodrama as theatrical – and juridical. The diegetic and extradiegetic spectators are necessary as witnesses, playing a role as jury in the unfolding of the drama of justice that involves the relations between women and the law.

In using the ambience of Naples, *Assunta Spina* also reveals how the Italian cinema utilizes geography to locate the spectator in a regional landscape, paralleling the uses of everyday life, work, family, and social institutions such as the law courts to enhance the sense of familiarity and hence of realism. Bruno connects this type of *vedutismo* to a sense of the city's "prominent scenic quality and its street energy."[34] These shots serve more than others to convey a sense of a panoramic gaze exhibited also in paintings and photography of the city. The shots are also intimately wedded to melodrama and to theatricality, revealing the city as an integral feature of Italian life in regard to negotiating the various aspects of the conflicts attendant on daily existence.

These early melodramas are instructive as well for what they have to say about cinema spectators of the time – who they were, what the films assumed about their knowledge and what they liked, and also what they could tolerate. Sorlin reminds us that Italian audiences, like other early national audiences, were "educated" into becoming spectators. The process of filmgoing was a gradual coming to terms with the magic of cinema from the early encounters with the mixed media of cinema and the theater, circus, and magic shows to the longer melodramatic and spectacular historical narratives that assumed prominence in the teens with such films as *Cabiria, Assunta Spina, La caduta di Troia,* and Caserini's *Gli ultimi giorni di Pompeii,* among others. In relation to the reception of these films, Sorlin cautions us that:

> We must accept the fact, even if it does not square with our habits, that spectators liked narratives based on major events easily comprehended and remembered, gaps or elisions of minor incidents or even of explanations did not perturb them, and they thoroughly enjoyed the magnificence of the outdoor pictures, the skill in staging massive scenes and the art of the actors.[35]

In short, audiences were receptive and familiar with the "theatricality," the grandiose narratives and style of the films: "Enjoying tear-jerkers was a cultural attitude."[36]

This "cultural attitude" depended on what Antonio Gramsci has termed the "common sense of folklore," a way of regarding the world that is based on "the conditions of the cultural life of a people."[37] These comprise

> various strata, the fossilized ones which reflect conditions of past life and are therefore conservative and reactionary, and those which consist of a series of innovations, often creative and progressive, determined spontaneously by forms and conditions of life which are in the process of developing and which are in contradiction to or simply different from the morality of the governing strata.[38]

Gramsci (for more on whom see Chapter 6) was addressing the formation of a popular culture that drew unashamedly on residues of the past but shaped these according to the tastes of the new media and exigencies of modern life. These melodramas, rather than subjugating their audiences to a monolithic sense of the ideology of nationalism, were more complex: They were educating audiences to the dramatic changes being wrought by the growth of a mass visual culture that could plunder all aspects of history, art, and politics.

Thus, it seems off the point to argue either for or against the idea that Italian cinema was already inherently fascistic, was merely a nationalist medium, or, conversely, merely an escapist opiate of the masses. Indeed, the cinema was intimately tied to a new politics of style and vision that eclectically incorporated nationalist images, conceptions of power identified with images of masculine leadership, virility, and power, and utilized the figure of woman as the source of exchange value, the basis and rationale for community and propriety. However, given the disjointed and fragmented sense of folklore, the ambiguous and polysemous nature of the visual image, and the excessive nature of the theatrical text, what is more evident is the creation of values and ways of looking that eludes one-to-one correlation between film and politics and gives rise instead to what I have described elsewhere as a "politics of style."[39]

This politics of style assumes that audiences were more engaged in a process of detaching themselves from the old world of representation, morality, and belief. The preoccupation with theatricality is characterized by

> a principle of indeterminability, of indiscernability: we no longer know what is imaginary or real, physical or mental, in the situation. . . . It is as if the real and imaginary were running after each other, as if each was being reflected in the other around a point of indiscernability.[40]

Hence, without celebrating the audience's liberation from the world of representation, we might do better to explore the possibility that the new folklore of cinema did foster the conditions for Fascism but in ways that transcend simplistic concepts of gullibility, escapism, and total belief on the part of audiences in the reality of the images viewed.

CHAPTER TWO

National History as Retrospective Illusion

I talian Fascism is identified with the years 1923–45, from the consolidation of the regime to its defeat. Numerous accounts trace its evolution to the immediate post–World War I era and to latent and long-standing dissatisfactions inherent to Italian culture and society, between different classes and political parties, arising from economic, social, and political conditions endemic to the interwar era. Much has been written about the rise of Fascism, tracing it to a significant and changing moment in capital formation, to ultranationalism, to anticommunism, to the status of interwar European politics, to the trials and tribulations of modernity, and to the failure of the Left. In any assessment of the character of Fascism, however, the popular media are key.

Benito Mussolini's role as Il Duce (modeled partially on the personality and politics of Gabriele D'Annunzio) was central to the movement and regime. Starting as a socialist but later abandoning his ties to socialism, Mussolini was impatient of liberalism and of intellectualism. An advocate of revolutionary action rather than reflection, he surrounded himself with individuals and groups, later called "The Fascists of the First Hour," who by means of intimidation and force undertook to alter Italy. Integral to the Fascist's evolving program were increasing the power of the state, enhancing the image and power of Italy as a nation to be reckoned with internationally, destroying the socialists and communists, breaking the power of the labor unions, and moving Italy into the modern world through an emphasis on increased capitalist productivity, imperialism, colonialism, and war.

Toward these ends, the regime sought to win the hearts and minds of the people, to alter existing patterns of life by intervening in education in the attempt to "Fascistize" young people, developing a number of social institutions: the ONB (Operazione Nazionale Balilla) for young boys and girls, the GUF (Gioventù Universitaria Fascista) for university students, and the OND (Opera Nazionale Dopolavoro) for the organization of leisure-time activities, as well as the ONMI (Opera Nazionale per la Maternità ed Infanzia) for the promotion of motherhood. In the arena of print, radio, and cinema, the regime sought also to shape the national culture in what it perceived to be the desirable aims of Fascism.[1] Despite its aims, Fascism was never able to totalize Italian culture and society (although it could employ coercion), because of internal oppositions between Right and Left within the party and the government, and because it never had a coherent sense of direction. There was never total adherence: The desire for profit conflicted with ideology, and the emphasis on tradition (the land, motherhood, home, and family) conflicted with the increasing modernization of the culture.

Filmmaking was central to the regime's objectives of shaping the culture according to the objectives of Fascism; but the Italian film industry was in a precarious state after World War I, its once dominant and influential role having been reduced to a mere shadow. Several factors contributed to this crisis in film production: lack of organization and integration on the part of the industry; improvising rather than taking stock of new social and economic realities; the staggering costs imposed by the system of *divismo,* tied to the great expense of historical and melodramatic spectacles; the loss of the foreign market, most particularly to competition from the United States (what Brunetta has described as "the long march of Hollywood in Italy"), which established the preference on the part of Italian audiences for American narratives and actors; and the resistance to adopting new cinematic forms, new technologies, and reconstituted forms of organization to capitalize on changing social and cultural conditions.[2] The Unione Cinematografica Italiana (UCI) was formed in 1919 to encourage investment and to regulate and stimulate production, but little substantive change was evident. The films being produced were largely remakes and poor ones at that, and the financial situation worsened. By 1923, production had fallen to fifty films.[3]

Committed to the notion of cinema as a weapon in the service of Fascism, L'Unione Cinematografica Educativa (LUCE) was formed in 1923 as a cooperative venture for the production of documentaries and newsreels that were to be shown in commercial film theaters along with the feature films. The organization was founded for purposes of using the cinema largely as a medium of education and propaganda. Nationalized in 1925, it was, in effect, a variation on Soviet agitprop, creating films to be screened in theaters and in traveling trucks (auto cinemas), bringing cinema to the people, especially to rural areas where there were no theaters. The films produced by LUCE covered a wide variety of topics, touching on all aspects of agriculture, industry, sports, culture, health, and education. In contrast to commercial filmmaking, where a conflict between state control and private initiative was evident, LUCE was tightly tied to the government and the party. Their personnel were bound to the dictates of the regime, portraying the successes of Fascism even in the last dire years of World War II.

In the arena of commercial film production, in the ongoing political and cultural tension between profitability and ideology, commerce often took precedence over Fascist propaganda. According to Elaine Mancini:

> [W]hile the policies of LUCE were understood and clearly followed
> . . . in the commercial industry no such understanding existed. . . .
> [F]ew feature filmmakers seemed to be members of the Fascist Party,
> despite enticements to join. Second, the response to governmental
> policy in the commercial film industry varied according to the differ-
> ent personalities. . . . In short, unpredictable reactions prevailed;
> while the government encouraged conformism, the film industry
> seemed to encourage individualism.[4]

If the films of LUCE, such as *Camicia nera* (Black Shirt, 1933), are revealing
for their adherence to propaganda, the commercial films offer a portrait that
is more mixed and contradictory, ranging from those like *Vecchia guardia*
(*The Old Guard,* 1934) and *L'assedio dell'Alcazar* (*The Siege of the Alcazar,*
1940), which seem closely aligned to the ideology of Fascism, to such films
as *Il cappello a tre punte, Sorelle Materassi,* and *Ossessione,* which appear
critical of Fascist attitudes. Moreover, the bulk of the films produced during
the era, including the so-called *telefoni bianchi* (upper-class comedies named
for their inclusion of a white telephone in the boudoir) are not easily relegated to the position of mere frivolous and vacuous texts serving the Fascist
cause by diverting audiences from political and social realities. The comedies,
the historical spectacles, and the costume dramas – in short, the sound films
of the Ventennio (the almost twenty years of Fascism) – are often comparable
in technique and perspective to many of the films produced in Hollywood,
a source of inspiration for Italian commercial filmmakers.

The regime was slow to intervene and support the ailing commercial film
industry, though certain individuals, most notably Stefano Pittaluga, sought
to redress the crisis in production through more centralization, a balance between foreign and indigenous films, and the encouragement of new directors.
Furthermore, there were ineffectual attempts to stem the tide of foreign films,
particularly Hollywood films, and one of the biggest threats to the industry
was apparent with the coming of sound on film. The problems connected
to the transition to sound were not entirely economic but also aesthetic and
ideological. On the positive side, sound provided the much-needed opportunity to assess necessary changes in film models; it gave rise to many debates
in books and journals about the new possibilities for cinematic expression
in forms of narrative and uses of image, dialogue, and music.

By the 1930s, though progress was slow, new directions and signs of an
upswing in this precarious moment for Italian film were evident. While many
companies went under, while audience receipts dropped, while taxes on film
profits were considerable, and while it was impossible (and unprofitable) to
curtail non-Italian films completely, slowly and with the help of the regime –
but without nationalization of the industry as had been advocated by Luigi
Freddi, director of the Office of Cinematography under the Ministry of Pop-

ular Culture (Minculpop) – signs of melioration were evident. Sound on film was enhanced by the introduction of musicals, with an especial emphasis on popular music. New recruits to the film industry were experimenting with new models, such as the literary works of Luigi Pirandello, which were being adapted for the screen with his cooperation.

Alessandro Blasetti, a young filmmaker who challenged the conventional and grandiose style of the historical epic and melodramas with such early sound films as *Terra madre* (1930) and *Resurrectio* (1931), was to become a major director of films during the era and beyond. Influenced by Fascism, as he acknowledged, his early films focus on the dramas of agrarian life, the conflicts of and debilitating aspects of modernity, with careful attention to characterization, mise-en-scène (it was not unusual for large segments of his films to be shot on location), and a penchant for a montage editing reminiscent of pre-Stalinist Soviet cinema. With the coming of sound, the silent-film diva slowly gave way to the working girl, the palace to the working-class home, and the gladiatorial arena to the department store (though historical spectacles were still an important genre during the 1930s and early 1940s). If Blasetti was the cinematic poet of tradition and of *strapaese,* with its focus on the ideology of ruralism and agrarian life, Mario Camerini was the chronicler, albeit not uncritically, of the city and of modernity identified with the ideology of *stracittà.* One of the directors in the cinema of the Ventennio popular for both his comedies and melodramas, Camerini was influenced by Hollywood and the French cinema (in particular, Jean Renoir's *Boudu sauvé des eaux* [*Boudu Saved from Drowning,* 1932]).

Innovations in cinema production were slowly effected by the Fascists: the Venice Film Festival was established in 1932, and a film school, the Centro Sperimentale di Cinematografia, was created during the mid-1930s. The period saw the appearance of new directors, scriptwriters, and technicians, many of whom had bolted to other countries during the disastrous twenties but returned in the thirties (e.g., Goffredo Alessandrini and Amleto Palermi). A steady rise in the number of Italian films was concurrent with a decrease in the number of non-Italian films in the theaters between 1930 and 1939. During the war, the numbers of imports, especially from Hollywood, decreased dramatically. In the arena of censorship, while little new was added to the list of prohibitions, the regime was by the 1930s more watchful, specifically in relation to politically seditious subject matter. (Camerini's 1935 film, *Il cappello a tre punte,* was excised as a result of scenes that appeared too critical of reigning practices.) In general, most scholars of the cinema of the era agree that the commercial film industry was "relatively free from government control and intervention."[5] This is not say that filmmakers did not exercise forms of autocensorship, but the bottom line for a lot of commercial production was to make the films profitable at home and, if possible, abroad.

According to Walter Adamson and others, there was no coherent political viewpoint at any time from the inception of Fascism in 1922 through 1932,

> when the first attempt to state a fascist "doctrine" was made. On the contrary, fascism made a fetish out of being an "anti-ideology," just as it was an "anti-party". . . . [I]f we nonetheless take it as a political doctrine in the strict sense, we are apt to miss many of the mythic and performative elements (rituals, styles) that most clearly link it to the culture out of which it grew.[6]

Like other national cinemas of the era, the cinema under Fascism ransacked earlier historical moments – the Roman Empire, the Renaissance, the Risorgimento, and World War I – to create a pastiche of elements drawn from popular folklore, literature, theater, opera, and current events. As Gianfranco Mino Gori explains, the historical film was a genre dear to the hearts of Fascist ideologues, since grandiose analogies could be made between Italy's glorious past and those of contemporary Fascism.[7]

The cinema's uses of "factual" history are a major source of the "mythic and performative elements" endemic to Italian culture during the Fascist era. However, in identifying the relation between past and present, one is confronted by the difficulty of defining cinematic uses of the past against factual notions of history. One is also confronted by the problem of how to read and understand the nature and effects of performance, the rituals and styles alluded to by Adamson. In the case of the Italian cinema under Fascism, which produced a goodly amount of historical films, it is tempting to ascribe its particular uses of history as monolithically serving Fascist culture and society. The sense of history communicated is fictive and eclectic: It is also affective, inflected by the structures of melodrama concerning the efficacy of action, questions of justice, and considerations of power.[8] The historical films proper, rather than being tailored to a political program, follow genre requirements in their treatment of narrative, creation of character, and evocation of place and time. In addition, they exceed any "messages" in their uses of spectacle. They reveal not one but a range of models – monumental, antiquarian, and critical – taking the forms of the historical film, the costume drama, the adventure film, and the biopic. These forms are altered depending on the filmmaker's predilections, the genre employed, the particular historical moment selected, and the point in time in which the films are produced (i.e., early or late in the lifetime of the Fascist regime).

Some of these films appear to be celebrating a glorious national past, not uncommon to other national cinemas, portraying the past as a locus of spectacle, a site of visual pleasure. In others, the past is a source of nostalgia, a place of fantasy, and a judgment on the present. The common denominator resides in the ways affect is mobilized in the uses of narrative, image, and sound. These historical films focus on the energetic and zealous efforts of exceptional individuals to direct events of the nation in the name of the people, on the struggle to attain power, and on the violence generated from this struggle. The drama of the imperiled nation and the clash between insider and outsider, loyal leader and traitor, legitimacy and illegitimacy are central. In these ways, the films are not so different from British Empire films or the Hollywood western. The signs of a nationalist rhetoric and symbology, with its reliance on melodramatic conventions drawn from nineteenth-century literature and opera, are evident.

The historical film and costume drama are operatic, relying on motifs characteristic of Verdian opera. Regarding questions of an Italian national-popular culture and its relation to the operatic, Antonio Gramsci wrote,

> Verdi's music, or rather the libretti and plots of the plays set to music by Verdi, are responsible for a whole range of artificial poses in the life of the people, for ways of thinking, for a "style." "Artificial" is perhaps not the right word because among popular classes this artificiality assumes naïve and moving forms . . . a means of escaping what they consider low, mean, and contemptible in their lives and education. . . .[9]

The relationship between opera and the cinema of the era can be seen in such films as *La serva padrona* (1934) and *Giuseppe Verdi* (1938). The literal uses of opera are overshadowed, however, by the operatic character of many of the melodramas of the late 1930s and early 1940s directed by Mario Soldati, Renato Castellani, Ferdinando Maria Poggioli, and Amleto Palermi, who derived many of their scenarios from nineteenth-century literary works. Giuseppe Adami, who wrote the libretto for Puccini's *Turandot*, was also responsible for the scenario of such films as *Ballerine* (1936). Camerini had recourse to the literary text on which the opera *Il cappello a tre punte* was based, and Palermi's *Cavalleria rusticana* (1939), though operatic in its style, was also based on a literary text.

Interconnection among the novelistic, the operatic, and the melodramatic, rooted in nineteenth-century culture,

> begins with Cuoco and Foscolo and passes through Manzoni and D'Azeglio. . . . [We can identify] the aesthetics of astonishment, moral Manichaeism, and the rhetoric of excess . . . brought to extreme consequences (logical if not artistic) as functions of the *école du coeur,* of civic education, and of the democratization of morality and its signs.[10]

The style of these writers is marked by a straining toward sublimity, religiosity, and sensuality. The landscape and especially the ruins of the past are objects of reflection and semiotic markers for the psychic state of the characters, an elegiac, nostalgic locus of cultural aspirations and anxieties.[11] The operatic character of the cinematic text, with its fascination for spectacle drawn from the past, can also be identified in the uses of music and choreography, especially in the choreography of groups. The use of music as song and as accompaniment functions as a major expressive mode to create a sense of the ambience and convey the emotional valences of interactions between the characters. In the sense that Peter Brooks describes the "mute gesture" characteristic of melodrama in its attempt to express the ineffable and inexpressible, music is the carrier of the characters' attempts to convey what words cannot encompass.[12] Dance is also central, evident in the spectacle of balls, military formations, and festivals and serving as a means of choreographing group relations.

The operatic style most emulated is that of Giuseppe Verdi's work, with its emphasis on the motif of sacrificial leadership. The accent is on heroic service and self-abnegation. The melodrama functions in Manichaean terms, differentiating hero and villain. The forest, grotto, and cave are the archetypal loci for the dramas of conversion, conveying the magical quality of the filmic world. Magic, like religion, provides an index to the supernatural or spiritual character of the conflicts, associated with the overarching sense of the power of the protagonist's might and will. Linked to nationalistic themes, these operatic works situate the protagonist beyond individual and personal interests and identify his actions with the fate of the people in whose name the actions are undertaken. The paintings, tableaux, and statuary they reference are identified with the national culture and especially with its patriotic symbols.

The monumentalism identified with an operatic treatment in literature, theater, and cinema has its roots in nineteenth-century historicism. Friedrich Nietzsche, in his *Untimely Meditations,* has much to say about the theatricality and excessiveness of this type of historicizing, referring to monumental history as

> [the] masquerade costume in which . . . [the historians'] hatred of the great and powerful of their own age is disguised as satiated admiration for the great and powerful of past ages, and muffled in which they invert the real meaning of that mode of regarding history into its opposite. Whether they are aware of it or not, they act as though their motto were: let the dead bury the living.[13]

The portrait of the "great and powerful of past ages" has been a staple of the commercial cinema, exemplified particularly by the films that are set in classi-

Figure 11. A spectacle of Roman unity, *Scipione l'Africano*. (Courtesy New York Museum of Modern Art Stills Archive)

cal times. This type of history, closely identified with the teens through the 1930s in Hollywood and in Europe, only indirectly makes connections between past and present.

The Italian sound spectacle of the 1930s, *Scipione l'Africano* (1937), directed by Carmine Gallone, was indebted to a classical subject involving the events of the Second Punic War, 297 B.C. Created in a vein reminiscent of the earlier historical epics (discussed in Chapter 1) but modified to meet the demands of the sound cinema and the tenor of popular film of the decade, *Scipione* offers a cinematic spectacle to vie with the "epics" of D. W. Griffith and Cecil B. DeMille [Fig. 11]. The film deploys every aspect of melodramatic representation and technological expertise to provide a monumental and spectacular treatment of the past. In encyclopedic fashion, it conjoins familial relations, homosocial bonding, unrequited and doomed passion, relations between the Roman populace and the military forces, and an imaginative recreation of the decisive battle between Rome and Carthage. *Scipione* draws on the conventions associated with the historical film: paintings, murals, costuming, architectural models, large casts, ritualistic ceremonies, and elaborate choreography of crowd scenes. Relying on orchestrated uses of long and medium shots and frequent close-ups, the film links perception to action and action to affect, thus providing the necessary connections between the subsets of the film and the film as a whole:

> each of these movement-images is a point of view on the whole film, a way of grasping this whole, which becomes affective in the close-up, active in the medium shot, perceptive in the long-shot – each of these shots ceasing to be spatial in order to become itself a "reading" of the whole film.[14]

The narrative of *Scipione* focuses on the militant conflicts between Romans and Carthaginians conveyed through images of the Roman Senate, the Carthaginian camp, and battle scenes. The action, however, relies predominantly on the two protagonists – Scipio and Hannibal – who contend for power. The melodrama centers on the feminine figures, particularly Sofonisba (Francesca Braggiotti), whose character is also central to *Cabiria,* and a Roman woman, Velia (Isa Miranda). As is conventional in historical films, a title situates the time in which the filmic events will take place, alluding to the century-old rivalry between the two nations. The initial images are of a smoking field, then of the exterior of the Roman Senate with crowds gathered to await the arrival of Scipio (Annibale Ninchi). The spectacle of the masses is intercut with Scipio's arrival, the editing stressing his singularity by cross-cutting between him and the crowd, connecting him with yet also separating him from the Roman people.

The element of spectatorship is introduced via point-of-view shots, first in long shot, then in close-up, providing perspective on the scene by means of individuals and groups in the massive gathering. Similarly, in the scenes that follow in the Senate, shots alternate between the gathered senators and individual speakers as a debate ensues over the feasibility of Scipio's undertaking a campaign against Hannibal in Carthage. Spectatorship is highlighted through intercutting of the groups within the Senate and those without, serving to underscore the unanimity of sentiment between insiders and outsiders. The episode culminates with the appearance of the victorious Scipio, who is tracked by the camera as he emerges from the building and walks through the parted masses. The choreography of his movement in relation to the thousands of people is accompanied by singing and loud orchestral music.

Following the public spectacle that opens the film, the scene shifts to the home of Scipio and to his wife [Fig. 12] as she gathers her jewelry to contribute it to the Roman cause. Size and perspective are mobilized for effect. The Madonna-like image of the woman with her baby is contrasted to the image of Scipio in his uniform of a Roman warrior with his young son, also in uniform – a miniature version of the father.

Figure 12. Roman domesticity: Scipione's wife in *Scipione l'Africano*. (Courtesy New York Museum of Modern Art Stills Archive)

The images of domestic harmony are shattered in the following scene, as the Roman Velia and her child are taken captive by the Carthaginians. This introduces the melodramatic element of the defenselessness of women in the face of war, their sexual exploitation at the hands of the enemy. Hannibal, seeing her, desires her as his concubine, but she refuses to succumb to him and is ultimately saved by Scipio and by Velia's fiancé, Arunte, who also had been a prisoner of Hannibal. The film is built on escalating parallels and contrasts. Velia is contrasted to the seductive and tigresslike Sofonisba, Hannibal to Scipio, the Carthaginian senators and masses to the Roman senators and masses, and each army to the other. The contrasting montage visually stresses order and disorder, discipline and rebellion, desire and duty.

The affective, visually excessive, and hence highly theatrical character of the narrative resides particularly in the figure of Sofonisba as a Cleopatra- and Dido-like figure, a throwback to the femme fatale of the Italian silent cinema, whose power is so great that she can cause men like Massinissa (Fosco Giachetti) to forsake their principles. Her sensuality is conveyed through her costuming, makeup, languid gesturing, the exotic mise-en-scène, and her identification with fire and with poison. She is filmed frequently in close-up, especially for the scenes of her suicide. In a nocturnal sequence, an image of the restless queen on her bed is superimposed with an image of her dragged through the flames of burning Carthage, foreshadowing not only her end but that of her realm. After the defeat of Carthage, she commits suicide in a highly operatic scene. Beginning and ending with a wipe, the camera focuses on a cup of poison, a hand and its tapered nails wrapped around the chalice. The camera then captures her face in close-up as she expresses her desire as queen to die for Carthage. She drinks the poison, intense music accompanying her gestures. The operatic death scene is significant for the ways in which femininity is identified with fragmentation and dissolution. Once again, spectatorship is stressed as an old man comes in, witnesses her dying, covers his face, and exits.

The film appears to recapitulate motifs aligned to contemporary events in Italy in the mid-1930s: the exaltation of a wise and powerful leader, the emphasis on preparation for war (in Africa, even), and the highlighting of the importance of agricultural as well as weapons production to support the war effort. This meeting of past and present is consistent with the conventions of the historical film and is, in the case of *Scipione,* a sign of the eclecticism and ambivalent historicizing characteristic of the era's cinema. Aside from the affective power of the images of violence, suffering, and death conjured through the scenes of battle, the rhetorical uses of women and children are not merely devices for enlisting sympathy in the face of the bloodthirsty and arbitrary Carthaginians but are closely tied to the film's melodramatic structure and style. The binary opposition between the legitimate power of Rome and the barbarism of the Carthaginians is exemplified in the iconography of the choreographed daylight world of the Romans versus the chaotic twilight world of their African enemies.

Scipione, while tied to the silent cinema, adds new, self-reflexive elements in its visual acknowledgment of the importance of style, design, posture, and observation. History becomes a stage. The composition, choreography, the mise-en-scène – all point to the use of people as objects, machines, and geometric patterns [Fig. 13]. The spectator is bombarded with images and sound, as if invited to entertain the spectacle. Gesture and physical movement become a form of seduction, an invitation to enjoy historical pleasures, aided by the music that overwhelms the dialogue, geared toward enhancing sentiment and evoking admiration for the vastness and virtuosity of the cinematic canvas. However, the alternating scenes of high court intrigue, battle, and domesticity creates a bridge between the remote and the familiar.

James Hay suggests that "the feature that distinguishes Scipione from many of his counterparts in silent movies and that aligns him with a more petit-bourgeois ideology is his dual role as family man and as a statesman/warrior."[15] Scipio's ultimate return to the land and to his family naturalizes the

Figure 13. Choreography of the masses, *Scipione l'Africano*. (Courtesy New York Museum of Modern Art Stills Archive)

preceding violence. Nevertheless, reading the film with regard to the excess with which it surrounds the figure of woman – especially in relation to Sofonisba and her association with the all-consuming fire – these final domestic images invite speculation on the reception of such a film. Can this last image of order and domesticity be reconciled with the operatic (and familiar) spectacle of Sofonisba's disruptive femininity, also identified with nature?

What is not so straightforward are the conditions of the film's initial reception. This raises the nagging question of whether, in its uses of genre and spectacular uses of image and sound, the film exposes or masks its nationalistic ideology, or even whether its nationalistic orientation was a primary feature in its reception. Although well-received by critics, winning the coveted Mussolini Cup at the Venice Film Festival, and though a reading of the film in terms of its patriotic and nationalist images might confirm its consonance with Fascist ideology and its celebration of the regime, *Scipione* invites a more complex assessment. As is characteristic of popular cinema, its uses of the past are heterogeneous, fragmented rather than totalizing. The film's style –

its spectacle associated with its stars, its choreography of crowd scenes, its preoccupation with spectatorship, theatricality, and intertextuality – suggests a looser and more eclectic relation to audiences. The style speaks to the use of history as a realm of fantasy in a way, as described by Sue Harper, that "grants a freedom to the audience to maneuver its own way through narrative codes."[16] As Iain Chambers writes in relation to history and memory:

> There exists no simple and direct recovery of how things "really were," only of how things come to be remembered and translated, not what happened, but what is happening. So everything is both remembered and repressed, every testimony is flawed. . . . Memory, whether personal or psychoanalytical, or collective and historical, dwells in an ambiguous landscape.[17]

Scipione l'Africano exemplifies the slippery ways that history functions in the popular cinema. For this reason, it is difficult to fix the text as a mere reproduction of Fascist ideology. Although the film may evoke images of the leader, the drama of the imperiled nation, and the glorification of war, it complicates the history that it portrays through its reliance on spectacle, its uses of music, and its melodrama, confusing what is "real" with what is "fictional" and inviting uncertainty about the nature of historicizing through cinema.[18]

Not all historical films are cast in the monumental mold. The Italian films that focus on the classical era seem to have a predilection for the grandiose, but other historical moments were also portrayed in the cinema. For example, the Renaissance is the context for *Lorenzino de' Medici* (1935) and *Condottieri* (1937), whereas *1860* (1934), *Il dottor Antonio* (1937), and *Piccolo mondo antico* (*Little Old-Fashioned World,* 1941) take as their subject the Risorgimento, the nineteenth-century movement to combine discrete regions into a unified Italy. The subject of novels, dramas, poetry, and painting, the Risorgimento reaches deep into Italian cultural and political life, generating competing political and cultural attitudes about the formation of Italy as a nation. For some writers, the Risorgimento symbolizes a successful struggle for unity; for others it constitutes a failure in that revolutionary goals were betrayed by the subsequent hegemony of North over South. The rhetoric of the Risorgimento was invoked by the Fascists in their attempts to define their movement as a realization of a revolution begun in the nineteenth century.

Alessandro Blasetti was one of the most prolific and popular historical filmmakers of the Fascist era. After a long career in cinema extending into the postwar years, he died in 1987. Blasetti worked in a number of genres – comedy, melodrama, fantasy, biographical and historical films. Despite his avowed commitment to Fascism in the early years of the regime, his films reveal that they are foremost cinematic texts that resist the narrow prescriptions of propaganda even when they are most closely tied to Fascist motifs. In his films, there is no strident nationalism, though there is an emphasis on national unity. His settings usually valorize the country over the city, and the most sympathetic characters are usually peasants, working-class, or displaced and marginalized figures.

Blasetti's *1860* is his unique attempt to find a film language suitable to convey his conception of the Risorgimento from the perspective of Sicilian peasants and on the soil of Sicily. The actions of the film are geared to the anticipation of Garibaldi's victory at Catalfimi. According to Blasetti, the narration is consonant with Fascist ideology – the emphasis on the unity of town and country and a populism that links classes and different regions, and the creation of a culture that exemplifies the overcoming of differences. The film draws on several art forms – painting, music, and literature – as well as on popular patriotic motifs. The Risorgimento is seen as a national melodrama through the eyes of its peasant protagonists, Carmeliddu (Giuseppe Gulino) and Gesuzza (Aida Bellia). The film, a combination of location and studio settings, of professional and nonprofessional actors, offers further verification of the compatibility between realism and melodrama.

According to Angela Dalle Vacche, "In representing the Risorgimento, Blasetti confronted a dilemma previously tackled by the Macchiaioli painters, how to revitalize the historical classical scene with the insertion of elements drawn from daily life and regional genre paintings."[19] Roberto Campari also discusses how the film relies on the paintings of Giovanni Fattori as well as on images derived from Sergei Eisenstein.[20] Along with the insertion of images from paintings and the creation of scenes in the style of nineteenth-century painting, Blasetti created through the action and the music an operatic text that invokes the rhetorical tropes of nineteenth-century opera, in contrast to the actual performance of an opera on film. The term "operatic" stresses the combined effect of character, image, and music to create the sense of scope of events and their melodramatic intensity in the service of heroic narratives of the nation and of power. The stylization of opera is further evoked through the emphasis on the southern Italian landscape as background, the choreographed character of the shots, and the highly stylized use of montage. In the cinematic representation of historical events, the bond between spectator and produced history is based on the effective marshaling of visual and auditory images derived from paintings. The film validates Pierre Sorlin's conception of cinematic history, which

> looks a bit like school history. . . . Classical history films were artefacts which attempted to reenact, recreate, dead events. The scenery had to be accurate and to conform to the models already offered by

pictures or engravings. . . . Actors recited elaborate texts which were
lectures on history and encapsulated what was considered the "spirit" of an epoch.[21]

The strange conjunction of artifice with the emphasis on accuracy, the co-
habitation of the fictional and the "authentic," is a major characteristic of
opera and of historical/costume films, revealing cinematic representation as
both "possible and fallacious." The historical film demands to be read in complex fashion through the treatment of its various artifacts, its borrowings from
the other arts, and the various ways in which it deploys music. From the
opening moments of the film, the film enunciates its rhetorical concerns. The
music functions throughout the film as signifier for the intense emotions invested in a struggle for national unity. The music will also be identified with
nature and with the innocence of the Sicilians, and as a bridge connecting
nature and the revolution.

The orchestration serves as a bridge to the setting, connecting landscape
to revolution. Variations in tempo, volume, and intensity enhance contrasts
in mood, character, and moral position. The images of the landscape assume
a mystical significance, reinforced by music, that seems to transcend their spe-
cificity, becoming part of the film's dialectical structure, particularly evident
in the film's portrayal of the opposition between the foreigners and the Sicilian (soon to be Italian) population. In addition, the use of chiaroscuro lighting distinguishes the enemy from the clear images of the heroic villagers. The
choreography also differentiates between the unnaturalness of the Austrian
mercenaries – their rigid mechanical movement in columns – in contrast to
the more fluid and random movement of the Sicilians, movements that are
identified with nature.

The visual and auditory distinctions paint a melodramatic canvas in
which the lines are clearly drawn between friend and foe, patriot and inter-
loper. The assignment of horizontal and vertical positions is metaphoric. The
images of reclining and rising, like movement and stasis, become important
as a way of measuring progress, but are also proleptic insofar as the notion
of rising is associated with the notion of the Risorgimento. The enemy is also
identified with jarring sounds, abrupt interruptions, entrances and exits,
whereas softly played patriotic music identifies the Sicilians. To enhance the
stages of the conflict a voice-over describes the course of events, losses and
gains. The voice-over, like the voice-of-God narration in documentary, is maintained throughout the film, commenting on changes in the action and providing an oracular sense, explanation, and historical authority. The film does
not depend on suspense; the outcome is known both by virtue of its historical subject matter and through its use of paintings and patriotic Italian theme
music. The emphasis falls on a realization of the already known, a rehearsal

of events that are drawn from history, but a history that requires repetition and heroic embellishment.

A moving camera records the panorama, the sense of the forces arrayed, and the rhythm of events. The camera movements are accompanied by loud or soft orchestral music, depending on the rise and fall of action. The use of tableaux, characteristic of operatic performance and of historical films, militates against the very naturalness the film seeks to espouse. The immobile image of Carmeliddu and Gesuzza when they are first observed, lying affectionately next to each other until awakened at the priest's request to serve the cause, is a painting that comes to life. Their movement, too, seems choreographed rather than random. The various groups of villagers are also drawn from pastoral paintings, as are the later scenes in the church. The rhythm of the peasant's lives is marked by tableaux of collectivity that are disrupted by the enemy. Time is related to the future and to the anticipated arrival of Garibaldi announced at the outset, and also to the desired return of the past in the present.

The costumes by Nino Vittorio Novarese are instrumental in developing the class and national opposition that the film pursues in relation to the peasants, the Bourbons, and the middle-class intellectuals that Carmeliddu meets on his journey to Garibaldi. As befits her peasant status, Gesuzza is dressed simply, but she is filmed in a highly stylized manner. Despite her apparent similarity to the other women, she is frequently distinguished from them as an icon of familial and conjugal devotion through the use of low camera angles and of close-ups. Carmeliddu, shot in similar fashion, is an icon of national purity and devotion in relation to the other men and to Gesuzza. The Bourbons are encased in their tightly fitting, ornate uniforms, whereas the Sicilian men are seen in their rough-hewn shirts and fleece pants, which, like the rocky landscape they inhabit, suggests primitiveness. The peasants are presented as childlike and inarticulate. Their treatment is reminiscent of Gramsci's critique of Manzoni's peasant characters in *I promessi sposi.*

The barbarism of the Bourbons is conveyed by their wanton killing of a young boy, a victim in this Manichaean struggle between good and evil. The child is a significant figure in the films of the Fascist era in such films as *Vecchia guardia,* a signifier of martyrdom, and a vehicle for the legitimization of vengeance (see Chapter 9). The slow movement of the horse that brings the boy's body back to the village conveys a further reproach to the inhumanity of the enemy. The music swells as the animal approaches the waiting priest (Gianfranco Giachetti). The priest's slow and methodical laying out of boy's body under the impatient observation of the Bourbon officer heightens the sense in which the church is the aligned with the people, that the cause for which they fight is (to quote one Italian critic of the time) "sacred." In the church scenes, the music is ritualistic and the tableau of the people chanting their prayers reinforces the motif of unity between church and emergent state. Carmeliddu's departure is accompanied by lyrical music. His boat journey serves metaphorically to connect Sicily, his origin, to Genoa, his destination. The passage of his journey is interrupted several times with scenes of battle between Bourbons and peasants, culminating in the brutal roundup of the peasants by their captors, underscoring the urgency of Carmeliddu's journey. Carmeliddu, unconscious, is rescued from a watery grave by a French ship, which brings him to port. Water shots will be reiterated on the return journey that brings Garibaldi and his men to Sicily. The journeys on the water, accompanied by the musical score, function as a bridge, linking music to images of landscape, and individuals to a political destination.

The spoken language and dialect differentiate the various individuals and groups involved in the conflict. Linguistic differences highlight regional ones, and language is central to this film of national unity, serving several functions. The coexistence of spoken Italian, German, and French functions as a reminder of foreign domination. For example, Carmeliddu is unable to understand the French who saved him. Significantly, unlike in neorealist films, the Sicilians for the most part do not speak the Sicilian dialect. On the rare occasions that they speak, they use official language, as if marking their assimilation into the future national landscape. In fact, many of the scenes shot in Sicily do not rely on dialogue. The film distinguishes between the plain style of communication of Carmeliddu, in particular, and the ornate style of communication of the middle- and upper-class intellectuals he meets on his arrival in Civitavecchia. His role as silent subaltern is evident when he listens to men arguing about the number of French troops present, the atrocities committed against women and children, and the destruction of churches.

Later, he is also audience to men of differing political persuasions arguing over the best course of events for the emerging nation – union between church and state, monarchy with Victor Emmanuel, or a republic headed by Mazzini. These differences are to be resolved in the victory of Garibaldi, which will be identified with the triumph of the monarchy under the house of Savoy. Carmeliddu breaks his silence only to ask others on his journey penetrating questions about Garibaldi's identity. His demeanor and questions underscore his peasant origins and, hence, his lack of sophistication [Fig. 14]. His simplicity and directness distance him from the political machinations and from the sophistry of the various political groups struggling for control, and his difference keeps him from quarrelsome intellectuals. He is identified by his single-minded commitment to Garibaldi as a man of action.

The specifically contemporary perspective of *1860* can be seen in the valorization of action over thought, reminiscent of Gramsci's discussions of common sense as the "popular philosophy of the masses . . . an element of cohesive force exercised by the ruling classes and therefore an element of

Figure 14. Carmeliddu (Giuseppe Gulino), *1860.* (Courtesy New York Museum of Modern Art Stills Archive)

subordination to an external hegemony."[22] The commonsense rejection of thought and, hence, the rejection of difference, serves in this context to underline the impossibility of making difference disappear except by coercion. In its melodramatic treatment of the various groups, the film only exposes the depth of dissimilarities. The uses of Risorgimento history come more clearly into focus as that earlier history is read as the authentic origin for the Fascist emphasis on national unity, and especially as a basis for overcoming oppositions between North and South.

The final scenes are reminiscent of the battle paintings shown at the beginning of the film. The film choreographs the movement of the two groups, the Bourbons and the Garibaldians. Interspersed are scenes of Carmeliddu, seeking Gesuzza, whose father had kept her away from the battle through subterfuge. Also intercut are images of flowers and trees, signifying rebirth, juxtaposed to scenes of battle [Fig. 15]. Shots of the Italian flag are accompanied by the ever-swelling theme music. The Garibaldians sing as they go to fight, and music (especially the sound of trumpets) is skillfully edited to advance or retard the various lines of group movement. The sound is interspersed with moments of silence. An elegiac tableau is intercut with scenes of intense fighting as Gesuzza comes across a dying soldier – a boy shown earlier with his mother at the men's departure for Sicily. Gesuzza cradles his head and, as the boy dies, Carmeliddu comes running to her, shouting, "Italy has been saved." The film ends with the waving of banners, a painting of the famous battle, and the playing of the national anthem, "Mameli's Hymn."

Through this fusion of the national anthem with this heroic painting, linking present to past and enshrining the actions of the men involved, the film becomes self-consciously identified with other artworks as well as with other historical moments. Drawing on the heroic traditions associated with the Risorgimento and the mythic figure of Garibaldi, the film does analyze the discourse of nation but enacts it as a public melodrama, pitting the forces of national and ethnic identity against the demonic forces of empire associated with a foreign culture. However, as with *Scipione,* the question of the film's strict confinement to the ideology of nationalism and, more particularly, of Fascist nationalism once again emerges. Its visualization of historical events, its operatic quality, its uses of music and painting point in another direction, namely, to the instability of memory that "can be attained by different paths to reveal diverse stories. . . . It can also be the site of amnesia."[23] In short, rather than fixing the Risorgimento past, the film reveals this past as mutable.

In other European cinemas and Hollywood, the First World War is often presented as a tragic waste of the lives of young men. For Fascist ideologues, however, "the Great War was considered the decisive turn toward the new Italy," since it catalyzed the new forces and revealed the "profound will" of the country and its "immense moral resources."[24] Closely linked to the genre of the war film, the melodramas produced under Fascism that address heroism and combat in the Great War often invoke history in their attempts to create a world where sacrifice and death cannot merely be contemplated and feared but can even appear as desirable, being sanctioned by historical precedent. Goffredo Alessandrini's *Cavalleria* (1936) is exemplary of the romanticism and melodrama identified with World War I. However, the film's melodrama works against an oversimplistic reading of the film as bearing obvious traces of Fascist ideology.

The melodrama focuses on the familiar scenario of an irreconcilable conflict between romantic love and service to country. The narrative traces the protagonist's conversion from an impossible love for a woman to the cause of the nation even at the expense of his own life. Often identified with religion, the process of conversion entails a turning away from worldly and sensual concerns toward "higher" spiritual goals. In the case of certain of the historical films and especially those associated with the Great War, an element of religiosity is evident. This religiosity, however, is not that of the church but appears to be of a secular religion, wherein the state assumes the exalted po-

Figure 15. The decisive battle for national unity, *1860*. (Courtesy New York Museum of Modern Art Stills Archive)

sition normally reserved for divinity. As Dana Polan argues, "If, as the war discourse will often argue, an individual gets out of place because he/she has internalized incorrect beliefs and values, then a potent narrative recovery from the violence of this bad internalization will be one in which an individual converts to a new and proper set of values and beliefs."[25]

The affective dimensions of conversion narratives arise largely from the transformation of relationships from an erotic register of heterosexual desire to one of homosocial bonding, often leading to an apotheosis of the protagonist through his relinquishment of world attachments and his martyrdom. The terms of this transformation will be conveyed through the style, especially through the binary distinction between interior and exterior worlds by means of an operatic emphasis on music, dance, and social rituals in opposition to the images of nature and technology. A film idol of the time, Amedeo Nazzari, plays the dashing Solaro, a cavalry officer and later a fighter-pilot, who falls in love with a young noblewoman, Speranza (Elisa Cegani) during the war. The spectacle exploits images of horse shows, cavalry exercises, and elegant people. The aristocratic world is displayed as glamorous: salons, ball-rooms, and exquisitely costumed bejeweled women.

Speranza is torn between her loyalty to her family and her love for Sola-ro. Solaro is split between duty and love, but with the help of his command-ing officer, Captain Ponza, he comes to accept duty. Ponza believes that his men, particularly brilliant officers like Solaro, must accept the seriousness of their military commitments. The striking aspect of Solaro's character is his lack of rebelliousness. His willingness to accept his superior officer's orders, his acceptance of the need to renounce Speranza, and his discipline and self-control are offered as a model of heroism. His conversion to and immersion in duty and service are eroticized in terms of his filial type of relationship to his superior officer. Solaro, not Speranza, is the film's specular object of de-sire: He is filmed as lover, as dashing aviator, and as doomed hero.

The agent of Solaro's conversion is Speranza. Through the impossibility of their union, the film reverses the usual polarity between life and death, making his death an entry into a higher form of existence. His identification with the land is equated to the nation that, in his death, he has regenerated and with which he merges. The stages of the hero's conversion are formulaic and ritualized, marked specifically by stages of separation from the female. He must first suffer the pains of unrequited love, then reconcile himself to the futility of his desire, to which is attributed the taint of effeminacy. He must find a masculine object worthy of emulation to replace heterosexual at-tachments. This substitution involves him in an Oedipal relationship with a significant paternal guide, who signals his regeneration. His new life is associ-ated with the isolated life of the flier, a glamorous image identified with the sky and with nature. Paradoxically, regeneration is identified with a symbolic or actual death. The protagonist is no longer passive, chained to the past and to his desire, but a liberated man of action. The airplane sets him apart from others, above the earth like a god. It also identifies him with the mechanical and not the human.

The melodrama draws on fundamental romantic tropes, predominantly involving the tension between desire and inevitable loss. The initial obstacle to love is familial: Speranza must accede to a marriage of convenience to save her family from economic disaster, and her father's illness, the threat of his imminent death, forces her to conform. A masochistic aesthetic underpins the relationship of Solaro and Speranza, deriving from a suffering that seems willfully directed toward the obstruction of any type of gratification.

The film stresses spectatorship in the scenes of musical soirées and balls as well as in the cavalry shows, military maneuvers, and close-ups of the pro-tagonists. The narrative relies on a bifurcation between domestic and military worlds. It is is imitative of *War and Peace* in its focus on the world of the

Figure 16. Romance and war: Captain Solaro (Amedeo Nazzari) and Speranza (Elisa Cegani) in *Cavalleria*. (Courtesy New York Museum of Modern Art Stills Archive)

aristocracy, tragic love, and on an opposition between nature and social conventions [Fig. 16]. The most ironic image in the film is of flowers: Solaro's relationship to Speranza is symbolized by an exchange of flowers, culminating in the image of a field of them where Solaro is buried. The flowers signify passion, life, and hope, like Speranza's name, but also indifference to life, the supremacy of death through heroism. Solaro's burial in the field of flowers fuses images of love, war, and heroism.

The ending, rather than maintaining the divide between masculinity and femininity, merges them. Solaro's death and union with the soil can be read in two ways: Polemically, it can be seen as the fulfillment of a virile commitment to war and nationalism; yet in Solaro's identification with the feminine imagery of a return to the earth and to fecundity, his character can be seen rather as subverting strict masculine identification. Ironically, Solaro becomes what he sought to escape.

Much as in Klaus Theweleit's description of the German soldier-male and his relation to women, the figure of woman is presented as derealized:

relationships with women are dissolved and transformed into new male attitudes, into political stances, revelations of the true path, etc. As the woman fades out of sight, the contours of the male sharpen. . . . It could almost be said that the raw material for the man's 'transformation' is the sexually untouched, dissolving body of the woman. . . .[26]

The theatricality of the film is most evident in its choreographed and stylized acting, its costuming, its emphasis on an aristocratic mise-en-scène and entertainment, and, above all, its reliance on woman as spectacle that serves to unsettle and make undecidable the character of the male protagonist and his role in "history." *Cavalleria* seems to elude a strict reading of its ideological connection to the Ethiopian invasion that the regime undertook to advance its expansionist and colonial aspirations. However, the historical films of the Fascist era thrive on the ability of the feature cinema to undermine a strict recognition of politics, of historical verisimilitude, and of strict identification between the events dramatized from the past and their relevance for the contemporary audience. According to Pierre Sorlin,

> We are tempted to ascribe to Fascism such features as the reverence for women, the importance of family life, the dependence of women and the overvaluation of nationalism. In fact, the same characteristics can be found in pictures made in Hollywood or in democratic European countries.[27]

As in Hollywood films of the era, what stands out more than these films' attempts to create consensus is the ways they are part of a process of unsettling the belief that history is the repository of truth and the final court of appeal. Instead, they have become part of a movement characteristic of modernity where – thanks to media, among other cultural forms – history has become malleable, even indeterminate. The focus of attention has moved to the spectacle, to the action, to the luminescence of the stars, and to the capacity of melodrama to shift concentration away from the history of World War I.

The history that these films offer bespeaks a recognition both of the fragility of historical events and of the role of cinema at the time to produce another politics, a politics of style, commensurate with the theatricality sought by the regime in its ceremonials and rituals and that cinema was capable of creating in another register. In other words, if adherence to the regime is too simplistic an explanation for Italian Fascism, the increased role of mass culture, in particular, provides more adequate index to the complexities of modern life, in which media are less important for the messages they transmit and more powerful for their role in destabilizing attitudes and beliefs. Perhaps this is closer to what is meant by "fascinating Fascism."

The historical films of the Ventennio are not carbon copies of each other or mere blueprints for Fascist ideology. Even when appearing to use history for polemical ends in the interests of tracing the movement toward national unity, with their emphasis on the greatness of the Italian past and the role of exceptional individuals in the forging of the appearance of national consensus, they are largely preoccupied with a sense of history as theater and with cinema as the medium for visualizing and animating a mythical past. In this respect, they are also revealing texts for understanding how history is constructed. Their emphasis on visualizing "the people," their penchant for melodrama, their invocation of other arts of the past and present – opera, painting, and architecture – their choreography and iconography speak to a fascination with spectacle wherein history can be considered as masquerade and where the official and philosophic dimensions become a pretext for the films, rather than their substance.

CHAPTER THREE

Challenging the Folklore of Romance

The largest output of films in the 1930s and early 1940s was of genre films – historical films, costume dramas, biopics, musicals, operatic films, melodramas based on novels, and comedies. Genre films are structured around familiar scenarios focusing on the folklore of romance. Popular customs and rituals concern courtship and marriage, gendered behavior, social legitimacy, authority, and contested power. On the subject of romance novels, Robin Pickering-Iazzi writes:

> Much of the pleasure of reading formula stories, whether detective novels or romance novels, derives from the repeated discovery of what the reader actually knows and anticipates, as conflicts, which may be aroused at both the textual and subjective levels, are then engaged and finally resolved in a satisfying manner at the novels' end.[1]

While narrative repetition is important to the pleasure of the text, also important in the genre cinema are its nondiegetic elements: its uses of spectacle, iconography, the topography of space, and embedded topical allusions that produce uncomfortable emotional responses and even militate against a satisfactory resolution despite the "happy ending." The folklore of romance entertains the possibility of failure, mobilizing affect toward ends that may also be consonant with what the spectator knows but that may lead in the direction of cynicism and skepticism rather than affirmation or identification. Narrative strategies, images, dialogue, or music are embedded in cultural matrices that cannot be completely controlled by the filmmakers.

Many of the genre films produced during the Fascist era are not seamless. Though they are hardly radical examples of a critique of the status quo, they reveal irreconcilable conflicts that their resolutions cannot completely mask. The films in their eclecticism, self-referentiality, and theatricality reveal that they are recognizable as a form of folklore that draws on the spectator's knowledge – not only of their anticipated and predictable formulas but also of their artifactual nature itself. Moreover, the genre films are challenging because they are *not* totally predictable, both owing to their contradictions and because their formulas allow for some flexibility or tampering. By the late 1930s and early 1940s, there are even more examples of discontent with the status quo. Two films discussed in this chapter, *La corona di ferro* (1941) and *Sorelle Materassi* (1943), are exemplary instances of an oblique critique of the failure of romance that implicate structures of power, romantic delusion, and national conquest. These films are set alongside two films produced over a decade later – *Senso* (1954) and *Il generale Della Rovere* (1959) – that extend and make more apparent their critique of the union of the folklore of romance with that of nation.

After 1937 and increasingly by the early 1940s, films came to be identified with greater discontent with the regime, a lessened adulation for Il Duce, and indications of anxiety about the future. The war in Ethiopia, the Italian-German alliance, the preparations and then involvement in a broader war, and the racial laws all helped to fuel dissatisfaction. More and more, the panegyrics presented in newsreels and documentaries were a source of cynicism, if not of laughter. Although censorship remained intact, and overt critique could produce repercussions through silencing, rustication, and even imprisonment, there were, nevertheless, signs of disquiet even among former adherents to Fascism and among the general populace. In this respect, Blasetti's *La corona di ferro* (*The Iron Crown*) is instructive. Ostensibly the film seems politically innocuous, employing familiar aspects of genre allied to spectacle to create a "fairy tale." Legend and folklore have served as major sources for cinematic narration: as a way confronting interdiction indirectly through moral parable, a means of bypassing censorship, and an exercise in producing an affective and deterritorialized relationship to images, tearing them from spatiotemporal coordinates.[2]

Ostensibly set in the thirteenth century, the film draws on motifs from folklore: the good and bad father-king, the sleeping beauty awakened by her prince, the Arthurian legend of the sword in the stone, the noble young man who lives among the animals and is initiated through trials into civilized society, terrifying giants of superhuman strength, the threat of incest through misrecognition, contending suitors for the hand of a princess, and the salvation of an ailing kingdom. The romance motif is tied closely to regeneration of the land. What could seem more harmless than a film set in this earlier time and preoccupied with magic? The spectacle relies on ornate costuming, a lavish mise-en-scène for the court and for outdoor shots. Although seeking to create the aura of an earlier age, *La corona di ferro* conveys a sense not of an actual, historic time and place but of "once upon a time." Moreover, a parable is obvious in the film's focus on the abuses of power in a world of violence and deception. The tale of the wicked king, a usurper of authority, and of his subsequent overthrow sits uncomfortably close to contemporary social events.

After a title that announces the purported time and place of the events, the narrative plunges into a scene of war and violence with the wounding and death of King Licinio and the usurpation of his crown by his brother Sedemondo (Gino Cervi). Sedemondo is confronted by a messenger from the pope, bearing an iron crown and asking permission to pass through the land. According to legend, the crown remains wherever injustice and corruption prevail. Seeking to rid himself of the crown, Sedemondo takes it to the gorge at Natersa and it sinks into the earth, ordering a slave to remain and kill others who seek to enter and reclaim it. Sedemondo, besotted by his power, rejects knowledge about the consequences of his actions. He is challenged by the prophecy of an old wise woman (Rina Morelli) in the forest who predicts that his wife will bear him a girl, whereas Licinio's wife will give birth to a boy. She also prophesies that, when grown, the two will fall in love with tragic consequences, and that the young man will ultimately wrest the kingdom from him. Sedemondo returns home, however, and receives the news that his wife has given birth to a son – the babies have been switched to protect the boy. Believing that the prophecy was erroneous, Sedemondo declares that the girl, Elsa, will be raised as his own, a sister to his (alleged) son, Arminio. Soon, though, signs of strife between Sedemondo and Arminio become apparent as the child rebels against the king's cruelty, and Sedemondo orders that the boy be taken to the gorge by a slave and killed.

Twenty years pass: Elsa (Elisa Cegani) lives imprisoned in the castle, and Arminio (Massimo Girotti) has grown up in the wild, a companion to lions. A tournament has been announced by Sedemondo, a means to find a worthy husband for Elsa. It becomes the event that will lure Arminio back to the kingdom of Kindaor and lead to the overthrow of Sedemondo. Through the magical agency of a stag who beckons, Arminio leaves his natural and isolated world, enacting the scenario prophesied by the old woman.

A combination of Tarzan and Robin Hood, Arminio makes his way out of the forest, saving a group of abused slaves along the way. Here he comes across someone who frees the stag that has been directing him. More adventures befall Arminio as he allies himself with this person, Tundra (Luisa Ferida), whose identity and gender initially are a mystery. Only when the two protagonists fight one another does he discover that Tundra is a woman and a leader of the people enslaved by Sedemondo. She urges him to assume the role of a champion for her oppressed people at the tournament.

Meanwhile, Elsa, the proverbial princess imprisoned in a tower and forbidden to leave her quarters, is shown languishing on her couch at Kindaor [Fig. 17]. A ceremonial scene follows in which the king greets the various suitors and receives their gifts. Elsa is lavishly clothed for her first presentation to the public. However, she complicates the scenario by exchanging clothes with a waiting woman and exits the palace, whereupon she meets Arminio, although she keeps her identity secret.

Figure 17. The martyred princess Elsa (Elisa Cegani), *La corona di ferro* (*The Iron Crown*). (Courtesy New York Museum of Modern Art Stills Archive)

The tournament is choreographed in a fashion to vie with Hollywood adventure films, with processions, banners, drummers, and patterned formations, and stressing ritual encounters – recalling also the style of Blasetti's earlier *Palio* (1932). The leading contender for Elsa's hand is Arriberto, a Tartar prince, who overcomes the other suitors. Sedemondo, not without affection for his daughter and responsive to her antipathy to the suitors, offers land and riches in exchange for Elsa's hand. The Tartar threatens violence if he does not get his due, but Tundra arrives in the nick of time to aid Arminio in defeating him. Arminio, greeted as the champion, announces that rather than assuming his rights as victor, he respects her right to choose. Tundra, unhappy over the possibility of a union between Elsa and Arminio, refuses to be friendly with Elsa. Later Elsa and Arminio meet in a palace grove, while an angry Tundra eavesdrops.

At a bacchanalian feast, Sedemondo reveals that he does not intend to keep his new promise of sharing the kingdom with Tundra, and Elsa struggles with her jealousy of Tundra. Again fate intervenes as Arminio discovers on Elsa a scar similar to his own – both having been inflicted by Sedemondo when they were children. Now the threat of incest emerges, since the lovers believe they are brother and sister. Distraught, Elsa rushes to the gorge at Natersa, where she is fatally wounded by Sedemondo's slave – learning before she dies, however, that she is not Arminio's sister. A battle then threatens between Sedemondo's men and the enslaved followers of Licinio, but the earth splits, dividing them, the iron crown appears, and peace is restored.

In the conventions and motifs of the adventure film that specializes in heroic feats, the emphasis is on the salvation of the family, the restoration of the benevolent paternal figure, and the importance of establishing legitimacy and continuity. In the contrasts between the claustrophobia of the kingdom, with its ornate but imprisoning gates, and the vastness and openness of the natural setting, the film visualizes the conflict between oppression and resistance, paralysis and action. The imagery dramatizes the tension between unity and disorder, stasis and movement, the individual and the masses. Folklore, melodrama, and spectacle meet in the ways the narrative relies on the visualization of binaries: Sedemondo and Licinio, Arminio and Sedemondo, Tundra and Elsa. Scenes of war, combat, and aggression punctuate the film, culminating in the death of Elsa, the innocent victim of Sedemondo's illegitimate usurpation of the throne. In this threatening world, the woman becomes the martyr as well as the instrument of reconciliation.

The prophetic role of the old woman in contrast to the willful actions of Sedemondo shifts the focus from suspense to irony, which lies in the highlighting of the motif of vision. The audience knows from the outset of the film what Sedemondo refuses to see: that the woman's predictions will be realized. The use of spectacle underscores the destructive consequences of his willing blindness. The film's preoccupation with vision, especially in relation to knowledge and power, is also manifest in its frequent recourse to the magical imagery of veiling and exposure, in Arminio's misperception of Tundra as a man, and, above all, in Sedemondo's efforts to conceal and obliterate any evidence of his illegitimate actions. Thus, while the spectacle serves to enhance the filmmaker's ingenuity in creating a make-believe world, it also presents a dual relationship to the act of seeing: *La corona di ferro* ties the vision motif, if only indirectly, to the ability of the cinematic image to conceal yet, paradoxically, also to expose misrepresentation and abuse of power. In this respect, members of the audience might have recognized the pedagogical elements in the film, involving a questioning of the role of spectacle in relation to power.

La corona di ferro won the Mussolini Cup at the Venice Film Festival in 1941 for the best Italian film,[3] but it was not without its critics. Significantly, Goebbels excoriated the film for having a pacifist perspective: Clearly, the potential for such a reading was not lost on him. Given the outbreak of war and the steadily declining fortunes of the regime, the text – particularly Sedemondo's having usurped rightful authority and enslaved the people – could indeed be (and has been) seen as subverting Fascist ideology. The adventure format, however, tends to operate on a most conventional level as an "escapist" entertainment film, and can be regarded as innocuous. *La corona* conforms to Brian Taves's description of the historical film genre, wherein "History is reduced to mutually opposing personalities, away from complex, ambiguous socioeconomic forces and political systems, substituting such dramatically appealing motivations as a tyrannical despot's desire for riches and power."[4]

Thus, audiences might appreciate the film's theatricality and spectacle, whereas the "historical" and "political" dimensions might be assimilated or rejected. This is not to suggest that the politics of such films is irrelevant but rather to complicate the ways in which contemporary politics must be seen in affective terms. Costume dramas, with their folkloric characteristics – their stylization, binary structure, formulaic treatment, and emphasis on magic – bear comparison, more than overtly historical films (e.g., *1860*), with Hollywood formulas for politicizing history. The reception of such a film thus becomes more problematic than its designation as innocuous escapism at one extreme or simple moral platitude on the other. The adoption of a genre mode with its penchant for fantasy does not preclude the film's critique of the present. By combining spectacle with the thematic treatment of power, the film's politics are less censurable.

More important, *La corona di ferro* reveals its preoccupation not only with issues surrounding the usurpation of power but with questions concerning the role of cinema, self-consciously focusing on the power of the visual image to conceal but perhaps also to reveal. Not only does the film adopt the conventional narrative as a cogent critique of power, but its reflexivity in the excessive and reiterative use of images of imprisonment, violence, and the image of a book becoming a film, reinforce the film's preoccupation with visualization and its effects. Its emphasis on vision is pronounced particularly in the case of Sedemondo: in his refusal to recognize the validity of what is shown to him, his arbitrary and destructive treatment of others, and the devastating effects of his use of force and violence.

Whether the preoccupation with vision of *La corona di ferro* was intentional on the part of the filmmaker or characteristic of general signs of cultural malaise is impossible to determine. However, these characteristics are not unique among the films in Italy of the late 1930s and early 1940s. Such films as *Il cappello a tre punte* (which enraged Mussolini), *Gelosia, Ossessione,* and *Sorelle Materassi* are also preoccupied with issues of vision in relation to the theatrical, arbitrary, and destructive uses of power by a masculine figure.

La corona was made at a time when a debate was waging as to the nature of and direction for the Italian cinema. In the film industry, there were signs of desire for change – an ennui, if not disgust, with the dominant forms of film production. Journal articles in such periodicals as *Cinema* revealed a predilection for films displaying realist tendencies and a turning away from genre production and what was regarded as its "artificiality." Certain filmmakers (e.g., Mario Soldati, Renato Castellani, Ferdinando Maria Poggioli) turned toward nineteenth- and turn-of-the-century fiction to create texts that were identified as "calligraphic," because of their ostensible preoccupation with style more than content.[5] These works, dependent on such writers as Antonio Fogazzaro and Emilio De Marchi, were at first commended then later rejected by critics because of their formalism and their seeming disregard, even criticism, of their contemporary social environment. However, a closer look at the films based on these novels reveals their dismissal from Italian film history as unwarranted, since they are indicative of a desire for a change of direction in cinema. Like the Blasetti film, these works operate by indirection, requiring a careful analysis of the ways the style and the uses of history speak clearly, if obliquely, to the cultural situation.

In a striking, theatrical, and unsettling vein, Poggioli's *Sorelle Materassi* (*Materassi Sisters*) is a dissection of the sexual politics of power and the power of sexual politics, suggesting that it, like the Blasetti film, has its own pedagogical designs on the audience that involve an inversion of romantic expectations and of blissful consensus. Moreover, the film can be seen as an investigation of cinematic spectatorship in its preoccupation with vision. Ostensibly, it is a portrait of a society gone berserk, where accumulation, venality, hypocrisy, and exploitation are commonplace. The film portrays a woman's world comprising three seamstress sisters, their assistant, a cook, a maid, a princess, and an American woman from Argentina. This haremlike environment is invaded by a man, Remo (Massimo Serrato), the nephew of the Materassi sisters, whose presence transforms the home into bedlam. Based on a novel by Aldo Palazzeschi, the film begins on a street where a car turns into a gate bearing the sign, "Materassi Sisters." Women are gaping out of windows as the car arrives at the home of the seamstresses. The visitor, a priest, goes to a workroom where he finds two of the sisters, Teresa (Irma Gramatica) and Carolina (Emma Gramatica), telling them that they are to be honored by a visit to the pope for their services in making priestly vestments. In a highly stylized scene of the sisters at the Vatican, the sisters walk down a long hall decorated with murals and paintings [Fig. 18] until they reach an ornate door, and the pope is announced. They kneel as he blesses them and others. Upon return home, they are observed by neighbors from windows and the street. The element of voyeurism is central to the film in its recurrent use of mirrors and windows. The opposition between inside and outside, looking and being looked at, is reiterated throughout the film.

In contrast to the scene of work rewarded, Remo is seen on a train, traveling in a first-class compartment with a third-class ticket. Confronted with this

Figure 18. The sisters visit the Vatican, *Sorelle Materassi*. (Courtesy New York Museum of Modern Art Stills Archive)

discrepancy by the conductor, he is saved by a sympathetic young woman who pays the difference between the tickets. When Remo arrives at the Materassi house, he tells the women a sad story of maltreatment at the hands of an uncle, while leering seductively at a young woman, Laurina. Teresa and Carolina invite him to stay with them; the third, youngest sister, Giselda, adamantly refuses to have a man in the house. Six months later, Remo is still with them, and the two sisters rave about their nephew to the priest, calling him a "perfect saint." They wait on him servilely and refuse to believe anything negative about his behavior. When a mother comes to the house to complain of Remo's taking advantage of her daughter, Teresa and Carolina angrily send her away. Remo's triumphs over women include the sisters, a sculptress, the maid, Niobe, and Laurina. In the hope of placating Remo, the sisters buy him a car after having bought him a bike and a motorcycle. His rise in this world is marked by graduation from two wheel to four, handlebars to horsepower.

The sisters' relationship with Remo reaches a new level when he, pressed to pay back a loan, asks them for the money. Despite the fact that their property is totally mortgaged, he insists that they sign a promissory note. They refuse, and he locks them in a closet, pocketing the key. Ultimately, the sisters sign the note. At an automobile showroom where he now works, Remo waits on a client, a rich American woman, Peggy (Clara Calamai), and makes a sale. She insists on going for a test drive, and he takes the wheel. The car runs out of gas because she has put sugar in the gas tank. He has met his match, in more ways than one. At the Materassi house, the sisters, huddled in a blanket, wait for news of Remo, and a telegram arrives, announcing his marriage to Peggy. A dissolve reveals a group gathered on the street by the Materassi establishment to watch the arrival of the newlyweds, observed from the window by the sisters. Later, at the church, where again a crowd of spectators is assembled, Peggy appears radiant as a bride. Teresa and Carolina arrive next – also dressed as brides, to the amusement of the crowd. After the wedding, the two sisters, still in their bridal finery, learn that Remo is leaving them [Fig. 19]. In a scene that borders on the surreal, the sisters are left like deserted brides. He bids farewell as the camera pans to the window from which the aunts look out at a fireworks display.

The satire develops through excessively stylized characterization. Each character – especially Teresa, Carolina, Giselda, and Remo – is drawn in caricature. The sisters' speech, gestures, and movement convey self-imprisonment, obsession, and inability to hear or see. They are prisoners of their romantic infatuations, and Remo the focus of their impossible desires. The consummate exploiter of women, he is portrayed as entrapped in a fetishized relation to the world, a caricature of the commodification of social connections. To say that he is cruel and sadistic would make him a melodramatic villain; what negates such an identification is the film's portrait of the sisters, who are equally fetishistic with Remo.

The film's pedagogy is closely tied to the power of looking. Teresa and Carolina observe the world through their window. They observe Remo's every movement, even when what they see is designed to make them look ridiculous. Giselda observes her two sisters and Remo through peepholes. The crowds watch the comings and goings at the Materassi house, amused at the events they see. The sisters are voyeurs, gratifying their desire through viewing photographs and especially through constant scrutiny of their nephew. The number of spectators on the street, which increases as the film progresses, serves as an ambiguous and ironic surrogate for the external audience, a distancing device that permits sardonic laughter. By extension, the external audience is implicated in the voyeurism.

Looking serves as form of distanciation, which undermines identification with the characters and underscores the film's obsession with vicarious experience, a characteristic identified with the cinema. Looking also serves as a way of highlighting the disjunction between desire and attainment, heightening the sense of their incommensurability. Seeing is not aligned to acting. The shifting perspectives inhibit the stabilization of any particular spectator-

Figure 19. The Materassi sisters in their bridal finery: Teresa (Irma Gramatica) and Carolina (Emma Gramatica) with Remo (Massimo Serrato) in *Sorelle Materassi*. (Courtesy New York Museum of Modern Art Stills Archive)

ial position: Whereas an unchanging perspective might ensure an affective involvement with any one character, these shifts disperse attention among the various characters and direct it toward the situation. The treatment of spectatorship in the film is triangulated, moving from the characters to the internal audience and external audience.

The characters' mechanical gestures and responses are like dream condensations, contributing to a sense of the derealization and abstract nature of their world. The objects in the film – the clothing, the bicycle, the motorcycle, and the car – are more substantial than the people. The characters' metamorphosis into puppetlike creations and their interchangeability with objects dramatize the film's preoccupation with power, exemplified by the characters' manipulation of each other and with the role of money as the medium of domination, indifferent to any human interaction. Teresa and Carolina seek to control Giselda and Laurina, Giselda to undermine that control through her own machinations, and Remo to control his aunts. His mastery over them is predicated on his ability to play on their desire to possess him and the threat of his withdrawal of affection. The force that animates their interactions among themselves and with others is fear of isolation. Locked into their sexual fantasies, waiting for someone to free them, their desire for affection plunges them into degradation, violence, and exploitation.

Through Remo's protean and disingenuous character, the film probes the excessive and destructive side of bourgeois attitudes toward family and respectability. Economics and sexuality (money, cars, and sex) are the terrain on which the game of dominance and subordination, deceit and manipulation, is played out between Remo and the sisters. If he is the women's object of desire and their fetish, locomotory objects are his fetish. Motor vehicles become signifiers of his sexuality. They are corollaries of his inability or unwillingness to confront human needs, and of his exploitation of people for the acquisition of material goods. In *Sorelle Materassi,* basic thematic elements of many of the films that address familial and, hence, national virtues are overturned – the sanctity and security of family relations, the elevation of industriousness, and the imperative of loyalty and service.

The melodramatic conflicts are orchestrated in the sisters' aggressive and competitive relationship with each other, in their "adoption" of and conflict with Remo, and in their competition with Peggy, who wins Remo. The petit-bourgeois world they inhabit can be read in the sisters' conspiracy with Remo to maintain the ideal of being "useful" even to the point of tolerating verbal and physical debasement. The mannered style of acting and the claustrophobic mise-en-scène create an alienating effect, producing an uncomfortable relationship to the events viewed. The ending of the film is an ironic commentary on the fantasy of the happy ending: Remo is successful in finding a rich woman to gratify his economic and sexual aspirations, and the sisters are freed of his tyranny – but they are once again alone, illusions intact, as at the beginning, before Remo's arrival.

The sister's situation obliquely invokes the war, pointing to the scarcity of men away fighting in Greece, Russia, Africa, and even in sections of Italy. The interactions between Remo and his aunts provide an unsettling portrait of masculinity as violent and exploitative, one counter to official legitimation of virility, sexuality, and power. However, the binarism of melodrama is undermined by the excessiveness of representation in the women's desperate attachment to a dominant masculine figure, their endowing that person with great power, and their willingness to endure any humiliation to maintain that relationship. All the characters dramatize the desire to possess, to manipulate, and to dominate through the obsession with money, respectability, and the terrifying fear of isolation. The lingerie and linen, the house, the vehicles, the photograph, and the clock that signifies Remo's absence and the sisters' longing for him – all these objects testify to the film's exploration of the commodification of desire.

More than many other films of the early 1940s, including *Ossessione, Sorelle Materassi* makes visible the grotesque and theatricalized character of

dearly held values enshrined in folklore – the self-sacrificing nature of feminine maternal behavior, the sanctified haven of the family, the phantasm of
masculinity and femininity, and the destructive desire to master and to be mas-
tered. The American, Peggy, is no exception: She merely turns the tables, augmenting the chain of exploitation, inviting reflection on marriage as another
dimension of the exchange of commodities and of the transformation of the
human into inanimate objects. Everyone is corrupt but none beyond empa-
thy. The film offers the remote possibility, through its focus on spectatorship,
that seeing, not merely looking, might offer an avenue of escape, if only for
the audience. In its focus on obsession, consuming but ungratified desire, and
misperception, pathos is tempered by the characters' opaqueness and invul-
nerability. Nothing enters to disturb this enclosed and histrionic world except
the possibility of recognition, and the only locus for such perception remains
with the external audience.

Thus, this film reveals a tendency, even prior to the neorealist movement,
to experiment with forms of filmmaking that were sensitive to new formal
and thematic concerns, and especially with tying questions of cinema to ethical questions. However, film criticism and filmmaking were to move in other,
less surreal and less formal directions. They turned toward American literature, including such writers as John Dos Passos and Ernest Hemingway, for
a different source of stylistic and philosophic innovation. They turned also
to the writings of Giovanni Verga, whose work was identified with *verismo,*
a movement toward a more objective and naturalist description of the world.
By considering different models, filmmakers such as Rossellini and Visconti
sought to turn the film industry away from the production of films that they
regarded as deleterious to the health and well-being of Italian culture.

Despite films such as Poggioli's, the mythology of a radical rupture between
the Fascist era and postwar Italy was promulgated immediately after the war,
resulting in the condemnation of the films produced under Fascism. It is customary to identify the films of the immediate post–World War II era as "neo-
realistic" and to regard them as addressing "[t]he mood of the time[, which]
was downhearted . . . a discrepancy between material losses, which were not
catastrophic, and the impression, widely expressed in papers, talk, and films,
that the country had gone through the greatest disaster it had ever experienced."[6] In the cinema, there was a tendency to look back at the Fascist era
with a general contempt and to see the film production of that time as complicit with the regime. The filmmakers were "driven by the desire to stamp
out what was perceived as the Fascist threat; their hope was that it would be
possible to start the whole business of cinema afresh."[7] Judging by the master
texts of neorealism such as *Roma, città aperta (Open City,* 1945), *Sciuscià
(Shoeshine,* 1946), *Ladri di biciclette (The Bicycle Thief,* 1948), *La terra trema* (The Earth Trembles, 1948), and *Umberto D* (1952) – a number of which

involved screenwriter-theorist Cesare Zavattini – there appeared to be a particular animus against historical films, particularly those that were filmed in the highly theatrical genre style of the years of Fascism.

Favoring a documentary or quasi-documentary look, loosely structured narratives involving the tragedies of ordinary people, and the use of nonprofessional actors, not stars, the films of the late 1940s and early 1950s focus on contemporary conditions and the imperative for social change, presenting events from "a resolutely anti-establishment stance."[8] As important as the specific moral clarion to see the world differently through the cinema was the necessity to put in place a style of filmmaking that would profoundly alter film. Roberto Rossellini's *Paisà* (*Paisan*, 1946) is one of the film texts identified with this new film form. Beyond using location settings and nonprofessional actors, the film is organized around six episodes that take place during the last days of World War II and encompass all sections of the country. It was loosely scripted, conforming to the improvisational nature of neorealist films, and "[l]ikewise, characters, plot, and locations were continuously and sometimes drastically changed – to correspond more closely with the people and places" the filmmakers encountered in their travels through Italy.[9] For the most part, one can see the great emphasis on the Italian landscape and also the film's dramatization of movement through that landscape. The Italian milieu assumes a major role as the film dramatizes the deep divisions wrought by Fascism and the war – in language, customs, gender, age, and race.

In the first episode, the burden of cultural and political difference is carried by "Joe from Jersey" and Carmela, the young Sicilian woman who has agreed to accompany the American detachment to an alternative route that bypasses the minefields scattered throughout the countryside. Through the encounter between the American and Sicilian, differences are gradually surmounted, but the anticipated romance that burgeons between the two is thwarted by their deaths from sniper fire. The second episode takes place in Naples, a city devastated by war, and concerns a young street boy, Pasquale, who attempts to "purchase" a drunk black soldier, Joe (Dots M. Johnson). Racial and language differences are central to this episode. The boy, seeking to hide his acquisition, takes him to a puppet show, where Joe, witnessing a battle between the Crusaders and the beleagured Moors, confuses fiction with reality and disrupts the performance by rushing to defend the black puppets. Ejected from the theater, Joe falls asleep, and the boy steals his boots and flees. Joe, who we now learn is an M.P., sees Pasquale several days later and orders him to return the boots. He forces the boy to take him to his home, only to learn that he and other homeless people live amid rubble in a cave. Despite language barriers, Joe inchoately comprehends that the devastation of the boy's world is not dissimilar to his own in the United States [Fig. 20].

Figure 20. A common fate? The boy (Alfonsino Pasca) and the M.P. (Dots M. Johnson) in *Paisà* (*Paisan*). (Courtesy New York Museum of Modern Art Stills Archive)

The burden is on the spectator to understand what is inaccessible to the characters. In their confrontations with the enemy or, for that matter, with their compatriots, the characters are confronted by a conflict between their learned and habitual responses to events (as is the audience) and with the failure of expectations. In relation to the failed folklore of romance, Joe and Carmela are not redeemed by love; the M.P. and the young boy are not united in their common misery. In the third episode, Francesca, a young prostitute, nourishes the impossible dream of being the lovely and uncontaminated woman that Fred, a G.I., had encountered upon his first arrival in Rome on the day of Liberation. The episode takes place six months after the arrival of the Americans. Francesca picks up a drunken G.I. and takes him to a hotel, where he babbles about changes than have transpired in the city. Through a flashback, it becomes evident that Francesca herself was the young woman with whom he had earlier fallen in love. Shamed by her present condition, she quits the room, leaving her address with a woman to give to Fred. She then transforms her appearance to coincide with her earlier image, only to discover, as she stands in the rain awaiting him, that she is abandoned. (Fred has torn up the address.) This episode contains several of the thematics building in the film – the cities as violated women, now prostituted; the failure of language (the flashback shows each learning the other's language); the disparity between the alleged Liberation and the subsequent daily life of the Italians – all of which call into question the romantic view of love and war.

The film reiterates a tension between a belief in commonality and a dramatization of the many intellectual and affective obstacles that stand in its way. Not only is this problem posed in terms of the events in the film; these events are, in turn, a major problem addressed to the audience and its assumed cinematic expectations. In the fourth episode, the quest of Harriet White, a young American nurse in Florence, to find her lover, the partisan leader "Lupo," is also a drastic truncation of familiar expectations: that Harriet will find her lover; that her friend Massimo will reach his family; and that observers to the conflict – such as the British soldiers who sit on a hillside looking through binoculars at the Florentine architecture while the battle wages – can comprehend the nature and complexity of the war and its destructiveness. The cultural gulf in the fifth episode, between the worldliness of three war chaplains and the narrowmindedness of the Franciscans whose secluded monastery they are visiting, is treated seriocomically. The monks do not know how to accept the presence of a Protestant and particularly a Jew in their enclosed world. The horrors of war and intolerance of difference are not comprehended in this episode; they constitute an *aporia,* a limit, that has not been confronted by the cloistered Italians. The final episode, in the Po Valley, portrays the activities of the partisans with their American OSS aides, culminating in a brutal retaliation by the Germans, who line up the partisans and push them one by one into the river to drown, and also kill any who try to save the men. The film ends with a dispassionate voice-over: "This happened in the winter of 1944. By the beginning of spring, the war was over."

In many of the episodes, Rossellini positions characters as observers. Children in the second and third episodes provide an oblique perspective on the American presence. The man on the roof reading a map and tracking the conflict in the fourth episode presents an incongruous response to the actual fighting taking place in the streets below. The altering gazes between the chaplains and the monks in the fifth episode punctuates their differing situations. In the final episode, groups of people look uncomprehendingly, even scornfully, at a floating dead man marked "partisan." The absence of commonality is intensified by the image of a crying child amid the corpses – one who is not "rescued" but merely scrutinized by two partisans.

Because of the seeming accessibility of the images of the urban landscape, the ravages of war, the ragged children on the streets, the images of rubble, the triumphant arrival of the American troops, and the ubiquitous and threatening images of the Germans patrolling the streets of Florence, *Paisà* seems to invite a comparison with numerous war films; yet a comparison with this genre falters.

The encounters of the film's characters frustrate simplistic readings, creating confusion in the viewer as to their actions. They are limited in their comprehension and capacity to act. They are childlike, drunk, or somnambulistic, overwhelmed by their own immediate ends, and unable to grasp the disparities inherent in their situation between expectation and realization.[10] Instead of the movement-image – a way of looking at the world that can be termed "organic" in that it creates a sense of unity between the parts and the whole text – we have the time-image, in which there is no longer a sense of synthesizing time and space, perception and action. Instead, situations are dissipated, producing "a serial rather than an organic form of composition."[11] Characters are presented in ambulatory terms, sleepwalking through the cinematic world, unable to act or react, and the spectator too becomes implicated in uncertainty and unpredictability. In particular, "The image becomes a space for reading: seeing and hearing as decipherment rather than following an action, a legible image to be read, a lectosign, rather than an action-image to be absorbed or reacted."[12] In short, the folklore of romance concerning gender, family, nation, and heroic action are placed under scrutiny.

This transformation in the cinematic image is evident prior to neorealism in such Italian films as *Sorelle Materassi,* where a focus on action is replaced by a focus on spectatorship. In fact, the excessive nature of many of the melodramatic and historical texts calls attention to the work of spectacle in collusion with spectatorship. Thus the time-image is evident even before the neorealist films of the immediate postwar years and continues well into the 1970s in the cinema of such directors as Luchino Visconti and Federico Fellini, among others. Although the films of these directors may not rely largely on nonprofessional actors, a documentary look, or scenes of ordinary or even contemporary life, their uses of history, melodrama, and narrative, their reliance on other visual arts, and their operatic character exemplify the time-image in their critical focus on the image itself and its open-endedness. Their films avoid grandiose and affirmative celebrations of Italian history, portraying instead a world resembling that of *Sorelle Materassi.* Through an emphasis on theatricality and performance, on the power of illusion and its relation to sexual politics, they offer a pedagogy for the audience that, in its ironic uses of spectacle, is critical of representation. Visconti, particularly in his consistent focus on performance, offers images of a decomposing world.

Visconti has been quoted as saying, "Verdi and Italian opera were my first love. My work always betrays a touch of the operatic whether in my films or in my plays."[13] Visconti's florid style lies in his dependence on painting and on the operatic, if not on opera itself.[14] From *Ossessione* to *La caduta degli dei* (*The Damned*, 1969), Visconti's film work has been identified not only with the operatic but also with the uses of history and spectacle. Two of his films deal directly with the Risorgimento: *Senso* (*Wanton Countessa*, 1954) and *Il gattopardo* (*The Leopard*, 1963). In the former, the text opens with a moment from Verdi's *Il trovatore* presented in the Teatro Fenice opera house in Venice. The production becomes an occasion for patriotic demonstrations on behalf of Italian unity and rebelliousness against the Austrians. This episode leads directly to the mainspring of the plot and to the relationship between the Countess Livia Serpieri (Alida Valli) and her Austrian lover, Franz Mahler (Farley Granger), through whom the failure of the Risorgimento is enacted. Visconti uses the operatic to expose the romanticism of nationalism, particularly the tension between the politics of family and of nation.

Visconti's comments and those of his critics notwithstanding, how valid is an attempt to link film, opera, and historicizing? That Italy has been the home of major composers and singers and that Visconti was a director of opera are hardly sufficient grounds for making such linkages. Angela Dalle Vacche has cautioned that the "connection with opera is an appropriate but limited one" in accounting for the penchant in Italian cinema for a "spectacular-allegorical style," though she identifies the operatic style of Visconti's historical treatment as Rankean history, a history of "great men, crucial battles, and memorable events."[15] Dalle Vacche's comments are also a reminder of the eclectic character of both opera and cinema, their tendency to cannibalize other arts. This characteristic alerts the film critic to the need to examine the multifarious ways in which spectacle - not merely narrativity and thematics - functions to bridge "the interface between the body and history."[16]

The Visconti text relies on visual opulence and aural stimulation, but in such a manner that the spectacle becomes the means of undermining the melodramatic sentiments and actions of the characters. Instead of drawing the spectator into a fascination with character, *Senso,* through its use of camp and parody - traits that would characterize many of Visconti's other historical films - visualizes a world in a state of decay and disintegration. *Senso* returns to a motif prevalent in many films of the Fascist era, namely, the loss of a capacity to discern the virtual from the real, which is connected to the pedagogical role of film. This pedagogy offers itself as an allegory whereby the romance of the couple and the romance of nationalism are intimately tied - in fact, mirror each other. The film has a dual trajectory, looking back on a double past, the moment of the Risorgimento but also, for those who can read this second connection, to Fascism.

The characters in *Senso* move through the narrative as if actors in a Verdian opera gone awry. After the opening scenes at the Teatro Fenice, the remainder of the film also has all the characteristics of an opera - doomed love,

Figure 21. Romance and betrayal: Countess Livia Serpieri (Alida Valli) and the Austrian officer, Franz (Farley Granger), in *Senso*. (Courtesy New York Museum of Modern Art Stills Archive)

betrayal, and revenge set against the opulent background of palaces, gardens, battle scenes, and lovers' trysts [Fig. 21]. Millicent Marcus has aptly described the use of spectacle in the film as follows:

> Not only in the opening scene, but throughout the film, *Senso* inhabits the boundary line between life and theater. . . . Indeed, the Risorgimento itself becomes a melodramatic performance with heroes, villains, and high-minded principles requiring a theatrical scenario of its own. . . .[17]

Marcus acknowledges Gramsci's relevance to the view of history enacted in the film (as well as in Visconti's *Il gattopardo*), where the mythology of the

Risorgimento is exposed to criticism, if not ridicule. In his notes on Italian history, Gramsci explores the concept of "passive revolution," that is, change that comes from above that does not radically alter the political life of the nation in the direction of popular struggle but betrays attempts to alter the power structure and constitutes a victory on the part of the ruling class to reconsolidate its power.[18] The Risorgimento, described in the usual terms of producing the unity of the modern Italian state, was a "revolution" that ensured the aristocracy, in collusion with the moneyed middle classes, would gain control of the state. In the language of the writer Tomaso di Lampedusa, whose novel, *Il gattopardo,* dramatizes this scenario of power, "Everything changes so that everything can remain the same." However, this Gramscian scenario in *Senso* is wedded to the folklore of romance and to its undermining by the female protagonist and her confusion between life and theater. "History is never scenery."[19] The operatic romance constructed by the protagonist doubles for history and both decompose for the spectator.

Senso, based on the novel by Camillo Boito, revolves around two failed romances: one personal, the other, national. The first dramatizes the gradual degeneration of Countess Livia Serpieri from a patriotic supporter of unification to an obsessed woman abjectly in love with an Austrian officer. The officer, Franz, has used her for his own personal ends to maintain a life of libertinism and parasitism – an attribute of his class, as he acknowledges. He thus treats her the same as those Italians who, like her husband, are more concerned with privilege and profit than with patriotism. *Senso* compounds ironies in contrasting the noble ideals of Verdian opera with the increasingly squalid portraits of Livia and her husband scrambling for personal advantage. The trajectory of the film resides in how "history interlocks with private life, while the body erotic breaks through the body politic."[20]

Livia begins as a beautiful figure of desire in the opening scenes at the opera in her décolleté gown and jewels. From her initial attraction to Franz, the narrative follows the contessa through her gradual reduction to a camp follower, forced to experience abasement at his hands as he extorts money from her and openly parades his affairs with other women. Once on this path, Livia moves through the dank Venetian landscape, the serpentine streets, oblivious to her surroundings – a somnambulist, like the sisters in *Sorelle Materassi.* Increasingly her obsession is evident in her unkempt appearance, a counterpart to the Venetian landscape. Deprived of appearing as a truly heroic figure or even as a desirable melodramatic heroine, she becomes instead a distorted mirror-image of Leonora, the operatic heroine of *Il trovatore.* The literal mirror shots that punctuate the film, reserved mainly for her, can in fact be read as her entrapment in the virtual world of theatricality, of the melodrama she ironically disavows as belonging properly to the opera but that later becomes her prison.

Livia's unacknowledged masquerade as romantic heroine is finally ended by Franz, in whose apartment she comes face to face with a young prostitute (whom she thus also distortingly mirrors). Franz rips off the veil covering Livia's face, exposing the ravages of time, and confronts her with her own corruption, which mirrors his drunken and dissolute state. He taunts her, calls her an aging and ridiculous figure, and mocks her gullibility and folly. In the end, she is a vindictive opera heroine, misplacing the source of her hate and rage and causing the death of her Austrian lover. The contessa is no innocent, however: She has participated inexorably in her operatic downfall.

Parallel to this excessive descent into personal humiliation are scenes of a second failed romance, in which the supporters of Italian independence are defeated militarily at the Battle of Custoza. These sequences do not glorify war in the national interest but present it in terms of carnage and, even more, as a prolegomenon to the disasters wrought by Fascism – another connection to the Gramscian analysis of passive revolution. The military battle was not the worst defeat of the national romance of Risorgimento, however; nor was financial support of the enemy the only betrayal. As Bondanella describes: "The Risorgimento was betrayed not so much by passionate women like Livia Serpieri as by others of her class who twisted the noble aspirations of Italian patriots to ignoble class-oriented ends."[21]

In this film, which alternates between inside and outside, the theater and the home, the battlefields of war and of class, it is not the specific historical events (including those excised by the censor) that occupy center stage but the idea of historicizing. The world of spectacle conveyed through the many artistic analogues in the film, including painting and opera – detailed by Angela Dalle Vacche in her analysis – is described by her as follows: "With Visconti, the interplay between reality and appearance at the heart of the neorealist style escalates into the conflation of history with opera and opera with history. At the same time, history gives in to national passion, while private desire seeks to contain history."[22] Critics identified *Senso* with earlier films whose antirealism they regarded as violating their notion of neorealism, and they were concerned about the filmmaker's relations to Italian history and to contemporary cinema. According to Dalle Vacche, "Visconti's obsessive historicism is symptomatic of an inability to overcome the legacy of the past."[23] But what does this mean? Is the director, in fact, mirroring his own entrapment, or is something more powerful at work in *Senso*'s recourse to the past that contradicts this autobiographical reading? Is the film really a "betrayal" of neorealism in its recourse to the remote past and to an "obtrusive" style, its uncritical indulgence in its "dazzling, sensual surface" thus "more of an unqualified aesthetic delight than of ideological disdain"?[24] Or is its dazzling but progressively sordid surface a sign of a critical engagement with the role of representation and its relation to past uses of cinematic historicizing?

Putting aside for the moment intentionality, Viscontian biography, critical psychologizing, and philosophic applications of historical paradigms, a more useful exploration of *Senso*'s fusion of romance and history leads to an exploration of the relation between art and politics. *Senso* provides a gloss on cinema in its uses of stars (e.g., Alida Valli and Farley Granger), in its elaborate mise-en-scène, and in the sound montage of Verdi, Bruckner, and popular German songs and lieder. The film draws on other arts to make evident that the issues treated in the text relate not *merely* to the Risorgimento but also to Fascism as well as to the present. Performance and spectacle were as endemic to Fascism (and modernity generally) as painting and opera were to the Risorgimento. In short, it is impossible to separate *Senso*'s theatricality from generally received notions of historical representation.

Visconti's film, then, is a way of addressing through spectacle the uses of the past and their implications for understanding national mythology. The text, which takes melodrama as its target of critique, is heavily invested in probing the character of theatricality. Performance is conveyed through every dimension of the film – the opera, its stars, the reiteration of a familiar narrative common to the novel, the opera, and the cinema – suggesting that the film probes, even undermines, the notion of the veracity of art and of its effects on behavior.

In this respect, there is no doubt that Visconti, with regard to Alida Valli's portrayal of Countess Livia, operates with one of the most central and resonant forms in Western representation: the figure of woman as exchange object and as source of cultural value. Her role as inevitable betrayer is guaranteed within the history of representation in Western culture. Visconti's film does not offer us a "progressive image of woman" as some would desire; instead "woman" becomes a catachresis, "the untruth of truth," exposing the unexamined relation between history and fiction.

In its treatment of the failure of the folklore of romance, Visconti's film also seems an ironic commentary on the return of the cinema of genres. The cinema of the 1950s provides evidence that war against Hollywood and the Cinecittà of the Ventennio was evanescent, a paper tiger. Despite the international popularity of films such as *Roma, città aperta, Ladri di biciclette,* and *Sciuscià,* the 1950s saw the return of the cinema of genres, the return of old stars and the rise of new ones (such as Gina Lollobrigida, Sophia Loren, Silvana Mangano, and others), numerous remakes of earlier films, and the licensed influx of scores of films from Hollywood. More particularly, the Catholic Church played a prominent role in this resurgence.

Although the church had always harbored an ambivalent attitude toward the morality of Hollywood, particularly during the years of Fascism, in the postwar era Catholic observers left no doubt as to their preference for the productions of Hollywood over the output of Italian neorealism.[25] Though still critical of certain areas (e.g., divorce, treatments of sexuality), there was no doubt that many Catholic authorities preferred "the entertainment values and cosmopolitanism of Hollywood."[26] A number of factors – the victory of the conservative Christian Democrats, censorship, economic conditions, and organized pressure to "embrace a more optimistic, healthy, and constructive attitude"[27] – contributed to the emergence of an Italian cinema that departed from the philosophic ideals of the exponents of neorealism, as expressed in their criticism, which was both ideological and aesthetic, and in the films that were identified with it. In Brunetta's words,

> As the various phases unfolded in which the cinema-goer was pro-
> gressively liberated of the germs of Fascist cinema first and then of
> their neo-realist equivalents, a process of renewal was set in motion
> involving new events and new personalities which gathered momen-
> tum in dramatic fashion as time went on.[28]

This "renewal" was Janus-headed. On one side, filmmakers such as Visconti and Fellini were increasingly identified with an "art cinema" recognized as such internationally. They were "auteurs who experimented with cinematic language," and the reflexivity of their works contained either direct or oblique references to cinematic spectacle. On the other side, the auteurist films, as Christopher Wagstaff has underscored, "depended on the general vigor of the Italian production sector, particularly at the popular level."[29] The renovated cinema of genres and of spectacle brought new activity to an ailing cinema, created new movie theaters, and new audiences; on the other hand, it en-sured that the culture of Americanism had entrenched itself and with it, the values it endorsed. For some, these values may have been identified with Fas-cism. Nonetheless, film was restored to its pedestal as a mass medium with the immense popularity of such films as *Catene* (1949), featuring the film star Amedeo Nazzari (a clip of which is inserted into *Nuovo Cinema Paradiso*), treating the melodramatic motifs of "death, blood, and family."[30]

In discussing these films, identified as "rosy neorealism," it would be re-ductive to regard them as pale imitations of melodramatic predecessors, car-bon copies of melodramas of the last years of Fascism. The melodramas, com-edies, and historical films that began to mushroom in these years introduced new personalities and complicated earlier genres. The films offer a "subver-sion of predictable plots,"[31] the "subversion" specifically entailing a concern through style and acting with the cinematic medium itself. In their excessive treatment of narrative conflict, their hybridization of genres, their assimila-tion of certain dimensions of neorealist forms of filmmaking, and their self-consciousness in the treatment of the medium, the films offer a challenge to the critic in understanding the character of cinematic culture. There are connections to be found between the concerns of the "art cinema" and the Italian popular cinema from the mid-1950s through the 1970s.

In discussing two films that depart from the earlier canons of neorealism – De Sica's *Miracolo a Milano* (1950) and Rossellini's *La macchina ammazzacattivi* (1952) – Peter Bondanella writes:

> Both films are highly self-conscious treatments of the interplay between reality and appearance, and do not provide evidence, as many critics would have it, that a political and economic crisis in Italian society was systematically ignored in the cinema on account of political or financial pressure on directors or producers, who supposedly displayed a cowardly willingness to make films for escapist entertainment rather than for progressive social change.[32]

Many of the films of the 1950s do not evade "social issues." The melodramas and the comedies address changing responses to gender, sexuality, the family, urbanization, social corruption, and history. They introduce the role of the personality in the context of changing conceptions of social and cinematic performance. The "interplay between reality and appearance," while not always addressed in reflexive fashion, has escalated beyond the films of the 1930s and early 1940s.

Robert Rossellini's *Il generale Della Rovere* (1959), like Visconti's *Senso,* links the historical moment of Fascism to the question of role-playing and visualization – and hence to the role of cinema. This was a film that Rossellini disliked, considering it "too well constructed."[33] Certainly in terms of its narrative content, the film is related to the popular cinema of genres and its folklore involving the romance of heroism, which might also implicate his own earlier films, especially *Roma, città aperta* (*Open City*). However, despite the conventionality of the themes, "all is not what it appears on the surface."[34] The films stars Vittorio De Sica, an international figure known for his acting as well as his directing. He is known, moreover, for directing such canonical texts of neorealism as *Ladri di biciclette* and *Sciuscià.* De Sica's international reputation as director and actor adds another dimension to *Il generale Della Rovere,* compounding the problematic of distinguishing the virtual from the real. As Emanuele Bardone, De Sica plays a swindler, gambler, and confidence man who inhabits many identities. He is Colonel Grimaldi, the fictitious identity he has assumed to present himself as the "savior" of victims of the Nazis for a price. Then he becomes General Della Rovere, an identity he is forced to assume to save his life when his shady schemes have been exposed to Colonel Müller (Hannes Messemer), head of Nazi operations in Milan [Fig. 22].

Figure 22. The swindler as hero: The incipient general (Vittorio De Sica) and Colonel Müller (Hannes Messemer) in *Il generale Della Rovere*. (Courtesy New York Museum of Modern Art Stills Archive)

Müller too plays a role, one not dissimilar to that of Erich von Stroheim as Rauffenstein in Renoir's *Grand Illusion*. In short, these two characters, who could be seen as protagonists in a melodramatic scenario, undermine the affective drive of melodrama. As critics have noted, the film evokes Rossellini's earlier *Open City* in its focus on the issue of loyalty and duty to the Resistance in the face of torture and sacrifice. The role of De Sica also carries echoes of his roué role in his own *L'oro di Napoli* (1954), and his identification with Naples is announced early in the film when he tells Müller, whom he has just met, that he is from "somewhere between Naples and Rome."

De Sica's role is protean. He becomes whatever is expected of him – supporter of the Nazis to the Germans, defender of Italians to those who seek his help to save relatives, romantic figure to those women he exploits for money – emerging finally as a hero of the Resistance and devoted husband of the Countess Della Rovere and father to the general's children. One way of reading the film is to regard the protagonist as finally undergoing a conversion to heroism as a consequence of his encounters in prison, his witnessing the torture and suffering of his fellow Italian prisoners. This view is of course sanctioned by the dialogue, by changes in his actions, and especially by his refusal to accept Müller's offer of a way out if he turns informer. However, to turn the film into a conversion drama not only reduces the complicated network of relations that surround his character and Müller's but also minimizes the importance of role-playing upon which the film insists. Everything turns on the fact that he remains an actor to the end, the major difference residing in the role that he chooses to play.

The film offers no revelation of his "true" identity: He dies an impostor. The only person who knows of his acting is the German officer, who has not been a good director of the drama he has produced, underestimating Bardone's capacity for play-acting. The film does not equate heroism and authenticity; in fact, it works in an opposite direction, undermining their strict correlation – a way also of undermining the melodramatic longing for realism while it thrives on excess in its inability to reconcile desire and moral imperatives, the social and the spiritual, the "surface of things" to "truer, hidden reality."[35] There is no hidden world in the film, but the issue of *how* we see seems central.

The film offers the traditional form of heroism in the figure of Bianchelli, who looks very much like the heroic priest, Don Pietro, played by Aldo Fabrizi in *Open City*. His words "I didn't talk" echo the priest's refusal to break under torture in the earlier film. Also, the figure of Müller contrasts to the melodramatic role of the Nazi Bergmann (Harry Feist) in *Open City*. Unlike Bergmann, Müller does not bear the signs of effeminacy, of deliberate cruelty. His character has the same ambiguity as De Sica's. In his role-playing, through many encounters with Bardone, with the Countess Della Rovere, and in his stated objection to the Nazi South West command of reprisals, he seems to be a kinder, gentler Fascist; yet given his obsession with the role he has given Bardone to play as General Della Rovere, he does not shrink from torture and violence. His play-acting is thus a modification of the portrayal of cinema Nazis, a correction of Rossellini's own earlier portraits of Nazis, a repudiation of simplistic forms of realism, and, especially, an indication of another conception of realism that involves a more direct address of its artificially constituted nature.

Of De Sica's character, Bondanella writes, "Bardone is a problematic character, an ambivalent antihero more suited to the uncertainties of a new age than to the immediate postwar period when back-and-white moral choices seemed possible."[36] Extending this comment to the cinema of the 1950s, we can say that De Sica's character (like that of Messemer) is the product of the marriage of neorealism with genre cinema. The style of the film is equally ambivalent: It bears the signs of neorealism in its emphasis on marginal figures like the character of Bardone; it portrays a landscape of the city that evokes the destruction of wartime; it includes documentary footage of the bombing; and yet the prison shots look more like a Hollywood crime film. The effects of Americanization are certainly evident in the blonde Valeria (Giovanna Ralli), one of Bardone's many mistresses and an imitation of the blonde sexpot so central to 1950s Hollywood (and British) commercial cinema.

The film continues the concerns of many films of the last years of Fascism as well as those of neorealism in its overriding emphasis on form rather than conventional content, and especially in its questioning of realism, using the genre film as medium. It is not a "war film," a historical film, a satire, or a dark comedy. Reenacting the Fascist era, it is a film that ponders the nature of reality as conveyed through the medium of cinema. Thus, it is a critical combination of various genres with the cinema of neorealism, submitting them to the larger issue of veracity and directing attention toward oversimplifications in the use of the cinematic image, and hence in its stance toward realism. Fascism is no longer merely a historical moment in the history of Italian culture and cinema; it is a way of looking at the world that becomes complicated by the persistence of a belief in the possibility of unadulterated and absolute truth. In this respect, *Il generale Della Rovere* exemplifies the characteristics of the time-image discussed earlier in the context of *Sorelle Materassi*. Taking as its central motif the issue of simulation and dissimulation, adopting as its protagonists two figures who are to the end engaged in role-playing, the film offers "a conception of history which simultaneously calls up the comic and the dramatic, the extraordinary and the everyday."[37]

This conception entails a recognition that characters do not act, they are acted upon. The protagonist of this cinema is no longer the hero, but Bardone, the swindler: This type of character "provokes undecidable alternatives and inexplicable differences between the true and the false."[38] The cinema takes up the banner of neorealism in a different register; realism becomes the truth of falsity, the impossibility of simple explanations, actions, and solutions, implicating the spectator in different reflections on history. Before sounding a premature death knell for neorealism, we should be cognizant that it produced and crystallized important changes in Italian cinematic culture – as in *Senso* and *Il generale Della Rovere* – in its acknowledgment of the passing of a world where filmmakers and audiences could believe in the truthfulness of the image. The "crisis of representation" begun in the Fascist era with films that openly acknowledged their fictionalizing, the struggle over the truthfulness and transparency of the cinematic image, would be challenged in both the genre films of the 1950s and 1960s as well as in the art cinema.

CHAPTER FOUR

Comedy and the Cinematic Machine

I n the customary divide between the cinema of the Fascist years and neo-realism, an opportunity is lost to understand the cinema's conception of itself as major force in Italian culture, as well as also to reconsider continuities and discontinuities in the history of Italian cinema. According to Ernesto G. Laura,

> the so-called "Italian-style" film comedy is different from other types of film comedy to be found in the history of the medium. . . . It is not only a question of a well-defined Italian landscape or of language or of even dialects, but of an intimate relationship with the customs, events, periods and problems of contemporary Italy.[1]

This chapter undertakes an examination of the permutations of cinematic comedy from the films of the 1930s to the present, focusing particularly on how various expressions of comedy are intimately tied to constructions of the nation, history, work, gender difference, and conceptions of the cinematic apparatus. Italian comedy takes a variety of forms: romantic comedy, musicals, comedian comedy (as exemplified in the work of such comic stars as Totò, Macario, Vittorio De Sica, Alberto Sordi, Nino Manfredi, and Roberto Benigni, among others), *commedia all'italiana* (related to the *commedia dell'arte*), parody, burlesque, and satire. The chapter explores how memories of Fascism and of the war are still intrinsic to the cultural life and politics of Italy, and how comedy is a major medium for recollection and criticism.

To gain an appreciation of the workings of Italian film comedy, it is necessary to return to films of Fascist era. Too often these comedies have been dismissed by critics as "white telephone" films – labeled pejoratively for the assumed presence of white telephones in the boudoirs of the rich and for their assumed "escapist" tendencies. In this manner, a large body of film production has been, until recent years, relegated to oblivion. Thus, the possibility for gaining an understanding of the connections between the cinema of the Fascist years and the cinema that succeeded it has been severely restricted. The comedies of the 1930s are, according to Christopher Wagstaff, the product of the machinery of genre, and comedy has a long history, going back to ancient Greece, in which maidens have tried to marry above their station, goals have been reached by deception, and mistaken identities have created untold chaos.[2]

The films are concerned with theatricality, role-playing, disguises, and dissimulation, and dramatize strategies for survival – some drawn from folklore – that are at times successful, at other times not. The comedies are not inane; They provide clues to the preoccupations and conflicts of the culture under Fascism.[3]

Many of the comedies of the 1930s and 1940s explore theft and deception as a precondition for acceptance of a more settled and respectable, if not modest, form of existence. However, their mode of reconciliation is ambiguous, a form of craftiness that appears to cancel out the more malevolent and melodramatic dimensions of manipulation and control, though the strategies are not transparent. In particular, Wagstaff identifies two types of comedy: the *commedia brillante,* derived from Austro–Hungarian theater and film comedies, with its brittle dialogue and its focus on the comedies of misrecognition; and *commedia sentimentale,* with its focus on a more emotional, domestic, even melodramatic view of the conflicts experienced and resolved for and by the protagonists.[4] The comedies offer more than conventional treatments of narrative and character. Through their creation of character and often innovative uses of setting, they offer clues into the films' relations to – *not* evasion of – social reality. Even more, they call attention to the medium, to the film as artifact and to the artificial character of the world they create. They do not necessarily serve overtly as a means of resistance to the status quo, but they do dramatize problems endemic to the cinematic apparatus.

The films manage, through theatricalization, impersonation, and disguise, to involve audiences, often cynically, in a bifurcated rather than completely naturalized and unified sense of the filmic world and hence of the culture. This enables a more complicated and conflicting range of responses to the familiar social conflicts posed in relation to courtship, marriage, or work. In the confrontation of the changing and often threatening terms of modern existence, survival is identified with ingenuity and dissimulation, and one of the things the comedies address is the common sense of "acting a part." While highlighting the snares and pitfalls of masquerade, the films also portray a culture that comes to depend more and more on visualization, particularly through cinema. One of the major conflicts in most of the comedies seems to be the tension between naturalness and artifice, and often it is artifice that is valorized as a means for negotiating conformity and desire.

La segretaria privata (1931), directed by Goffredo Alessandrini, was identified with its female protagonist's theme song, "Come sono felice [How

Happy I Am]" – the Italian equivalent at the time of the Roosevelt era's myth of "Happy Days Are Here Again" and a counterpart to the regime's emphasis on moving into modernity. The film focuses on the aspirations of petit-bourgeois figures struggling to attain an economic and social foothold in the middle class, though only a few are chosen. A version of *Privatseketärin* (Private Secretary), the film bears some of the marks of the German original in the use of music and in its characterization. The film fuses Hollywood, Hungarian, and German popular comedies of the 1930s, with their emphasis on female workers: shop girls, secretaries, typists, and department store clerks.

La segretaria opens with an image of a suitcase, before the camera travels to the image of the female protagonist, Elsa (Elsa Merlini). The train, a familiar cinematic image of modernity, arrives at the station, and men swarm to help Elsa with her suitcase; but a nattily dressed man with spats calls a taxi for her, expecting a "reward" for his assistance. She rides off – alone. The suitcase functions in hermeneutic and proleptic fashion to identify Elsa as the film's "baggage," raising the question of who will carry her away and under what circumstances. The feminine "baggage" is the fiction on which the film rests. She is the baggage of folklore, especially of the Cinderella narrative.

At the Pensione Primavera [Fig. 23], Elsa joins other working-class women also waiting for an opportunity to "strike it rich." They complain of the food, regimented life, and poor salaries, while the owner, like a headmistress, reminds them that payment for their room and board is overdue. Undaunted, Elsa is optimistic, hoping to earn her "mille lire al mese" (one thousand lire a month), and the following day she seeks employment. At an office of a bank, she sees women applicants turned away by the porter, Otello (Sergio Tofano), and she too is sent off. Again refusing to succumb to blighted hopes, she captures his attention by talking to him about music, especially opera, enhancing the film's reflexive allusions to theatricality and particularly its operatic dimensions. He asks her what music she prefers, and, sizing up the situation correctly and resourcefully, she responds, "Verdi." When she informs him that she likes *Otello,* she wins him over, and he tells her that he is the director of a chorus. He invites her to a concert, but she says pathetically that if she does not get a job she must return to the country. When he learns her name, he identifies her with Elsa in Wagner's *Lohengrin.* Given these signs of shared interests in opera, Otello takes her to the head of personnel (Cesare Zopetti), and she is hired because she is a potential object of seduction.

The office is a model of modern regimentation, desks equidistant from each other and lined up in symmetrical rows. Like a general reviewing his troops, the head of personnel inspects the typists – a not-uncommon Fordist image in comedies that feature workers. This unattractive image of discipline also serves as a sign of ambivalence in relation to the workplace and the role of women within it. At first, Elsa is ebullient about her work; then through a

Figure 23. Elsa Merlini as Elsa in *La segretaria privata* (Private Secretary). (Courtesy New York Museum of Modern Art Stills Archive)

series of dissolves, her look of joy alters to one of fatigue. She finds a seductive note from the head of personnel among her papers. He grows annoyed with her evasion of him and begins to find problems with her work, forcing her to work longer hours. During one of these late sessions, she is discovered by Berri (Nino Besozzi), president of the bank, as he leaves his office. Unaware of his identity, Elsa complains of her situation, and he sits down and helps her finish her work. In the process he finds that the mistakes attributed to her are those of the head of personnel, mistakes she has tried to correct. He invites her to dinner, and they end up at Otello's concert at a restaurant-club. There Otello conducts a group of singers in a medley of songs, and when he spots Berri in the audience, Berri signals to him to remain silent about his identity. The festive evening ends with Otello singing again as the camera pans a happy audience. In the taxi after, Elsa tells Berri how happy she is, and the scene cuts to Otello on the street, drunk and staggering, but singing about how happy he is.

Happiness turns to melodramatic conflict when Berri tries to seduce Elsa by inviting her to his house, and she is driven to defend her embattled virginity. At the boardinghouse, while other women are seen kissing their escorts good night, Elsa merely shakes Berri's hand and enters the house, where she again breaks into song. The final shot of this episode is of the women's shadows at their windows as light after light is extinguished.

At work the following day, the typists work under the strict surveillance of the head of personnel, and Elsa is berated for being late. She now recognizes Berri as the boss, and confusion mounts as Otello and Berri machinate to have Elsa come to Berri's house to take dictation. When Elsa arrives, she is greeted by the majordomo. Berri's home is an advertisement for the latest in modernist geometric furniture and interior design. He offers her refreshments and acts seductively toward her. When she slaps his face and exits, he says, "She loves me." She does not appear at work the following day, however, and Berri calls in the head of personnel and tells him to order Elsa back to the office or be fired. The man goes and begs her to return to work, but she refuses. Finally, Berri arrives at the pensione, confesses his love for her, and proposes marriage. While the other women vie to get a view of the romantic scene, Otello peers at the couple through the keyhole. The film ends with him conducting the women spectators in song, celebrating Elsa's success.

Similar to Hollywood comedies of the era, made during the early years of the transition to sound, *La segretaria* indulges "in a favorite Depression fantasy: the poor working girl, trapped in her dingy life, suddenly gets the chance to spend the rest of her days with a rich and handsome prince."[5] The film is characterized by its upbeat qualities, the liveliness of the songs, and the sense of collective optimism even among the other not-so-fortunate women at the pensione. Elsa, like her American counterparts, is a resourceful and independent character; but she is exceptional in contrast to other women of her class in her shrewdness about sexual morality, the key to her success. Her commonsense attitude of saving her virginity until marriage is central to her gaining the attention of the bank president.

Otello's role as a conductor of a glee club introduces the film's reflexive elements. He is the director of the action, finding Elsa the job, keeping silent about Berri's identity, and even impersonating him at one point. His identification with musical entertainment serves as a surrogate for the film's director, making impersonation and the upside-down world of carnival the sine qua non of success. Otello introduces the element of spectacle that underpins the entire film not only in his directing of the singing but also in calling attention to the element of *looking* that introduces and closes the film. Elsa is the object of surveillance: The head of personnel looks her over; she and Berri enjoy the spectacle of Otello's performance; and the young women at the pensione observe her with admiration and envy.

The final episode at the keyhole (an analogue for the cinema?) with Otello and the young women is a visual motto for the film in its highlighting of the pleasure of looking, particularly gazing at images of success. The aforementioned theme song, "Come sono felice," bears relation to Hollywood forms of Depression entertainment. The film valorizes the pleasures associated with the commodities made possible by capitalism in its focus on the elegance of clothing, automobiles, modern and sumptuous decor, and on the banker as the dispenser of equity and happiness. In the process, the film also sells itself as entertainment through the image of its star as the conduit for happiness and optimism. Thus, it might seem that *La segretaria* validates the notion that it is pure escapist fare designed for "little shop girls" who "go to the movies" to gratify their fantasies.[6] Such a reading maintains the assumptions that audiences, particularly female members of the audience, are totally swept away by the dreams of love and wealth, and that romance comedies are unashamedly given over to ideology: *La segretaria* not only portrays the drudgery, humiliation, and cramped lives of the working women at the pensione – a fate from which Elsa escapes – but stresses, in the face of economic and social constraints, the necessity of ingenuity and wit for personal survival that she characterizes.

Even more, however, *La segretaria* raises questions about the nature of the "cinematic machine." It seems clear that the film is not unaware of its devices, either of the role of cinema as a "dream factory" or of the importance of fusing fantasies of upward mobility with certain realities: the limits and exigencies of daily life in relation to work, the position of women as workers outside the home and exploited by their employers, and the role of marriage as a way out of social constraints. Moreover, the film is predicated – perhaps not intentionally, but culturally and generically – on a view of cinema as a mythical instrument capable both of redeeming ordinary life and as of serving as a "machine to kill bad people" (or, at least, maim and render them ineffectual). However, the cinema was far more important in inaugurating a new relationship to the world predicated on its power to refashion that world. Like advertising, fashion, and the rituals of public life, cinema introduced audiences to the world of the hyperreal, and may thus be regarded as instrumental (before discussions of the postmodern) in creating uncertainty about boundaries between the fictional and the "real."

One of the most well-received and profitable forms of comedy in the 1930s and early 1940s comprised the sentimental comedies made by the team of director Mario Camerini and stars Assia Noris and Vittorio De Sica (both audience favorites), such as *Gli uomini che mascalzoni . . . , Il signor Max* (see Chapter 11), *Batticuore,* and *Darò un milione.* The popular Noris and De Sica promoted an image of stardom that combined ordinariness and exceptionality, much as the films themselves fused the quotidian aspects of social life with the exotic. Unlike *La segretaria privata,* these films, though flirting with the world of the upper classes and with upward mobility, do not always resolve their narratives in favor of wealth and escape from the banalities of working-class existence: In *Gli uomini che mascalzoni . . .* (*Men Are Such Rascals,* 1932) and *Il signor Max* (*Mr. Max,* 1937), the protagonist played by De Sica remains within his working-class milieu. However, the more satiric *Darò un milione* (1935) and *Batticuore* (1939) do end with the female protagonist joining the ranks of the upper classes. That this form of comedy was viable, durable, had a profitable life, and crossed national boundaries is evident in the popularity of Camerini's comedies that focus on working-class characters. His films are similar to Victor Saville's *Sunshine Susie* (1931, another film based on *Privatsekretärin*), and numerous Hollywood comedies of the era where the world of typists and clerks is temporarily transformed into melodrama and finally redeemed through comedy. These texts rely on the devices of impersonation, misrecognition, and chance to sustain the tension between fantasy and everyday reality. As important as the delivery of the female protagonist from her humdrum existence is the fact that not every character is redeemed.

The carnivalesque as an image of an inverted world is fundamental to comedy and satire, and many of the comedies of the era are set within this context. Familiar behavior is suspended; roles are interchanged and reversed. Instead of impersonation, there is masquerade. Instead of collectivity and community, there are romantic coupling and escapism as the protagonists flee this world at film's end. In *Darò un milione* (*I'll Give a Million*) – which also stars De Sica and Noris, and won a prize at the Venice Film Festival – comedy depends on a familiar hypothetical question designed to overturn existing social roles: "What would happen if you met a millionaire who was willing to bankroll you?" This hypothesis sets in motion the narrative machinery that facilitates a momentary upsetting of expectations, allowing different and even critical perceptions of the situation to emerge. *Darò un milione* is hardly a legitimation of the status quo.

Blim (Luigi Almirante), a hobo reminiscent of Boudu in Renoir's *Boudu sauvé des eaux* as well as of Chaplin's tramp, is shown on the shore of a river. He has tied a weight to his leg and is wading into the deep water. The scene shifts to a nearby ship, where a tuxedoed man, Gold (De Sica), has been standing on the deck, aimlessly looking through binoculars until he observes the hobo seeking to end his existence. Immediately, Gold jumps into the water and swims to shore to rescue him. The men struggle, but Gold restrains Blim. The scene then cuts indoors to an elegant room where people are gathered by a radio listening to news of Gold's disappearance. Elsewhere, the hobo and the millionaire sit outdoors by a fire. Gold hangs up his own clothes to dry as Blim observes him, ogling wet money also hanging out to dry. Gold tells the beggar that he "will give a million" if he could find a person who was interested in him for reasons other than his money. The men fall asleep, and

Figure 24. The carnivalesque in *Darò un milione* (*I'll Give a Million*): Assia Noris as Anna. (Courtesy New York Museum of Modern Art Stills Archive)

when Blim awakens the next morning, his clothes are gone, and so is Gold; but the millionaire's clothes and money remain.

Now at the circus, Gold sees, on a sheet hanging up to dry, the shadow of a woman (as if in a shadow show). He looks again and is confused by the appearance of a heavy-set woman, who is not the same as the first shadow figure. Finally the first shadow-woman is revealed – it is Anna (Assia Noris) [Fig. 24] – and a crisis occurs that brings the couple together: "Bob," a dog and mathematical whiz, escapes down the road following a cyclist, and Anna and Gold give chase. Blim, meanwhile, has taken his story to the newspapers, informing them of the millionaire's offer. A lengthy sequence shows the editor's interview of Blim, introduces plans for capitalizing on the story, and culminates in the image of a layout with the headline, "I'll give a million to whoever makes a disinterested and generous gesture toward me." The sequence follows the circulation of the newspaper, people reading it and then passing on the information to others – thus emphasizing the notion of the media as purveyors of information (or rather disinformation). Beggars are shown now helping each other in the hope that one of them is the millionaire. Blim, however, has been trying to escape from the clutches of the newspaper editor, who has him confused with another hobo in bed with his wife.

Back at the circus, the stage is set for a lottery. The scene is crowded with equestrians, acrobats, floats, and beggars, as a billboard with a million-lire note painted on it is lowered to the ground. The spectacle in this scene involves a musical number miming the confusion between beggars and millionaires. The lottery is held, and Gold's number wins, highlighting chance or coincidence. When the beggars discover that Gold has the winning number, they douse him with water, and Anna takes him to her room to help him dry his clothes. While Anna irons his clothing, she finds a diamond ring. He offers it to her, but she refuses. Suspicious, she interrogates him, wondering why he doesn't work. Then the manager enters and, thinking Gold has compromised Anna, expels him from the circus. Gold returns, but when he observes her talking to the manager (by means of the same shadow technique as earlier in the film), he grows mistrustful.

Outside, Gold's "abdication" of life-style and offer of riches have turned the world upside down, destabilizing relations and producing greed masked as altruism. Gold decides to return to his ship. Finding Blim, he voices his disillusionment with people. (The world-gone-mad is beginning to normalize, however, as the greedy begin to return to their habitual bad treatment of beggars.) Gold tells Anna that there is no reason to pursue him, since he is not the millionaire. As he prepares to embark for his ship, she tells him good-bye and presses ten francs into his hand. This gesture melts his anger. He kisses her and says he has finally found a generous friend. Bringing her aboard ship, Gold places his ring on her finger.

The scene cuts to the beggars and Blim having their own party. Blim takes the money that Gold had left him and spends it on rides for the beggars, and the film ends on this saturnalian note.

Like most satire, *Darò un milione* relies on role-playing, role reversal, irony, and burlesque. The circus becomes a synecdoche for society, where different classes converge. Gold, like his English name, is the force that sets these agencies into motion and also disrupts their normal functioning. Furthermore, the narrative suggests that the vision of a transformed society is illusory. The exceptions to this view reside in the notion of pleasure exemplified by the beggars who, with Blim, enjoy the amusement rides at the end, perhaps an ambiguous comment on contemporary cultural predilections for bread and circuses to divert the masses. Dressing, undressing, and the exchange of clothes reinforce the various disguises, impersonations, and role reversals that take place. At the outset, Gold exchanges outfits with Blim; later, clothing comes to be associated with Anna, who is a maker of costumes. Her slip becomes an object of contemplation by Gold as she irons his clothes. Another recurring image, central to the film's concern with the attempt to unite materialism and spirituality, is of shadows. Gold twice encounters Anna through her shadow, as if to connect her to the illusory nature of the screen. Although the film does not allude to the cinema as a medium of deception, in its emphasis on the role of spectacle via the circus and in its play on shadows and on misrecognition, it does highlight visual perception and performativity. Given its heavy emphasis on role-playing, *Darò un milione* also seems less as a celebration of romantic love and more a reproach to the status quo as it dissects and uses masquerade to expose masquerade. This film, like Camerini's others, appears to be uneasy about spectacle and spectatorship. A platonic preoccupation with the illusory nature of appearance, a suspicion of looking, governs the text. In its treatment of femininity, the film seems to equate woman with spectacle, and spectacle with hypocrisy and deception – a motif that seems particularly apt in relation to the politics of Fascism.

Similarly preoccupied with impersonation and with fantasy, Camerini's 1939 film *Batticuore* is a satire on the world of the upper class and pretenders to that world. It adopts a range of melodramatic and comic devices to explore complicated relations among property, theft, and the law. The film is set in Paris, providing typical touristic shots of the city. Then, in voyeuristic fashion, a camera outside moves to peer into a window. Inside, a teacher (Luigi Almirante) lectures and tests his pupils, using a stuffed mannequin evident as the focus of testing and interrogation. Later, on the street, Arlette (Assia Noris) and a young man discuss their teacher's assignments and his expectations; they talk about gaining employment. So far, the scene seems innocuous, suggesting nothing disreputable; but the narrative takes an unexpected turn as Arlette's colleague approaches a fat, cigar-smoking man and tries to pick his pocket. The affair backfires, and the victim calls for help. People gather, while Arlette and her companion escape.

Later, Arlette rejoins "Professor" Comte and his other "students" at his school for thieves as he lines them up to stage scenarios of successful theft. He drills them through various stealthy movements designed to ward off arrest. Arlette is singled out to go through certain paces. The group then practices picking the pockets of a mannequin. For their final exercise, they pretend they are riding on the bus, plying their trade. At their "graduation" party, Comte further inspects Arlette to ensure she is professional. He has her practice an alibi should she get caught, namely, that she is basically an honest and virtuous person, has never had any run-in with the law before, and begs leniency. He prophesies a promising career for her.

After a failed attempt to find legitimate work, Arlette finds herself on an elevator with a well-to-do looking man who wears a jeweled stickpin. A series of cuts between close-ups of her and of the stickpin leads to a shot of the man – minus the pin that she has stolen. Seeking to evade her victim, she enters a movie theater featuring a Fred Astaire–Ginger Rogers movie (one of the two direct allusions to media in the film) and sits, only to find the man seated next to her. She replays her innocent-victim routine with him while the onscreen film enacts the same scenario, underscoring the film's preoccupation with the confusion between life and theater. The man, Count Maciaky (Giuseppe Porelli), orders her to come with him to the Stivonian Embassy.

We next see Arlette in fashionable clothes (provided by Maciaky) as she enters the grand hall of the embassy. The count tells her to dance with Jerry, Lord Salisbury (John Lodge), an English nobleman, and to steal his pocketwatch, which bears the photograph of the Stivonian ambassador's wife. During a television broadcast that gets scrambled – the second allusion to media in the film – Arlette removes the woman's picture from the watch. She then places the watch in Jerry's pocket, thinking that he is unaware of her machinations and impersonation.

After the ball, Jerry insists on escorting her home. Hoping to escape him, she pretends to take a room at a hotel. She exits to find him waiting. He invites her to a restaurant and tries to get information from her about the "secrecy he sees in her eyes." They have their photograph taken, and once more Jerry comments on her eyes, telling her she does not "look like a sinner" – again highlighting photography and its relation to "truth." When they exit, he kisses her, and they are observed by the Professor, who is in the bushes, disguised. Jerry tries to catch him, but all he finds is a discarded beard. Arlette returns to the hotel and actually takes a room.

The next day, Jerry calls her, but she says she cannot see him, as she does not have her baggage from Stivonia. At his residence, Jerry tells his butler – the very man whose pocket Arlette's companion had earlier tried to pick – that he is in love with Arlette but plans to teach her a lesson. He then goes to see her and has several new outfits brought to her. She accuses him of trying to seduce her, but after he reassures her, she agrees to spend the day with him. She has also received a threatening note from Maciaky to return the borrowed clothes or be exposed, but the note was accompanied by a bracelet.

The Professor arrives, takes the bracelet, and in return gives her money to pay her bill. Hoping to escape Jerry, Arlette leaves, but she sees him on her way out. She tries to dissuade him from any future relations, saying that he knows nothing of her past, but he is undeterred. In the lobby, too, is her former companion in crime, jealous of Jerry's attentions. When Jerry discovers that his watch is missing, he thinks Arlette is the culprit; but her erstwhile accomplice, incompetent as always, is caught by hotel security. Jerry insists that the young man be punished, and the scene shifts to police headquarters, where Arlette tries to confess to her crimes. When Count Maciaky is called to testify, he surprisingly asserts that nothing was stolen and shows that he is in possession of his stickpin. Moreover, when Jerry's pocketwatch is pried open, it is revealed that the only thing in it is the photo of Jerry and Arlette taken earlier. The two are reconciled, and she begins to recount a narrative of her life. The film ends with wedding festivities, where the Professor and his students enjoy the opportunity to fleece the rich guests; however, they agree it is a special day and decide to return the stolen items.

Camerini's seemingly "light" (and thus underestimated) comedy touches on basic social structures as they are implicated in Italy's contemporary society. The film's ostensible escapism resides in its playful amorality, its use of parody, and its employing romance to reestablish customary morality at the end, masking the more serious notion that "property is theft." Although the film reproduces conventional voyeurism, allowing a peek into the world of wealth and luxury, its mechanisms of spectatorship are such that its view of the life of the other half exposes its moral imperfections. From the opening shots, the issue of looking is highlighted. The inside–outside images underscore the notion of hiding, then exposing, what goes on inside this society. The audience is playfully indicted as a voyeur and then invited to participate in this hide-and-seek. Looking as a form of surveillance and discipline is emphasized, as each of the characters controls the other through their gaze: the Professor his students, the thieves their victim, the count and Jerry the scrutinized Arlette. Through this emphasis, and in linking looking to crime, the film undermines any simplistic notion of escapism and opens a window onto the complexities of popular cinema, particularly in its willingness to share with the audience knowledge about its strategies.

The recognition of the image as currency appears central to Camerini's film, offering a meditation on representation as unstable specie circulating through many and untrustworthy hands. Impersonation or performance is thus more than a self-reflexive device: As in so many melodramas of the era, it begins to resonate with supplementary, politicocultural meanings, raising the question of authenticity, of truth. *Batticuore* even undermines the truthfulness of confession, as Arlette's attempts to tell the truth are finally thwarted by Jerry, the count, and the police.

Camerini's comedies are not naïve about the power of the cinematic image. In their various explorations of theatricality – whether acknowledging the necessity for social survival of blurring the boundaries between art and life, the value of withholding information, and the need for impersonation (even theft) rather than authenticity – they provide insights into the complex character of cinema, which thrives by generating a sense of the image as real and desirable while also conveying its fictional status. In their stylization and their self-conscious attention to the powers of theatricality, these comedies demonstrate that they cannot be relegated to a limbo of escapism in which the audience passively consumes dream images. Rather, the texts work to enlist the audiences in the work of constituting a world that is both familiar and estranging. By calling attention to performance, these films find a meeting ground with the spectator, even if it is often only one of cynicism. They subvert political platitudes and truisms about the uniformity of consensus by underscoring the ubiquity and inevitability of the artifice of performance as endemic to art and to social life.

In reaction to what they considered the triviality and escapism of the genre cinema under Fascism, filmmakers and social critics sought to discredit such formulaic types of filmmaking by inventing freer, less stylized, and more contemporary cinematic forms that they deemed more realistic. Their objective was to create a new pedagogy for film, one that addressed the ravages of war, the persistence of Fascism in postwar Italian institutions, and the possibility of reeducating spectators to the need for a new cultural politics. Of the films of the late 1940s and their impact, André Bazin wrote:

> [D]oes one not, when coming out of an Italian film, feel better, an urge to change the order of things, preferably by persuading people, at least those who can be persuaded, whom only blindness, prejudice, or ill fortune had led to harm their fellow men?[7]

For many critics it was necessary to reject the films of the 1930s and 1940s as being too closely tied to Fascism – a perennial anxiety that haunts Italian cinema. This anxiety led many commentators on Italian cinema to forget the cinematic productions of that era, and has also led critics to underestimate connections between the films of the 1930s and those of the postwar period. However, as Christopher Wagstaff indicates, "Neorealism's depiction of the ordinary, everyday life of typical Italians owed a lot to the narrative strategies accumulated in the 1930s and 1940s for comedy films (the genre most often used this type of social setting)."[8] In addition, these earlier comic and satiric films were not blind to social excesses but expressed them within the bounds that censorship circumscribed.

During the heyday of the films identified with the neorealist movement, there was a tendency on the part of "overzealous progressive critics . . . to place neorealist directors within an aesthetic impasse"[9] by insisting on a fidelity to authentic locations, a documentarylike look, nonprofessional actors, and an avoidance of artifice associated with genres. However, it became clear that such strictures were constraining and, what is more, did a disservice to the attempts to understand the very basis of neorealism – namely, its insistence on an *exploration* of reality. In critical commentaries on Italian cinema, one still finds accounts that narrate the demise of neorealism. Such accounts rely on a rigid view of the neorealist style and its preoccupations, freezing these productions into a particular time frame too narrow to accommodate Italy's cinematic past as well as the changing concerns of neorealism. The ethical and investigative spirit of neorealism was not abandoned; rather, there was a greater exploration of the conditions and nature of realism in more complex and philosophic terms, often in the vein of comedy and satire.

One of the most complex cinematic commentaries on cinema and photography and their relations to social reality is the comedy *La macchina ammazzacattivi* (*The Machine to Kill Bad People*, 1948–52) by the filmmaker of the canonical *Roma, città aperta*, Rossellini. *La macchina* employs a mixture of professional and nonprofessional actors, documentary and studio footage, fantasy and everyday reality. In its style and its fusing of realism and illusionism, the film relies on standard techniques of the popular commercial cinema: Flashbacks, montage editing, dissolves, wipes, and superimpositions are all used in its investigation of the townspeople and the miracles that befall them. Focusing on a surrogate for cinema (this time, photography) in its probe of myths of the omnipotent visual image, the film includes a wide range of social types and social conflicts; but its primary impetus is to interrogate the nature of representation, particularly concerning the filmmaker's power and the nature of ethical responsibility in filmmaking.

The film's theatricality is announced immediately by the image of a hand inserting a model of a town, suggesting a comparison between the film and the stage. The comedy begins with a group of American men and their families. The men, veterans of World War II and of the fighting in Italy, are plotting ways to make money by turning the ruins of a castle on the mountain (also the site of the town cemetery) into a luxury hotel. One of the company, a young woman, notices a sign that reads "long live Saint Andrea," that day being a festival to honor the saint. As the Americans drive on the tortuous winding road to the village, they hit an old bearded man, who mysteriously disappears when they try to find his body. He reappears in the next scenes walking on the town streets and looking like a figure out of religious painting or icon – alerting the spectator to his mysterious, even magical, role. The parallels between his image and that of the saint are the first clues to his ensuing importance. The camera returns to his image several times during the lengthy shots of the religious procession held in honor of the patron saint. Other characters are introduced, most notably Celestino Esposito, a photographer (Gennaro Pisano) who might be considered the film's surrogate director in collaboration with the old man. Close-ups of the town worthies are intercut with views of the procession. The camera returns several times to the town moneylender, Amalia, who is an object of the other spectators's surveillance and negative comments.

The middle section of the film is introduced through a visitation to Celestino by the old man [Fig. 25]. Echoing a biblical motif, in particular of Mary and Joseph seeking room at the inn, the man asks for a night's lodging. From here on, the film in a series of episodes portrays the follies of members of the community, involving parental abuse, memories of Fascist officials, and, above all, economic competition and greed by individuals, businessmen, and the mayor and other town worthies. Celestino's humble shop is covered with photographs of these townspeople, which the old man examines. Their conversation is interrupted by a young couple, Romeo and Juliet, who are plotting to run away from their rich feuding parents and request the willing aid of Celestino. The old man asks Celestino why he is willing to violate the dictum "Thou shalt honor thy father and his mother" by assisting the couple, and Celestino recounts his story of being displaced by Agostino, the town policeman, in the affections of a woman. Moreover, through Celestino's account, shown in flashback, the old man learns that Agostino was a confirmed Fascist. Upon discovering this, the old man says, "We'll fix him," and asks for a photo of Agostino, muttering that the town really needs assistance. Not comprehending, Celestino responds that what they really need is Saint Andrea. The suspicion, long since planted, that this old man is himself the saint soon seems confirmed: After he instructs Celestino to photograph the photo of Agostino, the actual figure of Agostino is found miraculously frozen in a Fascist salute.

Now a series of "miracles" occur in which the townspeople are punished for their greed and indifference to each other. The next miracle involves the appearance of town boats loaded with fish after a long period of unsuccessful fishing. Instead of rejoicing, however, the wealthy Del Bello and Cuccurullo, fathers to the escaping lovers, quarrel bitterly over price as the townspeople look on. Miracles continue to happen, the next being the arrival of a letter for the mayor indicating that the Ministry of Public Works has given the town eleven million lire. Quarrels quickly escalate among various representatives of the town, each trying to arrogate the money for his own ends. Celestino attempts to intervene and explain the miracle, but he is ignored by all. No one, not even the priest, seems to be interested in his news. Greed runs rampant. Amalia, the moneylender, appears and tells the town council that the money is hers, since everyone is indebted to her; she plans to use it for a monument to her dead husband. Even the workers machinate to get the money. Disgusted with these visions of greed, hypocrisy, and lack of community identification, Celestino decides to take revenge. Gradually he begins to exercise power, copying photos of the townspeople and thereby "exterminating the wicked" despite the town doctor's warning that "as soon as one goes another takes his place." After accidentally photo-freezing the doctor, Celestino decides to punish himself in the same fashion for his abuse of the camera's powers. He is stopped, however, by the reappearance of the old man, who is revealed to the photographer as an incompetent devil who had "hoped to make a name for himself." Celestino convinces him (at the price

Figure 25. Celestino (Gennaro Pisano) and his visitor in *La macchina ammazzacattivi* (*The Machine to Kill Bad People*). (Courtesy New York Museum of Modern Art Stills Archive)

of becoming mortal) to revive the dead, and the film ends with the scene of the miniature stage set and the voice-over intoning, "Do good but don't overdo it and think twice before you punish anyone." Thus, the audience is invited to contemplate connections easily taken for granted between morality and cinematography.

The role of artifice is central: in the image of the hand itself at the beginning and end ironically reminiscent of Michelangelo's *Creation,* linking the film to religious painting but also to the creative aspects of vision through artifice. The central role played by photography reinforces the film's preoccupation with reproduction and with recording, characteristics of mass media as opposed to painting. Another intertextual allusion, this time to music, is to the opera *I Pagliacci* and its ironic notion of "la commedia." According to Peter Brunette, "the theatrical elements foreground the artificiality of the narrative, of course, and the status of *La macchina ammazzacattivi* as filmed artifact is appropriately underlined by continuous dissolves, a uniquely cinematic device."[10] The difficulty that critics have had with the film resides in its eclectic character, its fusion of fantasy, documentary, and documentarylike images. The film is an exercise in style whose eclecticism, pastiche, and fusion of realism and fantasy contribute to its examination of the heterogeneous and improvisatory nature of cinematic representation.

La macchina, by exploring the moral and political implications of cinema, probes the character of the visual image and renders it more ambiguous than in classical realist cinema and more complex than in earlier examples of neorealist social critique. The film seems to focus on the position of the creator, the production process, and the technology, satirizing the expectation of a direct correlation between image and reality and between intent and practice. It would seem that the filmmaker is not interested in establishing and affirming univalently a "link between the man and the world." Rather, "Rossellini loses interest in art, which he reproaches for being infantile and sorrowful, for reveling in a loss of a world: he wants to replace it with a morality which would restore a belief capable of perpetuating life."[11]

The criticism of the film, which faults Rossellini for mixing fantasy and realism – and, even more, for not distinguishing between the oppressors and the oppressed – does not address its more complex analysis of the role of filmmakers: They are neither saints nor moralists, and when they adopt these positions, they do as much harm as the evils they try to eradicate. Comedy thus serves to investigate and challenge doctrinaire and authoritarian positions. In the words of Peter Bondanella:

> While creating an elaborate joke with Celestino's self-delusory activity, Rossellini emphasizes a fundamental characteristic of filmic art. In a comic manner he tells us that photography (and by extension, the cinema as a branch of this art form) is incapable of separating good from evil or of readily distinguishing reality from appearance. ... Nowhere is there any clear distinction between diametrically opposed metaphysical or ethical positions. The camera, viewed as a means of acquiring knowledge of social reality by overly optimistic neorealistic theorists, has been reduced to a fallible and neutral instrument. . . .[12]

These comments apply as well to overly optimistic views of cinema from a number of ideological perspectives, including those concerning Fascism. The film's focus on the role of cinema (*la macchina*) is not a prescriptive or even merely descriptive one. Rather, it serves to examine the role of illusion, particularly as it relates to the reductive ways in which many films (and much film criticism) still hold to the canons of realism as positing a link between the world and the spectator. *La macchina ammazzacattivi* plays at undermining that position, enabling a different and more critical view of cinematic illusion.

Peter Brunette writes, "One of the most interesting things about the film is that it is cast in the form of the *commedia dell'arte* (a form that was also to interest Renoir), and thus largely concerned with broad character types rather than sharply individual psychological portraits."[13] The stylization and typification endemic to this comedy can be seen as enhancing its investigation of visual representation as well as establishing comedy "as a form of documentation."[14] Bondanella, too, suggests that "the links between Rossellini's film and the *commedia dell'arte* lie . . . in the film's reliance on vivid comic action, visual effects, humor, and a conception of film character based on the comic masks typical of this theatrical tradition."[15] These techniques serve as an alternative to the rigid strictures of the cinema of neorealism, where characters "are determined by their social surroundings."[16] In the satiric treatment of the working-class characters, whose behavior mirrors that of the middle classes, the film also turns away from an uncritical partisanship with workers – another feature that drew ire from leftist critics. The film had committed itself to exploring the potentially destructive nature of individuals with access to this powerful medium, so all forms of criticism were now opened to investigation. This included simplistic judgments about the cinema under Fascism.

In ways consonant with *La macchina*, Federico Fellini has criticized prescriptive notions of film, political engagement, and forms of reception. *Amarcord* (1974) proffers memories of cinema as inherently tied to the culture of Fascism. According to James Hay, "Fellini's *Amarcord* presupposes that images (whether those we fabricate ourselves, perceptually, or those fabricated for us, artistically or commercially) are an essential component of social interaction and knowledge."[17] Regarding the film's treatment of "social interaction and knowledge," and particularly of memory, Fellini remarked:

> Mine is not a nostalgic memory, but one of refutation. Before delivering a judgment, one must first try to understand: reality can't be contemplated aesthetically, but reviewed critically. *Amarcord* is an awkward film. How many films have you seen which have given you the same picture of Fascism, the same portrayal of Italian society of that period as much as it intends to suggest the danger of any intention – in a less naïve and clumsy but more ominous way – of returning to the same society. Fascism is like a threatening shadow which doesn't stay motionless at our backs. . . . Fascism always lies waiting in ambush within us.[18]

Fellini's observations can be said to characterize the ongoing anxiety in Italian culture about the character and ever-present threat of Fascism. Moreover, this anxiety emanates, as Fellini suggests, from the refusal on the part of intellectuals and artists to think critically about the nature and role of Fascism.

Not alternating between documentary realism and fantasy, as did Rossellini's film, but remaining within the parameters of fantasy, caricature, and even satire, *Amarcord* picks up the issue of the role of the artist and of illusion, challenging notions of realism as political truth. The film does not adhere to a single narrative line; it is not a narrative but an excursus on narration. Employing a number of characters, adopting the town's lawyer as a historian, directing focus away from a conventional protagonist who is the agent of the film's actions, dispersing attention over a field of figures, creating a loosely linked, episodic, and even circular structure, the film does not lend itself to a "message" or to a reenactment of conventional rescue or redemption fantasies. The spectator instead becomes aware of a number of simultaneous events adding up to a very fragmentary and nonpolemic portrait of life in a small town during the Fascist era, and of the various and different elements that comprise this cinematic community. While the film acknowledges folly and cruelty, even violence, its does not become a machine to kill bad people.

The film is neither history, nor biography, nor allegory; it is an encyclopedic foray into the nature of cinematic spectacle. The spectacle is composite in origin – drawn partly from folklore, as in the early scenes portraying the rituals governing the coming of spring, the bonfire of the burning of the witch. During this episode, *Amarcord* provides a sense of the various (and selective) elements that constitute a collective memory of that earlier period. However, if there is any element that can be singled out as governing these episodes, it is the role of cinema: "As a cultural exploration, *Amarcord* dramatizes the American cinema's subtle yet pervasive effects on the sensibilities of a relatively provincial movie public."[19] In the opening scenes the viewer is made aware of the key role played by the town's movie theater and its advertisements for Hollywood films. With the entry of Gradisca, the town's Greta Garbo, and of the movie theater owner, the town's Ronald Colman, the importance of Hollywood is made so manifest that it becomes meshed with the world of the everyday. Moreover, the bonfire itself becomes another oblique examination of the role of spectatorship, as the camera roams over the gathered audience, probing their responses to this visual spectacle.

Even in the scenes that take place in the schoolroom (as well as in the group photograph of the assembled teachers and students), the emphasis is on spectatorship. Each of the teachers is portrayed as a caricature, and the students function as spectators, laughing at and undermining the pedantic tirades on history, religion, mathematics, language, and art. Both public and private life are contaminated by the penchant for theatricality. The visit of Fascist *federale* produces an orgiastic sense of the event, involving processions, athletics by boys and girls, a fanciful wedding smiled upon by a large and grotesque image of Mussolini where, in Peter Bondanella's terms, "the entire population seems anxious to become a collective, unthinking entity under Il Duce's benevolent gaze."[20] The boy Titta's (Bruno Zanin) home life, too, becomes a comedy when Aurelio discovers that his son had urinated on the hat of a townsperson during the showing of a western at the cinema.

Each of the characters – Miranda, her favored brother, Aurelio, the grandfather, the maid, Titta and his brother – reenact familiar scenarios of family life, all playing a role for each other. Even the scenes in the church where Titta and his friends go for confession are not exempt from theatricality, as Titta invents stories for the priest, who is more involved in flower arrangement and the prurient narratives Titta recites. The contrast between what Titta tells and what he fantasizes is also instructive, since, knowing what is expected, he allows his private thoughts to drift to the movie theater and his encounter with Gradisca, who is enthralled not with him but with a Gary Cooper film.

In its recollection of the past, the film does not neglect to invoke memories of the town's early history, its architecture, and especially the prominent role played by the Grand Hotel, symbol par excellence of luxury and Americanness. "For the young Titta, the Grand Hotel," writes Hay,

> is an almost sacred shrine whose faced conceals exotic characters (a prince or Caliph) and erotic mysteries (his uncle dancing until dawn with a voluptuous Nordic vacationer). The Grand Hotel is, for the provincial community, its touchstone with a more cosmopolitan set – with that which comes from beyond.[21]

It is to the Grand Hotel that Gradisca is brought (as recounted by the lawyer-narrator [Luigi Rossi]) to reenact a fantasy that looks like a reincarnation of a Gary Cooper film, in which the characters are dressed in elaborate uniforms and move like automata. It is to the Grand Hotel, too, that a caliph arrives with his harem, and where we have a reenactment of an Orientalist musical with an ungainly Biscein, the peanut vendor, as the narrator and recipient of all of the dancing women's attentions.

Similarly, the ballroom dancing of the expensively clothed Fascist guests at the Grand Hotel reproduces the lavish upper-crust settings of films of the era. Certainly the town's gathering at the seaside to witness the arrival of the *Rex*, Fascist Italy's answer to the large seagoing ocean liners of other European nations, is another ironic homage to the power of spectacle and modernity identified with the 1930s and with Fascist shows. However, the castor-oil treatment meted out to Aurelio at the hands of the Fascist authorities, the family visit to Uncle Teo at the mental institution, and the death of Miranda seem to depart from the metacinematic scenario, except that they too have an aura of theatricality about them that derives from Fascist ritual as well as from family ritual.

A major cinematic aspect of the film involves movement: movement within the frame and out of frame; the editing of shots in a way that emphasize the passage of time; of time, like the cinema, as movement. From the opening of the film, movement is highlighted: the puffballs at the beginning (and end), the snowflakes, the mad circling of the cyclist, the emphasis on other forms of locomotion (e.g., the car races, the movement of the characters as they promenade, and the reiterative focus on dancing). The style of filming also highlights movement, with the camera circling, swirling, and zooming. The film moves through various layers of time: antique and modern, pagan and Christian, dream and "reality," one spring to another, and one generation to another. If there is a protagonist in Fellini's film, it is time, exemplified by this sense of constant movement, a movement that produces repetition but also the possibility of another, possibly different beginning. Time is what identifies the characters' folly and also their limited understanding of their world, but it is also what humanizes them:

> The child in us, says Fellini, is contemporary with the adult, the old man, and the adolescent. Thus it is that the past which is preserved takes on all the virtues of beginning and beginning again: it is what holds in its depths or in its sides the surge of a new reality, the bursting forth of life.[22]

In its emphasis on theatricality, *Amarcord* challenges the conventional dichotomy between reality and illusion, calling attention to the ways they are connected rather than separate. Theatricality in *Amarcord,* as in the films of Visconti and Pasolini, assumes a different valence, involving an affirmation of the power and the delusory nature of the cinematic image, and the necessity of (in)sight to aid the spectator in thinking differently. In the filmmaking of Rossellini and Fellini, there is a constant striving to work against the grain of formulaic images while at the same time acknowledging their character and sway. These directors' comedies also identify the importance of rethinking Fascist culture through the commercial cinema, a preoccupation they share with their generation and with later generations of Italian filmmakers.

La vita è bella (*Life Is Beautiful,* 1997), produced, written, directed, and acted by Roberto Benigni, employs comedy (as does Rossellini's *La macchina* and Fellini's *Amarcord*) to present a portrait of life under Fascism. The film goes beyond most existing treatments of Fascism in Italian cinema, however, by addressing the treatment of the Jews. Unlike De Sica's *Il giardino dei Finzi-Contini* (*The Garden of the Finzi-Continis,* 1970), which portrays their treatment melodramatically, *Life Is Beautiful* confronts the subject of the Holocaust with comedy; and central to the film's conception of the deadly seriousness of comedy is Benigni's comic persona.

In the tradition of other comic actors (e.g., Charles Chaplin, Jerry Lewis, and Woody Allen in the American cinema and Totò, Alberto Sordi, Nino Manfredi, and Maurizio Nichetti in the Italian), Benigni has a clearly defined persona that carries over from film to film. This persona is characterized by frenetic and spastic physical movement, a range of facial expressions, and rapidly delivered dialogue. Slapstick and especially struggles with machines are inherent to his confrontation with the world. His persona relies on misperceptions by others, especially representatives of the state, who attribute guile and even malevolence to his ostensibly innocent and inept actions. In *Life Is Beautiful,* Benigni's persona becomes a serious reflection on Fascism and particularly on racism.

The film begins in 1939 in Northern Italy and, much as in Fellini's *Amarcord,* presents a portrait of life in the Fascist era, including images of the civil bureaucracy, the school, and the sumptuous Grand Hotel where the protagonist works for a time as a waiter. Guido Orefice (Benigni) is a Jew who seeks to open a bookstore. The racial issue – initially absent – assumes prominence in the latter half of the film. At first, his Uncle Eliseo is attacked by hoodlums; later Eliseo's horse is painted green and identified as "un cavallo ebreo" (a Jewish horse); and finally Guido, his child Giosué, and his Christian wife, Dora (Nicoletta Braschi), are taken away to a concentration camp. If the first part of the film allows Benigni full rein to exercise his comedic talent through a "fable" to expose the meanness, hypocrisy, materialism, and racism of life under Fascism (particularly striking in his impersonation of a school inspector who lectures on the "Aryan body " and on the beauties of the Italian ear and belly button), the second half of the film mingles comedy and tragedy as Guido and his son confront survival in the camp.

Certain motifs carry over from the first half to the second. Initially, the reiterative allusions to Schopenhauer's "will to power," learned from Guido's friend Ferruccio, serve largely to enhance the ultimately successful romantic scenario between Guido and Dora. Later, these allusions play a critical role in dramatizing the life-threatening encounters of Guido and son in the camp, and the father's strategies for ensuring his son's survival. Offenbach's "Barcarolle" from *The Tales of Hoffman* is repeated in both sections of the film, at first identified with cultural life under Fascism and with Guido's courtship of Dora. Opera is once again used to highlight cultural values that have been mangled by the Fascists and Nazis. Later when Guido plays the "Barcarolle" on the Victrola, sending the music through the camp – providing an opportunity for Guido to communicate with Dora – it takes on another, more serious dimension: Amid the atrocities, it calls attention to the coexistence of culture and barbarism. Similarly, the reiterative role of riddles associated with Dr. Lessing (Horst Buchholz), whom Guido meets first at the Grand Hotel, initially appears as a game. When Guido again encounters Lessing as the camp doctor, he hopes that the memory of their shared game will provide a means of escape for him and his family. He discovers instead that games are deadly. The doctor's obsession with solving riddles precludes any concern with physical reality. If Guido is preoccupied with his survival and his son's, the doctor is totally indifferent to the needs of the body (earlier to his food, later to his charges in the camp). In these ways, the familiar conventions of comedy once again take on a darker cast, calling attention to the abuse of the body and the disregard for and willful destruction of material needs.

As in *Amarcord,* comedy is not offered as mere entertainment; it is an alternative mode for confronting, not rationalizing, cruelty and suffering, a way of thinking differently about the conditions necessary for survival in extremely adverse conditions. The film presents the audience with a historical situation regularly dispensed through newsreels and fiction films that focus unremittingly on the enormity of the horrors of Fascism and the Holocaust. *Life Is Beautiful* makes no pretense to realism, to presenting events "as they really were." Instead, through the seriousness of comedy, the film invites the audience to ask different questions, about the survivors, rather than merely providing another memorial to the dead.

A key aspect of the film's comedic treatment is the relationship between the father and his young son. The images of the child among the men, the perspective offered by his accurate view of events in contrast to his father's fictions, and the nature of the "game" set up between the adult and the child provide a less formulaic treatment of events at the camp. This game extends to the role of cinema: It is clearly not a machine to kill bad people, but it does offer an opportunity for another reflection on fiction and reality. The comedy also functions to mitigate sentiment, as in the scene where Guido translates the Nazi's orders into language designed for Giosué's ears. The liberation of the camp by the Americans serves ironically as a fulfillment of Guido's promises to the child about winning a tank; it also highlights the film's preoccupation with the role of riddles, in this case the inexplicable riddle of survival in the face of horror. The anticipated "happy ending" often glibly assigned to the comic form is circumvented in Guido's death. The family does not emerge intact, only the child and mother survive. As in the Tavianis' *La notte di San Lorenzo (The Night of the Shooting Stars,* 1982), the audience learns – but not until the film's end – that these events have been recounted by Giosuè as an adult, thus indicating that history is inevitably subject to "re-vision." Moreover, the film reveals, as do so many Italian comedies, that Fascism and war remain central to Italian culture and politics, and that film comedy remains a dominant form for rethinking the past.

CHAPTER FIVE

The Landscape and Neorealism, Before and After

G eography and the political and cultural values attached to different regions and locales – specifically, the role of borders – are of major consequence for an understanding of national formation as it is communicated through the media. As John Dickie writes, "A great deal of national self-esteem or aspiration is invested in territorial integrity and, more generally, in the imagining of the geographical space with which the nation is deemed to be coterminous."[1] In Italian literature and cinema, geography has been identified with numerous and often conflicting conceptions of the landscape.[2] For example, major metropolitan centers such as Rome, Milan, and Naples have served as signifiers of national identity and modernity. Such portraits of the urban landscape expose the constituted and contested character of, and the different values assigned to, conceptions of the Italian nation.

The history of the Italian nation can be read through visually graphic representations between urban and rural life that rely on distinctions among various geographical and cultural boundaries. Architecture, painting, and statuary are identified with different historical and cultural moments as well as with the landscape of the ethnicized male and female human body. Although actual maps (often inserted into cinematic texts) indicate regional landmarks and differences among the various locales, another form of mapping is also evident in the parallels drawn between the landscape and the iconography and behavior of its inhabitants. In particular, distinctions between the northern and southern landscapes of the nation are common in the iconography of the Italian cinema.

Not only has geography served as a means for identifying national borders and their expansion; it has served as the locus of internal ethnic aspirations, delineating different groups and their relation to political and cultural power. The Risorgimento gave rise to the mythology of a national unity despite the existence of various ethnic and linguistic groups, and significant economic, political, and cultural differences among regions: "Paradoxically . . . the way that the representatives of the new national order conceived of the South as alien to an Italian nation was part of the process whereby it was incorporated into the Italian state."[3] This way of thinking persists and is integral to the rhetoric and ambitions of the Lega Nord today, with its emphasis on northern "independence" and its familiar articulations of difference from the South. The Italian cinema thrives on affirmative and critical narratives and on images of the Risorgimento and its legacy. In particular, Antonio Gramsci's writings on the "Southern question" identify a long-standing aspect of Italy's conceptions of national incorporation, dependent on representations of the country and the city. Gramsci wrote:

> The poverty of the Mezzogiorno was historically "inexplicable" for the popular masses in the North; they did not understand that unity had not taken place on the basis of equality, but as a hegemony of the North over the Mezzogiorno in a territorial version of the town-country relationship – in other words, that the North concretely was an "octopus" which enriched itself at the expense of the South.[4]

The implications of this North–South division make themselves felt on a number of fronts in the cinema – in conceptions of race, ethnicity, tradition, language, and modernity. Other cultural and political divides are manifest in perceptions of peasant as opposed to urban life, of agriculture versus industry, and of country compared to city (*strapaese* vs. *stracittà*). These distinctions were mapped in terms of regional entities and naturalized and disseminated throughout the remainder of the nineteenth century and the twentieth via literature, painting, photography, journalism, popular culture, and the broadcast media.

Visual and verbal representations of landscape have a long tradition in the arts. Long before images of city and countryside were produced in the cinema for the Italian public, there already existed, in Italy and throughout Europe, paintings that memorialized the architecture and landscapes of imperial Rome; but classical Rome was not the only period to be visualized by (and for) Italians. Florentine and Neapolitan urban as well as pastoral landscapes were also subjects for the painter's brush, and later for the camera. A reading of American, British, and European literature reveals a mythology of Italy communicated through the literature of tourism, a mythology that identifies Italian cities as part of international lore and curiosity. Writers such as Henry James liberally employed the Italian landscape in their melodramas involving the encounter between the "new world" and the decadent world of Europe. German writers such as Heine and Goethe saw Italy as not only a source of culture but as an escape from the rigidities of northern existence. Later, Thomas Mann's *Death in Venice* (and Visconti's 1971 film based on this work) situated the city as the source of illicit (and decadent) desire. Interest rose, especially in the late eighteenth century and in the nineteenth, in the sights of everyday life, street life, and in images of urbanization.

Although the fascination with the ruins of time has solicited the attention of writers and painters, artists have also been drawn to changing and modern visions of older cities. Such portraits involve contrasts with the surrounding countryside and images of the various social classes and regional "types" that are part of this landscape. The long-standing motif of the connections between the rural and urban landscape are integral to images of war, of land and naval conflicts – refracting images of moments of heroic national struggle in the many eighteenth- and nineteenth-century portrayals of the naval fleets and battles in the Bay of Naples, for example, as well as in paintings devoted to memorializing the Risorgimento. From the silent cinema to the present, images of war have been a staple of Italian cinema, as seen in films such as *Senso*. Most important, World War II contributed to the remaking of images of the nation through the destruction as well as reconstruction of the Italian city and countryside, and to the dissemination of mass-produced images of Italy and her populations.

Travel literature, too, has contributed to the creation of mythologies concerning various European cities, whether as the cradles of European civilization, cultural metropolises, nostalgic exemplars of a "vanished" world of culture, or fascinating sinks of crime and iniquity. The nineteenth- and early twentieth-century European Grand Tour, largely the domain of the upper and moneyed classes, has given way to large-scale tourism with its packaged tours, tour guides, picture postcards, and mass-produced souvenirs of Italian sites. The touristic attractions of the cinema of the 1890s were tied largely to images of urban life in the major cities of both northern and southern Italy. During the last years of the nineteenth century and the first decades of the twentieth, photography studios that reproduced city life in photographs and films flourished; and in early cinema, the landscape functions in its own right, not merely as a narrative enhancement. In writing about the travel genre in early American cinema, Charles Musser states that one-shot images of place "indicate that these images could be made to carry rich and often disturbing meanings – assumptions about imperialism, racial and cultural superiority, sexism and Social Darwinism."[5]

Classical and contemporary Italy is part of the European, if not the visual, imagination of the world. The cinema did not invent the metropolis but inherited a multitude of historical, political, and aesthetic values associated with rural and urban life. Concomitantly, views of the city and of the countryside are intimately related to a tradition of pastoral painting and drawing but also to notions, often critical, of urban life. Urban life became identified with mobile populations: These moved not only from the country to the city, but within the various cities, and from one nation to another. The emigration of populations has been a standard feature of modern life since the mid-nineteenth century.

The cinema has been a major disseminator of images of real and imaginary places, augmenting and altering a sense of place. The cinematic experiments of the 1920s, as exemplified by the films and writings of Lev Kuleshov, demonstrated the possibilities of "creative geography": fostering the "illusion of spatial and temporal unity by cutting together five separate shots taken at five separate places and times."[6] The cinematic use of landscape does not merely record existing reality, therefore, but significantly alters our sense of "real time" and space.

In Italian cinema, as Giuliana Bruno has discussed, geography conveys "a conglomerate of diverse regional and local forces that express differences in language as well as in history and culture."[7] Not only were the images of cities part of a repertoire of cultural values, but they were a resource for early cinema in its "ability to *show* something," and this "something" was drawn from familiar regional images. As to the fascination with place, the cinema drew on a preexisting folklore associated with familiar or exotic places. The actualities of the first decade of the twentieth century, in such vignettes as Promio's views of Venice,[8] were highly dependent on city scenes, especially those identified with religious values, regional and touristic familiarity, and cultural splendor.

With greater attention to the fusing of exhibition and narrative, the importance of historical and cultural sites does not disappear. In some instances, cityscapes and landscapes function in representational terms, providing points of extension and even equivalence for character and narrative events. In other instances, the city assumes its own character as a counterpoint to the aspirations and actions of the characters. For example, in *Assunta Spina*, the Neapolitan landscape draws frequently on familiar views of the Bay of Naples, obviously serving to situate the events within very specific and familiar landscape shots (see Chapter 2). In the 1930s, two films in particular are significant for adopting Naples as protagonist: *Napoli d'altri tempi* (*Naples of Former Days*, 1938) and *Napoli che non muore* (*Naples That Never Dies*, 1939). In each case, the city is identified with popular culture associated with Neapolitan music. This conjunction is in part attributable to the cinema's discovery of the potential of sound to evoke a sense of regional character and to align these images to national integrity and creativity.

In *Napoli che non muore*, a melodrama, images of the city familiar to the tourist – photographs of Mount Vesuvius, the bay, the *lungomare* (sea front), and the restaurants and places of leisure – are abundantly scattered throughout the film. The perspective of the city is fused with the romantic relationship between a Neapolitan man and a French woman, Anne (Marie Glory), and the narrative focuses on the connection between the domestic interior of a middle-class Neapolitan family and traditional conceptions of the woman's position as wife and mother. The Frenchwoman regards Naples as a place of play and sexual license, but she is finally educated into the consequences of flouting her conjugal and maternal responsibility. Through the threatened loss of her child brought about by her neglect, she learns that the city is not the romantic picture-postcard world that she had envisioned. The film's bias against such a superficial encounter with the city is evident in its transposition from the urban and modern landscape to the domestic one. According to James Hay, "One of the intentions in this film is to debunk the notions that Naples, i.e. Italy, is simply a playground for decadent high society . . . to reveal the *true* Italian society that lies beneath Naples' glittering facade."[9] This "true Italian society" is tied to gendered images of the city. Anne seeks to penetrate the masculine space of the city and must be converted to accepting her womanly place within the family. However, through the attractive images of the city presented to the spectator in contrast to the restraining and disciplinary images of the domestic scenes, the film offers an ambiguous and unresolved image of the place of woman in the city and, by extension, in Italian culture. Anne's foreignness serve more largely to underscore the alien, that is, problematic position of woman in the Italian society tied to late-Fascist nationalist rhetoric about "French decadence" that becomes identified in the film with the Fascist woman as mother.

In Palermi's *Napoli d'altri tempi,* again the filmmaker provides familiar images of the Neapolitan landscape, but here the identification with the building of the funicular and the views of the bay are interspersed with street scenes of working-class as well as upper-class life. The city of Naples is embedded within the framework of Italian history and within the myth of national unity. It is the site for the conversion of a young man, Mario (Vittorio De Sica), into his proper role as artist, citizen, and family man. The opening shots of Naples are accompanied by music. A group of people is assembled waiting to ride the funicular and anticipating a popular Neapolitan song that will commemorate this occasion. The film's encomium to popular music is introduced by intertitles, identifying the importance of music as intrinsic to the cultural and social life of the city of Naples. In conjunction with the music, the funicular becomes "an anthem of social change for an emerging national-popular culture."[10]

Among the group of observers is Mario, destined to become an important composer of Neapolitan ballads and, like the filmmaker, the creator of new images of this culture – but only after he is properly initiated into this role. Images of Mario are intercut with images of the sea and of Mount Vesuvius accompanied by sounds of Neapolitan popular music, contributing to a sense of Neapolitan cultural life as "natural." An intertitle introduces the departure of troops to Africa as Mario, among the cheering crowd, sings a song marking the occasion, thus linking Naples to the broader canvas of Italian history. Among the group of onlookers is Maddalena (Emma Gramatica) who will become his fairy godmother. Unbeknown to him, she is the sister of his deceased mother, another form of "history" tied to images of family and domesticity that the film situates within the Neapolitan landscape.

The question of familial identity is a mainspring of the narrative that will carry Mario from obscurity to fame, transforming him from an orphan of uncertain class and regional affiliation to a man with a genealogy and a community. This community, it is also revealed, has a history, and this history is tied to national aspirations. Maddalena and the Cavaliere Baracchi (Giuseppe Porelli) live in the past, recollecting another time in Naples when Italian soldiers had gone to fight in Africa. That past, however, will play a key role in the film's present, tied as those events are to the fate of Mario.

At that earlier time, Maddalena's sister had been engaged to a young man who died in that war. Now, Maddalena undertakes to trace their child, Mario, but learns at the orphanage where he had been placed that he now has a different last name. He has become a composer but in order to support himself works in a grocery store. When, having traced him to this locale, Maddalena appears and asks for Mario Sposito, he informs her that his name is Perla. Undaunted, she informs him that she has a piano he can use. After initial reluctance, he accepts her offer. The delivery of the piano becomes a festive and musical occasion not only for Mario but for the entire neighborhood, highlighting the sense of community that prevails among the Neapolitan working classes.

Maddalena, with the aid of Baracchi, takes a position in an upper-class house, where she furthers her plans for Mario by enlisting the daughter, Maria (Elisa Cegani), in advancing his career. Experiencing difficulty in selling his music to agents of publishers, they urge him to present his songs at a party given at Maria's house. Reticent about performing before this well-dressed, upper-class gathering, he begins by playing familiar popular songs by other composers. Their response is indifferent until he plays his own Neapolitan song, "Napoli mia," whereupon they become attentive and enthusiastic. Excluded from this upper-class gathering, another audience, Ninetta – a young neighborhood woman who is enamored of Mario – listens from the street with her family. This scene, like many throughout the film, highlights the importance of audience as the imagined community that validates the conjunction between the city and its music.

As in *Napoli che non muore,* there is an emphasis on an antagonism between interior and exterior views of the city that will later be reconciled. Here the antagonism resides in a tension between social classes. Mario's rise to fame parallels his growing attraction to Maria – though her Aunt Bettina (Olga Vittoria Gentilli) disapproves of Mario, planning for Maria to marry a wealthy suitor. Maddalena, too, is unhappy about their relationship. Having discovered a note from Mario to Maria, she tries to convince him of the impossibility of marriage to Maria. Both she and Ninetta have recognized changes in his behavior toward his own class. Naïvely, he insists to Maddalena that Maria can live without her luxuries. However, after a final meeting with Maria, again at the seaside, he acknowledges their class differences and bids her farewell.

Melancholy after Maria's departure from Naples, Mario works compulsively at his songwriting, determined to leave the city. Maddalena, attempting to deter him from leaving, reveals their kinship and his mother's identity. In place of Maria as his wife, he has now acquired a surrogate mother, one identified with him, with Ninetta, and with working-class culture. The film's final sequences are festive. As at the beginning, there is a crowd scene on the street, and once again Neapolitan music is heard and celebrated – but this time it is Mario's "Napoli mia" being sung by his people, in a scene conjoining the protagonist to Neapolitan popular music, popular music to Neapolitan history, and that history to the role of the family and nation. Having achieved his objective of being a composer, integrated into family and Neapolitan life, Mario walks along the street with his fellow citizens, arms linked, singing.

The "resolution" of the film, which relies on familial and conjugal union, is fused with the idea of entertainment as being specifically a compensation for personal loss. The public space of the city is tied to performance and performance to individual and, hence, to national identity. Naples becomes central to the process of forging community, and the urban community is identified in terms of national aspirations. In the film, the city is the locus of trial and of discovery, a synecdoche for Italy and for an identification with nature through the emphasis on the sea and the mountains. The image of the funicular serves to forge a connection between nature and mechanical and cultural production. Finally, the importance of the past is legitimated in the image of the rejuvenated Neapolitan community.

The city plays a crucial role also in other dramas produced in the 1930s. In these films, characters are often mired in a life of misery and banality but, through a series of encounters, discover the folly of trying to live beyond their means and come to recognize that, to quote Brunetta quoting *The Wizard of Oz*, "There's no place like home." In some instances, "home" is identified with domestic life as a haven against the threats and depredations of the city. In particular, if the characters aspire to upper-class luxury and leisure, they learn the virtues of family and simplicity, as in Mario Camerini's *Rotaie (Rails,* 1929), *Gli uomini che mascalzoni . . .* (1932), and *Il signor Max* (1937). If they are trapped in poverty, leading to prostitution in the case of women, they are ultimately relocated in places of domestic security.

Camerini's comedies and melodramas are set in Rome or Milan primarily, and his portraits of the cities are tied to an ambiguous vision of modernity that neither celebrates nor condemns urban life but presents both its dangers and its fascination. The city streets with their humming traffic, ubiquitous automobiles and trams, movie theaters, nightclubs, and other places of entertainment, department stores, large and opulent hotels, and a world of fashion – these offer images of a society where those not armed to resist its lures can easily be led astray. The city is a seductress, identified with commerce, cosmopolitanism, luxury, and leisure, and what rescues the young protagonists is the family as haven, as a source of protection and common sense. In Palermi's *La peccatrice* (The Sinner, 1940), the title character, having been brutalized by urban life, leaves the city for the country and finally returns to her maternal home. More than mere backdrop to the narratives of these films, the city is a character in its own right, coming to be associated with history, culture, social life, aspirations to national unity, and conflicts between tradition and modernity. (In some ways, these films are indebted to Hollywood cinema, a cinema of youth and modernity, also struggling with the lures of modern life in opposition to tradition.) If, in the genre films of the 1930s, a city like Naples functions as a site of spectacle and as allegory (becoming a signifier for national aspirations *or* serving as a place of retreat from those aspirations), there is no doubt that the sense of place in these films is fundamental to their self-conscious role as entertainment – a role necessitating engagement with a sense of national belonging in the public and the domestic arena.

This preoccupation with the city does not diminish in the post–World War II era. If anything, the city plays an even more prominent role but with a different treatment that uses the urban landscape to convey a sense of dislocation. Naples continues to be a major protagonist in postwar cinema, first in neorealist films that portray the hardships of life, such as *O sole mio* (1945) and *Io t'ho incontrata a Napoli* (I Met You in Naples, a 1946 remake of *Assunta Spina*), and later in *Due soldi di speranza* (*Two Cents Worth of Hope*, 1952), *Processo alla città* (*City on Trial*, 1952), *Un marito per Anna Zaccheo* (*A Husband for Anna*, 1953), and De Sica's *L'oro di Napoli* (*The Gold of Naples*, 1954). Neapolitan life is seen in images that highlight dislocation, unemployment, graft, and political corruption.

De Sica's *L'oro di Napoli* is an anthology of four different stories based on the writings of Giuseppe Marotta. Scripted by De Sica and Cesare Zavattini, the film satisfied no one, though Brunetta asserts that it displayed extraordinary creative energy, had a fine sense of ambience, and was rich in humor and melodrama.[11] The first episode starred the comic actor Totò (whose films were set largely in Naples). *L'oro di Napoli* opens with a touristic view of the bay, accompanied by Neapolitan music, and an intertitle reads, "Here is a bit of that love of life, patience and eternal hope that goes to make up 'the

Figure 26. Saverio (Totò) parades through the streets of Naples, *L'oro di Napoli* (*The Gold of Naples*). (Courtesy New York Museum of Modern Art Stills Archive)

gold of Naples' . . . ." There is a mist shot of Mount Vesuvius. Moving from these panoramas, the first episode begins at a cemetery, with Saverio (Totò) praying over a grave. It quickly becomes evident that he is a recruited and paid mourner for a Mafia boss, Don Carmine, who has come to stay in his house and who is terrorizing him and turning his small children against him. The camera follows him home, showing images of Naples as he negotiates his way through crowds, passes the stalls of street vendors, and traverses its squares and narrow streets. The interior of his home is modest, but he clearly does not live in poverty: His apartment has several rooms and a balcony, from which he can see the square below.

After an unpleasant and threatening encounter with Don Carmine, Saverio, dressed in eighteenth-century attire, enters the street on his way to perform an ancient celebratory ritual at the opening of a grocery store. Followed by a band of children and adults [Fig. 26], he makes his way to the store, where he utters the ritualistic words of welcome for the crowd and sings a Neapolitan song until interrupted by Don Carmine and his cohorts. When he learns that the don is ill, he throws him out of the house with enthusiasm, dropping his clothes from the balcony to the street below and watching them scatter. The episode ends ambiguously when Don Carmine, learning that his assumed heart trouble is only indigestion, returns to ruin the family's celebration of his departure. Three things stand out in this episode as a prologue to the others: the views of Naples from balconies and streets, the emphasis on walking in the city, and the importance of street spectators as an audience for dramatic events.

The next episode of Neapolitan city life stars Sophia Loren as Sofia, the wife of a pizza maker with his own pizzeria. Sofia's roving eye gets her into trouble when she forgets her emerald ring at the shop of a young man with whom she is having an affair. The episode is a darkly humorous search for this ring, which Sofia tells her husband must have fallen into a pizza. He is then willing to wake up neighbors, pester the priest, and even harass a distraught man whose wife has recently died to regain the valuable jewelry. At last her lover, by means of gesture, informs Sofia of the ring's whereabouts. When the young man claims to have found it in his pizza, the ever-present crowd extols him for his honesty. The husband, however, does not recall that man having bought pizza, but again Sofia lies, saying she forgot to record the sale. The episode alternates between interiors and exterior. The narrow streets with their shops become a place for work, encounters with customers, and song, where crowds of neighbors participate vicariously in the drama of the missing ring. A parallel is made between cinema and urban life, between crowds and spectatorship, with the city a place of fantasy and danger.

The third episode stars De Sica as a decadent aristocrat, Count Prospero B., suffering under the control of his wife, who has forbidden him to have any money because of his penchant for gambling. His flat is large, filled with paintings, statuary, and valuable antiques (which he is caught trying to steal by his wife and Giuseppe, the servant). He tries desperately to get money for his gambling with a "baron," bribing his servant with promises of doubling his salary after his wife's funeral, but to no avail. It turns out that his life is a tissue of illusions, however, since he is on his way to play not with one of his aristocratic cronies but with the young son of the concierge. These scenes portray him, despite his elegance, as vain, childlike, obsessive, impotent, and brutal as he bullies the boy, Gennarino, who keeps winning. He offers Gennarino his estate, his clothes, his tinted glasses, and ends by abusing him verbally. The final shot is a close-up of the pathetic child caressing his cat.

Although each episode takes the spectator to a different neighborhood in Naples, it is evident that *L'oro di Napoli* eschews the familiar guidebook views of the city (except at the beginning of the first episode and, as we shall see, briefly but ironically in the fourth). The third episode, aside from its exterior views of the apartment house, is restricted to interiors of the aristocrat's opulent abode (briefly) and of the rather sparse and shabby apartment

Figure 27. Framing the prostitute: Teresa (Silvano Mangano) and Don Nicola (Erno Crisa) in *L'oro di Napoli*. (Courtesy New York Museum of Modern Art Stills Archive)

where he and the boy plays cards. Contrary to the upbeat images of Naples as a city of music and popular festivals, then, this film presents the city as a place whose interiors reveal hypocrisy and desperation.

The episodes grow progressively darker and more violent. In the fourth and final one, a prostitute, Teresa (Silvana Mangano), finds herself selected to be the wife of a wealthy bourgeois, Don Nicola Giraci (Erno Crisa), "owner of four shops" [Fig. 27]. The initial scene shows Teresa being given a festive farewell by other women in the brothel, who are enthusiastic about her new life. She is taken by Don Ubaldo, agent for Don Nicola, in a horse-drawn carriage to the Galleria Umberto I, where she is to meet her fiancé. This scene offers the spectator familiar and sustained images of one of the Neapolitan architectural landmarks, a place that becomes a signifier of commerce involving women and the family. She and Don Ubaldo enter the gallery, where they pass people walking by the various shops, and he takes her into a café. Teresa wonders why Don Nicola has selected her, and Don Ubaldo seeks to divert her curiosity. With the arrival of Don Nicola, the mystery deepens rather than clarifies, and the three take a ride in a car to the church where the marriage is about to take place. Here the Neapolitan streets and architecture are visible, particularly the imposing seventeenth-century church, where a crowd of well-wishers is gathered. The church is filmed in terms of its exterior splendor, thus reinforcing disjunctions between the grand exteriors of Naples and its claustrophic and dehumanizing interiors, to be revealed at his family's home, where the servants are supervising the wedding party.

The tension between Teresa's high expectations and her groom's coldness is set in contrast to the gaiety and effusiveness of the assembled guests, who sing while an orchestra plays. Slowly, Teresa moves through the rooms, meeting Don Nicola's mother, who has "more jewels than the shrine at Loreto." The bride's uneasiness grows as she finds a photographic portrait of a young woman in the room to which Nicola has assigned her, then observes him in tearful conversation with an elderly couple (the woman's brooch bears the same portrait) as he urges money on them. Finally, in direct conversation with him, she learns that she was selected because she was a prostitute: Thus Nicola does penance for having rejected the young woman of the photograph, who "killed herself for me." Teresa's role, he says, is to make him suffer, to remind him of his sin, which he hopes will ultimately be made public. She pleads with him, saying, "Why should I make you suffer? I only want a little gentleness. Am I not a woman?" After shouting outside the door to his room, which he has locked, she packs her things and walks through the house to exit onto the dark street, stopping at a lamppost, a venue associated with urban prostitution. From her perspective, the audience sees the deserted square and the exteriors of menacing buildings, conveying a sense of the impersonality and desolation of urban life, often visible in other De Sica films. The wind can be heard. She looks back to the house and forward to the deserted square; then she returns slowly to the house, knocking loudly to be admitted until, in long shot, the door closes ominously on her and the film.

L'oro di Napoli does not present a "rosy" view of contemporary life and of the upper and moneyed classes. The comedy progressively turns to pathos with its increased focus on the helpless and exploited members of the community. The "love of life" to which the intertitle alludes at the film's outset complicates and ironizes the meaning of city life, a life that involves domestic discord, loneliness, hypocrisy, obsession, and, as epitomized by Don Nicola, a perverse sense of justice. Although Naples is central to its narrative, *L'oro di Napoli* is not a melodrama in which the city becomes the villain; for simplistic renderings of urban life to be made complex, the city must be seen in conjunction with the class and gendered perspectives of the characters and the narration. Naples serves as a signifier for Teresa's plight. It too has been prostituted; it too has suffered a fate similar to her exploitation by Don Nicola and his family. Commerce and money are more than economic transactions;

they function in affective terms as the incentive to work out guilt, rage, and blind vindictiveness.

The city has been the source of countless films, from the historical spectacles of silent cinema to the films made during the sound era under Fascism. The treatment of the city, however, underwent a progressive transformation, first in the films in the immediate aftermath of the war, and later in the 1950s. In the postwar era, Rome, like Naples, continued to capture the imagination of filmmakers and audiences alike. Though Rome is still the inspiration for many films, the portraits of that city and of urban life have become much more complex and heterogeneous. Even where a film invokes touristic and painterly images of the city, as in Lina Wertmüller's *Film d'amore e d'anarchia,* there is a tension between the characters' situation and the world in which they move. Shots of the city, while clichéd, are evident as clichés. Characters move in the urban environment like somnambulists or homeless waifs, seeking to act but failing (as in *Ladri di biciclette* and *Umberto D*). The relation between character and the environment is one of encounter, where the characters are largely observers, "prey to a vision, pursued by it or pursuing it, rather than engaged in an action."[12] The presence of children in many of the neorealist films can be attributed to the child's "motor helplessness . . . which makes him all the more capable of seeing and hearing."[13]

Critics have commented on Rome as protagonist of Rossellini's *Roma, città aperta.* Peter Brunette has written, "Rome stands for the rest of Italy . . . before us at all times throughout the film, either directly, as visual background, or indirectly suggested through its particular social relations reenacted in the interiors."[14] The narrative, characteristic of films that treat the time-image, has been a source of controversy for critics who would like to see Rossellini as departing from neorealism. The film appears to employ "conventional narrative elements. . . . All of the characters are tightly intertwined for maximum efficiency, and the result is a complex and thickly populated fresco."[15] The destiny of the characters is tightly interwoven: Pina's death, the perfidy of the Nazis in collusion with Marina that culminates in the deaths of Manfredi and Don Pietro. What is important are the consequences of the Nazi occupation, the distinctions between betrayers and their victims, and how these are tied to the history and character of the city as a synecdoche for wartime Italy.

Although the characters are cast in the traditional mold of heroism and cowardice characteristic of conventional melodrama, in the final analysis, the melodrama is overwhelmed by the very complexity of the "fresco" of the city and its inhabitants. There is a tension in the film between the scenes involving Pina, Francesco, Manfredi, and Don Pietro and those involving the Nazis, the latter identified with Hollywood sets and stylization and the former identified with neorealism. The harsh style of the former is closely tied to the

Figure 28. Women up against the wall: Pina (Anna Magnani) resists the SS in *Roma, città aperta* (*Open City*). (Courtesy New York Museum of Modern Art Stills Archive)

role of the landscape, what Robert Kolker has attributed to "the cinematography, the framing of the characters amidst urban or country squalor, in ruined tenements or desolate town squares."[16] Though the wanton torture and killing of the priest and the engineer can easily be read as an affirmation of the Italian resistance to political oppression, and though the Nazi behavior can be identified with the unmitigated evil of the Germans, there are many ambiguities and unresolved issues that provide another level of interaction with the film beyond a familiar narrative trajectory. This involves the complexity of Rossellini's style, which makes less determinate and transparent any understanding of motive and action.

The film's innovation resides in its interrogative stance toward heroism and villainy. The characters' actions are always complicated by the urban milieu. An excess disturbs the film, causing critics to struggle with questions of narrativity and realism, and this excess connects to the disturbing questions surrounding the Roman landscape. Why is it that Pina loses all restraint when Francesco is taken away, a loss of restraint that leads to her death [Fig. 28]? Why is it that Marina's betrayal, seemingly amenable to "explanation" on the

Figure 29. Torture and martyrdom, *Roma, città aperta* (*Open City*): Major Bergmann (Harry Feist) waits as Manfredi (Marcello Pagliero) is prepared for interrogation. (Courtesy New York Museum of Modern Art Stills Archive)

level of narrative analysis – dissatisfaction with her life, with the war, and with Manfredi's indifference – is identified with and complicated by a form of somnambulant behavior attributable to her drugged state and to Ingrid's material (and sexual?) seductions? Are these women's roles to be regarded as merely another conventional instance of the identification of femininity with transgression and social decadence? Moreover, in the portrayals of the martyrdom of Manfredi and Don Pietro, are we offered another conventional image of masculine heroism capable of convincing the audience of the possibility of political and social regeneration? The film does not answer these questions. Contrary to traditional narratives that depend on conversion, action, and resolution, *Roma, città aperta* takes a more complex turn that situates the characters and events within the synecdoche of Rome as the nation. The map of Rome, revealed by the German commandant, Bergmann [Fig. 29], the images of the Roman skyline, Pina's death and the scenes of the subjugated populace on the streets, the image of the young boys observing the death of Don Pietro, and the final images of Saint Peter's situated within this distant panorama are the focal points of the film's interrogation, raising questions about the future and the fate of the people in this environment rather than a clear "message" of hope or even of despair.[17]

The projection of the city landscape becomes an object of reflection and investigation that alters a conventional reading of the film as being narrowly tied to the fate of individual characters. The map at the Nazi headquarters, like the skyline of Rome, is an ironic reminder of the gap between a knowable world and its impossibility, even intolerability. The landscape of Rome stands in a central relation to the suffering of the characters and in relation to the forces that entrap them, and as such it is an invitation "to think, even to believe, not in a different world, but in a link between man and the world, in love or life, to believe in this as in the impossible, the unthinkable, which nonetheless cannot but be thought."[18] *Roma, città apertà* complicates traditional cinematic uses of the city, creating uncertainty about the relationship of the characters to their milieu.

Like the other canonical, most frequently cited and written-about films identified with the urban setting in the immediate postwar neorealist cinema, *Ladri di biciclette* (*The Bicycle Thief*) also relies on the city of Rome and uses it in dynamic fashion in relation to the major characters, Antonio Ricci and his son, Bruno. Millicent Marcus has written at some length about the kinds of associations the images of Rome elicit, particularly commenting that Bazin's description of the film as "a walk through Rome" is not limited to topography: The film is a walk through Rome's social institutions – police, church, and trade unions.[19] It also offers images of life in poorer neighborhoods. Marcus writes that

> De Sica's Rome . . . is a fragmented, decentered space with few familiar landmarks and no sense of cohesion. . . . Rome is presented as a maze, full of endlessly twisting and turning streets that dead-end or lead into yet more labyrinthine byways, and Antonio's movements are as aimless and random as the streets themselves.[20]

Marcus not only identifies the major dimensions of this film, but locates the crux of neorealism in the unsettling effects of the time-image on narrative form and meaning, from the perspective of classical modes of cinematic storytelling.

The plot line of the film can be (and has been) reduced to one sentence: An unemployed man finds a job, pawns through his wife's agency their matrimonial sheets to obtain a necessary bicycle, which is then stolen, and which he unsuccessfully tries to regain by seeking throughout Rome for the thief. This summary serves to reinforce the commitment of the scriptwriter (Cesare Zavattini) to the notion of neorealism as relying on a film loosely centered on the lives of the poor to realize the cinema's potential to portray everyday life.

In *Ladri di biciclette,* the focal point is neither the interior of the home (though it does show the interior of the Ricci home once and the thief's and the fortuneteller's apartments), nor the interiors of the various social institutions where Antonio goes to seek redress for the theft or to find the thief. Instead, the action is largely on the streets – a place of constant mobility. From these streets, the film presents views of Rome distinct from the usual touristic images of the city. Moreover, when these unfamiliar places are visited, they are presented not as monumental, exotic, and unusual but as banal. Sorlin writes: "Ricci enters the city three times. . . . On none of these occasions does he go through Roman Rome or classical Rome and he never goes past an ancient monument."[21] One of the more striking moments takes place when father and son walk along the Tiber and buildings, imposing and remote, can be seen looming in the distance. Mira Liehm has noted that the "film's imagery concentrates on the representation of a man trapped in closed spaces."[22] Yet there are a number of scenes that focus on open, exposed, and threatening space – most notably when, after treating Bruno brutally, Antonio loses sight of the boy and is confronted with a remorse-inspiring view of the Tiber, where a drowning boy has been rescued. Similarly, at the beginning of the film, the spectator is made aware of landscape through views of the unfinished apartments that constitute the neighborhood of the Val Malaina. The scenes of Antonio riding to work also offer the suggestion, though ultimately ironic, of a sense of space, movement, and destination in an environment that constricts the potential of space.

The spectator is also given a sense of repetition and sameness – in the views of the flea market where Antonio and his friend Baiocco, along with Bruno, attempt to find the stolen bicycle; in the exteriors of the new city dwellings; and in the shabby housing in the Via Panico, where Antonio ultimately confronts the young man (wearing a German cap from the war) who has taken his bicycle. When Antonio and Bruno take shelter from the rain under an arch, the German-speaking priests who are also sheltering themselves offer another instance of the alienating and incomprehensible sense of the persistence of the past. The shots of the rows of pawned sheets (one of the most quoted and familiar images in the film) and the rows of bikes seen in the redemption center reiterate the sense of a world where difference is suppressed. The many and various images of the Roman landscape shift the spectator's attention away from the characters as objects of identification, pointing instead to the intersection between those characters and their world and complicating any understanding of motivation. Existing in the midpoint between the North and the South, as in *Sciuscià,* the city is the quintessential milieu to portray the dislocations of postwar life and the uncertainty of identification with everyday sights and sounds.

Most particularly, the behavior of the various people that Antonio and Bruno encounter in their attempts to find the stolen bicycle paints a further portrait of a depersonalized and inhospitable climate. The policeman is gruff with Antonio, deciding a political demonstration is more worthy of attention; Antonio's request for assistance at the trade-union hall is curtly cut off; the middle-class helpers at the church seek to silence him so that they can get on with their service; and the men on the street, angry and menacing after Antonio's desperate attempt to steal a bicycle himself, is mollified only by the presence of Bruno. The film ends ambiguously as the father and son are swallowed up in the urban crowd, the scene fading into darkness.

In contrast to prewar narratives that feature urban life – *Il carnevale di Venezia (Carnival in Venice), Palio* set in Siena, the Naples-based films discussed above – *Ladri di biciclette,* like *Roma, città aperta,* presents modernity and its ties to urban life in terms that reveal disjunctions between landscape and character. The search for the stolen bicycle becomes a pretext to examine the Roman world, a means for entering into a new sense of the cinematic image where the onus is removed from the central characters to control the action. Instead, in constantly moving through the landscape, the characters expose disjunctions between time and space, history and memory. Their movement takes on a different quality, as traditional forms of meaning assigned to narrative are displaced by an open-ended treatment of space, its multiple points of association, and the confounding of past, present, and future. Spectatorship shifts from an anticipation of action and purposeful resolution to an awareness of chance and contingency and of the illusory and dreamlike nature of the cinematic image. Robert Kolker has described the resonance of the imagery in this film as "*milieu gathering,* the expansion from direct concentration on the central character to his immediate world."[23]

Rome once again is the protagonist in *Fellini's Roma,* which is no more an action film than *The Bicycle Thief* and *Umberto D* and extends the neorealist preoccupation with time and contingency. According to Peter Bondanella,

> Fellini's city is a city of illusions and myths – it is the center of Italian cinema, the headquarters of the Roman Catholic Church, as well of the Italian government, and Fellini seems to view religion, politics, and cinema as human institutions relying upon the manipulation of images and myths.[24]

Unlike historical films, *Fellini's Roma* is not a paean to a classical past but a pastiche of different views of Rome derived from the director's own memories, previous Italian films, and images of contemporary Rome. The film be-

Figure 30. Federico Fellini directing *Roma*. (Courtesy New York Museum of Modern Art Stills Archive)

comes, as do many of his others, a meditation on the cinematic image as the arbiter of a virtual "reality" where the sense of place, the city with its evocations of ancient Rome – its frescoes, statuary, architecture – is laden with memories of different moments in Italian history [Fig. 30]: cinematic historical spectacles from the silent era, early Roman art, Fascism, and the 1970s.

By bombarding the spectator with past and present images of the city throughout its various episodes, the film draws on a bank of images of the Eternal City drawn from literature, painting, tourism, and, of course, other films (including Fellini's). Central to the film is its nonnarrative structure: We are not given a definitive fictional character whose melodramatic conflicts are interwoven with the life of the city. Instead, the primary actors in this film are the director and his audience, who wander about the city together. If there is any unity, "the only unity of Rome is that of the spectacle."[25] Spectacle in Fellini is not significant for its own sake but governed by its multilayered relation to geography, history, psychology, archaeology, and, above all, to a sense of the excessive and theatrical – qualities evinced in the brothel scenes and, even more so, in the outrageous and memorable fashion show sponsored by the ecclesiastical authorities.

Fellini's film makes more cogent the sense of cinema as having moved from being a medium of action to one of reflection, and in this case the object of reflection is the city. *Fellini's Roma* is a nonfiction fictional film, a nondocumentary documentary, a nonethnographic ethnographic film. Eschewing a "story," it tells a story but in terms that make the spectator conscious of what is normally taken for granted in cinema: namely, that the sense of locale and its relation to history is more than a chronological and moral judgment of events that occurred in the past. In the views of Rome, past and present coexist; the film fuses the historical past through its treatment of time.

The modern dimensions of the city are not any more "realistic" than those portions of the film that conjure up images of the past. For example, traffic jams take on an a dreamlike quality, and the image of the motorcyclists acts as a visual and auditory refrain, as in *Amarcord.* This image of the motorcycle gang that circles the sites of classical Rome is one of a number of episodes and images that call attention to the persistence of the past in the present but as witnessed through a modern perspective. This episode is "Fellini's modern version of the ancient barbarian hordes invading the Eternal City."[26] That Fellini relied largely on re-creating his images of the city in the studio rather than concentrating on location shooting is more than a piece of technical information: It suggests that uppermost for him is the sense of the enclosed and highly artificial character of the visual medium. There is no reality that is "outside." The images of Rome – through the alternation between the exterior of streets, monuments, and buildings with the interiors of the pensione where the young man (the narrator) stays when he arrives in Rome – undermine any sense of an opposition between the external milieu and domestic life.

The many shots of the director are not merely self-reflexive; they are a constant reminder that these images are drawn from memory, diluted by time and forking in may directions. Fellini's own childhood memories are "fictionalized" through the bizarre view of a play about Julius Caesar and the images of children in a classroom viewing slides of ancient Rome. The film also presents images of a silent historical film featuring classical Rome. Later the spectator is also shown views of Fascist spectacles. The scenes in Rome of the young man's arrival at the pensione, with its array of eccentrics, its scenarios of familial relations that are hardly idealized, and the inclusion of Marco Landi, who claims to have acted in Mario Camerini's films, reinforces associations with the Fascist era. The film moves from the house to the street and to a restaurant [Fig. 31] with its different perspectives on social relations. Thus, the spectator is constantly reminded of several pasts: Fascism, the war years, the ancient world, and the fleeting present.

The introduction to the present is by way of a lengthy episode of Fellini and his crew filming the *autostrada* (motorway), which is itself a mélange of cars, police motorcyclists, animals dead on the highway, images of classical

Figure 31. Outdoor life in the city, *Fellini's Roma*. (Courtesy New York Museum of Modern Art Stills Archive)

ruins, vans with sports fans waving flags for their Neapolitan soccer team, leftist demonstrations, and tourist vans with Americans. Maintaining the fluid shift between past and present and a sense of world in movement and change, the film reverts to a variety show during the war in the 1940s, which provides a sense of the popular culture of the time: dancing acts including an imitation of Fred Astaire, comedians, a presumed amateur show, and a trio of singers offering the popular music of the day. In its aggressive interactions with the stage acts, the audience is foregrounded, and the film highlights the reception of this form of popular entertainment through the acts interrupted by dissatisfied and rowdy men and through the announcement of a Fascist military victory not so enthusiastically received by the audience. The whole performance is then interrupted by an air raid, which allows a further opportunity for the film to indicate divided attitudes among the populace about Fascism and the war.

Ephemeral and passing images of a world are underscored, nowhere so poignantly as in the episode in which a filming crew of Germans (filmed by Fellini) are taken underground where a subway is being constructed and where the frescoes of early Rome circa two thousand years ago are uncovered [Fig. 32] only to disintegrate as the air hits after centuries of entombment – a breathtaking realization of the film's central preoccupation with time and the cinema. A parallel concern of the film is that the cinema, similar to other instruments of modernity, has a dual dimension, offering both a virtual image of the passage of time and a record of its evanescence. The scene in the brothel, bizarre and surreal – part of the young man's memories of the war – is another instance of the landscape of Rome seen from a perspective of the world as a "grotesque circus performance."[27]

In the scene that follows, in which the Roman aristocracy attends an ecclesiastical fashion show, the film outdoes itself with its presentation of a cornucopia of images portraying the decadence of the Catholic Church – its consumerism, addiction to fashion, and religious sycophantism. The priests' plastic clothing is ultramodern, and skeletons grace the runway in elaborate bridal finery. After the procession of the various models and of a float that features a version of the *danse macabre,* there follows a brilliant sunburst image of Pius XII that brings the aristocratic and churchly audience to its knees in homage as they regard this "image" in orgiastic ecstasy. This fusion of past religious rites and imagery with a modern fashion show is yet another instance of the film's acknowledgment of the residual dimensions of the past dressed up to accommodate to contemporary myth and ritual.

Another saturnalian episode now takes place in the present in the Festa de Noantri in Trastevere. Here young and old, tourist and Roman, and personalities such as Gore Vidal and Anna Magnani mingle as again the film focuses on the life of the city, the rituals of eating, dancing, and group singing. Another ritual is also evident as we see the police seeking to clear the area of young people on drugs. In the final shots of the film, tracking cyclists moving through various sections of Rome, the camera reveals more views of nocturnal Rome in the piazzas, statuary, churches, and the Coliseum until the group disappears onto the highway. At times, the buildings and statues appear to be moving too, so that nothing seems to stay fixed – an analogue to the ways the film has presented a dynamic vision of the "city of illusions" (in Gore Vidal's comments) where all the social institutions are portrayed as "makers of illusion." Thus, Fellini has once again managed to orchestrate a film that violates our expectations of cinema in the forms that categorize it: as narrative form, as genre, as documentary, as travelogue, as political text, as avantgarde, as popular culture, as autobiography, and so on. The film is all these things by virtue of its insistence on cinema – as in Deleuze's notion of cinema as something that is not merely a technology and artistic form but a central feature of modern thought that has, if not altered, at least refreshed our thinking about the constituted nature of the world and of cinema as reinforcing its virtual and theatrical character.

Figure 32. Under the city, *Fellini's Roma*. (Courtesy New York Museum of Modern Art Stills Archive)

Beyond the focus on specific metropolitan centers such as Rome and Naples, a consistent feature of Italian cinema is its representations of Il Mezzogiorno, or Italy south of Naples. Gramsci had written that the South can be described as an area of extreme social disintegration. His observations focused on divisions between northern industry and southern agrarianism not as two separate entities but as interrelated, and evidence of the fragile sense of Italy as a unified nation. Of treatments of southern Italy, John Dickie writes:

> The South has been made into theatre for "the shock of diversity," whether provoking moral indignation in the spectator or a fascination for the picturesque. . . . Journeys to the South have been woven into the mythos of the foundation and crisis of the nation. . . . From street-corner prejudices to journalistic and academic discourse, the very diverse and changing problems within the South, such as those related to underdevelopment and organized crime, have too often been thought of as the problem of the Otherness of the South, seen as an unchanging whole without differences.[28]

The cinema has disseminated images of the Sicilian landscape with implied or overt portraits of the political, cultural, and social landscape, portraying a land given over to corruption, brigandage, and archaic and destructive rituals and traditions in such films as Visconti's *La terra trema* (The Earth Trembles, 1948), Lattuada's *Il mafioso* (1962), Rosi's *Salvatore Giuliano* (1962), his later *Cristo si è fermato a Eboli* ([*Christ Stopped at*] *Eboli,* 1979), and the Tavianis' *Kaos* (1984). *Salvatore Giuliano,* set in the stark, mountainous, and impoverished landscape of southern Italy, uses an investigative style related to documentary to focus on collaboration among Sicilian terrorists, the Mafia, and the Italian government. *Il mafioso,* a fiction film, assumes a more encyclopedic investigation of the landscape of Sicily in relation to work, family life, social conventions and rituals, and collusion between North and South.

In content and style, though critical of the treatment and exploitation of the South, *Il mafioso* reveals the difficulty of portraying the complexity of the "Southern question" without falling into the position of reproducing the southerner as Other. The film visually develops distinctions between the physical and cultural landscapes of Milan and a Sicilian village, Calamo, where the protagonist, who works in a large Milanese industrial company, returns for a two-week visit to the village of his birth in Sicily. The film opens with lengthy close-ups and long shots of the factory, with men working on the machines. The workers are shot as body parts, displaying their arms and torsos as they work on the various machines. Long shots reveal the vast and impersonal extent of the industrial works, with high-angle shots of a man in a white coat inspecting and checking the timing of the workers for safety and efficiency. The man, Antonio Badalmente, played by comic actor Alberto, is a "chronometrist," a time expert. Time will play a major role in this film, which connects the history of North–South relations to the contemporary situation, the regions to each other, and both to the United States and to the Mafia.

Orchestrating several narratives and focusing on several locales, *Il mafioso* is a work of ethnography as well as a portrait of the Mafia in Sicily. A lengthy prologue, develops the contrasts between North and South in a number of ways. The views presented of landscape are not only of the factory – its physical makeup, its bureaucratic character, its Fordism, its hierarchialization, its supermodern look, and its assimilation and transformation of southerners – but also of the busy and crowded life of the streets – the numerous cars, traffic jams, imposing buildings, modern apartments, huge malls, and the large train station. Contrasts are also set up between dark-haired Antonio and his blonde wife, Marta, as well as their fair children, Cynthia and Caterina. The film is not indifferent to questions of gender in its portraits of the sexual division of labor within the couple (and particularly in the domestic and familial relations portrayed when they reach Sicily). In Milan, he is portrayed as indifferent to Marta's complaints about fatigue and as insisting on leaving certain tasks to her. She, on the other hand, is critical about making this trip to his parents in the South, further evidence of domestic conflict but also of cultural difference. Additional differences will develop throughout the film as she plays the role of an "outsider," viewing with trepidation the Sicilian landscape and the customs of Antonio's family and the villagers.

Il mafioso devotes extensive time to images of landscape from the boat and the train on the journey South, filmed both from an enthusiastic Antonio's perspective as well as from that of a less eager Marta. As the ship approaches the Straits of Messina, the camera pans the sea and the distant landscape, and Antonio, looking ahead, says to her, "There's Sicily." She, in turn, comments on Italy "slipping away." He responds by asking, "Isn't this Italy too?" His enthusiastic verbal (and ironic) commentary accompanies the images of transmitters, of industry and technology, as he says, "You can already smell the oranges and the lemons." Through views from a car, the landscape changes gradually to a more barren vista without buildings and with little vegetation. The road is modern but bumpy, and Marta comments again, "It's obvious we have left Italy behind." The next view is of a village as Antonio shows his children a painted Sicilian cart, and he describes the scene (from Tasso) showing Rinaldo at the battle of Roncisvalle. His idealized view of village life is that it is "happy and carefree," although subsequent scenes undermine his ebullience. When they see a funeral, he waxes enthusiastic about tradition, extolling the customs of the people sitting by the corpse, eating and drinking. However, when he asks about the cause of death, he is told the man died "from two pistol shots" – thus introducing the theme of violence, which will increase and culminate in his own brutal actions.

The view of the family upon their arrival is no longer from his perspective but from the camera's (and ours) as the viewer is invited to contemplate familiar images associated with Italy: old women in black with heads covered; a young woman, Rosalia, with dark hair and a mustache (similar to Rosalia in Germi's *Divorzio all'italiana*); various uncles and neighbors; and a crowded house replete with icons, photographs, religious paintings, and a traditional silver bedstead. The ritual of eating is underscored by close-ups of heaping plates of food, gossip about men in the village, and singing. Marta's presence is registered with silence and suspicion as the women observe her blondeness, her reluctance to eat much, and her smoking. She now becomes the conduit to the traditionally negative image of the South. In her remoteness, she allows for a distanced, though negative, assessment of the family and of Antonio's excessive idealism about home. She begins to experience the outsider's uneasiness about what is not being said and expresses a need to have interpreted the veiled language that she hears. Antonio translates the less innocuous events, but does not clarify more fundamental aspects of the social relations she encounters. For example, he explains that the term "sitting" refers to unemployment, but he offer no any explanation for other customs such as rituals of ostracism and revenge.

A walk on the street with Antonio and family allows Marta (and the audience) to view the ancient character of the buildings (earlier we were shown the old cathedral and the mountain beyond). Everywhere she sees signs of death as she and Antonio go to meet his patron, Don Vincenzo. From Marta's perspective, each of the houses is shown with a plaque commemorating a dead relative, and Antonio explains that "It's a tradition. We never forget our dead ones." Throughout the film, information about events is accumulated largely through instances of visual and verbal innuendo, but the confrontation with the Mafia is deferred until midfilm, by which time the audience has been given a sense of the village milieu and of the spoken and unspoken behaviors of its inhabitants. For example, in greeting former colleagues, Antonio asks about the whereabouts of one of the villagers, Filo, and is told that the man "betrayed his friends," for he "goes about agitating among the workers." Thus when Antonio sees Filo on the walk to Don Vincenzo's, he ignores him; when Marta asks why, Antonio lies and says he did not see him. The motif of vision is once again reinforced – her views of the village and his. Further exposed is the split between the modern life he has acquired in Milan and the power of the secrets and silences surrounding traditional life in the village. Everything about the village – the ancient streets, the interiors of the houses – is set in contrast to the mechanistic modernity associated with the city of Milan, highlighting "the clash between modern customs and a more ancient code of conduct that resists and survives in an era of transition."[29]

When arriving at Don Vincenzo's villa, the couple is at first turned away unceremoniously: A churlish woman at the locked gate grabs the package Antonio is to deliver to the don and walks away. When finally they are admitted to the compound, which resembles a feudal palace, their first encounter with the don confirms that he is not merely an powerful, upper-class figure in the community but the head of the local Mafia, waited on by a senator, a priest, and criminal associates. The gift turns out to be a silver heart with the names of victims destroyed by the Mafia, and the don says, "Our friends in America do things in a big way." However, a name is missing on the list, and the audience is informed as to the task Antonio, even before he left Milan, had been assigned – to kill. Connections between northern industrialists and southern Mafiosi are made explicit, as are those between southern Italy and the United States. Whereas the images of the landscape portray differences, actions reveal collusion.

Don Vincenzo presents himself as able to understand and respond to the needs of the "people." He refers to bad "contracts" – other people's plans that run counter to his wishes to build a dike in the area. In the name of benevolence, he says that he wants to leave the dike as his memorial for the "poor people" who need the water. Thus, his role as paternal figure is associated with profit and protectionism. His lavish villa is a ornamented with classical architecture and outdoor frescoes, and he sits on a high bench like a king. Antonio, finally arriving after having been recalled by the don, greets him as he would an aristocrat or church prelate, kissing his hand. More significant, the audience learns, is that Antonio's position in the North was due to the don's influence, and given the don's bestowal of favors for profit, he is going to ask for repayment, an expression of "gratitude." Again, communication proceeds through indirect discourse, as noblesse, servility, and pomp veil the commerce and violence upon which the don's power over the people rests.

The audience is also provided other views of the physical and cultural landscape, involving Antonio's father's bargaining for a plot of land that Antonio wants to buy for a vacation home for himself and his family. The owner initially was asking fifty lire per square mile but now is asking two hundred, knowing full well that he can extort this amount. In a scene that borders on Boccaccio-type satire, a friar with a divining rod is seen claiming that water buried on the land explains the increase in price. Whereas Antonio seeks to reason with the owner, the father becomes shrill and fights with the man over the accusation of being called a "cuckold," which he tells Antonio is also a slight on his mother, who is thus a "whore" – a desecration of the cult of honor based on the veneration of the southern woman. When Antonio asks his father, "Do you want to turn this into *Cavalleria Rusticana*?" (invoking the writings of Verga and the opera), the father calls Antonio a "woman" and rides off.

In a subsequent scene in the village market, with its jewelry, clothing kiosks, and a pistol-shooting stall, Antonio learns from one of the don's henchmen what it is he must do. He is reminded of his status as a "special son" who, during the post–World War II era, a period of "chaos, hunger, and the black market," had carried "messages" for the don. Despite the services he performed at that time, he still "owes" the don payment for his job in Milan, and Antonio will acknowledge his "respects" for Don Vincenzo, which are greater even than what he owes his father and mother. Respect and loyalty are identified with economic exchange and social protection and linked to his performing an act of violence that will confirm his masculinity.

The film relentlessly pursues the enigmatic character of Southern culture. In a beach scene reminiscent of Pasolini's documentary *Comizi d'amore,* Antonio and his former friends discuss the "isolation" of the southerner, which one man claims is due to "economic and social problems," whereas another says it is not a problem of communication since "we communicate among ourselves." The problem, says another man, is communicating with "others and especially females." Once again, the question of women and Southern life comes to the fore as the men (who have built a sand sculpture of a nude woman with large breasts) ask Antonio about women in Milan, and he briefly describes an affair with a woman before Marta as the men listen avidly. However, when the men gaze at Marta, who comes into view in her bathing suit, Antonio gets annoyed, announces "I'm still Sicilian," and walks off protectively with his wife. The question of masculine honor is tied to the female body as male property. The violence attendant on this position is underscored visually as the men brutally destroy their sand sculpture.

The remaining scenes involve Antonio's paying his debt to the don by killing a man in New York, thus fulfilling the codes of paternalism, masculinity, and honor. Antonio returns to the village, rejoining his wife as if nothing has happened. The film ends with images similar to those of the opening scenes: Antonio in his white coat, returning the pen he had mistakenly appropriated before his visit and being told, "the world would be better off if there were more people like you." Antonio is seen again using his chronometer, checking out work at the factory. Thus, the film provides a broad vista on the "Southern question" and attempts the impossible task of integrating the economic situation of Southern life with the vestigial remnants of familialism, subordination of women to the codes of honor, the segregation of those who work against custom, and the role of the Mafia as integrally associated with landlordism, patronage, and violence. Moreover, the North is not exempted from this analysis, since the Mafia is part of Northern industrial life.

The film also portrays, through the character of Marta, marked distinctions that are part of the profound cultural differences between the two regions despite their interdependency. Through Antonio, the film addresses the disjunction between the idealization of traditional aspects of life inherited from the past and the inadequacy of these images in the context of the actual conditions to which the populace is subjected. In regard to the uses of landscape, the film sets before the viewer visual contrasts of these regions, contrasts that are intimately tied to the portraits of character and their industrial and rural habitats. History is invoked through the images of the modernity of the North and the quasi-traditional environment of the South – which appear to be remote from each other but are actually mutually interdependent – and through the knowledge that the Mafia has its roots in the postwar era and is linked to the role of the Allies. Though the narrative involving Antonio's payment of his "debt" to Don Vincenzo resuscitates images of criminal violence associated with the Mafia, the episodes in Milan are integral to the film's portrait of the "Southern question." Inevitably, the film falters in its evocation of stereotypes of the southerner, though it provides a sense of their persistence in the cultural lexicon of Italian cinema that involves images of the land, architecture, domestic life, and the interface between urbanity and myths of rural life.

CHAPTER SIX

Gramsci and Italian Cinema

T he memory and effects of Fascism, the war, and the Resistance were central to national concerns for postwar intellectuals of the Left, as seen in the films that were identified with the "golden age of neorealism." To these anti-Fascist, pro-Resistance leftists, it was important to create films that focused on the necessity for cultural and political change. Such films challenged the genre approach, with its assumed escapist tendencies, its penchant for spectacle (identified also with Hollywood and Americanism), and its depoliticized concept of cinema. Neorealist filmmakers advocated an engagement with contemporary social problems in a cinematic language that was investigative. However, as David Forgacs indicates, of the 822 films that appeared between 1945 and 1953, "films by directors associated with neorealism in the widest sense accounted for . . . less than a third" of production.[1] These films were largely unsuccessful commercially, "box office flops at home."[2] Their demise resulted in part from the return of Hollywood products, the ongoing intervention of the Roman Catholic Church through censorship, the consolidation of power by the Christian Democrats, and the economic encouragement of and support for films that promoted "positive" images of Italian life. Moreover, filmmakers themselves began to question the tenets and constraints of neorealism, seeking forms of cinematic expression that, directly or obliquely, addressed the advent of the consumer society and reexamined the political role of culture. In the films of the late 1950s and 1960s, also considered a "golden age" of Italian cinema, the preoccupation with cinematic style and the reintroduction of historical subjects became a source of investigation for many of the filmmakers who were, in greater or lesser ways, influenced by Gramscian thinking.

The name of Antonio Gramsci is as important for cinema as it is for Italian political thought. No other figure's ideas played such a large role in the development of the post–World War II Italian cinema. Gramscian issues may not have been as obvious in the cinema of the immediate postwar era, but they dominated the cinema of the late 1960s to the 1970s. His influence is most evident in the works of such filmmakers as Luchino Visconti, Bernardo Bertolucci, Mario Monicelli, Ermanno Olmi, Pier Paolo Pasolini, and the Taviani brothers. Gramsci's concern for economic and political change was intrinsically tied to the role of culture and education. In his analysis of cultural politics, he discussed literature, theater, opera, serial fiction, journalism, legal

149

forms, painting, and, to a lesser extent, cinema. In all of his writing, the emphasis on the importance of pedagogy is central, but, for him, pedagogy was not pregiven, authoritarian, or moralizing. He saw it rather as a process of developing critical skills conducive to transforming commonsense knowledge inherent to subaltern groups, and, thereby, effecting a transformation from common sense to good sense. For change to occur he thought that the subaltern must first develop the intellectual means to analyze and understand the power of common sense, which he describes as follows:

> Every social class has its own "common sense" and "good sense,"
> which are basically the most widespread conception of life and man.
> . . . Common sense is the folklore of philosophy and always stands
> midway between folklore proper (folklore as it is normally understood) and the philosophy, science, and economics of the scientists.
> Common sense creates the folklore of the future, a relatively rigidified phase of popular knowledge in a given time and place.[3]

These ideas are crucial to an understanding of his conception of intellectuals, their role in analyzing the existence of obstacles to new forms of knowledge, the relation between knowledge and action, and the ways culture functions to maintain or to alter institutional power in the interests of ruling groups. His ideas are also important for understanding the historical landscape of Italian cinema.

Born at Ales, Sardinia, in 1891, Gramsci became a major architect and intellectual of the Italian Communist Party (PCI). He went to elementary school in Sardinia, during which time his father was arrested, ostensibly for administrative malfeasance (1897–8), and in 1903, Antonio left school to help his family. He returned in 1905 to secondary school, where he began to educate himself about socialism. In the years following his graduation, he became more involved in socialist politics while attending a *liceo* in Ghilarza, Sardinia. He was awarded a scholarship to study at the University of Turin in 1911, where for two years he studied linguistics despite the health problems that were to plague him all his life. By 1915, he had left the university to become a journalist and organizer for the Socialist Party (PSI). An advocate of revolutionary struggle, he was active in establishing factory councils for the promotion of worker activism and education. Increasingly disaffected with the PSI, he became one of the founders of the Italian Communist Party. In 1922, he went as a delegate for the party to Moscow, where he was selected for the executive committee of the Comintern. Once again he became ill and spent time in a sanatorium. During this time, he met Julia Schucht, who became his wife.

When the Fascists came to power, Gramsci continued to work for the party and to write and organize against Fascism. In 1924, the same year as the murder of the socialist deputy Giacomo Matteotti, Gramsci was elected to Parliament; but then in 1926, under a new set of decrees promulgated by the regime, he was arrested, transported south, and then in 1927 transferred to a prison in Milan. After a trial in 1928 sentencing him to twenty years in prison "to keep this brain from functioning," he was sent to a prison near Bari. There, in ill health, he obtained the desired permission to write, and kept the many notebooks on a variety of intellectual and political subjects that are known as *The Prison Notebooks*. In 1932, five years before his death, his sentence was reduced to twelve years and four months, but his health was deteriorating rapidly. He spent the remainder of his sentence in and out of a clinic, dying in 1937, the year his sentence expired. Thanks to his sister-in-law Tatiana Schucht (and to a few other friends and colleagues), he was able to get many of the books he required for his writing. Due primarily to her efforts, the notebooks were gotten out of prison, placed in a bank vault in Rome with the intent of having them delivered to Moscow, where they were housed until the end of World War II. These notebooks, published finally in 1948, were to have a great influence on the thinking of many Italian intellectuals of the Left and on postwar filmmakers. They were more widely disseminated in the 1960s.[4]

The notebooks, like Gramsci's preprison writings, reveal the range of his intellectual and political interests. They particularly reveal that he was not a Marxist in the tradition of the many economistically minded thinkers of the 1930s. Not that he ignored the importance of economics, but his theoretical and pragmatic concerns went far beyond a simplistic corporatism and institutional reform to embrace the necessity of cultural change that would empower subaltern groups, enabling them to direct their own affairs rather than subjugating them to the edicts and dictates of traditional elites, a situation particularly characteristic of Italian cultural and political history.

In particular, the "Southern question" remained a central and abiding concern, still relevant for understanding political and cultural conflicts in Italy central to Gramsci's analysis of Italian history and particularly of the Risorgimento as a "passive" or failed revolution (a theme reiterated in such films as *Senso, Il gattopardo,* and *Allonsanfán*). In Gramsci's terms, the South has been portrayed as "the ball and chain that prevents a more rapid progress in the civil development of Italy."[5] Gramsci's writings on the South address "the complex of feelings created in the North about the South" that were part of his personal legacy, having grown up on the island of Sardinia. Gramsci was not merely documenting and commenting on what is legion in studies of Italian cultural and social history: He was attempting to analyze these conditions for the purposes of charting conditions for change.[6] Toward that end he sought to identify the constituent elements in that failed revolution that were repeated with variations under Fascism and in contemporary Italy. Recognizing the celebratory nationalist myths associated with the Risorgimento as a "revolution" that united Italy, he sought to identify the ways in which the notion of unity was, in fact, the establishment of a limited hegemony on the part of a minority: political moderates, the monarchy and upper classes, industrialists, and intellectuals, producing a revolution from above and relying on what he identified as "transformism," the process whereby excluded groups are assimilated into the conservative political spectrum.

His emphasis was primarily on understanding how the subaltern can achieve hegemony. Toward that end, he felt that education was essential and particularly important for the creation of a group of intellectuals who could understand and counter the power of those intellectuals who contribute their economic, political, and technological services to the state, thereby perpetuating the status quo and obstructing the creation of new intellectual strata and hence new social forms. In emphasizing the importance of education, Gramsci was not saying that subaltern groups are not intellectuals; They have their own sense of the world, of what is wrong and of what is needful for survival, but their ideas are not, in Gramsci's terms, coherent and critical. Their world is that of common sense, which is in his terms tied to folklore that is "not elaborated and systematized because the people, by definition, cannot do such a thing; and it is also multifarious, in the sense that it is a mechanical juxtaposition of various conceptions of the world and of life that have followed one another throughout history."[7] A study of folklore is necessary to create a critical sense of language, history, and politics for the purposes of assuming leadership. Common sense, while useful in the short run, is a passive response to events, and the impetus toward change requires the acquisition of ideas and skills that will enable subaltern groups to resist assimilation into the status quo as well as splintering, to understand power, and to act in their own interests.

In discussing the vexing historical problem of the Italian South, Gramsci had explored the ironic fact that there was no sense of unity between the workers in the North and the peasants in the South, the consequence being not only the ongoing suppression of southern but also the assimilation of northern workers into the reigning hegemony, even when this was not in the best interest of either group. In films that were made by Visconti, Bertolucci, Pasolini, Olmi, and the Taviani brothers, there is often a Gramscian emphasis on southern Italy, and, if not on the South, then on peasant and industrial groups in the North. In the works of these filmmakers, there is also

1. a focus on the ambiguous, if not treacherous, role of members of the upper classes and especially of intellectuals, who, even when they begin by identifying with subaltern groups, are largely led to identify with the groups in power or to abandon their zeal for change and become alienated or cynical (e.g., *Allonsanfán*); and
2. a preoccupation with rethinking history from below, in what we might now term "unofficial history."

One finds a return to the past either through a use of the historical film (e.g., *Senso, Il gattopardo, 1900, L'albero degli zoccoli* [*The Tree of Wooden Clogs*]) or through a treatment of contemporary events in such a way as to evoke echoes of the past and of a world different from that presented, by filmmakers who regard subaltern groups from a sentimental vantage point (e.g., as either victims of a harsh, indifferent, and exploitative economic and political order or as militant heroes in behalf of revolutionary change). The world of the subaltern in Visconti's *La terra trema* or in Pasolini's *Accattone* and *Mamma Roma* is not Manichaean and melodramatic, posing a simple distinction between past and present, worker/peasant and landlord/industrialist. Instead the filmmakers offer images of a world where the protagonists are portrayed in terms of Gramscian common sense. These films draw on a folklore that dramatizes age-old customs and folklore conducive to survival of the tragic obstacles the characters encounter in a world hostile to their interests.

The trajectory of these films is not toward success and resolution of conflicts but rather along a painstaking, often tragic, dramatization of the conditions of the characters' lives and their responses to them. In those instances that posit class conflict and choose to set the films in the past – in the Risorgimento, in the pre- or post-Fascist environment – the films pick up the Gramscian concern to analyze the persistence of past forms of belief and action in the present. In those set in a contemporary context, there is also a preoccupation with forms of common sense that signals a conflict with good sense. This emphasis, which probes the immersion of the subaltern classes in a way of life and thinking, differs from conventional cinematic renditions of social life as exemplified is such films as *1860* (see Chapter 2).

In *Il gattopardo* (*The Leopard*, 1963), Visconti ventures into a region explored by Gramsci, one that has offered a perennial challenge to Italian writers and filmmakers and has been used for a variety of ideological purposes – Sicily. *La terra trema* (1948) and *Rocco e i suoi fratelli* (*Rocco and His Brothers*, 1960) are Visconti's previous cinematic forays into this region. The melodrama with which *The Leopard* invests the sense of Sicilian identity (in contrast to northern Italian identity) is reminiscent of the tensions dramatized but then mediated by Blasetti's *1860*. At stake in *The Leopard* is the history of a region colonized by Austrians, Spaniards, and then Piedmontese, which continues to this day to pose a cultural, social, and economic problem in relation to the notion of Italy as a unified nation. This "Southern question" addressed by Gramsci also involves the issue of the North as an "Octopus which enriched itself at the expense of the South. . . . [I]ts economic-industrial increment was in direct proportion to the impoverishment of the economy and agriculture of the South."[8]

In *The Leopard,* the alliance of Don Fabrizio and the House of Salina with Don Calógero and the House of Savoy constitutes another form of political and economic betrayal – of Sicily and of its subaltern classes – as well as of Italian unity. The film dramatizes the further colonization of Sicilians (which appears in Blasetti as a form of liberation) through a portrait of "the subordination and victimization of the native."[9] In this context, Marcus comments,

> Official histories presuppose that Italy was always an organic whole whose unity was suppressed by foreign domination until its popular liberation in 1870. Such a fiction conceals the reality of imperial conquest by the House of Savoy, which managed cleverly to identify its own dynastic interests with those of the mythic totality.[10]

This view is celebrated in Blasetti's film and critically dissected in Visconti's.

Viscont's style is dependent on a high degree of collaboration with musicians, actors, scriptwriters, set designers, and costumers. This ongoing partnership produces a sense of the visual and thematic continuity of his cinematic world. *The Leopard* was the result of collaboration with the composer Nino Rota and the photographer Giuseppe Rotunno. As is usual for Visconti's films, Piero Tosi did the costumes. The script, based on the Di Lampedusa novel, was coauthored by Suso Cecchi d'Amico, Enrico Medioli Pasquale, Festa Campanile, Massimo Franciosa, and Visconti himself. The lead actors were international stars: Burt Lancaster and Alain Delon. The Italian cast had worked with Visconti before and were familiar faces in Italian cinema: Claudia Cardinale, Paolo Stoppa, Massimo Girotti, and Rina Morelli, among others. The Di Lampedusa novel was the inspiration for the work, though there is no doubt that, as in other of his films, Visconti embroidered elements from his own personal history into the text. Although the operatic style of *The Leopard* is tied to familiar conventions of the historical film, there is also the incorporation of opera itself, through the ironic use of music from Bellini and Verdi, to dramatize the machinations of power, the thematics of succession, family continuity and disruption, inheritance and the role of romance. The violation of classical film narration, the slower pace of the narrative, and the excessively mannered mode of posturing by the characters function as distanciation, as commentary, and as object for critical contemplation. The slowing down of the action undermines fascination with public performance and ritualized actions. The central conflict in *The Leopard* – from novel to film – is the antagonism, then collaboration, between the aristocratic and bourgeois family. Regarding the emergence of the bourgeoisie, Gramsci had written:

> The revolution which the bourgeois class has brought into the conception of law, and hence into the function of the State, consists especially in the will to conform (hence ethicity of the law and of the

State). The previous ruling classes were essentially conservative in the sense that they did not tend to construct an organic passage from the other classes to their own, i.e., to enlarge their spheres 'technically' and ideologically; their conception was that of a closed caste.[11]

In the aristocratic mode, the iron rule of the aristocratic patriarch, the necessity of arranged marriages, and the acceptance of familial duty rather than of romance are the rule. Hence Don Fabrizio (Burt Lancaster) must endure his wife's "Gesu Maria" when they have sex, and seek sexual gratification outside conjugal bonds. Whereas the prince wants no ties to the new nation-state, Angelica (Claudia Cardinale) and Tancredi (Alain Delon) are the cynical harbingers of the new order of social class, the Italy that men like Chevalley (Leslie French) seek in idealistic terms to inaugurate as an instrument of change. Reminiscent of the Fascist abuses of the state in the name of "law and order," this couple is the new ruling elite. If chivalric honor was the domain of the aristocracy, law and order are the province of the bourgeoisie. Angelica and Tancredi prefigure the emergence of civil society, with its assumed division between public and private spheres. Although the new class appears to have greater freedom in its domestic affairs, it has in fact abrogated its prerogatives in the interests of a regulated society, the much-vaunted law and order extolled by Tancredi as a stay against anarchy.[12]

Geoffrey Nowell-Smith has commented on the importance of Gramsci's writings to an understanding of the film.[13] In his writings on Italian history and in those on the state and civil society, Gramsci speaks of the "crisis of hegemony, or general crisis of the state,"[14] characterized in the novel by the defeat of the Garibaldians as well as by the expanding domination of the ruling class under the combined class forces of Don Calógero Sedara (Paolo Stoppa) and Tancredi in the name of the monarchical state. The drama of this class collaboration, is also evident in the Visconti film in the domestic intrigue that makes this collaboration possible. The melodramatic affect resides in several related areas: in the portrayal of the aging and misguided prince who is loath to renounce power; in the ambition of the ambitious Don Calógero, determined to buy his way into the upper classes; in the opportunism of Tancredi, willing to kill others for power; and in the figure of Angelica, Don Calógero's daughter, content to romanticize and capitalize on this state of affairs for her own ends. Of all of the characters, Fabrizio is the most complex, as both betrayed and betrayer. He is the baritone to Tancredi's tenor. Although he is the villain, he is sympathetic and attractive by comparison to the others, perhaps because he can cynically reflect on and illuminate the terms of that betrayal. The film was an opportunity to study this character.[15] The role of Don Fabrizio, like that of an operatic protagonist, is highly stylized and mannered. His character is largely conveyed through one-on-one interactions with the others: Padre Pirrone (Romolo Valli), Don Ciccio (Serge Reggiani), Tancredi, and

Figure 33. The House of Salina in church, *Il gattopardo* (*The Leopard*). (Courtesy New York Museum of Modern Art Stills Archive)

to a lesser extent, the princess (Rina Morelli). In these "duets," his rhetorical range is revealed. He appears always to be onstage even in the moments when he is most isolated: observing others at the gathering for the election results, regarding himself in the mirror, and praying alone on the street in his final brief soliloquy. His figure is especially linked to the ritualistic moments in the film – the initial scene of the family at prayer [Fig. 33], the processional entrance to the church at Donnafugata, the church service, the stately dinner for Don Calógero, and the ball scene. The use of language as sound to heighten the spectacle and to enhance the web of relations and themes, rather than to produce any intrinsic or incremental meaning, is evident in the family scenes at prayer, in group novel reading, and in the priest's chanting of prayers at the inn.

The numerous mirror images underline the nature of the prince's misrecognition wherein he sees reflected a delusory image of his wholeness and power. Fabrizio's melancholy gazing into the mirror at the ball reveals the fracturing of this self-image.[16] In terms applicable to the Visconti film, Gilles De-

Figure 34. Life as spectacle: Angelica (Claudia Cardinale) at the grand ball in *Il gattopardo* (*The Leopard*). (Courtesy New York Museum of Modern Art Stills Archive)

leuze has written: "the mirrors are not content with reflecting the actual image, but constitute the prism, the lens where the split image constantly runs after itself to connect up with itself."[17] In linking cinema to the other arts, Deleuze says,

> If we consider the relations between theatre and cinema in general, we no longer find ourselves in the classical situation where the two arts are two different ways of actualizing the same virtual image, but neither do we find ourselves in the situation of a "montage of attraction." . . . The situation is quite different: the actual image and the virtual image coexist and crystallize, they enter into a circuit which brings us back constantly from one to the other.[18]

In *The Leopard* (as in *Senso*), the interpenetration of art forms – as in the film's operatic culmination at the grand ball – underlines that "life has become spectacle" [Fig. 34]. Past and present, virtual and actual, real life and spectacle all blur into their opposites. This "theatricality" divides, making everything a reflection and an object of reflection: "the aristocratic world of the rich, the former rich: this is what is crystalline, but like a synthetic crystal, because it is outside history and nature, outside divine creation."[19] Surrounded by art, the aristocrats "demand freedom but a freedom which they enjoy like an empty privilege."[20] Fabrizio lives in a decomposing world – a *Götterdämmerung*. History is important; it is "never scenery. It is caught obliquely in a low-angled perspective in a rising or setting ray, a kind of laser which comes and cuts into the crystal, disorganizes its substance, hastens its darkening and disperses its sides."[21] The most important aspect of these crystals of time is "the revelation that something arrives too late."[22] The paintings, the uses of Bellini and Verdi, and the operatic nature of the film contribute to this sense of decomposition and "too-lateness," most tellingly revealed in the glances exchanged between Angelica and the prince at the ball.

The Leopard also embeds cinema history. In histories of Italian cinema, Visconti is identified with the development of neorealism through his 1942 film *Ossessione* and his later *La terra trema* (1948), although both films also depend on the operatic.[23] With *Senso,* Visconti moved to larger-scale production, utilizing American funding and American actors in a return to the historical spectacle, with its expensive trappings, lavish costumes and settings – a film form that the neorealists had so disparaged.[24] Yet *Senso* and *The Leopard* hardly qualify as conventional historical films. In their particular appropriations of opera, their resistance to binarism, mythology, and notions of progress, and their use of irony, they become a commentary on the kind of operatic historical film represented by Blasetti's *1860. The Leopard,* with its "essentially operatic spirit, dependent on large gestures, operatic design, and melodramatic movement,"[25] is able to exploit such features to offer a multifaceted and critical sense of history that mitigates the monumentalism characteristic of national discourses. The film is instead a critical reflection on the vicissitudes of the Italian nation-state, with its ties to family and property – an exercise in complicating and blurring the boundaries associated with official historicization and its relation to opera and cinema. *The Leopard* dissects the commonsense character of popular representation on film and opera, which assumes a common fund of beliefs and goals and is mistrustful of analysis, intellect, and contemplation. The film's self-conscious use of history in collusion with operatic themes and techniques contributes to a critical engagement with questions of politics and power, particularly with the failure of popular struggle.

Appearing in the same year as *The Leopard,* Mario Monicelli's *I compagni* (*The Organizer,* 1963) reveals another facet of the Gramscian concern with the history of political struggle in Italy and with the relation of intellectuals

Figure 35. Demonstrators in *I compagni* (*The Organizer*). (Courtesy New York Museum of Modern Art Stills Archive)

to workers. The film returns to an earlier time, the 1890s, and to a strike by workers in a textile mill in Milan [Fig. 35]. Utilizing photographs and socialist songs from that period, the film, contrary to many traditional political films of the Left, does not commemorate a victorious strike but investigates one that fails. Focusing on the vicissitudes of the workers as they confront the possibility of starvation, and emphasizing the power of the bosses to threaten them by means of scabs, strikebreakers, bribes, and the militia, the film probes the problems confronting the workers: their vulnerable position by virtue of the level of their organization, the manifold obstacles to unity, and the need for education in order to gain better practical and theoretical insights into their condition and the possibilities for altering it.

The workers are presented neither as passive victims nor as unblemished heroes of the hour. Their portrayal is geared to indicating the reasons for the strike's failure, which must also be attributed both to their disorganization and to the powerful forces arraigned against them. A number of vignettes dramatize the trajectory of the workers' struggles: their initial mistrust and fear, their later enthusiasm for the strike and its potential political benefits, and finally, the combined bribery and physical violence on the part of owners and managers to thwart collective action. Other elements in society are shown as sympathetic to the strikers – the young soldier who shares his food with a striker's family, the railway guard who averts his eyes as the workers steal coal to stay warm, and the prostitute who befriends and houses the "organizer," Professor Sinagaglia (Marcello Mastroianni) [Fig. 36], when he is being hunted by the police. Ultimately, with the breaking of the strike, the professor is led off to jail, one of the leaders leaves town, and the future fate of the workers returning to the plant is uncertain.

The professor struggles to define his role in relation to the workers. A member of the middle classes, he has at great expense to his personal life – separation from his wife and two sons, impoverishment, harassment by police – committed himself to the socialist cause. However, he is presented not as a "savior" of the people but as a declassed intellectual who is himself learning about the forces that conspire with and against the workers. He is not the only intellectual in the film: Omero, the schoolteacher fired by his superior, has been supportive of the strike. The film's concern with education is manifest in the relation between Omero and his younger brother, as the dismissed teacher insists on the young boy remaining in school.

Among the socially divisive elements portrayed are women's position in the family's rejection of their prostitute daughter; the workers's inability to talk to and their fear of the manager and the owner; the traditional animosity between northern workers and southerners who come to work in the factories; and the workers' vulnerability to personal favors, as when the manager bribes one of them by paying for physical care for his sick wife. In the film, the workers are reminded by the manager that he, like them, is salaried, thus rationalizing his impotence in communicating their requests for shorter working hours. Of the technocratic class of the North, Gramsci wrote, "In the North, the dominant type is the factory 'technician,' who acts as a link between the mass of the workers and the management."[26]

I compagni is not merely a "document" about the 1890s but an ongoing investigation (relating to the 1960s) of major Gramscian positions: What is the relation of the intellectual to the workers? How is the viewer to understand the conflict between traditional values and the emerging conditions that are the inevitable concomitant of modern, industrial life? What is the connection between education and politics? What role does history or an understanding of the past play in understanding social and economic relations? What are the blind spots inherited from the past that keep the workers vulnerable to verbal and physical coercion? What stylistic options are available, particularly in the idiom of the 1960s, for creating a political cinema? In its satirical characterizations and focus on thwarted expectations, this film works against the grain of conventional political images, and of heroic conceptions of historici-

Figure 36. Incomplete "pasteup" of advertisement for *I compagni* (*The Organizer*), with Marcello Mastroianni's name missing. (Courtesy New York Museum of Modern Art Stills Archive)

zation, providing the opportunity for rethinking political cinema. It is reflexive in its uses of music and political symbols, suggesting that although they may resonate affectively, they do not necessarily produce different and more critical forms of politics.

Ermanno Olmi's *L'albero degli zoccoli* (*The Tree of Wooden Clogs,* 1978), also set in northern Italy in the nineteenth century, is consonant with a Gramscian analysis of the relations between culture and politics. Focusing on peasant life, the film dramatizes in specific terms conditions in the Bergamask countryside at that historical moment. The text adheres to certain aspects of neorealism in its use of nonprofessional actors, location shooting, a minimal narra-

tive, the character of everyday existence, the deflation of melodramatic portraits of victim and aggressor without minimizing the hardships of peasant
life, and its avoidance of overt politicizing. Through its visualization of an earlier world, Olmi's text "contrasts the simple Christian steadfastness of his peasants to the insensitive cruelty of their superiors, reminding his viewers of the
many virtues that have been lost in the rapid transition from an agrarian,
peasant culture to one based upon rapid industrial development and urbanization."[27] In the images of the film, the land itself plays a major role in the
shots of the fields and of the peasants plowing, planting, and harvesting [Fig.
37]. Repeated shots of the tree-lined roads provide an eloquent commentary
on the vulnerability of peasant life that culminates in the landlord's eviction
of Batisti's family for his cutting down a tree to make clogs for his son to wear
on the walk to school.

In portraying the peasants, the film does not make them either primitive
or exotic. Through the many scenes of work, especially in those of the grandfather, Anselmo, planting his tomatoes, the spectator learns of the useful and
necessary knowledge that underpins survival in these conditions of hardship.
However, these are not scenes of squalor. The intertitles describe the homestead, which houses from five to six families, and explain that a large portion
of the livestock and the farm equipment belong to the landlord. Two-thirds
of the harvest are also his, but rather than highlighting his power directly, the
film chooses to portray the interactions among the families and less among
the ruling powers. For example, the eviction is handled through the bailiff,
without dialogue. Batisti's loading of his cart to leave the homestead is shown
through images of the other families silently observing his departure, but the
harsh punishment on the part of the landlord is not lost on the spectator.

Consonant with the Gramscian critique of common sense, the film addresses the mode of survival that inheres in this world, especially the role of
religion. When the unfortunate beggar comes to the various families for food,
he is not turned away, but given food despite the meagerness of their diet.
When the widows' cow becomes ill and the vet urges her to destroy it, she
prays in the chapel for a miracle, gets water from the stream and tends the
animal, who recovers. The miracle is thus not divine but resides in the faith
and persistence of the woman in the face of hardship. However, religion is
not presented univalently as a positive force. In the portrait of the priest,
Father Carlo, one sees also the ways in which he encourages resignation
through Christian belief and ritual, and the importance of charity and love
rather than resistance.

The film begins on a Gramscian note as Batisti and his wife are told by
the priest that they must send their son, Minek, to school. The motif of education as a means of escaping rural life is central to the film, though, once
again, treated by indirection. Batisti points out to the priest that he needs the

Figure 37. Peasants in the field, *L'albero degli zoccoli* (*The Tree of Wooden Clogs*). (Courtesy New York Museum of Modern Art Stills Archive)

boy to help him in his work, but Father Carlo tells him that the boy is gifted and that getting Minek an education is serving the will of God despite the difficulties this might entail for the family. However, as a result of Minek's breaking his clogs as he walks to school, an act that drives Batisti to cut down a tree, the family is driven from the land, thus confirming his initial skepticism about the blessings of schooling for his child. Still, the film is concerned with pedagogy: in Minek's teaching his parents what he learns at school, in the grandfather's education of his grandchildren about the nature of the earth and planting, in the transmission of customs from one generation to another, and in the reliance on common sense and folklore for survival.

The film becomes a form of pedagogy for the viewer in offering an alternative and antisentimental version of this world, where the peasants are shown to be immersed in the contradictions of their servitude. On the one hand, they struggle within the limitations of their conditions to survive; on the other, they are indifferent to the political struggles for democratization that are taking place. This is evident when, during a festival where a speaker orates about progress and the need to fight against the abuses of privilege, one character is less involved with the speech than with a coin on the ground, stealthily picking it up and hiding it in the horse's hoof, only to find it gone later. When Maddalena and Stefano visit a nun in Milan, they are witness to the street demonstrations between soldiers and political agitators, yet they are more preoccupied with life in the convent. Moreover, when Batisti is driven from the land, the peasants accept with resignation the likelihood of starvation and squalor that has befallen him and his family. One of the most telling moments in the film involves the killing of the pig. Writes Bondanella:

> We are shocked by the blood and gore of the scene, but for the peasants, this seemingly cruel execution of a docile animal represents a necessary part of their daily lives. And even when they are forced to kill their animals, the peasants obviously feel more affection for their livestock than the landlord feels for the peasants.[28]

Such episodes are further indication of the film's refusal to render the lives of the peasants exotic and idealized.

The style of *L'albero degli zoccoli* relies heavily on visual tableaux and music. The images and sound (and also the uses of silence) convey the texture of rural life. The repetitive character of the world is reinforced by the reiterated images of the tree-lined roads and the field, the views of the homestead, and the reliance on rituals relating to harvesting, births, storytelling, and marriage. Bach organ music underscores these ritualistic moments, as does the frequent introduction of folk music. The landlord is identified with opera as he listens to Rossini's *Barber of Seville* while the peasants bring their maize to the bailiff to be weighed. The film, organized by the various episodes that rely on the passage of the seasons, does not focus on one protagonist but disperses its focus among the various families and their separate tribulations. By avoiding the usual expectations of classic narrative, which emphasizes the heroic and exceptional individual, the film through its style makes an oblique comment on conventional political cinema, where the emphasis is on the radical imperative of struggle, resistance, and revolution.

The films of the brothers Paolo and Vittorio Taviani dramatize many of these concerns from the vantage points of historical and contemporary perspectives. Whether directly influenced by Gramsci or not, their films, along with those of Pasolini, are germane to issues raised by Gramsci in relation to national history and culture. Through the medium of the feature film, the Tavianis' texts address the nature of "organic" versus traditional intellectuals, especially the roles they play in political struggle. The Tavianis' exploration of subalternity touches on familiar conflicts in Italian society, centering particularly on questions of regionalism and the problematic history of North–South divisions. With respect to their films' reenactments of the past, the Tavianis' work can be said to explore, not monumentalize, historic images and issues relating to contested positions over popular memory.

Whether selecting the recent past and the political struggles during the 1960s for representation, as in *I sovversivi* (The Subversives, 1967), the more remote internecine conflicts during World War II in *La notte di San Lorenzo* (*The Night of the Shooting Stars,* 1982), or the nineteenth-century struggles for unification as in *Allonsanfán* (1974), the Tavianis' treatment of history is predominantly interrogative, analytical, and ironic, not melodramatic and nostalgic. In the process, in all of their films, and in their own roles as film-makers, the Tavianis explore the role of film along with other forms of cultural expression. They are consistent in portraying the struggle for cultural self-expression and engagement on the part of both their upper-class and peasant protagonists in ways that reveal an indebtedness to Gramscian conceptions of common sense.

The Tavianis' concern with language in the Gramscian sense is not confined to linguistic structural questions but entails an engagement with questions of national identity, regionalism, familialism, emigration and diaspora, social class, and sexuality. In short, language represents for them, as for Gramsci, a confrontation with fundamental and critical aspects of cultural representation, an issue that has been important to many Italian filmmakers since World War II.[29] Their films are political in terms of Gramsci's sense of cultural politics, where emphasis on social and political change involves a rethinking of the composition, history, and discourses of (and about) subaltern groups. The Tavianis seek to awaken the spectator to the imperatives for change, but they are not polemicists; they have no program. Rather, they use their cinema to experiment, to raise questions about Italian history, about the role of intellectuals, the workings of common sense, and about film culture itself – especially by exploring the politics of film, and, more specifically, the form of filmmaking designated as "neorealist."

The uses and abuses of history are central to the Tavianis' films, and bear a close relation to a Gramscian concern with historical analysis. In his discussion of "historico-political analysis," Gramsci found that

> a common error consists . . . in an inability to find the correct relation between what is organic and what is conjunctural. This leads to presenting causes as immediately operative which in fact operate only indirectly, or to asserting that the immediate causes are the only effective ones. In the first case there is an excess of "economism," or doctrinaire pedantry; in the second, an excess of "ideologism." In the first case there is an overestimation of mechanical causes, in the second an exaggeration of the voluntarist and individual element.[30]

In the spirit of the Gramsci quotation, the Tavianis, in developing their film language, are looking to avoid the extremes of "economism," of reducing characters and events to "mechanical causes," and of determinism; at the same time, they seek to avoid reductive "ideologism," which would emphasize individual volition, uniqueness, and freedom from cultural restraints.

Though the Tavianis' films are recognizable in an international idiom, they can best be understood within the context of Italian cinema, from the post–World War II era to the present. Italian films of this epoch have addressed political issues, perhaps in more sustained, direct, and intense fashion than in other European cinemas. However, as the Tavianis are aware, the audiences for their films today are different from earlier audiences, especially those of the immediate postwar era. They find that

> there's a certain amount of cynicism setting in among the Italian populace. It's a great crisis, one involving the questioning of values, many hopes that were never realized, myths that have fallen forever, a very difficult economic situation, a time of flux.[31]

Recognizing the need to address this new audience, the Tavianis made their films an arena of research for social transformation, especially at a time when commitment to political alternatives was waning. Their explorations have a precedent in the history of contemporary European cinema. Many of the French New Wave filmmakers turned to the auteurist aspects of Hollywood, singling out such filmmakers as Alfred Hitchcock, Sam Fuller, and Nicholas Ray to establish the possibility of creating a personal style in the midst of the "studio system." In particular, being critics too, they explored ways of deconstructing classic narrative, and the spectator's role within that system, in an attempt to call attention to the cinema and to the ideological nature of cinematic expression. Their work in documentary films, as well as the impact of neorealism, allowed them to work eclectically and self-consciously with narrative, gestural language, imagery, and sound.

In the films of the Tavianis, a recognition of the relationship to neorealism is indispensable for understanding the forms of Italian political cinema. Of their relationship to that film movement, they had this to say:

> When we started our first film we realized that neorealism was degenerating. It had become an expression of petit-bourgeois, heavily naturalistic stories. So, when we embarked on our career in the cinema, we wanted to depart from neorealism, to make it react to something new and something old. . . . In this sense, we felt that we were burying a beloved father. Although this "father" is dead and buried, he remains a strong influence in our memory.[32]

This "strong influence" can be seen in the Tavianis' choice of subjects for their films: Italian history (especially the history of Fascism), peasant life, regionalism, continuing conflicts between urban and rural existence, generational and family conflicts. The Tavianis were also aware of the pitfalls of a neorealist aesthetic as articulated by its practitioners and critics, especially Cesare Zavattini and André Bazin. The ideology of neorealism – its common-sense orientation (in Gramscian language), if not consistent with its emphasis on the dispossessed; its special pleading on behalf of materialism (albeit not Marxist, for the most part) and of humanism – posed problems as the Tavianis explored possibilities for a political cinema.

Increasingly, the Taviani brothers experimented with style by veering more toward examinations of the bourgeoisie and away from the strictures of documentary forms of filmmaking and from the unexamined adherence to melodrama and sentiment. However, the Tavianis' departure from neorealism was, like that of Jean-Luc Godard, more of an adjustment than a rupture. While maintaining the neorealist sense of context and the importance of location shooting, the Tavianis most diverge from the neorealists in their treatment of narrative and in their film language, which is closely tied to modernist practices. Their preoccupation with language as both an instrument of oppression and a potential vehicle of change is their particular means for providing an implicit critique of neorealism and for addressing issues that are endemic to Italian culture and society. The Tavianis have acknowledged the importance of Roberto Rossellini's *Paisà* in shaping their sense of World War II. Rossellini's film and other neorealist films, as Millicent Marcus suggests, provided "a way of rethinking the entire event and of beginning to give it meaning for the future."[33]

In the 1960s, filmmakers sought a cinematic language that was critical of social institutions – and of cinema itself as an institution – as instruments of conformity. In that exploration, neorealism was acknowledged as a problematic precursor. The modernist political cinema, which evolved and was exemplified in the work of such filmmakers as Antonioni and Godard, placed greater emphasis on the spectator and on strategies for making the spectator aware of the cinematic experience. Distanciation, self-reflexivity, and montage ruptures between image and sound were strategies adopted to call attention to cinematic language as constructed rather than given.

Concerning the limitations of neorealism as an effective medium for communicating with contemporary audiences, the Tavianis have said:

> In postwar Italy, during the neorealist period, the feeling was that good and evil were very distinct things which could clearly be distinguished from each other. As the years passed, good and evil became more difficult to distinguish from one another; they seemed to blend. . . . Those who came out of the neorealist movement found themselves constrained to find new instruments, new tools to express themselves. And that's how the cinema of the Sixties came about.[34]

Unwilling to abandon the social concerns of neorealism, but equally unwilling to perpetuate the notion of access to a seemingly unmediated reality, the Tavianis have continued to experiment with various modernist techniques in order to disrupt what they interpret as the spectator's easy assimilation of the filmic events in classic cinema.

The presence of melodrama in neorealist representation has not been given the attention it deserves. The challenge to neorealism derives from the same critical impetus that led the neorealists to challenge the cinema of genres with its commonsense and folkloric dimensions. When the Tavianis refer to the clear-cut division between good and evil that seems so often to characterize many neorealist films, they are referring to the issue of melodrama's affective excessiveness, its clearly drawn demarcation between victim and oppressor, its fixed conceptions of subaltern identities, and its tendencies to totalize questions of social justice. As recent research has made clear, melodrama is not just another genre or a film style; it is a worldview and an integral dimension of many representations of history.[35] By narrating the trials and tribulations of its protagonists, melodrama seeks to account for human misery in ethical terms and, based as it is on humanist assumptions of the individual over the collectivity, melodrama produces a history of oppression from which the victim must either be saved or to which he or she succumbs. In the Tavianis' work, melodrama is tempered and complicated as the films come to develop Gramscian strategies for identifying how common sense, not individual idiosyncrasies, reproduces a familiar image of social relations. For them, culture must be examined not in terms of individual effort but in relation to the structures and strictures that individual groups inherit, inhabit, and either legitimate or seek to resist.

Padre padrone (*Father Master*) orchestrates Gramscian concerns, especially the question of language as intimately and specifically tied to cultural and political differences relating to the long-standing North–South issue. The film explores commonsense strategies of survival through the legitimation of, as well as resistance to, regionalism and familialism. Made for television, the film appeared in 1977 and received international attention and acclaim. Among the Tavianis' productions, it is exemplary for the ways in which it adopts a neorealist style yet at the same time radically and ironically modifies it through such strategies as the flashback, voice-over commentary, dream sequences, and sound–image montage. The film interweaves fact and fiction in its incorporation of the actual, adult Gavino Ledda (by then a professor of linguistics and author of the book *Padre padrone*) with the fictional one: Ledda's presence at the outset of the film not only complicates the relationship between fact and fiction but also raises issues of education, modernization, and the role of organic intellectuals (including the "authors" of the film) as necessary but contradictory elements in the transformation of peasant life.

Padre padrone is set in Gramsci's Sardinia, one of Italy's poorest regions, and the Sardinian landscape is integrally identified with the struggles of the peasants to survive. Like the Gavino of the film, Gramsci grew up in this environment and was later to use his own knowledge of the Mezzogiorno in analyzing transformations in Italian culture and society. The experiences narrated by Gavino Ledda in his book and re-created on film reveal a similar fascination with the Sardinian world and the ways in which it represents an important aspect of Italian political and cultural life. In unsentimental fashion, the film examines obstacles to and possibilities for change in this rural part of Italy. By situating the perspective on events in the eyes and ears of the young Gavino and of the film's narrator, the grown and educated Gavino, *Padre padrone* undermines an omniscient narration. By intermingling the fictional character and the actual individual to complicate perspective, the film works to defamiliarize traditional associations with peasant life – a technique that makes it possible to experience the narrative in less clichéd and melodramatic terms. The peasants are portrayed as intelligent, struggling human beings confronting their harsh environment with a knowledge of their world necessary for physical survival. This is not to say that they have a critical awareness of the terms of the potential for change, but that common sense – the complex mélange of information based on knowledge they have acquired about their environment, respect and fear of the past, adherence to traditional practices, superstitions, and family loyalties – is mobilized as a mode of protection. According to Robert Kolker, in *Padre padrone,*

> No one mood is permitted to wear itself out, and no one opportunity is missed to manipulate the viewer's perspective and the tone of particular events, and to comment upon them in the imagery or on the sound track in a manner that is not quite psychological, sociological, or directly political, yet manages to combine these three modes of inquiry. . . . We are engaged and yet asked to keep our distance, and we learn with some force of an exotic and appalling way of life through a film that is somewhat exotic in mixture of styles and levels of discourse.[36]

Kolker's reference to exoticism is crucial in relation to the Tavianis' representation of peasant life. Conventional treatments of peasants are usually characterized by voyeurism: The spectator is invited to gaze at an unfamiliar and exotic world that remains alien and fascinating in its remoteness. The style of the Tavianis' film, specifically the variation of perspectives, makes the spectator aware of differences between conventional treatments of peasant life – ethnographic and commercial melodramatic narratives – and the portraits these filmmakers present. *Padre padrone* unsettles a fixed and unified interpretation of the characters and events by pitting the point of view of the child against that of the adult, by the uses of montage that create a tension between image and sound, and by the self-conscious focus on different forms of language (verbal, visual, and gestural), none of which assumes an easy access to the characters and their context. However, the most striking way in which *Padre padrone* affords a different portrait of peasant life is through its concern with education, an issue that is central to Gramsci's focus on the nature of the subaltern and the problematic of social change.

The Tavianis have said that Gavino's father and the hills of Sardinia "represent a brutally paternalistic conditioning process in Gavino's school of hard knocks."[37] The key terms in their statement are "conditioning" and "school of hard knocks." In this film, peasant life is seen as a form of education, far different from city life and from traditional notions of schooling: In the scenes with his father, the boy is taught, harshly, what he needs to know to survive and be productive in this environment. This perspective further breaks down the alienating aspects of rural existence. Peasant life is not mindless but represents a traditional form of learning that must be challenged in order for change to take place. In this respect, the film does not idealize nature and agrarian life; rather, it contrasts them with urban life and notes the exigencies of modernity from which even remote areas like this cannot escape. The knowledge of the subaltern that served well for survival in one context is now, through the portrait of Gavino and his conflict with his father, subject to interrogation.

Applicable to the ways the film treats knowledge is Gramsci's assertion that "all men are intellectuals . . . but not all men have in society the function of intellectuals. There is no human activity from which every form of intellectual participation can be excluded."[38] In the film, when Gavino is wrenched out of the classroom by his father, a contrast is made between the kind of knowledge represented by his father and that of the school. This sets up a contrast, sustained throughout the film, between the father's obsessive commitment to the position of a pastoral *padrone* and Gavino's increasing consciousness of the modern world. However, the father's behavior is not arbitrary: In terms of common sense, his actions are based on his traditional belief that formal education is not necessary and might perhaps even be detrimental to the life of the shepherd. The boy, removed from verbal language and books, is transported to a world of sounds in nature [Fig. 38].

The father's is a traditional world in which survival depends on generational continuity, submission to paternal dictates, and a mistrust of professional and conventional intellectual pursuits. It is not bereft of worldliness and does not imply that the peasants lack a philosophic sense of the world. Rather the question is posed whether traditional commonsense positions are most conducive to an understanding of psychosocial conditions and thus presumably of alternative forms of behavior and action. Through strict discipline, the father initiates Gavino into the skills necessary for becoming a shepherd.

Figure 38. Gavino Ledda as a youth (Fabrizio Forte) in Sardinia, *Padre padrone* (*Father Master*). (Courtesy New York Museum of Modern Art Stills Archive)

The young child receives his education in isolation from his mother, from other children, and at times even from his father. This separation from human contact makes the boy acutely conscious of the sights and sounds of nature. In relation to his psychic and physical needs, he mitigates his loneliness and is initiated into sex by observing the animals – as well as other young shepherds buggering them. The film also dramatizes his desire for pleasure and knowledge against the constraints of his culture. For example, Gavino is introduced to music through two itinerants who sell him an accordion, which he tries to play and then destroys in frustration when he cannot produce the sounds of music. In these episodes Gavino does not merely submit to his conditions: He becomes aware of the severity of the world that has been imposed on him. Kolker comments on the particularly harsh thrashing that the father gives the boy:

> The camera frames the two in a perfect image of a pietà and the father's singing is joined by other voices on the sound track as the camera drifts away from the two figures to the countryside. The viewer is permitted to experience revulsion at the beating, relief at the father's show of concern.[39]

The act is thus seen not as sadistic but as inherent to this type of existence, in which the father is doomed blindly to repeat his own history. The double vision of the film - apparent in the contrasts between Gavino and his father, music and language, language and silence, as well as isolation and community - is always present and indicative of a conflict over folklore and history, common sense and good sense.

Gavino's rebelliousness is not unique; it is characteristic of the other young men from his part of the country and of the changes affecting Italian rural life and Sardinia in particular [Fig. 39]. The army, where he discovers the power of language, intervenes to alter what might be a repetition of his father's life. The language he acquires is verbal, technological, and artistic. He learns to speak, read, and to construct a radio by following directions. By acquiring a new language and skills, he is forced to come to terms with a number of differences from his past involving social class and regionalism. His decision to go to the university provokes a confrontation with his father in which Gavino is the winner, but the victory is not clear-cut, as in a film that celebrates upward mobility.

Though Gavino has fought against the constraints of this world - such as familialism and the harsh patriarchal society represented by his father - he does not totally sever his ties. His decision to return to Sardinia signifies not only his sense of belonging and commitment to his culture but also his ambivalence about his identity: "In Sardinia, his sense of rootedness serves him as a kind of scourge, by which he can muster a sense of dynamism and mission."[40] Gavino, through his acquisition of education and his (and the film's) emphasis on the importance of language as a means of controlling (not being subordinated to) one's world, becomes representative of what Gramsci termed the "organic intellectual" - a creation of modern rather than traditional societies who occupies an organizational position in relation to his or her class. For Gramsci, the absence of language signifies imprisonment, a form of chaos in which the entire community (but particularly the young) are contained by the triple structures of patriarchy, class, and generation. The attainment of language, on the other hand, enables individuals and groups to make sense of their world and, possibly, to transform it. Gavino, through his experiences of the world beyond his rural environment, including his subsequent education, is not only able to understand and articulate his situation but also is in a position to transform his earlier environment, rather than become a spokesman for the professional class to which he now belongs. Language becomes a means of escape not only for him but for others in his village.

The film closes but does not resolve the conflicts. The now-educated Gavino is both alienated from but still very much a part of this world to which he returns. He dramatizes how the problems of modernity and of economic and social transformation are dynamic and present themselves in new and still

Figure 39. Gavino Ledda as an adult (Saverio Marcone), *Padre padrone* (*Father Master*). (Courtesy New York Museum of Modern Art Stills Archive)

problematic forms. Thus, the film orchestrates unresolved issues involving language, history, the changing and also static dimensions of subaltern life, the importance of intellectuals (both characters and filmmakers) in bringing these conditions to light, and the role of cinema as a means of developing a popular culture critically responsive to the contemporary world.

The cinema of Pier Paolo Pasolini (1922–75) offers a perspective on modernity and capitalism from the vantage point of subaltern groups. Pasolini was challenged by the work of Gramsci but struggling to develop his own conception of cultural politics more suited to changing economic and cultural conditions. In many ways, his literary works, journalism, philosophical writings, and films displayed Gramscian concerns with exploring the cultural and political landscape in an attempt to understand life under the shifting forms of capitalism. His wide-ranging reading included an ongoing preoccupation with the forms of and relations between high and popular culture, including Euripides, Sophocles, Dante, Boccaccio, Chaucer, Bach, Vivaldi, Renaissance painting, the Bible, Hollywood, early Italian cinema, popular music, and street folklore. His complex portrait of the world in his writing and films entailed mixing styles, disrupting expectations, challenging clichés, and offending audiences – Catholic, Marxist, middle-class, and gendered. Though his predominant focus was on Italian culture and politics, he became increasingly sensitive to the ways the Italian situation was not unique but part of a larger pattern of global economics – a political and hence cultural transformation in the latter part of the twentieth century of a world "wiped out by global capitalism."[41]

Whereas his early films, *Accattone, Mamma Roma,* and *Il Vangelo secondo Matteo,* focus largely on the subproletariat, his later films are intricate dissections of the increased bourgeoisification of marginalized groups, leading him afield to such countries as Africa, the Middle East, and Asia to locate the character of preindustrial forms of life that were rapidly disappearing under the impact of late capitalism. Accused of being naïve in his elevation of the sexuality of subaltern groups, of colonizing "the disenfranchised Other to fulfill his own dreams,"[42] Pasolini is difficult to situate in terms of conventional film and politics. In a Gramscian vein, he began by exploring the world of the subproletariat in his quest to find a language to address, albeit ambivalently or rather ironically, those aspects of subaltern life that stand in contrast to conventional notions of family, masculinity, identity, and sexuality. His portraits are not idealizations: The characters are thieves, pimps, prostitutes – disingenuous, cynical about authority, verbally and physically brutal, very much in the vein of neorealism – but, as Viano writes,

> neorealism relied on the plenitude of the represented image, that is, on its hoped-for mono-semic status. Inevitably, the audience was thought of as unified, as an undifferentiated mass bound to experience a common (because natural) reaction in the face of a universal signifier.[43]

Pasolini "drives the wedge of difference into neorealist plenitude. *Accattone* makes the image the site of an ambivalent decoding."[44]

The key words are "difference" and "ambivalent," and they can be linked to Pasolini's Gramscian perspective. The world as portrayed in classical cinema is a closed one in which assumptions about the nature of reality, and about the consonance between signification and truth or falsity, are rampant. In Gramsci's thinking, it is precisely the given nature of common sense and of its folklore that is in need of critical elaboration. Similarly, in Pasolini, one must find the difference in the usual assumptions of commonality and sameness. More cogently, one cannot assume that "seeing is believing." To the contrary, language (verbal and visual) is ambivalent, protean, and polysemic, and the guiding principle of Pasolini's filmic vision is to enhance the sense of this ambivalence for demystifying common sense in the interests of new perspectives – not absolute truths, but a way of thinking differently.

There are no unified narratives in his films, just different histories, affects, beliefs, and actions – fragments of a world torn from familiar contexts. There is a lack of motivation on the part of the characters, a blurring of the lines between the fiction and the "real," a preoccupation with theatricality, even camp, through the allusions to other works of art and the antinaturalistic acting and uses of mise-en-scène, thus highlighting the constructed, not essential and absolute, nature of the image and its referent. In this fashion, the focus shifts from the meaning of images to how they are deployed in the interests of either conformity and sameness or of thinking and seeing differently. Pasolini's films, from beginning to end, are metacinematic – preoccupied with the role of cinema as an apparatus of thought, of intellection. In this respect, they adhere to the Gramscian notion of the necessity of critical elaboration and particularly the importance of demystifying common sense, cliché, and habituation. In exploring and dramatizing subalternity, they introduce a different sense of subaltern life that is desentimentalized, avoiding either romanticization or demonization.

In Pasolini's *Accattone* (1961), a number of strategies are evident that will remain throughout his later films, though with differing emphases. These include the uses of language that are not mimetic but are designed on a number of levels to convey a sense of affect, of emotive reaction, a link between the human and other animals and of the various senses (synesthesia), as well as the prerational or irrational nature of communication. In short, in the uses of language we have not "a language of cinema but a language *for* it."[45] Equally important is the emphasis on a journey and on movement: In each of the films (perhaps derived from Pasolini's Dantesque inheritance), the characters are seen on the road, moving constantly from one place to another, precluding the conventional sense of locating the character within a familiar milieu. The landscape is circumscribed to the world of the *borgata,* or hamlet; and though later films expand the geography, opening up new mythic and psychic vistas, even in *Accattone* one is made aware of the mythic dimensions of the landscape and hence of the characters. For example, from the outset Accattone's jump into the Tiber as a consequence of a dare evokes already the Dantean *Purgatorio* (alluded to in the intertitle at the beginning of the film), the jump being more than a literal event, signifying his (and the audience's) immersion into another dimension of reality, one that relies on Christian symbolism, iconography, music, and hermeneutics.

The early shots of *Accattone* are pictorial, stressing art and artifice. Accattone is portrayed in the same frame as a statue of an angel, and his posture is similarly statuesque; the other young men too are presented in various poses. Throughout the film, the text will slide from a seeming naturalism of the milieu to other strata of perception, involving the mythic landscape identified with Dante and with another strata of time identified with these lumpen-proletarians [Fig. 40].

The narration involves a young man, Vittorio, "Accattone," who derives his livelihood by pimping, primarily for Maddalena. She has been responsible for betraying her former pimp and having him sent to jail, but he gains revenge on her and has her brutally beaten. Bereft of funds and seeking new forms of support, Accattone befriends a young woman, Stella, trying at first to introduce her to a life of prostitution. In the face of her willingness to sacrifice herself for him, however, he relents and finds work loading scrap iron. Later, rejecting that kind of life, he turns to theft. Chased by the police, he dies violently when his motorcycle crashes into a truck.

As can be seen, the narrative is quite straightforward; what is not are the ways in which the text plays with the mythic dimensions of the events portrayed. By linking Accattone with the figure of Christ, the text complicates the audience's perspective on the nature of the characters, tying their fate to the world of dream, hallucination, and tragedy (not sociology). In Naomi Greene's terms, Pasolini's film "denounced social misery and yet somehow ennobled it."[46] The references to religion, especially in the names of the women – Maddalena and Stella – deindividualize the characters, much as the protagonist's name is transformed from Vittorio to the generic Accattone (literally, "beggar"). Similarly, the landscape ironically fuses with Dante's archetypal journey toward redemption, deindividualizing place. However, the film is not a moral parable involving the conversion of a character from a life of decadence to a life of spirituality. It is rather part of a quest to find a language that can challenge reigning morality, even that of the Left, raising but not answering questions concerning a social group that is conventionally reductively dismissed, treated sentimentally, and judged. Through the parallels with the story of Christ (which will also find their way into *Mamma Roma* and *Il Vangelo*), Pasolini will ennoble (but not heroize) his lower-class figures. He can show them in their contradictoriness, as victims of a social order but not passive and, above all, not deprived of dignity and complexity.

The main focus in this film is not on the narrative but on the pedagogical (and poetic) possibilities of cinema. Vision is stressed in a number of ways. For example, as in the opening scene when Accattone plunges into the Tiber, the spectator is offered images of his body cross-cut with that of the sculpture of an angel on the bridge. The parallels between the figures in the film and the paintings of Masaccio and of other fifteenth-century artworks are not mere decoration; they too are part of the Pasolinian pedagogy, which juxtaposes past and present. Moreover, the repeated close-ups of him and of his friends and shots of their bodies in motion or in stasis invite questions about their identity for which the film resists any simplistic answers. The repeated emphasis on vision serves both to undermine the conventional invisibility of

Figure 40. Pasolini (in glasses) on the set of *Accattone*. (Courtesy New York Museum of Modern Art Stills Archive)

these figures within mainstream cinema, and, more important, to offer a different vision of the world. The characters are not merely to be gazed at by the spectator, however: They are engaged in a surveillance of one another. Accatone spies on Ascenza, his ex-wife, and on his small son, on a mission to get money. Stella, newly initiated into prostitution, observes the prostitutes on the road. The most striking allusions to vision involve the policeman's eyes in extreme close-up as he surveys this criminal world.

This emphasis on vision as polyvalent marks the character of subproletarian life as one of constant surveillance. Even more in relation to the meta-cinematic dimensions of the text, the connections among theft, visualization, and cinema serve to focus attention on the ways that the film itself is a thief, stealing images from other arenas and appropriating them "to another regime of signification."[47] In connection with both visualization and its relation to intellectual perspective, the film remains within the Gramscian orbit. Naomi Greene reminds us that Pasolini is not a judge or a moralist ("the moralism that Pasolini deemed 'horrendous'"), and neither was Gramsci: "for Gramsci, the critic's task is not to judge a work of art but to explore its 'hidden ideologies' – to see what political and historical tendencies they call into question on the part of writer and audience."[48] Questions of form, style, and language are neither ends in themselves, a form of aestheticism, nor political platforms. Rather, they are a resource for deciphering representation and its ties to the existing hegemony.

Similarly in *Il Vangelo secondo Matteo* (*The Gospel According to St. Matthew,* 1964), Pasolini once again draws on the figure of Christ but directly [Fig. 41]. Using the words of the Gospel, the film again creates a portrait that conforms to Gramsci's emphasis on questions of leadership and the role of intellectuals; above all, it explores a pedagogy of culture through the cinema. Utilizing episodes from the birth, preaching, trial, and crucifixion of Christ, and tying them to images of Renaissance painting (as in *Accattone*), earlier cinematic versions of the life of Christ, and the Sicilian landscape [Fig. 42], the film aims to link the past to contemporary history and emphasize cinematic narration. The critical and political role of religion as the common sense of subaltern groups is central. (African-American spirituals mingle with baroque music on

Figure 41. Otello Sestili as Judas and Enrique Irozoqui as Jesus in *Il Vangelo secondo Matteo* (*The Gospel According to St. Matthew*). (Courtesy New York Museum of Modern Art Stills Archive)

Figure 42. Panorama, *Il Vangelo secondo Matteo* (*The Gospel According to St. Matthew*). (Courtesy New York Museum of Modern Art Stills Archive)

the sound track.) In particular, by situating the film in underdeveloped areas in Sicily rather than filming it in Palestine, Pasolini was able to "find parallels and analogues in the present."[49] *Il Vangelo* seems to offer a last gasp in his films of the Gramscian emphasis on the need to create a "national-popular culture" based on "the conception of the nation-state as a site of a potential hegemony of intellectuals connected to the working class."[50] In its focus on the relation between Christ and the Sicilian peasantry, the film also reveals problems associated with the presentation of the people as "meek and passive followers."

This view of the peasantry seems to bespeak a portrait of an "intellectual who, despite an intense desire to be 'organically' linked to the people, cannot breach the immeasurable gap between them." In fact, Pasolini's films were in the late 1960s and 1970s to express an increasing discomfort with Gramscian conceptions of cultural politics. He told Oswald Stack, "the idea of Unity taking place through an integration of the popular language is an illusory one."[51] He, like many other intellectuals, confronted the progressive development of new forms of cultural expression that were tied to increased monopolization, the now-global character of capitalism, the failure of the counter-cultures of the 1960s, and the commodification of all forms of social life, especially of sexuality, which he tied to new forms of fascism. Gramsci's legacy has had to meet new and disturbing economic, political, and cultural exigencies in contemporary Italy.

CHAPTER SEVEN

History, Genre, and the Italian Western

F rom biblical epics, costume dramas, Roman spectacles and biopics to the numerous films that have sought to unravel the nature and effects of the Fascist era and of World War II, historical concerns have animated Italian film forms and various historical genres and constituted a staple of the national cinema despite stylistic and political differences. The appearance of the Italian western in the 1960s on the heels of the resurgence of Roman and biblical spectacles is another manifestation of a return to past history and of the prevalence of genre production in the Italian cinema, despite brief attempts to move in a realist direction. The so-called spaghetti western shares some concerns with the "art cinema" identified with Fellini, Rossellini, Antonioni, Visconti, Pasolini, and Wertmüller.

In part, due to the cold war and the economic and political intervention of the United States, Europe was transformed from a devastated wartime country to what has been dubbed an "economic miracle." In commenting on this time, Pierre Sorlin writes that filmmakers found "no necessity . . . to bring in social issues since neorealism had already introduced them to the cinema."[1] Nonetheless, the thematics addressed in films of the 1950s and 1960s, whether comic, melodramatic, or working in countercultural directions, do involve "social issues," such as urban anomie, industrial (*not* wartime) blight, familial disintegration, divorce, marriage, and new sexual mores. This period was rich in films with historical settings drawing on such diverse contexts as ancient Rome, the Middle Ages, and the eighteenth and nineteenth centuries. Italian modernist filmmakers, such as Fellini in *Fellini Satyricon* (1969), offered their versions of history in film. Although Italian national cinema has always been tied to international production and dependent on international modes of dissemination, the 1960s can be characterized as a moment when cinema broke loose of its national moorings, financially and culturally, participating in what is now described as globalization.

The emergence of the spaghetti western belongs to this moment. It began slowly and crested in the late 1960s and early 1970s. Before Sergio Leone's *Per un pugno di dollari* (*A Fistful of Dollars*, 1964) "some 25 westerns had been produced at Cinecittà."[2] Though internationally associated with Leone,

Italian westerns were also made by Sergio Corbucci (a.k.a. Stanley Corbett, known for such films as *Django* [1966] and *Il mercenario* [*The Mercenary,* 1969]), Enzo Barboni (a.k.a. E. B. Clucher, director of such popular films as *Lo chiamavano Trinità* [*They Call Me Trinity,* 1970]), and Tonino Valerii (*Il mio nome è nessuno,* a work discussed later in this chapter). An extensive discussion and analysis of the individuals involved and of the films, their modes of production, themes, style, and politics, can be found in Christopher Frayling's *Spaghetti Westerns.*[3] The Italian western can be characterized by its eclecticism, drawing on different genres, national film traditions, international casts, a combination of comedy and melodrama, and an innovative approach to the cinematic medium. According to Frayling, who acknowledges and attempts to account for this eclecticism, an understanding of international as well as national film culture is essential for an understanding of the films. Leone has cited the importance to his work of such films as *Yojimbo* (1961), *Sanjuro* (1962), *Shane* (1953), and *Vera Cruz* (1954).[4] This citation is important to underscore the international character of the genre and to confound the notion that the Italian western was a mere appendage of Hollywood.

One layer of history subtending the Italian western involves the concept of "western-ness": what the designation "the West" signifies, how this signification circulates throughout European and Asian culture, and how it inflects and is inflected by other indigenous forms. From their earliest manifestation in the silent era, the historical film in general and the western in particular have been closely linked to nation formation, and this link persists even when the uses of history are aimed at undermining discourses of nation. In the analysis of the impact of Americanism on European culture today, there are two major contending positions that can account for this phenomenon. In one view, the weighty presence of U.S. films and television can be taken as prime evidence for the ubiquitous and devastating nature of North American economic cultural imperialism. Alternatively, Americanism can be interpreted as selective appropriation of the host culture on the part of the foreign culture for its own uses. It can signify, for better or worse, a greater global interdependency, which reveals a historical, hence changing, relation to the circulation of capital. One of the major contributions of Frayling's study is the way it suggests how global interdependency is inscribed in the Italian western.

In examining the culture of Americanism, it is necessary to understand its "third meaning," not as signifying either the geographical United States or Europe, but as a trope for a phenomenon that has existed since the turn of the century and undergone various permutations. In the 1880s Nietzsche wrote:

> There is something of the American Indians, something of the ferocity peculiar to the Indian blood, in the American lust for gold, and

the breathless haste with which they work – the distinctive vice of the new world – [which] is beginning to infect old Europe with its ferocity and is spreading a lack of spirituality like a blanket.[5]

Nietzsche's comments reveal, as Gramsci's do later (if in a different vein), that Americanism was a force to be reckoned with in accounting for transformations in European culture. It is significant too that Nietzsche cites the lust for gold (presumably referring to the gold rush of 1849) as an important factor in Americanism. His comments, in conjunction with Frayling's discussion of the importance of the influential writings of Karl May (1842–1912), foreground two thematics that are part of the European construction of North America: the "noble savage" and gold.[6] That these themes persist is evident in the German westerns of the late 1950s and 1960s, starring such international actors as Stewart Granger along with German casts.

Italy's ties to America are bound to the effects of waves of Italian emigration to the United States and Latin America in the late nineteenth century. This was intimately linked to economic and political problems in Italy exacerbated by the Risorgimento, relating especially to stark inequities between northern and southern Italy.[7] In general, regional antagonisms have played an ongoing role in the cultural and political life of Italy. Antagonisms, not always overt, have been manifest in relation to the distribution of economic and political power, the hierarchialization of regional characteristics, linguistic differences, condescending attitudes on the part of northern intellectuals toward southern culture, and especially the association of the South with primitivism, brutality, and brigandage. The differences revealed that Italian unification was less a revolution, despite the heroization of Garibaldi, than a political containment of the Italian South by the North.

The move westward by many Italians beginning in the nineteenth century – first from Abruzzi and Calabria, later from Sicily – carried with it profound changes for those regions as well as for the families that it often parted (but who might be privy to news from across the ocean). America figures prominently in the Italian cinema; conversely, Italy has also figured prominently in Hollywood. The drama of emigration appears in such films as Brignone's *Passaporto rosso* (1935), which bears resemblance to the western genre. The 1930s comedies of Mario Camerini contain American themes and characters. Postwar dramatizations of Americans in Europe are prominent in films by Rossellini, De Sica, and Giuseppe De Santis. More recently, the Tavianis' *Kaos* and *Buon giorno, Babilonia!* (*Good Morning, Babylon!*, 1987) address the effects of emigration. Therefore, it is not at all unusual or surprising that the Italian westerns have assimilated and appropriated Americanism to their own ends. In the Italian films, there is a congenial union between the themes and styles attributed to the North American western, involving the American continent, both north and south of the border, and portrayals of Italian life – in representations of the Mezzogiorno in particular.

The emphasis on landscape, on demographic mobility (westward); the focus on brutality, brigandage, revenge, and criminality; the decomposition of villages, the ambiguous role of the Catholic Church, and the stark competition for economic power – all are conditions that inhere in Italian folklore but can be grafted to prevailing representations of Americanism. (This grafting is not restricted to the western genre but is also evident in that of the crime film.) However, the Italian westerns are not polemic or doctrinaire; rather, they are interrogative about political issues involving notions of power, economics, nation, and cultural identity. On questions of politics and representation, Leone has said:

> We have no right to prick the political conscience of our contemporaries. We are not *magisters.* The films we made ought to make people think. We are professional "exciters." But we are not directors of conscience. The audience should be allowed to draw their own conclusions.[8]

Leone's words recall a similar comment by the German filmmaker Rainer Werner Fassbinder: "I like to make my audiences think and feel." Independent of authorial intentionality, the "audience" is not monolithic, and it will draw what it can or what it desires from the text. Leone's comments acknowledge his recognition that audiences cannot be coerced into responding "properly," but the reaction against tendentiousness need not be construed as being against politics or history – just against the imposition of forms of historicism and forms of politics. Hence, there seems to be – again referring to Gramsci – a different notion of pedagogy at work in Leone's films as social text. His film *Giù la testa* (*Duck, You Sucker;* or, *A Fistful of Dynamite,* 1971) reveals an engagement with Gramscian issues in ways similar to the films discussed in Chapter 6. Whether intentional or not, this genre film can be seen as sharing thematic concerns with the "art cinema."

Born in Naples in 1929, Leone came to filmmaking by way of a family that was professionally involved in the cinema. His mother was a film actress; his father, Vincenzo Leone, was a director remembered mostly for his silent films under the name of Roberto Roberti, though he did direct a handful of sound films. The actress Carla del Poggio recalls seeing the young Sergio Leone following his father around on the set of *La bocca sulla strada* (The Man on the Street, 1941), which also starred the popular star Armando Falconi.[9] In the silent era, Leone's father had worked on several films with the diva Francesca Bertini. The elder Leone later ran afoul of the Fascist bureaucracy, forcing him and his family into rustication. The memory of Fascism was to resurface in the films of his son Sergio, and in those of Sergio's contemporaries. Aside from visits to the set with his father, Leone's first work in cinema in the 1940s was, according to the actor Aldo Fabrizi, as assistant to well-known directors such as Mario Camerini, Carmine Gallone, and Mario Bonnard.[10] In the post–World War II era, when neorealism was in full sway, Leone worked as an actor in a bit part in *Ladri di biciclette* (1948). However, his career was not to be in acting but directing. After apprenticing himself to various Italian directors in the 1950s and working in various capacities as an assistant to Hollywood directors, Leone turned to directing his own films.

Leone worked on about fifty films in a supportive capacity until 1959–61, when he directed or codirected such historical spectacles as *Gli ultimi giorni di Pompei* (*The Last Days of Pompeii*), *Il colosso di Rodi* (*The Colossus of Rhodes*), and *Sodoma e Gommorra* (*Sodom and Gomorrah*), all costume films, made inexpensively, featuring international casts and abundant physical action. Films such as these (Leone was not the only practitioner) seemed a throwback to earlier Italian silent film spectacles (e.g., *Cabiria*, various incarnations of *The Last Days of Pompeii*) with heroes like Ursus and Maciste, thus forging a link with the popular cinema of the past as well as with Hollywood epics such as *Ben-Hur* (1959) and *Spartacus* (1960),

In this much-neglected genre,[11] the focus on power, masculinity, and materialism is variously related to the thematics of many other Italian and European melodramatic and comic films of the era. Emphasizing conflicts between "insiders" (representing institutionalized authority) and "outsiders" (representing the struggle for freedom and recognition), the films are intertextual, drawing on either biblical or ancient Greco-Roman times for their dramatizations of power conflicts between tyrannical figures and oppressed groups. The protagonist as outsider – as Jew, as slave, or as both – works to solidify the embattled community in its fight against hostile forces. The genre subtends the Italian western, sharing a preoccupation with history, adventure, and masculine derring-do. They are also similar in their use of international stars (especially lesser-known Hollywood actors and stars with declining careers), their inexpensive mode of production, and their overt use of physical movement – crowd scenes, acrobatics, choreography, torture, striking combats, and other violence.

These historical adventure films of the 1960s are also related to the Italian western in another way: In their use of international casts, multilingual personnel, dubbing, and locations set all over the world, the films signaled the increased internationalization of filmmaking – particularly, Americanism as the metaphor for globalization. This globalization went beyond the actual mechanics of assembling the films to concerns shared across national boundaries: the preoccupation with historical representation, the cultural merging of East and West on the level of cinematic forms, a greater recognition of hybridization and of the powerlessness of masses. It is possible to see in those films from before 1968 a commonality of antagonisms toward prevailing power structures, a concern with militarism and its deleterious effects, and a mistrust of the state.

Rather than being clones of Hollywood films, the Italian westerns represent a crisis of cultural representation that was taking place worldwide. During the postwar era, the Japanese made inroads into the West with the films of Akira Kurosawa. The genre system associated with so many popular national cinemas, from Hollywood and Britain to Japan and India, was undergoing a transformation due to economic, cultural, and political factors. Older genre forms were being injected with more social, even critical though not necessarily revolutionary, content. "Art" forms were competing with popular ones, and a new hybrid form was emerging that drew on both art and mass production. Not only did genre boundaries become blurred, but the images of old established stars gave way to new and different national and international icons (as we shall see regarding the stars who emerged from the Italian westerns). Thus, the filmmaking of this era reveals that "Americanism" is a phenomenon larger than the geographical and cultural boundaries of the United States and its cold-war domination, coming to represent worldwide transformations and conflicts. The uses of history in this era – whether of feudal Japan, the India of the zamindars, ancient Rome, or the American West – signal this contest over power.

When Sergio Leone and his team of actors, musicians, camera operators, and technicians undertook the series of Italian westerns that were to make such an impact on popular filmmaking, they were not without precedent. They were operating within a cultural climate congenial to the themes and styles of their work.

The western is a literary and cinematic form that has received a surplus of commentary in American studies and, more recently, in film studies. In the influential studies of the film western – Jim Kitses's *Horizons West* and Will Wright's *Six Guns and Society* – mythology has been subjected to the rigors of structuralist analysis, which schematizes and codifies the elements of the narrative according to the variant expressions of myth and of genre.[12] Still, the status of the discourse of history haunts discussions of the western, revealing, as with other forms of cinematic representation, an increasing attention to forms of historicizing, in fact, a preoccupation with reinterpreting the past and, in particular, a focus on threats to the masculine persona and body.

In Fenin and Everson's study *The Western,* there is a bifurcation between the history of the settlement of the American frontier and the mythology to which it gave rise. Fenin and Everson complain that "reconstruction of historical events was and still is changed to suit the script," and they refer to the lack of "realistic pictures" and "authentic traditions."[13] On the other hand, Kitses argues that westward expansionism is inscribed in the larger ideological project of nation formation and that "the western is American history," though the idea of the West is "an ambiguous mercurial concept."[14] In his study of Clint Eastwood, Paul Smith addresses the ways in which the concept of the "real" has now shifted from the earlier binary conflict between two notions of history, one real and the other fantasmatic, to a conception of a "cultural and social imaginary" that subsumes the division between the real and the fictional, allowing for a more flexible and less monolithic conception of genre.[15] While there is little doubt about the variability of the forms adopted by the western (which can allow for Italian, German, Japanese, and Indian production), the notion lingers that these forms are a North American property. Smith's formulation of the notion of a social imaginary comes closer to redressing the complaints about lack of historical accuracy in the popular cinema and the western in particular, opening the way for rethinking notions of myth and ideology that are all-encompassing, abstract, dismissive of counter-memory, and useless for entertaining the historicity and heterogeneity of popular culture.

In discussing the Italian western, it has become customary to draw parallels between that form and the Hollywood western as produced by John Ford in such films as *Stagecoach* (1939), *My Darling Clementine* (1946), and *The Man Who Shot Liberty Valance* (1962). Films such as *Shane* (George Stevens, 1953) and *Vera Cruz* (Robert Aldrich, 1953) are also frequently cited. Discussions of the North American western stress certain abiding elements of structure, theme, and style. One of the most prominent motifs is the foundational narrative, the struggle to create a civilization in the wilderness, as in *Stagecoach.* This foundational narrative entails, along with the drama of forging a community, a struggle between the individual and the collectivity, the motif of "moral regeneration," and the archetypal conflict "between nature and civilization."[16] John Cawelti additionally cites the presence of conflict between European and/or eastern values and the frontier, but the "basic premise of the classic western was a recognition of the inevitable passing of the old order of things, reflected in the myth of the "old West," together with an attempt to affirm that the new society would somehow be based on the older values."[17] According to Cawelti this formula was not suited to the exigencies of the post–World War II world and even less to the "more polarized social and political atmosphere of the 1960s."[18]

Much stress has been laid on the importance of community in the western in relation to a savior figure who, for reasons of altruism, revenge, romance, or profit, becomes embroiled in the society for a period of time, either staying or moving on after his goals are accomplished. The protagonist may enter the community as an agent of transformation but may ultimately choose not to be assimilated into it (as in *My Darling Clementine*). Conversely, the community may indeed assimilate the hero, as in *The Virginian* (1946) or *Stagecoach*. The relationship of the male couple – the protagonist and his sidekick, who work in tandem for or against the community – is also a familiar convention. Earlier forms of the western are imbued with more idealistic notions of nation, which disappear in the postwar era and with the cold war. Genre lines begin to blur, even to the extent of grafting the crime genre and film noir onto the western. Psychosocial treatments become evident: A transformation in the protagonist can be seen particularly through the more sympathetic treatment of the outlaw. In place of the idealistic hero is the professional protagonist doing a job, coincidentally "in the right place at the right time," as exemplified by such films as *The Wild Bunch* and *Butch Cassidy and The Sundance Kid* (both 1969). This "job happens to be fighting whether for the law or against it."[19] Representatives of the law are presented more ambiguously. These transformations during the 1960s and 1970s are indicative of the genre's sensitivity to contemporary conflicts and changing social patterns.

Like these later Hollywood westerns, Leone's films are characteristic of changes in genre production and of political and cultural antagonisms identified with the 1960s and 1970s. They have broadly engaged with the moral concerns in their dramatization of protagonists who struggle to survive in societies hostile to change and to collective practices. The films interrogate masculinity and its discontents, its complicity with violence and power, and they pose, though do not resolve, ethical dilemmas about the forms of power. Their concerns seem similar in many ways to the historical investments of the Tavianis' films – especially *Padre padrone* (1977), which orchestrates problems of language, patriarchy, subalternity, masculinity, the family, social power, and clashes between rural and urban life as well as tradition and modernity.

Central to Leone's films, and those of other directors of the Italian western, is landscape. The films rely on a certain dry and dusty desert landscape that comes to signify "the West" but provides an arena of open space for action. This milieu is less associated with the domestic space – though there is a contrast between open, contested public space and closed domestic space in *Per qualche dollaro in più* (*For a Few Dollars More*, 1965) and *C'era una volta il West* (*Once Upon a Time in the West*, 1968) (a film that particularly capitalizes on this disjunction). The images of towns such as Tucumcari, Agua Caliente, Sweetwater, and even El Paso convey the sense of dirt, grime, and poverty that could apply as easily to the industrially undeveloped terrains of Latin America, Africa, Sicily, or Sardinia as to the North American West. The ubiquitous fly (the most notorious example seen in the opening of *Once Upon a Time in the West*) serves as a synecdoche, a specific marker of the annoyances and discomforts inherent in this life and also of the physicality of the characters.

The attention to the minutiae of this world merges with the most distinctive dimensions of Leone's films: (1) the choreography of movement, (2) the stylized use of faces, and (3) the aversive uses of sound, as in the grating of wheels, the extra-loud noise of oncoming or departing trains, the omnipresent buzz of flies, and sounds of eating, belching, and farting. These sounds merge with the orchestral ones so that it is often difficult to know which is "natural" and which is "manufactured." The music also other identifies the films' hybridity: Chanting, orchestral music, whistling, harmonicas, guitar music, the pipings of a flute or piccolo, and choral and instrumental themes mingle to provide a complex narration that is more than mere support to the narrative or simple atmosphere or filler. The operatic quality of the Italian western not only has its roots in the "horse opera" but is similar in many ways to those films by Visconti and Bertolucci that are profoundly tied to opera.

Critical work on the Italian western has singled out Ennio Morricone's music for analysis (and praise).[20] The scores for Leone's films serve a number of functions – affective commentary on a character's actions or state of mind, mockery, cliché, leitmotif, thematic continuity – and, hence, comments on reiteration, variation, or ironic reversal. The music is a major carrier of the historical excess that creates the sense of openness and heterogeneity of narration. As in opera, there is a union between verbal and gestural language and the music. Where there is dialogue, it is often restricted to one-liners – something Clint Eastwood will employ to advantage in both his western and non-western films (in the infamous "Go ahead, make my day"). There is a sense too that the dialogue, composed as it is of clichés, truisms, proverbs, one-liners, and commonsense wisdom, works with the music and sound to punctuate, mock, comment on, or correct the banality of language. In many instances, the sparsity of dialogue is a sign that this world is one of action and less of verbalization. Leone's films draw especially on traditions from Italian theatrical and film comedy. The importance of farce, slapstick, and satiric allegory are evident in such films as *Once Upon a Time in the West* and *Duck, You Sucker.* Moreover, the residual elements of the *commedia dell'arte* are evident in character typification, the uses of gags, stylized gestures, *lazzi* or physical and verbal tricks, and repartee. Frayling has noted the relations between the Italian art of puppetry and the staging of the action in the Italian western. (Puppetry is not restricted to these films but is spread throughout Italian cinema – in the melodramas and in the *commedia all'italiana.*)

In the musical scores and in the choreography of body movement generally, the films also evoke the characteristics of comic opera and its penchant for oratory and mock solemnity.[21] The fusion of history, melodrama, and comedy and the attention to character, imagery, and music in Leone's films are reminiscent of such films as Visconti's *Il gattopardo,* which are also eclectic. The Leone films validate the connection between folklore, melodrama, and the operatic that is central to popular representations of history. The affective strategies of melodrama and opera are conveyed in the iconography, body movement (especially in the choreography), gesture (from both heroic and comic opera), and in the use of intense close-up. particularly of the face. Bodies in motion are a hallmark of the films. Substituting for the ballets of grand opera are the choreography of the shoot-out, images of men riding through the landscape or of processionals, and scenes of ritual – as when Jill and the other mourners observe the bodies of the dead McBains as in *Once Upon a Time in the West* or in the various rituals of violence interspersed throughout the film. The camera movement – pans, tilts, the use of hand-held equipment – conveys the sense of a world of energy and motion, a world of bodies that collide. The music also serves to render the affective intensity of these physical interactions. The choreography, moreover, calls attention to the body politics of the films – more to the sexuality of the masculine body than to the feminine – since femininity seems confined to the few instances where women are fantasized or dreamed about, or when the homosocial relations suggest traces of tenderness in the brutal and violent environment.

Heterosexual romance is not a central motif of these films, and heterosexual relations are subordinated to the motif of homosocial bonding. The relations between men – Colonel Mortimer and Monco in a *For a Few Dollars More,* Cheyenne and Harmonica in *Once Upon a Time in the West,* Tuco and Blondie in *Il buono, il brutto, il cattivo (The Good, The Bad, and the Ugly,* 1966), and especially Juan and Sean in *Duck, You Sucker* – are central and complex, involving a form of coupling that is ambivalent. Their relations are based on economic competition but also on something else that entails grudging admiration and respect, if not affection and tenderness. Sex between men and women is circumscribed in this environment and when present is likely to be coercive and brutal. When women are present, they are either carriers of economic value as kept women, prostitutes, heirs to property like Jill in *Once Upon a Time in the West,* or figures of nostalgia. Maternal figures are conspicuously placed in the background. Eroticism is conveyed more largely through scenes of eating, sparring, or killing.

The face in close-up, much identified with Italian westerns, contributes in many ways to an understanding of the physical world in the films. The faces serve as a means to interrogation of the subject's character, and the close-ups are not reserved for the protagonists alone but are dispersed, associated with antagonists and silent observers of the action. Frequent and tight close-ups also contribute to the tragicomic nature of the situation, since characters are identified by their unshaven faces: dirt, moles, and, in some cases, spittle that is clearly visible. In the early part of *Duck, You Sucker,* the agonizing close-ups focus on one part of the face, either the leering eyes or the masticating mouths filled with the crushed and oozing food. The alternation between full-body shots and close-ups serves to underscore a conflict between the head and the body, between intelligence and force – a primary tension in Leone's films – and questions about the dominance of one over the other.

The body mechanics are reminiscent of physical movement in Pudovkin and Eisenstein. They also recall the comic choreography of Chaplin – an icon of Americanism for many Europeans. Body movement in the films can be fruitfully identified with the Italian tradition of the *commedia dell'arte.* Discussing the role of the body in the *commedia* in contrast to opera, Angela Dalle Vacche comments that

> the body of the *commedia* seems more in tune with a bustling street life caught unawares, even when performed indoors. The body in the *commedia* also expresses a paradox. While it refers to the slow-moving, deep structures of daily life, it is in constant motion. The body in the *commedia,* with its agility of a dancer and with its careful choreography, nonetheless produces an effect of spontaneity. By virtue of movement, the body in the *commedia* resembles more a living document than a still monument.[22]

These observations can be applied to the ways in which Leone films mix the melodramatic and the comic, the monumental and the everyday. The politics of the body communicates the tell-tale constraints of the effects of producing the conforming body, and does so via an eruption of unruly antagonisms that signify the impossibility of total submission. The physical action in the Leone films, their emphasis on trickery and on violence, recalls the *lazzi* of the *commedia* as the characters engage in a range of physical actions and verbal wit to antagonize and outsmart their opponents.[23] Gordon describes the *lazzi* as referring to "comic routines that were planned or unplanned," and they "allude to any discrete or independent, comic and repeatable activity that guaranteed laughs for its participants."[24] The *lazzi* were associated with "athleticism and clowning, tumbling, stilt walking, diving, and tightrope balancing."[25] For example, the most obvious instance of a *lazzo* is a scene in *The Good, the Bad, and the Ugly:* Clint Eastwood is cleaning his gun as Eli Wallach's hired assassins attempt to sneak up on him; yet with great agility and sang froid he manages to dispatch them all. In the same film, the repeated gag of Tuco and Blondie taking turns at hanging each other and then shooting through the rope, causing the character to fall, recapitulates in humorous fashion the double-crossing tricks that Eastwood and Wallach play with each other. *Once Upon a Time in the West* and *Duck, You Sucker* are filled with repetitive gags and reversals based on fast movement and legerdemain.

A more bizarre episode of this trickery occurs in *A Fistful of Dollars*: The Man with No Name inserts himself between the Rojos and the Baxters, propping up two dead bodies to lure the warring groups into fighting with each other. The play with a repetition of physical objects as vehicles of recognition, revenge, and trickery can be seen in the use of the physical armor in this film or in the use of the watch in *For a Few Dollars More,* which recapitulates and foregrounds motifs of memory and revenge. The repetition of routines throughout the films works, as does the music, to highlight ironic reversals as well as changes over time. They also work more seriously to create a sense of an unstable world where ingenuity is essential to survival.

The typology of the characters in the Italian western also bears resemblance to *commedia* types. For example, vestigial remnants of the braggart captain (the offspring of Plautus' miles gloriosus) can be seen in such figures as Tuco in *The Good, The Bad, and the Ugly,* Cheyenne in *Once Upon a Time in the West,* and in the rivalry between the two bounty hunters – Colonel Mortimer and Monco (literally, "maimed") – in *For A Few Dollars More* [Fig. 43]. The pairing of figures, their competitiveness, and their exchange of qualities are also reminiscent of the relations between *zanni,* the various clowning figures. The *zanni* of the *commedia* (sometimes referred to as John, since Zanni is a nickname for Giovanni), according to Allardyce Nicoll, "appears as a stupid booby, but more commonly he mingles with his folly an element of wit, an element of liveliness, of good fun, of grotesquerie."[26] The figures of the Dottore and Pantalone, the older professional men who should be wise but who are pedants or betrayers or sunk in folly, are often interchangeable.

The comedy that arises from the Italian westerns has a resemblance to the popular philosophy that Gramsci suggests passes for wisdom; It appears to serve as a guide for action, only to reveal its inadequacy in contexts that require innovation and wit. If common sense as folklore involves a stylized and naturalized commitment to past actions and behavior, the melodramatic and comic treatment of character and situation in the films serves to foreground historical excess, allowing these historical elements to be examined, if not understood, within a present context. The heavy dependence on physical action, on the body, and on faciality sets up tensions between historical stasis and dynamic movement and change, between mechanization and spontaneity, and between containment and the release of energy. Physical action in a Leone film can signify static repetition and routine mechanization, or it can signify mental alertness.

The world that is provided in the Italian westerns is not one of simple heroes and villains. Common sense is not defeated but is shown in its contradictory dimensions: as a form of wisdom in the short run and as more questionable knowledge that requires interrogation in the long run. Clint Eastwood's comment in *A Fistful of Dollars* that "Every town has a boss. When

Figure 43. Clint Eastwood as Monco in *Per qualche dollaro in più* (*For a Few Dollars More*). (Courtesy New York Museum of Modern Art Stills Archive)

there are two around I'd say there's one too many," is conducive to an understanding of the wisdom necessary for survival, but it also raises more questions than it answers: Why can't there be two? How does one know who is the boss? The statements may adequately characterize the competitiveness and violence that results from two bosses – the Rojos and the Baxters – but the resolution, getting rid of both, while solving one problem, introduces more fundamental problems about power. There is no doubt that the pragmatic assessment of power works in immediate terms both to describe and to diagnose problems that are integral to survival, as *A Fistful of Dollars* dramatizes. The uses of past history, the road taken by the films, does not lead to a future that is mapped but to an ambiguous future, an open one like the roads that the protagonists often take as they ride out of town as alone as when they arrived.

Leone's films have encouraged allegorical readings, and *Duck, You Sucker* is an exemplary film to explore the multilayered texture of his films: It orchestrates many Gramscian issues relating to Americanism, common sense, the role of intellectuals, the nature of subalternity, the characteristics of passive revolution, and, above all, the ways in which history informs these issues (see Chapter 6). From the opening moments of the film, when Juan attempts to hitch a ride in a passing stagecoach, concealing his identity and the objective of his journey, the film presents a number of questions that are characteristic of the investigative form of Leone films: Who is this man? Why is he at this deserted stop along the road? How long has he been here? Why is he important enough to open the film? The film will play with questions relating to his identity. He is obviously not a minor character: Those who recognize the name Rod Steiger from the film credits will know that this is an important role, though they may not know what course his story will take [Fig. 44]. Familiarity with other Leone films alerts the spectator to the possibility that appearance is not a reliable guide to character identification. For example, when he first appears, Juan Miranda is the silent subaltern, and a lengthy sequence plays with a number of familiar images of subalternity: He is passive, verbally abused, and humiliated, and the bodily lumps he receives at the hands of the drivers are matched by the cruel treatment he receives from the patricians grouped inside the coach. As the camera dissects their faces, the group becomes an Eisensteinian montage of leering eyes, drooling mouths, and tearing teeth, thus transforming them into images of the beasts that they consider peasants to be, establishing the negative character of the upper classes and of the church.

The tables are turned when the stagecoach is attacked by Juan Miranda's gang, his "family" of sons and his father. In one sense, Juan still fulfills the passengers' and perhaps the audience's expectations of peasants in his cruelty, his indifference to life displayed in his casual shooting of one of the passengers, his thievery, and his rape of the woman on the coach. The film does not present a sentimentalized view of peasants.

Juan, turns out to have a genealogy: He introduces his father and informs the passengers that his mother had "the pure blood of the Aztecs which was before your people"; Juan's numerous sons, however, are from different mothers. Thus, the question underpinning this episode and the entire film (and others by Leone) is "Who are you?" The answer involves more than the individual's proper name: It is a positional question in relation to access to knowledge and to the exercise of power.

In introducing another "John," John H. Mallory or Sean (James Coburn) [Fig. 45], the film presents another set of reversals that will characterize the

Figure 44. Juan Miranda (Rod Steiger), the reluctant revolutionary in *Giù la testa* (*Duck, You Sucker*). (Courtesy New York Museum of Modern Art Stills Archive)

Figure 45. James Coburn as Sean in *Giù la testa* (*Duck, You Sucker*). (Courtesy New York Museum of Modern Art Stills Archive)

seesaw relationship between the two characters. Sean appears like a magician or a trickster, materializing from the smoke of the explosion he has produced. The question of sameness is articulated by Juan, to whom Sean offers a partnership in sharing the loot from the banks that they will rob: "My name is Juan and your name is John. That is destiny." Sean's abrupt entry into the narrative raises even more questions: What is an Irishman doing in the Mexican countryside? Why is he riding a motorcycle in this barren and uninhabited environment? Why is he causing explosions? In interactions between Juan and Sean, differences between the two men become evident: One is an intellectual, the other a peasant; one is a reader of books, the other is hostile toward readers of books; one is a committed revolutionary, the other a brigand. The contrasts raise the problem of detecting sameness and difference that animates the film – in relation to character and history. Are the two men with the same name in different languages the same or different, and what is the importance attached to differences? What are the similarities and differences between the Mexican revolution, the Irish, or any revolution (including the Risorgimento)? What is revolution? And what constitutes relations among men in situations identified as revolutionary?

More questions concerning sameness and difference arise from Juan's comments on revolution: What is the difference between robbing a bank and making revolution, when revolution results in maintenance of the status quo, of existing property and social relations? What is the difference between the character of Dr. Villega (Romolo Valli), a physician committed to the revolutionary cause, and traditional heroic portraits of revolutionary leaders? The film's interrogation of political struggle is problematized through this figure: Villega is an intellectual and an organizer. As a physician, he serves the cause by saving the lives of his political allies. He is also capable of killing his enemies in cold blood, as when he dispatches the government soldiers on the train who threaten Juan. Yet he becomes a betrayer: Unable to withstand torture, he informs on his comrades.

Villega's appearance, when first seen on the train, borders on the comic: He wears a black suit like that of a priest, a crisp white shirt, a white hat with a black band, and a pince-nez. Giving the aspect of a mild, middle-class, bookish man, he continues to be absorbed in his book even after he has dispatched the government men. Although his character is not broadly comic, it is satiric. Like the Dottore (doctor) of the *commedia* and of opera, he too is characterized by his "bookish affectations and his academic excesses."[27]

Though Villega does not appear as a clown or blatant fool, it becomes obvious as the film progresses that his aspirations to leadership depend more on his status than on his knowledge of people and events, and that he is as self-serving as the others. Distinctions among the characters, though, are not clear-cut: Villega shrinks from battle and informs on his colleagues because of his fear of bodily harm; in this respect, he contrasts with Sean, with the

Mexican officer, Guttierez, and with other Leone characters who do not fear physical confrontation. Juan, however, shares the doctor's tendency toward cowardice, although the peasant's attitude toward violence is based on profit and shrewdness, whereas Villega's (like that of the braggart captain of the *commedia*) is motivated by glory.

Another seriocomic aspect of *Duck, You Sucker* arises from the motif of confusion, which Sean articulates this way: "Where there's confusion a man who knows what he wants stands a good chance of getting it." This is another of those proverbial bits of common sense that invites examination. Confusion comes to stand in for the blurring of boundaries between characters and the contingent dimensions of political struggle. Its dominant metaphor appears to reside in the imagery of the explosions generated by Sean, producing confusion and the inability to see clearly, but emblematized in the reversal of events that turn out contrary to expectations. Both comedy and melodrama are closely tied to narrative confusion. Predicated on conceptions of victimization, of order restored, of innocence vindicated, and on the expectation of justice, melodrama's affect is generated from the precariousness of social identity, the fear of loss of position, the disappearance of moral and ethical boundaries, and disjunctions between expectations and outcome. The melodramatic moments in the Leone film are concerned with death – evident in the horrible Goya-like scene in which Sean and Juan witness the devastation of the revolutionaries in the grotto, and also when Juan confronts the death of his sons. The melodrama of loss is also generated through the scenes of masses of people gratuitously shot down by the troops.

Sean's adage "Revolution is confusion" solidifies the link between the melodramatic and comic elements in the film, the most notable being the robbing of the bank, which was to turn Juan into a rich man but instead makes him a poor hero. His commonsense political philosophy as expressed to Sean is, "My country is only me and my family." This characterization of nation suggests to Frayling an incorporation of Italian regional and national discourses in Leone's films, perhaps a particular instance of the "amoral familialism" attributed to southern Italians.[28] In a verbal moment unusually lengthy for a Leone film, Juan lets loose another barrage of invectives against the revolution:

> Don't tell me about revolution. The people that read the books they go to the people who don't read the books and they tell them the time has come to have a change and the people who read the books sit around the big polished table and talk and talk and eat and eat but what has happened to the poor people. They're dead.

This scene is important because it dramatizes – not merely in Juan's words (which resemble the peasants' attitudes toward revolution in *1900*) but in the nature of interactions between Sean and him – the divide between intellectuals and subaltern groups.

The Gramscian distinction between organic and traditional intellectuals (see Chapter 6) seems to underpin Juan's commonsense characterization of intellectuals. Sean generally tries to silence Juan, laughing at him, maintaining his superiority. (In writing of the role of laughter in the *commedia,* Nicoll says that not only do the *zanni* engender laughter by their appearance and mode of speech, but also by their own "love of witty laughter" and their "cruel, libidinous, cynically witty, and self-seeking actions,"[29] which bespeak a tenuous sense of superiority that later proves to be questionable.) After Juan's diatribe, however, Sean throws his copy of Bakunin's *Patriotism,* a major anarchist document against the power of the state, into a muddy puddle, and this time he does not laugh or even smile at Juan's words.

In the next scene, Juan remains with Sean to fight the *federales,* shouting at him, "You listen to me, you piece of shit. You think you are the only man in the world who has balls. Well, you are wrong. I have the balls and I stay." Sean now laughs again at Juan, whose bravado invocation of masculinity appears to be mixed with notions of *onore* and machismo, suggesting that his motives are no less contradictory than Sean's. Juan's reference to his genitalia notwithstanding, his speech does not explain why he remains with Sean in this dangerous venture. Is the homosocial bond stronger than their ideological differences? (Juan seems to have somewhat relinquished his earlier obsession of exploiting this "firecracker," as he calls Sean). Alternatively, are we to believe that Juan has been infected by Sean's revolutionary attitudes?

The next episodes, involving the destructiveness of the troops, representatives of the state, evokes connections with the cinema of the post–World War II era. The figure of the blond, blue-eyed Mexican federal officer looks more like the familiar representation of the Nazi in cinema than an officer from the early part of the century. The way he is filmed in his armored transport seems to have more connection with a World War II Panzer commander than with a military officer from 1913. Moreover, his appearance in his impeccable uniform, his effete attention to his bodily needs, the close-ups of him sucking an egg and later brushing his teeth, also suggest parallels with the portrayal of the Nazi officer in Rossellini's *Roma, città aperta.* Does the Leone film also contain a similar implication of effeminacy, that the federal officer has "no balls," to use Juan's designation of masculinity? Does the film, therefore, imply that sexual politics in the form of the failure of masculinity can be brought to bear on the question of violence on the part of those who represent the authority of the state? The scenes of the torture and shooting of the revolutionaries while the federal officer sits observing the massacre from behind the wheel of his vehicle, rain on the windshield (the informer, Villega, at his side), also connect this episode to *Open City.* However, while there appear to be some parallels, there is also an important difference: Whereas Manfredi, the engineer, and Don Pietro, the priest, do not break down under torture and inform on the people, Dr. Villega does. *Duck, You Sucker* attaches several more elements to Rossellini's portrayal of the Fascist state and its barbarism, as well as reflecting on the lessons of history – especially the betrayal of the Italian Resistance in the postwar era. In relation to revolution, the film interrogates notions of heroism, suggesting either that representations of heroism are too idealistic and dissonant with the actual confrontation of power or, in contrasting Villega and an Irish informer (presented in Sean's flashback) with Sean and Juan, that critical recognition of complicity, betrayal, and bodily needs, if not foolhardiness, is a requisite in political struggle.

In the final moments of the film, a number of further reversals occur. When Sean, in hand-to-hand combat during his pursuit of the federal officer, leaves himself out in the open, he appears to be ignoring his own dictum to "Duck, you sucker." This act seems to be either particularly foolhardy, the essence of romantic heroism and martyrdom, or a suicidal gesture. Why does he choose to die with the commander? There is a great deal of the operatic involved in this final death scene. While he is breathing his last, Juan is ministering to him, trying to keep him alive. Here their relationship can be characterized as a form of male love. There is little posturing, mockery, or boasting – only Juan's tender and vain ministrations and Sean's lapsing into a flashback, where he is once again in the Irish countryside and kissing the young woman we'd seen in an earlier flashback. Cumbow reads this ambiguous moment as "a Leone effort to recapture lost innocence – to return perhaps to the sweetness of life 'before the revolution.'"[30]

Duck, You Sucker does not nostalgically enshrine the history it probes. History does not become myth; nor is it abandoned for an ahistorical realm of "once upon a time." Any "once upon a time" in a Leone film is no untroubled, pastoral world in a golden age. The repeated concern of his films with the question of identity – represented by Frank's repeated statement to Harmonica "I have to know who you are" in *Once Upon a Time in the West* – can be taken as emblematic of a preoccupation with knowledge. Any answer is always partial, and the knowledge may produce failure rather than unqualified success. The essence of this knowledge is related to history, and particularly to the meaning of "experience." Since the trajectory of the narratives seems to be not resolution but investigation, the narratives – and the "confusion" they dramatize – do not shrink from portraying the indeterminacy of this contest for knowledge.

Different moments in history collide: 1913, the 1940s, and the present. Different cultures (European and American) and different forms of filmmaking are also invoked. The issues raised by the film are closely tied to difficult questions about politics that rose to the surface globally in the 1960s and

1970s and continue to garner theoretical attention. The film emphasizes the connection among the banks, money, and political corruption, and Juan invokes Americanism by articulating a desire to escape to the United States ("Which way is America?" he asks Sean) – a haven for immigrants and a bastion of capitalism, government corruption, and anticommunism. *Duck, You Sucker* appears particularly apt for the early 1970s, when competing notions about revolutionary change were everywhere evident in Europe and in America, and where confusion – not necessarily unproductive – seemed characteristic of the times.

Though it is often the case that popular cinema of the 1960s and 1970s gets shortchanged in relation to auteur cinema, there is evidence that certain films identified with the spaghetti western (or with horror) are quite self-conscious about their status as cinema and are actively involved in exploring the nature of the cinematic medium and the role of spectatorship. For example, *Il mio nome è nessuno* (*My Name Is Nobody*, 1973), directed by Tonino Valerii, although not an instance of the cinema of poetry in the mode projected by Pasolini, is a sophisticated examination of the properties of the western genre as transported into the European context and its relation to historicizing and, particularly, cinema history. In his brilliant study of this genre, Christopher Frayling has stated, in relation to its popularity, that it came about as a result of "attempts by the industry to 'seize' a 'mass audience,'" and by the receptiveness of that audience to these films, which they must have regarded as portraying "significant changes in Italian social life."[31] Among these changes are increased urbanization, a growing cynicism about social and political life, and a greater sophistication on the part of the audience. The Italian western was an international form; it was not a carbon copy of the Hollywood western (which was itself becoming more internationalized), though it acknowledged the role of Americanism. Into its treatment of the familiar conventions of the genre, it introduced allegory, examining relations between history and myth, politics and power, the individual and the masses, Fascism and modernity, and, simultaneously, the status of the cinema.

My Name Is Nobody illustrates how, in its uses of allegory, the spaghetti western focuses on questions of history reinforced, yet sometimes also undermined by the cinematic medium: The film "can be read as an exploration (in retrospect) of the relationship between the Italian western (especially Leone's films) and cherished myths of the Hollywood genre."[32] From its first moments, *My Name Is Nobody* rehearses the conventions of the western: Three men are shown riding into a small town, raising dust as they do, and finally arriving at their destination – a barber shop – where they gag the barber and his son. The interplay of sound and image offers a counterpoint to the familiarity of the event in the use of close-ups, the alternation of inside and outside shots, the absence of dialogue, the loud ticking of a clock (always in the western one is reminded of time), and the interruption of their action by a cutaway to Jack Beauregard (Henry Fonda) getting news of a ship, the *Sundowner,* on which he plans to sail in a couple of weeks. Throughout the film at key intervals, a messenger from the ship's ticket agent, and then the ticket agent himself, will inform Beauregard of the date of sailing and of a necessary deposit of five hundred dollars. Beauregard's response is merely, "No hurry," indicative of his indifference to time.

What becomes evident from these opening moments, then, is the motif of time, of repetition, and of difference in repetition. Through an ellipsis, we now see Beauregard being placed in the barber's chair by one of recently arrived men, and – still without dialogue, while the clock ticks away loudly – the camera probes his face and shows the positions of the other men. The man proceeds to lather, then to shave Beauregard until, through camera movement, we are drawn from Beauregard's face to his gun in the man's crotch, thus confirming the threat of this encounter. After this slow and lengthy prologue, the action moves quickly as, with one shot, Beauregard destroys his "barber" and his two cohorts without. When, upon their release, the real barber's son asks his father, "How did he do it?" the barber responds that "there is nobody faster than him" – thus adding to the element of duration the idea of speed. The rhythm of the film and the actions of its characters will revolve around velocity and slowness. Moreover, the question of identity – a staple in the western, and especially exaggerated in the Italian western – emerges through the names of the characters. "Nobody" is the one who will acquire an identity through his association with Beauregard. "Beauregard," as the French indicates, is the fine-looking, the ideal appearance that must be maintained to keep the tradition of the western alive.

In keeping with its contrapuntal techniques, the film shifts from Beauregard to Nobody (Terence Hill) [Fig. 46] as he fishes with an insect as bait, accompanied by the theme music, playing loudly, that will be associated with him. The emerging motif of looking is evident as Beauregard rides up, stops, and himself observes the scene. After successfully catching his fish, Nobody exchanges looks with Beauregard, and the play on Beauregard's name now assumes greater prominence, emphasizing not only looking but having a good appearance. Though the Italian western often relies as a major motif on the quest for gold and the greed, competition, and violence it produces, in this film these take a back seat to the interchanges of looks between Nobody and Beauregard. Nobody attaches himself to the older man, and in their first face-to-face encounter, we are made aware of Nobody's designs on Beauregard. Confronting his "hero" in a ramshackle restaurant, Nobody, like a movie fan, leisurely recites Beauregard's gun battles – specifically, the number of men, their names, and the places where they were killed – all while holding a basket containing a ticking bomb (from Beauregard's enemies outside, who await the desired explosion) and well aware of the time allotted for the bomb to

Figure 46. Terence Hill (alias Mario Girotti) as "Nobody," *Il mio nome è nessuno* (*My Name Is Nobody*). (Courtesy New York Museum of Modern Art Stills Archive)

go off. The question of style, of "going out in style," will be central to No-body's creating a proper scenario for Beauregard, and in particular, his plan to have Jack confront and destroy the 150 men of the "Wild Bunch" (the first reference to Peckinpah). The issue of style also relates to the film's metacin-ematic character: Nobody is the film director who seeks to orchestrate events for Beauregard, his star, and those events must be staged in style – in the style of the western at its best – to do honor to its legendary status.

Now comes the first of several images of the thundering ride of that "Wild Bunch," accompanied by their Morricone–Wagner Valkyrie leitmotiv, the in-evitable allusion to the operatic quality of the western, and Nobody asserts his project of turning Beauregard into a legend, of having him "written up in all the history books," of memorializing him. History is linked to recording, to seeing, to the role of memory. "I see it all clear as a crystal," says Nobody. Elaborating on the importance of vision of brilliance and clarity, Beauregard responds wittily to Nobody by telling him, "You shine like a door in a whore

Figure 47. Henry Fonda as the "legend" Beauregard in *Il mio nome è nessuno* (*My Name Is Nobody*). (Courtesy New York Museum of Modern Art Stills Archive)

house," to which Nobody responds, "I like folks to see me." The obvious reiteration of mirror images – in Nobody's use of a mirror to look at himself and, later, to warn Beauregard, and still later in the extended play in the carnival's mirrored House of Horrors – reinforces the film's preoccupation with the notion of reflection, extended to that of the deceptive nature of the image and its problematic relation to actual events.

Always evident in the film's metacinematic discourse is the extratextual role of Fonda as a Hollywood legend [Fig. 47], as well as Italian actor Terence Hill's (pseudonym for Mario Girotti) international popularity for his role as "Trinity" in a series of films (e.g., *They Call Me Trinity*). Thus, another subtext of the film emerges: namely, the passage of the form from Hollywood to Italy through the actors. Nobody, the creation of the western, is indeed a clown in the tradition identified with the *commedia dell'arte*. His persona relies on physical and verbal gags, on his use of wit and humor, as much as physical action to outsmart his opponents: when he deflates the "tall man" who is really a midget, when he frees the black men from the pie-throwing booth, when he (in an extended scene) outdrinks and outshoots his competitor. In these scenes too, Nobody plays to an audience and calls attention to the importance of being seen – another mark of the theatricality identified with the Italian western in contrast to that of Hollywood.

Sitting aboard the *Sundowner* (another allegorical reference to his and the western's demise), Beauregard writes a letter to Nobody after his legend has been reinforced (at Nobody's instigation) by his single-handedly killing the "Wild Bunch," and after his death has been simulated (with his permission) by Nobody on the main street of a town in the presence of all its inhabitants and a photographer. In the letter, he affirms Nobody's parable about the "birdie, the cow, and the coyote," which had earlier eluded him but which he now interprets as "folks that throw dirt on you aren't always trying to hurt you, and folks that pull you out of a jam aren't always trying to help you." (The film's uses of aphoristic one-liners – e.g., "If the risk is little, the reward is little" – highlight the folk wisdom upon which the western genre relies and that this Italian western seeks to examine.) The film ends with Beauregard writing, intercut with Nobody dodging other "nobodies" who seek to make a name for themselves by killing him, and Beauregard's voice narrating the contents of his letter. The last shot of the film places Nobody in a perilous situation reminiscent of Beauregard's earlier "close shave" – in a barber chair, vulnerable to the "barber's" razor but with his hand poised to crush the man's testicles – thus leaving open the question of the continuity of the genre.

The film's aforementioned focus on mirroring and reflecting, related to its consciousness of itself qua film, and of film as illusion. also assumes a pedagogical function vis-à-vis its emphasis on belief – on the importance, as Beauregard writes, "of that illusion which made my generation tick." Throughout, the element of time (the time of the film and the film's allusions to time) are tied to change – encapsulated in Beauregard's letter, where he distinguishes between his generation and Nobody's ("I guess it's your time not mine"). The world of Beauregard's generation was one of open spaces, "lots of elbow room," and the ethos was one of tolerated violence. Now space has shrunk, and violence is "organized." The time of the gunfighter as hero is over. His letter is an elegy to a lost world and to a disappearing form of cinema. The generational differences between the two men are linked to distinctions between the Hollywood and the Italian (and international) western and to a cinema no longer governed by the action-image but by time-image.

The film indicates that the subject matter of the popular cinema has been folklore, legend, and mythology; but *My Name Is Nobody,* in its elegiac focus on memory and the creation of myth (with Nobody as the director of Beauregard's role), is an excursus on the passage of history: The cinema now is a reflection on its past and on its precarious future.

La famiglia

The Cinematic Family and the Nation

Viewed from stereotypic and monolithic notions of the role of patriarchy, the subordination and silencing of women, and the interpretation of consensus as unchanging adherence to dominant values, the Italian family is often viewed as a major obstacle to change. It is regarded and portrayed as endemic to the traditional life and backwardness of Italy and especially of southern Italy, an instrument of unmitigated oppression on the part of the Roman Catholic Church, of the Fascist regime, and, later, of Christian Democratic ideology and practices. The family has played a key role in the configuration of Italian national identity tied to the regulation of marriage and divorce, conceptions of gender and sexuality, health, morals, and procreation. It has also been crucial in the dissolution of traditional values and behavior.[1] The family has been the property not only of Italian popular culture but of American-Italian culture, associated with generational differences, with the notion of passion and revenge, and with the Mafia. It is an object of veneration and obsession, the material of melodrama, and also the butt of humor.

The history of the Italian family in the fourteenth and fifteenth centuries was, contrary to the folklore of family life, rather varied, "making it quite difficult to identify a single type that could be reasonably characterized as the Italian family."[2] Not only are there regional variations, there is variation within regions. These depend on economic activities and family practices, and involve class differentials, status, the land, and agrarian and urban forms of life. In particular, the role of the church from Roman times to the present has to be considered as a major factor in marriage and in the bearing and rearing of children. Also central to conceptions of the family is the role of the state in establishing laws governing adultery, rewards and penalties for childbearing and child rearing, property rights, and gender responsibilities. In relation to gender difference, the male, not the female, was considered the source of procreation, and women's chastity was tied to a conception of family honor that remained intact for twenty centuries, first as a major source of legal jurisdiction, later as a social offense. In modern times, as historians have established, there is no uniform concept of family life. Increasingly, changes affecting the role of property, of women, and of differential living arrangements have become evident. Contrary to the romanticized mythology of the extended family, family life in coresidential arrangements was largely dependent on regional economic conditions: The family was less a source of emotional nurturance and more of "an unsentimental mechanism for productive and reproductive ends."[3] While the economic dimensions of family life may be acknowledged, such issues as the position of the father as provider-lawgiver and the mother as physical and emotional nurturer, the responsibilities of the parents to their offspring, and the relation of the family to the state and to other social institutions are much more contentious. Differences attributed to family life among different social classes and regional ethnicities, through both popular culture and critical writings, have raised the question of the application of uniform or middle-class standards to other classes and regional groups. Prior to cinema, painting had been a source of images of the family. Nineteenth-century portraits afford abundant examples of middle-class life in images of fathers and sons, mothers and sons, filial portraits and images of congregated families, attesting to a sense of propriety, property, and responsibility; much rarer are images of the working-class family. However, the twentieth century compensated for that disparity through painting, photography, and the cinema.

In *A History of Contemporary Italy,* Paul Ginsborg writes, "Attachment to family has probably been a more constant and less evanescent element in Italian popular consciousness than any other."[4] He asserts, however, that analyses of the role of the family are "more complex and one-sided" than many writers on the subject have acknowledged. Challenging Edward Banfield's notion of "amoral familialism," with its exclusive focus on the centrality and politically retrograde character of family allegiances in the life of southern peasants as major obstacles to social change, critics have sought to examine the family not as a source of backwardness but as a social and cultural construct "strategically used in changing circumstances and to express different interests."[5] The family has been a hotly contested area of social and cultural life, one subject to the control of the Italian state as well as of the Roman Catholic Church. Although, over time, "there have been massive changes in family life following from new employment patterns, education, and the diffusion of feminist aspirations . . . the church has tried to hold constant some moral principles through an uncompromising affirmation of basic teachings."[6]

The church's position reveals that ideas of family cannot be separated from considerations of gender and sexuality involving procreation, hetero- and homosexuality, relations of power within the family, and legal relations between the family and the state. The church has remained steadfast concerning the "sexual act" for propagation not pleasure, resistance to birth control, and opposition to homosexuality but has experienced defeats in relation to divorce and abortion. Legislation in the 1970s "marked the end of an era in which the governance of family life had been a matter entirely for the family itself: now the silence and secrecy of the domestic sphere were being broken."[7] Laws contested the husband's place as legal head of the family and pro-vided for the equal rights of conjugal partners in relation to each other and to their offspring. Though the law decreed juridical equality for family mem-bers and allowed and made provisions for the dissolution of marriage, it is clear that aspects of family ideology persist in the struggles of various gay and lesbian groups to challenge vestigial conceptions of normative sexuality.

From its earliest years the Italian cinema has played a role both in the dis-semination of representations of myths and folklore of family life and in the exposure of conflicting and contradictory portraits of the family involving the authority of the paternal figure, courtship and sexual relations, conceptions of masculinity and femininity, and the character and role of children. Portraits of *la famiglia* seem bilateral at best: The family appears ideally to be a source of order and stability, and a force for national unity. On the other hand, it also appears a tenuous haven from the depredations of the social order; a signi-fier for social fragmentation; a critique of gendered and sexual roles; and a myth in need of demystification. The numerous representations of family in the Italian cinema are largely characterized by conflict, ambivalence, and by reference to a larger social fabric that exceeds the domestic sphere.

In her discussion of the media and the position of women in the family under Fascism in the 1920s through the early 1940s, Victoria De Grazia has exposed the contradictory effects of social and political life of the era as they relate to the family. Whereas official views of the regime emphasized the im-portance of tradition, the sanctity of family life, the commanding role of the husband, and the imperatives of reproduction and maternity, the actual situ-ation was more complex. The lures of modern industrial life were a counter-weight to domestic imperatives. In particular, the role played by mass culture, through radio, cinema, and journalism, was "an empowering force for young working-class and lower middle-class women."[8] Images of modernity, partic-ularly associated with freer and more mobile images of women, collided with more stable and sedate familial ones. Similarly, advertising presented a world of commodities associated with travel and adventure that offered attractive images of escape from humdrum routine. An examination of the commercial films of the Fascist era corroborates an uneasy relationship between old and new, traditional and modern views on the family. Cinematic treatments of family life are also a window on the commonsense character of consensus.

In silent cinema texts such as *Cabiria, The Last Days of Pompeii,* and *Quo Vadis?,* the family is presented as being under siege – through natural catastrophe, the threat of barbarian, non-Christian cultures, and the deca-dence of the imperial order – although, in the final analysis, the moral order triumphs through the regeneration of the family identified with national as-pirations. However, as we have seen, the threats to the family that must be constantly renegotiated involve the unruly nature of femininity and its per-ceived connection to social disorder. In *Assunta Spina,* we are given a portrait of a family with an absent mother, a vision of a willful and transgressive woman who does not conform to conventional patterns of sexual purity, submissiveness, and maternity. In *Assunta Spina* and *Cabiria,* the diva is the antithesis of the maternal figure with her assumed commitment to service and nurture. The melodramatic tenor of the films, their focus on the attractiveness and intensity of the diva is an index to the always threatening and potentially destabilizing role of woman in the family, offering an image of pleasure that might not be mitigated by the conventional "resolution."

With the coming of sound, a number of texts presented portraits of the endangered family as a threat to the nation, none more cogent and popular than in the films of Mario Camerini, Amleto Palermi, Alessandro Blasetti, and Vittorio De Sica. Even in the monumental historical film *Scipione l'Africano,* war is being conducted in the name of Roman familial and national virtues, with the family threatened by Carthaginian barbarians. As we saw in Chapter 2, Scipio's heroic virtues present him as the savior of women and children, thus mitigating the sense that his warlike prowess is one of ambition pure and simple. The family is closely tied to the formation of the nation, and, as Étienne Balibar writes,

> the modern family . . . is the sphere in which the relations between individuals are immediately charged with a "civic" function and made possible by constant state assistance, beginning with the sexes which are aligned to procreation. This is also what enables us to understand the anarchistic tone that sexually "deviant" behavior easily takes on in modern national formations.[9]

In dramatizations of the family, a tension between this "civic" function and the threat of deviance runs like a fault line.

Camerini's comedies and melodramas, especially such films as *Il signor Max, Come le foglie* (Like the Leaves), and *T'amerò sempre,* revolve around transgressions of family life. The comedy *Il signor Max (Mr. Max,* 1937) focuses on the protagonist's desire to partake of the splendor and luxury of upper-class life, thus spurning his working-class position and, thereby, the values and everyday patterns of life associated with the family. Living in two identities as Gianni, a modest newspaper vendor, and Mr. Max, a pretender to wealth, the protagonist attempts to live up to the high style of his upper-class cronies. Scorning the simple virtues of his working-class family, he seeks romance with Lady Paola – until he discovers that "there is no place like home"; then he abandons his pretensions and finds a woman of his class who embodies the virtues of nurture and service. However, the film does not elevate the image of the family to which he returns, but presents it as a modest alternative to the upper-class decadence he has witnessed.

Central to exploring the dangers and crises that threaten the life and well-being of the family is the role and behavior of woman: Feminine transgression opens to the threat of (and the fascination with) social dissolution; it is also the necessary hinge for entertaining forms of restabilizing domestic order. Camerini's melodrama *T'amerò sempre* (*I'll Always Love You*, 1933) deals directly with threats to the family and with its rehabilitation, focusing on the plight of an unwed mother and her attempts to resist repeating her mother's fate. Adriana (Elsa De Georgi), the major protagonist in this drama is a solitary female who, through willfulness, impulse, or the threatening and oppressive character of working-class life, violates expectations of female purity. The imagery evokes prevailing representations of femininity as exemplified by the propaganda and advertisements of the time. In its opening scenes, the film bears a resemblance to documentaries produced by LUCE for the edification of women in their requisite roles as producers for the nation.[10] In a maternity ward, scores of babies are photographed as nurses tend newborn infants. The camera pans a line of newborns in their cribs, providing a curious vision of regimentation, clinical hygiene, and modern care.

The melodrama draws on familiar conventions: the vicissitudes of the orphan in the impersonal world of the city, with no familial identity or social support; the lower-class woman at the mercy of parasitic, immoral, and violent aristocrats; the unwed and unprotected mother seeking to fend for herself and her child in a threatening environment; the dangers of prostitution that confront dependent women; and the appearance of a masculine "savior" of motherhood, and hence of the sanctity of family. Consonant with Camerini's other films, the visual codes are an index to the sexual and social-class dimensions of the narrative. The plight of the unwed mother is intimately tied to this image of the home as less-than-perfect sanctuary from the depredations of the world of work and upper-class leisure. In certain ways, the film seems to parallel the propaganda of the regime in its insistence on the return of women to the family, on the importance of reproduction, and on the imperative of the proper responsibility of mothers to guard and care for their children. The vision of Adriana's mother's tragic end, along with Adriana's aggressive treatment at the hands of an unscrupulous aristocrat and his snobbish sister, underscores the necessity of proper familial support and nurture from childhood to maturity. "Promiscuous" feminine sexuality appears to be the danger, the absence of proper guidance and care for girls its cause.

The lack of social constraints on gender and sexuality reinforces the imagery of the dangers of unconfined feminine sexuality, subject particularly to social exploitation in the form of prostitution, that threatens to undermine the role of woman as "a moral human being"[11] – the role she is expected to assume in maintaining the cohesiveness of the family as reproducer of future citizens of the nation. In the Fascist education of women as mothers, their role as national reproductive agents means a denial of desire, a dematerialization of their bodies, and their transformation into an abstract entity known as the mother. The projection of femininity, however, is slippery, for while the appeal to motherhood is usually couched in terms of the inherent naturalness of reproduction, it is feminine "nature" that is threatening and hence in need of cultural intervention in the form of surveillance, discipline, and masculine support. Such support is provided by Mario (Nino Besozzi), who defends her against the importuning and manipulative behavior of the count, who had earlier refused to acknowledge his paternity of her child. The maternal melodrama in the film thus addresses the contradictions inherent to femininity and evokes Fascist discourse of women, but *T'amerò sempre* is not hermetically sealed; it is no mere reflection and celebration of Fascist ideology concerning women's place in relation to domesticity. As James Hay maintains:

> Marriage may redeem her past and her social stigma as an unwed mother, but Camerini has already satirized the rituals of petit-bourgeois family life in the earlier scene at Mario's home. And herein are the contradictions of the movie's ideology. The audience is encouraged to enjoy and accept lovers who are misfits but who, in their rejection of the fads of upper-crust society, appear quite stable.[12]

The portraits of the family and of the beauty salon where Adriana and Mario work both underscore the role of role-playing and artifice. In the family, satire emerges from characters who conform to stereotypical familial behavior: Mario's mother, eager for her son to marry; Mario's sister and her fiancé, an overenthusiastic couple contrasted to Mario and Adriana; and the inevitable, embarrassing showing of photographs of Mario as a child. The salon offers another form of artifice in the marcelled and heavily made-up women who frequent the shop and are identified with another form of regimentation: conformity to social conceptions of femininity. Mario and Adriana are misfits in both the domestic and work worlds they inhabit. She, as an unwed mother, is hardly a domestic model of femininity, and, unlike the count and Mario's brother-in-law to be, Mario is modest and unassuming, hardly an example of aggressive virility. The role of artifice and ritual thus imply an awareness of the constructed nature of gendered roles and also a gentle critique of their constraints. The film problematizes notions of naturalness pertaining to the family at the same time that it offers, through Mario and Adriana's union, the possibility of a different form of attachment, though still within the sanctioned orbit of the family. Thus, rather than merely presenting a unified and reiterative image of prevailing Fascist ideology, the film reveals irreconcilable differences and contradictions concerning representations of the family.

Whereas Camerini's film problematizes connections among the family, sexuality, and social class, Blasetti's *Terra madre* (*Mother Earth*, 1930) offered a

Figure 48. Paolo (Gino Cervi) getting breakfast in *Quattro passi fra le nuvole* (*Four Steps in the Clouds*). (Courtesy New York Museum of Modern Art Stills Archive)

version of family life more closely tied to the ostensible ideals of the Fascist regime. Made in the early years of sound cinema, the film dramatizes the regeneration of a padrone whose estate he has placed in the hands of absentee landlords. He ignores the needs of his tenants in favor of his romance with a woman who represents the acme of modern urban life, devoted to American-style music, leisure, and sexual promiscuity. Only when his estate is endangered, and after he realizes the domestic (e.g., natural) virtues of Emilia, the daughter of one of his tenants, does he return to his responsibilities as paternal figure to his people (and, eventually, to children he will have with Emilia) and acknowledge his ties to the land as "mother earth." The film's common sense relies on the myth of woman's identification with the earth, with procreation, and with renewal, qualities assumed to be natural and that are the basis of family and essential to the regeneration of the national community.

Blasetti's later film comedy *Quattro passi fra le nuvole* (*Four Steps in the Clouds,* 1942), identified with the emergence of neorealism, offers a vision of urban familial life as claustrophobic and conflictual. The protagonist, Paolo (Gino Cervi), is seen in a darkened apartment in Rome, preparing his own breakfast before he sets out for his daily routine of work as a traveling salesman [Fig. 48]. His wife is never shown but is heard offscreen complaining and giving orders. As visual correlative of his situation, a pot of boiling milk overflows on the stove. On the bus, he meets a young woman, Maria (Adriana Benetti), another of the unwed mothers who grace the screen of the era. She regales Paolo with a tale of woe and convinces him to come home with her to the country for the day and pretend to be her husband. In this role he meets her family, especially her father, whose values are cast in the traditional mold of a paternal tyrant. Through the comic and carnivalesque confusion that results from the young couple's role-playing, her family is transformed, becoming more accepting of her plight. By contrast, the vision of the urban family remains dark and antagonistic when the protagonist returns home from his sojourn in the country. The contrast between the two styles of life, urban and pastoral, is not resolved, but the film has introduced various elements that stand as threats to domestic unity: marital alienation, paternalism, promiscuity, and the conflict between tradition and modernity. Blasetti's film is a further indication that the films of the era were becoming increasingly preoccupied, even critical, of idealizations of the family.

In a more melodramatic and somber vein, Vittorio De Sica's *I bambini ci guardano* (*The Children Are Watching Us,* 1942) dramatizes a family riven by strife as a consequence of the mother's promiscuity and the father's impotence. The mother runs away from home, the husband commits suicide, and the boy is sent away to a boarding school, where he is completely alienated from his mother. Neither the father nor the mother is presented in the traditional melodramatic terms of good and evil. The husband is rigid and pompous as well as vacillating and powerless in the face of his responsibilities. The wife is torn between her responsibility to the child and her obsession with her domineering lover. The child, Pricò (Luciano De Ambrosis), is the victim of the violence of the gendered and familial conflict that he encounters in his home and in the world of the upper classes when he goes on a holiday with his temporarily reunited parents [Fig. 49]. The events are presented largely through the boy's perspective, whereby family life is portrayed in terms of dissolution seen through the portraits of the women. They are either, like the adulterous wife, disaffected with conjugal relations and heedless of their maternal role or, like the grandmother, obsessed with their authority and power over the family. The men, meanwhile, are either weak or overbearing. Thus the child, finally bereft of his father and rejected by and rejecting of his mother, suffers from indifference and neglect. The image of the family is closely tied, as in Blasetti's *Quattro passi fra le nuvole,* to images of urban life as visualized by the claustrophobic apartment house and its uncongenial tenants; but the countryside, where the boy finds himself constrained and controlled by the grandmother's tyranny, is also threatening.

The film can be regarded from two vantage points: as a legitimation of the narrative of the nuclear family and a critique of the failure of "family val-

Figure 49. Pricò (Luciano De Ambrosis), severed from family, in *I bambini ci guardano* (*The Children Are Watching Us*). (Courtesy New York Museum of Modern Art Stills Archive)

ues" as promulgated under Fascism. Given its obsessive preoccupation with framing, surveillance, the impersonality of urban life, and images of hostile communities in the apartment house and at the beach, it can be perceived as a portrait of a world in disintegration, dramatized most cogently through the image of a dysfunctional family that is either the source of the social malaise or the consequence of an anomic, fragmented, and hostile environment. The events are filtered through the vision of an "orphan" for whom the romance of family life is a nightmare, connected as it is to other destructive social and cultural forms. Overarching the film's conventional family-melodrama scenario is a preoccupation with the disjunction between the appearance of normality and the impossibility of conforming to its images.

Visconti's *Ossessione* (1942) offers an even more striking challenge to traditional conceptions of family life associated with Fascist ideology. This film, more than any other, has been connected to the rise and perspective of neorealist filmmaking in its use of professional and nonprofessional actors, its scenes shot on location, its focus on socially marginal characters, and, most important, in its challenge to the genre filmmaking of the time. However, it also utilizes domestic melodrama to portray conjugal, sexual, and social antagonism, offering the spectator images of a dislocated, authoritarian society. The narrative, based on the novel *The Postman Always Rings Twice* by James M. Cain – another instance of the role of American influences in the 1940s – is a familiar one. A nomadic figure, Gino (Massimo Girotti) appears at a trattoria cum service station, becomes enmeshed in the dreary lives of the couple who own the establishment and whose relationship is marked by the husband's boorishness, his expecting his wife to wait on him, and her disaffection with his unattractive appearance and gross behavior. Seduced by the wife, Giovanna (Clara Calamai), Gino begs her to escape with him; but she, attached to the security of home and income, finds herself unable to leave. The claustrophobic and dark images of the trattoria stand in opposition to the recurrent images of the open road, symbol of the nomadic life upon which Gino reembarks alone. During his wanderings Gino meets Lo Spagnolo (Elio Marcuzzo), who travels from town to town performing. Lo Spagnolo offers a way out of Gino's obsession – companionship, suggesting even the possibility of a homosexual relationship, and freedom from his doomed heterosexual romance. Later, complicit with Giovanna in the murder of her husband, Gino finds himself obsessed by guilt and tortured in having to confront the domesticity that she imposes on him yet he finds himself unable to resist. He has a second chance to escape when Lo Spagnolo appears at the trattoria, but Gino rejects him violently. A final opportunity presents itself when he and Giovanna visit town, she to collect the insurance money. Meandering, he meets Anita, a dancer and also an itinerant, with whom he spends an uncomplicated afternoon; but the possibility of a liaison is precluded when he returns to Giovanna.

The film dissects the social and sexual relations that underpin idealized fantasies of heterosexual romance leading to marriage, probing the craving for financial security and social conformity that are identified with violence and a loss of freedom. *Ossessione* focuses, as do other films of the early 1940s (e.g., Poggioli's *Gelosia*), on the disruption of familial harmony by sexual passion. The difference between the Visconti film and many of the films critical of Fascism resides in its encyclopedic treatment of psychosocial relations. Although it begins with a chance but eventually fatal encounter – the basis of many melodramatic and operatic scenarios – the film gains momentum by enlarging into a number of episodes that orchestrate but do not resolve the conflicts posed: homosocial bonding, heterosexual romance, the enforced claustrophobia of domesticity, the role of the law in overseeing and controlling social behavior, and the role of art as escape. Once again, the much-vaunted concern in Italian culture with family solidarity is subject to critique.

The problematic nature of the cinematic family intensifies during and after the war. In the films of neorealism, portraits of family life are couched in terms of survival under conditions involving the ravages of war, broken homes, single-parent families, unemployment, and homelessness: In De Sica's *Sciuscià,* for example, one of the boys, Pasquale, is an orphan; the other, Giuseppe, is betrayed by his family. In his *Ladri di biciclette (The Bicycle Thief)*, the family is intact but threatened by Antonio's lack of employment. The mother, Maria, is instrumental in helping the father reclaim his pawned bicycle so that he can work; but she then disappears from the film, which thereafter concentrates on the theft of the bicycle, Antonio's quest for the thief, and the vicissitudes of his relationship to his son, Bruno. The film develops affective relations between father and son, focusing on the ways that Antonio's reaction to loss and his desire for reparation and economic security assume characteristics of the indifferent and hostile milieu in which he finds himself. His obsession finally reenacts the aggressive behavior of the subproletarian world to which the other bicycle thief and his cohorts belong. Ironically, his behavior also comes to resemble the indifference and depersonalization of prevailing social institutions – the police, the trade unions, and even the church.

The film's treatment of familial relations opens a window onto changing conceptions of family in the cinema and, more broadly, the character of cinematic representation. First of all, as in *I bambini,* the emphasis is affective, displaying a concern not only with economic issues but with the quality of familial relationships implicated in and threatened by social forces. Second, though the film maintains a continuity with the emphasis on the importance of family as a source of nurturance and mutual support, *The Bicycle Thief* has shifted from a prescriptive and formulaic mode to one that is interrogative. The film raises more questions than it resolves in its investigation of the institutional pressures that Antonio confronts as he seeks to regain his economic livelihood and masculine respect through his recovery of the bicycle. More than *I bambini,* however, *The Bicycle Thief* detaches itself from familiar political positions, immersing the spectator in the ambiguity of social relations that violate conventional sentiments about the family and children.

In particular, Antonio's behavior as paterfamilias is first registered as befitting the conventional and expected paternal role as family provider. As the film develops, however, his actions reveal this behavior as inevitably reproducing the indifference and callousness of his society, as revealed in his treatment of his son, Bruno. The film ends ambiguously with an image of father and son holding hands after Antonio has been exposed in his own unsuccessful bid to steal a bicycle. As the screen darkens, he and Bruno disappear into crowd. Critics have suggested that this ending reaffirms the father–son relationship through the son's "miraculous" act of forgiveness, suggesting, again, that familial bonds are a source of spiritual sustenance in a hostile world. Such a reading places great emphasis on the redemptive power of love and of the family as the potential site of altruism and selfless devotion, in contrast to the hostile social milieu. More important, though, the film has dramatized the limitations of conventional family relations, revealing that the family is part of a larger social milieu from which it derives its identity for better or worse.

Figure 50. 'Ntoni (*center*) in *La terra trema* (The Earth Trembles). (Courtesy New York Museum of Modern Art Stills Archive)

Visconti's *La terra trema* (The Earth Trembles, 1948) maintains this director's focus on domesticity as a major locus of social conflict. Based on Giovanni Verga's *I malavoglia,* the film focuses on the fate of a Sicilian family as the son, 'Ntoni Valastro [Fig. 50], defies traditional ways of life and seeks to improve their economic existence. His plans of mortgaging the family home in order to modernize the family's fishing business lands him and the family in conflicts with other fisherman and with the middlemen who profit from their labor. As a consequence of his actions, the Valastros lose their new boat in a storm, their home, and their livelihood, and 'Ntoni is forced to become a laborer for others instead of becoming independent and wealthy as he had planned. The film orchestrates familial relations within the context of economic, cultural, and political issues endemic to the life of the larger Sicilian community and to the internal and external threats to its survival. It is not, however, a polemic on the family. Its focus on the Valastros dramatizes how the family is not an isolated institution but at the intersection of conflicts concerning marriage, tradition and modernity, economic pressures, class differences, and the demands of the community.

Figure 51. The endangered family: Anna (Yvonne Sanson) and Carlo (Amedeo Nazzari) in *Tormento.* (Courtesy New York Museum of Modern Art Stills Archive)

At the film's outset, the family is presented as close and mutually supportive; by its end, the family has disintegrated. 'Ntoni, now aware of the folly of his bourgeois aspirations – aspirations that were tied to the integrity of the family – returns to his life as a fisherman with the blessing of his mother and with a resigned attitude toward his world. In many ways reminiscent of the rural world of Olmi's *L'albero degli zoccoli,* the film stresses the mythical, folkloric dimensions of life in this society, focusing more on the ritualistic aspects of life, on the traditional dimensions of family roles, than on overt opposition to existing social and economic structures. It does, however, portray the pressure on the family to change in the face of new economic conditions and, at the same time, the powerful hold of tradition, which does not guarantee harmony and may even be the harbinger of more conflict. *La terra trema* casts a critical eye on notions of cultural and political change, interrogating political and aesthetic forms that propose simplistic notions of individual agency.

The films of the 1950s are heavily invested in portraits of endangered family life. The popular film *Tormento* (1951), directed by Raffaello Matarazzo, melodramatizes the travails of a married couple, Anna (Yvonne Sanson) and Carlo (Amedeo Nazzari) [Fig. 51], who are, as in a folktale, the victims of a malevolent woman, Anna's step-mother. Through her machinations, every obstacle possible is placed in the path of the couple. He is unjustly accused of murder and imprisoned, and Anna undergoes economic hardship and is forced to relinquish their child. The family is finally reunited only after all these obstacles are eliminated. In the filmmaker's earlier *Catene* (1949) too, economic, juridical, and psychological obstructions to the integrity and continuity of the family drive the narrative. The popularity of such films derives, in part, from their ability to make contact with the changes attendant on post–World War II social life. As Sorlin has written about these successful Matarazzo melodramas:

> [H]e did not change the plots but shifted the dream from the terrible nightmares of sex and violence which had tormented audiences for years to concrete expectations. Fears were still there but softened by a reassuring background. Italy was becoming decisively industrialized, and could get rid of her old family concerns.[13]

As befits melodrama, the films draw on immediate conflicts involving the integrity of the private sphere: marriage, work, forms of entertainment – in short, the struggle for personal survival. The family melodrama has a dual valence. It can dramatize obstacles to survival but can also present them in ways that do not threaten the fragile social order.

In the 1950s, Roberto Rossellini directed Ingrid Bergman (then his wife) in *Viaggio in Italia* (*Strangers,* 1953), a film that explores the disintegrating marital relationship between an upper-middle-class couple during their "voyage to Italy." Earlier in the decade, Michelangelo Antonioni had offered his version of marriage in his *Cronaca di un amore* (*Story of a Love Affair,* 1950), which also veers away from a portrayal of working-class and peasant relations to focus on the upper classes and to provide an insight into the new world wrought by Italy's economic miracle, a world of "the high bourgeoisie, of wealth, fashion, and, fatally fast cars."[14] In its treatment of the couple's relationship, *Cronaca di un amore* dramatizes the estranging effects of modernity within the context of middle-class life. Particularly cogent in the motif of the husband's quest to discover his wife's past is its parallel to the film's concern to complicate the nature of relationships, to distance the spectator from "hope, either from a change in the environment, or pockets within it: faith, the family, love, affection."[15] Like *Viaggio in Italia*, Antonioni's *Cronaca* is further evidence of the 1950s preoccupation with the tenuousness of the domestic sphere.

Of the many films that focus on Italian familial life, Pietro Germi's *Divorzio all'italiana* (*Divorce – Italian Style,* 1961) and *Sedotta e abbandonata* (*Seduced and Abandoned,* 1964) address the complexities of family life and especially the thorny issue of *onore* in the context of Southern customs and sexual politics. Produced and directed at a time before the passing of divorce legislation, *Divorzio* is, nevertheless, not a simplistic satire on then-existing obstacles to divorce. The absence of divorce is rather the pretext to examine intersections among marriage, patriarchy, femininity, and masculinity, and their roles in the legitimation of traditional Sicilian culture. The film is also an instance of the character and popularity of *commedia all'italiana,* which is related to the earlier *commedia dell'arte.* As Bondanella writes,

> Flourishing at the height of what has been termed the "Italian economic miracle," the *commedia all'italiana* lays bare an undercurrent of social malaise and the painful contradictions of a culture of a culture in rapid transition. Moreover, the sometimes facile and optimistic humanitarianism of neorealist comedy is replaced by a darker, more ironic and cynical vision of Italian life.[16]

As is often the case with comedy as opposed to melodrama, its more serious aspects are minimized, ignored, even neglected. In the case of *Divorzio all'italiana,* in its very style the film offers an encyclopedic treatment of Italian life through the lens of familial relations and of the role of cinema in disseminating images of the cultural milieu.

The characters, especially Ferdinando, known as Fefé (Marcello Mastroianni), and his wife, Rosalia (Daniela Rocca) are florid, their movements choreographed in an overstated manner and the delivery of their lines highly stylized. Fefé's reiterative primping before his mirror, his sucking in of his lips, his various affectations – dark glasses, hair-net, slicked-down hair, plucked eyebrows, and assumption of various exaggerated poses – visualize his self-preoccupation, fulfilling his satirization as a decadent and desperate down-at-heels aristocrat. Similarly Rosalia's actions and appearance, embellished by a mustache, are designed to convey the theatricality of her role, first as simpering wife, then as a virago, a besotted paramour to her married former lover, Carmelo, and a wily betrayer of her husband – a theatricality enhanced by the voyeuristic shots that govern Fefé's different perspectives on his wife. In Rosalia's and Fefé's interactions in bed, at the beach, and, above all, in their promenading together through the main street of the village [Fig. 52], the couple offers an image of the hypocrisy of marital life. His fantasies of having his wife boiled in a large soap-making kettle, of burying her alive in the sand at the beach, of having her killed off in public by the Mafia, are merely a prelude to the actions he initiates to get rid of her.

The extended family portrayed includes Fefé's sister, who is courted by the local undertaker; his father, who is a womanizer; and another family headed by Fefé's uncle, who actually owns the family house now, Fefé's father having gambled away his patrimony. In the house also lives Angela, Fefé's cousin, played by Stefania Sandrelli, who becomes the object of Fefé's desire, the motive for his setting in motion a divorce, Italian style.

The main line of the narrative, Fefé's plans to kill Rosalia so that he can be freed of her oppressive demands and gratify his desire for Angela, is interwoven with a number of episodes that reveal the hypocrisy of family life and of conjugal incompatibility. The bedroom scenes dramatize the games attached to conjugal sexual relations, both in Rosalia's importuning to be told how much he loves her and in Fefé's later importuning when he decides to trap her in an illicit relation with her former lover. He pretends to have renewed sexual desire for her only to have her plead the proverbial headache. The scenes where Fefé discovers his unmarried sister in a clinch with her suitor, thus violating the stricture of premarital sexual abstinence, also underscore the repressive sexual politics governing courtship and the family. The pivotal drama, however, is that of Mariannina Terranova, a servant who kills her unfaithful fiancé in the name of honor. She is defended by a lawyer who spells out the code of honor, describing it as "a complex of moral and civic attributes" that makes "a person respectable and respected in a social environment." Her trial sets in motion Fefé's plan to rid himself of the burden of Rosalia. In Fefé's reading of the penal code, he learns that a husband who kills his wife for dishonoring the family through illicit carnal relations receives a sentence from three to seven years, and he weighs this slight sentence against the sentence of a lifelong marriage to Rosalia.

In introducing the importance of the penal code, the film indicates that the law conspires with community morals to maintain intact the concept of *onore,* and that violence is justified in the name of family respectability. The film also indicts the church, as in the scenes in the cathedral when the priest thunders his support of Christian democracy, family values, and the necessary rejection of "sin" and "illicit" sexuality. In fact, after a showing of Fellini's *La dolce vita* (1960), where the town gapes at the gyrating voluptuous body of Anita Ekberg ("the luxurious mammal" as Don Rosario describes her), the priest blames Fefé's cuckolding on the cinema. The Communist Party (shown twice in the film) is portrayed as ineffectual in ameliorating social practices, given the resistance of the community to change. When a communist orates about democracy and women's rights, he confronts the powerful sway of the code of honor, as the workers to whom he speaks refer to women as whores. Once again, the film reveals that the position of women as chaste is central to male dominance and, further, to the integrity of family life.

The film's treatment of family is not confined to the domestic sphere but expands to include a range of social institutions – the law, the church, political parties, and the Mafia. In this respect, the role of the street is central to the film. The people, especially the men on the street, are not mere passive

Figure 52. The family on parade: Fefé (Marcello Mastroianni) and Rosalia (Daniela Rocca) in *Divorzio all'italiana* (*Divorce – Italian Style*). (Courtesy New York Museum of Modern Art Stills Archive)

witnesses to the drama of honor that Fefé has directed: They are part of the staging. Family life becomes a form of theater, directed by the community. The film stresses the controlling dimensions of the townspeople's observing the family drama, as well as their judgmental role in determining the extent of the "crime" and of its "punishment." The emphasis on spectatorship illuminates the double standard that determines distinctions between public appearances and permissible private peccadilloes. Though it is possible to violate sexual codes, such a transgression must remain secret: Once it becomes known, judgment must follow. The emphasis on inside and outside, private and public, conveyed through shots of windows where characters look out and others look in – as when Fefé and his father run to the toilet to peek out of the window at Angela in her bedroom – also reinforces the theatricality of events. This theatricality underscores the role and power of honor as a social performance that is meant to control individuals through the response of the community.

Opera is integral to the text, enhancing the satire. The courtroom is fused with the theatrical plans of Fefé, who directs the performance of infidelity that is to culminate in violence and the intervention of the courts. Several times, operatic music underscores the lawyer's orations. When he and Rosalia attend a performance of *L'elisir d'amore*, Fefé puts his wife on display, and the code of honor is identified with the melodramatic motifs of outraged dignity, betrayal, and death. Opera is not the only cultural text circulating the code: newspapers, oratory and rhetoric, and even cinema contribute. Thus the emphasis on clichés is central to an understanding of the film's satiric treatment of the sexual code of honor that prevail. Rosalia's behavior in her relationship to Fefé – and, later, to Carmelo – is a compendium of clichés about romance. Angela's letters to Fefé are a parody of adolescent clichés. Romanticism itself becomes a vast cliché, not only in the dialogue of the characters but in their posturing. The film suggests that the fetishizing of sexuality, its romanticization, breeds habituation, hypocrisy, and violence. *Divorzio* does not relent in its exposé of the illusions of love everlasting, and the last shot of the film reveals Angela languidly stretched out on the deck of a boat with Fefé as the camera glides to the hands of a young man, presumably their guide, caressing her feet.

Through its satire the film makes clear that family honor is not the cause of familial or community discord but rather the sign and effect of many other complex factors, among which are sexual purity clothed in the aura of romance and political control on the part of the church, the Mafia, and other conservative interests. These interests find their expression (though not exclusively) in the elevation of masculine, namely patriarchal, prerogatives (exemplified by Angela's father beating her, violating her privacy by reading her mail. and forcing her examination by a midwife to establish her virginity). However, as *Divorzio* makes clear it is not only the men who wield power and work to maintain the status quo: The women are complicit in reinforcing, when expedient, the repressive aspects of family life. Rosalia, Mariannina (Carmelo's wife), and even Angela play an active role: No mere victims, they are subversives whenever possible, engaging in dramas of betrayal, threatening the men with cuckoldry, and, in the final analysis, resorting to violence.

In this satire, sex as property and conjugal propriety subtend the inevitable marital infidelity, the hypocritical games that all of the characters are called upon to play. In short, the film provides the viewer with a map to trace the lines of containment or escape. Finally, it is important that the film is told in flashback, allowing the major perpetrator of the "crime" not only to narrate but also to portray himself as victim. His voice-over, fused as it is with the words of the lawyer, ironically becomes a collective voice, like the definition of honor itself. This is visualized at the end when we return to the present and he is greeted like a hero by the townspeople.

The family is not an isolated unit but intimately connected to other social institutions, to economic life, and to more immediate conceptions of sexuality and the body (of the individual and of the nation), as exemplified in the films of the 1960s. Dino Risi's *Il sorpasso* (*The Easy Life,* 1962) is an eclectic film that contains echoes of a number of film genres – *commedia all'italiana,* U.S. beach movies of the 1960s, melodrama, and the road movie.[17] The film portrays the family from two vantage points: the traditional (and extended) family, seen when Roberto visits his relatives, and the family of "the easy life," seen through Roberto's indifferent and unceremonious relations with his former wife and daughter, sugesting his strong attraction to the young woman. Through the dual perspectives of the quizzical, uncertain, and dispossessed Roberto (Jean-Luis Trintignant) and the cynical and reckless Bruno (Vittorio Gassman) in their frantic voyage from Rome to the Riviera, the film offers a critical dissection of various aspects of the Italian social and cultural milieu of the 1960s: the hastened tempo of life, frenetic and alienated leisure activities, and attitudes toward Americanness, tradition versus modernity, work, technology, and sexuality (hetero-, homo-, and asexual).

In an equally encyclopedic vein, but in documentary form, Pier Paolo Pasolini set out to produce an investigation of Italian culture and politics in *Comizi d'amore* (1964) that can also be traced to sexuality and its relation to conceptions of family life, intimately tied to conceptions of the nation. The investigation connects sexual and gendered issues to considerations of Italian legal practices. The film draws on the observations of writer Alberto Moravia, psychiatrist Cesare Musatti, and other intellectuals (including Oriana Fallaci and Camilla Cedernato) to pose certain hypotheses about resistances to change in the Italian social structure. The film, "a portrait of prejudice and conformism . . . also illustrates how widely Italians differ: southerners and northerners, peasants and bourgeoisie."[18]

The documentary techniques utilized in the film are aligned to cinéma vérité, adhering to its more reflexive orientation rather than adopting an objective perspective on the very complicated subject of sexuality and its relation to other social phenomena. Pasolini's persona in the film as the interviewer is as ambiguous as the answers to his questions given by the subjects he chooses to interview. Maurizio Viano says that the film does not have much sociological value: As an interviewer, "Pasolini talks too much and ends up suggesting what the 'correct' answer should be. . . . The value of *Comizi d'amore* is to be found in the documentary representation of men and women, young and old, wearing masks."[19] Throughout the film the viewer is made aware of the interviewer and of the presence of the camera as an opportunity for posturing, for "wearing masks" [Fig. 53].

In the opening scene, Pasolini asks groups of children in both Naples and Palermo if they know where "babies come from." Individuals, extremely aware of the situation, smirk at each other as they most often answer, "from the stork," or provide equally mythical answers. What is important in their comments is not merely the perpetuation of the folklore of childbirth but the hypocrisy, the secrecy, and the constraints of living in a cultural situation where one can neither speak nor act on what one knows. Instead a code of silence prevails, carrying with it a double standard: a conformity to prevailing values in public and a different behavior in private life. The children's behavior suggests that they are toying with the filmmaker, and Pasolini, as interviewer, persists in forcing them to confront the question, as if wanting to ensure that the character as well as the content of their responses registers on the viewer. The film is as important for its style as for the subject matter of the interviews, since the technique calls attention to the question of whether filmmaking produces "truth" or is another instance of posturing, of theatricality and illusion.

Interspersed with their interviews are Pasolini's encounters with various individuals. Following the initial episode, the filmmaker enlists the aid of Moravia and Musatti in discovering how it might be possible to learn people's views on sexuality. The division of the film into episodes allows for the filmmaker to travel to different parts of Italy and interview different groups on the "sexual problem": homosexuality, sexual deviance, marriage, divorce, the role of women, and the effects of the Legge Merlini (Merlini Law), which abolished brothels formerly run by the state. The film ends ironically with scenes of a marriage in northern Italy that highlight the perpetuation of romantic notions of marriage, the economic investments on the part of families, the couple's momentary stardom in the eyes of the community, and the community's investment in the ritual. This final episode focuses in its voice-over on the question of what the future holds in store for the couple.

Whether the interviewees are athletes, young female workers, participants at a dance, women at the beach, peasants in the field (in both North and South), subjects on the street, or a train conductor and a group of male passengers, their responses seem largely to fall into clearly demarcated categories: There is the recognition that things have changed, that traditional customs and patterns of life have changed for the individual, though there is division about whether these acknowledged changes are for better or worse. There seems to be agreement that sex is important, though differences are evident concerning its importance. For example, one of the athletes interviewed says that sex "is important but not critical." The viewer is aware too

Figure 53. Pasolini conducts an interview in *Comizi d'amore* (*Love's Meetings*). (Courtesy New York Museum of Modern Art Stills Archive)

that many of the responses are consonant with the teachings of the church concerning the family and procreation, though the church is not singled out as a target. In the vein of religious teaching (and perhaps with undertones of Fascism), one interviewee (with his son sitting on his shoulders) vehemently insists on the importance of the family to society and the nation in ways that echo the anger of older men on the train, who insist that the new morality and "unnatural" homosexuality in particular should be severely dealt with as inimical to notions of masculinity and procreation. Most generally, in the responses, there seems to be a resistance to homosexuality, ranging from "disgust to pity" (as one of the four entitled sections suggests). What these episodes make clear is that these articulated values of the family and procreation are central to notions of conformity and prejudice. The unexamined and only obliquely invoked issue for all involves a belief in "abnormality," the widespread refusal to confront the threat of "deviance" as central to the maintenance of the status quo.

Reinforcing the feminist discussion on the beach concerning the position of women are scenes in a southern Italian town, where the men reiterate the necessity of women's traditional position yet maintain that women are not inhibited from speaking. When the townswomen are finally urged to speak, they validate that their lives are still determined by gendered, sexual, and familial constraints, and they share the men's judgments on "promiscuity." The film touches on all the major aspects of sexual conformity – chastity, virginity, honor, marriage, divorce, prostitution, and homosexuality – but its investigative mode does not simplistically set up modernity in opposition to tradition. Though the film focuses on limitations of past forms of behavior, it also, through the interviews with people in the city, indicates where modernity, acknowledged by most of the speaking subjects as inevitable, has not produced more "liberating" views on the subject of sexuality. This position is especially evident in the debates on the street about the Legge Merlini and its positive and negative effects on prostitution, as articulated also by several prostitutes.

It would be an injustice to the complex issues raised by the film and by its style to interpret it as a polemic for freer sex and for enlightened relations concerning marriage and divorce: In its confrontation with the various respondents, *Comizi d'amore* does not have a tendentious and sociological agenda so much as a philosophic one involving the question of knowledge. Gramscian concerns are very much in evidence. Consistent with Pasolini's other films, the focus is on the problematic role of knowledge, the persistence and power of commonsensical and therefore fragmented and often uncritical views of the world, as well as on the nature of a certain mode of theatricality, wherein playing received roles seems more advantageous than questioning their efficacy. The film is concerned with knowledge as power and with arriving at an analysis of the persistence of beliefs about family, sexuality, and gendered beliefs rather than with a reformist notion of eradicating "prejudice."

Pasolini's film offers no solutions, though it suggests that thinking differently is an imperative to altering power relations in society. The style also suggests that the audience is necessary to the processes of this interrogation. Through dialogue and close-up, the external audience is made aware of the disjunction between what the interviewees say and how they act, as they laugh at questions, smile coyly, wink at or nudge each other – even refuse to talk. Thus, it is possible to see that the speakers know more than they care to say, that they have access to other forms of knowledge that they do not articulate. This makes it difficult to label what they say as mere lying, though perhaps it is more appropriate to see it as a form of acting, learned as inherent to conformity.

Portraits of the family did not diminish in the Italian cinema of the 1980s and 1990s: If anything, the cinematic family became even more burdened by the past and by political imperatives. The politics of family life is central to Bertolucci's *La tragedia di un uomo ridicolo* (*Tragedy of a Ridiculous Man*,

1981), which traces the effects on a husband and wife of the kidnapping of their son. The father, Primo Spaggiari (Ugo Tognazzi), is a wealthy owner of a cheese and sausage factory. The wife, Barbara (Anouk Aimée), a French-woman and former art student, has surrounded herself with paintings in their lavish home. Their son, Giovanni (Ricardo Tognazzi), has been involved in left-wing causes that are identified with terrorism. The film focuses on a phenomenon of Italian political life that began in the 1960s and continued to the 1980s: the disaffection with existing political compromises identified on the Left with "the roiling frustration many young leftists felt with the Italian Communist Party's move away from revolutionary commitment . . . and out of a certain Catholicism of many of the same young Communists who saw in the figure of Christ a model of anticapitalist renunciation and revolutionary democracy."[20] On the Right, "terrorism" grew out of both a collusion with the state and an enduring conviction that only Fascism could promote civil order in the face of the unrest fomented by movements for social change. Bertolucci's film focuses on youths associated with the Left but is ambiguous concerning the nature of their politics. The tactics of the young radicals in the film involves kidnapping and subsequent requests for ransom.

In *La tragedia di un uomo ridicolo,* the son, not the father, is kidnapped, and the film situates the nature of the politics of terrorism on its periphery. As Robert Kolker writes, the film concentrates "not on the politics and actions of terrorism, but on the politics of its 'victims' and on the psycho-political space that exists between the political activist and the political reactionary."[21] The film opens on the father's birthday, and events are narrated through his voice-over. Surrounded by gifts, he reflects on his past and contemplates the present. In one of the several mirror shots where he confronts the image of himself as a "ridiculous figure," he nonetheless indulges his self-satisfaction with his role in life. Shortly after this introduction, however, the father learns of his son's kidnapping and the request for ransom. For both the husband and wife, money becomes the terrain on which they enact their differing conceptions and expectations about their son's return. The father, who anticipates an enormous ransom to retrieve his son, is reluctant to waste the money if the boy is already dead, whereas the wife spends her time assessing their possessions to calculate the amount that will be required to pay the kidnappers in order to save him. Although they are anguished over paying the ransom, "there is something wrong with the cool ferocity with which they make the attempt; it is somehow devoid of passion, too full of self-righteousness."[22] The obsession with money becomes the vehicle to dramatize their lack of engagement with each other and with their son. The kidnapping sets in motion deep generational differences between the father and son. Primo's character is further revealed in the self-congratulatory way he presents himself as a former partisan and son of the working class. He also postures as a hip modern man, dancing to rock music with the maid in the midst of his misfortune.

As a caricature of the self-made man, he sees no contradiction between his earlier politics and his present position as a member of the ruling class. In his encounters with his workers, he is condescending, willing to seduce his son's young female friend Laura, and contemptuous of Adelfo, the young would-be worker-priest. The kidnapping, in which they are both instrumental (along with Giovanni himself), seems to be more pedagogical than vicious, serving to expose the father's "ridiculousness," his blindness to his position, and his complete misrecognition of the character of his son's politics and those of his son's political colleagues. While he thinks to take them for fools and ultimately to regain the ransom money, they, in turn, have anticipated his actions and turn the tables on him, exposing his self-serving plans. In a scene reminiscent of Pasolini's *Porcile* (*Pig Pen,* 1969), the kidnap plan to ransom Giovanni (narrated by Primo) is intercut with images of a stable with grunting pigs, a dead pig hanging and dripping blood, and another pig in a machine being flayed. This scene underscores Primo's brutality, his willingness to slaughter his son for his own gain. By means of these images, the film exposes that more is at stake than the issue of family – particularly, a father's betrayal of his son. The brutality of the capitalist (the former leftist turned entrepreneur), obscured in sentimental family melodramas, is starkly visualized as inextricably tied to an economic and political context. Kolker comments how the film portrays "a more subtle killing: of conscience, of the ability to make connections between political, the moral and the financial: of the domestic and paternal imperatives that reactionary ideologies always preach."[23]

The game between Primo and the "kidnappers" centers on the uncertainty of whether the son is dead or alive. In pragmatic, businesslike fashion, Primo succumbs too easily to the tantalizing financial possibility that his son is dead and hence anticipates and plans for the return of the ransom money he and his wife have raised. By contrast, Barbara refuses to even entertain the possibility that Giovanni is dead. Her portrait, however, is not idealized. She is fascinated with her image as a distraught and bereft mother, and performs like a chanteuse and auctioneer for decadent members of the aristocracy to gain the requisite funds. Much as she has surrounded herself with paintings at home (against which she is frequently situated), she has aestheticized the crisis. However, it is she who makes sure that Primo's plot is foiled. Thus, as in a comedy, the son is returned and the family is "united" with the young people in possession of the ransom money. The film is rich in ironies: The son who was "dead" returns to life. The wife who had appeared crazed and deluded was after all able to see. The husband who prided himself on his political genealogy has, completely unwittingly, betrayed his political past.

La tragedia is also rich in intertextual allusions to painting, to music (both operatic and rock), and to other films – namely, in its visual allusions to the images and motifs of other political films. The film invokes the texts of

Figure 54. Carlo (Vittorio Gassman) in the opening family photograph of *La famiglia.* (Courtesy New York Museum of Modern Art Stills Archive)

Godard, Pasolini, Visconti (and Bertolucci himself, e.g., *Il conformista,* 1970), filmmakers who complicate familial relations, their connection to the delusions of the ruling classes, generational differences, and the role of cinema in orchestrating these concerns.

In a fictional and more directly historicized treatment, Ettore Scola's 1987 *La famiglia (The Family)* focuses exclusively on familial relations in encyclopedic fashion, weaving them with questions of social class, sexuality, intellectual life, psychology, and economics. The film covers eighty years of Italian history, from 1908 to 1986, and through this period lays bare profound cultural and social changes on the perspective of the Italian family. As Bondanella notes, "The patriarchal family has traditionally represented the focal point of Italian life, but much of its strength has been eroded by the evolution in Italian society and morality that Scola's film narrates."[24] The film begins as it ends, with a photographer taking pictures of a family gathering. Initially the grandfather of the family, Carlo (Vittorio Gassman), presides over three unmarried daughters and a married one, who has just given birth to a boy of the same name, Carlo [Fig. 54]. The film ends with this grandson, Carlo (also played by Gassman), now a grandfather himself, surrounded by a new generation of family.

The photographing of the family – like the pictures on the wall of the apartment – are part of the film's reflexivity, its self-conscious concern with art and with the film itself as portraiture. The film remains consistent in its emphasis on recording. The family is the source of its own mythologies through its recording of its history, and the filmmaker's chronicle is involved in reproducing this record. In this way, the film complicates our understanding of reality, of history, as produced rather than as a reflection of a preexistent reality. Similarly, the film complicates our understanding of *la famiglia*. The treatment of history, although chronological, is selective and dispersed among several characters rather than tightly knit and controlled thtough the perspective of one. The film is not a melodramatic narrative that focuses on the vicissitudes of one family member; rather, it is organized episodically to chronicle moments in the history of this whole bourgeois family.

That family history is narrated in part by the younger Carlo, in the present, recounting in voice-over the circumstances of his birth and tracing events in the life of the family to the present time. His grandfather was a professor at the University of Rome; his father, Aristide, was an official at the Ministry of Education; and Carlo becomes a high-school teacher, later a professor himself. The family, thus identified with learning, is also shown to have artistic leanings: Carlo's father was also a painter, and his mother, who had studied singing, sings him and his brother to sleep with operatic arias. (Thereafter, his brother Giulio writes a novel, which Carlo neglects to read until fifty years later.) When the family is gathered at the festivities for Carlo's baptism, the camera pans and studies their faces as his mother sings, in French and Italian, the plaintive air "Plaisir d'amour." (The film's references to painting, opera, popular music, photography, and eventually, television – including a televised vignette from Marilyn Monroe's marriage to Arthur Miller – are, as in Scola's other films, a recognition that the family is not an isolated institution but intimately tied to other social and cultural establishments.)

The film treats the passage of time and memory; hence its use of a narrator and of flashback. Carlo's voice-over narration also absolves the film's treatment of history as focusing on the world inside the home: The history within is, after all, tied to the external world. Moreover, the narration, like the claustrophobic concentration of all the action within the walls of the apartment, underscores the film's preoccupation with history from the perspective of family life. The narration is punctuated by shots of the apartment's central corridor, which not only separates the rooms but records the passage of time: The corridor, like a stage set, is largely empty to begin with; then it is inhabited, usually by the appearance of children, who create bridges among the different generations and their different concerns.

The female side of family life is presented in the film's portrait of the three unwed sisters – Margherita, Luisa, Ornella – who argue constantly, threatening to kill themselves (reminiscent of Poggioli's *Le sorelle Materassi*). Their quarrels are a reiterative motif in Carlo's growth to manhood and accepted as a fixture of family life. Though these figures play a subordinate role, they are emblematic of the older generation and of the frustrated responses of its women to the lack of social alternatives, particularly for those among them who were unmarried and dependent. The sisters provide a contrast to the next generation of women, especially Beatrice and Adriana.

The portrait of the old Carlo is less psychologically nuanced than that of his sons. He remains distant as a strict patriarch, known by his authoritarian stance, his cultural values, and his stern morality; however, there is a disjunction between the image of himself he offers to his sons and the suggestion of a certain eccentricity. Neither of his sons carry themselves with the same assurance and authority. A major motif in the life of the family is the combative relationship between the two brothers, Carlo and Giulio, the latter singled out by his father as the weak one, whom Carlo must look after.

Carlo's adulthood is introduced through his giving literature lessons to a young woman, Beatrice. He corrects her reading of the critic De Sanctis, insisting dogmatically that De Sanctis did not "attempt" to unite literature and society. The outside world enters the home as Beatrice indicates the rise of Fascism by reference to one of her professors, Tabanelli, who holds that the purpose of art is to "serve the nation." Fascism and its impact on the family are further developed through the character of Enrico, who rails to Carlo that they must do something to stop its spread, though Carlo is less concerned. Enrico will later be a journalist for an anti-Fascist paper in France, go to fight Franco during the Spanish Civil War, and die, leaving a wife and daughter.

These events are not shown directly but relayed, like all of the news that involves the world outside the house, through the telephone, telegrams, or letters. This strategy is an instance of the film's recognition of connections between modernity and the media that have altered family relations. Even more, the strategy ironically underscores the enclosed nature of family life, where public events enter the domestic sphere from the outside as if disconnected from the private dramas. At this point in his life, Carlo meets Adriana, Beatrice's sister, with whom he falls in love almost immediately when she arrives to tell him that Beatrice cannot attend her lesson due to illness. However, Adriana does not succumb to his passion and desire for her to stay with him; instead, she chooses to go to Paris to study music – yet another instance of changing patterns concerning women's role, changes that Carlo in his romanticism refuses to acknowledge. The two fight over his unwillingness to let her go, he asserting in conventional fashion that she would stay if she loved him. They have an angry farewell on the stairs of the apartment – one of several they will have throughout the film. Thus, Carlo's negative attitudes toward the question of women and their independence is underscored, and in the next episode, he is seen married to the more conventional Beatrice and with two children (in the corridor), Paolino and Maddalena.

His continuing romantic attachment to Adriana is dramatized when she calls the family from Paris and he conjures up a radiant image of her, one of the many fantasy moments in the film. It is also through a phone call that news of Enrico's anti-Fascist activities is received, and immediately thereafter, Carlo's Uncle Nicola appears wearing the uniform of a *squadristo* and creating a crisis in the house: He plays hide-and-seek with Paolino, but as the child follows him – responding to each question "Where are you?" that he is right there – Nicola unthinkingly ignores him. The boy becomes terribly upset and has to be put to bed by his grandmother, who sings an aria from *La Bohème* to him. In its understated way, this episode conjoins the public and the private, the family and social institutions. Nicola's behavior is emblematic of the Fascist world outside in its callous cruelty and lack of awareness of what has gone wrong.

The film also introduces the increasing signs of modernity via the technological appurtenances that appear in the home. The family listens to a concert by Adriana gathered around the radio. Later Carlo and Adriana, visiting while the family is on holiday, will watch the sinking of the *Andrea Doria* on the television. At the end of the war, Carlo is back at his job at the high school and teaching (like his grandfather) at the university. Enrico has died in Spain, but Giulio returns from military service in a state of shock and refuses to leave his room. Carlo is unsympathetic to his brother's condition, forgetting his father's order to look after him. Again, instead of creating an official and monumental history of Italy, the film, through the lens of the family, stresses the nature of everyday life from the vantage point of middle-class existence. Although not a polemic on the rise and fall of Fascism, *La famiglia* manages, through its portrait of family conflict, indifference, and hostility, to suggest connections between the public and the domestic spheres. The consequences for the family of the war are also indicated by reference to its reduced economic situation. When Adelina, the former maid, comes to visit with groceries, she notices that the family has had to pawn its silver and piano to make ends meet, and that its food is ersatz and meager. Giulio's problems are also solved in the return of Adelina, who cares for him as if he were a child. The two are married, and now another change is marked in that the family has absorbed a former member of the working class.

Carlo's character and the history of his generation and of his family come into clearer focus as Adriana comes to visit with her French fiancé, Jean-Luc (Philippe Noiret). Through the encounter between Carlo and Jean-Luc, Carlo's discontents about his marriage and his politics are revealed, as is his lingering attachment to Adriana. Jean-Luc describes life in Italy as exhilarating for Italians, who are now compelled to confront new challenges. Carlo disagrees with everything Jean-Luc says about changes in Italy, fights with his wife, and leaves the table in a rage. The changes that Carlo resists involve women who work, young men like Paolino who cannot find a niche in the work world of their parents, and separation and divorce among the younger members of the family. The apartment itself appears larger as the family gets smaller. Carlo's mother has died, then one by one his unmarried sisters die, the young people leave home, and finally Carlo is alone after Beatrice's death. The film's last episode takes place at Carlo's eightieth birthday. There he confesses to his brother that he did not read Giulio's manuscript "The Waste" until recently and experiences remorse because it was a beautiful book and he had judged it without reading it and lied to Giulio about its poor quality. The film has taken the viewer through almost a century of familial and political events, births and deaths, domestic and public disasters and changes. Instead of alternating between public events and their impact on the interior life of the family, it has offered a view of everyday life and dramatized how the conception of family is responsible for and responsive to the world beyond. Uppermost is the notion of the middle-class family as a constant source not only of a sense of community but also of antagonisms. These emerge in different forms with each new generation, posing the question of the fate of the family – and of the larger culture to which it bears a relation – given the pressures it is portrayed as increasingly having to confront.

Films produced in Italy in the 1980s and 1990s focused more and more on the family as an index to political, cultural, and aesthetic changes, seeing these transformations as connected to emerging gender and class differences in the social positions of men and women, to new conceptions of sexuality that are not always salubrious, and to generational conflicts between parents and children that betoken profound differences and misunderstandings. These changes are indicative as well of the dissolution of conceptions of the family as the basis of the Italian nation, its history, and its representations of citizenship, continuity, and morality.

CHAPTER NINE

A Cinema of Childhood

R epresentations of childhood and adolescence have played a major role in Italian cinema. Figures of childhood, tied to representations of the family, serve as a window to another, less familiar, way of exploring and viewing the social landscape. Evolving since the cinema's beginnings, the cinematic child and adolescent have functioned variously as signifiers of innocence in a corrupt world, melodramatic images of martyrdom tied to the disintegration or regeneration of society, figures of nostalgia for a lost past, signs of generational warfare in society, and as means of providing a different and distanced perspective on familiar social situations. This chapter explores the role cinema has played in disseminating and interrogating images of the young.

Sometimes the young person is the unknown, a tabula rasa to be written on by social forces, a medium for cultural common sense. At other times, he or she is the locus of knowledge, offering a perspective that challenges the common sense of the adult world. In some instances, especially in films of the interwar era, the child, more often than the adolescent, is an unknowing victim, whereas in neorealism, he or she is a knowing victim. In the former narrative, the child is viewed through the lens of the adult world; in the latter, the child as knowing victim governs the perspective. In all instances, the child is an index to cultural knowledge – who has it and how it is shared with the audience. Some films involve portraits of the child within the family as an index to domestic stability or conflict, but a significant number focus on schooling and on the various ways in which young people are either temporarily or permanently in conflict with authority. A smaller group of films involves the world of young people who live on the street, dramatizing their implied or direct relation to existing social life.

In order to appreciate the discursive ways in which young people are represented in the visual arts and particularly in the cinema, it is necessary to rehearse some of the ways in which childhood was represented in earlier cultural forms. In the Middle Ages, as Philippe Ariès has written, "the idea of childhood did not exist,"[1] or at least it existed in quite different terms from those of modernity, judging by paintings and printed manuals. Not that people did not recognize the presence of infants and children, but they did not examine that childhood was a category very loose defined. While there was a recognition of children's need for affection, there was generally little distinction between children and adults. Childhood as a specialized area of sociological and psychological focus was nonexistent, though there was certainly a sense of the importance of the younger members of society and a concern for their nurture. For example, in paintings prior to the Renaissance, distinctions between childhood and adulthood were imprecise, since "as soon as the child abandoned his swaddling-band, he was dressed just like other men and women of his age."[2]

Images of the child are found in the Middle Ages in religious paintings of the Virgin and infant Jesus, as well as in mythological paintings, most often in the figure of Cupid, or in illustrated manuscripts as angels "singing and playing musical instruments."[3] Generally, the attitude that seemed to prevail was that infants and babies were anonymous and hardly distinguishable from the adults to which they were likened. For example, in relation to games, village festivals, and "wedding feasts and dances," children were presented as little adults. This attitude was to undergo a change by the seventeenth century thanks to the writings of the humanists and, furthermore, to the emergence of a different attitude toward childhood promulgated by the Jesuits, who "who were to dominate the education of the aristocracy and the richer middle-class . . . based on the concepts that childhood was innocent and that it was the duty of adults to preserve this innocence."[4] Such practices as discipline, separation of the sexes, and instruction in morality and chastity were increasingly inculcated as a means of maintaining this belief in youthful innocence.

Conceptions of childhood changed with the advent of modernity. By the Renaissance, group forms of (male) education were developed, rather than individual instruction by a parish priest or monk, although young boys were not segregated by age. However, by the seventeenth century, distinctions among different ages began to emerge evident in young people's clothing, in their behavior, and in their forms of education. Increasingly too the preoccupation with the sexual behavior of the young was monitored by parents, religious counselors, and physicians. For the rising middle classes, the child became an object of portraiture, investigation, and social concern. By the eighteenth and nineteenth centuries, changing notions of the family, social class, sexuality, medicine, normality and abnormality, and demography were to introduce new categories and problems governing the concept of the child.

Many of these changes were inspired by the new materialism, although among the lower classes the situation had not changed significantly: "Among the poor the old attitudes lingered on – poverty bred proximity, and so forced adults and children to share the same world."[5] Increasingly, childhood became an area of intense interest touching questions of the psyche, sexuality, and initiation into responsibilities. Moreover, increasingly, a distinction became evident between childhood and adolescence. In particular, education became a major force in the definition of and initiation into patterns of work, sexuality, leisure, and national identity. Foucault writes that "Around the schoolboy and his sex there proliferated a whole literature of precepts, opinions, observations, medical advice, clinical cases, outlines for reform, and plans for ideal institutions."[6]

Also, though the childhood of the poorer classes was considerably shorter than that of the middle and upper classes, some change was evident by the latter half of the nineteenth century, due both to liberal reforms that stressed the importance of literacy and to new forms of production that increasingly rendered obsolete industry's need for certain kinds of cheap (child) labor. These changes were, of course, determined by particular economic exigencies, particularly in rural areas. However, the demand for specialized skills, because of the increased importance of technology, tended to reinforce the prolongation of childhood and adolescence and thereby mandate and reinforce fine-tuned distinctions between youth and maturity. As J. H. Plumb reminds us, "After World War II huge segments of the population, female as well as male, remained in the educational system to twenty-one and beyond, and the number increases every few years."[7]

The social revolutions of the twentieth century were central to considerations of the role of youth, insofar as young people are confronted by antagonisms between the necessity of their coming of age and the irrelevance of large numbers of their group to productive work and any other form of social utility except consumerism. Increasingly, the popularization of childhood and adolescence as a problematic area of social concern was evident in the clinical literature, creative writing, and various arts of the nineteenth and early twentieth century, focusing on the need for forms of education that prepared young people to meet the needs of their society in relation to the family as well as the broader society and nation. Hence it is not surprising that in fiction, in manuals on education, and in the cinema, the milieu of the school is emphasized, not only as a place of detention, boredom, physical and mental suffering but also as a place where social amelioration is necessary to produce a different social order.

In the twentieth century, in particular, the young were both courted and abused, studied and reviled, blamed for the degeneration of moral values and focused on as a pivotal force in the regeneration or degeneration of national values and morality. In the period before World War I, the image of youth was still tied in many ways to the morality, social values, patriotism, religiosity, and conformity that were inherited from the previous century. In the interwar years, radical changes were in evidence, involving challenges to authority, to modes of discipline, to accepted forms of sexual behavior, and to parental control – a situation not unfamiliar to present attempts to explore the position of young people in society.

The relation between youth and modernity can be brought even more sharply into focus if one examines the rise of Fascism in Italy. Youth was a primary target for its ideologues and planners, and sufficient evidence has been mounted to describe the ways that Italian Fascism divided its youth groups along the lines of gender and age, and even more regarding the ways it sought to identify Fascism as a youthful movement in its revolutionary zeal and in its idea of the need to rejuvenate Italy. Not only did Fascism reiterate the notion of being fruitful and multiplying in the interests of the nation, underscoring the need to expand the population, but it connected the concept of youth to vitality, and vitality to modernity. The photographs of the era, its advertisements, and its newsreels intensified the sense that children were in every way the backbone of the regime. It must be noted, however, that many of the "reforms" concerning youth were made with the approval of the Catholic church, which had served ongoingly as the promoter of the family and of education for the enhancement of Italy as a Christian society. This is not to say that children were granted the status of adulthood and of decision makers: The reforms in education, the emphasis on the family and reproduction, and the focus on a "new Risorgimento" identified with Fascism all subordinated youth to larger social interests. However, as has so often been articulated in recent years, Fascist public policy and spectacle were only one side of a complicated situation, since Fascism never succeeded in totally organizing the populace and gaining total adherence. A look at the documentaries produced by LUCE, which highlighted the relation of youth to education, the military, and to sports, reveals not only the propagandistic aims of the regime but a portrait of a world that does not seem far removed from other European and American images of youth as the hope of the future.

In the post–World War II era, the situation altered due, in large measure, to the experiences of war, dislocation, family upheaval, and widespread poverty. Given the greater emphasis in neorealism on social misery, the image of the child is presented less often within a sheltered environment and becomes a window, a witness to and an actor in, economic and social suffering. (This image will remain even to the 1990s with such films as Gianni Amelio's *Il ladro di bambini* [1992].) However, with the victory of the Christian Democrats in 1948, and then later in the midfifties with the beginning of the so-called economic miracle, there was a concerted attempt to revert to more traditional, middle-class images of the family and youth and to repudiate the images of poverty and social malaise portrayed through the immediate postwar cinema. Films (and posters for them) reveal an uneasiness about the containment of youth and the future of the family. In the literature and films of the "*anni di piombo* (the leaden years, signifying terrorist activities from the 1960s to the 1980s)," as Beverly Allen has described, we see that in the portrayal of young terrorists "they relinquish their subjective location within the body politic they are attacking both by their so-called perversions and with the lead of their bullets and bombs. Not only are they not children anymore, they are also not Italians."[8] What often emerges is the notion of youngsters as a contested terrain, an indication of a society that regards its young as potential consumers – and, ironically, in the very process of consumption, a threat to social order.

The Italian cinema's portraits of children offer insights into the ways popular culture disseminates the common sense of folklore. In discussing the Neapolitan silent films of Elvira Notari, Giuliana Bruno comments on the filmmaker's uses of Gennariello, a street urchin drawn from prefilmic Neapolitan folklore. (He is a figure later invoked in the *Lutheran Letters* by Pier Paolo Pasolini, a filmmaker whose stories, writings, and films were intensely addressed to the struggles of the young, especially to youth of the underclass.) Gennariello is a street child (played in Notari's films by her son Edoardo) who is "poor but fundamentally honest, sympathetic, uneducated but smart, intuitive, and street-wise character who often came to people's aid."[9] Here in her dramatization of the street life and sufferings of the poor, Notari's films are at a remove from the idealizations and innocence of childhood, suggesting that the films of De Sica (e.g., in *Sciuscià*) and Rossellini (e.g., in *Paisà*), with their streetwise children, have a precedent in earlier Italian cinema. Like the characters in these later films, Notari's Gennariello "is the quintessence of the good warm-hearted side of the Neapolitan urchin, a typical visualization of a *lumpenproletarian* youth who lives in the streets and in the poor homes of Naples but is neither a delinquent or corrupted."[10] One might also add that he does not resemble the images of dire victimization evident in *Cabiria*.

The early sequences of *Cabiria* place much on the family prior to the eruption of Mount Etna. Traditional images of the child Cabiria as innocent and playful are evident as she sits in the garden playing with Cresa, her nurse. Scenes with her family invoke a sense of harmony, as evidenced in paintings and Roman sarcophagi of family groupings. However, what is stressed after the volcanic eruption and Cresa's attempts to save the helpless child – who is ultimately in danger of being thrown as a sacrifice into the fiery statue of Moloch, along with other children – is the notion of the young child as an innocent whose purity is threatened by barbaric forces. (This scene is also serves as a reminder of ancient rituals of the disposing of young females, who were considered unproductive.)

These early vignettes of the rescue of Cabiria set the stage for the film's implicit dramatization of the difference between the civilized Roman culture and that of African barbarism. That Cabiria is saved by the noblewoman Sofonisba, a pagan, complicates this binary distinction. Although there are few scenes of interaction between Cabiria and Sofonisba, the identification of Sofonisba with passionate excess leading to her suicide contrasts with the child-like, that is, innocent and virginal, way in which Cabiria's role is conceived even as an adult, dependent on her family, her nurse, on Sofonisba, but above all on the physical powers of Maciste and the chaste devotion of Fulvius. Thus, the film seems to provide a safety valve whereby Italian (and upper-class) femininity can be seen in the traditional context of the national imagination, tied to images (as at the end of the film) of the glorification of Romanità – a conception of the Italian nation identified with its glorious Roman past that the Fascist regime was to exalt. In this way, the character of Cabiria, presented through images of her childhood and of her childlikeness, is identified with the notion of woman as innocent but potentially endangered figure, to be redeemed like the nation itself.

During the Fascist regime the figure of the child, especially the boy, assumes importance not only in the films produced by LUCE but through the coordinated efforts with youth groups, which were organized by age. These films, largely documentaries, focused on children's pastimes, organized sports, and eradicating juvenile delinquency. According to Elaine Mancini, they were "designed to instill the Fascist spirit, to teach ideals and to enforce discipline."[11] Of the fiction films that feature youth, one of the few that directly addressed the coming of Fascism was a popular film, Blasetti's *Vecchia guardia* (*The Old Guard*, 1934), in which a young boy, Mario, becomes a heroic martyr to the Fascist cause. The film revolves around the struggles between the socialists and Fascists, socialism being identified with incompetence and disorganization in relation to all the social organizations – municipal government, health care, and the schools. The film focuses not only on the communal bonds among the Fascists, which will lead them triumphantly to the March on Rome, but also on family life. Their aggressive, militant activities, presented in various scuffles with socialists in the shops and on the streets, are justified in terms of the mismanagement of government and industry, the disregard for the care of the sick and the young, and the paralysis of education – all attributed to the Socialist Party.

The pivotal role is played by young Mario, an adolescent whose family is convinced of the efficacy of Fascism, as is he himself. Presented as precocious, Mario loves to repair clocks. (The notion of time is doubly presented in the film: through his youth, symbolizing the coming of a new, modern, and better order, and through his association with the repair of timepieces, identified with the new time of Fascism.) The film presents him as eager and bright, as committed to the values of the older Fascists, but it also uses him as a melodramatic figure in that he becomes the sacrificial victim to the callousness and indifference of the socialists, who would frustrate significant social changes. The film was not received unproblematically, since representing earlier Fascist history carried the danger of "raking up unwanted memories" for those in authority.[12] Mancini sees parallels between Blasetti's film and the German *Hitlerjunge Quex* (1933), though Blasetti claimed not to have seen the latter. Their similarities may reside mainly in the appeal to and emphasis on youth as a source of social and political transformation, not in their styles.

The Blasetti film opens with a titled prologue that exalts *squadrismo* (marauding bands of black-shirted adherents to Fascism terrorizing the populace) and situates the time of the narrative as preliminary to the March on Rome (1922). The arrival at a medical clinic of a truck bearing an older man injured by the socialists introduces the motif of justifiable violence in the interests of the "new" as opposed to the "old" guard. It is at the clinic that we meet one of the major protagonists of the film, Dr. Cardini (Gianfranco Giachetti), whose son, Roberto (Mino Doro) is a Black Shirt.

Returning home after a particularly strenuous night fighting the enemies of Fascism, Roberto finds his younger brother, Mario (Franco Brambilla), working on a clock. (The young boy's penchant for machines will symbolize the emergence of the modern order identified with Fascism.) Mario reveres his older brother, and the family is a model of domestic unity, in contrast to disruptive external forces. The mother is submissive and totally supportive of her sons, whose physician father will ultimately join them in their struggle to realize Fascism. The other important woman in the film is Maria (Barbara Monis), a neighbor who is a schoolteacher and Roberto's fiancée. Her role as teacher is fundamental to the film's emphasis on pedagogy as central to reorganizing Fascist culture.

The film is not silent on expectations of productive work and orderly workers for the new world identified with Fascism. At Dr. Cardini's clinic, the physician is hampered by the refusal of his employees to submit to the necessity and discipline of work. Instead they go on strike, with no regard for the necessary services performed by the hospital. The implication, however, is that the workers are less to blame than are the leaders of their union, who are in league with socialists. The local government is corrupt: The officials turn a deaf ear to Cardini's requests for help, spending their time at public events such as festivals, or in plain idleness.

The aggressive tactics of the *squadristi* in "ameliorating" this hopeless situation are portrayed in a barbershop scene, where a Fascist, Aristide, gets revenge on a socialist by shaving off half his beard while others look on and laugh. Violence erupts as a group of provoked socialist agitators throw rocks through the window of the barbershop, and a young boy is injured, thus "proving" their aggressiveness, indifference to young people, and the disruptiveness of their opposition to the Fascists. The legendary castor-oil treatment is meted out to one of the socialists when he goes to the pharmacy to get medication for laryngitis, and later castor oil is given to the hospital workers, who are thus "urged" to return to work.

In parallel fashion, education is also under siege, since the town supervisor has canceled classes and locked the school. However, Roberto, Maria, and another man reopen the school, having gotten the keys from the custodian. The climax of the conflict among Fascists, socialists, and bureaucrats occurs in a street battle where Mario is shot, a martyr to the Fascist cause. His death becomes the rallying point for the Fascists. The boy's body is draped with the Fascist banner and an elegiac scene follows, focusing on the mother's and Maria's bereavement. Mario is given a hero's funeral that mobilizes the community, The Black Shirts march through the streets, singing, "Today no one stays at home, Mario is with us." The film ends in a spectacle of lights, flags, and patriotic music, a prefiguring of the Fascist March on Rome.

Vecchia guardia offers a call to unity and aggressive collective action against socialists and the bourgeoisie, legitimated by young martyrdom. The rhetoric appears aimed at the film audience, drawing on the affective appeal of violence against young people seen as victims of a malign bureaucracy. The audience is asked to witness the repeated images of disorganization and subversion represented by the authorities in the local governing bodies, the factories, the schools, and by the socialists in particular. These perceived threats culminate in the death of Mario, which functions as a means of rallying the community against its enemies. The impact of his death, seen as martyrdom to the cause of Fascism, is underscored through the reiterated images first of women and then of the entire community grieving. Young people are thus central to the Fascist mission, and their violation a justification for retaliation. The clock that Mario seeks to repair, identified with the new time of Fascism, can now only be fixed by the Black Shirts and by the community that stands behind them. The affective appeal of the film rests with the child, a victim of a pernicious and unhealthy world in need of regeneration. He is a model of devotion to family, precocious and perceptive about the future, and a reproach to those who do not understand the call for a social awakening.

Two later feature films, one comic, the other melodramatic, offer different and more complex portrayals of young people: Rafaelle Matarazzo's *Il birichino di papà* and De Sica's *I bambini ci guardano*. Both made in the last years of the war, they use the child as a window through which to gaze reproachfully on the failure of social and familial unity. *Il birichino di papà (Papa's Little Devil*, 1943) has been identified as a comedy that undermines Fascist ideology and its practices,[13] and in its linking of the school to the family, it also draws on melodrama. The film centers on the socially disruptive actions of a young girl, Nicoletta (Chiaretta Gelli), who is not innocent of the machinations of the adults. The film can be read as a critique of educational policies, particularly as they affect young girls subject to the discipline of the school authorities; but the film, rather than focus solely on the school, also links the vicissitudes of young people to the family. An examination of the "subgenre" of schoolgirl films from the 1930s to the 1940s reveals changing relations to forms of consent and coercion that can be connected to prevailing educational practices as promulgated first by Minister of Education Giovanni Gentile and later by his successor, Giuseppe Bottai.

Since education was a high priority for Fascism in the regime's attempts to Fascistize youth and especially to domesticate young women, it is not surprising that the era's films should focus on the school as source of dramatic conflict. However, an examination of such school films as *Mädchen in Uniform* (*Girls in Uniform*, 1931), *Zéro de conduite* (*Zero for Conduct*, 1933), and *Tom Brown's School Days* (1940), among others, reveals that the school film is not unique to the Fascist era. Involving threats to young people – and, hence, threats to conceptions of the family and the nation – this subgenre has been a cinematic form that crosses national boundaries. The necessity of affective investment in the process of the socialization of the young is not restricted to Fascism but inheres in all forms of nationalism insofar as these are connected to the role of the family and of education.

Common to all of these films that feature the vicissitudes of young people in the school setting is melodrama. Ironically, it is through melodrama that one can locate the strategies for consensus building and also the impossibility of total adherence. Identifying these tensions is not a matter of excavating hidden discourses but of tracking how melodrama and its "structures of feeling" are part of a "constant reworking of values . . . elements of a wider and more general signifying system" that inheres in the social text.[14] This signifying system is not purely formal and abstract but produced out of a social "symbology" that draws on familiar and contradictory folkloric elements circulating in the culture at large.

Il birichino di papà is a pastiche of traditional and contemporary images, drawing on the school, the family, femininity, and youth. In orchestrating these various elements, the film is reminiscent of Hollywood cinema, with its focus on youth, its emphasis on familial values, its uses of spectacle, its populism, and "its celebration, in *modern* images, of spiritual community and conservative values."[15] But the incorporation of Americanism can be read bivalently, to accommodate to Italian and even Fascist values or, conversely, to their critique. Nicoletta, the protagonist of *Il birichino*, is a counterpart to Deanna Durbin, a youthful Hollywood star, associated with the movie musical, who was popular with Italian audiences of the time and with a cinema that was identified with and celebrated youthfulness. Durbin's persona is a source of misrule and reconciliation within her films' narratives: Her character functions to unsettle the hardened structures of family and social institutions and to inject the illusion of spontaneity and freedom into the reigning order of family and social institutions by including the world of entertainment. The emphasis on the expressive dimensions of song links entertainment to the utopian desire for the management of crisis, but in the process the terms of the crisis are made manifest as well. In Materazzo's film, the rebellious character of its youthful musical protagonist is addressed in the context of the repressive functions of the educational system.[16]

The film opens with light and frenetic music conjoined to images of carriage wheels, horses' hoofs, and of a young girl in the carriage singing. This opening stresses movement and energy, attributes that will be associated with Nicoletta, in contrast to the constraining and static views of the adults who seek to control her life and behavior. (These images will reoccur at the film's end.) The scene then shifts to a large house, seen from outside and then from within. (Opposing images of inside and outside are central to the film.) Nicoletta's father and aunt are arguing about her lack of conformity to prevailing conceptions of femininity. The father, Leopoldo, calls her "Nicola" (a boy's name) and defends her right to act like a boy, though he regards his other daughter, Livia (Anna Vivaldi), as representing a more acceptable form of feminine behavior and appearance. Thus, youthful femininity is at stake in the unraveling of the dramatic conflict and tied to the film's exploration of both family and school life.

The family is in a state of disorder, awaiting the arrival of the aristocratic Della Bellas, whose son Roberto (Franco Sanderia) is betrothed to Livia. The first view of the Della Bella family – mother, son, and daughter – in their car on the road presents them as conforming to the prevailing image of upper-class snobbery. The daughter, Irene, complains about having to visit the country and predicts that Robert will be bored with Livia. Their car is sent off the road, however, when passed by the singing Nicoletta in her carriage – foreshadowing her later conflicts with and victory over them.

The Marchesa Della Bella, highly critical of Nicoletta's behavior, recommends that the girl be placed in a school where she can be disciplined and where the marchesa, being connected with the school, can survey the girl's progress. One of the incidents that motivates the marchesa's suggestion is Nicoletta's discussion of a horse giving birth. Shocked, she insists that the girl be properly disciplined to enter society, and that this school is just the place for such a preparation. Nicoletta gets momentary revenge when a rolled-up rug she sends down the stairs reaches its destination – the marchesa.

In her room, Nicoletta complains to her father about Livia's going to live at the marchesa's, but he tells her "to be a man" – that is, to submit to authority as he does. Their conversation is interrupted by fireworks that Nicoletta has arranged in Livia's honor – another proleptic sign of the trouble to be engineered by the girl.

Nicoletta goes off to the school, despite her father's misgivings and her nightmares about the school. In images reminiscent of scenes from Sagan's

Mädchen in Uniform, a film critical of the Prussian quality of German upper-class schools, *Il birichino* focuses on the regimentation of the girls, showing a montage of feet, bodies, and systematized movement. According to Reich, the images of the school "reek with militaristic connotations," which she finds in the use of shadows, the choreography of the girls' regimented movement, and the clicking sounds of their heels.[17] In class, Nicoletta fails to answer teachers' questions and is repeatedly given a "zero." In contrast to the class-room scenes, the girls are also shown less formally, singing and lounging about until the moment of leisure is disrupted by a teacher. Nicoletta is called to the office: There she finds her sister, who complains to her about her trou-bled relations with Roberto. Nicoletta, in turn, complains about the school, explaining that she does not cooperate with her teachers because she does not want to give them any satisfaction.

A scene of Livia and Roberto quarreling reveals domestic strife between the couple as a consequence of his womanizing. Familial conflict is paralleled in the ensuing scene by conflict at school, instigated by Nicoletta. An audi-ence is assembled outdoors to watch the students perform as they parade out of the school building, singing a song in praise of the curriculum. Nicoletta, however, is perched on a window ledge outside the building and, in full view of the assembled audience, is singing loudly and energetically about the op-pressiveness of school life. Her father, one of the guests, is unperturbed by her youthful prank, but the principal is not pleased, and Nicoletta is confined to the infirmary. She escapes, leaves school, and goes to her sister's house. En-tering the house, she finds Roberto in a compromising situation with Maria-nella, his former fiancée. Nicoletta gives Roberto a tongue lashing and goes upstairs to pack Livia's clothes. Determined to remedy her sister's situation, she calls Giulio Marchi, a lawyer and family acquaintance, who agrees to help her and Livia.

The film's denouement takes place at the Della Bella home, where the lawyer informs the gathered family of Livia's plans for divorce and of Nico-letta's demands that she be allowed to withdraw from school. Roberto prom-ises to reform, and he and Livia reconcile. Nicoletta is permitted to leave the school and to return home. Thus, her resourceful actions in behalf of her sis-ter and herself are rewarded. The treatment of this unconventional young girl has served as the vehicle to probe existing social practices within permissible bounds.

Il birichino di papà is a critique of the repressiveness of school disci-pline and of the repression of young people. It is also, as in films by Camerini, a critique of upper-class decadence, irresponsibility, and cruelty, especially in the flouting of the integrity of the family. The marchesa is the bridge between the school and the family, linking them in their oppressiveness. By contrast, Leopoldo is representative of a more enlightened paternal attitude toward familial relations and, in particular, toward unconventional feminine behavior. Within his family, Nicoletta is permitted her rebelliousness and her flouting of rigid gender typing of girls.

The paternal family, with its benign character of Leopoldo, is likely to be read as less repressive than the maternal one, identified as it is with the rigid and sadistic marchesa and her daughter, Irene. Significant in this juxtaposition is how the film can be seen to represent, on the one hand, a critique of authoritarianism, the repression of youth, and the constraints on feminine behavior, and on the other hand, a reaffirmation of patriarchy as less repressive and more enlightened, as offering (an illusion of) freedom. This reading seems to capture both the sense in which the film offers a critique of the status quo represented by institutions but also remains within the parameters of familialism, offering both an apparent critique of Fascist practices while adhering to the traditional position of the family, though in more benevolent terms. It is in this context that the role of melodrama in relation to comedy becomes important. The melodrama in the film arises from Nicoletta's persecution at the hands of a woman – the marchesa – and the youthful protagonist is also female. Thus, the androgynous child Nicoletta presents an unsettling and unresolved image of femininity that exceeds conventional cinematic portraits of young girls within the context of the family and the school.

In De Sica's *I bambini ci guardano* (*The Children Are Watching Us,*1942), the melodrama focuses again on problematic female figures, and particularly on feminine perfidy, but much of the film's perspective arises from the gazings of young Pricò at antagonistic relations between his mother and father and at brutal and eroticized relations between his mother and her lover. As its title suggests, the film insistently explores the role of looking, and in so doing it includes performances (such as a puppet show and later a magic show), refers to the movies, and finally portrays the world that the child sees as a bad melodramatic film. Pricò is cast initially in the traditional mode of helpless victim in a world that comprises interfering and hostile neighbors, sexual infidelities, hypocrisy, and upper-class snobbery. His caretakers are indifferent to his needs, and it is through this neglect that he observes the hypocrisy of the adults. In particular, after the mother disappears with her lover, Roberto (and not for the first time), the housekeeper, Agnese, takes Pricò to an aunt's shop, where he sits and observes the women workers giggling about their various sexual exploits. Later, he hears the aunt berate his father for his conjugal inadequacies. The father takes Pricò to the home of his grandmother (the father's mother), a tyrannical matriarch who disapproved of her son's marriage and now disapproves of the boy, who is "like his mother." The grandmother leaves Pricò in the care of a young woman who is more interested in her affair with the pharmacist then in tending to Pricò's needs.

The boy falls ill, and his illness becomes the pretext for the mother to return to the family. The reunited family takes a trip together to the seashore, but this offers no idyllic counterpoint to the previous events; instead it intensifies the suffering and isolation of the child and alters his perceptions of the adult world. When the father, who must return to work in the city, leaves his family, once again the mother's lover tracks her down, and before Pricò attempts to run away he observes his mother and Roberto embracing on the beach. Wandering alone, unable to get a ticket back to Rome [Fig. 55], almost mangled by an oncoming train, accosted at night by a drunk, he is finally returned to his mother by two police officers as an audience at the hotel observes the drama. The boy returns home, alone, his mother again having gone off with Roberto. Unable to manage himself and the child, the father enrolls him in a church-run boarding school, where Pricò is seen framed by the stairwell as he gazes down pitifully at the retreating figure of his father, who returns home and commits suicide. The final shots in the film are of Pricò and the priest as the boy's mother and the housekeeper come to see him. He rejects his mother, embraces Agnese, and disappears into the large and depersonalized space of the building.

Pricò, played by Luciano De Ambrosis, is an ethereal-looking child, shot frequently in close-up. He is identified with his toys (a scooter, a rocking horse) and with a caged bird in his room – but these serve as a vision of reproach, since they are seen at those moments when he confronts his mother's infidelities, her theatricality, and her disappearance. The boy is portrayed as a passive recipient of the cruelties of this world but also as a conscious spectator to its hypocrisies and betrayals. The film has all the characteristics of melodrama – familial conflict, secrets, victimization, illness, suicide, and betrayal – as it dissects a world where so many of the values held dear to Fascism seem to be unraveled: the sanctity of the family, male virility, and collectivity among the neighbors.

Although the mother is the source of much of the conflict, in her obsession with Roberto and presumed inability to resist his blandishments, the role of the father is not simply drawn as victim to her callousness. He is portrayed as pompous, officious, vacillating, and ultimately helpless; a hint of his having been under his mother's iron rule emerges in the scene at her house. Toward the end of the film, he broods over yet another disappearance by his wife. Now he becomes childlike himself, and the boy more the adult. Pricò's troubled movement through the narrative highlights the ambiguity about how much he knows. Through the unrelenting shots of his watching what transpires among the grownups, the audience shares his perspective on events, blurring the division between childhood "innocence" and adult awareness.

Moreover, the film's emphasis on secrecy, central to melodrama, is filtered through the child, revealing once again that what is at stake in presentations of childhood is the character and status of knowledge. Secrecy or the with-

Figure 55. Pricò, alone and desperate after witnessing his mother with her lover again, in *I bambini ci guardano* (*The Children Are Watching Us*). (Courtesy New York Museum of Modern Art Stills Archive)

holding of information in the film, the refusal to expose what one knows, is clearly identified with the child (or with marginal groups that are identified with children). This film raises a number of questions about childhood: Are children indeed innocent and unaware? Are they unready to receive information regarding adult behavior? Are they untrustworthy in maintaining family secrets? The emphasis on secrecy as complicity is most evident when the mother asks Pricò to withhold from the father her lover's visit to the house and his striking the boy. Withholding information becomes central to an understanding of the child's position, since it not only indicates that he is not an innocent tabula rasa but also underscores the hypocrisy that is endemic to this world. By viewing the events from the child's perspective, through Pricò's gaze, the film presents a less familiar view of childhood, shifting concern from the melodramatic conflicts of the adults onto the child. Instead of regarding Pricò as the object of the gaze of others, he becomes the active carrier of knowledge within the film, forcing critical attention onto the hostile environment in which he is placed.

The uses of landscape in the film also interact with the child's perspective to indicate the aseptic, impersonal world (as in the shots of the apartment house and of the school) inhabited by the child, opening out to a broader commentary about social relations than melodramatic assignment of guilt. The spectator is conscious also of spatial relations in the way contrasts are developed through size: The boy's smallness is set against the enlarged exteriors, where he seems to be engulfed and where the question of responsibility appears more amorphous. Finally, the film ends ambiguously: The characters disappear without the text providing a suggestion of resolution; the tragedy is unmitigated, the family such as it is now is not reconciled, and the boy is completely isolated. More than the film's adhering to the familiar technical descriptions of neorealism (location shooting, nonprofessional actors, etc.) these techniques suggests that the film has moved from the classic forms of film melodrama into a different place more fully developed in two other of De Sica's films – *Sciuscià* and *Ladri di biciclette.*

In discussing the European postwar cinema, Colin McArthur writes that "a recurrent image . . . is of children moving through the ruins of war-torn cities." *Sciuscià* and *Ladri di biciclette* bear the "manifest influence of Italian Neo-Realism on their overall look, and the foregrounding of children as protagonists . . . all of these films offer images of the war-torn fabric of their respective urban milieux."[18] *Sciuscià,* although often considered the inferior text of the two, is an important one to examine for understanding Italian cinema's ways of looking at the world, and particularly how the cinema uses children to create a different perspective on events. *Sciuscià* is set in Rome in the immediate postwar era, and the young boys, Pasquale and Giuseppe, are reduced to living on the streets, to eking out a living often by shining shoes (hence the title, an Italian approximation of "shoeshine"), by black-market deals with American servicemen, and by shady deals engineered by family members. It is the latter that proves tragic for the boys, sending them to reform school and finally tearing them apart as a consequence of corrupt and indifferent authorities – police, lawyers, judges, and prison officials.

The film offers no reassuring images of domestic life. The children in the narrative are all orphans or outcasts, of little interest or concern to the adults. The film begins deceptively with an image of openness and with the two boys riding a horse through a suburb of the city as other children follow them shouting with delight. The sense of movement and freedom is underscored, the association being with the exuberance of youth, and the boys' attachment to the horse, Bersagliere, is evident, as is the camaraderie of the children despite the conditions of hardship in which they live. In contrast to *I bambini ci guardano,* one gets very little view of domestic interiors. We see the stable where they and the horse sleep, the crowded quarters that families share in one building, and, of course, the inside of the reform school.

Figure 56. Framing the children in *Sciuscià* (*Shoeshine*): Giuseppe's mother (Irene Smordoni), Giuseppe (Rinaldo Smordoni), and Pasquale (Franco Interlenghi). (Courtesy New York Museum of Modern Art Stills Archive)

The blackmail swindle set up by Giuseppe's older brother lands the boys in reform school. He promises that they will be shortly set free through the efforts of a lawyer; however, the situation demands that the boys have faith in the system, trust that they will be freed, and not reveal anything about the blackmail scheme that could get their elders in trouble. Events turn out differently, since the coercive tendencies of the reformatory officials have not been taken into account by the boys or their families. Ultimately Pasquale is tricked into betraying Giuseppe by an official who, using another child, pretends to be beating Giuseppe to get him to talk. From then on enmity exists between the boys, an enmity that leads to new alignments, to violence, and ultimately to the accidental death of Giuseppe as he is chased by Pasquale. Inexorably one tragic incident piles upon another, and there is no way to reverse the events, to provide a resolution to the accumulated misunderstandings. As for the adults outside the reform school, they are either totally indifferent to the plight of their children – as is the mother of the sick child, Napoli – or, more concerned for those offspring who can provide materially for the family, as is Giuseppe's mother [Fig. 56].

Attitudes associated with idealized middle-class notions of affection between children and adults are noticeably absent in the film. The children have only one another to rely on, and with life in a house of correction, these bonds of solidarity begin to break down. The film moves from shots of openness to ever-constraining images in the reform school (the only open place being the courtyard in front of the cells, where the officials and guards lecture or rail against their wards). The bright light of the opening sequence gives way to darker shots, and the film ends at night. The children become the lens through which various social institutions are viewed: the bureaucracy of the police; the ridiculousness, indifference, and lack of preparation on the part of the lawyers for the children's defense; the pedantry of the judges; and the behavior of the reformatory officials, which De Sica links to Fascism. In this milieu, boys either take on the brutal character of the authorities or are destroyed by reformatory life.

The vignettes provided of postwar Italian society that focus on the boys are inextricably tied to images of landscape and architecture. In particular, space is no longer an index to a consonance between the characters and their milieu: Landscape becomes a character in its own right, signifying the boys' destitution, the absence of a literal and cultural home, and underscoring their complete lack of control over their world. The initial image of childhood freedom, the boys joyfully riding their horse in the open air, gives way to images that reveal the illusory nature of that freedom. The suburban landscape changes to views of the city, with the boys at work on a crowded street, shining the shoes of G.I.'s. The darker and threatening dimensions of their lives are shown in the shots of the cramped dwellings, in the stark views of the reformatory, and, above all, in the ponderous architecture of the building that houses the court where the boys are tried. The film's treatment of the events derives from the focus on the boys both as spectators to this world and as bearers of the film's pathos in the scenes of their brutal treatment at the hands of the authorities. The images inside the reformatory and those inside the courtroom collapse conventional distinctions between inside and outside: The boys are dwarfed by the massive and constraining architecture, as they are by the authorities – not only the reformatory officials but also the lawyers who "defend" the boys and the judges who sentence them.

Constraining images from inside the corrections van taking the boys to the reformatory, as well as of the institution itself, are set in ironic contrast to the interspersed images of the open road, where the boys earlier rode their horse (and where the horse will lope away from the final scene of disaster). The film's preoccupation with the children's perspective on events becomes manifest as alternating shots reveal a young girl, Nannarella, seen first in close-up then in long shot against the urban locale, as the boys gaze disconsolately at her through the bars of the vehicle. Nannarella becomes the mute testimony to the harsh treatment of the boys as they are carted away and, later, as they are treated in the courtroom. We thus have in this film a further permutation of the idea that the "children are watching." The use of children as spectators in the courtroom scene, besides enhancing the sense of theatricality identified with forms of institutional life, underscores the incongruity between their perceptions and those of the adults who manage their world. Once again it is the child who bears the knowledge of the situation, whereas the adults are blind. This compounds and complicates what is presented on the screen. (So does the blurring of distinctions between youth and adulthood as the boys increasingly imitate the behavior of their elders.) These children are not innocent: They have seen, and the audience sees through their eyes, the cruelty and indifference of the post–World War II world. As a consequence of their vision, it becomes difficult to regard the film in conventional melodramatic terms, since what the children see is an indictment of the clichés of childhood. Mira Liehm has stated that

> a structural weakness of *Shoeshine* stems from the incongruity between the authenticity of scenes shot in actual settings and those staged in the studio or composed in the traditional manner (close-ups of innocent childish faces: close-ups of little hands whose fingerprints are being recorded, the composition of the scene showing Giuseppe's mother's visit to the prison, etc.).[19]

But what Liehm identifies as a "structural weakness" is at the heart of a film that self-consciously resembles a typical prison picture, with its conventions and clichés.

The transposition of the adult conflicts identified with prison dramas onto the young boys introduces a disturbing element. Rather than constituting a "weakness" in the structure, the "incongruity" between realist and genre styles shifts the focus to issues of spectatorship and to issues concerning "authenticity." The film is as much about conceptions of cinema as it is about the tribulations of the children; it is about clichés and the puncturing of clichés. In its use of landscape and of children, the film creates a portrait of a world governed by clichés, but one in which these clichés are thrown into crisis.

Sciuscià appears to have designs on the audience other than the mere recording of the miseries of daily life. The invocation of cinema in the final moments of the film – in the boys' responses to the newsreels involving the actions of the Americans in the Pacific theater of war and to the slapstick of the comedy film – is only one indication of its preoccupation with cinematic representation. It must also be noted that the film challenges the theatricality of a large portion of the cinema, with its emphasis on spectacle and melodrama, that preceded it in the Fascist years. *Sciuscià,* by emphasizing contingency and accident, compounding judgment, and focusing on the role of spectatorship, undermines melodrama in favor of open-endedness. This open-endedness is conveyed by situating the protagonists as ambulatory, as meandering through the landscape in "aimless movement" that does not result

in definitive action. Through the "voyage form," the spectator follows the characters as they confront the indifference of their world.[20] The use of the child
as protagonist is crucial, since "in the adult world, the child is affected by a
certain motor helplessness, but one which makes him all the more capable
of seeing and hearing."[21] The children in neorealist films are more acutely at-
tuned to observing that it is impossible "to pursue a course of justice."[22]

In *Ladri di biciclette* (*The Bicycle Thief*), De Sica continued to use the child
as a conduit to challenge prevailing assumptions about cinematic illusion.
The film follows the peregrinations of Antonio and his son through the streets
of Rome to find the thief who stole his bicycle, which he needs for work. The
child, Bruno, is witness to the effects of the bicycle's loss; through his eyes,
the audience sees Antonio become obsessed to the point of brutalizing him.
In the innumerable discussions of this film, emphasis has been placed on the
father–son relationship, threats to its integrity, and the gradual overcoming of
these threats. The interactions between them are indeed crucial to an understanding of the unconventional ways images function in the film. Still, it is
the gaze of the child – a motif in many films by De Sica and screenwriter Cesare Zavattini (also including *I bambini ci guardano, La ciociara, Miracolo
a Milano, L'oro di Napoli,* and *Sciuscià*) – that contributes to the nuanced
sense in which *Ladri di biciclette* is less a record of cinematic reality than an
investigation of cinema as the medium for different insights about the world.

The film's Rita Hayworth poster is, as several critics (e.g., Marcus) have
suggested, an indication of its preoccupation with the character of cinematic
reality – Hollywood's and its own. In the Hollywood cinema, the focus is on
the efficacy of action, the promise of rewards for hard work and persever-
ance. *Ladri di biciclette* dramatizes the loss of familiar domestic, urban, and
ethical landmarks to recognize, label, and judge. The film offers nothing by
way of materially compensating Antonio for his loss. However, the perceptual
burden of the film rests with Bruno. Through his gaze, the audience is invited
to observe Antonio's struggles with obsession, rage, and finally the desperation that leads him, in turn, to steal a bicycle. Bruno does not fit the conventional image of childhood. He is neither an innocent, nor inarticulate. He is
in many ways more adult and certainly more prescient than his father, though
he is helpless to deter Antonio from his goals. In following his father through
the city, his knowing gaze, registering different moments of Antonio's behavior, provides the opportunity for the audience, as in *Sciuscià,* to view an
alternative to the conventional and sentimentalized portraits of father–son relations. Equally important, Bruno also serves as the displaced object for Antonio's anger, allowing the audience to see the father through the eyes of the
child as assuming the character of his milieu, becoming as indifferent and
even as aggressive as the social institutions the two encounter on their journey. De Sica's filmic children are a major break in the clichéd sense of child-

hood, a harbinger of new forms of presenting youth in the postwar cinema or at least of complicating the nature of childhood and adolescence.

Increasingly in the films of the 1950s and 1960s, children continue to play an important role. In such 1950s films as *Tormento,* they are the victims of a world where violence, hypocrisy, infidelity, and conjugal discord are preeminent. In other films, the child may serve as a silent observer or a neutral filter for events. For example, in Antonioni's *Deserto rosso (Red Desert,* 1964), in which dialogue is quite sparse, the child, Valerio (played by Valerio Bartoleschi), says little, yet his presence is evident throughout as an enigmatic aspect of the film's preoccupation with vision. He becomes merely another cipher in the film, one more indication of the struggle of his mother, Giuliana (Monica Vitti) to see and recognize the world in which she is immersed, a world that has thrown her into psychic disequilibrium. Her son's world, however, is not cast in the mold of the conventional melodramatic childhood, violated at the hands of indifferent, disturbed, or cruel parents. His own neurosis, exemplified in his momentary (feigned?) hysterical paralysis, is more adult than childlike. Although he says little, his silence is eloquent. His presence calls into question the nature and role of verbalization and reinforces the image of the cinematic child as inscrutable but disorientating. In a lesser vein, his neurosis mirrors that of Giuliana.

His mother's recounting to him, during his immobility, the images of a young girl on a deserted island in a lush and beautiful natural environment is another reminder of a fantasmatic world that stands in direct contrast to the polluted industrial environment of Ravenna. However, this scene is not a parable of maternity, of the desire for a return to a pastoral world, or of a "solution" to the estrangement of the family and the mother's malaise. There is no return to a simpler world that is misidentified with childhood innocence and pleasures basking in the bosom of parental love. The son's role reveals that the film is not concerned with reigning clichés of family and childhood. He is not a melodramatic reproach to his disorientated mother; rather, he serves to dissolve images of childhood.

Films of the 1970s returned to the Fascist era and to the war, using the child as a filter through which to reconsider the past. For example Fellini's *Amarcord* (1974), while creating an encyclopedic portrait of life under Fascism in its explorations of the role of the cinema, the family, the school, and the church, focuses heavily on the world of the adolescent. The young boys are neither idealized nor presented as melodramatic victims (of Fascist oppression). Instead they are caricatured as concerned with their own pleasures, their sexual desire, affectively but not intellectually in rebellion against their parents, teachers, and priests, indifferent to the politics but not the spectacle of Fascism. The portrait of Titta (Bruno Zanin) is the primary vehicle for the film's exploration of youthful fantasies about movie stars, sexuality, and adventure. He is identified with the hazy lines between reality and cinematic illusion that the film attributes to the culture of the 1930s. Titta provides a sympathetic but also critical insight into the travails of growing up at that time. The death of his mother is a particularly poignant counterimage to a world devoted to spectacle. Through his character, the film provides an antidote to conventionally monolithic and public images of Fascist culture. In effect, the adolescents become a different and less familiar window to this provincial world, revealing the absurdity, vanity, and unthinking complicity of everyday life under Fascism. In Marco Bellocchio's *Nel nome del padre* (*In the Name of the Father,* 1972), young people are also highlighted in relation to education, and connections are forged among generational conflict, authoritarianism, and submerged memories of Fascism. Linking the years of Fascism to the present, the film investigates the submerged cultural and political past that plagues present society and also invokes the role of cinema to make parallels and probe differences between past and present.

In Italian cinema of the 1980s, the child as spectator (if only through the recollection of an adult) is evident in the Taviani brothers' film *La notte di San Lorenzo* (*The Night of the Shooting Stars,* 1982) [Fig. 57]. This film too returns to the years of Fascism and World War II as a woman, Cecilia, recollects her experiences as a child during the massacre of the village of San Martino. (The film is based on the destruction wreaked on the filmmakers' village of San Miniato, which the Tavianis had earlier attempted to record in their first film, a documentary short.) Like the postwar films previously discussed, the film does not follow classical lines of narrative; it is not a melodrama; and it does not single out particular characters to exalt their actions. In line with other films by the Tavianis, *La notte di San Lorenzo* poses problems associated with specific historical events and offers an unconventional form for interrogating those events. In particular, the film challenges myths of Italian national unity, conceptions of Fascism and its effects, and the role of official history as the conduit for "truths" about Fascism and World War II. Most significant to our discussion, the use of the child again becomes the means whereby the film seeks to undo certain myths.

The film is an exploration of folklore that has accumulated around the war, regarding the Resistance and especially relations with the Americans and Germans and among different Italian political factions. The Tavianis do not regard the moment of the war and the role of the various Resistance groups as a "battle of foreign forces for the military fate of Italy, but as a civil war to determine its political future."[23] Toward these ends, the child Cecilia (Micol Guidelli), through prelogical forms of knowledge – magic, superstition, folklore – serves as a spectator, an unconventional commentator on the events that ensue. Through her eyes (but guided by the knowledge that the film is a flashback and tainted by adult memory), the audience views the conflicts of townspeople over the decision to leave the town in anticipation of the perfidious

Figure 57. The Tavianis directing *La notte di San Lorenzo* (*The Night of the Shooting Stars*). (Courtesy New York Museum of Modern Art Stills Archive)

bombing of the cathedral by the Nazis. Repeatedly, the notion of a united front against Fascism is demystified. In portraying their encounters along the road as they seek to find a haven with the Americans, their contact with Resistance fighters and with Black Shirts, and their sojourn in another town, Sant'Angelo, where they finally hear the news of Allied victory, the film draws on the antagonisms inherent to Italian life (regional, class-based, familial, and political) that are embedded in the myths of Italy as a nation – particularly the long-standing myths of that "golden" moment during the war repeatedly rehearsed in neorealist films and writings on the Resistance. The perspective of the child creates a sense of indeterminacy as to the reliability of such narratives and redirects the focus of the film once again to the question of knowledge – unsettled, thanks to children and childlike adults.

There are in fact two children in the film: Cecilia in flashback and her own child, an infant, who is seen at the beginning and end of the film. The inarticulateness of the infant in the present serves to underscore the ambiguity of the relationship of the past to the present and of the present to the future. The flashbacks to Cecilia as a child raise questions about that past, how to understand it and how it relates to prevailing narratives on film. In her memories, Cecilia recalls first of all how, during the wedding ceremony of Corrado and pregnant Bellindia, she scanned a painting of the harrowing of hell – identifying her vision with the devil's crossed eyes and providing a humorous proleptic commentary on the events to come, whose portrayal may be the result of skewed vision. For a moment the camera lingers on the child in close-up, a reminder of the fact that she is the creation of her older self.

By using memories of childhood, the film can subvert "the neorealist claim to an objective, authoritative cinematic approach."[24] In another sense, the film has not subverted so much as complicated the role of the child, as we have seen in the discussion of the films of De Sica earlier in the chapter. In particular, if we accept that "what purports to be individual reminiscence is really that of the collectivity,"[25] *La notte di San Lorenzo* identifies that collectivity not so much in the mere reminiscences of others as in the idea that history is neither sacrosanct nor seamless, and certainly not transparent. One can never assume a direct access to the truth, and the emphasis on folklore underscores the collective (not individual) and fragmentary (not unified) nature of knowledge. The uses of folklore are identified with childhood, and the child's perception, rather than being a flaw, serves to undermine traditional and official accounts of events.

Conventional notions of childhood are flouted through the six-year-old child, Cecilia. The film's uses of folklore are tied to her perspective and, by extension, to the film's critical portrayal of received and conventional knowledge. The child is first associated in the church with a painting therein of the "Dies Irae," the Day of Judgment, a recurrent motif in the film that associates this biblical allusion with the concrete events of the war and with implied questions concerning the shape of the future. Throughout the film, ironic links are made through Cecilia's gaze between the biblical and classical allusions invoked and the events taking place. The most striking instance of this collision between ways of seeing is the brutal encounter between the Fascists and anti-Fascists in the wheatfield. Viewed through the eyes of the child, the scene emerges as a fantasy but also as an unwitting unmasking of heroism, given the disjunction between the spectacle of the epic warriors and the image of the scruffy men in the cornfield. The child's uses of the *filastrocca* (a traditional magical incantation for protection), connected to Tuscan folklore, parallels the old man's recitation of Homer. These invocations of folklore and epic soften the critique of the past by suggesting the partial nature of common sense rather than its falsity. Ritual, folk tale, and superstition are connected to strategies for survival, and the film does not minimize the life-and-death nature of the internecine struggles recounted; rather, it uses folklore ironically to force a rethinking of the past.

Through using this unwieldy and unreliable form of narration, *La notte di San Lorenzo* can connect the past to the present (the frame of the film and the relation of Cecilia to her own child) and project onto the infant a number of questions concerning the shape of the future. The death of Bellindia and her unborn child becomes a further exploration of the forces in the past contributing to the betrayal of the people, particularly the church. The identification of Cecilia's child as an infant underscores the sense of uncertainty about the future articulated by the adult Cecilia in her anxiety (and the film's) concerning the possibility of a repetition of the past in the present. Again, the child plays a pivotal role in situating the film's explorations of history. Significant too is the artificial setting for Cecilia and her infant, tinted blue like a greeting card of the Nativity, framing the film in an allusion to folk images associated with popular culture and with religion. Interlaced through the film are allusions to images of beginnings and dire endings, Creation and the Last Judgment. The "Dies Irae" and Verdi's *Requiem* are associated with images of mortality. The child is identified with individual birth and death, with questions of cultural death and regeneration and with the fearsome possibility of repetition of the past.

More recent films continue to focus on childhood and adolescence, as exemplified by *Mery per sempre* (1989), *Nuovo Cinema Paradiso* (1988), *Il ladro di bambini* (1992), and *Io speriamo che me la cavo* (1993). These films reveal that the dramatizing of children continues to function as a social and stylistic commentary on Italian culture in both historical and contemporary terms. The internationally popular *Nuovo Cinema Paradiso* (*Cinema Paradiso* in its U.S. release) reconstructs the social life of a southern Italian village from the years of Fascism and the war to the present, again using memories of childhood to offer a different image of the past as purveyed in conventional histories. The film ties the life of the community to the role of cinema and to changes that take place in cinematic production and reception from the Fascist years to the present through the perspective of a young boy, Toto, obsessed with the moving image. His initiation into the magic of cinema adulthood is through the projectionist, Alfredo, his surrogate father.

The film offers an encyclopedic view, at times critical, at other times nostalgic, of Italian culture through its focus on film. It is a narrative of growing up in the provinces, a portrait of the effects of war on the family and community, a look at the controlling and censorious role of the church in relation to morality, a history of Hollywood and Italian films, and an elegy for the passing of childhood and of the cinema in its heyday. The child serves a number of roles: He is guide to a different version of the past, one seen through the projections of cinema rather than through the school, prison, or even family. His childlike fascination with and enthusiasm for the cinema becomes the analogue for identifying the power of cinema, its hold on audiences. Cinema belongs to the magic of childhood, to fantasies of escape, and to romance, in contrast to adulthood and contemporary life.

The film *Mery per sempre* (Always Mery) focuses on a reform school and the antagonistic relations between teacher and youngsters. The school, as we have seen, is not an unusual setting for featuring young people; nor, for that matter, as we have seen with *Sciuscià*, is the reform school. From the 1940s to the present, the attraction to films that feature "social problems" has continued unabated in Italian cinema, focusing most often on adolescents and teenagers, increasingly on delinquent and marginal youth. The fascination with youth derives from a number of sources: the legacy of neorealism that often singled out young people as societal victims; the political events of the 1960s that posed youthful radicalism as either a promise or a threat; the events of the 1970s and 1980s identified with political terrorism and often specifically linked to youth; and the targeting of young people as an audience and as consumers. The films of the 1990s are exemplary of the persistence of portraits of young people as both source and effect of the failure of social institutions, and dramatize efforts to redeem youth and those institutions.

Mery per sempre follows the conventional trajectory of portraying a young teacher in Palermo who is naïve about the life of the poorer classes. It is he who receives the education through his growing interest in the histories of the young people, despite obstacles they and the school administration throw in the way. As suggested by Angelo Restivo, "the figure with whom the audience is asked to identify is the anguished schoolteacher . . . whose own sense of identity is thrown into crisis by his encounter with the youth."[26] The element of difference in this film from conventional melodramas of conversion and service (both on the part of the young people as well as the teacher) is the introduction of gay sexuality. Mery is a boy who prefers to look and act like a woman and who prefers men as objects of desire. This complicates the narrative, as the teacher also learns and seeks to instruct others about sexual as well as class difference. The film reaffirms that the focus on children is a pretext for reconsidering questions of social knowledge, its nature, who possesses it, and toward what ends: The child bears the burden of transforming the adults. Likewise, *Il ladro di bambini* (*Stolen Children*) is concerned with the rebelliousness of young people; the conflict between them and representatives of the law, which is indifferent to their condition; and the education of a *carabiniere* (police officer and army corps member) through conflict and contact with them [Fig. 58].

Lina Wertmüller's version of the school film, *Io speriamo che me la cavo* (*Ciao, Professore!*, 1993) also takes place in the South and uses third-grade children as a vehicle for illuminating aspects of social and economic life in the Neapolitan environs. Education again becomes the locus of ideological concerns tied to questions of sexual politics and regionalism. Once again, children as representatives for subaltern groups serve as the instrument for educating the teacher about important differences between North and South. The film's structure is reminiscent of *Mery per sempre,* though it leans to the comic rather than to the purely melodramatic. Professor Sperelli (Paolo Villaggio) finds himself in a situation alien to his conceptions of social life: Through computer error, he was sent to the southern town of Corzano rather than to

Figure 58. *Il ladro di bambini* (*Stolen Children*): Rosetta (Valentina Scalici) and Antonio (Enrico Lo Verso) (Courtesy New York Museum of Modern Art Stills Archive)

the northern town of Corsano. Nothing is organized according to his expectations. The school is run by a janitor in league with the Mafia, not by the principal, who is too busy having babies. The children prefer to work than to go to school and are resistant to his pedagogical objectives for them.

As in *Il ladro di bambini,* the children ultimately instruct and initiate the adult. The turning point in his relationship with them occurs after, in a rage at the troublesome young Rafaello's insubordination, he slaps the boy and is mortified over his having resorted to violence, which he identifies as the cause of the "troubles" in the South. However, the boy's mother thanks him, and the children gain greater respect for him. The film seeks to work against regional stereotypes but at the same time it inevitably falls prey to them. The children are attractive and precocious, offering a range of types: the fat boy, Nicola, the seductive Rosella, the sleepy Gennaro, the poorly Tomasina, and the tough, defiant Rafaello. The vignettes of children are filmed in close-up and are extensive. In the vein of neorealism, the film uses professional and nonprofessional actors (the children) and a combination of location and studio shots. Moreover, the integration of landscape shots with the vignettes of the young students serves to link questions of region to the children's social world. The reiterated landscape shots – of the sea and of the countryside in the trip to Caserta – set up a familiar contrast between the beauty of the region, a haven for tourists, and the painful struggles of the inhabitants to survive economic inequities and social rituals of stagnation.

Wertmüller's film reinforces the roles that children, particularly those from marginalized groups, are called upon to play in the contemporary Italian cinema. They have become the sources of local knowledge, superior to the adults. They act as their caretakers or as windows onto the limitations of the adult world. In contrast to the adults, who are inured to their environment or unable to control their lives, the children are clever and able to negotiate with constraints – or, in certain cases, they are victimized. The children are also capable of distinguishing adults who, like Professor Sperelli, are educable from those they must merely rebel against or manage for their own ends.

As we have seen, children are used by filmmakers as a strategy to expose the conventional and clichéd character of the adult world and provide a different perspective on contemporary life. However, films such as *Io speriamo che me la cavo,* like *Nuovo Cinema Paradiso,* are also prey to their own clichés in their portraits of the precocity of youth and in attributing to children the ability to speak truth – long a tradition in representations of childhood.

CHAPTER TEN

The Folklore of Femininity and Stardom

W omen occupy a precarious position in the Italian cinema, both as filmmakers and as subjects of works by male filmmakers. Only within the past two decades have studies begun to appear analyzing the position of women in Italian culture – in literature, cinema, other visual arts, and even in advertising. Victoria de Grazia's *How Fascism Ruled Women* examined the position of women during the Fascist era, paying attention to how women were represented through radio and cinema. Giuliana Bruno's studies of the silent cinema have focused on the works of a female filmmaker, Elvira Notari. Bruno's collaborative effort with Maria Nadotti to investigate various dimensions of women's role in the Italian media have highlighted feminist concerns about the history, character, effects, and changing perspectives governing women's representation in Italy. The exploration of gender requires an understanding of what is meant when the name of "woman" is invoked. How are perceptions of Italian culture and society shaped by beliefs in the "truth" of "woman"?

Despite certain commonsense meanings, there is no universal and absolute meaning to the appellation "woman," Binary distinctions attached to "masculinity" and "femininity" derived largely from biological distinctions between the "sexes," and conceptions of gender are largely determined by their social, legal, and cultural construction. For this reason, a study of cinema is a primary means for deriving the cultural character, force, and changing dimensions of circulating representations of femininity. Cinema is a cultural encyclopedia drawing on various strata and artifacts in the culture, both "high" and "low": novels, poetry, painting, music-hall entertainment, popular magazines, the sights and sounds of the city, classical and popular music, conceptions of the human body, of health and disease, religion, juridical practices, and writings on psychology. The folklore directly tied to the figure of woman entails a mixture of tradition and modernity. It is an archive of the past altered to suit contemporary conditions.

Throughout the following discussion of representations of women in Italian cinema, the term "femininity" is used in identifying how the figure of woman exceeds conventional conceptions of male and female. Resisting fixed identification, femininity is synonymous with uncertainty, with that which is disruptive to the world of the masculine protagonist and to the social order. Its threat and its power lies in its protean character. Although femininity takes many forms through the portraits of woman – as femme fatale, mother, wife, entertainer, prostitute – these forms are often united in representing the feminine as a threatening and problematic force. Even in texts that seem to present the figure of woman as a source of creativity and nurture, there are cracks that reveal how contradictory, fragmented, even fantasmatic, are the portraits of the feminine.

Rearding the position of women in Italian society, Luisa Passerini writes that, particularly in the context of changes resulting from political pressures, especially those exerted by feminist and lesbian and gay groups since the 1970s, "Italy remains a country in which gender relations are still formed in the mould of underlying masculinism – old-fashioned or newfangled, covert or manifest – and this masculinism both sustains old traditions and invents new ones."[1] The task of this chapter is to disentangle old from new, covert from manifest, and traditional from new forms of expression concerning the uncertain aspects of gender representation in Italian cinema in relation to femininity (even in cases where the director is a woman). The figure of woman appears in a number of guises – maternal, conjugal, social transgressor, and so on – in films by both male and female directors.

A number of films, from the silent era to the present, feature a repertoire of mothers and maternal surrogates. One also finds single women, often entertainers, bereft of lovers, languishing for companionship – specifically, conjugal relations – but fated to isolation by virtue (or the assumed lack therein) of their careers. Women of color are more rare, though not absent: One sees them especially in the films of the Fascist era (e.g., *Il grande appello* and *Sotto la croce del sud*) but also in such recent films as *Lo zio indegno* (*The Sleazy Uncle*, 1989). Often, women of color are central to the transformation of the masculine protagonist and then peripheralized and finally eliminated from the narrative. Other feminine characters are barred from the realization of desire by their social class and, in more recent films, by their refusal or inability to conform to social expectations. Narratives featuring an unwed mother have her doomed for a time to wander with her child, subject to social ostracism and often driven to crime and prostitution until redeemed or destroyed. Usually a figure of self-sacrifice, the mother renounces her own desires in behalf of her offspring – though there are also significant instances where the mother seeks to impose her desires onto her offspring (e.g., Pasolini's *Mamma Roma*). The maternal figure, as paragon of self-abnegation or as errant and destructive, is inescapable. Even when the mother is not directly invoked, the scenario of maternity guides the narrative, images, and relations among characters.

Figure 59. The incarnation of the diva: Sofonisba (Francesca Braggiotti) in *Cabiria*. (Courtesy New York Museum of Modern Art Stills Archive)

The maternal figure (often not yet an actual mother but a mother-to-be) does not always appear in isolation: Often she is juxtaposed with another, more transgressive figure – the femme fatale, the ungovernable woman, the woman bent on eluding the men who would seek to dominate her. Among the repertoire of feminine figures of the silent era is the femme fatale, exemplified in such films as *Cabiria* in the figure of Sofonisba [Fig. 59], the incarnation of passion, defiance of the social order, and finally of self-destructiveness. She is found in the historical dramas, where the emphasis transcends domestic constraints, the action is situated in an aristocratic context, and the women, given their upper-class status, have had access to social power. When this power is destroyed, its destruction is traced to the woman's refusal to conform to expectations; whereas Sofonisba's counterpart, Cabiria – dependent, constantly threatened, submissive, and attached to a strong masculine figure – endures and is "saved," returning to Rome with her future husband, Fulvius, under the watchdog eye of Maciste.

Melodramas of the silent cinema often present their central female characters, if not women generally, as an endangered species. A notable exception is *Assunta Spina,* whose protagonist is a variation on the femme fatale. Emblematic of the lower-class woman – passionate, vulnerable, and trapped within the confines of her class – Assunta is transgressive in relation to conventional notions of marriage and the family. The film does not gloss over the perils that confront working-class women, their fates tied to the demands of masculine honor, its inevitable violence, and the concomitant intervention of the law. However, by portraying Assunta as a woman who does not conform to an image of fidelity and single-minded devotion to one man, the film situates her as "the product of a friction between assertion of the self and a need for the other."[2] In her unaccountable flouting of convention (seen in her becoming the mistress of Don Federico), and particularly in the film's emphasis on her being the destructive force in the lives of the men she encounters, Assunta exemplifies the many other "infamous women" who inhabit melodrama. Her character is testimony to the impossible demands made on (or inevitably invoked by) femininity, most dramatically illustrated when the woman, either voluntarily or as a result of chance, does not conform and submit to the sanctioned order.

With the rise of Fascism and the advent of the sound cinema, representations of femininity underwent certain permutations, specifically involving questions of urbanism, of tradition versus modernity, maternity, familial demands, and of the increasing pressures engendered by drives for consensus. If there was articulated a fantasy of the coming into being of a "new man," there was also an attempt to produce a "new woman" as "counterpart." Magazines, newspapers, documentaries by LUCE, and commercial feature films were increasingly devoted to this project, aligning it particularly with government campaigns to enhance the birth rate as well as with the battle to restore the primacy of the family, presumed to be under siege.[3] The emphasis on the valorization of motherhood corresponded with the devalorization of feminist aspirations. Toward the ends of making motherhood attractive and profitable, the regime offered honorific titles and monetary incentives. Of the character and effects of maternity practices under the regime, de Grazia writes:

> This pattern of relegating women to domestic duties, while diminishing their authority in the family, will come as no surprise to anybody familiar with how modern welfare states operate. What distinguished fascist Italy is perhaps only that the state's claim to promote a mod-

ern maternity was so vigorous, while government services were so unevenly administered. The fascist family services offered the allure of the modern without its underpinnings. They set new standards, interfered with old customs, and stigmatized traditional practices. Yet they failed to provide the wherewithal for women to feel empowered by a modernized maternal craft - either as the providers or as the beneficiaries of new services. Italian mothers of all classes were made to feel inadequate, anxious, and dependent.[4]

These comments have a bearing on the cinema of the Fascist years, which disseminated images, whether melodramatic or comic, of women as mothers - images that conform to often unsuccessful attempts to reinforce traditional gendered differences based on philosophical and political writings. As Lucia Re points out,

If we want to gain a less limited understanding of all the levels and complexities of the cultural construction of gender in the Fascist era, we need to consider the ways in which the hegemonic discourse of the regime finds philosophical as well as political and ideological grounding in its *theories* of gender.[5]

Examining the writings of such philosophers as Giovanni Gentile, Re probes the ways in which the theorization of sexual difference must be accounted for in relation to modernity and yet also to tradition, with its insistence on motherhood as "something innate, original, and essential to woman."[6] Re explores writings on modernism and avant-gardism that denaturalize the biological and maternal through techniques of estrangement, irony, and satire. At the same time that there was a drive toward totalization, there were inevitably indications of fissures in the cultural fabric.

The composite and contradictory tension between tradition and modernity is further explored in Karen Pinkus's *Bodily Regimes,* an examination of advertising under Fascism. Pinkus not only complicates the battle of the sexes but also makes it quite central to Fascist struggles for hegemony. Writing that "Fascism brilliantly exploits the inextricable, reciprocal exchange that pertains in any state formation between the body politic and the formation of the individual body,"[7] she documents the collusion among capitalism, modernism, and the production of desexed bodies, which aids in an understanding of the treatment of the female body. She underscores the fact, however, that sexuality in Fascist terms must be understood as actually moving beyond gender in its derealization of the body, affirming and denying it simultaneously: "At times, the body seems to erase any traces of its own gender - to masquerade or cross dress - as a security measure, almost as if to escape the controls of the regime."[8] Seen in this way, gender function is not transparent. Films of the era offer a number of instances where the female body is a site of contention. This contentiousness is evident in the iconography of the actors and in their theatricality, which calls attention to femininity as performance and, in the process, serves to "derealize" conceptions of the "natural" body. Since the popular cinema thrives on the sexual politics of femininity for the creation of spectacle, for narrative complication, and for affective value, an examination of its protean forms of femininity yields insights about the always contested nature of its production, reception, and consensus.[9]

The star system has been a major feature of commercial filmmaking, inextricable from representations of femininity. It is an index to the mode of industrial production, providing information about the personnel responsible for making films in relation to issues involving choice of actors, styles of acting, types of narratives, relations among producers, directors, actors, and camerapersons, and economic considerations involving questions of labor, salaries, and profits. The emergence of the star system is tied to the rationalization of the industry and to other commercial forms – styles of dress, cosmetics, hairdos, advertising, and forms of entertainment. The star is a highly paid worker in the film industry and also a salesperson for consumable items that are part of the visual texture of the cinematic world; yet, these practical, business-oriented considerations are intimately tied to cultural values. According to Christine Gledhill,

> [The star is a] product of mass culture, but retaining theatrical concerns with acting, performance and art; an industrial marketing device, but a signifying element in films: a social sign, carrying cultural meaning and ideological values, which expresses the intimacies of individual personality, inviting desire and identification; an emblem of national celebrity, founded on the body, fashion, and style; a product of capitalism and the ideology of individualism, yet a site of contest by marginalized groups.[10]

The persona of the star – through cinematic roles, visual images, and reportage on his or her personal life – is a commodity whose value is closely tied to the national imaginary and its cultural values: standards of physical beauty, social class, gender identification, fashion, morality, sexuality, and politics. The problematic at the heart of any analysis of (male or female) stardom, then, is to recognize the striated and variegated sources of its construction, circulation, appropriation by various groups, sensitivity to changes in the culture, and, above all, how the economic and the cultural are complicit in the formation of its value.

In the Italian cinema of the teens the reign of the diva was "a reflection of a way of life of a particular social class and of the film world itself, as if the actors had taken themselves for the roles they were playing"[11] The enticement of members of the nobility to the studios and the focus on the production of certain types of upper-class drama were part of the film industry's effort to "restore its prestige."[12] The moment of *divismo* coincides with a number of political and cultural developments inherent to the teens and twenties, including the aftermath of large-scale emigration from Italy, the attempts at colonizing Africa, and the unprecedented growth of industrialization and of movements for economic reform, including the rise of socialism. This was a period that saw challenges to traditional sexual politics as woman's domestic and public roles were debated and challenged by socialists, liberals, and radicals.

Largely associated with the early cinema (as discussed in the Introduction), *divismo* differs significantly from the treatment of star-actors associated with sound cinema. These differences are due to the historical moment of its appearance and to the unique character of the silent cinema:

> [B]y exploring commonplace milieus under the ingenious guidance of the camera, the film . . . extends our comprehension of the necessities which rule our lives: on the other hand . . . it manages to assure us of an immense and expected field of action. . . . The camera introduces us to unconscious optics as does psychoanalysis to unconscious impulses.[13]

Divismo distinguishes the exceptional and the charismatic, even supernatural, qualities associated with the diva. Among her many characteristics, the one major quality is her decadence, which is identified with the world of passion, transgression, and unattainable desire. An embodiment of the "European culture that precedes the First World War,"[14] the diva belongs not only to early cinema but particularly to its manifestation as a "hysterical cinema," one that is invested in the affective character of the visual image and its relation to a particular style of existence. The diva is removed from the world of ordinariness. A corporeal being, she conveys the raging and conflicting passions that drive her to suicidal or murderous actions. In her acting, her gestures, her languid and sensual movements, her nuances of facial expression, and her attitudes that scorn conventional life, the diva embodies the enigmatic character of femininity, its "mystery," elusiveness, and threatening nature. She brings to the cinema an operatic fascination with eroticism and violence. Her figure can also be considered a surrogate for the popular cinema itself. as a form of spectacle, the body of woman substituting for the body of film – also mysterious, appealing, and identified with sexuality and violence. In particular, the moment of the diva "incarnates the behavior of a class that has lost its political and economic hegemony, but remains a model and point of reference for all of European theatrical and cinematic culture."[15]

L'ultima Diva (The Last Diva, 1982) focuses on the image of one of the major divas (Italian: *dive*), Francesca Bertini, whose accomplishments the film records; it is also a commentary on *divismo.* Excerpts are included from her films as well as from others of the silent era. (Appropriately, the film begins and ends with moments from *Sunset Boulevard,* an homage to the diva of silent cinema and an analysis of her figure and her fate.) Through the comments by Bertini and by Italian film critics, the viewer gains a sense of the connections between the film texts and the role of the diva, both on the screen and off. Emerging from Bertini's commentary and from her onscreen presence is an image of the diva as a persona highly histrionic in physical appearance and gesture with an intense self-preoccupation, a scorn for the commonplace, and a striving for control over others.

The theatricality of the diva can be inferred from the exotic or provocative titles of the various films with which Bertini and other *dive* were associated – *Inferno, La serpe* (*The Serpent*), *La contessa Sara* (*The Countess Sara*), *La signora delle Camelie* (*Lady of the Camellias*), *Fior di male* (*Flowers of Evil*), *Rapsodia satanica.* The identification of the cinematic diva with the operatic one is also important, since the same emphasis on fatality, sensuality, loss, and power is shared by both. Also in common is the emphasis on the mute gesture identified with music, which, in conjunction with the visual image (and, in film, the intertitles) approximates the unspeakable suffering and ecstasy with which the diva is identified. (Bertini even avers that "one of her great performances in 1918" was in *La Tosca* – a role she played opposite Gustavo Serena, her director and coactor in *Assunta Spina.*)

That the diva lost her privileged position after the First World War was due to a number of factors, some economic, others cultural and political. The competition of Hollywood cinema, which attracted audiences in the 1920s, made serious inroads on the economic vitality of the Italian film industry. The continuous and outrageous salary demands of the *dive* were thus ruinous to producers and studios at a time of shrinking box-office receipts. Furthermore, the films that were being imported provided new kinds of cultural images identified with Americanism and geared to youth, to modern images of life, and to "ordinary" images of femininity associated with typists, clerks, and saleswomen, in contrast to the exotic diva and the narratives with which she was associated.

Though the diva lingered in a few melodramas that featured the femme fatale, the star came to take her place – an example of how images bend and alter with changing economic and cultural imperatives. The interwar era saw a proliferation of genre films – historical and biographical films, costume dramas, comedies, musicals, melodramas, and war films – and stars were cultivated in the image of Hollywood. Also evident are attempts to accommodate to new images generated by Fascist rhetoric and public spectacle that were geared to more contemporary situations. Profitability outweighed ideology, and the stars were largely constructed through popular images derived from magazines, advertising, and the "long march of Hollywood" in Italy.[16] For example, parallels were drawn between Assia Noris and Carole Lombard, Chiaretta Gelli and Deanna Durbin. Even where the Italian star does not have a specific Hollywood counterpart, one can see an indebtedness to qualities of the U.S. star system in the emphasis on youth, physical beauty, trimness, identification with quotidian life, and modernity.

Although Miranda, like the diva of silent cinema, is glamorous and fashionable in appearance, her acting is less histrionic. Miranda was often compared to Marlene Dietrich.[17] She is identified with the role of entertainer (as is Dietrich) in such films as *La signora di tutti* and *Zazà.* In both, her blonde and statuesque beauty sets her apart, making her the fatal object of others' (both feminine and masculine) desire as a consequence of their captivation once having gazed upon her. The fate of her character is to be isolated, often destroyed. Although she is not an icon of domesticity, many of her roles focus directly on her desire for marriage and motherhood, from which – by circumstance, not her volition – she is barred.

La signora di tutti (*Everybody's Lady,* 1934), directed by Max Ophuls, is a film that doubles as melodrama and as a metacinematic commentary on the cinematic apparatus and stardom, linking stardom to femininity. It is full of images associated with the movie industry and particularly the machinery that belongs to the creation of stardom. The film focuses on publicity posters featuring the name Gaby Doriot (Miranda), artifacts associated with the business of filmmaking, such as phonograph records, and interviews. The industry's economic dimensions in relation to stardom are highlighted when, early in the film, an agent and a film producer argue over the star's salary. The movie studio is filmed as crews race wildly about doing costuming, makeup, and sound. Gaby is as yet invisible, a prefiguration of the film's interest in the star "as a construction, as the sum total of a disembodied voice and an image (the two sensory registers of the cinema)."[18] Significantly, the film that Gaby is to make is also called *La signora di tutti.* The title itself describes a major aspect of stardom, the notion of the star as "everybody's woman." Visibility, particularly the appearance of the star, will become a major preoccupation of the film, focusing on how the star is materialized through the narrative.

The first image of Gaby is on the operating table, semiconscious after a suicide attempt, at the mercy of another kind of director, her doctors, who are investigating her body in their attempt to restore her to life (and to the screen). An intimidating machine that looks like a camera is lowered to anesthetize her. Gaby's situation is analogized to a surgical situation in which the "patient" (e.g., the star) is helpless, rendered passive by technology. The scene decomposes and recomposes into a flashback view of young women singing in a chorus. The episode focuses on her having been the object of the music director's passion and on her responsibility for his disappearance, as the school officials assert in chastising her. She is withdrawn from school and subjected to the discipline of her stern father. The narrative of stardom has been set in motion by the focus on the folklore identified with the female star persona: sexual precociousness, mishandling by adults, subjection to a cold father, and deprivation of a maternal image.

Prohibited from socializing, she enlists the aid of her aunt and gains permission for her sister, Anna, and herself to attend a party given by a young man, Roberto Nanni (Memo Benassi). Before the party, she is seen scrutinizing her image in a mirror as she drapes her body with fabric and naïvely asks the mirror if anyone will dance with her. Her dressing for the party is the first of a number of succeeding scenes where she is seen emerging in outfits more fashionable and hairdos less constrained than those in the school scenes, with makeup that highlights the contours of her face, giving her an aura of elusiveness and mystery. The party becomes the first step in unraveling the events in her rise to stardom. Dancing first with Roberto, then spinning off on her own, she becomes "dizzy," as she describes it to him (while the camera takes a 360° pan from her and returns to her). This "dizziness" is another of the many instances that situate her as the "object" of the narrative but not its agent. Roberto, called to his invalid mother's side, leaves Gaby alone in a room with a clock. A close-up of the clock is accompanied on the sound track by the repeated word *vergogna* (shame). The dimension of time is thus accentuated – both clock time and the time of memory, related to the affective time of cinema. The film's blurring of past and present enhances the sense of moving from real time into the mythic time of memory and fantasy, where the star exemplifies this "dizziness" in temporal perception.

Gaby's rise to stardom is further enhanced by her relationship to the Nanni family where, once again, she is the source of a tragedy that will deprive her of any hope of domestic happiness. Gaby's fatal fascination for men will intervene and contribute to the formation of her tragic persona, which becomes identified with the folklore of stardom. Alma, Roberto's mother, will function as a surrogate mother to her, opposing Gaby's rigid father. Gaby's life can be likened to an opera scenario, and opera will be identified with the events that lead to Alma's death and link Gaby to the world of the operatic heroine. Her relationship with Leonardo, Alma's husband and Roberto's father, emerges as a parallel to the operatic scenario they had witnessed together at La Scala, prefiguring Alma's death, Leonardo's suicide, and, ultimately,

Gaby's demise. Alma's death, counterpointed as it is to the moment of Leonardo's declaration of his passion for Gaby, reinforces a central motif of the film as it centers on Gaby: the identification of desire with mistiming, misrecognition, and death.

La signora di tutti seems to parody the narratives of stardom, involving the trajectory from obscurity to success and the failure of wealth and position to gratify the romantic desire. Moreover, the film focuses on the role of "publicity" as an essential component in the creation of the star. Gaby is interviewed and has the opportunity to "tell her story"; but as the reporters talk about Leonardo's demise and her relationship to him, what is accentuated is the importance of recounting events for the purposes of publicity, which entails creating a narrative of "happiness" and "success." The emphasis on the star's manufacture through publicity is recapitulated through the photographs and the poster of her that we see prominently displayed at the end. This portrait of stardom reveals its dependency on commerce, particularly in the star's exploitation at the hands of agents and producers. As the producer says after learning of Gaby's attempted suicide, the machinery of publicity must "continue and continue." Moreover, this publicity must also be tied to a melodramatic scenario that highlights the endless obstacles to fulfillment, as the film-within-the-film reveals.

All of the melodramatic codes are evident: paternal interdiction and brutality; ungratified desire; the elimination of the maternal figure (Alma) and with her the possibility of familial unity; the obsessive and adulterous attachment of a masculine figure for a younger woman, leading to violence and to a fatal end both for him and for the object of his desire. In addition, the role of secrets, misinformation, and chance, producing discord for all involved, is connected to the melodramatic (and operatic) preoccupation with bad timing. The elements of looking and performance are reiterated throughout the text – surveillance is imposed by her father, men gape at her behind the walls of her garden, she is scrutinized at the party. From the first moments of her flashback, the camera singles her out from the other young women. Repeatedly her face is shown in close-up, as if to wrench her image out of the filmic events and present it as a spectacle in its own right. Various transformations in her image occur, through costuming and makeup, effected by her surrogate mother, Alma. Her awkward school uniform and plain dresses give way to increasingly glamorous attire, comprising ruffles and veils and slinky close-fitting dresses, such as the black gown she wears to the opera with a glittering overcoat. Gaby is metamorphosed into a figure of fashion and glamour.

The film restricts the amount of dialogue that Gaby speaks directly, focusing on a temporal disjunction between the events and her comment on them; the world exists in flashback and in memory. She is identified not with action but with somnambulism, isolation, memory, and loss of consciousness. Her relations with others are characterized by a loss of will, movement without direction, a continuous state of disconnectedness exemplified by the final scene of her telephone conversation with Leonardo [Fig. 60], in which the phone is left dangling. In fact, the narration of her "history" transpires through the narcosis or dream state of the star detached from the chronological events of the narrative. Gaby's late entry into the narrative and the fact that her narration is divorced from her consciousness and from any localized speaker seem to underscore how stardom is more a hallucination or dream (like cinema) than a corporeal entity. Not only does the film probe the phenomenon of stardom through Miranda's portrayal of the character Gaby, but it also made a star of Isa Miranda, who would go on to play a number of roles that were variations on her image in this film.

Mary Ann Doane, who has suggested that the character of Gaby is a reincarnation of the diva of the silent cinema, writes:

> The tradition of the *diva* and the melodramatic mode that it entailed was competitive with, and gradually marked a change of direction from, the fascination with the costume dramas and historical epics. . . . Events of import were now constrained within the closed and claustrophobic sphere of a privatized space, their sole determinant the inexplicable but inevitable sexuality of the woman.[19]

But Gaby is *not* a diva; she is a star, differing from the diva most notably in the very paralysis of her character, in its passivity. The film thus presents an important distinction between the phenomenon of stardom and that of *divismo:* The dominant characteristic of the diva is her ability to generate a sense of force, energy, and volition. The diva is closer to the stage actor, where "the actor identifies with the character of his role." The star appears more the creation of a cinematic apparatus that, as Walter Benjamin has described, is "composed of many separate performances."[20] Gaby's portrait, according to Doane, is "devoid of intention or motivation; she floats from experience to experience without motivation."[21] This is not the powerful Bertini or Lyda Borelli. This is no Garbo or Dietrich. This is a newer image of the star controlled by the medium rather than controlling it. She fulfills Parker Tyler's description of film stars who "seem to be sleepwalkers, the mirage of souls incarnate, their own shadow selves rather than real women."[22] Thus, the star is the consummate image of value, a construction that exposes the material of celebrity, fame, wealth, and glamour. The "tragic" dimension is the price she pays in being relegated to the realm of shadows.

Film melodramas featuring women as entertainers escalate in the latter part of the Ventennio, offering problematic images of femininity. These films sug-

Figure 60. Isa Miranda as "Everybody's Lady," *La signora di tutti.* (Courtesy New York Museum of Modern Art Stills Archive)

gest a crisis of representation inextricably tied to the figure of woman. In *Il carnevale di Venezia* (*Carnival in Venice,* 1940), directed by Giuseppe Adami and Giacomo Gentilomo, the central character is Ninetta, played by the lyric soprano Toti Dal Monte. Ninetta, though an opera singer, is not a successful stage performer; she works as foreman in a tobacco factory.

The film contains a mélange of operatic arias (with orchestral work by the Royal Opera of Rome), folk songs, and ballet (performed by the Corps de Ballet of La Scala). The factory scene is introduced by music as Ninetta and the other women sing at their work; however, conflict erupts as she warns one of them to perform better or be reported. In response, the woman taunts Ninetta about her daughter, Tonina (Junie Astor), revealing that she is carrying on with Paolo, Count Sagredo (Guido Lazzarini).

Also figuring largely in the film is the city of Venice: More than backdrop, it is central to the spectacle and theatricality of the text. The film poses oppositions between success and failure, working-class life and upper-class aspirations, and Venice's visual splendor is set against domestic conflict, specifically in the context of problematic mother–daughter relations. Tonina, disaffected with her family and neighbors, runs away to see Paolo, and her flight is not discovered by Ninetta until after the family is dressed for a feast. Stoically, Ninetta goes with her father, Montini, to the festival. When he asks her to sing, she refuses at first but relents after he commands her not to expose her feelings publicly. When she performs a traditional lullaby that Tonina (in the audience with Paolo) recognizes from her childhood, the daughter decides to return to her mother and finds her praying before an image of the Madonna. Determined to succeed, Tonina makes an attempt to practice her own singing. Paolo, zealous for Tonina to perform, plans for her to appear in Venice as "the nightingale of San Marco." Her performance is threatened when she loses her voice, but Ninetta, concealed, sings in her stead as her daughter mouthes the words. The audience is wildly enthusiastic. Distraught, Tonina seeks to reveal the deception, but Paolo, ignorant of the substitution, prevents her from doing so. The final shots of the film are indoors, with Ninetta alone at the piano until joined by her father. Montini tells Ninetta that only he knows she was the singer. Leaning against her father, Ninetta responds, "But he'll marry her." Tonina will marry well, and the secret of her fraudulent performance will be safe.

Il carnevale di Venezia offers an affectively intense and ambiguous version of maternal femininity, reenacting the melodramatic motif of a mother's total devotion to her daughter to the point of self-abnegation, subordinating her own career to further her daughter's ambitions. By concealing her daughter's lack of talent, she succeeds in realizing Tonina's marriage to a nobleman. The film does not reconcile talent, success, and domesticity. Rather, creativity is subordinated, for both mother and daughter, to work and to the domestic sphere. Though the film has classic elements of the opera and the musical film – romance, spectacle, the struggle to succeed in the world of entertainment, and self-reflexivity about performance and spectatorship – its treatment of spectacle does not overwhelm the conflicts; rather, while celebrating performance, it reveals a disjunction between performance and social life.[23] The festive aspects of carnival that usually function as vehicles for undermining conventional behavior and restraints are complicated and diluted by Ninetta's fraudulent act of ventriloquism and by the image of her isolation at the end.

In the final analysis, Ninetta not only "gives up her child to the social order," but in so doing she negates her own identity[24] – a feature central to maternal melodramas. The film can be seen to reiterate the pathos of a film like *Stella Dallas,* where maternal desire is "displaced onto the daughter."[25] In *Il carnevale* as in *Stella Dallas,* the mother's "sacrifice" must be kept silent. The film's silences – like Ninetta's – argue for the text's working on commonsense assumptions shared with the audience, playing with the subordination of the public to the private sphere and of self-expression to self-suppression. The viability of the private sphere is maintained by suppressing truth, by keeping the secret of impersonation intact. The mother–daughter relationship remains ambiguous through the conspiracy of silence. What is not ambiguous, however, is the film's insistence on the role of performance and ventriloquism – not authenticity – as integral to femininity.

Renato Castellani's *Zazà* (1942) is an exemplary text for perceiving the ways that "cinema seduces its viewers by mimetically exacerbating tension in an orgy of unproductive expenditure."[26] The film features Isa Miranda as a chanteuse who is suspended between career and romance. This opposition is too schematic, however, since *Zazà* – like the films of Josef von Sternberg to which it has been compared – is a complex portrait of what Gaylyn Studlar has described as the "visual pleasure of unpleasure."[27] Woman appears as malcontent, disrupter of the family, and corrupter of socially sanctioned behavior – not merely as its victim. The pleasure of the text, particularly for the female spectator, derives from the complex portrait of a female protagonist who, while aspiring to the world of domesticity, cannot be accommodated within it. The film reveals the sadistic power of the text as it seeks to dominate her and her struggles to elude that control.

Instead of reinforcing mechanisms of control in relation to femininity, the film opens a window onto "abjection, fragmentation, and subversion of self-identity."[28] Neither a closed ideological document nor an anti-ideological celebration of subversion and counterhegemony, the film oscillates between control and dissolution. Characteristic of the scenarios of melodramas (often disparaged as "woman's films" or as "tearjerkers") that focus on beleaguered femininity, *Zazà* offers the familiar narrative of a woman who falls in love with a married man and relinquishes him for the sake of his family. However, this narrative is insufficient to account for the film's treatment of femininity. At stake is a more subtle representation of the cultural position of the woman that involves the terrain of spectacle, associated particularly with the female body [Fig. 61]. The film portrays Zazà as the object of men's admiring gazes, but it also portrays her own gaze as it focuses on remote though seemingly desirable images of family life.

Zazà reiterates the tension in the woman's film between desire and self-sacrifice, the incommensurability between the world of entertainment and that of domesticity. The film's complex interplay of pleasure and desire is the legacy of romanticism, provoking contemplation on the inevitable, necessary, spectacular, and pleasurable aspects of suffering and renunciation. The aestheticized suffering provides pleasure in its acknowledgment of the impossibility of gratification. The focus on the female protagonist's role as an image captured for the consumption of others has dual implications: First, by appropriating it for common consumption, the film frames her image and thus seems to contain the threat of her disruptiveness. However, the strategies of containment through framing make specific its restrictive and disciplinary conditions. The ways in which she is filmed – strikingly framed either in the mirror, in the window, or in performance – repeatedly isolate her as an ob-

Figure 61. Woman as spectacle in *Zazà*. (Courtesy New York Museum of Modern Art Stills Archive)

ject for the inspection of others, particularly by highlighting an image of femininity dissociated from the familiar world of family life. The film's identification of femininity with the maternal role, and maternity with the family, could be read as yet another form of disciplining wayward femininity [Fig. 62]. However, the opposition between the world of entertainment and domestic life is not a simple reiteration of the injunction for women to be fruitful and multiply but instead undermines this expectation, presenting the woman as an object of pathos.

By constantly differentiating and isolating Zazà through its emphasis on specularity, the film places her in an ambiguous position that frustrates narrative recuperation of the feminine position as wife and mother. In this film, the estranging character of femininity reveals a world where power (includ-

Figure 62. Domestic fantasies: Isa Miranda as mother in *Zazà*. (Courtesy New York Museum of Modern Art Stills Archive)

ing that of the filmmaker over his feminine subject) cannot be considered apart from sexuality, and where female desire is isolated from conventional images of family and religion. In the case of *Zazà*, the role of femininity becomes ambiguous: It can be regarded as yet another instance of the disciplining of a wayward and recalcitrant female; but it can also be seen as pointing up the impossible and spectral position of femininity outside the conventional boundaries of heterosexual union and maternity by highlighting her role as an entertainer and isolating her from the familial scenario.

The star system and genre narrative of the 1930s and 1940s were subjected to negative criticism by neorealism, which declared its opposition to Hollywood cinema and offered different images of femininity. The figure of Rita

Hayworth came to represent the artifice and conventionality of the Hollywood form of production. Ironically, neorealism ultimately produced its own stars, as witnessed in the international celebrity of Anna Magnani; but her image is distant both from that of the diva and from the cultivated image of glamour associated with the commercial cinema. Although Magnani also acted in roles during the Fascist era, most notably in *Teresa Venerdì* (*Doctor Beware,* 1941) and *Campo de'fiori* (Field of Flowers, 1943), her comedic image in those films can barely be identified with glamour. Her acting credits in both Italy and the United States are impressive, and she would, after World War II, become an icon of Italianness and femininity. The basis for her international celebrity derived from the role she played in *Open City*, though her fame grew in the 1950s along with that of other emerging icons of femininity – notably, Sophia Loren, Silvana Mangano, and Gina Lollobrigida. How does one account for her popularity in a neorealist and not a genre context? Moreover, what connections are there between Anna Magnani and these other stars, who were identified with glamour?

Giovanna Grignaffini suggests that though neorealism as a school seemed remote from the mass market of cultural production, it nonetheless had an impact on subsequent film production and especially on the determination of star formations. Citing *Riso amaro* (*Bitter Rice,* 1949) as the important film that formed a bridge between "the neorealist experiment and the popular cinema of the 1950s,"[29] Grignaffini says that this film, with its emphasis on "landscape and the human presence in it, rather than constituting a radical break with neorealism, became the basis for the commercial cinema of the 1950s and beyond."[30] The transition was effected through the focus on the human body, in this case particularly the female body, in which

> human beings are represented as *operators* of the landscape, in the
> sense that they both receive and regulate its modulations, the geo-
> graphical as well as the anthropological; human beings and the land-
> scape are then, in turn, represented as *operators* of a new national
> identity and physical characteristics, bodies, and gestures, restored to
> an immediately legible transparency, also become landscape.[31]

Stardom is tied to questions of national identity and geography. Stars are identified with particular locales, rural and urban spaces, and physical and linguistic characteristics. The association of the figure of woman with the land and, by extension, with the nation is a central feature – and one often taken for granted rather than analyzed – of the pervasiveness and power of folklore as communicated through changes in the images of stardom. Commenting on the elusive connections between the body of woman and the landscape, Gillian Rose writes:

Desired but lost, space seems to stand for nothing other than the inaccessible plenitude of Mother. Place becomes the feminized Other
in the discourse of humanist geography, idealized as Woman, spoken
in terms of the (lost) Mother.[32]

Rose's comments are relevant for understanding the physical transformation that occurred in the images of the stars in the 1950s and beyond. The
Italian postwar cinema was involved in redeeming Italian "reality" from the
ravages of Fascism and World War II, and the figure of woman as a signifier
of the regenerated nation plays a role in this reclamation. Magnani's ample
body, disheveled look, husky voice, and passionate acting is identified with
her role as Pina in *Roma, città aperta (Open City)* a role that speaks to long-
standing folkloric connections between woman and the devastated nation.
She becomes the personification of Rome.

Pina's death in the Rossellini film is allegorically connected to the violation of Rome by the Fascists and to its requisite salvation in the future. Pina
can be identified with her working-class origins, her "fallen condition" in her
role as an "unwed mother,"[33] her unkempt appearance, "her status as a *popo-
lana* whose identity is very much bound up with her community," and her
"colloquial language."[34] Thus, whereas the other female characters in the film
(Marina and Ingrid) are remnants of the Fascist genre cinema, Pina offers a
different version of femininity, one that comes to be identified with the Magnani star persona. She is the embodiment of a new, but nonetheless theatrical, type. She offers the illusion of

the female body, intact and uncontaminated by the look of Fascist ideology, a creature of the earth, rich with joyous sensuality, generous
in its proportions, warm and familiar: a body-landscape, along whose
outline would read the future of a nation that has to start again from
scratch.[35]

Magnani's image reveals the new forms that representation and performance
were to take after neorealism and because of it. Her superb mastery of roles
relies on the illusion of her authenticity, that the image we see on the screen
is "an ontological identity between the actress and the role she is playing."[36]

Thus, Pasolini's choice of Anna Magnani to play the title role in *Mamma
Roma* (1962) is based on her identification with the city, first established by
her role in *Open City,* confirming Grignaffini's linking of landscape, the urban
landscape, and the human in the form of the female body. In *Mamma Roma,*
the presence of Magnani invokes the indelible memory of her role in the earlier film and specifically of her identification with the city of Rome. Once
again, we see a focus on her female body and to a lesser extent those of the

other prostitutes; and once again we see that she is identified with the maternal figure [Fig. 63]. However, by contrast with the "saintly image" of Pina, in the Pasolini film what we see exposed are the ways this maternal and sanctified image is theatrical, the product of the history of feminine representation in the cinema. Critics have recorded tensions between the director and the star, he trying to mute the excessive affect that was inherent to her cinematic personification, she falling back on the qualities with which she has been identified and for which she has been lauded. Reflecting on the experience of working with Magnani, Pasolini recounted how

> At a certain point, I thought that the Magnani of *Roma, città aperta* could pass wholly into my reality, but this did not happen because Anna Magnani remained effectively within her own consciousness as an actress, her independence as such, and rightly so.[37]

The film involves the struggles of a country woman, a prostitute, with her young son, Ettore. Mamma Roma eventually takes him to Rome, where she creates for him a "respectable" environment, setting him on the path of the bourgeois virtues of education, work, upward mobility, and proper marriage. She is in error about escaping her past on two counts: First, she does not anticipate the reappearance of Carmine, her former pimp, which returns her to the streets. Second, she finds that Ettore's identification is with the boys on the street, with sexuality, and with the pleasures of fighting and thieving – she cannot recreate him in her desired image of the bourgeoisie.

From the first moments in the film, where we see her dancing and singing in a scene visually reminiscent of *The Last Supper,* we are made aware of the film's use of Magnani's stardom to challenge cherished Italian cinematic fictions – involving images of the lower class as basically benevolent – with which she was associated. *Mamma Roma* is not a neorealist film. As Viano asserts, "Pasolini strips the mask of the universal, monocentric perspective from which the neorealists saw reality."[38] Thus, landscape does not function in the same ways as in a neorealist text. Like everything in a Pasolini film, the emphasis is on an antinaturalism that offers, in Viano's terms, "a certain realism." In directing his actors, Pasolini's general tendency toward cinematic language is to present it in stylized terms, to reduce the amount of affect that might be expected in melodramatic and sentimental terms. Profoundly preoccupied by the relations between "truth" and the various "fictions" assigned to truth that are, in effect, the residual dimensions of folklore from earlier times, Pasolini's films are intensely involved with exploring the theorems that can help expose fictions that are granted the status of the real.

In the character of *Mamma Roma,* the female fiction is familiar: It is tied to the folklore of the countrywoman come to the city, the possibility of gain-

Figure 63. Anna Magnani as the title character in *Mamma Roma.* (Courtesy New York Museum of Modern Art Stills Archive)

ing a new identity, and of realizing this identity through her son. The film is another journey through the streets of Rome, often darkened, occluded, and desertlike, as when she walks the streets accompanied by changing clients and homosexuals. These scenes not only disrupt a realist sense of landscape but also derealize the characters, marking their encounters as yet another instance of the film's revealing the actors' theatricality, undercutting sentiment and unsettling the spectator's response. If Ettore's movement through the film is likened to that of a "sleepwalker,"[39] so too is Mamma Roma's. If this somnambulism is for the young man "the best visual translation of a state of non-participation in normal, waking life,"[40] his mother's streetwalking is in a similar vein, reinforcing the impossibility of her aspirations for herself and her son. By exposing the falsity of the movement of the characters, the film (and Magnani's role in particular) exposes clichés that, in the context of a realistic, action-oriented cinema, would appear as natural truths.

In this respect, Magnani's image – a carryover from her other films and what earned her status as a star – is also exposed as a performance, one more instance of the star as a sleepwalker. Her presence in *Mamma Roma* evokes her starring roles in such films as *Il miracolo* (*The Miracle,* 1948), *Bellissima*

(The Most Beautiful, 1951), and Hollywood's *The Rose Tattoo* (1955, Academy Award, Best Actress) in the intensity of her acting, her nervous movement, changing facial images, and range of emotional responses to events. Her star image, a composite of a number of conflicting feminine positions – motherhood, prostitution, violated and defiant femininity, and even a certain androgyny – is inscribed in her role as Mamma Roma. When she sings in the aforementioned opening – detached from the others at the table in a tableau-like moment in a setting with no depth – Mamma Roma is performing for herself, her son, and the others. This opening prefigures the subsequent scenes in which she performs – her tango dance with Ettore, her appeal to the priest to help her find a position for Ettore, her admiring gaze at her son as he works in the restaurant (a job she has engineered by means of a charade), her denunciation of Ettore for his attachment to Bruna (a young woman of the streets, free with her sexual favors), and her attempts on the road to separate her son from his cohorts.

These episodes appear like a parody of maternity and of Magnani's brand of theatricality and affective excess associated with her character's ambition, guilt, and rage. In a realist context, the intensity of her rage and grief would reinforce, bespeak, and produce identification with her victimhood. However, those qualities with which Magnani the star is identified – uniqueness, intensity, sexuality – sit uncomfortably in a film that seeks to lift the veil from the various forms of representation identified with realism and its penchant for the melodramatic. Magnani's role functions in dual fashion: First, it serves to unmask forms of maternal femininity that identify it with the values of family, respectability, work, and religion (of the Madonna in particular). As Viano writes, "Far from representing the glory of Italy, the word 'Roma' is at first uplifted by the association with mother – indeed one of the sacred signifiers in Italian culture – and then degraded as the name of the prostitute."[41] Second, her role functions as an oblique meditation on the apparatus of stardom. Thus Pasolini's film tears away clichés, but his use of Magnani, to return to Grignaffini's observations, does not redeem the figure of Italy through the body of the woman; rather, it exposes the fraudulence of any attempt at symbolization and national recuperation.

Magnani is finally not an uncomplicated, earthy, joyous, and sensuous creature but a prostitute. She is not a nurturing, self-abnegating mother, though she might seek to adopt that role. Instead the viewer is confronted with how the film's perspective and style frustrate such a position. This film, like so many others by Pasolini, can also be considered metacinematic in the ways that it is preoccupied with the role of cinema (and here stardom) as a vital force for undermining conventional cinematic, cultural, and political values. In its style and subject matter, *Mamma Roma* indicts existing forms of filmmaking for their complicity with the commercial film industry and their imbrication in the other financial structures that determine the world of commerce. This film, by one of the most vocal critics of the cultural politics of Italy, is an unrelenting unmasker of sentiment, of the unrealism of neorealism, and of the increasing commodification of western culture in which the star plays such an integral role.

By contrast, such films as *Catene* and *Tormento,* along with other melodramas of the popular cinema, capitalize on the conflicting and conflicted role of femininity in the context of a very popular form of family melodrama in which, according to Sorlin, "blood and mystery intermingle with daily concerns."[42] The films' popularity at the box office was due to the tenuousness of government subsidy that displayed an animus toward the "pessimistic" cast of neorealist texts (perhaps reflecting audience reaction too), demanding an "optimistic, healthy, and constructive attitude."[43] The films, often identified as "rosy neorealism," were not a total departure from neorealist concerns in their focus on familial conflict, on daily life, and on working-class protagonists. In these films, however, in contrast to those of the neorealists, the woman assumes greater prominence.

De Santis's *Riso amaro* (*Bitter Rice,* 1949) is one of the financially successful films produced in the vein of modified neorealism. The film is a mélange of different genres: musical, woman's film, crime film, and docudrama. Along with its attempts to create a documentarylike approximation of the world of workers, the film relies on melodrama and on the stock figures of the crime genre. By extension, it examines the world of the photo romance (and the world of commercial cinema that animates it). The alternation between melodramatic and documentarylike scenes of the rice workers sets up a contrast between the fiction involving the stars – Silvana Mangano, Vittorio Gassman, Doris Dowling, and Raf Vallone – and the less glamorous sequences involving the *mondine,* the women working the rice fields, played by nonprofessional actors. The film's treatment of its female protagonist, Silvana (Silvana Mangano), has been identified by critics with the "puritanical, not to say misogynistic" treatment of women "characterized by neorealism."[44] Looking like a parody of a Hollywood star, Silvana's sexual attractions are highlighted as she gyrates her limbs and entire body for assembled spectators. Silvana is what Silvana Mangano will become: the embodiment of the female star persona in the 1950s, an incarnation of the fan magazines and of romance [Fig. 64] – though the narrative punishes her by death for her desires.

Bitter Rice begins with a voice-over describing the nature of rice cultivation in Italy, its geography, and its uses of itinerant female labor, shown gathering to board a train for the rice fields. Despite its appearance of a documentary with voice-over narration, it turns out that the voice describing the workers' departure for the rice field is that of an on-air radio announcer, thus introducing a reflexive element into the narration. The documentary-type footage shifts to melodrama in the style of the crime film. Walter (Gassman), a con artist, seeking to escape the police, boards the train with his accomplice, Francesca (Doris Dowling), who will join the women in the fields. Silvana, a beautiful and unscrupulous worker, lives in her body and for her pleasures. An avid reader of the photo romances, she seeks to escape from this banal world of work to America – an instance of the film's conjunction of mass culture with Americanization.

The first view of her is as she dances a boogie-woogie, gyrating her body voluptuously before an admiring crowd. Reminiscent in appearance of a film star, sensual, and eager to escape this life, she attaches herself to Francesca, who has been enthralled to Walter, serving as his "moll" and suffering the indignities of his manipulative and abusive treatment. Learning about a stolen necklace that Francesca hides in her bedding, Silvana becomes a thief herself, taking the necklace that comes to represent for her the glamorous life she desires. The film centers on the tragic effects of her desires. As Francesca gradually becomes deglamorized and identified with the *mondine,* Silvana slips deeper into her fantasy of wealth, aligning herself with Walter. "In her fantasy," writes Antonio Vitti, "Walter appears to be the Prince Charming of the *Grand Hotel* she reads."[45] Several times throughout the film, images from the photo romances are displayed, but these – like the twice- stolen necklace that turns out to be fake – are emblematic of the unattainable and ultimately self-destructive life she desires.

Silvana's character is identified with Americanism and Hollywood cinema. She serves as a commentary on commodity culture and on cinema and popular-romance literature as the purveyor of the deadly fantasies that enthrall her (and, presumably, audiences for the commercial cinema) and lead her to death. In many ways, the film returns to a motif of the previous generation, the politics of style so identified with the cinema under Fascism, but for purposes of criticism. By contrasting the two women, making Silvana the besotted embodiment of Americanism and (deglamorized) Francesca the moral center of Italian working-class collectivity, a traditional image emerges of the Italian woman as preserver of the family and of social order.

Significantly the cinema of illusion is identified with the image of woman: Images of femininity are the means to distinguish between creative and harmful visions of representation, desirable and undesirable images of Italian culture and society. (This popular cinema of illusion would once again gain the upper hand over the following decades in the resurgence of the genre film and the star system.) Although *Riso amaro* adopts a "puritanical" stance toward Silvana, her image was to become an indication of changing attitudes toward sexuality. In the hands of other filmmakers, woman's body was to signify another attitude toward the "redemption" of physical reality aligned with conceptions of the nation redeemed from the taints of twenty years of Fascism.

Figure 64. The postwar woman in Italian cinema: Silvana Mangano as Silvana in *Riso amaro* (*Bitter Rice*) (Courtesy New York Museum of Modern Art Stills Archive)

Although much has been written about Federico Fellini as a renegade from neorealism, he regarded neorealism as "a development" rather than a "closing of the movement. . . . Now what was needed was the knowledge of humanity, by turning those same eyes on the inner man."[46] His work was, in his view, not an abandonment of neorealism but an extension of its concerns. While Fellini's work cannot be easily categorized, there is no doubt that the films identified with his signature display an array of feminine figures: marginalized women, prostitutes, movie stars, artists, feminists from *La strada* (The Road, 1954) to *Il Casanova di Federico Fellini* (*Fellini Casanova*, 1976), and *La città delle donne* (*City of Women*, 1980). Fellini's contribution to the folklore of femininity is based not on realism but on the role of fantasy that governs sexuality and artistic creativity. In *La strada*, the pivotal character is Gelsomina (Giulietta Masina), a mediating figure between two extremes of masculinity and two different notions of performativity (read: artistic creation): The agile Il Matto (Richard Basehart), a high-wire artist, is identified with spirituality, with scorn for the world of materialism and banality; the strongman, Zampanò (Anthony Quinn), with physicality, unreflective materialism, and brute force.

La strada is a "conversion" film. Zampanò's transformation at the end is a consequence of Gelsomina's transformation through her encounters with Il Matto. The characters in their typification owe their existence in part to the *commedia dell'arte:*

> Il Matto belongs to the Arlecchino family with his motley costume, wit, refinement and acrobatic skill. Zampanò, instead, is a descendant of Pulcinella in his churlishness and utter lack of grace. Whenever they come in contact, they cannot help but perform their *commedia dell'arte* routines, enacting in their offstage lives the very roles they play in the circus tent or the makeshift arena of the roadside show.[47]

The form of the film, as in most of Fellini's oeuvre, involves movement in space that is actually a correlative for movement through time. Very much the heritage of neorealism, the film is not a conventional narrative: There is no "plot." The road of the title comes to represent the way the film moves through the character's various encounters with each other and with others along the way. It comes to signify, as in the archetypal conception of the journey, the acquisition of knowledge and insight of different orders and degrees, involving feminine and masculine, physical and spiritual, sensual and suprasensual perception. However, this knowledge is not codified. It is not didactic, despite the famous speech about the pebble spoken by Il Matto and reiterated by Gelsomina, and it is incumbent on the film's spectator to reflect on the significance of the characters' actions and speeches. The characters assume mythic proportions as they become identified with the four elements: Their actions lose individuality and gradually depart from a familiar frame of reference associated with realism. Beginning with Zampanò's purchase of Gelsomina (whose name means "jasmine") from her rural and needy family, the two begin their journey on the road [Fig. 65]. This road can be aligned with the Dantean sense of a movement through various aspects and conditions of "the divine comedy." The literal movement on the road entails a spiritual movement to a form of enlightenment that could be translated, in noninstitutional religious terms, to a form of grace. However, this grace, in Fellini, is not sentimentalized: It involves a sense of loss, an awareness of death, a recognition of pain, violence, and cruelty enhanced and illuminated by the fates of

Figure 65. Giulietta Masina as Gelsomina and Anthony Quinn as Zampanò in *La strada*. (Courtesy New York Museum of Modern Art Stills Archive)

Il Matto and Gelsomina, who finally play a part in Zampanò's wordless communion with the sea and the sky at the end.

The figure of Gelsomina, who enters onto this harsh road out of necessity (though later she chooses to remain with Zampanò until Il Matto's death), is ironically related to Petrarch's Laura and Dante's Beatrice and to mythic reenactments of woman as a figure of redemption. *La strada* raises the *commedia dell'arte* to a divine comedy. Gelsomina's role as agent of conversion is tied to a long-standing conception of femininity as a creative force identified with the sea, as inspiration (literally associated with life as movement), and as a pedagogue of a special kind. Her childlike qualities link her to a prerational, prelinguistic world. In resisting language, she appears to share certain qualities with Zampanò; in his case, however, there is a disdain for words in favor of physical action and force. Through the course of the journey, her interrogation and observation of Zampanò, her conversations with Il Matto, and her dialogue with the nun at the convent, Gelsomina enters into language and seeks to communicate with the resistant Zampanò. Then, after the death of Il Matto, she begins to abandon words, becoming inarticulate herself and unable to respond to Zampanò's prodding questions.

In her appearance, in contrast to the other women with whom Zampanò has sex – the redhead in the trattoria, the cook at the wedding party, the women at the circus – Gelsomina is ethereal, identified with Il Matto and with androgynous sexuality. Although she is forced to have sex with the strongman, the sexual act is part of her resigned initiation into the world. In the trajectory of feminine characters in the film, she is the most dreamlike and fantasmatic: child-adult, asexual, identified with nature and with commerce, a token of monetary exchange (a substitute for her sister, Rosa, also named for a flower). She exists in a liminal, in-between space: between Il Matto and Zampanò and between nature and culture, identified as she is with transformation (through her encounters with the two men) and with natural objects along the road. Thus, among the many philosophic issues invoked by the film, the issue of femininity is crucial: *La strada* draws on the cultural lexicon of images of femininity that are part of myths of birth into culture, knowledge, and creativity.

Vittorio De Sica, not involved with the particular intellectual or political concerns that animate the films of Fellini and Pasolini, continued to direct films that mounted a humanistic critique of social institutions largely through melodrama, comedy, and the use of stars. As a director, De Sica has been identified with a form of the woman's film in texts as early as *Teresa Venerdì,* and especially those involving Sophia Loren, who appeared in his *L'oro di Napoli (The Gold of Naples,* 1954) (as did Silvana Mangano), *La ciociara (Two Women,* 1960), and *Una breve vacanza (A Brief Vacation,* 1973). Loren was his most successful and popular female star, another icon of Italian womanhood but one who is more identified than Magnani with conventional conceptions of exuberant femininity: beauty, curvaceousness, and mammary appeal. Having grown up in Pozzuoli, near Naples, she has been frequently identified in films and interviews as a Neapolitan. Two films directed by De Sica, *L'oro di Napoli* and *Ieri, oggi, domani,* explicitly identify her with Naples. In *La ciociara,* also directed by De Sica, she is identified with the South, embodying certain stereotypes of that region – a dark beauty, animal vitality, sensuality, explosive emotion, and a fierce maternal passion. For her role in this film, Hollywood gave her an Oscar.

Loren began her career as winner of a beauty contest, then was brought to the attention of one of the judges of yet another contest, Carlo Ponti, who became her mentor, sending her to acting school and preparing her for a career in film. Her life was to be dramatically altered by her relation to Ponti, whom she married in 1957 only to discover that their marriage was not legal in Italy. These events became part of the international tabloids as her career grew, especially after she won the Academy Award for *La ciociara.* Loren's biography is a star biography, from humble beginnings to dizzying heights, relying on scandal – an inevitable ingredient when, as with Loren, the emphasis is placed on sensuality – to enhance and underscore the threat of her sexuality (bolstering the transgressive dimensions of the female star image) and, through publicity, to bring it into line with prevailing sexual standards. Hence, Sophia's identification with motherhood, her several attempts to have a child, and her eventual success in birthing conform to the ways "[m]otherhood and family are routinely stressed"[48] in Italian cinema and through its female stars. The scandals involving Loren serve, as in film melodramas, to associate the star's image with the conflict between conformity and resistance. Her fame carried beyond national borders as she, following Gina Lollobrigida, brought the "Italian woman" to the forefront of international attention at a time when the challenges to domestic values and femininity (as well as masculinity) were under scrutiny in the cinema. Loren also demonstrates how "Americanism" was no longer the property of the United States but closely tied to the global-ization of culture, where national commodities like stardom are packaged for the international market. In her persona, Loren remains "Italian" by virtue of her identification in films and publicity with the Italian milieu and in her phys-ical appearance, her uses of her body, gesture, Italian accent, and her associ-ation with Mediterranean life.

De Sica's *La ciociara* situates the narrative in a specific moment of Italian his-tory, the Second World War, and the film explores the effects of war on two women, a mother and her daughter. Based on the Moravia novel of the same name, this narrative too takes place on "the road" as the mother and daughter contend with conditions of survival in war-torn Italy in 1943. Their journey from Rome to the countryside involves a number of encounters that permit the dramatization of the atrocities of war from the vantage point of the two women. One focus of the film is the romanticized image that Cesira (Loren) maintains about her relationship to her daughter, patterned on religious ico-nography and theatricalized notions of the maternal role that jar with the events wrought by Fascism and war.

Beginning in the streets of Rome, revealing the effects of an air raid, the film moves to Cesira's grocery, where the bombs' impact upsets her daughter, Rosetta (Eleonora Brown). The girl has an attack that appears epileptic (and, as it turns out, proleptic). Cesira revives her, talking of leaving Rome until the war is over. Her would-be lover, Giovanni (Raf Vallone), whom she asks to mind the store in her absence, coerces her to have sex, reminding her that her marriage was not one of love but of convenience: She married an older man to escape her life of poverty in the South, and has prospered under Fas-cism. Cesira is a pragmatic creature, devoted to commerce and survival, but her conceptions of motherhood involve fantasies of sexual purity and pro-priety for her daughter. She and Rosetta take a train south but decide to dis-embark when they learn that the tracks have been bombed. When the two get off the train, they ready themselves for a long walk. Male passengers gaze admiringly from a window as Cesira glides seductively away.

Renting a room from a woman whose two sons have fled the war, Cesira is accosted by two Fascists, looking for deserters, who attempt to fondle Rosetta. Back on the road, the two women experience strafing from German planes and see an old man killed. When they arrive in the village at a wedding anniversary celebration, the talk around the table reveals that her relatives are largely indifferent or even sympathetic to the Fascists, their sentiments exposed by the anti-Fascist Michele (Jean-Paul Belmondo) whom no one can understand. The family is primarily concerned with survival not politics, heedless to Michele's warnings about the Germans. An insistent motif of the film involves the indifference of the peasants to analysis of their plight until they experience Germans atrocities firsthand. In the midst of disaster, Cesira's first thought is for her daughter's safety, protecting her from the ravages of men. She fantasizes a husband like Michele for the young girl. This obsession with security in the face of the contingencies of this wartime world is central to Cesira's blind spots and a contributing factor to the rape of her daughter. The irony is compounded by the fact that had they remained with others to learn of Michele's fate, they would not have found themselves in the bombed-out church at the mercy of the Moroccans who rape them both.

Helpless in the face of her daughter's violation, Cesira shouts at a group of Americans in a tank, blaming the Allies for this disaster as Rosetta stands by in shame. No further words are shared by the two as they sit in a truck that takes them on their way home, stopping at the town of Fondi to rest. Here Rosetta goes out with Florindo, the driver, enraging Cesira when the daughter returns with the proverbial nylon stockings as payment for services. Having learned that Michele is dead, Cesira insults her daughter, berating her for her behavior and especially for her indifference to what has transpired. Rosetta's impassive stance collapses when Cesira tells her of Michele's death; the girl begins to sob and Cesira cradles her, asking for forgiveness. The film closes on an iris shot of the mother holding the daughter in a pose reminiscent of a pietà [Fig. 66].

In *La ciociara,* looking functions to reinforce "mainstream visual alignments of the film in accordance with the industry requirements imposed by [Carlo Ponti] in the casting of his wife as Cesira."[49] In fact, it is the film's ironies and contradictions, including the uses of Loren's star persona, that are most revealing in relation to portraits of femininity. Her presence enhances the theatrical dimensions of femininity, making it emerge not as an exploration of motherhood so much as a masquerade of maternity, underscoring its destructive dimensions. The issue of the gaze is tied to the requirements of classical cinema and, throughout the text, to questions of property and commodities, compounded by Loren's acting and physical appearance. Her shapely figure, clinging clothes, and sensual walk are tied to the commerce of cinema. Loren invites the spectator's gaze throughout, from the film's earliest moments, in her self-absorption and in the reiterated shots of her from the

Figure 66. The two women in *La ciociara* (*Two Women*): Cesira (Sophia Loren) and Rosetta (Eleonora Brown). (Courtesy New York Museum of Modern Art Stills Archive)

perspective of men. Loren's presence reproduces the problematic of femininity as that of being visualized and desired. This motif persists in the scene where she and Rosetta detrain and elicit the admiring looks of the men, including the young Germans, leaning out of the window.

Michele's glances at Cesira also enhance the desirability of Loren's image, which exceeds the narrative requirements, and everywhere in the text the looks of others reinforce the power of that image. Her preoccupation with money and security resonates in a text that is implicated in the value of the erotic female body. The scenes of Cesira grooming her daughter, her satisfaction in gazing at Rosetta in proprietary fashion, are no more innocent than Giovanni's lustful gazes at Cesira that culminate in his possession of her body. Thus, the economic value of Loren's cinematic image is invoked and actually reinforced by her character, who is constantly involved in looking appraisingly at objects and people, her daughter among them. The film resonates with the pleasure of looking, which is always threatened by its conversion to violence. The preoccupation with appearance is constantly compromised by the desire to possess. Cesira's violation is inevitable given that the film obsessively connects sexuality, looking, and violence.

Not only is rape central to the diegesis, it is predictable. On a conventional level the war is seen as rapine, the generator of atrocities. Furthermore, the woman's body is traditionally the signifier of the ravished nation, and Cesira being imagistically associated with the pastoral landscape, the rape of women is identified with the rape of the land. The film relentlessly anticipates and orchestrates violence to the female body, and the rape involves both mother and daughter – but with a difference. Cesira is accustomed to the commerce of the world and to force that must be negotiated, and thus her rape is a confirmation of the ways of the world. Rosetta's rape is of another order for Cesira: Contrary to her worldliness and commonsense realism, she has nourished the fantasy of her daughter's purity and intactness as if it were possible to escape the depredations of Fascism and war that have been revealed. However, the poignancy and complexity of the film resides in its refusal to reduce Cesira to a mere victim. Her fetishizing of her daughter's body, associated with the reiterated images of the Madonna and Child, are in direct contrast to her own sensuality, materialism, and will to survive. As the surrogate for Italy as a vanquished and bleeding land, she is also complicit with the bloodletting in her refusal to visualize, hear, and recognize the signs of her own accommodation to political realities, her blindness to the fact "that no human life is above historical contingency."[50]

The daughter's rape provides a crude awakening both for Cesira and for the audience. The fantasy of escape and forgetfulness is smashed in the violence perpetrated on Rosetta and in the subsequent scenes where the young woman succumbs to the commerce of sex. However, Cesira still cannot accept the violation of her daughter and displaces her rage about the rape and its effects by becoming abusive toward Rosetta. The final moments of the film – the wordless, weeping embrace of mother and daughter and their framing as a pietà – do not offer a "solution" to the dilemma. Ironically, they recapitulate the image of the mother and child but in a context that opens up the possibility of rethinking cherished icons of femininity and maternity. The highly stylized images are a reminder, as is Loren's star persona throughout, of another layer of allegory: the role of art, and cinema in particular, to enhance and possibly expose their "powers of the false." Though the film may not satisfy a desire for an alternative, noncommercial text that can bring out the political and narrative complexities of the novel, it offers a powerful portrait of the historical uses and abuses of femininity in Loren's enactment of the maternal role. A more realist text might have shrouded the constructed and contradictory aspects of femininity and of maternity; but De Sica's text exploits these illusions to reveal how powerfully they serve as destructive clichés.

Loren's star image is tied to cosmopolitanism and to Italy's economic miracle associated with the "new consumerism" at home and the successful export of commodities abroad.[51] The media's consumption of images is inextricable from the "consumption of meanings and symbols of the most diverse kinds."[52] Loren's star image must therefore be understood as disseminating a range of meanings that impact on conceptions of traditional sexual mores, involving greater freedom in sexual behavior, challenges to Catholicism (with its emphasis on familialism, maternity, reproduction), increased physical mobility (changes in domicile, tourism), youthful rebellion, dress codes, and fashion.[53] One of the best films to gauge the polysemous character of Loren is *Ieri, oggi, domani* (*Yesterday, Today, and Tomorrow,* 1963). Comprising three segments, in which she plays three different characters in three different time frames, from the postwar era to the 1960s, the film offers clues to the dimensions of her star persona. In the first segment, "Adelina of Naples," she is again, following her role as the pizza seller in *L'oro di Napoli*, identified with the city of Naples and with lower-class life, offering a reprise of her initial designation as a woman of lower-class origins consonant with her biography. She is, as consistent with her offscreen life, again transgressive, involved with illegal black-market activities and hence with the law, since she owes money to the city authorities and must either pay or go to jail. Maternity is her means of flouting the law: She learns that if she remains pregnant, she cannot be put in jail. She walks the streets, hair awry, sporting her big belly, shouting in raucous voice to her neighbors, ordering her husband, Carmine (Marcello Mastroianni in a subordinate role), to perform sexually, and accumulating seven children – far too many to be contained in her tiny dwelling. When Carmine can no longer perform, however, she turns against him, taking him to the physician, who describes him as run down and in need of rest. She tries to seduce their friend, Pasquale, to increase the family, but relents and finally decides to go off to jail.

At this point the community, sympathetic to her and hostile as ever to authority, takes up a collection to pay her fine, while the lawyer succeeds in getting her a pardon. Loren's role – in the references to her origins, troubles with the law, and attempts to have children – is tied to her star persona. Her bouncing bosom and swaying body are designed, as Pasquale says. to "bring out the animal." In her release from jail, Adelina herself becomes a star, attracting reporters and crowds on the street as she rides through her neighborhood, cheered by all. These events – set before the economic miracle – serve to highlight an earlier time of economic hardship, familial bonding, and community solidarity that were identified with neorealism but that center now on the dominant role of Adelina/Loren.

The second episode, "Anna of Milan," links Loren to the prosperous image of Milan in the 1960s and is indicative of another side of her star persona associated with glamour, wealth, and the fast life. Her voice is heard on the sound track, reciting the endless and boring responsibilities of an upper-class existence. The events take place on the wide streets, business areas, and highways of Milan, a major locus of Italy's economic miracle. Renzo (Mastroianni again) emerges from a small car and gets into a Rolls Royce. Anna is about to enjoy the transgressive pleasures of adultery. Driving her Rolls without regard for others on the road, she is dressed in a Dior outfit – tight-fitting black dress, fur-trimmed coat, raking hat – and ostentatious earrings, snake bracelet, watch, and rings. Her hair is smartly coiffed and she is heavily made up. Inviting him to drive, he swerves to avoid hitting a young boy selling flowers on the road, thereby smashing the car into a truck. She then berates him for his helplessness in not being able to change the tire and for using her costly coat to kneel on. Finally, she flags down an expensive sports car and leaves Renzo on the highway to wait for a mechanic. The Loren image in this episode is linked to wealth, commodities, fashion especially, and mobility. She is an emblem of the sixties – beautiful, stylish, and unattainable – and of the new prosperity: The wife of an industrialist (in real life, a cinema magnate), seeking pleasure but revealing, in the final analysis, her attachment to the material appurtenances of her life.

The final episode, "Mara of Rome," introduces yet another image of Loren tied to the new sexuality and the greater freedom in cinema to explore prostitution in the 1950s, 1960s, and 1970s. This image of Loren – a union of the Madonna and whore, of seduction and chastity – is linked to the new consumer society (as in the previous episode) and its threats to traditional Italian institutions (obliquely to the family, more directly to the Catholic Church). In the first view of Loren, she is merely draped in a sheet as a young priest-to-be, Umberto, gazes at her longingly as she, through her gestures, encourages his attention while "innocently" parading her charms. When her doorbell rings and her "client from Bologna," Rusconi (Mastroianni) arrives, we get further corroboration from him that she is "a goddess of beauty," an "imperial highness." Through him too, she is seen in the various roles she is called upon to play for her clients: child, mother, and sex object. Through the two men's fascination with her, the audience is invited to explore the sources of Mara/Loren's appeal to men (and to themselves). The linking of religion and sexuality is initiated first through Umberto's desire for her, and in his decision not to take priestly vows. Once having seen her – her appeal is so overwhelming – abstinence is impossible. However, as penance for her transgression against him, Mara temporarily withholds her body from men. Rusconi, who sees her as the embodiment of his fantasies of sexual gratification, must succumb to her transitory vow of abstinence. A creature of economic shrewdness, preoccupied with the "respectability" and the marketability of her image, she brags about the substantial money she earns and tells Umberto's grandmother that she chooses her clients "very carefully": They are all sons of tycoons.

The most revealing insight concerning stardom emerges when she, in lieu of sex, strips for Rusconi. This moment becomes a striptease in which Loren offers the enticing image of her body for gaze, not for his appropriation but for the movie audience [Fig. 67]. Her undressing for Rusconi (and for the cam-

Figure 67. Sophia Loren's "striptease" as Mara in *Ieri, oggi, domani* (*Yesterday, Today and Tomorrow*). (Courtesy New York Museum of Modern Art Stills Archive)

era) captures the quintessence of cinematic femininity and stardom. The film, through the metaphor of striptease, introduces a major characteristic of the star: The spectator may look, but there is no way to realize the desire set in motion by the image. The expensive image of the star has no substance, revealing how its economic value is based on its illusory nature. Stardom appears to bear no resemblance to a material system of exchange; it is merely to be looked at and desired, much as Rusconi watches Mara perform for him. However, this final episode, like the film overall, has evocatively suggested connections between the economics of filmmaking and the role of the star as a conduit through which this desire flows and produces profit. In addition, "Mara of Rome" suggests links among economics, stardom, and prostitution.

The films of Michelangelo Antonioni have been identified with the figure of woman and with one feminine figure in particular: Monica Vitti. Antonioni began work in cinema during the Fascist era as a scriptwriter and was later associated with the critics of the journal *Cinema*. His early work as director utilizes aspects of neorealism, but, like Fellini, he became identified with a form of filmmaking that seemed to many to be a betrayal of neorealism in subject matter and style. In the sixties his films were noted as the harbinger of a new, "minimalist" mode of filmmaking: self-reflexive, auteurist, related to modernism, and concerned with form. *L'avventura* (1960) more than *Il grido* (*The Outcry,* 1957) brought his work into international prominence. His films are exemplary of the paths neorealism was to take in the hands of directors (e.g., Fellini and Pasolini) in the 1960s. Rather than forsaking that cinematic form, his films, like theirs, were a realization of the possibilities opened up by the neorealist aesthetic. In their abandonment of conventional modes of narration, begun by Zavattini–De Sica and Rossellini, the films probed changing relations between character and milieu in a context appropriate to the far-reaching cultural and social transformations wrought by industrialization and the "economic miracle."

Antonioni's films focus largely on characters in movement though the landscape, often on a journey. They emphasize different registers of the passage of time and the inscrutable and enigmatic nature of character. Their inconclusive endings can be identified with the canonical works of neorealism, but their departure from that school derives from their focus on questions of sexuality (treating both masculine and feminine figures), not as a polemic on class differences and conflict, not as a sociological text per se on the new economic and social formations developing in Italy, but as an intricate analysis of a new, emergent culture. The images of that culture are not conveyed through melodrama; nor are they conventional portraits of interactions among the characters. The films work through analogies with other art forms, an exploration of milieu, and through the characters' dehumanization. Antonioni's films are an exploration of a culture of visualization, of how the world and the body are to be understood in terms of cultural signs rather than in purely physical terms. In Peter Bondanella's words, "Antonioni's originality lies precisely in his de-emphasis of the dramatic potential of the film plot with its traditional problems, complication, and eventual resolution, all developed through some notion of psychological conflict between well-defined figures."[54]

Monica Vitti was identified largely with the films of Michelangelo Antonioni, and their association reveals an aspect of stardom that has a lineage in the history of cinema: the symbiotic relationship between male director and female actor evidenced in the relationships of von Sternberg and Dietrich, Rossellini and Magnani (and then Ingrid Bergman), Ingmar Bergman and Liv Ullman, Fellini and Giulietta Masina. Vitti became the representative of Antonioni's alienated female protagonists and garnered international attention in

Figure 68. Monica Vitti as Claudia in *L'avventura*. (Courtesy New York Museum of Modern Art Stills Archive)

such films as *L'avventura, La notte* (*The Night,* 1961), and *Deserto rosso* (*Red Desert,* 1964) – films belonging to a different mode of filmmaking than either the neorealist or postwar genre films. Antonioni's films were associated with a directorial signature, with philosophical and conceptual issues, the transformed and transforming nature of postmodernity, and a focus on form and technique. These films posit a different relation to actors and acting.

Vitti's acting is understated and minimal, relying on the union of camera movement and mise-en-scène, creating an aura of ambiguity, undermining clear outlines of the character's subjectivity yet conveying a sense of crisis. Her blonde, pale, thin, and willowy appearance is complemented by her designer clothing [Fig. 68], closely tied to the feminine fashions of the 1960s as part of the films's general focus on the texture of the upper-class, highly industrialized, and commodified world that is at the heart of Antonioni's complex examination of the relation between technology and artistic technique. Vitti's film image can thus circulate in the world of the jet set, of high fashion and mobility, yet operate differently than that of the conventional star turn. If Vitti's role appears as somnambulistic, it does not reinscribe the role of the star as commodity. Rather, her image is part of an interrogation of the cinema and of visualization that the director has undertaken to analyze. She is depersonalized as part of a larger framework where depersonalization is intrinsic to the texture of the world portrayed. Hence, Monica Vitti's image bears little resemblance to that of such stars as Anna Magnani, Sophia Loren, or even Mariangela Melato (see the upcoming discussion of *Film d'amore e d'anarchia*), who are identified with effusive affect and familiar female subject positions (even where the role is a caricature).

L'avventura offers the viewer an instance of intellectual cinema where the problems and questions are more important than a neat "message" or description of what the film is "about." Assisting the spectator in the "adventure" of cinema, the film utilizes the figure of woman as a puzzle (one of the characters we meet is Patrizia, who spends her time doing puzzles) and connects woman to looking and, therefore, to spectatorship. The presence of paintings, their connections to the characters and the mise-en-scène, and the introduction of Goffredo (Giovanni Petrucci), a young painter, enhance the enigma of the role of looking in the film. Relations among the characters – familial, marital, commercial – are also enigmatic. The word "why" recurs as they confront one another with questions that are never adequately answered.

Aboard the yacht on which a group of wealthy Italians (and one less affluent friend, Claudia) are cruising off the coast of Sicily, the question of looking becomes complicated in relation to the characters and to the spectator, underscoring the sense of the indeterminacy of vision. Repeatedly, the characters are uncertain about what it is they see, whether sharks or boats – Anna (Lea Massari) even confesses to her friend Claudia (Vitti) that she made up the story about the sharks – but the larger level of visual uncertainty entails Anna's disappearance on the island where the group stops for a brief exploration of its landscape. The characters wander on the rocky hills, calling Anna, and inventing different scenarios of what has happened to her; but equally cogent are the ways in which they survey one another and how the camera becomes an alternative commentator on the landscape and on the characters' interrelations. Uppermost is the fact of the missing body of a woman and of Claudia as an observer to the main crises in the film, including a guilt-laden interaction between Anna and her father before embarking, Raimondo's attempts on the yacht to seduce Patrizia, and finally, at a hotel, her betrayal by Anna's lover, Sandro (Gabriele Ferzetti), in his sexual liaison with a voluptuous starlet, Gloria Perkins (Dorothy De Poliolo).

The core of the film presents the mystery of femininity as it involves depiction of the woman's body. It is not a conventional crime detection film, though it shares with that genre its focus on the mystery of the missing "body" of a woman and investigative efforts to track the clues to its disappearance and to materialize it. Anna's disappearance serves as a meditation on conventional cinematic representations that seek repeatedly to render the world visible and hence knowable. The mystery of seeing is not solved but gives rise to philosophic and problematic questions concerning vision and its relation to culturally constructed conceptions of gender and sexuality and, particularly, the resistance to distinguishing between absence and presence, sameness and difference. The film struggles to see and think about the world differently at the same time that it reveals the tendency to remain rooted in repetition. For example, the two women, Anna and Claudia, are brunette and blonde, respectively. They are different in gesture and appearance – and yet the substitution of one for the other is at work in Claudia becoming the object of Sandro's desire so soon after Anna vanishes. In a later scene between Patrizia and Claudia, blonde Claudia puts on a brunette wig and Patrizia a blonde one, and they comment on how different they look. In that same episode, however, Goffredo's paintings of nude women all appear to be the same.

Thus, the characters' quest to find Anna is analogous to the director's (and the viewer's) struggle to distinguish the contours of this modern world, with its residues of the past often visualized through painting. For example, the painting on the walls of the San Domenico Hotel of a woman with an old man – perused by a young woman (the aforementioned Gloria) who is, at the same time, regarding Sandro – elicits a number of questions concerning the role of looking in the film. In commenting on this painting, P. Adams Sitney writes:

> Merely as an expensive baroque object the painting contributes to the opulence of the hotel. As an image of an old man sucking at the breast of a young woman it is a curiosity, all the more interesting because of an indication of a sight off the canvas. In the sexually charged environment, it mediates a failed seduction. . . . In this film of ellipses that parades one loss of meaning or certainty after another, the painting and its multiple interpretations allegorizes the status of cinema.[55]

The loss of meaning or certainty is particularly cogent because it is tied to the integral relationship between the woman's body and artistic/cinematic vision. Antonioni's film draws on but does not make explicit or resolve the dilemma of femininity, its constructed nature, its connection to desire, and its undecidable character. *L'avventura* poses it as an enigma that has become more evident in the context of cinematic investigation.

Landscape and architecture also play an important role in relation to the film's investigation of cinema's power to elicit an interrogation of reality rather than reiterate commonplace interpretations of social and sexual relations. The island and Anna's disappearance signify more than a portrait of modern "alienation" and more than a simple opposition between nature and culture. The island – in contrast to the crowded and menacing streets of the cities, evident particularly in the look of the men who ogle Claudia as she waits for Sandro, or in the mass hysteria of those who witness the spectacle of Gloria

Perkins's exhibitionism – seems to constitute a ground zero. As such, the island signifies how conventional forms of interaction are pushed to their limit and introduces the major investigative axis of the film – the crisis of representation, involving a reassessment of relations between men and woman and their sense of their milieu.

The return to the city and to the landscape of the South after the extended search on the island are more than a commentary on urban life: They afford the opportunity for the characters (and the viewer) to continue their exploration of the social and sexual body. The architectural landscape of Noto (near Syracuse) is presented as a contrast between past and present, emptiness and crowding. The past is evident in the shots of the massive baroque church, but the town offers another, less monumental, portrait of the present. Claudia, waiting alone on the street as Sandro enters a hotel to follow up on a reported sighting of the missing Anna, is initimidated by groups of men who ogle her and attempt to surround her. This episode reinforces the film's investigation of sexual politics and its inextricability from the investigation of the female body.

There are several allusions in *L'avventura* to melodrama and to sentimentality, but the film distances itself from conventional melodrama, intent as it is on self-consciously examining conventional assumptions about sexual relationships. In *L'avventura,* and even more in *Deserto rosso,* Antonioni "is not an author who moans about the impossibility of communicating in the world. It is just that the world is painted in splendid colors, while the bodies which people it are still insipid and colorless. The world awaits its inhabitants, who are still lost in neurosis."[56] The allusions are aligned to the imperative of rethinking the conventional romantic positions assigned to the woman's body, sexuality, and modernity. *L'avventura* parallels poststructuralist attempts to rethink the language inherited to describe the world, and of its intimate connection to the figure of woman as a cultural creation illuminated through the illusory and evanescent properties of cinema.

The films of Lina Wertmüller offer still another perspective on femininity in the Italian cinema. In particular, *Film d'amore e d'anarchia (Love and Anarchy,* 1972) orchestrates in encyclopedic fashion connections among women, sexuality, history (particularly the history of Fascism), and politics. Though not identified primarily with feminist politics, Wertmüller's films have probed issues of concern to Italian feminists. The 1970s were a decade of "explosive growth and proliferation of collective practice and experimentation. . . . Italian feminism was experimenting with a political practice closely linked to a female experience of knowledge, both individual and collective."[57]

Wertmüller's works focus on female experience within the context of larger institutional structures – the state, working-class organizations, the church, the cinema – that reinforce and legitimize traditional social practices.

She is sensitive to the history of these institutions and how they are implicated in heterosexism. However, she has been chastised by feminists for adopting a style of comedic satire that presents women in grotesque and vulgar terms and relies on social stereotypes rather than developing a film language more conducive to female experience.

Before directing her own films, Wertmüller worked in the theater, then for a time as assistant to Fellini. She became associated with Giancarlo Giannini, who was to become a major component of her films, when he acted in a play she directed. *Film d'amore e d'anarchia* takes place largely in a brothel and is a highly stylized film in the vein of Fellini. The characters typify certain attitudes and values; the setting too is antirealist and charged with allegorical significance. Though this film is not a feminist tract, it does situate the position of women as central to an understanding of the history of Fascism and its relation to contemporary politics on film. The narrative involves a northern Italian peasant, Tunin (Giannini), who is apolitical but identifies with the brutal death of his anarchist friend, Michele Sgaravento, at the hands of the Fascists. As a result, he contacts anarchists in Paris, returns to Rome, and seeks out Salome (Mariangela Melato), a high-priced prostitute with a hatred for the Fascists. She welcomes Tunin, inviting him to have sex with her, to hear her history of a time prior to her becoming a prostitute, and to share a meal with the women in the brothel. There Tunin meets Tripolina (Lina Polito), with whom he falls in love; she will, in part, be responsible for his failure to accomplish his mission of killing Mussolini.

Through the images of the brothel and the urban and rural landscape, the film will make connections between sexual relations and Fascist politics. Like so many films of the 1970s that return to that earlier history, Wertmüller's is concerned with offering a psychosexual accounting of Fascism as opposed to a purely historical analysis. In particular, the film links the rise of Fascism and the failure to defeat it to gendered and sexual conditions. Choosing to concentrate on the analogy between women and prostitution – the sale of the female body and its sexual commodification – the film excludes any portraits of other aspects of woman's position as mother, daughter, and wife. Thus, there is minimal focus on women outside the brothel except in the opening scene in the countryside and in a later rural outing by Tunin, Tripolina, Salome, and Spatoletti, her hypermasculine client and the head of the Fascist police. The bordello is Wertmüller's strongest and most antiromantic indictment of women's historical position. Millicent Marcus writes that

> In keeping with a long literary tradition, Wertmüller has made this house of prostitution a figure for Italy in all her anguished history of foreign conquest and moral compromise. . . . Fascism is simply the latest in a series of clients who have enjoyed the willingly surrendered virtue of this desirable, irredeemably fallen land.[58]

The identification of Italy with the figure of woman and prostitution reiterates long-standing connections between women and the nation, with women as the medium of economic and political exchange. In this respect, the film is harsh in its treatment of women, making them the victims of national hegemony but also identifying the terms of their complicity. Hence the conjunction of love and politics entails the sense of how women have been exploited as well as how they have collaborated in perpetuating their domination [Fig. 69].

In the visual presentation of the bordello – its mélange of classical, modernist, and Orientalist kitsch art – can be seen the cultural artifacts that reinforce and communicate the image of woman as sexual object. The melancholy and romantic songs that the women sing around the table convey the myths of love and romance that subtend the selling of woman's body. In Salome's room, mirrors capture not only the self-enclosed nature of this world but the imposed narcissism that is part of the folklore of women in relation to their bodies. The names of the two female protagonists, Salome and Tripolina, allude to myths and fantasies relating to women. Salome is identified with one of the archetypal seductresses of Western culture; Tripolina, with the exoticism of Africa (and of Italy's colonial ambitions in Libya) as well as with the image of Rudolph Valentino in *The Sheik* (1921). Although there is a distinction between Salome's commitment to the demise of the regime and Tripolina's single-minded love for Tunin, the two women are alike in their enslavement to fantasies of romance. If one is tempted to accord greater virtue to one or the other, the film cancels out their differences at the end. However, this cancellation is not a mere moral judgment but a recognition of the power not only of romanticism but of the forces of violence in the world, which Tunin and Salome have underestimated.

The role of Spatoletti (Eros Pagni) is central to the outcome of the film. An incarnation of Mussolini and the Fascist emphasis on virility and physical power, he is also a representation of the excesses of hypermasculinity. The brothel exists because the culture adheres to the necessity of subjecting women to virile domination. As Bondanella writes, "Spatoletti continuously associates political power and sexuality. Italy is metaphorically seen as a ravished woman, dominated by sexual and political adventurers like Mussolini and Spatoletti."[59] The film is mindful, however, of the economic context that supports his political power. The viewer is made aware that economic exchange in the bordello is predicated on the continued patronage of clients, which entails maintaining a high-class establishment – the best of foods, as Madame Aïda boasts – and an appealing physical environment, most evident in the modernist works of art on display in the brothel and in the spectacle of the women parading before the men as in a beauty contest. The mirrors, paintings, and sculpture in the brothel, like the protofascist architecture on the streets where Spatoletti and Tunin find themselves after the day in the country, en-

Figure 69. Women and Fascism: Mariangela Melato as Salome in *Film d'amore e d'anarchia* (*Love and Anarchy*). (Courtesy New York Museum of Modern Art Stills Archive)

hance the sense of this Fascist world as a garish theater. These images indict Fascist culture (and its persistence in the present) as complicit in the prostitution of social *and* cultural life. However, the emphasis on prostitution is a constant reminder of the economics of culture and, in particular, of the collusion among money, sexuality, and artistic representation.

The distinctions between Tunin and Spatoletti are important to the gendered and sexual distinctions satirized in the film. The two characters reveal conflicting conceptions of masculinity. In describing their differences at the end of the film, Millicent Marcus writes:

[T]he two men become visual embodiments of their opposed political positions. Spatoletti is the very image of Fascist order with his slicked-back hair, his impeccable white uniform pulled tightly over his muscular body, his forward-leaning aggressive posture, and his polished rhetoric of interrogation. Tunin, already the victim of Fascist manhandling, is in total physical disarray, with his tousled hair, his loose sackcloth shirt, his slumping posture, and barely audible, but nonetheless infuriating responses.[60]

Tunin's ungainliness and naïveté may draw the spectator into assuming that his role (like his association with nature) is a reliable index to the film's point of view. He is not a hero; but the spectator is made aware – through Salome's narrative of her own history, including the death of her unfortunate lover, Anteo Zambon, at the hands of the Fascists – that Tunin is an embodiment of Anteo (a name ironically identified with one of the rebels against the gods in mythology), both in his appearance and in his eventual fate.

There are moments where the film offers another vision to this brutality, though it is tainted by the myths of romance that the film is seeking to undo. These are seen in the encounters in the country and in the later lovemaking between Tunin and Tripolina (whom he has renamed Ricciolina, his "curly locks"). For a time, it appears possible that love might triumph; but the women's subsequent fight over waking Tunin, their mutual succumbing to love (and hence to feminine stereotypes), expose another myth: that love is transforming. Instead, the film shows that the counterpart to Spatoletti's hypermasculinity is hyperfemininity couched in the language of love and nurture.

The film's dissection of politics employs several strategies to convey the complexities of Fascism in relation to past and present. Its major strategy relies on exposing the brutality of Fascism as founded on forms of economic exchange that involve trafficking in women's bodies. The metaphor of prostitution, beyond commercial exchange, involves a cultural aesthetics that capitalizes on the woman's body, nudity, clothing, and maquillage. Dressing and undressing become the film's way of exposing the naked aspects of brutality and commerce that are covered over by artifice. Finally, the film dissects heroic and romantic narratives. If the text undoes images and narratives of heroic resistance, it does so in the context of their complicity with a sexual politics that has long involved idealized conceptions of femininity that conceal its exchange value under the rubric of "love." In short, if Spatoletti exemplifies the brute force of masculinity and a corresponding aesthetic of virility and power, Tunin exemplifies problems with the humanist ideal of individual agency and resistance. The problematic that the film cannot resolve is the position of femininity so anomalous that even the female characters cannot fathom it. Still, the film suggests that sexual politics is at the basis of Fascism.

In a film made a decade later, *Sotto . . . sotto . . . strapazatto da un anomala passione* (*Sotto, sotto,* 1984), Wertmüller takes another look at the "woman question," focusing this time on the issue of lesbianism, which becomes the *pretext* for dramatizing women's position in Italian culture. As in her *Film d'amore e d'anarchia,* the exploration of gendered relations is uppermost, though this time situated in a contemporary context. The role of history is never absent, tied as it is to a range of issues central to Italian Catholic culture. Feminist critics have had difficulties with the film, finding that it "denies the existence of lesbianism and slyly circulates pernicious stereotypes about it."[61] Lucy Fischer has written that *Sotto . . . sotto* is "more about the *fantasy* of lesbianism than about lesbianism itself – a subject about which Wertmüller seems uneasy. . . . The director also shows her hand in the lesser weight she assigns to the female characters."[62] Such a reading suggests that the film is (or should be) *about* lesbianism and that there is a fixed and available lexicon of lesbianism upon which the director should have drawn. One of the difficulties in addressing the films of Wertmüller is that often the critics do not situate the film within the context of Italian culture and history: They do not examine the gendered portrayals in the film within the problematics of a national cinema. Another, though related, problem resides in the ongoing confusion about how to read the film through the lens of comedy and satire, which perforce entail caricature, exaggeration, and distortion. The film is interested in exposing the folklore and fantasy that govern perceptions of women. As in *Divorzio all'italiana,* femininity is seen as bound to the cult of machismo and *onore* identified by many with southern Italian culture.

Sotto . . . sotto purports to examine the position of women in Italian culture from the vantage point of the history of cinema: It is laden with references to Hollywood and Italian cinema, and includes a reference to French cinema (Gérard Philipe in *Le Diable au corps* [*The Devil in the Flesh,* 1947]) and a more general one to "poor" Rainer Werner Fassbinder. Opening with a view of a television on which *Casablanca* is playing, close-ups of Humphrey Bogart and Ingrid Bergman enable the introduction of two of the present film's major protagonists, Ester (Veronica Lario) and Oscar (Enrico Montesano), quarreling about whether Bogart and Bergman are "gay." A number of allusions to film stars are interspersed: to Anna Magnani and Sophia Loren, to Stefania Sandrelli in *Divorzio all'italiana,* Ingrid Bergman and Cary Grant in *Notorious,* Monica Vitti in *Deserto rosso,* as well as to Richard Burton and Liz Taylor. Moreover, one of the episodes, in which Oscar is seeking to find the presumed lover of Ester, takes place at Cinecittà, and the narrative is a compilation of many of the films referenced, as well as of Wertmüller's own films. Like much of Italian cinema, and especially Italian comedy that addresses sexual politics, this film focuses more on caricatures of femininity than on the female characters as "realistic" embodiments of "correct" heterosexual or lesbian positions.

In *Sotto . . . sotto,* as in the other films cited, the question of what women are and want is as ephemeral as all the writings about and cinematic portraits of them. Thus this film, in its problematic presentation of femininity, reenacts the "truth of untruth" about women, elaborating on the various ways in which knowledge about them is inextricably tied to cultural fantasies, and that these fantasies require a demystification of representation in the Italian context. In its invocation of other films and of television, *Sotto . . . sotto* locates a major source of feminine and masculine fantasy in the media. If the film seems unbalanced in its portrayals of women, this may reside, in part, in the director's preoccupation with the various cultural, religious, political, and social institutions that support and reinforce masculine hegemony over women.

One of the most interesting and frequently denigrated aspects of the film involves its uses of setting – architecture and statuary. Lucy Fischer is critical of the film's deployment of landscape. She notes that the scenes at Bomarzo have an "eerie and magical quality," such that the issue of lesbianism is relegated to the realm of witchcraft and dream: "This sense of lesbianism as witchcraft undercuts any serious portrayal of its possibility for women."[63] The archaic statues and the old towerlike house (where the women kiss and later talk about an "impossible" escape to Lesbos) are reminiscent of fairy tales (e.g., "Rapunzel") or *A Midsummer Night's Dream.* As for the scenes in the city, Fischer describes them as augmenting the film's "fantasmatic quality": "The section of Rome that Oscar and Ester inhabit is a composite of ruins rather than a credible neighborhood."[64]

This criticism seems to derive from a predilection for a more realist treatment of character and landscape that would allow greater scope for the film's portrait of lesbianism. The film, however, is primarily concerned with the powerful forces in Italian culture that not only annihilate women's desire but are reminiscent of Fascist politics. In the context of satire, these are drawn quite broadly to reveal their persistence and perniciousness:

> One of the characteristics of *commedia all'italiana* is its exposure
> of an undercurrent of social malaise and the painful contradictions
> of a culture in rapid transformation. Moreover, the sometimes fac-
> ile and optimistic humanitarianism typical of neorealist comedy is
> replaced by a darker, and more ironic and cynical vision of Italian
> life.[65]

Sotto . . . sotto seems cast in this mold, focusing more on the general texture of Italian life than on redeeming individual characters and situations. All of the characters are flawed, and the spotlight seems to be shifted over to these powerful institutions. In this context, the Catholic Church is heavily satirized for its opposition to new forms of knowledge as well as of social organization, as these involve the family and the position of women. When the priest lectures on the Bernini statue of Saint Teresa, he underscores the fact that he is talking about the spiritual not carnal dimensions of her adoration of Christ. The thought of any "carnal" relations except for procreation are precluded by the priest's parading traditional lore about women and sexuality.

The church is also satirized for defining and determining the character and direction of sexual desire. Most crucial to the sexual politics of the film as it relates to Catholicism is the scene where Oscar goes into the church to seek guidance from the priest, whom he identifies with patriarchy, ritual, and violence – ironically, many of the characteristics displayed by Oscar in his treatment of women. An argument ensues over whether Oscar will make the sign of the cross in the confessional, and he refuses, saying that it would not be sincere, as he is follower of "historical materialism." The satire is double-edged: Oscar's words confirm that the church reduces "the people to ignorance," yet he threatens to bring back Fascism ("We'll go on being Fascists again"). The scene exposes both Oscar and the priest as implicated in Fascism in their authoritarianism and recourse to violence. The priest, in his anti-communism, makes fun of the Communist Party, calls Oscar a subversive, and threatens to call the police. Oscar refuses to describe himself as a proverbial "lost sheep" and takes refuge in being "endowed like a bull."

Consistently, the film highlights the clichés that Oscar mouths about women and men, stressing his belief in "normality," rejecting "unnatural" same-sex love, reiterating his fear of and rage at the possibility of being cuckolded, calling all women whores, and resorting to verbal and physical violence as his masculine prerogative. At one point, though, after inveighing against homosexuality, he confides in Amilcare (Mario Scarpetta) while cradling the man's head. Several times, the film suggests that the behavior of the men carries homosocial connotations. In the final episode of Oscar's raging like a bull and attacking the women, his Fascist leanings are reinforced as he mocks freedom, equality, and democracy, but then says before his physical assault that he will be modern, even postmodern – interpreting modernity as having sex with both of them.

The film ends ambiguously with the pathetic image of Oscar in an ambulance, asking Ester, "Do I have to bleed to death to make you care for me again?" and a dissolve to the landscape of Rome at night. It is clear that Wertmüller's position toward femininity is as anomalous as the film's title: From the perspectives of Italian history and culture, the situation of women, despite changing attitudes toward homosexuality, marriage, and divorce, is still governed by antiquated and traditional (mis)conceptions and resistances to sexuality derived from the past, and particularly from the church and Fascism. This accounts for the overriding attention to Oscar as exemplary of these attitudes. In general, the film's greater focus on the men and relegation of the women to the fantasmatic speak less to Wertmüller's fashioning "a work that reveals certain tendencies she might not have wished to disclose"[66] than to her fashioning a work that reveals the overwhelming constraints on developing an understanding of woman's position. In the words of Patrizia Violi,

> We know that the female seems to be precisely that which is removed from language, that which is repressed in discourse, therefore that which is "unspeakable." Indeed, if we try to define it, we can only arrive at a negative formulation: "a woman is something that cannot be."[67]

Not only from Wertmüller's film but from all the film's discussed above, it is clear that the question of "woman" reveals itself as imbricated in forms of representation that acknowledge not only its "unspeakability" but also its reliance on existing modes of language – verbal, gestural, cinematic. These require a different conceptual and analytic framework for understanding the sexual politics that continue to govern the dominant role of heterosexism.

CHAPTER ELEVEN

Conversion, Impersonation, and Masculinity

An examination of the films produced in Italy over the course of this century reveals changing perceptions of the masculine figure. Even the most blatantly masculinist texts reveal that the portrayals are not seamless and unitary, but expose the bricolage of their construction, how they are a compendium of different and often conflicting cultural data. The films are a trove of information concerning how the folklore of gender is created from the fabric of cultural common sense. This common sense relies on folklore drawn from popular and canonical literary works, paintings, other films, politics, economics, and popular psychology.

The folklore of masculinity is based on assumptions of difference between the two genders embellished, legitimated, and disseminated in social, legal, and cultural forms. Masculinity must be understood as having a parentage similar to femininity but different effects in relation to social and cultural power. If femininity is an abstraction with no intrinsic meaning but available to be endowed with value and significance, masculinity has been assumed as the standard of measurement for its value. Producers and consumers are complicit in the creation of cultural commodities, sharing in their value creation. These commodities produce monetary as well as social value as a means of fashioning the folklore of consensus. Although the profit motive is constant, the production process is hydra-headed, utilizing constantly changing strategies to ensure circulation and consumption. Considerations of sexuality and gender are fundamental components in the production, circulation, consumption, and determinations of social and cultural value.

The concept of masculinity is central to the production of social meaning via forms of representation and representativeness providing the semblance of a subject who ostensibly participates willingly, and out of necessity, in the dissemination and maintenance of social and cultural forms. Images of masculinity circulate primarily at the level of gender differentiation, but this in turn reaches into domestic and public spheres, into the division of labor, touching on questions of sexuality and reproduction, and, at the most abstract level, of social order and chaos. Cinema and now television and video are major forces in the production, counterproduction, and reproduction of masculinity.

Attempts to identify an originary or homologous source (e.g., biological conceptions of gender) for the role that sexuality plays in the construction of social value usually end up in a morass of essentialism and reductionism. They mystify the power assigned to sexuality and obfuscate how affective value circulates and signifies in multiple fashion so as to seize and harmonize different and even dissident constituencies. Value "does not wear an explanatory label. Far from it, value changes all labour products into social hieroglyphs."[1] The production and the consumption of the text of masculinity, while presupposing a homogenous community, reveal both attempts at unification and fractures and fissures that belie such unity available to the critic through an examination of the character of "social hieroglyphs."

The Italian cinema during the Fascist era constructed its conceptions of masculinity sometimes parallel to and often subtly in divergence from the ideology of masculinity promulgated by the regime. Such construction is evident in the theatricality of the portraits, obvious in the highly choreographed and stylized images of masculine characters in the genre films. Theatricality, a politics of style that makes itself evident *as* style in contrast to intrinsic meaning, was inherent to Fascism, with its self-conscious awareness of strategies for creating consensus not merely through the public spectacles staged by the regime to garner the hearts and minds of the people, but specifically through the use of cinema as a medium for creating believable, if conflicting, images of the world. Though the audience may not accept the "truth" of the image, it does produce a dilemma about the relation between itself and "real" life. Correspondingly, in the case of portraits of masculinity, the artifice of the medium opens up the possibility of its tenuous but nonetheless powerful nature. In other words, the "imaginary" character of the portrait, rather than simply being dismissed as unreal, becomes key in questioning the basis and nature of reality.

One of the major cultural and political figures of the 1920s and 1930s was Gabriele D'Annunzio (1863–1938). A writer, a personality in an age when the "personality" as we now experience it was emerging, D'Annunzio's influence extended to the cinema as well as to politics, particularly the public performances of Benito Mussolini. According to Jared Becker, "In many ways, D'Annunzio is the pivotal character . . . for it is he above all others who orchestrates the shift from a nineteenth-century culture of nation-building to a culture of radical nationalism and imperialist aggression."[2] Becker names D'Annunzio "Italy's most original architect of Fascist ideology"[3] and illuminates the style and character of the poet's works (themes relating to racism, nationalism, colonialism, homoeroticism, mass culture, antidemocracy, and imperialism) – concerns endemic to Europe in those decades and not exclusive to Fascist Italy.

D'Annunzio's fascination with virility, masculine power, and sexual excess are part of a mythology that has its connection to Fascism; but it belongs more largely to a certain historical moment between the wars when national honor was closely tied – especially in Italy and later in Germany – to a sense of national defeat and loss of power in relation to western politics, to the sense of failure of traditional views of democracy, and to the hostility toward "Bolshevism," liberalism, reformism, intellectualism, and traditionalism. One of the major issues confronting Italy during the interwar period was the question of modernization and modernity, the conflict between adherence to traditional patterns of economic, social, and cultural life and the pressures of capitalism and industrialization, commented upon by Antonio Gramsci in his notes on "Americanism and Fordism."[4] This particular tension is closely tied to conceptions of masculinity in relation to the elevation of national ideals of honor, expansionism, and war.

In the silent cinema (and D'Annunzio's contributions to the nationalist motifs of *Cabiria* have been often noted), the predilection for historical epics and costume drama is as much due to the mythology of the leader, his role as national savior, as it is to the penchant of popular cinema for spectacle. In particular, *Cabiria* has been described by Sorlin and others "as a nationalist manifesto." The figure of Maciste, played by the immensely popular Bartolomeo Pagano, is an image of physical power (presented as benevolent). This image was to become familiar in Italian politics and cinema of the era (and return in the peplum epics of the 1950s and 1960s). Sorlin illustrates the similarities in appearance between Mussolini and Pagano by juxtaposing their photographs.[5] Furthermore, the historical dramas of the silent era focus on the excesses of unchecked power contained by these defenders of the nation, whose physical power is tempered by responsibility to violated femininity but unleashed in all its strength against barbarians. In the numerous costume dramas, the redemption of the classical world, with its threat of natural disasters (e.g., volcanic eruptions) and its emphasis on the excesses of imperial power (e.g., the madness and cruelty of emperors such as Nero), rests on the broad shoulders of the masculine protagonist, who is a servant of state power, a savior of women and the family, and a defender of the social order.

The cinema of the 1930s does not abandon these historical narratives (e.g., *Scipione l'Africano*) with their heroes but often ties their motifs more closely to contemporary events, particularly those that address expansion into Africa either through direct colonization or war. An exemplary film in this respect is *Lo squadrone bianco* (*The White Squadron*, 1936), a colonial narrative of conversion set in a wartime milieu. In this film, directed by Augusto Genina, Captain Santelia is the prototype of masculinity in iconography and gesture, suggesting that the "'true' body of the fascist is the phallic body, existing in a state of preparedness for war."[6] The captain is filmed from various angles in a posterlike, statuesque pose, identified with toughness and choreographed gestures. His heroic stance, his body mechanics, might appear ridiculous were it not for the reinforcement of his appearance through the mise-en-scène, in the alternating shots of him with the image of his subservient troops, and the melodramatic character of the narrative in the conflicts between Santelia and one of his men. In particular, the drama of conversion is dependent on the antagonisms developed between the captain and the playboy, Mario Ludovici (Antonio Centa).

The film begins with a car hurtling forward in the darkness, shot in the chiaroscuro of film noir. This scene is intercut with images at a country estate, where elegantly dressed socialites – among them Cristina (Fulvia Lanzi) – are entertaining themselves at a party by eating, flirting, and dancing. The driver, Mario, finally arrives at the party and is castigated for his lateness by Cristina, with whom he is madly in love but who toys with his affections, both now and in the ensuing scenes. Dejected, he impetuously decides to join the "White Squadron" in Libya and departs for Africa. There he encounters a life of discipline and sacrifice for which he is unprepared. Different models of masculinity, both in contrast to his socialite friends, are presented to him through two dedicated officers, Captain Donati (Olinto Cristina) and Captain Santelia (Fosco Giachetti). Donati is shown as paternal and humane to the men in the squadron and also to the Arab servants, whereas Santelia is a disciplinarian and superpatriot. His motto is, "Death in combat is the most glorious end of a true soldier." He does not fraternize with the men but stands apart, often in the shadows, scrutinizing them.

Santelia, it becomes evident, is contemptuous of Mario's casual attitude toward army life and voices doubts about his competence and commitment as a soldier. El Fennek, Mario's Arab aide, is puzzled by Mario and his relationship to Cristina, whose photo the aide examines with amusement, if not contempt. Mario treats his life at this outpost in the desert casually, brooding over Cristina and allowing himself to be waited on. Intercut with scenes of his interactions with the other men are shots of Cristina with her fashionable friends, dancing and enjoying herself, receiving Mario's letters and placing them unread in her purse. The squadron receives combat orders, and the men ready themselves for a mission against the Africans. Their departure is shot from various angles and distances as the men are reviewed by Santelia. They mount their camels and set off to the accompaniment of martial music. En route to combat, at Captain Santelia's orders, the men stop to pay homage at the grave of a dead comrade, Bettetini – another indication of Santelia's single-minded devotion to Italy's imperialistic mission in Africa, in contrast to the attitude of Mario.

Mario becomes ill. Though warned to be judicious with the water ration, he persists in drinking. The captain, learning of this illness from El Fennek, comes to see Mario and expresses concern about his health. (The metaphor of health plays a central role in dramas of conversion.) Mario, in his feverish state, fantasizes images of Cristina; but finally he takes a silver cigarette case she has given him and buries it in the sand. A sandstorm arises, and the men are in danger of dying from thirst and exhaustion. Mario hallucinates, telling Santelia, who is tending him like a parent, that he wants his respect. He emerges from his dark night of the soul, a follower of and believer in the captain. Together, the men meet the enemy in a battle. At the base to which they will return, Cristina, who has arrived with some visitors, waits to see Mario. As yet there is no news of survivors of the battle. When at last we see Mario he has taken the dead Santelia's place, and in appearance and action is a reincarnation of the captain. He rejects Cristina's advances, telling her he is no longer the same person: The Mario she knew is buried with Santelia.

In this drama of conversion, the paternal figure is linked not to stark generational differences (though Santelia is somewhat older than Mario) but to psychological ones regarding the difference between feminine and masculine behavior and the rejection of heterosexual pleasure. Homosocial relations triumph as the "romance" between the two men moves from hostility to fusion, founded on the exclusion of the feminine figure and of any signs of behavior identified with softness and femininity; yet the progress of their relationship, leading to their ultimate convergence, evokes language similar to heterosexual romance. Femininity, thus, is not totally eradicated: It is transformed and rendered acceptable through its transposition into a wartime scenario. Cristina's shift from seductress and object of desire into mere spectator to Mario's conversion into a leader of men would certainly seem to validate descriptions of the Italian Fascist body as armored against woman. (Such treatments of women, however, are not unusual in the other national cinemas of the era.)

What may be unusual is the extraordinary emphasis on discipline and its relation to the leadership principle to the exclusion of other relationships. The protagonists' relationship is intensified by its being set into this monumental, eroticized, and exotic landscape, into a world of "primitives," and associated with a form of primal nature that is harsh and punitive but beautiful, as evinced by the aerial and long shots of the rippling dunes and the vastness of the terrain. One civilian's comments that the events of Mario's return are like a novel seem apt both from the perspective of exposing the fiction of the events and, more significantly, in regard to valorizing the necessary dimensions of theatricality, melodrama, and posturing inherent to masculine conversion. The excessive portrait of the men takes on the character of impersonation that could be said to adhere to, as well as evade, the "controls of the regime."[7] Giachetti's and later Centa's posturing as the hero of the hour is drawn to the point of caricature.

The folkloric elements of the film reside in the stages of Mario's conversion, patterned after religious conversion: his initial immersion in an erotic and aimless existence, his trials and illness in the "desert," his awakening to a disciplined, self-abnegating, self-denying form of existence through contact with Santelia, and finally his assumption of the captain's position and stance, becoming the ideal soldier as exemplified by Santelia. The motif of male bonding constitutes the other folkloric element: It serves as a mirror for Mario to affirm his image and demarcates a world where women are excluded.

Many folkloric motifs are evident in *Il fu Mattia Pascal* (*The Late Mathias Pascal,* 1937), a film offering another, satirical perspective on masculinity that might serve as a critical commentary on *Lo squadrone bianco.* Based on the Pirandello novel, *Il fu Mattia Pascal* is patterned on folk literature and, like *Squadrone,* follows the stages of the drama of conversion, where the protagonist, through adversity and enlightenment, gains a new identity. The film begins deceptively as a pastoral idyll. Mattia (Pierre Blanchar) is romantically attached to Romilda Pescatore (Nella Maria Bonora), whom he is about to marry. An appearance of rural harmony is shattered by the harsh realities of money and familial aggression. Signora Pescatore (Irma Gramatica), Romilda's mother, is the archetypal bad mother from fairy tales – greedy, grasping, and tyrannical. Significantly, neither Romilda or Mattia have fathers, reinforcing the notion that Mattia inhabits a woman's world. Immediately after the wedding party, the mother-in-law confronts Mattia with a bill for the festivities, completely disregarding that his mother has paid her 50,000 lire for the couple's housekeeping – all the money that she has in the world. By contrast, Mattia's mother is the good mother, completely devoted to her son and willing to go to any lengths to please him. The disrupted wedding feast is a prologue to a series of misfortunes that beset Mattia and his mother, following the motif of trials associated with the folklore of conversion.

Very quickly, Mattia learns that Romilda is similar to her mother, and her first act on the wedding night is to refuse him the wedding bed. With his own mother destitute (thanks to Signora Pescatore), Mattia goes to work as a librarian, where he is further exploited. The coup de grâce comes when his mother is dying: Signora Pescatore not only forbids Romilda to go to Signora Pascal but arranges with the mayor for a pauper's funeral. The characters in this world are thus highly stylized and divided between victims and aggressors: The women associated with the village are domineering and exploitative; Mattia, identified with his self-sacrificing mother, is passive and unable to combat the aggressiveness of his mother-in-law and his wife.

The element of contingency, central to the conversion narrative, now intervenes: Mattia wanders off after the funeral and, in a haze, finds himself on a train. Good fortune follows as he heads for Marseilles and, on the advice of an old man (the proverbial wise man of folklore), ends up in Monte Carlo, where he wins at roulette. The contrasts between city and country, provincialism and cosmopolitanism become increasingly apparent: The countryside is aligned to oppression, the urban world offers a chance of freedom. With his winnings, Mattia returns home determined to reclaim Romilda and make Signora Pescatore a "slave to him." He is unaware, however, that he has been declared dead: The body of a drowned drunkard has been identified as Mattia Pascal, and the real Mattia arrives home in time to view his own funeral. Thus he becomes a spectator to his old world and his life of impersonation begins.

Having shed one identity, he goes to Rome, to the Luxor Hotel, where he assumes another as Adriano Meis from Milan. It turns out that there is already a Meis family at the hotel, but he is unable to manufacture evidence of his relationship to them. Fortunately, he also makes the acquaintance of a spiritualist, Signorina Caporale (Olga Solbelli), who directs him to a boardinghouse where he meets Luisa (Isa Miranda), and she and "Adriano" fall in love. However, Count Papiano, who also resides in the hotel, having learned that Adriano has no identity papers, threatens him with exposure; moreover, he steals Adriano's money. Mattia, once again cast adrift, tries to "kill" his alter ego by drowning but relents and returns home to his former life. There he learns that Romilda has remarried. Her new husband is a provincial official and, seeking to avoid embarrassment, gets Mattia identity papers as Adriano Meis. As Adriano he returns to Rome, is reunited with Luisa, and, having outsmarted Papiano, tells her, "Io sono . . . Io sono . . . Il fu Mattia Pascal." Thus, he finally has an identity that is validated. He has escaped from the tyranny of the past and entered into a "new life."

The stages of Mattia's transformation are consonant with the imagery of conversion: youthful naïveté and oppression, a journey to enlightenment, the "death" of the old life, the struggle to obliterate the past, and, finally, rebirth. The structure of the narrative is dependent on a strict dualism: two mothers, two absent fathers, two women with whom he is involved romantically, two drownings and two false suicides, the protagonist's two identities, and the two worlds they inhabit – the countryside and Rome. The figures he confronts are binary as well: mother figures good or evil, male authority figures tyrannical or sagacious, women cruel or benign who either oppress or save him. Characters from folklore and fairy tale include the classic maternal shrew, the counterpart of the witch; the cruel decadent aristocrat who malevolently obstructs the protagonist's progress; vulnerable "orphans" (both Luisa and Mattia) who find an identity and romance; and the aforementioned wise old man who points the way.

The symbolism of the journey and of water are typical of the trajectory of conversion narratives. Spiritualism, as represented through Signorina Caporale, also reinforces the magical and folkloric aspects of the narrative. The protagonist's first "death" takes place in the country and his "rebirth" is associated with Monte Carlo and Rome. His second death in the city is only provisional since, after his return to the country to legitimize his new identity, he appropriates his former and only provisional role more fully. Money, equated with sexuality and power, is the instrument of his oppression, the means whereby Mattia is controlled but finally the means whereby he assumes power. In his new sense of self, he can subordinate the women from his past and, ironically, "march" on Rome. The "happy ending," like the rest of the film, is a fantasy. In the protagonist's journey toward the acquisition of a "proper" name and identity, the film provides a critical, even reflexive, blueprint of the conversion narrative. Moreover, the fiction of Mattia's death and rebirth are less the preconditions for a new and higher form of life than they are a satiric commentary on moribund forms of social life. In its excessive reliance on stylization, coincidence, and magic, the film proclaims itself as artifice, invoking an audience that can entertain its ironies. In its use of caricature and stark character contrasts and its repeated emphasis on forms of looking – such as Mattia contemplating his own image in death and his repeated surveillance by others – the film complicates the folklore of masculinity, revealing it as determined by necessity and contingency.

A different portrait of masculinity emerges in the popular comedies of Mario Camerini, one that focuses on social class and the protagonist's aspirations to wealth and power that will be restrained. *Il signor Max* (*Mr. Max,* 1937) features Vittorio De Sica in the title role as a Roman newspaper vendor, Gianni, and as a would-be upper-class gentlemen, Mr. Max (naming himself after the camera that he carries with him on the cruise). The comic confusion begins when he undertakes a cruise as a consequence of the largesse of a well-to-do friend. The cruise gratifies his fantasies of becoming a gentleman. On his way to board the ship, he encounters two women who are also going aboard. In particular, he is attracted to Lady Paola (Rubi Dalma). Gianni recognizes the disparity in their backgrounds immediately when she asks him if he plays bridge, to which he too quickly answers, "no," betraying his lower-class origins. Seeing the shocked expression on her face, he adds, "not tonight," and thus begins his attempt to acquire the accoutrements and habits of the upper class. Using his limited funds, he overspends on shaves, haircuts, and, above all, on a bouquet of orchids for Lady Paola. He returns home early and broke.

The family home is modest, with a picture of Mussolini in evidence on the wall. Despite his uncle's castigation of his behavior, Gianni is determined to play the role of Max, and a montage sequence traces his crash education into upper-class life in his learning bridge, tennis, golf, and foreign phrases. At the newsstand, he sees Lauretta (Assia Noris), the governess for Lady Paola's sister, Pucci. She is astounded by the similarity between Gianni and Signor Max, but he disguises himself by his Roman accent and his loose bodily deportment. Realizing that he can once again find Lady Paola through Lauretta, he follows her car on bicycle, but in his recklessness to keep up with her, he crashes into a taxi. Concerned, she gets out of her car and, along with a policeman, assists him into a pharmacy to be treated. Determined to get her address despite her coyness and refusal to provide the information, Gianni tells the policeman that he will need her as a witness, and thus once again he is back in business as Max. He goes to the Grand Hotel, the ultimate in art deco setting, where the guests are expensively clothed in the latest fashions. He arrives dressed elegantly in evening clothes, ascending the stairs, nonchalantly smoking a cigarette. By contrast to Gianni's looser deportment, even awkwardness, Mr. Max holds his body stiffly and speaks in a drawling manner laden with verbal affections.

Back at work at the newsstand, his partner assists Gianni in acquiring a riding habit: Gianni has agreed to go riding with his friends from the cruise, and his playing at being an international playboy requires a costume befitting a member of the leisure class. Once again Lauretta appears, though Gianni is quite indifferent to her wholesome and modest appearance. However, his uncle, after a brief conversation with her, decides that he likes her and invites her to a concert sponsored by the Dopolavoro (the after-work, leisure organization established by the regime). She accepts readily. In contrast to the bored, alienated images of upper-class life in the sophisticated world of hotels and nightclubs, the concert hall focuses on images of collective life. The choral singing (with Gianni in the chorus) becomes an expression of community values. The uncle manipulates Gianni into dancing with Lauretta, and she, now enamored of him, asks him to come to the station to say farewell – as Pucci's caregiver, she is slated to travel with Lady Paola. She is unaware, of course, that Gianni is Max and that he too will be traveling on the train.

At the station, Gianni's play-acting (and De Sica's) is put to the test as he works frenetically to maintain both identities. At first, as Max in stylish coat and hat, he walks past an unsuspecting Lauretta (who stands on the platform awaiting Gianni) and entrains. Then he descends from the other side of the train to assume his identity as Gianni. He enlists the aid of his partner (selling newspapers at the station) to take his place on the train temporarily, giving him the overcoat and hat, and directing him to stand with his back to the window to look like the already boarded Max. Then, divested of his outer clothing, Gianni approaches Lauretta as himself, tells her good-bye, and pretends to walk away. She enters the train, his partner detrains, and, unseen by Lauretta, Gianni climbs on board to reassume his identity as Max.

The final phase of his flirtation with upper-class life occurs as he sits at table listening to Lady Paola and her friends gossiping about divorces and remarriages. When he takes part in a bridge game, he bids poorly, angering Paola, and exits from the game. He bumps into Lauretta, who is in tears, having been subject to Pucci's tantrums and verbal abuse. He tries to comfort her, and she talks of her life, her loneliness, her affection for Gianni, and, carried away, he tries to kiss her. She slaps him despite his insisting that he is Gianni. Called on the carpet by Lady Paola after Pucci makes a scene, Lauretta quits. Overhearing that she is returning to Rome, Gianni also changes trains, and he and Lauretta meet again at the newsstand where he has preceded her. The two declare their love for each other, though Gianni teases her (or gets revenge for the slap?) by asking her if she has ever kissed a man. At first, she claims she is a "good" woman, but then confesses that she kissed someone who looked like Gianni. Gianni does not confess his impersonation, and when he arrives home with her he is counseled by his uncle not to tell her about this escapade. Lauretta is received into the house, and the door closes on the family, like a curtain falling, leaving the audience outside. Once again, secrecy prevails in the interests of family harmony and masculine superiority.

In following the conventions of romantic comedy, the heterosexual couple is properly matched. Through the Gianni/Max duality, the film sets up the contrast between different masculine life-styles relating to work and to leisure – one sedentary, the other nomadic; one productive, the other parasitic; one associated with family and community, the other with exclusiveness and boredom; and one identified with effeminacy, the other with masculine responsibility. De Sica playing Max in contrast to Gianni ascribes a putative effeminacy along with snobbishness to upper-class men. By comparison, Gianni is more "virile" but also more immature, in need of guidance by his uncle. The film is not a celebration of masculinity; instead it offers a modest, even chastened, image of the petit-bourgeois male as initiated into assuming domestic responsibilities. The "secrecy" behind doors that close on Gianni and Lauretta is a bond, a shared knowledge, between the audience and the filmmaker that the happy ending is a forced closure rather than a resolution on the part of the film. Moreover, it leaves open questions concerning the construction of the "home" and the disciplining of Gianni into familial responsibility. The other "secret" that mars the "happy ending" is Gianni's withholding from Lauretta the knowledge of his impersonation, thus also suggesting barriers to an idyllic and reciprocal relationship. The presence of secrets suggests a certain cynicism.

The films produced in the Fascist era that addressed masculinity were not carbon copies of one another. They reveal that there were a number of accommodations available in the representation of masculinity and its relation to power. In particular, it has been customary to single out several films that suggest disaffection with the regime in the early 1940s – for example, De Sica's *I bambini ci guardano,* a film that focuses on paternal suicide, familial disintegration, and a young boy's isolation. However, conspicuously missing from the list of films selected as harbingers of neorealism are many works by Ferdinando Maria Poggioli, whose films exemplify a group of melodramas produced in the last years of the regime that focus primarily on a masculine protagonist obsessed with power, destructive of others and of himself. In Poggioli's *Gelosia (Jealousy,* 1943) the spectacle of masculinity as developed through the character of Antonio (Roldano Lupi) is rendered through a range of figurative elements: animals, a crucifix, clothing, and lighting. The lighting and the use of symmetry and asymmetry invite reflection on the illegibility and obscurity of this world.

The film begins with two riders on horseback. The scene is dark to the point of obscurity, though it becomes evident that one rider is the hunter, the other his prey. One man, the one who has been singing, falls to the ground, but the identity of the other is not clear. In the following scene, the police enter a house. A man, heard proclaiming his innocence, is dragged out and arrested. Antonio, the Marchese di Roccaverdina, is approached by a lawyer who seeks to enlist his help to save Neli, one of Antonio's peasants and the man accused of murdering Rocco Curcione. The lawyer informs Antonio that there appears to be no apparent motive for the murder, since Rocco, once a womanizer, became a changed man after his marriage to Agrippina (Luisa Ferida). The new widow tells Antonio of her plight, but he treats her summarily. The Baronessa di Lagomorto (Wanda Capodoglio), who runs the affairs of the estate, then confronts Agrippina, concerned that the peasant woman will resume her one-time relationship with Antonio, if not become his wife.

The trial scene is highly choreographed and filmed from Antonio's perspective. Witnesses attest to Neli's innocence. A sign reading, "The law is equal for all," is posted in the courtroom and serves as an ironic indicator of the travesty of justice to be enacted. In a night scene that borders on Gothic horror, Antonio, wearing a cape with which he partially covers his face, passes through a corridor (containing a statue of Christ) on his way to seek absolution from the priest. He confesses his long-standing affair with Agrippina and that he had arranged the marriage between her and Rocco, ordering him not to consummate the marriage. Tortured by jealousy, he had finally murdered Rocco. The priest counsels him to make reparation and to confess his crime, for an innocent man will die because of him. Scornfully, Antonio responds that he is a Roccaverdina and above the law. He reminds the priest that he is constrained by his priestly office from revealing the confession.

Antonio, beginning to feel pangs of guilt, writes a note of confession to be given to the public prosecutor and contemplates shooting himself; but he is interrupted by the arrival of Zosima, who has come, at the instigation of the baroness, to collect money for charity. Filmed standing in the doorway as she leaves, as if on the threshold between life and death, Antonio takes the suicide note and burns it. Shortly thereafter, he proposes to her, expressing the hope that she will help to banish the ghosts in his life. Antonio is no sooner married, however, than he begins again to seek out Agrippina. Zosima complains to her mother that Antonio has become melancholy. When Antonio learns that Zosima has agreed to care for one of Neli's children, he becomes enraged, shouting at her that he does not want a reminder of an unpleasant situation. No longer submissive, she tells him that she has had enough of his behavior, alluding not only to his silences but to his relations with Agrippina.

Antonio's growing discomfiture is portrayed in another night scene when, in a candlelit room, he begins to hallucinate the sound of horses' hooves. He gets up and goes to Zosima's room. but her door is locked. When she opens it, saying that she locked it out of her fear of him, he repentantly proposes that they take a trip together to the country. Their trip is marred, however, by their meeting a peasant who asks Antonio permission for his son to marry Agrippina, which he angrily refuses. Immediately thereafter, Zosima informs him that Neli has died in prison. Agata, Neli's wife, now comes to the house with her children and exhorts them to remember that their father was innocent, and she curses the murderer of Rocco. In Antonio's darkly lit room, a shadow of a cross and his own shadow are visible on the wall superimposed onto images of the murder and of the priest in judgment. The music is harsh and dissonant. Antonio becomes delirious and, as Zosima tends him, he raves about the sound of the horses' hooves. Following this night, Zosima leaves for good, but Agrippina returns. In his room, toward the end of the film, he sits paralyzed in a chair, oblivious to everything.

The darkness of the opening shots is highly expressive of the pervasive atmosphere of the film. The obscurity of the night scenes foreshadows the obscurity of Antonio's actions – his brooding intensity, the uncontrollable nature of his jealousy, and the violent force of his obsession. These night scenes, as he descends into guilt, hallucination, and madness, reinforce his ambiguous and shadowy interior world, magnifying the nature of his fixation. He is also filmed from the rear as if to obstruct any clear access to his state of mind and motivation. Furthermore, the film's reliance on symmetry reinforces the compulsiveness of his behavior and is particularly evident in the recurrent shots of the corridor decorated with a statue of Christ (which Antonio eventually orders removed). Antonio, vampirish in a long cape, stalks through this corridor at night on his way to confession. The last shots of the film also take place in the corridor, ending on a somber note as a priest and young acolytes chant prayers for the withdrawn Antonio. Although his violence is over, there is no consolation for the havoc that he has wrought.

Antonio's incipient madness is identified with suggestions of diabolism in his uneasy relation to the crucifix, his satanic suffering that admits of no mitigation, and his paralysis, his inability to escape his monomaniacal fixation. The contrasting portraits of Zosima and Agrippina highlight the familiar conflict between the idealized upper-class maternal figure, associated with religion and the family, and the sexualized peasant figure [Fig. 70]. Both women are, in their own ways, the victims of Antonio's inability to accept the privileges and responsibilities of his social class. His aristocratic position is his license to exercise his power over his wife, his mistress, and his peasants.

Religion functions in the text as an ironic correlative to Antonio's arbitrary and excessive behavior. Rather than enhancing the positive and transformative character of religion, the priest underscores its impotence in the

Figure 70. Antonio's (Roldano Lupi) obsession, Agrippina (Luisa Ferida), in *Gelosia* (*Jealousy*). (Courtesy New York Museum of Modern Art Stills Archive)

face of the protagonist's refusal to be accountable to the law or to religion. The melodrama has looked at the world upside down. The protagonist's madness and disintegration is not a sign of repentance; rather, Antonio's ravings reinforce the sense in which all boundaries are undone and unrestrained desire has become rampant. As Klaus Theweleit writes, "These men experience their affinity with power as 'natural.' To them, powerlessness means the threat of permanent exclusion, both from justice and from pleasure. Their every action becomes an *assertion of themselves;* they are always in *opposition*."[8] *Gelosia* offers a vision of masculinity at the limit. The film does not soften or mitigate the abuse of power but suggests that Antonio's abuses are closely tied to his contempt for the law, his hatred of women, and his feelings of superiority to his peasants. In many ways, the film speaks directly to and critically of Fascism in its manipulation of the law (and religion) for its own ends, in its subjugation of women, and in its elevation of the male leader to a position of absolute power.

The post–World War II films are similarly preoccupied with dramatizing masculinity in relation to power, portraying the arbitrary exercise of power but also probing the means of resisting it. An exemplary instance of a belief in another form of opposition devoted to questions of social justice and ethical behavior is Roberto Rossellini's *Roma, città aperta* (*Open City*), where the two major masculine figures, the engineer Manfredi and the priest Don Pietro, exemplify the high-minded ideals of anti-Fascist Resistance, identified not only with the communist Left but with Christian morality. Through the harassment of the populace encapsulated in the wanton shooting of Pina (Anna Magnani), the film dramatizes the grim effects of the Nazi occupation of Rome, allowing for the opportunity to portray through Bergmann, the head of the Gestapo in Rome, and his assistant, Ingrid, the consequences of unchecked power identified with Fascism and Nazism.

A paean to the Resistance, the film offers a religious belief in the possibility of combating this power, of freeing Rome (as a synecdoche for Italy) from the years of blighting totalitarianism based on force, including physical torture, and on corrupting the vulnerable by appealing to their desire for love and security. If, as Millicent Marcus suggests, "the protagonist of the story is Rome itself, as a place, and as an historical entity"[9] – citing the map used by the Nazis and the one used by the Resistance – the city is anthropomorphized through the major figures. The city of Rome is a violated woman, embodied in the violated bodies of the dead Pina and the corrupted Marina. Redemption and resurrection is only possible through the sacrifices, the heroic martyrdom, of the two men. Masculinity is portrayed as identified with passion, with the sacrifice on the cross in the name of humanity, whereas femininity is identified with the despoliation of a city in need of regeneration.

The film offers idealized images of masculinity. In contrast to the Nazis and Fascists, Manfredi and Don Pietro are identified with moral responsibility to the community. Their actions are possible because they cannot be bribed (like Marina), but even more they are portrayed as having a commitment to a higher cause, and they choose death rather than betrayal. In the scenes of torture, the torturer insists on their talking, offering to spare their lives if they become informers; but as in the case of the barber in *Il generale Della Rovere* – whose last words are, "I didn't talk" – the emphasis is on the virtues of self-discipline, silence, altruism, belief in a capacity to transform the world through collective action, and particularly in the vindicating power of history. Specifically in relation to questions of sexuality and gender, the film, through the roles of these two men, relies on familiar and normalized images of masculinity. These two are juxtaposed to Bergmann, whose image, as many critics have noted, suggests effeminacy – an ominous hint of deviant sexual practices. Similarly, in the case of the women, Magnani projects a deeroticized nurturing image, whereas Marina, in her person and in her environment, projects an aura of decadence. In the case of Ingrid, her identification with lesbianism as masculinized also reinforces the film's attempts to realign "natural" images of masculine and feminine behavior.

If the films of the Fascist era, excepting the last years of the regime, were more largely preoccupied with the construction of a redeemed masculinity, those of the post–World War II era focused on flawed portraits. Increasingly in both melodramas and the comedies, one sees a dissection of conventional and clear-cut ethical, gendered, and sexual values. In the case of *Il generale Della Rovere* (1959), Rossellini returns to the Second World War but with a less pronounced sense of the union of Christian and communist beliefs and of an intrinsic understanding of ethical action. If the earlier film had probed the complexity of realism, identifying it less with the external dimensions of style (e.g., location shooting, the use of nonactors, a loose sense of narration) and more with its possibility of genuineness in relation to moral truth and clarity, *Il generale Della Rovere* gives us a masculine protagonist who is identified with masks, duplicity, and manipulation. If *Open City* equates the two martyrs with authenticity, *Il generale Della Rovere* is preoccupied with performance and its effects. In this film, created in the aftermath of failures on the part of the Left resulting in the hegemony of Christian Democracy, the access to truth is murkier, like the lighting that Peter Brunette has identified with "the stylized *film noir* of a movie like *Fear* [*La paura*], rather than the serviceable 'natural' flatness of *Open City*."[10]

Il generale Della Rovere's focus on a swindler become hero is not the only distinguishing mark of the new masculine protagonist: It also signals a different, less starkly binary treatment of melodramatic conceptions of good and evil, heroism and villainy. The preoccupation with "acting" and its significance serves as an indication of a world where the nature of truth is elusive, where roles are not indications of reality, where impersonation yields a different and more complex access to truth. De Sica assumes the protean identities of Bardone become Grimaldi and Grimaldi finally become Della Rovere. This transformation underscores the importance of performance rather than authenticity. Also, by using De Sica, the film capitalizes on his stardom, his position as icon in the Italian cinema. Thus, the problematic relation of the cinema to truth is enhanced by an actor playing an "actor." Masculinity, like heroism, is exposed as a masquerade, but the idea of impersonation takes on different connotations, necessitating a rethinking of one's expectations of what is "natural" and "real."

The burden the narrative imposes on the viewer is to rethink the conventional binary between fiction and fact, between acting and being, imposing a more severe test in terms of how to evaluate the visual image. In particular, connections between myths of masculinity and conventional notions of intrinsic virtue subtending heroism, leadership, and power are put to the test. The audience continues to be "swindled" by this swindler who assumes the role of the "real" General Della Rovere, but this "fiction" thus enables another aspect of reality to emerge: namely, that representation is based on fiction and that thinking differently entails the recognition that roles assumed to be natural are in fact forms of "untruth," relying on the instability of our perceptions and judgments.

In the 1950s, familiar conceptions of masculinity were resurrected with the reappearance of the genre cinema and particularly with the comedy, adventure, and historical films so popular with Italian and international audiences. The peplum epics and the spaghetti westerns are an index to the cultural imaginary of that period and especially to the complex character of masculinity that emerged. It has been fashionable to refer to the 1950s as a time of "crisis" in relation to masculinity; but there has never been a time when masculinity and femininity have not been in crisis, either with each other or independently. The crux is to locate difference in the ever-present though deepening signs of a crisis in representation, particularly masculine representation, over the course of cinema history – a crisis that has its counterpart in the Italian popular cinema.

The figures of Ulysses, Ursus, Maciste, Spartacus, and Hercules are familiar characters in the popular cinema of the 1950s, and are especially popular for producers of and audiences for Hollywood and Italian cinema of the 1950s and 1960s. The appearance of these films are evidence of the increasing internationalization of cinema. The films are also indicative of changes of style in the genre conventions, in the use of locations, and in the types of actors employed. Although the spaghetti western has received its measure of critical acclaim (though not without its detractors), the peplum epic has been treated more cursorily. (Its name is from the Latin *peplum*, a full upper garment worn by men, but identified in these films as a short sleeveless and draped tunic, belted at the waist, worn by both male and female characters.) Only recently – with the particular critical attention paid to the idea of gender as performed not pregiven, to the notion of theatricality, and to the changing role of the body as a locus of value – has it been possible to examine masculinity in its various permutations and to begin to dissect its character as a contested terrain and, hence, as offering insight into the changing folklore that reveals the complicity between economic and cultural forms.

In 1957, *Le fatiche di Ercole (Hercules;* a.k.a. *The Labors of Hercules)*, was a huge success, bearing every imprint in its style of commercial and formal indebtedness to Hollywood as well as to the earlier historical films of the silent era. Its genre, the peplum epic, was "set in classical antiquity or in a distant but indeterminate past time and populated by buxom and inarticulate damsels in distress as well as by heroic musclemen protagonists."[11] These films, according to Bondanella and to Gian Piero Brunetta,[12] were international coproductions, utilizing actors (often lesser-known) from the United States, Great Britain, and France who were then to become international stars. Histories of world cinema mention these films only in passing, usually in derogatory terms, "though more than 170 films, approximately 10% of Italian film production between 1857 and 1964, belong to this genre."[13] The problem confronting historians and critics of Italian cinema is how to account for the films' popularity with audiences.

Relying on allusions to Greek mythology and Roman history, the texts are replete with classical names familiar to even the most rudimentary student of classical times (Hercules, Penelope, Ulysses, Caesar, Nero, etc.) and thus offer an aura of erudition. In accounting for these films, critics have cited a number of sources. For one, the Catholic Church, not comfortable with the critical content of neorealist texts and their unflattering portraits of contemporary Italian society, were equally critical of "immoral" postwar Hollywood films, with their representations of independent women and rebellious youth, and negative images of family life, and sought to control, through censorship and publicity, the influx and the effect of these films. Moreover, the victory of Christian Democracy weakened the position of the Left in political and cultural life. Giulio Andreotti, then under secretary of state, cast a jaundiced eye on those films that, he felt, concentrated on "the negative effects of all these images of poverty, of unemployment, of thieves, bicycles and tramps."[14] (Thus, while there were reservations about the Hollywood cinema, with its "absence of truly Christian principles, the lack of spirituality and the predominance of materialism and paganism in American film,"[15] Hollywood films were ultimately preferable to the kind of cinema exemplified by neorealism.)

In the 1950s and 1960s, changing economic and cultural conditions saw the diminishing influence of the church as a result of far-reaching changes in Italian life: social and cultural mobility, the economic miracle that, in Paul Ginsborg's terms, transformed Italy from "a peasant country . . . [to] one of the major industrial nations in the West," which affected the sociocultural life of the nation, involving the family, patterns of sexuality, and the position of men, women, and young people.[16] The "rule of the international market economy, more than the power of local elites" was to determine perceptions of social life.[17] In particular, Americanism was not only ensconced in Italy but was to play a major role in shaping the cinema of the future. Thus, the peplum epics were – like their counterparts, the spaghetti westerns – a curious anastomosis of images and attitudes toward tradition and modernity as well as national identity. Portraits of sexuality especially constitute a major innovation, inflecting the iconography, gesture, and specific narrative conflicts in these films.

Ercole e la regina di Lidia (Hercules Unchained, 1959), like so many of these films (e.g., *Le fatiche di Ercole* [1957], *Ercole al centro della terra* [*Hercules in the Haunted World,* 1961], *Ercole alla conquista de Atlantide* [*Hercules and the Captive Women,* 1961], *Ercole contro Roma* [*Hercules against Rome,* 1964], *Ercole contro i figli del sole* [*Hercules against the Sons of the Sun,* 1964], *Maciste e la regina di Samar* [*Hercules against the Moon Men,* 1964 (note the interchangeable hero)], and *Ercole, Sansone, e Ulisse* [*Hercules, Samson, and Ulysses,* 1965]) poses the conflict between legitimate and illegitimate power. The film stresses the egregiousness and arbitrariness of the tyrants, Polyneices and Eteocles, brothers who refuse to abide by the rules of sharing the throne of Thebes. Hercules is to be the agent of justice.

The film opens with a mature Hercules, recently married to blonde Jole and now accompanied by her and young Ulysses on the road to Thebes. On their journey they confront different threats to their safety, most of which are confronted and resolved by the physical strength and wiliness of Hercules. For example, when he confronts the giant Antaeus, played by Italian-American boxer Primo Carnera, the physical encounters are cast and choreographed so as to distinguish between brute power and sport, the latter illustrated in terms of the hero's verbal and strategic superiority to the giant, whom Hercules "reduces" to human size. The spectacle of the male body is fundamental. As Ina Rae Hark writes:

> Extreme forms of this display occur in the appropriately named spectacular, where the genre's cultural settings (biblical, Greco-Roman) allow for both male and female fashions that reveal considerable flesh; moreover, in these cultures homoerotic practices are widely acknowledged and the punishment of criminals or conquered foes is a highly elaborated public show.[18]

The roughness of Antaeus' body and his unkempt condition contrast with Hercules' smooth chest and bulging muscles, his scant costume enabling his chest, arms, and legs to be fully exposed. Nonetheless, in his costuming, in the conjunction of his muscular body with the folds of the garment, the sight of the ornate belt that cinches his waist, and the draping of the peplum over one shoulder, a suggestion of androgyny is invoked. This is further developed in the trial involving his drinking of the "waters of forgetfulness," which cause him to forget his marriage, his duty to save Thebes (where Jole has been left, allegedly in good hands), and his responsibility for the younger Ulysses.

In finding himself in the land of Queen Omphale, Hercules succumbs totally to her sensual blandishments, becoming her sexual plaything [Fig. 71]. She is a man-eater who thinks nothing of killing off her sexual playmates with the appearance of a new prey. Hercules is now filmed in languid positions on a couch, where he is massaged by Ulysses and by Omphale's maidservants, having given himself over to drink, eating, and sexual pleasure with her. Through Ulysses, he learns that in a cave are Egyptian workmen who, at the orders of the queen, preserve the bodies of her former lovers in a mysterious formula that makes them look like wax figures in a museum. if Hercules does not recover his memory and hence his physical power, he will become like the others, despite Omphale's asseverations of love. He does return to his former self and regain his strength, realizing with remorse that he has endangered Thebes by his long absence. As a consequence of the return of his memory and strength, he fights off Omphale's soldiers and gains her permission to leave the island. Like Dido in the *Aeneid,* she then commits suicide, jumping into the boiling concoction that was designed for her love slaves.

Figure 71. The body in *Ercole e la regina de Lidia* (*Hercules Unchained*): Hercules (Steve Reeves) overcome by Queen Omphale (Sylva Koscina). (Courtesy New York Museum of Modern Art Stills Archive)

Returning to Thebes, Hercules with the aid of his men gains entry to the walled city, destroys wild tigers with his bare hands, and saves his wife. Both Polyneices and Eteocles are killed. (The two brothers offer antithetical but parallel images of masculinity: Eteocles with his marcelled curls and fringed bangs, his ornate costumes, and his exaggerated gestures, suggests yet another variation on the feminized masculine body that bears a parallel with the tyranny of Queen Omphale, whereas Polyneices is swaggering, rough, and verbally aggressive.)

The largest portion of the narrative is devoted to Hercules' sojourn with Omphale, the scenes of battle alternating with scenes of erotic enjoyment. Throughout the film, it is evident that the battle scenes and those of sensual surrender are linked by the focus on the temptations, visual pleasures, and threats to masculinity of ungoverned sexuality, thus aligning the film with sexual morality while permitting a view of the delights of sensuality. In talking about the young men of "today," Laertes, the father of Ulysses, remarks, "Today, the young men think only of their pleasure." The emphasis on sex in the film is not at all exceptional for the films of the era – in those films critical of the "commodification of sexuality" as well as those more congenial to sexual subjects. The peplum epics are an indication of the emergence of the "sexy film" which, writes Bondanella, "heralded the imminent arrival of other apparently now permanent developments in Italian culture: Magazines containing softcore and hardcore pornography, special theaters for pornography."[19] However, these films need to be examined from a perspective that does not reduce them to mere generic repetition, sociological fodder, identity politics, or the "escapist" character of the mass cinema: In their treatment of masculinity, their foraying into the dangers and pleasures of sexuality, and their obviously over-the-top forms of theatricality, they offer images of a culture trying to anastomose traditional values (through their recourse to the past in conjunction with conventional morality) to the fascination, inevitability, and profitability of new commodity forms that entail the cultural commerce of the body, both male and female, and of sexuality. In particular, these films designate the male body as spectacle, an object of examination and seduction for male and female viewers alike.

If the peplum epics present the male body as an object of exhibition, opening up the possibilities of the greater commodification of the body and sexuality that reigns to the present time, another route to the exploration of masculinity is offered by the *commedia all'italiana* and its dissection of Italian sexual politics. Masculinity in relation to the position of the paternal role and its effects on the family, its imbrication in the network of Italian social relations, more particularly in the context of Sicily, is painfully dramatized in the dark comedy *Sedotta e abbandonata* (*Seduced and Abandoned,* 1963), directed by Pietro Germi. The film dramatizes the effects of the code of honor on Agnese (Stefania Sandrelli), one of Don Vincenzo Ascalone's (Sarò Urzì) four daughters, but the narrative centers on the father's role as engineer of the events that lead ultimately to the marriage of the "dishonored" Agnese.

The film presents "a chilling vision of how traditional social values can destroy an individual, especially a woman with a mind of her own."[20] In the process of upholding the respectability of the family, the father destroys himself as well. Beginning with the "seduction" of Agnese by Giuseppe "Peppino" Califano (Aldo Puglisi), the fiancé of her sister, Matilde, the film dramatizes the effects of Don Vincenzo's discovery of Agnese's deflowering (thanks to his wife, who presents him with a note she has recovered, after Agnese had tried to throw it away, of Agnese's confession to Peppino of her feelings of remorse). From this point on, Don Vincenzo is out to settle accounts, and often victimizes his daughters in the process. He enlists the aid of the midwife (an act reminiscent of *Divorzio all'italiana*) and of a clinic to establish that Agnese is pregnant. He then forces Peppino to break off the engagement with Matilde and contemplates various strategies to uphold his honor – consulting his lawyer cousin to discover the least costly path through criminal law – and decides on simply having his son, Antonio, shoot the recalcitrant Peppino, who does not want to marry a dishonored woman like Agnese even though he is the cause of her degraded status. That murderous plot failing –

Figure 72. Men's rituals in *Sedotta e abbandonata* (*Seduced and Abandoned*): Giuseppe Califano (Aldo Puglisi) honors Don Vincenzo (Sarò Urzì) before the dishonored Agnese (Stefania Sandrelli). (Courtesy New York Museum of Modern Art Stills Archive)

thanks to Agnese's warning the police, to Antonio's ambivalence about doing the deed, and to the northern policeman's detachment from the mores of the South – the question of how Don Vincenzo might restrain his rage, vindictiveness, and barbarism is highlighted.

Thus despite the film's many images of Agnese – locked in her room, violated by being forced to undergo a physical "inspection," beaten by her father, verbally abused by him and by Peppino, and driven to the point of madness at the end – the center of the film is the paternal role and the ways in which his position is sanctioned by the community. (His power is derived, as he himself acknowledges, from his contacts with officials involved in the law, in the bureaucracy, and in the church.) With Don Vincenzo at its head, the family parades itself before the town for their observation and approval. As in *Divorzio all'italiana,* the family is always onstage, performing for each other and for the community [Fig. 72]. Don Vincenzo's physical appearance and gesture are crucial to an appreciation of the role of father: Rotund, solid in girth, with a walk that bespeaks power and ownership, he rules over his family by means of his intimidation of, and scorn for, the world of females that he controls. Surveillance is a key factor in the control and maintenance of sexual roles. At the dinner table when we first see him, he mocks a courtship letter that Peppino has sent to Matilde. When he discovers Agnese's incriminating note, he explodes into a rage (later likened to the explosions that take place in the quarry he owns).

Although completely obsessed with the role of his daughters' sexual purity and its importance to the family's standing in the community, he is not himself averse to womanizing. Outside of the home, he and his cronies ogle women on the street and in the bar, and he presents himself to them as a man who understands something about the sexual practices of "real men," thus dramatizing the double standard that exists between men and the women in the community. However, his position is not entirely unsympathetic, since the film presents the ways in which his behavior is controlled by the values and actions of the community: His performance is for their benefit, and the concept of honor is, as in *Divorzio,* presented for their approval, functioning as a theatrical performance for the other men. As Marcus writes about the father's actions, "Don Vincenzo is the stage director par excellence who takes full advantage of the dramatic possibilities for spreading abroad an idealized family image at variance with the private truths which threaten to dishonor the Ascalone name."[21] The depth of his commitment to honor is seen in the deathbed scene, the fruits of his emotional expenditure in achieving the marriage between Peppino and Agnese. A lonely death is preferable to delaying this long-sought alliance.

The other masculine figures in the film – Peppino, Antonio, Baron Zappala, and the older men in the town – are also ironic portraits of the nature and effects of the code of honor linked to reigning conceptions of masculinity. The townsmen are voyeuristic and verbally as well as physically threatening. Antonio, inept, pathetic, reluctant to carry out his father's command to kill Peppino, is manipulated and brutalized by his father. Baron Zappala, an impoverished aristocrat with bad teeth that, according to Matilde, make his breath stink, lives in the ruins of his ancestral palace and tries twice, unsuccessfully, to hang himself. Peppino, a facsimile of Don Vicenzo's values, is browbeaten both by his family and by Don Vincenzo. Sharing the other men's double standard that a man may behave seductively toward a woman whereas a woman's duty is to resist his advances, he seeks to run away from both families rather than accede to marrying Agnese. He is cowardly but also brutal, ambitious but also lazy – another instance of the juvenilization of the men that characterizes their imprisonment in the code of honor, which the film suggests is at the basis of masculinity and its role in relation to the family.

The film's focus on the body is partly expressed in the unattractiveness of the men and women: Their bodies are corrupted through corpulence, self-mortification, and numerous physical ailments. Agnese and her sisters are exempt from disfigurement, but the film suggests that immersion in this diseased way of life entails an inevitable deformity of body and spriit. (Initially, when Agnese confesses her indiscretion to the priest, he tells her to mortify her flesh, underlining the notion of "carnal" sin; this leads to her sleeping with rocks in her bed.) Peppino, having locked himself in his room to escape from his family, talks to his image in the mirror, reiterating his self-disgust. (The enforced examination of Agnese's body by the midwife at Don Vincenzo's order also underscores how the code of honor relies on physical as well as psychic scrutiny.) When Don Vincenzo visits his lawyer cousin for advice about how to remedy his injured honor, the cousin's wife, Carmela, lists a long string of physical ailments to which she is prey. After Don Vincenzo orders his son to shoot Peppino, the doctor comes to visit to Antonio, who has gotten a boil on his nose and is running a fever of 104°. (The father is indifferent to his son's ailment, only wishing to accomplish his murderous objective.) Although Don Vincenzo replaces the missing and decaying teeth of Baron Zappala (described as otherwise good-looking), the baron, offended in his dignity, later throws his new teeth away. The notion of honor is even likened to a physical defect: In seeking to discover what tragedy has befallen him, Don Vincenzo's cousin asks if it is a "tumor," and Don Vincenzo responds, "No, honor." This links further the notion of honor and masculinity to a disease that eats at the community, and visualizes its effects on the bodies of the men who feel called upon to uphold its value.

Of all the Italian male stars – Amedeo Nazzari, Alberto Sordi, Nino Manfredi, Vittorio Gassman, Giancarlo Giannini, Roberto Benigni, even Vittorio De Sica – the man most identified with both national and international stardom is Marcello Mastroianni. He is known for such highly successful comic films as *Divorzio all'italiana, Ieri, oggi, domani*, and *Matrimonio all'italiana (Marriage Italian-Style,* 1964). He appeared in leading roles for all of the major Italian directors – Germi, Visconti, Fellini, Antonioni, the Taviani brothers – and is also known for his work in Hollywood and European films; but perhaps the quintessence of his star persona was most evident in his relationship and work with Federico Fellini.

Bondanella has written that "Fellini treated his actors as faces and potential images rather than performers. His casting was, as always based on the actor's image on the screen rather than any special dramatic talent."[22] In choosing Mastroianni for the leading role in *La dolce vita,* "Fellini wisely realized that Mastroianni's completely plastic face was capable of almost any kind of expression."[23] Over the years of working together, the personal relationship between the director and the actor became close. Commenting to Charlotte Chandler on their relationship, Fellini said

I am asked frequently if Marcello is my alter ego. Marcello Mastroianni is many things to many people. For me, he is not my alter ego. He is Marcello, an actor who conforms perfectly to what I want from him, like a contortionist who can do anything. . . . He's so natural. He's never nervous when he acts. The only time he is nervous is when he has to go on television and talk about acting.[24]

In an interview with Charlotte Chandler, Fellini recounted how he had explained to Mastroianni the reasons for choosing him over Paul Newman in *La dolce vita:* "I have chosen you because you have an everyday face," which he qualified by adding, "Very normal in a movie-star kind of way, I mean." He further recounted to Chandler how "Marcello also represents an ideal man. He's the man every woman would want."[25] In discussing Mastroianni's frequent persona in his films as an intellectual, he said, "He thinks, but he does not act very much."[26]

Although Mastroianni's star persona is perhaps most closely identified with the roles he played for Fellini, there are nonetheless certain aspects of his appearance and acting that are shared by his work as a whole: his theatricality, his seemingly always performing, his willingness to expose his imperfections and to engage in self-parody, his identification with the nonheroic or even antiheroic, his aura of failure and capacity for introspection – all of these added to his suave charm, ruggedly handsome, poised, and devil-may-care appearance. If he projected, as Fellini suggests, the "man every woman would want," this may derive from the union of his good looks with the quality of vulnerability. He is not, except in parody as in Fellini's *La città delle donne,* the supermale whose appeal resides in his physical power and masterfulness: In De Sica's *Ieri, oggi, domani* and Germi's *Divorzio all'italiana* he portrays exaggerated males whose masculinity backfires; in Bolognini's *Bell'Antonio* (1960) he plays an impotent husband; and in Scola's *Una giornata particolare (A Special Day,* 1997), he is a homosexual.

What is it that makes him a consummate instance of international stardom?[27] Perhaps his appeal resides in the protean dimensions of cultural conceptions of masculinity. He could play a decadent aristocrat as in *Divorzio all'italiana* [Fig. 73], or a self-deluding representative of the upper classes in *Allonsanfán,* an exaggerated portrait of a womanizer in *Ieri, oggi, domani* and *La città delle donne,* an anguished artist in *8½,* a heroic but beleaguered socialist organizer in *I compagni,* and a pathetic portrait of a paternal figure in Tornatore's *Stanno tutti bene (Everybody's Fine,* 1990), all the while maintaining his sexual appeal. Though he was married, his offscreen life was identified (as Fellini's has been) with many affairs, linking him to such female stars as Faye Dunaway and Catherine Deneuve.[28] His relationship to Fellini, which Mastroianni described as "a love affair without sex," also lent an androgynous element to his persona that certainly carried over into his screen roles in their parody of virile masculinity. Like Loren, with whom he was repeatedly paired, he communicated a sense of Italianness transportable to the international are-

Figure 73. Marcello Mastroianni as Fefé in *Divorzio all'italiana*. (Courtesy New York Museum of Modern Art Stills Archive)

na by projecting an image of physical attractiveness, geniality, and urbanity. His persona is that of a man for all seasons, appealing to different audiences and to both men and women.

From the vantage point of critical analysis of cinematic portraits of gender and sexuality, Mastroianni's performance in *8½* (1963) is an exemplary text to explore the protean dimensions of his star persona. The film, itself an instance of Fellini's metacinema (see Chapter 12), probes the "role of sexual desire and audience response in the cinema,"[29] and Mastroianni is able to complicate that image through a combination of parody, caricature, melodrama, fantasy, and memory. In *8½*, Marcello's role undergoes a number of permutations from the moment his image escapes the smoke-filled car in which he is trapped and ascends into the air, to the final scenes where he joins all the characters as at the end of the circus, where the performers (the characters in the film-within-the-film) join together with him in the ring.

Marcello as Guido is the consummate figure of power and desire – a film director who seeks actors for a film and situations in which to film them. He is a decadent, bored, and restless but attractive image of vulnerable masculinity who is a wielder of power and object of desire because he can create stars.

Constantly on the quest for new experiences, he confronts women whose images blur one into the other. However, his inaccessibility is an invitation to women and a goad to make him experience love for them. At the same time, he is a childlike man who lives in his fantasies – fantasies of childhood and youth, surrounded and tended by women, and of adulthood, surrounded by bevies of women who seek to rebel against, but ultimately succumb to, his whip. In episodes involving his wife, Luisa (Anouk Aimée), Mastroianni reenacts to perfection the image of the erring husband who is both threatening and attractive, challenging his partner to come to terms with his promiscuity – to convert him or to reject him. The allusions to his childhood and his punishment at the hands of the priests are also part of this image of vulnerability, since they are narrated from the perspective of his guilt-driven introspection.

His debonair appearance is enhanced by the international cast of characters who surround him, American, French, and Spanish, but also by the different accents and languages that are spoken. The seductiveness of his enigmatic character is also communicated by his well-tailored clothes, the scarf around his neck, the cape that he wears at times, the rakish hat, his dark glasses, and even the sheets that he wears in the baths and in the harem scene. Finally, the fact that he plays, as he has in other films, the role of an artist-intellectual, though flawed, enhances his persona, adding the image of intelligence to his other qualities, as well as the suggestion of voyeurism, as he sits by and observes the various women who pass through the scenario of his films and of his life. Though the role Mastroianni plays in this film is Fellini's invention and based on many aspects of the director's own character, the fusion of director and star does not obscure or eradicate the actor's persona; it adds another dimension. Such a fusion highlights a particular aspect of stardom involving the symbiotic relationship between stars and their directors: The director becomes a star through his or her actors. Mastroianni's image is a combination of ordinariness and exceptionality, characteristics identified by Richard Dyer as an important component of stardom. Mastroianni's ordinariness was exemplified in his vulnerability, his proneness to confusion; his exceptionality in his longevity, his graceful aging, his charm and good humor, his intelligence, and his belonging to the world of the talented, the rich, the eccentric, and the famous.

An actor that can be said to share some of the qualities of Mastroianni is Giancarlo Giannini [Fig. 74]. He achieved international renown in works by Lina Wertmüller based on the popularity of such films as *Mimì metallurgico ferito nell'onore (The Seduction of Mimi,* 1972) and *Pasqualino Settebellezze (Seven Beauties,* 1975), where he established a clearly Italian and even regional persona that makes him distinctive as an Italian star. However, unlike Mastroianni, and despite the plasticity of his face, he remains more narrowly an icon

Figure 74. Giancarlo Giannini as Tunin in *Film d'amore e anarchia.* (Courtesy New York Museum of Modern Art Stills Archive)

of Italian masculinity. In *Mimi,* as the eponymous Southern worker, his character ranges from an unkempt and downtrodden worker, unsuccessful sexually with his wife, Rosalia (Agostina Belli), to an image of raging masculinity caught finally in the familiar dilemma of upholding his honor (similar to Mastroianni in *Divorzio*). Mimi is forced to leave Sicily and find work in Turin as a consequence of his flouting the Mafia by not voting for their candidate. There he becomes romantically involved with the bohemian-Left radical Fiore (Mariangela Melato) to the romantic strains of *La traviata.* Once again the Mafia forces him relocate, and he returns to the South, to Catania, where he becomes even more a victim of the Mafia and finds himself deeply embroiled in the sexual politics of the Mezzogiorno: His honor is wounded by his discovery that his now-modernized wife has had an affair with Amilcare, a customs collector. Mimi decides to seek revenge by having sex with Amilcare's wife, Amalia (Elena Fiore), in a scene where size becomes a visual commentary on the implications of following the code of honor with its emphasis on virile masculinity: By means of fish-eye lenses, Mimi is seen to shrink before Amalia's enormous buttocks, which fill the scene, and he is reduced (as he is at the end of the film) to infantile proportions.

Mimi's physical appearance undergoes a number of transmutations as he moves from dark, swarthy, southern bumpkin to a more cosmopolitan image in Turin, taking on the characteristics, under Fiore's tutelage, of a romantic lover and idealist. Now vain, he wears a hair net, clips his mustache, examines his skin, and fulfills the image of the romantic operatic hero. Upon his return South, however, he undergoes another visual transformation as the prototypical Latin lover (accompanied by tango music and dance) only to be deflated by Amalia's overwhelming size in bed. In general, the image Giannini projects is one of malleability, tenuous sexuality, suggestibility, absent introspection, and meager cosmopolitanism – qualities not easily translatable to the demands of international stardom. These attributes are again invoked in *Film d'amore e d'anarchia,* where he is an awkward but well-meaning peasant with a self-destructive naïveté about the urban world and the politics of Fascism. Even in *Lo zio indegno,* Giannini as a nouveau-riche entrepreneur is cowed by the worldly behavior of his intellectual and unconventional uncle. In *Mi manda Picone (Where's Picone?,* 1984), he plays a sleazy conniver who hopes to extort money but finds himself (as Giannini's characters often do) outsmarted by the powers that be.

Conceptions of masculinity are at the core of Bernardo Bertolucci's *1900* (1976), a film that has been received with disappointment by some and enthusiasm by others.[30] The determining character of gender and sexuality are central to the film's examination of patriarchy, Fascism, and socialism in the context of the Ventennio and World War II. The film seeks in epic fashion to address questions concerning the uses and meaning of history, the nature of ideology, and the relationship among economics, politics, and culture. Bertolucci's *1900* "analyzes contemporary Italian history through family history by telescoping the events of this century into the juxtaposed chronicles of two different clans."[31] Its trajectory relies on doubling and mirroring or, as T. Jefferson Kline has described it, on "the play of repetition."[32]

This doubling or twinning in the film depends on many juxtapositions: distinctions between past and present, between Fascism and socialism, realism and antirealism, psychoanalysis and Marxism, cinema and other art forms, and the pairing of antithetical purposes of families, social classes, and of masculine and of feminine characters. Though focusing on the interrelationship of two families, the film is an unrelenting dramatization of homosocial relations between the two masculine protagonists, Alfredo (Robert De Niro) and Olmo (Gérard Depardieu), ultimately revealed as half-brothers. Through these characters, the film juxtaposes two colliding forms of masculinity tied to Fascism and anti-Fascism. It does also offer an image of a vibrant and active political woman in the character of Anita Foschi (Stefania Sandrelli), but *1900* remains preoccupied with questions of masculinity.

The film (in both its shortened and original form) is framed by the Liberation of Italy in April 1945; it reverts to a prolonged flashback to events at the beginning of the new century, a sustained focus on events leading to the rise of Fascism and its destructive effects, and, finally, defeat at the hands of the partisans and the Allies. The chronicling of the two families focuses on divergent views of paternalism, familial responsibility, masculinity, and sexuality. In the case of the Berlinghieris, the impotence of the old padrone (master), also named Alfredo (Burt Lancaster) – his inability to consummate his sexual desire for a young peasant woman – sets the stage for the more violent sexual acts later committed by members of the family, most notably by Alfredo (his grandson) and by the interloping foreman, Attila. Sexuality is the mechanism whereby the film seeks to probe the psychology of these masculine aggressors – not by isolating sexuality as the sole determinant of events, but by seeking to integrate it with the broader political issues involved in the rise of Fascism and in the fall of socialism.

When we first see Giovanni (Romolo Valli), the old padrone's son, he is already bridling against the authority of his father, harboring resentments toward the previous generation, and impatient to receive his patrimony. His father's demise, when it comes, signifies the death of the old feudal world, with its ties to nature, and the triumph of modernity, in the machine and capitalism. Once Giovanni assumes the role of padrone, he is ruthless in pursuing not sexual pleasure but the accumulation of money and property, gained at the expense of his peasants' welfare. A similar antagonism exists between the younger Alfredo and his father, Giovanni, and he too must wait for the time that he can assume control of the family. Alfredo is presented as likable but vacillating, afraid of confrontation and conflict. His passivity has its sexual and political implications. He is a searcher of pleasures with little gratification (like his uncle). In fact, Alfredo's wife, Ada (Dominique Sanda) is his perfect counterpart: Both are aesthetes; both recoil from violence yet, as voyeurs, seek it out. Whether their inaction is a result of an exhausted aristocratic line or the consequence of rigid paternal control, they are unable to act, paralyzed before the brutality that surrounds them.

Olmo appears to offer an alternative to Alfredo. Whereas Alfredo seems apolitical and passive, Olmo is active in organizing the peasants. He is identified with the struggle against Fascism, as are his peasant relatives, friends, and his activist wife, Anita Foschi (Stefania Sandrelli). The film probes the half-brothers' differences. According to Kolker:

[W]here Alfredo remains stuck within bourgeois patriarchy, Olmo is born free of it. Olmo is a speculative figure, a peasant unencumbered by the urban middle class and a nostalgia for the present. He is a bastard offspring of history, which he attempts to change.[33]

The case of Attila (Donald Sutherland) is yet another perspective on the film's probing of connections between masculinity and Fascism. Socially shunned by Alfredo and bridling against his sense of powerlessness, this foreman finds an ally and a springboard to power in his relationship with Regina, Alfredo's cousin (Laura Betti). He constructs his masculine identity through Fascism, in his defiance of the law and in his brutality to anyone who does not bend to his will. Attila, like his barbarian namesake, unleashes the forces of violence and political reaction, rallying the support of other reactionary forces in the community; but the most gratuitous forms of brutality are enacted by Attila. His smashing the body of a cat against a wall foreshadows his violence against a young boy who has been observing Attila and Regina at their sexual games in a shack on the estate: The boy is dragged into the shack and savagely beaten to death, his head bashed in. Attila's opportunism, rabble-rousing, and arbitrary violence identify him as the "new virile man" of Fascism, whose virility is identified with physical force and with death.

Attila's reign of terror is not suppressed by Alfredo who, with his father's death, becomes the padrone of the estate. In his vacillation, his passivity before Attila's acts of cruelty, and his incapacity to control the Fascists, he betrays his peasants. By contrast, Olmo appears to be the good father, aiding the peasants in organizing against the Fascists in the name of socialism; but in commanding the peasants to give up their weapons at the end of the war, on the orders of the Committee of National Liberation, Olmo too betrays the people, foreshadowing the demise of revolutionary struggle in the postwar era.

Thus, in *1900,* Bertolucci explores the causes for the failure of socialism, tying them not merely to the failure of formal politics but, as in his other films, to degraded forms of patriarchal power aligned to sexuality. When Alfredo and Olmo seek to have sex with a young epileptic female prostitute, Neve (Stefania Cassini), Alfredo regards this as a sexual "adventure" without any regard for her as an individual, whereas Olmo recoils from the encounter. Their relations in childhood repeatedly identify Alfredo as alienated from nature, in contrast to Olmo, who is associated with the earth. Alfredo remains trapped in aestheticism, uncomprehending or indifferent to power and politics.

The differing roles of each of these male figures within the social order are intimately connected to familial and class differences as well as to their treatment of women. The older generation, exemplified by the old Alfredo and Leo Dalco (Sterling Hayden), the peasants' spokesman, share certain qualities despite their differing class positions: Both are tied to the land and to a personal relationship with the people on the estate. Olmo's position in rela-

Figure 75. Two aesthetes, Alfredo (Robert De Niro) and Ada (Dominique Sanda) in *1900*. (Courtesy New York Museum of Modern Art Stills Archive)

tion to women, to Anita and also to his mother, is one of affective closeness. Moreover, from the beginning of the flashback portraying the childhood of Olmo and Alfredo, Olmo (like the peasants) is identified with trees, water, animals, and with a sense of his own body as he masturbates into a hole in the earth that he makes.

Alfredo's relations with Ada are based on yet another sexual and political configuration, involving his attachment to his Uncle Ottavio (Werner Bruhns), an aesthete, a hedonist, a homosexual, and a hater of the crude provincial life. Ottavio is identified with modernism and with urban life; however, Alfredo's role as padrone admits of no such escape, and his union with Ada appears to evoke his incestuous desire for his uncle. Ada's refusal to see, her literally playing blind, persists throughout their relations, causing Alfredo after his initial fascination to recoil and become brutal toward her; yet she is his counterpart [Fig. 75]. In another sense, he too plays at being blind: Although he deplores the acts of brutality brought on by Attila and the Fascists, he does nothing to intervene. Another aspect of his character that aligns him to Ada, causing grief to both, resides in their sexual ambiguity, which links them both to Ottavio and to decadentism but is expressed in their inevitable and escalating hostility toward each other.

Through the character of Attila, the film suggests that Fascist masculine sexual arousal is predicated on the destruction of the body, from pleasures derived from enacting (and witnessing) mutilation. Attila's relation to Regina is based on a common bond of violence, of violent acts against both the physical body and the body politic. His hatred of life is expressed not only in his brutality against the cat and the young boy but in his brutish beating of Olmo; in his gruesome murder of the aristocratic Signora Poppi (Alida Valli), whose house he and Regina have decided to own, despite her refusal to relinquish it to them; and in his barbaric shooting of a group of peasants.

Thus, *1900* has attempted to do what Visconti sought to do in *La caduta degli dei (The Damned,* 1969): to open up the analysis of Fascism by dissecting the psychodynamics of masculinity, reiterating too its focus on family, on relations between sexuality and power, and introducing – if ambiguously, in the spirit of Visconti – the exploration of homosexuality and femininity as imperative considerations for an understanding of the uses and abuses of social and political power. In Bertolucci's film, the overriding concern with socialism as an alternative to agrarian patriarchy and to Fascism underpins the investigation, suggesting not only the film's preoccupation with the rise and fall of the Fascist regime but also with exploring the obstacles to and possibility of socialist revolution. Bertolucci seems to follow a trajectory explored by Pasolini – namely, to conjoin masculine sexuality and politics – but his films move in a direction more closely tied to psychoanalysis and to an examination of identity formation than to performing a sustained exploration of the deformation of all forms of sexuality under capitalism. There still lingers in his work a quest for a "natural" form of masculinity.

A fin-de-siècle sense of aging seems to haunt some Italian films of the 1990s. Franco Brusatti's *Lo zio indegno (The Sleazy Uncle,* 1989), a melodrama–comedy hybrid, dramatizes a familiar motif from films of the past two decades: the relation of masculinity to aging and of aging to creativity. This emphasis on aging may result from the disappearance, through death and retirement, of a generation of directors and actors. It may also derive from the uncertainty as to the fate of cinema in the age of television, the fumbling attempts to define a European cineidentity, and the postmodern penchant for nostalgia.

Lo zio indegno focuses on an aging roué, played by the aging cosmopolitan star Vittorio Gassman. Gassman has made films in Italy and in the United States, though his Hollywood films were not as successful as his Italian ones. Though he has not attained international stardom, he has gained a reputation as an international actor. He is best known for such films as *Riso amaro,* in which he played a down-at-heels and brutal criminal exploiting women [Fig. 76]. In general, his most successful roles have marked him as a rake, a ne'er-do-well, or a flouter of social conventions: Those in *C'eravamo tanto amati*

Figure 76. Vittorio Gassman as the con man Walter in *Riso amaro*. (Courtesy New York Museum of Modern Art Stills Archive)

(*We All Loved Each Other So Much*, 1974; see Chapter 12), *Profumo di donna* (*Scent of a Woman*, 1974), and *Lo zio indegno* are variations on this persona. Less identified with working-class masculine figures, he is more likely to appear as a professional person, a lawyer, teacher, artist (or con artist). On screen he is appealing, even lethal, to women. Capable of playing aging or infirm figures, his attractiveness and seductive charm are still evident.

In *Lo zio indegno*, Gassman plays Luca, the dying sleazy uncle of the film's title, who haunts movie theaters to seduce young women with the line, "I could be your father." His character is complemented by his nephew, Riccardo, played by Giancarlo Giannini. Different from his characters in the Lina Wertmüller films, here Giannini as Riccardo is an extremely successful entrepreneur, the owner of an industrial cleaning company. He is married, with two children, and his conventional life differs radically from that of his uncle: Riccardo's home is an advertisement for the latest in furniture, electronic commodities, and an outdoor "barbecoo"; Luca, by contrast, lives in a hovel – overcrowded with books, scattered papers, and a dog who is as sexually arousable as his owner. Hinging on a contrast between cleanliness and filth in environmental, bodily, and sexual terms, the film traces the increasing fascination on the part of the once-reluctant Riccardo for his disreputable Uncle Luca, which leads him to invite the uncle to the seaside: Riccardo will attend a business conference and Luca will be free to play on the beach. Increasingly, his resistance to Luca undergoes a transformation as he surveys the older man's vitality, his zest for living, and his contempt for bourgeois rituals.

Luca is a poet with a modicum of international fame, and Riccardo, coming to his uncle's apartment while Luca is out, meets a group of international visitors who have come to do homage to Luca's work. To them he inveighs against poets, contrasting the disorderly and irresponsible poet's life to his own productive and lucrative existence. The allusions to cinema and to writing reinforce the film's investment in contrasting the antiseptic nature and banalities of bourgeois life to a radical and transgressive form of existence that seems suspect in the eyes of the law and of the wealthy middle classes. Luca, for example, is in every way politically incorrect: He refers to one of the women with whom he has been having sexual relations – a black woman he now wants to "sell" to a friend – as a "desert cat." (Her presence is interesting as an oblique, if unexamined, reminder of the presence of immigrants from Africa to Italy in recent decades.) The primary trajectory of the film, however, is the effect of Luca on Riccardo: This entails flashbacks to Riccardo's childhood and the revelation of his mother's affair with Luca, thus tying the uncle's representation to questions of memory. Luca is the catalyst bringing to light disruptive aspects of sexuality inimical to the commodified images of contemporary life seen in Riccardo's relations to his workers and his family.

When Luca is brought before a judge for stealing and selling a painting from Riccardo's house, we are given a rundown of Luca's refusal to conform to the law, his passing bad checks, his "obscene" behavior with women, his "corruption of minors," and his attitude toward work, which bears no resemblance to Riccardo's orderly, efficient, and profit-driven behavior. The film ends at a hotel, with nephew and uncle competing for the attentions of an opera singer. Riccardo finally seduces her but is unable to gloat: Luca, meanwhile, has died. The final images of the film are of Riccardo sitting on the hotel steps, looking out at his uncle's body on the sand. He begins to smile and slowly drinks the aperitif that Luca was to have paid for, since Riccardo has won the bet over who would win the singer's affections.

Lo zio indegno juxtaposes two images of masculinity: One, the uncle, belongs to the Italian cinematic imaginary and to a long line of masculine figures who, in Fellini's terms, constitute "the Italian [as exemplified by *Fellini Casanova*]: the indifference, the commonplaces, the conventional ways, the facade, the attitude. And therefore, it is clear why he has become a myth, because he is really nothingness, universality without meaning. . . ."[34] *Lo zio indegno* offers a more sympathetic portrait, with Riccardo as the instrument for resurrecting and inspecting that mythic figure, to whom he is the uncertain cinematic heir.

In looking retrospectively at the various ways in which masculinity has been represented in Italian cinema over the course of the century, several issues stand out: There is in the films an overwhelming preoccupation with the care and nurture of the male. In some instances he is naughty and inept but clever. In others, he is a swaggering body, a spectacle on display. In still others, he has been a political force, converted and committed to change. More recently, the masculine figure is a vestige of a glorious or heroic past that is now reduced to banality or a harbinger of new ways of thinking and acting. In all instances, as Fellini's quotation reveals, he is a performance, a "facade," an "attitude," indicating that, like Proteus, the male changes to suit cultural, social, and cinematic exigencies.

CHAPTER TWELVE

Cinema on Cinema and on Television

C inema's fascination with its miraculous exploits, ranging over space and time, can be traced to the very first films produced. As studies of early cinema and of the genre system (especially the musical genre) reveal, films are inevitably intertextual and, in many cases, even self-reflexive: They comment and reflect on themselves as well as on other cinematic texts. In some instances, this labor appears to be effaced, and the film seems to be offering a version of unmediated "reality"; but even here there are indications of the text's awareness of its status as text in its invocation of theater, photography, opera, and literature and its preoccupation with the antinomy between realism and illusionism. The Italian cinema offers us a fertile range of films that are revealing about the character and properties not only of Italian cinema but about cinema generally – histories of its resources and also of its limitations, its relations to the other arts, its hope for and despair of its role as an agent of change, and its conceptions and expectations of audiences. In short, among the various burdens that the films impose on themselves is their operating as essays on the cinematic apparatus.

One of the important figures in Italian literature and theater, Luigi Pirandello, was himself involved in filmmaking, and his novel *Si gira* (Shoot) – among other novels, plays, and essays on theater and film that he wrote – is a reflection on the cinematic medium. In that work, he expresses many of the issues that continue to engage students of cinema. One of these is the need to develop an understanding of the unique properties of the cinematic medium, involving the effects of photographing, the relationship and effects of linking images to each other, and particularly the "film as both an art form and as a *new* means of communication in a *new* society."[1] In his writing, both the style and the content adopt various cinematographic devices: montage, multiple perspectives, a concern with the fragmentary and elusive character of the novelistic and cinematic subject, and, above all, the quality of theatricality; that is, the illusionist nature of the fictions presented that undermine an unmediated and realist response to the narrative. As Manuela Gieri writes, "in any modern narrative, the critical issue is not so much *not* to tell a story, but how to denounce the 'fictionality' of the narrative construct."[2]

Pirandello's works on and in film (some have been the source of films in Italy, Hungary, Germany, and Hollywood) are not merely examples of art cinema as opposed to dominant commercial cinema but are a recognition of the changes wrought by the cinema on audiences in relation to the perception of the visual image. The character and effects of cinematic production inhere in all kinds of cinema whether the filmmakers have chosen to be explicit or indirect about the labor involved in creating a world through its technological apparatus. Pirandello's works exemplify metawriting and metacinema in their allusion to such devices as dream states, doubling or splitting, film-within-the-film, characters as surrogates for an "author," an emphasis on looking, a "preoccupation with states of mind,"[3] and the invocation of an audience. Pirandello's work stands as an exemplary case for the necessity of rethinking dichotomies about realism and illusion or antirealism. Though his uses of modernist devices call attention to the fictional nature of reality – and especially to the role of cinema as heightening the sense of language, particularly visual language – his concerns are not restricted to art cinema, but rather have had an impact on all forms of cinematic production. In the popular commercial cinema of the 1930s and 1940s, its reliance on generic conventions and theatrical excess, its intertextuality, and even its uses of reflexivity call attention to its constructed nature and place audiences in an uneasy relation to characters, events, and action.

In the sound cinema of the Fascist years, a theatrical motif persists in the so-called white telephone films, in Camerini's comedies and melodramas, in the "calligraphic" films in the late 1930s and early 1940s, and even in neorealism, whose films reveal attempts at negating the artifice associated with the genre system. Two films from the Fascist period serve to underscore theatricality and its relations to the character of the cinematic image, its construction, and its effects on audiences: Mario Camerini's *Figaro e la sua gran'giornata* and Mario Soldati's *Dora Nelson*.

The cinematic form most identified with escapism and with antirealism is the film musical, where song and dance are considered to be evasions from the hardships of life – failure, violence, unrequited interpersonal relations, and abuses of power. The prime characteristic of musicals is their emphasis on a show-within-the-film, which serves to present art as life and to celebrate performance over naturalism. Their antirealism is mainly identified in their foregrounding of theatricality, artifice, romance, and resolution of conflict. Their eclecticism is evident in their reliance on earlier literary, theatrical, and cinematic sources to meet the exigencies of the contemporary moment.

One of the first Italian sound films was *Figaro e la sua gran giornata* (*Figaro's Big Day*, 1931), a musical directed by Mario Camerini, which links life and art. Melodrama is present even in the comic scenarios, in their motifs as described above, and in their theatrical styles. As the title indicates, the film is indebted to Rossini's *The Barber of Seville,* but it also draws on a play by Arnaldo Fraccaroli, *Ostrega che sbrego!* The narrative is structured around the attempts of a waning baritone, Basoto (Gianfranco Giachetti), to insert himself into a performance of *The Barber of Seville* by a visiting opera troupe. His boasting of his once-great career is unmatched by his actual performance: While a braggart about his talent, Basoto cannot sing on key. On the other hand, Nina (Leda Gloria) – a victim of parental control and the focus of the melodramatic scenario – is abundantly talented, and Basoto and Rantolini, the manager, seek to enlist her as their Rosina against the efforts of her father and, later, of her lover Chiodini (Maurizio D'Ancora). Her life is also complicated by the refusal of her parents to entertain marriage between her and Chiodini. The dual lines of the narrative – romance and theatrical performance – meet in the trials and tribulations of Nina and her relationship to Chiodini, suggesting that "the symbolic wedding celebrates the ongoing relationship between film and spectator as much as it celebrates the union of the couple,"[4] and, further, the union of art and life.

The plight of the beleaguered and helpless feminine figure beset by irate parents and a jealous spouse, a traditional source of melodramatic and operatic conflict, is overcome – not only for the characters but also for the internal and external audiences – through artistic performance. *Figaro* blurs distinctions between life and theater by consistently calling attention to the role of spectatorship, involving several audiences in the film: the townspeople, the opera troupe, the parental figures, and Basoto and Chiodini as eavesdroppers to Nina's singing. The focus on "live entertainment" in *Figaro* (and musicals more generally) serves "to speak more directly to the spectator . . . maybe that's why so many musicals are about putting on a show rather than about making films."[5] In the context of entertainment, the misunderstandings, misrecognitions, deceptions, and prohibitions associated with "real life" appear momentarily suspended, relegated to an oneiric, fantasmatic world. This suspension does not necessarily mislead the audience, rendering it unable to distinguish between art and "reality." While the text offers a momentary respite from constraints, it never lets the audience forget that what it is watching is artifice, "entertainment." Nor does the text conceal conflict: *Figaro* offers an image of community in the contemplation of shared conflict and even of shared knowledge about the impossibility of reconciliation, save through entertainment. Moreover, as in the Hollywood musical, the film "seeks to bridge the gap [between audience and performance] by putting up 'community' as an ideal concept."[6] Escapism here can be construed as the transformation of life into theater, where all problems can be resolved [Fig. 77]; but the "coincidence" of the parallel between the opera and the film, the consequence of "putting on a show," has a more substantial and contradictory valence.

Figure 77. Life as theater: Nina (Leda Gloria) and Chiodini (Maurizio D'Ancora) in *Figaro e la sua gran'giornata* (*Figaro's Big Day*). (Courtesy New York Museum of Modern Art Stills Archive)

Though *Figaro* eschews a realist form of representation in favor of illusion, its reflexivity in calling attention to the parallels between art and life ironically suggests a lack of consonance between social reality and representation. Theatricality (in this case, melodrama), the acknowledgment of the necessity of performance, becomes a strategy for exposing and contending with, not denying, conflict. In the disruption of the final staging of the opera, sabotaged by Nina's father, the film seems to undermine the familiar strategy of ending with a union of successful stage performance and romance. The parallels between art and life have worked in a reverse direction, so that the conflicts besetting the characters have taken on the characteristics of the opera; the lives of the protagonists and of the townspeople are, in fact, more theatrical than the performance.

Of the many ways that 1930s cinema takes itself as subject, one involves the convention of an actress aspiring to a career in the movies. The scenario portrays her attainment of success in work and in romance after a series of vicissitudes and impersonations. This scenario dramatizes homologies between artistic and social performance. Mario Soldati's *Dora Nelson* (1939), a comedy that resembles Hollywood comedies of the era, centers on a poor young woman who, after a series of obstacles and misrecognitions is assimilated, as a result of her contact with the film world, into the world of the upper class. This Cinderella narrative is commonplace, but what is interesting about the film is its reliance on impersonation and doubling, a strategic device in comedy for challenging the primacy of "real" life over fiction. The film, a remake of a French text, hinges on dual identity, the similarity in appearance but difference in attitude between an upper-class woman and her lower-class counterpart.

From the opening moments of the film, through the device of a film-within-the-film, the spectator is thrown into confusion as to appearances. A group of gypsy performers are singing and dancing as a bemedaled officer greets the arrival of a princess. Suddenly, when the "princess" (Assia Noris) has a tantrum, it becomes clear that this is a film-within-the-film and that the woman is an actress. She is the titular Dora Nelson, the widow of a Russian ex-prince. At home, she berates her second husband, Giovanni (Carlo Ninchi), a wealthy industrialist, for being a bourgeois; her aspirations are tied to the aristocracy.

In the narrative's gesturing toward self-reflexivity and in its relations to theatricality, the director of the film-within-the-film is confronted by the fact that he needs to replace his star in order to finish the production. Fortunately, a look-alike, Pierina (also played by Noris), who happens to be a clerk in a hat shop, is found to fill the role in the film-within-the-film. Such doubling, characteristic of many of the comedies and melodramas, underscores the concern with sameness-in-difference that the films portray. Pierina is brought to the studio, outfitted, and made up for the part, though she is not eager to make a name for herself in the cinema. Not only are the two female characters doubled, but the plots of the film and of the film-within-the-film mirror each other. There the similarities end: Dora is the consummate diva, enemy of middle-class life, given to tantrums, and hostile to the burdens of maternity and family. She has a daughter who is engaged to a respectable young man (Massimo Girotti), but her lack of maternal concern and her willful behavior threatens their marriage. As one might expect, the confusion between the identities of Dora and Pierina escalates. Giovanni, who has come to the set to find his wife, instead finds Pierina and marvels at the visual resemblance between the two women. Desperate, he asks Pierina to play the role of wife and mother for a few days during the engagement festivities for his daughter so that the occasion will provide an illusion of a united and harmonious family.

Giovanni brings Pierina to the house, where she outdoes herself in performing the role of Dora, entertaining the guests, winning them over with her charm, and thus establishing herself as a performer in the domestic arena. The only person she cannot charm is the daughter, who is antagonistic toward her "mother." Pierina, experiencing the daughter's hostility, has a tantrum herself and angrily tells Giovanni that she wants to leave. They kiss, and the kiss seals their love, bonding them in the conspiracy of dissimulation. The festivities for the daughter are successful, and Giovanni tells Pierina that he is happy for the first time in his adult life.

The parallel plot involves Dora in nefarious dealings with the self-styled aristocrats and their hangers-on, as well as in shady financial machinations that make the headlines. (This distinguishes unproductive performance from productive.) Dora's intrigues are intercut with scenes of family life, culminating in the daughter's marriage and the newlyweds' departure on their honeymoon, which ends the necessity of Pierina's pretending to be Dora. Marriage and role-playing thus are fused. Pierina, realizing the hopelessness of her love, humbly informs the husband that nothing can come of their relationship because he is married. Seeing Dora return, Pierina hides, but before she can warn Giovanni, the melodrama is truncated: The chauffeur runs in bearing a newspaper that announces, "The strange case of the dead revived . . . the first husband of Dora Nelson, believed dead in a train crash, has been restored to life after eight years, and the marriage to the noted industrialist Giovanni Ferrari has been dissolved." The film ends with Giovanni and Pierina on the road in an open convertible. Stopping to observe the making of another film, starring Dora and her prince, they look at the actors, laugh, and drive off.

Though in its narrative of doubling and in its iconography the film seems openly to evoke the notion of cinema as a "dream factory," encouraging the assumption that the Italian cinema of the time was escapist, there is another dimension to the film, one endemic to the functioning of popular cinema and to its reception. This other dimension, as with so many comedies of the era, involves the film's reflexivity concerning cinema. The emphasis on role-playing, on the slippery line between acting and "reality," serves a dual and complex function: Not a disavowal of the narrative of upward mobility and of the selection of the fittest to receive the rewards of money and privilege, it does upset simplistic notions of the film as a mere carrier of an air-tight ideology identified as escapism, which assumes the diversionary powers of spectacles of the rich and famous. By setting up the film-within-the-film against the film itself, *Dora Nelson* shares with its audiences the knowledge of the fictional status of cinema and its narratives. In this manner, the film winks at the audience, confirming viewers' commonsense knowledge about narratives of romance and upward mobility – that they are "make-believe." The film's visualization of the movie set, its portrait of the fast life through Dora, its images of opulence in the scenes where Pierina impersonates Dora, and the blurring of the lines of vision through the device of doubling – all these suggest that the romance narrative and its familiar conventions are a pretext to explore and exploit spectatorship. The comedy lies less in the repetition of the Cinderella folklore and more in the shared joke between the audience and the film – that film viewing entails theatricality and, even more, that impersonation *is* life. Thus, the reflexivity is not in the service of "radicalism" or even of subversion, but instead offers tell-tale markers of how popular texts attend to the potential of audiences' knowledge of illusion and play.

The film makes distinctions among different forms of theatricality and the ends to which they are put. Though the preoccupation with exploring boundaries between reality and illusion, art and life, persists, the film seems to want to distinguish also among forms of spectacle. Pierina's acting in the interests of rescuing the family ultimately is "excused" and finally exposed as a benevolent and necessary act canceling out bad performance – as in homeopathic magic, where like drives out like. The emphasis on performance suggests that audiences' ability and competence to recognize cinematic conventions is increasing, and that cinema's relation to modernity involves a growing theatricalization of social life, including the public spectacles of Fascism. The film's reflexivity suggests a necessary decomposition of notions of the "real." Although not valorizing "authenticity" and realism, *Dora Nelson* reveals that it is not merely imposing a fictional construct on an innocent and unsuspecting audience; rather, it is engaged *with* the audience in acknowledging the social value (and profit) of cinematic fictions.

Neorealism was antagonistic to the type of commercial filmmaking exemplified by the films discussed above, in its style, choice of subject matter, and topical allusions to films; yet neorealist films communicate their own conception of the nature and status of the cinema. In *Roma, città aperta,* the physical traits and dress of Marina, Ingrid, and Bergmann, their melodramatic and stylized forms of acting in contrast to Pina, Manfredi, and Don Pietro – often condemned by critics as a residue from the earlier cinema – present a dichotomy between spectacle and realism, linking the former to Fascism and the latter to emergent forms of representation. The film is as much about resistance to commercial cinema as it is about resistance to the Nazi occupation. Too often the "realism" in neorealism has been construed as the unmediated reproduction of "natural" life rather than the codification of "conventionalized expectations." Filmmakers such as Rossellini were not naïve; their "realism" was an attempt to strain "against currently accepted boundaries of the realistic, close toward the dangerous unpredictability of the (represented) real."[7] In *Ladri di biciclette,* the striking contrast of its starkness to genre films, the references to moviegoing, and especially the poster of Rita Hayworth in *Gilda* that Antonio is hired to paste to the wall before his bicycle is stolen are not merely passing references to the "other" cinema but reminders of the colonization of Italian culture by Hollywood. The image of Hayworth, for example, opens up questions of spectatorship: "The Italian spectators' desire to have, or to look like, the epitome of American glamour, the icon of American economic and military supremacy simultaneously affirms and denies the essentialism of national and ethnic (as well as sexual) difference, placing him/her in the position of both colonizer and colonized."[8] This concern with Americanism and its impact on national identity play a central role in Italian cinema, ranging from outright emulation to ambivalence, to critical rejection.

Similarly in *Umberto D* (1952), cinema, specifically of the commercial variety, is invoked through the figure of the landlady (Lina Gennari) in her (and her guests') clothing and hairdos, reminiscent of movies of the era. Her engagement to the movie-theater owner is not gratuitous but makes still more binding the new world of Americanness she has entered – and from which Umberto (Carlo Battisti), a retired and impoverished civil servant, has been excluded. Her role amplifies beyond that of the melodramatic villain to become allegorical. Her penchant for opera, her operatic melodrama in her dealings with Umberto and her posturing with friends, is another indication of the illusionist character of her world. Her destruction of Umberto's old-fashioned room is testimony to the eradication of the Italian past in the interests of the new images of prosperity and consumption. The film accords with the neorealist ambition to produce a more acceptable national image through its attack on the cinematic values associated with Fascism.

A further reminder of the threat of the Americanization to Italian culture is evident in Silvana's preoccupation in *Riso amaro* with photo romances and with visions of glamour. Magazines function as a reminder of the deleterious effects of commercial cinema on the populace. In the films of neorealism, the concerns self-reflexively dramatized with film are indications of an attempt to reverse the current political and aesthetic course, increasingly identified with the economic miracle and with the abandonment of a transformational politics in the late 1940s and 1950s. The specific concerns gathered under the banner of "realism" were, in Manuela Gieri's terms, related to the notion that "to see, meant to understand, or at least the effort to understand . . . that it is possible to provide an unambiguous and reliable representation of reality."[9] In other words, neorealism in complex fashion acknowledged the power and threat of media. Media were a synecdoche for the social and national situation, identified with a threat to national integrity; ironically, these films had not abandoned the quest for a national idiom, expunged of the taint of Fascism. The neorealist films reveal, in retrospect, links between cinema and national identity, as well as a nostalgia for a different aesthetic and politics.

Arguments have been advanced for the "demise" of neorealism by the mid-1950s on the basis of political repression, the victory of the Christian Democrats, audiences' low tolerance for films of social and political persuasion, the economic vicissitudes of the film industry, and the emergence of Italy's economic miracle. These explanations account only partially, however, for the abandonment of many neorealist tenets by many filmmakers. Putting aside, for the moment, specific explanations for the directions the Italian cinema took in the late 1950s and onward, it is evident that neorealism was a symptom of the ongoing economic, social, and cultural transformations that were set in motion by the rapid modernization and capitalization of Italy. Equally important are the changes that were effected by globalization and specifically the Americanization of the world that were to have such an impact on Italian culture and cinema.

The issues set in motion by Rossellini and De Sica were later to take new stylistic forms consonant with the changing cultural and political landscape, as exemplified by the films of Michelangelo Antonioni. Though such Antonioni films as *Gente del Po* (1943–7) seemed to belong to the documentary style of neorealism, the film reveals an experimentation with form and subject matter: "[R]ather than the camera recording a subject, it is in search of a subject whose identity and outline elude it."[10] His subsequent films augment this heuristic approach to film form. The focus in the films is on more dispassionate, distanced forms of looking and formal elements that suggest the filmmaker's preoccupation with psychological motifs, a penchant for concentrating on female protagonists, and a concern for linking landscape in ambiguous ways to the internal states of his characters. In *Deserto rosso* (*Red Desert,* 1964), the emphasis on the urban landscape and on the somnambulistic movement of Giuliana (Monica Vitti) takes precedence over any sense of narrativity. Conventional narrative is obliterated as the motif of vision and its relation to a new way of thinking about cinema comes to the fore. Instead of an overarching "story," the spectator is given fragments of narratives that cannot be neatly organized and unified.

From its opening moments, with their lengthy shots of the refinery and of the waste deposits surrounding it – and the aimless wandering of Giuliana through this ostensible wasteland – the viewer is thrown into another realm of perception. The film cannot be reduced to a simple sociological reflection on the "alienation" of the modern person in the modern industrial world, though this concern becomes central to the film's investigation of cinematic perception. The confusion concerning the identity of the characters, questions as to what they are doing, the why and how of the resolution of certain social problems that must be contemplated – these give way to a quest "for new narrative forms for the cinema and not from 'life,' not in declarations of social and political faiths, but rather from within a new, 'modern' tradition of narrative."[11]

At stake is the relation between seeing and understanding, but in ways that suggest there is no immediate relation between the two and that the work to be done by the spectator touches the status not only of cinema but of modern thought, its limits and its possibilities:

> Antonioni does not criticize the modern world, in whose possibilities he profoundly 'believes': he criticizes the coexistence in the world of a modern brain and a tired, worn-out, neurotic body. So that his work, in a fundamental sense, passes through a dualism which corresponds to two aspects of the time-image: a cinema of the body which puts all the weight of the past into the body, all the tiredness of the world and modern neurosis; but also a cinema of the brain, which reveals the creativity of the world, its colours aroused by a new space-time. . . . He is not an author who moans about the impossibility of communicating in the world. . . . The world awaits its inhabitants, who are still lost in neurosis.[12]

As part of this dual process described by Deleuze, *Deserto rosso* forces the spectator to follow Giuliana through a familiar route of neurosis in relation to her husband, Ugo (Carlo Chionetti), her son (Valerio Bartoleschi), and her affair with Corrado (Richard Harris). She is suffering a "trauma" ascribed to the effects of an automobile accident and has tried to commit suicide. The focus, however, is not on the psychoanalysis of her "breakdown" but on the ways in which her state of mind reproduces the endless portraits of modern disaffection in literature and cinema belonging to the world of popular psychology and cliché. The film's insistence on landscape – of Ravenna and of the island in Giuliana's fantasy – and its insistence, as its title alerts us, on the color and texture of the world she (and the audience through her) envisions do not serve as symbolic keys to unlocking her character. Instead, character and landscape become a field for investigation, an invitation to rethink clichés about reality and use film as an exercise in seeing differently. Through its use of color, its connections to abstract art, and its formal concerns, the film challenges reductive forms of thinking about modern life and, by implication, about cinema. At the end, the film returns to the mother and child as again they wander through this landscape; but this time Giuliana, in response to her son's question about whether the poisonous yellow gas will kill the birds, indicates that the birds have learned to avoid it. Thus, the film is not advising quietism, offering a moral (though it might, in a different reading, be interpreted in this manner); rather, as Bondanella suggests, it is "an ecological film in reverse"[13] in its interrogating the reductive and inverted ways spectators assess the physical world (and its articulation in cultural documents), which inhibit critical insight. One of the snares of the film, one that it seeks to expose, is precisely the ways character is psychologized in an effort to make simple, causal connections between behavior and environment. Moreover, the film challenges the dichotomy between cinema and social world through its creation of an enclosed technological world from which there is no escape.

Commenting on Antonio's film, Pier Paolo Pasolini writes:

> In *Red Desert* Antonioni no longer superimposes his own formalistic vision of the world on a generally committed content (the problem of neurosis caused by alienation). . . . Instead he looks at the world by immersing himself in his neurotic protagonist, reanimating the facts through her eyes. . . . By means of this stylistic device, Antonioni has freed his most deeply felt moment: he has been able to represent the world seen through his eyes, *because he has substituted in toto for the world-view of a neurotic his own delirious view of aesthetics* . . . in Antonioni we find the wholesale substitution of the filmmaker's feverish formalism for the view of the neurotic woman.[14]

The "cinema of poetry," as Pasolini describes it, is a meditation on the medium of cinema that is at the basis of his own work as well, though subject to changing forms as he seeks to explore the relations between cinema and the emerging world wrought by consumer capitalism and its new forms of Fascism.

Like so many filmmakers of his generation, Pasolini began to question and then to move away from the neorealist aesthetic in literature and cinema, finding neorealism to be a "tape recording" of reality. Moreover, as Naomi Greene writes, "Scenes that the neorealists would have filmed in long takes in order to preserve the spatial relationships and 'correct flow' of things are seen instead in a disconnected disjointed fashion."[15] Highly stylized, Pasolini's choreographed, antinaturalistic and antisociological films comprise elements of past culture (an inheritance of Gramscian "common sense"?), and are "always involved [in] in a self-reflective meditation not only on culture and style but even on cinema itself."[16] However, rather than maintain a binary distinction between film and reality, Pasolini, in ways reminiscent of Godard, seems to insist that cinema is not a reflection of reality but the reality of the reflection. Regarding Pasolini's commitment to "realism," Maurizio Viano asserts that

Pasolini never participated in making a scapegoat of the word *real-ism* and was always careful to employ the word *naturalism* to indicate cinema's "impression of reality." In fact, he thought that film-makers could harness cinema's "impression of reality"' to a positive end and prompt the spectator to see that reality is like a film, that "reality" is not natural.[17]

Pasolini's *Teorema* (1968) takes as its "theorem" the fantasmatic and never-accounted-for arrival into a wealthy family of a young man (Terence Stamp) who seduces its members – father, mother, son, daughter, and maid – and succeeds in destroying their conventional and isolating relations to their world. The narrative is set in motion by a prologue which, set in an industrial area of Milan, presents the father (Massimo Girotti) as relinquishing control of his factory to the workers and driving away from the scene. Rather than following this episode by a sequence that clarifies or enhances his gesture, however, the film assaults the spectator with the sight of a volcanic landscape, an image of barrenness devoid of signification that will recur throughout the film (and in other Pasolini films) as a leap into an uncertain future. Moving backward in time, by contrast, the film provides glimpses of the family and of the various effects of the young man's visit on their lives. It closes with two stark images: the maid, Emilia (Laura Betti), partially covered in earth, a *mater dolorosa* weeping tears not of sorrow but of hope for the renewal of life; and the father in the volcanic desert, stripping himself of all possessions, including his clothing. Having depicted the various expressions of bourgeois socialization, enculturation, and deracination, the film traces effects on the characters of their divesting themselves of the constraints of their economic, social, and sexual roles. For all the characters but the maid, the effects are not only destructive but also revealing of the particular character of their entrapment: The son, Pietro (Andrès-José Cruz) forsakes his young schoolfriends and plunges into the role of an oppositional artist, painting signs against the "establishment," destroying any vestige of representational art, becoming an incarnation of the rebellious youth of the sixties. Lucia, the mother (Silvana Mangano), torn between religious consolation and uncontrollable sexual desire, takes to the road seeking sexual contact with young men. Odetta (Anne Wiazemsky), the daughter – whose life has been lived vicariously through an album with a prominent photo of her father and through her scanning of his image – is, after her contact with the stranger, unable to move, and she is taken away to a psychiatric institution. Whereas the other family characters are identified by frantic movement, Odetta is identified with immobility – a sign, perhaps, as Viano suggests, "of refusal rather than a mere psychotic attack."[18]

The film is not a "case study" of the individual characters, of neurosis and psychosis, of the effects of alienated life any more than is Antonioni's *De-*

serto rosso. The film is a "theorem" exploring what would happen if the seemingly "normal" and complacent lives of the bourgeoisie were challenged and overturned, and the various episodes suggest that the particular forms of the characters' reactions do not produce a utopian reaction but reveal the profound barrenness of their existence and their entrapment. However, the "theorem" resides not really in this scenario of pain and spiritual confusion but rather in the investigation of something else: a "living problem" not from within (the text or the characters within the text) but in the film's refusal to reduce the problems that it poses "to the exteriority of the physical world any more than to the psychological interiority of a thinking ego."[19] The visitor from the outside is the force that directs attention to something other than conventional sociological or psychoanalytic analysis, focusing rather on the problematic of the cinematic apparatus itself as the "outside" that enables the theorem to be realized and explored. Cinema is, in fact, the focus of the film even though, as in Antonioni's film, there is little direct allusion to it. The focus in *Teorema* is on the philosophical and ideological dimensions of seeing and hearing as a means to explore ways of thinking about the world (or, by implication, to occlude that possibility). *Teorema*, like most of Pasolini's films, is multilayered: It involves, at one level, a probing and rethinking of conventional Marxist positions on the nature and role of the bourgeoisie, particularly its changing character. On another, more important level, however, it is an exploration of cinema as an instrument of investigation, not solving but making palpable and frightening the implications of not *seeing* the problems and, hence, of not thinking.

The emphasis on the visitor's (and the external audience's) surveillance of the various family members and the maid, their consistent (and fetishized) scrutiny of his presence, the frequent allusions to cultural artifacts – painting, photographs, religious icons, books, popular music, and the reiterative image of the eyes, culminating in Emilia's peering through the earth that covers all but her face – suggest that the film assumes another layer in its allegorical treatment of the role of visual culture and of cinema in particular. The cultural crisis that the film poses is the crisis of meaning and belief. In seeking to destroy what is regarded as realistic and natural, the film substitutes a different mode not merely of filmmaking but of perception – one that, in Viano's terms, "will be the truth of a contingent relationship, a truth revealing as much about the object as about the knowing subject."[20] The role of the desert in this film and in *Porcile* (*Pig Pen,* 1969) is like a zero degree in relation to meaning, calling attention to the limitations of truth, especially as that truth is packaged and consumed through prevailing modes of cultural expression.

The 1970s were a time for the investigation of film language by philosophers, semioticians, cineradicals, and filmmakers. In particular, psychoanalysis and

Marxism became, for many Italian critics and filmmakers, the ingredients necessary for understanding the nature and impact of cinematic production and reception. For French filmmakers, the figure of Alfred Hitchcock and his uses of the horror and crime-detection film offered (and continues to offer) a resource for analyzing the cinematic apparatus as an instrument of violence, particularly violence identified with vision, and, moreover, the psychosexual basis of cinematic pleasure. The horror film is intertextual, drawing on other films and film conventions both in its style and in its allusions to the connections between seeing and the threats posed by what is seen. For example, *Profondo rosso (Deep Red,* 1975) – a film directed by Dario Argento and clearly influenced by Hitchcock – places great emphasis not only on seeing but particularly on parapsychology, with its reliance on other senses to intuit threats. Through the psychic "demonstration" of Helga Ulmann (Macha Méril), the film establishes that the threat of violence is not only in the viewing of acts of horror and mutilation but arises in the "head," in the feelings that are related to the affective dimension of thought in cinema. Helga does not "see" the murderer in the hall but she can "feel" death. The film thrives on disjunctions between vision and hearing but also on "bad timing" in relation to the anticipation of the act of murder and its execution. *Profondo rosso* is in the tradition of Gothic horror: What becomes important is the large and ancient house, which has been a site of mystery, secrecy, and violence, and the narrative turns on the quest of a character to return to the "scene of the crime" and, by extension, to bring the audience to confront the return of the past. The figure of woman is central to the narrative, whether as investigating presence or as responsible for the original and ensuing acts of violence.

In *Profondo rosso,* the person who wants to know is, significantly, not a visual artist but a musician, Mark Daly (David Hemmings). (Mark is also the first name of the central character in one of the major "horror" films: Michael Powell's *Peeping Tom,* a British film expressly concerned with the relation between film and fantasy, vision and violence.) The film's emphasis on music, its pounding rock sound track, underlines its concern with forms of knowledge in addition to spectatorship. Before we finally confront the perpetrator, we "hear" her voice. In fact, the reiterative playing of the children's song identified with the first act of murder is as important a clue as is the reiterated image of the murder scene. Mark realizes that his response to the murder scene was one of misrecognition: He initially took in the scene through what he assumed was a painting; but upon returning to the scene, he is forced to admit that what he took to be a painting was, in effect, a mirror – underscoring the film's investment in the precariousness and threat of seeing and of memory. The film thrives on partial clues that tantalize the audience yet are finally misleading. That the source of the violence turns out to be the mother of a homosexual young man perhaps suggests the Hitchcockian world of *Psycho.*

Profondo rosso draws the viewer into the familiar fantasy of the threatening power of woman that (particularly in horror films) must be appeased by her death – but only after the audience has witnessed the havoc created by her vengeful, if not insane, fury.

In its style, the film reiterates clichés of the horror film, reveling in the camera as an animating presence. Certain scenes are shot in a hand-held style, and the camera directs the spectator to the details of the murder scenario. Along with the obtrusive presence of the camera experienced through the highly choreographed visual detail, the emphasis on windows (visible or boarded), mirrors, and paintings also maintains the mystery of vision central to the film. As might be expected, close-ups of eyes are prominent. In addition, the spectator is made aware of design (as in early expressionist horror films): The repetitive images of ornate windows composed of highly decorative leaded panels afford a parallel to the clairvoyant's description of her thoughts as like a "cobweb" – also a familiar image in horror films.

Parallel to the "primal" scene of murder (a reversal of the child as victim), but contributing to the problematic of understanding what is seen, are the discovery that Helga was Jewish (as we learn from her funeral, where the mourners recite Kaddish) and the antagonism between Mark and Gianna (Daria Nicolodi) over the issue of women's liberation. In the case of Helga's death and the discovery of her Jewishness, the spectator is invited to make comparisons between these murders and the destruction of the Jews in the Holocaust. She is an émigré from Eastern Europe, although her name suggests that she is German. This is but one of the many paths that the film asks the viewer to observe, and the possibilities of making connections among the various clues become part of the film's dense allusive system. The conflicts between Gianna and Mark over who is the strongest and "will come out on top" becomes a tantalizing allusion to women's liberation – especially to the fact that women are not gentle as Mark says they should be – and offers a possible clue to the motives for the various murders.

Thus, *Profondo rosso* exudes an uneasiness with cinematic style and content in its play with the audience as to the properties of a form – horror – that continues to attract viewers. Horror films, like this one of the 1970s, gave way to the "splatter" films of the 1980s.[21] Argento's film – despite the gruesome ending that validates its title (the Italian original is twenty minutes longer and gorier than the American release) – still seems more interested in investigating the visual medium than in gratuitous images of violence. (Contrast the camp uses of violence in *Dellamorte dellamore* [*Cemetery Man*, 1996]). *Profondo rosso* makes claim to our attention since it also offers an essay into cinema spectatorship, treading familiar ground precisely because of its exploration of the as-yet-unfathomed nature of the links between knowledge and vision, cinema and violence, and the role of gendered difference in this equation. In the process of interrogating vision, the film also, by highlighting the connections between murders past and present, addresses the role of memory and (as in the conflation of a painting and a reflection) points both to its persistence and to the violence inherent in the memorializing of actions.

The present generation of moviegoers – the "fifth generation," as Pierre Sorlin refers to them – are accustomed to "the world in a box." What, though, have been the effects of television on the production and the reception of cinema? Sorlin writes that these audiences for television "did not despise television, they bought or hired videocasettes and CDs, and felt at home in the 'commercialised' culture. Unlike the members of the fourth generation, they were neither highly interested in the history or theory of cinema nor fond of intellectual, sophisticated films."[22] The effects of the growing imperialism of television has certainly taken its toll on films identified by the authorial signature. Elena Dagrada, in tracing the eventual rapprochement between television and cinema, writes that

> At first, there was a complete rejection on the part of critics, whose cultural background was predominantly literary and who were reluctant to get involved with an audio-visual medium, especially such a popular one. As time passed, however, the relationship began to change and become one of gradual acceptance. More recently it has even involved forms of courtship and mutual admiration.[23]

Considering that at least one-third of Italian film financing in the 1990s came from television channels, filmmakers can no longer remain indifferent or hostile to this different medium.[24] As far as cinemagoing was concerned, there was a severe drop in attendance, though audiences might see films on television. Critics who address the new relations between cinema and television reiterate familiar positions: There is nostalgia for the assumed homogeneous audiences for earlier films. There is disagreement about the televisual medium itself, whether it is a symptom of cultural exhaustion or whether its vitality resides in its cultural heterogeneity. As a consequence of the "world in a box," the cinema is no longer identified by "a unified series of pressing social concerns" or by a clearly identified and internationally known group of filmmakers. Differences from the cinema of commitment have led certain critics to "assert that Italian cinema is moribund (if not already dead)."[25] In the work of filmmakers in the 1980s and 1990s, the lamentation of the "death of cinema" in relation to television and other electronic media played a role much as the cinema earlier played in accounting for the morbidity of the live theater and of opera. The cinema continues to reflect on itself but in ways that indicate uncertainty about its character and status in the future.

One film that explores the many changes in Italian cinema is *C'eravamo tanto amati* (*We All Loved Each Other So Much,* 1974). In its style and allusions to other filmic (and televisual) texts, the film, rather than being an encomium to the cinematic medium, is a critical exploration of political failure, as is evident in the treatment of the three masculine protagonists. The subject seems again to be memory, in particular the memory of the Resistance and the high political and cultural hopes with which it was identified for all too brief a time. This "memory" is inseparable from the postwar role of cinema in generating these political hopes (in contrast to the present role of television, tied to an altered political and cultural milieu). From the first moments of the film, the identification of the cinematic apparatus with time is established as the spectator is presented with repeated shots of the trio of Antonio, Nicola, and Luciana arriving by car to bring poor Gianni his driver's license, which he had left behind by mistake. Similarly, the image of Gianni (Vittorio Gassman) exiting his house and going to dive into his pool is reiterated until stopped in time by a freeze frame, leaving him in midair. Through flashback, the three men are seen as young men fighting the Nazis, a fight identified with anti-Fascism, political radicalism, and community. By following each of the three men, the film then explores the ways in which this scene of unity was, after all, illusory – like the cinema itself. The war scenes are shot in newsreel fashion, appearing grainy, like a scene from Rossellini's *Paisà,* and ending with actual newsreel footage of the Liberation of Italy. The three friends part in 1946, as Nicola reports – Antonio to stay in Rome, Gianni to study in Pavia before he returns to Rome, and Nicola to teach in Lower Nocera. The early scenes of Antonio's (Nino Manfredi) life in Rome – his menial work at the hospital, his meeting Luciana, and his taking meals at the Mezza Porzione (Half Portion) Restaurant – are intercut with actual newsreel footage of the rise of the Christian Democrats (with the aid of American dollars and the purging of socialists and communists). Thus the heroic image of the Resistance, identified with the collective struggle for political change and with the cinema of neorealism, is progressively eroded as the world begins to take on the destructive traits of materialism, greed, and self-aggrandizement dissected in the films of Antonioni and Fellini.

Antonio's courtship of Luciana (Stefania Sandrelli), an aspiring actress, is developed through parallels with the theater. Luciana takes him to a performance of Eugene O'Neill's *Strange Interlude.* She has acted in other plays, including *Our Town* by Thornton Wilder, and thus the motif of Americanism is introduced as a reminder of its cultural influence, which can be traced to the last years of Fascism. The theatrical device in *Strange Interlude* of freezing the onstage action, so that secrets can be shared with the audience but kept from the other characters, is one that the film will adopt in its presenting the interior monologues of various characters. Consistently, the film inserts allusions to cinema, as in the introduction of newsreel footage of the elections of 1948, which serves to mark the transition from the immediate postwar world to that of the conservative era ushered in by the victory of the Christian Democrats.

Gianni comes to the Half Portion Restaurant, where he is treated like a hero by (and seduces Luciana away from) Antonio. The scene is interrupted by clips from *Ladri di biciclette* as Nicola (Stefano Satta Flores), a schoolteacher, narrates the importance to his generation of this film and other works by De Sica, Visconti, and Rossellini. He is fired by his school for his defense of the film against charges that it is "garbage." The scene evokes memories of life under Fascism, not only in the vehemence of Nicola's dismissal from teaching for his beliefs but also in his wife's pitiful plea for him to apologize so as not to lose his position. The episode registers reactions against the politics and aesthetics of neorealism. Significantly, the action is interrupted by a return to Gianni and Luciana. These interruptions are comparable to O'Neill's dramatic technique, but they also serve to call attention (as did the opening scenes) to cinema's ostensible and ironic power to mangle time and space.

The introduction of Romolo Catenacci (Aldo Fabrizi) is also intertextual. For those who remember Fabrizi as Don Pietro in *Roma, città aperta,* the obese hulk of flesh he has now become is a physical reminder of the passage of time and of his metamorphosis from an idealistic and martyred priest to a gangster. The imagery grows more Felliniesque with images of Catenacci's awkward, short-sighted, frizzy-haired daughter, Elide, of the vulgar and overstuffed artworks and furniture in his house, and of a huge roast pig descending from on high by crane at the feasts he sponsors. The dominant technique of the narrative has been one of splitting the action, forking into several directions, calling attention to the parallels and antitheses among the characters, to the passage of time, and to the changes that have transpired.

The motif of repetition and the downward spiraling of the action is further reinforced by Luciana being seduced again, this time by Nicola. Another allusion to cinema is inserted as he enacts for her the "Odessa Steps" sequence from Eisenstein's *Battleship Potemkin.* This seduction ends in her attempted suicide, though she is rescued by Antonio and Nicola. Following her suicide attempt, the film, which had begun in color, then reverted to black and white, shifts to a predominant use of color. Thus the first scene portraying a gathering of the Catenacci firm, to celebrate its creation of a housing project, is in black and white; the second, a New Year's ceremony, is in color. Though in both a roast pig is lowered onto a table, the color scene shows the pig draped in an Italian flag and amid a more affluent setting, reinforcing the passage of time and alterations in Gianni's relations to the Catenacci family. Gianni, now a member of the family and firm, is seen as the cynical but affluent husband of Elide and the mocker of his father-in-law. He has also taken it upon himself to modernize his wife, streamlining her appearance and introducing her to literature. Gianni and the family watch Nicola's appearance as a contestant on television, on a show that is a variation of the U.S. "64,000 Dollar Question." The episode introduces another aspect of Americanism, evident in the form of the game show and in the person of its host, Mike Bongiorno, a popular Italian TV personality. The scene is noteworthy for its focus on spectators, especially the Catenacci family, who eat as they watch television. The subject of the "quiz show" is the "history of Italian cinema": Cinema has become "history" as well as an informational commodity for television. Once again, De Sica's *Ladri di biciclette* is introduced, and Nicola as a devotee of cinema history attempts to answer the question of why Bruno cries in the film. By giving an elaborate explanation, and thus failing to answer, "Onions in his pocket," Nicola loses the contest. The world of television that is presented highlights the economy of space in the studio, the time constraints, the banalization of information, and the commerce of the medium.

In direct contrast, a scene of filming a movie is shown (reconstructed by Scola): Fellini (mistaken by a police office for Rossellini), with Marcello Mastroianni at his side, is directing Anita Ekberg's Trevi Fountain scene from *La dolce vita,* a landmark film in the Italian cinema and one that moved away from the neorealist school of filmmaking. Other cinematic allusions occur in the ensuing scenes: Black-and-white stills are seen of Monica Vitti in Antonioni's *L'eclisse* (*The Eclipse,* 1962) as Elide (Giovanna Ralli) – now slim, properly coiffed, dressed in the height of fashion, and seen in a brightly colored interior whose design and decor are emphasized – narrates that the film left her "stunned"; it captured the sense of female solitude. The motif of "solitude" centers on Elide's inability to communicate verbally and her total dependence on Gianni. Before the final encounter between Elide and Gianni, however, yet another film clip is introduced, this one from the Kim Novak–Laurence Harvey 1964 version of *Of Human Bondage,* dubbed in Italian and then redubbed with dialogue belonging to Antonio and Luciana – a further instance of the film's blurring the lines between life and film. The last scene between Gianni and his wife is also cinematic and is portrayed surrealistically: Elide, a ghostly image projected by his imagination, confronts Gianni in the automobile graveyard. In addition, a Dantesque scene, reminiscent of Fellini, shows a caged Romolo Catenacci brought down to earth in a way much like the roast pig lowered at the firm's celebrations. Gianni prophesies how the two of them are forever yoked.

When Gianni bumps into Antonio in a parking lot, they arrange for the three longtime friends to meet. This reunion, once again at the Half Portion [Fig. 78], underscores the growing differences among them. The film ends with a return to its beginning, as Gianni finally dives into the water with Nicola, Antonio, and Luciana looking on as if they were watching a film.

C'eravamo tanto amati offers a film version of a crucial thirty years in Italian history, a period that saw dramatic changes in Italian life. Moreover, it links memories of that era to questions of the cinema – neorealist but also

Figure 78. The three friends of *C'eravamo tanto amati* (*We All Loved Each Other So Much*): Nicola (Stefano Satta Flores), Gianni (Vittorio Gassman), and Antonio (Nino Manfredi). (Courtesy New York Museum of Modern Art Stills Archive)

postneorealist – that responded to and helped create the political, cultural, and cinematic changes the film portrays. Scola's film registers new forms of representation via the televisual medium that have further altered the cinema and history. The film, dedicated to the "late Vittorio De Sica," invokes unanswered questions concerning the relations between politics and cinema, and about the shape of the cinema to come.

Scola's film is not alone in it focus on the changing cultural role of cinema. Other filmmakers have presented their elegiac or nostalgic testaments of the passing of a cinematic culture. Giuseppe Tornatore's *Nuovo Cinema Paradiso* (1988) is a flashback to the postwar era and to a very specific focus on the role of the cinema then and in the present. The film may be said to be an elegy for a cinema that no longer exists. A major difference between *C'eravamo tanto amati* and the Tornatore film resides in how each views the cinematic past. The Scola film is primarily concerned with Italian cinema history, various film styles, the role of different auteurs, and the connections between the films it selects to show and changing moments in Italian culture and politics. *Nuovo Cinema Paradiso* focuses on a range of international films and seems committed to a view of Italian cinema as a source of fantasy, escapism, and consensus, whose passing it laments. Framed by the present, it is a flashback to the childhood of the narrator. It ends with the funeral of the paternal projectionist Alfredo (Philippe Noiret) and with the destruction of the town movie theater. In its retreat to flashback, the film leaves modern Rome and returns to a village in Sicily, dramatizing changes, from World War II to the 1980s, that made their impact on the region.

The events in the film are presented from the vantage point of Toto (Salvatore Cascio), a small boy totally obsessed with cinema, who manages to bribe his way into serving as Alfredo's assistant. Interspersed throughout the minimal narrative are shots of the local audiences as they experience a host of films: silent and sound, Italian, Hollywood, and European. One level of the allegorization of the history of cinema involves the morals of the community as supervised by the village priest, who scours the films for instances of indecorous sexual behavior. The film tracks the changing nature of the audiences and their greater sophistication, but also their major identification with the cinema, seen most vividly when one of the characters recites the dialogue of *Catene* along with the film. The plaster lion through which the films are projected, light streaming from its open mouth, is a reminder of the exotic artifacts associated with earlier cinema. The film attributes to cinema a powerful role as surrogate for family, superior to the dreary, even hostile, nature of familial life. Cinema becomes a bonding agent for the community, a relief from the drudgery of work, and finally an index to the changing nature of social life in Sicily. The tender relationship between Toto and Alfredo is predicated on their shared love for the moving image and its accoutrements – though when Alfredo is burned and blinded as a consequence of the flammability of early film stock, the film dramatizes the dangerous and evanescent quality of cinema as well as its constantly changing technology.

Filmmaking plays a key role in Toto's romantic obsession with Elena (Agnese Nano), whose image is seen and preserved through the film that he makes with his small Bell and Howell movie camera. Their relationship is thus intimately tied to the cinematic image and technology, and the death of this relationship is paralleled to the loss of the sense of a cinematic community, which is mourned by the film. The older Toto is a melancholy figure who, although a famous director, is, like the film itself, cathected by a vanished past. Though there is no future for him in his boyhood village of Giancaldo, there are memories. The film capitalizes on nostalgia, identifying the village with cinema's escapist potential by selecting clips from films that are largely popular and canonical. The changes in the physical landscape of the village parallel changes in the films, as well as in their audiences. Like a work of ethnography, the film, through its focus on the patterns of village life that are tied to cinemagoing, probes the alterations in patterns of thought and behavior that have transpired in Italian life.

Tornatore's romance with cinema continues in his 1994 film *L'uomo delle stelle* (*The Star Maker*). The film features a fake "talent scout" from Rome, Joe Morelli (Sergio Castellitto), who travels with his truck through various Sicilian towns and villages under the guise of finding talent for the cinema. (His adventures on the road also involve filming the funeral of a village personage, Dr. Mariano Guarneri, in a setting that recalls such films as *Divorzio all'italiana* and *Sedotta e abbandonata.*) He enters each town blaring through his loudspeaker a speech about having come to bring some lucky persons fame and fortune in film. Tornatore's camera lingers on scenes of village and countryside, from the perspective of Joe's truck, and gradually introduces the audience to this con artist's technique of "filming each person" and seeking the "faces" he claims to photograph (though somewhat later we learn he has no film in his camera): Joe gives his potential "stars" lines from *Gone with the Wind* to recite – and some of these hopefuls attempt to act out their own versions of the sections of the film involving Scarlett and Rhett. From many, though, he gets poignant personal histories of economic exploitation, family oppression, prostitution, homosexuality, Mafia violence, or criminality. A mother tries to pawn off her daughter on him by offering Joe her body; others tell him of World War II and the Germans. Uncle Leonardo, 112 years old, recalls Garibaldi, and another man, a Spaniard, tells him of the Spanish Civil War, his dialogue based on a song popular among the Republicans. Allusions to politics are also evident in the competing posters for the Communist Party and the Christian Democrats plastered on the town's walls.

Joe is a fraud, but people have confidence in him: Everyone wants to tell his or her story, to be recorded on film. A police officer asks to be filmed; bandits succumb to a screen test (and even pay); and a young orphan, Beata (Tiziana Lodato), who lives in the convent, begs to be filmed and to accompany Joe to Rome. Hearing her pitiful tale of how she earns her living cleaning people's houses and letting men look at her, Joe feels compassion and refuses her money, as well as her request to travel with him.

This Don Quixote of a filmmaker is finally robbed by a couple, the "Prince and Princess Montejuso." Abandoned on the road, he is discovered by Beata, who has followed him. After brutally raping her, he continues his work with her assistance (shades of *La strada*) until arrested for fraud by the policeman whom he had earlier "filmed." Looking on are a group of fisherman in a scene that evokes images from Visconti's *La terra trema.* After Joe's arrest, Beata, operating from his truck, earns her living as a prostitute; she later disappears. When Joe is released from jail, he returns to her village in an attempt to find her again; there he learns from a child that she is in a place for "crazy people." Beata does not recognize him; she repeats that Joe is dead. He claims to be "Joe's friend" and promises to return when he has found work. The ending is a montage of the images and voices of the various people who have recounted their stories throughout – stories that, contextually, will be lost because never truly filmed.

L'uomo delle stelle offers an opportunity to see the lives of Sicilians in the postwar era through the lens of the camera. Avoiding a static portrait of Sicilian life, it raises the issue of how much has changed in the region and yet has remained largely unaddressed by Italian cinema. The film, in the vein of *Amarcord*, attempts to recount the history of a specific moment through the role of cinema, and Fellini is evoked throughout in Tornatore's use of caricature and the journey through the landscape. (As noted previously, there are also parallels to *La strada*, with Beata as a Sicilian Gelsomina.) There are quotations from other films and filmmakers as well: Germi, Bertolucci (*1900* in the workers with red flags who seek to reclaim their land, *Il conformista* in the scenes of the asylum), Olmi's *L'albero degli zoccoli*, De Sica's *Umberto D*, and Tornatore's own *Nuovo Cinema Paradiso*. Once again, Rita Hayworth in *Gilda* appears in the oft-quoted posters, and a picture of Anna Magnani is visible among the photographs on his truck. These images, however, function in a context different from that of *Nuovo Cinema Paradiso:* As a surrogate director, Joe Morelli indicts the fraudulence of contemporary filmmakers (or of the film's own director?) for exploiting the region and its inhabitants and for failing to address its history.

Returning to find Beata, Joe is given a meal in the village bar-restaurant. He is ignored, but a crowd gathers around a television set with the logo "TV" visible – thereby introducing television as another determining factor in the fate of cinema in the last decades of the twentieth century.

Antagonisms and rapprochements between film and television were a dominant motif in the cinema of the 1980s and 1990s, not the least reason being the dominant role of media magnate Silvio Berlusconi in Italian politics; yet, as Sorlin cautions, "Berlusconi was much more a symptom than a cause."[26] In Western Europe as in the United States, television was well-entrenched by the 1960s, altering patterns of entertainment and political life. It has often been cited as one of the major causes of the decline of cinemagoing and of the influence of the cinema, and controversy continues unabated about its effects and who is to blame. In such films as *Intervista* and *Ginger e Fred*, both by Fellini, the monster is the "world in the box" itself. Television has posed a challenge to cultural critics, and responses to the medium have often sounded like rehashes of the early diatribes against the popular cinema, proclaiming its negative impact on practically every segment of society. Television has been blamed for the decline of family values, the dissolution of community, the rise of terrorism, the triumph of Americanism, and the resurgence of Fascism (among other things). Too often such critiques sound more like the earlier war of "high" art versus popular entertainment than a serious analysis of the changing character of contemporary culture as a consequence of TV and video. However, there are critical texts that seek to describe and analyze the character and impact of television and its relation to other visual media, particularly the cinema.[27]

A film that addresses relations between film and television is Maurizio Nichetti's *Ladri di saponette* (*The Icicle Thief,* 1989). The Italian title's mention of soap refers both to TV "soap opera" narratives and to television as a commercial medium for the selling of soap. (Clearly, both titles also cite a De Sica classic, adapted by Nichetti as a film-within-the-film.) The film undertakes to examine the medium of television from a number of vantage points. Television has become a museum for cinematic texts; but through the pompous commentaries that sometimes introduce them and the commercials that disrupt them, these texts are drastically altered, edited for time and content. The interruptions by advertising are a component of the television-watching experience, changing the viewer's relation to the cinematic text. Channel surfing and the muting of sound are indicative of a different relation to textual meaning and continuity and of the differences between television and cinema audiences. Television is shown to be a domestic medium and one of distracted viewing tied to child rearing, eating, and reading the newspaper.

The film takes place, in part, in a television studio as a female employee invites the spectator (standing in for Nichetti, the director, who is not yet seen) to follow her. The "journey" into television land will alternate among different sites: the television studio in Milan where Nichetti will supposedly be interviewed about his film; the film-within-the-film itself, which is to be aired; the commercial interruptions that disrupt the smooth flow of that film; and the living room in which a family receive various programs. These sites become progressively blurred as they flow into each other.

Nichetti, who looks like a hybrid of Charlie Chaplin and Woody Allen, does not conform to the conventional image of a powerful director: He is flat-footed, easily confused, and awkward in the extreme [Fig. 79]. Still, he is in the tradition of the auteur, having directed, written, and acted in the film, and having also directed and written the film-within-the film; he is even forced to enter the lattter to "save" his disintegrating narrative. In his confrontation with real-life film critic Claudio Fava, he learns that the critic is totally unprepared to introduce his film. Fava's condescending attitude toward the filmmaker reveals a penchant on the part of television not only for non-Italian films but also for older, more canonical works, which are reduced to clichés as Fava mouths the usual criticism about their self-conscious use of allusions and quotations and "modern sensibility." Nichetti's film manages to capture the way that "information" on television is compressed into sound bites for audiences. The living-room wife even asks to have the sound turned off, since she does not want to hear the "plot." Here, Nichetti offers a clue to the differences between film and TV: One can "edit" out the sound in television, reject what one does not want to hear, create a collage of different programs. In this respect, too, the film's critique of the mode of presenting film on television is underscored by an audience member's disaffection with programming style and her editing out unwelcome material.

When the film-within-the-film appears, it is, like the De Sica film, in black and white (though transferred to color television), but differences overwhelm similarities. Maria and Bruno may bear some physical resemblance to the actors in the De Sica film, but Nichetti is physically quite different from De Sica's Antonio. Moreover, Nichetti's film is already tailored for a contemporary audience: This Antonio does *not* get the job as in the earlier film and must look for work; Maria is spared the washing and pawning of the wedding sheets and her visit to La Santona, the fortuneteller. Most significant, the home becomes a locus of the action, whereas in *The Bicycle Thief,* once Antonio's bicycle is stolen and the quest for it begins, the domicile is never again seen. Moreover, Maria is portrayed as the dissatisfied housewife of soap operas: She seeks a life outside the home as a member of a singing group with two other women and is generally indifferent to her baby, who sticks its fingers into light sockets, gets trapped under baskets, and so on. In short, the "woman question" has altered the 1948 world as reconstructed by Nichetti, as has domestic discord. Bruno is witness to strife over the "cabbage," and he assumes a major role as cook and mass server to the priest, Don Italo. Here too the "purity" of the Ur-text is undercut, as Nichetti introduces and renames a character from yet another neorealist text – Don Pietro from Rossellini's *Roma, città aperta.* Furthermore, he makes the priest a comic figure, constantly confused about events. In the efforts to rewrite the De Sica film for a contemporary audience, the filmmaker has "corrupted" the text of *Ladri di biciclette* this much even before the first of several commercial breaks for "Splash."

In relation to the commercials, it is significant that the husband views television in distraction: His interest is random as he raises his eyes from time to time from his reading of the newspaper, largely focusing on the semiclad women who appear in the commercials or in the broadcast film-within-the-film. His wife is more attentive, noting that a certain commercial was made "eight years ago"; but the "soap sud" implications of the title now connect to the film-within-the-film as a rendition of a soap opera. In both the filming of the television-viewing couple and the film being shown on TV, the focus is on domestic discord. The preservation of family values – a cliché of contemporary society – seems to be satirized in the anomic relation among the family members and in the role of the priest, who diagnoses marital discord as the couple's problem, seeking to learn from Bruno what is "wrong" at home. This domestic focus underscores the melodramatic dimensions of both the film and film-within-the-film. As in a soap opera, the conflict changes for a mo-

Figure 79. Maurizio Nichetti in his *Ladri di saponette* (*The Icicle Thief*). (Courtesy New York Museum of Modern Art Stills Archive)

ment to concord, as husband and wife celebrate Antonio's new job; but, as in melodrama, this harmony cannot last for long. At this point, the film is disrupted by another commercial, which compels Nichetti to complain about the integrity of his work. This complaint is not without its irony, since the film-within-the-film is itself clichéd.

Now, for the first time, television invades the film-within-the-film as Bruno watches a young boy eat a "Big Big" candy bar and sings the appropriate jingle for Antonio and Maria. Antonio blames his wife for the boy's corruption on the "dumb songs" that she rehearses; she, in turn, blames the "radio." The film begins to move quite rapidly to blur the boundaries among the various aspects of the narrative: the film-within-the-film family and the television-viewing family; the theft of the chandelier and not of the bicycle, which was stolen earlier by someone else; the penetration of the film narrative by commercials and, conversely, the commercials by the film characters; the introduction of color into black and white; the total derailing of the film-within-the-film narrative by Bruno, who revenges himself on Nichetti for wanting to place him in an orphanage; the appearance of a young woman scantily clad in a bathing suit in a television commercial further complicates connections between television and film. She emerges from a car, but before the text can specifically identify the product being advertised, she dives into a pool and emerges (in color) in the film-within-the-film during a power outage at the television station. Antonio pulls her from the water, covers her as she is transformed to black-and-white, and brings her home. Heidi, as she introduces herself to Bruno and Maria, is played by actress-model Heidi Komarek. In desperation at the sight of her, Maria pursues the opposite course of diving into the lake and emerging in a commercial for "Vial Blu," a soap powder. Increasingly, characters come from or enter into the world identified with television production, and Nichetti's remake of *Ladri di biciclette* takes on the attributes of a soap opera, involving familial discord, adultery, theft, a murder charge, and a police investigation, all necessitating the director's entry into his own film-within-the-film in an attempt to straighten out the confusion and produce a happy ending (contrary to his original scenario).

Heidi's presence creates further comic effects. In her use of English and, haltingly, of Italian with a heavy American accent, she evokes connections between Italian and American television, if more broadly between Italian culture and that of America, reinforcing television's international dimension as well as its invasive character. Her relationship with Bruno becomes a joke about childhood, since he handles the presence of this semiclad, tall, willowy blonde better than Antonio does. Nichetti, seeking to reclaim his authority over the narrative, tells the two to stop changing the plot: "I'm the director here." Nichetti's confrontation of Antonio – the same actor playing both roles – further undermines textual boundaries, and the irony of his protest is evident. The director, clearly, is no longer in charge: The cultural, social, and economic text of television is more powerful than he.

The final image of the film – Nichetti trapped in the television, unheard as he begs to be let out – is a trope that works in several ways: It emblematizes the film director's entrapment in the televisual medium, and it signifies the world reduced to a television box to the exclusion of a world outside the medium. However, this ultimate image may have other valences. Working in two directions – the relation of film to television and of television to film – *Ladri di saponette* has become a metatextual commentary on how media must take into account changed attitudes toward realism and such matters as the "theft" of images and their emergence in new forms. In this sense, the film's ending may be an apocalyptic one; but it may also be seen as raising all-important issues concerning the future of the cinematic (and televisual) image (and of its creators), not only in the context of Italian cinema but more broadly in the arena of international media.

In a more antagonistic vein, Federico Fellini has taken on the television medium, culminating in his *Ginger e Fred* (1986). Reminiscent of the Frankfurt School's diatribes about mass culture, the film treats the world of TV with some humor and a great deal of satire. Fellini said this about the medium:

> Television talks to us, at us, when we are defenseless, even unaware.
> Its message of vulgarity and wrong values is transmitted to people

watching when they are on the phone, arguing with each other, over eating conversationless dinners. The best way to watch television is when you are asleep. . . . It has relieved of us of talking to each other. It can relieve us of thinking, that is, of the internal conversation in which each of us talks only with himself in his own head. The next invasion is of our dreams.[28]

Peter Bondanella accounts for Fellini's attitudes toward television this way:

Television represents a threat to the creative expression of the individual artist, in Fellini's opinion, not merely because it employs an impoverished technical language [which it does], but, more importantly, because it destroys the ritualistic nature of the cinematic experience, the sense of attending a church where images rather than words are communicated in a dreamlike language that projects our fantasies onto the silver screen in a fantastic and voyeuristic environment that we experience as a group rather than in the privacy of our own homes.[29]

Ginger e Fred is not Fellini's only film to address the aggressive nature of television. The oft-remarked scene in *Intervista* (1987) where the Indian spears become television antennas is one of the more striking visual moments in this film, one that is predicated on its own making and in which a Japanese TV crew serves to remind us of television's voyeuristic and intrusive nature. *Ginger e Fred* is much more than Fellini's vendetta against Italian television, with its numerous commercials that break the flow of a film – the bane of film directors, as is also evident in *Ladri di saponette*. Rather, *Ginger e Fred* addresses the shrinking of the world of cinema to the size of a box, the ubiquity of that box, and its desecration of cultural icons. This last is exemplified by the cartoon that utilizes the opening tercet of Dante's *Inferno,* transformed for commercial ends, to advertise and sell a Betrix timepiece. Thus the film attacks not only television's commercialism but its cultural vandalism. The televisual world is predicated on the reduction and simplification of verbal and visual language. The sense of largeness that so characterizes the cinematic screen in other Fellini films has been attenuated. The omnipresence of small TV sets – in every room, in the limousines, in the dining areas – is only one indication of this shrinking world; the prevalence of midgets becomes another. The world of cinema has suffered a diminution.

Commenting on the choice of Ginger (Rogers) and Fred (Astaire) as the bearers of the magic of the cinematic dream world, Fellini has commented, "In the 1930s, Fred Astaire and Ginger Rogers represented the American cinema for Italians. They told us that a joyous life existed. . . . In the world of Fascism, . . . [they] showed us that another life was possible, at least in America, that land of unimaginable freedom and opportunity."[30] How ironic that, in a film dramatizing the television homicide of cinematic images of that life, Fellini should have been sued (unsuccessfully) by Ginger Rogers. In adopting the figures of Ginger and Fred, the film focuses on the ways television cannibalizes every aspect of social life. Each person is a mirror of a famous person. Thus we not only have the central characters, Astaire and Rogers, but also look-alikes and sound-alikes for the Queen of England, Ronald Reagan, Bette Davis, and Clark Gable, among others. As with the lead roles – small-time performers, played by Giulietta Masina (Fellini's wife) and Marcello Mastroianni, who used to imitate Astaire and Rogers – we are given unattractive and aging versions of the "original" characters, whose lives are at an extreme remove from the "joyous world" that Fellini celebrated in the Hollywood cinema of the 1930s. Everything – the littered landscape, the sausage advertisements, the edible underwear, the hotel's paper-thin walls, the indistinctness of the architecture, the bags of garbage strewn across the landscape, and the banality of the expressed desires of the characters – conspires against pleasure.

Utilizing the framework of a variety show [Fig. 80], the film presents the world of television as an indiscriminate and pale parody of the riches of popular culture as exemplified by the earlier music hall and the genre of the musical film. For example, "Unlike the various routines in the traditional variety hall theater Fellini loves, television imitates the variety of the variety hall but completely distorts the individuality of the separate routines."[31] Instead of the pleasure of variety in its celebration of difference, the world is cruelly reduced to bizarre imitation void of imagination, and there is no postmodern *jouissance* in its new incarnation. The pathetic dancing of Ginger and Fred – often filmed in disconcerting long shot and marred by Fred's ungainly fall – underscores the crudity of their imitation, which hardly serves as an homage to the cinema, instead pointing up the lack of individuation and creativity of the variety-show format. In a sense, the film reminds us that "Now, that the new, all-devouring machine has adulterated everything, it is no longer possible to escape from a disturbing reality by finding refuge in past memories."[32] In this film, the "machine" has banalized and hence eradicated memory.

Finally, Nanni Moretti's *Caro diario* (*Dear Diary,* 1993) would seem to share Fellini's concern with the past and future of cinema and television, seeking a mode of expression that, in Deleuze's terms, is of "cinema, body and brain, thought." The film is divided into three sections, regarding which Gieri writes:

> In Moretti's life, the final episode, "Medici" ("Doctors") actually came first; the second episode, "Isole" ("Islands"), was scripted when he had recovered from his illness; the first, "In Vespa" ("On the Scooter") was shot as the movie *Dear Diary* was in the making and is thor-

Figure 80. Fellini on cinema and television, *Ginger e Fred*. (Courtesy New York Museum of Modern Art Stills Archive)

oughly scriptless. "On the Scooter" is literally a film and a life in the making as it emphasizes the ability to look at things in a fresh, new way, retrieving the enchantment of our first glance at the world and the awe that is typical of an age of innocence.[33]

Freed largely from the constraints of a narrative, Moretti uses himself as the instrument for thinking differently in and about images. In the first section, Moretti points out various Roman neighborhoods on his scooter, observing the architecture, street life, and dancing. In a movie theater he sees members of his generation, now professionals, self-indulgently lamenting that they have "compromised" their lives and have become co-opted and "ugly." When he returns to his scooter, Moretti yells, "I shouted the right slogans, and now I'm a splendid forty-year-old." Rejecting their self-flagellating and confessional position, Moretti seeks a different cinematic voice on his journey through the film in his rejection of narrative, his use of intertextual allusions, his critique of prevailing media, and his autobiographical stance.

Playfully, he recounts how he rang a doorbell and announced to a tenant of one of the apartment houses he has been admiring that he is making a musical about a Trotskyist pastry chef in the "conformist" Italy of the 1950s. His comments are accompanied by a Leonard Cohen song, "I'm Your Man." He approaches a young man in a red Mercedes to inform him that, unlike filmmakers who believe in the majority of people, he believes only in a minority. Continuing on his ride, he tells us that *Flashdance* changed his life, and we learn that he does not dance but watches the dancers. On his scooter, he moves to the music, waving his arms. This first segment is devoted to shaking loose from the prison house of conventional images and words, finding release in movement and music. In his confrontations with bystanders, pedestrians, and people in cars, we establish that he is – as Jennifer Beals, whom he meets, calls him – a bit "off," not exactly crazy. The next cinematic encounter occurs when he goes to see *Henry: Portrait of a Serial Killer* – a splatter film that represents the type of movie fare available in the summer. Uncomfortable during the viewing, he reads reviews of the film; then, in a fantasy, he goes to attack the pretentious critic who has written a review that exemplifies the celebratory and complex rhetoric of contemporary film journals (with phrases such as, "Henry is a prince of annihilation promising a merciful death." In this episode, Moretti attacks the banality and pretentiousness of critical language inherent to the cultural milieu. After leafing through yellowed newspapers announcing the death of Pier Paolo Pasolini, Moretti follows the road that leads to where that filmmaker was murdered, connecting the brutality and bloodshed on the screen to the social violence that Pasolini had sought to examine in his films and that, in the end, was turned on him. The motif of violence has a double valence, applying to the body of the dead filmmaker and, by extension, to the body of the cinema.

If the first section focuses on the cinema in various ways – as confession, as violence, as fantasy, and as music and dance – the second section explores the culture of television. Continuing his journey, Moretti travels to various islands (including Stromboli) in search of a story only to discover that there is "No place or character . . . to be found, since Eden is lost forever in the time and space of [the soap opera] *The Bold and the Beautiful*."[34] With his friend Gerardo, Moretti visits various couples whose relation to their children seems to emerge from a reading of the latest "how to" books on child rearing, and who are indifferent to anything *but* their children, producing little monsters who tyrannize the adults. In moving to Stromboli, where the wildness of the volcano recalls not only Rossellini's but also Pasolini's barren landscapes in such films as *Teorema* and *Porcile,* we see a world colonized by tourism, with its mania for building and modernizing. Gerardo, who earlier disavowed his interest in television, increasingly becomes obsessed with *The Bold and the Beautiful.* At the end of the episode, he leaves the island of Alicudi, shouting that television critic Hans Magnus Enzensberger is wrong: "Television is not the source of the problem. It does not corrupt the children" (though the visits to the various islanders seem to implicate the family in the world of soap operas). Underlying the humor of the various episodes in this section is the recognition that the world has indeed changed, thanks to modernity and to television in particular, and that it would be counterproductive and naïve to act as though it had not.

The third section focuses inward on Moretti's body. He uses himself not as a figure of pathos but as a text to be read in ways similar to the Pasolini segment – as engaging the question of the cinema of the body and the body of cinema. Without minimizing the seriousness of his lymphoma, the visits to the various physicians, the mounting shelves of the various medicines and suggested cures, are an indication of the difficulty of reading symptoms – a situation that has actually prevailed throughout the other two episodes. Just as the reviewer of *Henry: Portrait of a Serial Killer* has misdiagnosed the character of that film, just as the parents on the various islands misperceive the needs of their children (as well as their own), and just as television is taken as causal not symptomatic (by Enzensberger and Gerardo), so the medical establishment is used by Moretti as a trope to dramatize the confusion between symptom and causes, mistaking effects for source.

The implications of this metalepsis for the fate of Moretti's cinema are that, in the process of making *Caro diario,* he has also sought to diagnose the symptoms of a problematic culture, looking at the literal and cultural body of his own practices. *Caro diario* is more than a critique of film and television; it is an autocritique whereby the filmmaker has begun to forge a different type of cinema. Freeing himself from his past personae (played by himself, in this film as in others, under the name Michele Apicella), he prescribes his "cure" through movement in time, through abandoning past formulas and conventions, looking for a cinema of body and brain to come into being.

The Italian cinema of the postwar years was closely tied to conceptions of Italy's integrity as a nation even when, as in the 1960s, films were critical of directions on which the nation and the cinema had embarked. Cinematic energy continued to be devoted to Italy's self-image, as well as to her position in Europe and in relation to Hollywood. Increasingly. the films explored an unresolved and uneasy relation to the past, and were particularly engaged in a collective enterprise of questioning their cinematic inheritance. The Italian cinema bore the burden of seeking to understand the years of Fascism and to create a cinema purged of its taints. Moreover, it was an interrogative cinema that addressed the uncertain shape of the future. It had earned an international reputation as a cinema of auteurs with such figures as Rossellini, Antonioni, Visconti, Fellini, and Pasolini, whose films, despite stylistic differences, shared a common cultural heritage. It also gained international acclaim as a cinema of genres with such notable figures as Germi, Leone, and Monicelli even as it was involved in redefining the nature of the genre system, reasserting its roots in popular culture and earlier examples in the cinematic genres – comedies, westerns, and melodramas. It was a cinema that was largely (though not universally) political, one that even in popular films, through the *commedia all'italiana,* was critical of prevailing social structures and eager to push the limits of cinematic language. It was a cinema that ultimately relied on the star system through such figures as Marcello Mastroianni, Sophia Loren, Gina Lollobrigida, Silvana Mangano, Vittorio Gassman, and Nino Manfredi, among others. Italian film was also recognizable through its invocation of the national landscape as well as its iconographic urban settings; yet it has always been (and still is) tied to the United States, even if its Hollywood and American connection was double-edged. Last but not least, it was a cinema whose finances depended on producers, box-office receipts, television, and other sources of local and international revenue.

Italian film since the 1980s has been by no means a monolith, and certain changes are evident. Characteristic landmarks of the Italian cinema of the 1960s and 1970s have, at least in some productions, been eclipsed, and these changes are evident in the modes of production, personnel involved in filmmaking, and new styles of film forms and language. It is not so clear that Italy is a cinema of auteurs: The reign of the auteur now has a shorter half-life, though some well-known auteurs such as Lina Wertmüller, Bernardo Bertolucci, and Ettore Scola continue to make films. Some recent Italian filmmakers (e.g., Gianni Amelio, Giuseppe Tornatore, and Nanni Moretti) are known to target audiences outside Italy. Furthermore, the Italian cinema has had to confront its assimilation by the New Hollywood cinema, where filmmakers such as Scorsese have sought, in the spirit of homage and profit, to outdo their Italian models. Also, thanks to television and video, more filmmakers are self-taught, a fact that also contributes to the further dismantling of a commonly perceived cinematic culture.

In the assessment of Gian Piero Brunetta, stardom today in mass society is "unstable and precarious."[35] Italian stars have been replaced by television personalities, nonprofessional actors, and new faces. The role of stardom is questionable in the growing instances of independent film. The cinema of genres, dependent on specifically national discourses and conventional genre forms, is also becoming a remnant of the past – though there continues to be a passion for nostalgic films that rehearse the history of cinema, such as Tornatore's *Nuovo Cinema Paradiso,* which, like his later *L'uomo delle stelle,* may be said to be an elegy for a cinema that no longer exists either in Italy or internationally. The more recent *Il postino* and *La vita è bella,* which have had an international audience, revisit the national past as they confront the loss of mythified images of the nation and expose the presence of unsettling cultural and social boundaries.

As is characteristic of the centripetal or "polycentric" character of recent Italian cinema, dubbed by some as a "young cinema," a large number of films are preoccupied with the dissolution of boundaries – generational, sexual, gendered, and national. For example, the films *Il ladro di bambini, Ragazzi fuori* (1990), and *Mery per sempre* (1989) focus on generational and sexual differences and on the failure of traditional familial and social relations. Youth is portrayed as a tenuous force for redemption and a sign of social disintegration. These films, often set in the Italian South, focus on marginalized youth and involve older figures – teachers and police – who are forced to come to terms with the drug trafficking, theft, prostitution, and transsexual preferences of the young. These films bear some of the characteristics of neorealism: the avoidance of stars, the highlighting of dislocated characters in constant movement through space, and the emphasis on the connection between the social landscape and the "dead-end" lives of young people. These films situate the characters and their milieu in a place deprived of old or new national markers and locate them as part of a denationalized landscape that bears a resemblance to that of youth as represented in other European cinemas. Likewise, in their challenges to the boundaries of the nation, this "young" cinema does not address race and ethnicity with the same vitality as British cinema or even French cinema.

A film such as *Lamerica* (1994), directed by Gianni Amelio, is exemplary of films of the 1990s that forcefully call into question traditional national boundaries. Returning to the Fascist era by means of 1930s newsreel footage from LUCE, the state propaganda organization, *Lamerica* links the fate of Albania to that of Italy and, as the title suggests, to earlier myths of America. The film invokes a submerged and unpopular history of Italian politics in order to undermine any affirmative sense of national integrity and altruism. The two Italian entrepreneurs in the film have come to Albania in ways reminiscent of the Fascist exploitation of Albania in the 1930s. The man they choose as a front for their company is an expatriated Italian imprisoned by the communists who lives in the past – but one that bears an uncanny resemblance to the present in Albania and its relations to Italy. Among the many chords on which the film plays, the question of immigration is central. To the old man, "Italy has become a kind of 'America' for the Albanians fleeing the poverty and oppression of their homeland." Thus, the film revises the history of the nation and introduces unsettling questions about Italy's relation to the "other Europe" and to "America."

Another and more contentious film that revises postwar Italian history – one that has caused controversy in Italy – is the 1997 film *Porzus,* directed by Renzo Martinelli. This film returns to the Italian Resistance and rehearses events that took place half a century ago on the border between Italy and Yugoslavia. The events center on the massacre of noncommunist partisans, members of the Osoppo Brigade, by a group of communists who are members of the Garibaldi Brigade. The film is structured around repeated encounters between two men, Geko and Storno, and as a narrative of crime detection coupled to the genre of the western. Storno, one of the former partisans and a member of Osoppo, has assumed the role of judge as he interrogates and accuses the communist Geko of atrocities at Porzus – atrocities that most critics of the film remind us had also involved the brother of Pier Paolo Pasolini, Guidalberto, who fought with the Christian anti-Fascist forces on the border of Yugoslavia and died in the massacre. From a different direction than *Lamerica,* this film challenges and seeks to rewrite preexisting cinematic versions of the Resistance as exemplified by the films of Roberto Rossellini. In its revisioning and judging the past, *Porzus* is symptomatic of a dissolution of boundaries between Left and Right in the demise of the cold war.

Nanni Moretti has been instrumental in seeking to move cinema off its center in both auteurist and popular generic forms. *Caro diario* abandons both the broad historical panorama and conventional forms of storytelling, in the process casting a critical look at the relations between media and culture: the Roman urban context, life on the road, the speed of contemporary life, Americanity, splatter films, the youth-centered middle-class culture, health and medicine – and television.

Television has dictated the shape of the Italian cinema of the past decades: In Italy and other European countries, films have been (and are) part of television fare and are often subsidized by the medium; but what effect does television – with its specialization in information, live events, catastrophes, tabloid culture, and collective mourning – have on cinematic production? More and more, films have adopted a televisual style, if not its subject matter. Maurizio Nichetti's dour comedy *Ladri di saponette* is an interrogation that utilizes a televisual style to explore how television has destroyed old cinematic markers.

On the economic and global role of television, Jean-Luc Godard, in his familiar contentious manner, has commented:

> If I refer to my knowledge of movies, . . . movie-making was strongly tied to the identity of a nation. That's why there is no French television, Italian, or British, or American television. There can be only one television because it's not related to the nation. It's related to finance and commerce. Movie making at the beginning was related to the identity of the nation. . . . This is because when countries were inventing and using motion pictures they needed an image of themselves. . . . Today, if you put . . . people in one so-called "Euro-country," you have nothing; since television is television, you have only America.[36]

Italian cinema reveals that it is now enmeshed in a global identity crisis that involves the cultural, social, political, and aesthetic contours of the nation as communicated through film. Have television, multinational financing, and America sealed the fate of cinema, as Godard suggests, so that it is no longer possible to draw on conceptions of national identity? Or, conversely, in its polycentrism and challenge to traditional boundaries and borders, are there signs that cinema can offer images of new identities and communities within Europe? Many film critics make predictions – some dire, some hopeful – as to the shape of things to come and the role that Italian cinema might play in the future of Europe. The future, however, is uncertain. Italy is embedded in a network of relations – to the political and cultural climate of Eastern and Western Europe, of America, and even of other parts of the globe that are yet to be identified and evaluated.

Notes

PREFACE

1 Pierre Sorlin, *Italian National Cinema 1896-1996* (London: Routledge, 1996), 2.
2 Ibid., 4.
3 Giuliana Bruno, *Streetwalking on a Ruined Map: Cultural Theory and the City Films of Elvira Notari* (Princeton: Princeton University Press, 1993), 3.
4 Ibid., 4.
5 Étienne Balibar and Immanuel Wallerstein, *Race, Nation, Class: Ambiguous Identities* (London: Verso, 1995), 87.
6 Gilles Deleuze, *Cinema 2: The Time Image* (Minneapolis: University of Minnesota Press, 1989), 271.

INTRODUCTION

1 Christopher Wagstaff, "Cinema," in David Forgacs and Robert Lumley, eds., *Italian Cultural Studies: An Introduction* (Oxford: Oxford University Press, 1996), 216-33, at 219.
2 Giuliana Bruno, *Streetwalking on a Ruined Map: Cultural Theory and the City Films of Elvira Notari* (Princeton: Princeton University Press, 1993), 56.
3 Gilles Deleuze, *Cinema 1: The Movement Image* (Minneapolis: University of Minnesota Press, 1986), 121.
4 Walter Benjamin, *Illuminations,* ed. Hannah Arendt (New York: Schocken Books, 1976), 236-7.
5 Pierre Sorlin, *Italian National Cinema 1896-1996* (London: Routledge, 1996), 17.
6 Gian Piero Brunetta, *Storia del cinema italiano,* vol. 1: *Il cinema muto 1895-1929* (Rome: Riuniti, 1993), 29-30.
7 Elaine Mancini, *Struggles of the Italian Film Industry during Fascism, 1930-1935* (Ann Arbor: UMI Press, 1985), 12. See also Bruno, *Streetwalking,* 30-1.
8 Renzo De Felice, *D'Annunzio Politico, 1918-1938* (Rome: Laterza, 1978); Philippe Julian, *D'Annunzio: Adventurer, Poet, Lover of Genius* (London: Pall Mall Press, 1972); Lucia Re, "Gabriele D'Annunzio's Theater of Memory: Il Vittoriale degli Italiani," *Journal of Decorative and Propaganda Arts, 1875-1945* 3 (Winter 1987): 6-52; Jared Becker, *Nationalism and Culture: Gabriele D'Annunzio and Italy after the Risorgimento* (New York: Peter Lang, 1994).
9 Bruno, *Streetwalking,* 137.
10 Ibid., 141.
11 Benjamin, *Illuminations,* 236-7.
12 Brunetta, *Storia del cinema italiano,* vol. 1, 78.
13 Deleuze, *Cinema 1,* 97.
14 Pierre Leprohon, *The Italian Cinema* (New York: Praeger Publishers, 1972), 19; Peter Bondanella, *Italian Cinema: From Neorealism to the Present* (New York: Frederick Ungar-Continuum, 1993), 2-4.

15 Gilles Deleuze, *Cinema 2: The Time Image* (Minneapolis: University of Minnesota Press, 1989), 156.

16 D. N. Rodowick, *Gilles Deleuze's Time Machine* (Durham: Duke University Press, 1997), 152.

17 Ibid., 10.

18 Ibid., 11-12.

19 Gian Piero Brunetta, *Cinema italiano tra le due guerre* (Milan: Mursia, 1975), 15-28.

20 Mancini, *Struggles of the Italian Film Industry,* 33.

21 Ibid.

22 Pierre Sorlin, "Italian Cinema's Rebirth, 1937-1943: A Paradox of Fascism," *Historical Journal of Film and Video* 14(1) (1994): 3-13, at 3-4.

23 Philip Morgan, *Italian Fascism, 1919-1945* (New York: St. Martin's Press, 1995).

24 Victoria de Grazia, *How Fascism Ruled Women: Italy, 1922-1945* (Berkeley: University of California Press, 1992), 72.

25 Ibid., 81.

26 Ibid., 170.

27 Ibid., 279.

28 Ibid., 282.

29 Doug Thompson, *State Control in Fascist Italy, 1925-1943: Culture and Conformity* (Manchester: Manchester University Press, 1991), 32.

30 Leprohon, *Italian Cinema,* 86.

31 Ibid., 86.

32 Millicent Marcus, *Italian Film in the Light of Neorealism* (Princeton: Princeton University Press, 1986), 23.

33 Deleuze, *Cinema 1,* 205-15.

34 Ibid., 211-12.

35 Ibid., 207.

36 Ibid.

37 Ibid., 208.

38 Deleuze, *Cinema 2,* 145.

39 Ibid., 148.

40 Leprohon, *Italian Cinema,* 126.

41 Marcus, *Italian Film in the Light of Neorealism,* 29.

42 David Forgacs, "Cultural Consumption, 1940 to 1990s," in Forgacs and Lumley, eds., *Italian Cultural Studies,* 273-91, at 278.

43 Bondanella, *Italian Cinema,* 142.

44 Christopher Frayling, *Spaghetti Westerns: Cowboys and Europeans from Karl May to Sergio Leone* (London: Routledge & Kegan Paul, 1981).

45 Robin Buss, *Italian Films* (London: B. T. Batsford Ltd., 1989), 79.

46 Manuela Gieri, *Contemporary Italian Filmmaking: Strategies of Subversion - Pirandello, Fellini, Scola and the Directors of the New Generation* (Toronto: University of Toronto Press, 1995), 165.

CHAPTER ONE: EARLY ITALIAN CINEMA ATTRACTIONS

1 Tom Gunning, "Non-Continuity, Continuity, Discontinuity: A Theory of Genres in Early Films," in Thomas Elsaesser with Adam Barker, eds., *Early Cinema: Space, Frame, Narrative* (London: BFI Publishing, 1990), 56-63, at 56.

2 Ibid., 57.

3 Pierre Sorlin, *Italian National Cinema 1896-1996* (London: Routledge, 1996), 17.

4 Gian Piero Brunetta, *Storia del cinema italiano,* vol. 1: *Il cinema muto 1895-1929* (Rome: Riuniti, 1993), 19-20.

5 Sorlin, *Italian National Cinema,* 17.

6 Brunetta, *Storia del cinema italiano,* vol. 1, 29-30.

7 Pierre Leprohon, *The Italian Cinema* (New York: Praeger Publishers, 1972), 11.

8 Ibid., 12.

9 Giuliana Bruno, *Streetwalking on a Ruined Map: Cultural Theory and the City Films of Elvira Notari* (Princeton: Princeton University Press, 1993); Tom Gunning, "The Cinema of Attractions: Early Film, Its Spectator and the Avant-Garde," in Elsaesser with Barker, eds., *Early Cinema,* 86-95.

10 André Gaudreault, "Film Narrative, Narration: The Cinema of the Lumière Brothers," in Elsaesser with Barker, eds., *Early Cinema,* 68-76, at 71-2.

11 Dai Vaughan, "Let There Be Lumière," *Early Cinema: Space, Frame, Narrative,* 63-8, at 65.

12 Miriam Hansen, "Early Cinema – Whose Public Sphere?," in Elsaesser with Barker, eds., *Early Cinema,* 228-47, at 233.

13 Ibid.

14 Thomas Elsaesser, "The Institution Cinema," in Elsaesser with Barker, eds., *Early Cinema,* 153-73, at 156.

15 Leprohon, *Italian Cinema,* 16.

16 Brunetta, *Storia del cinema italiano,* vol. 1, 71-92.

17 Ibid., 195.

18 Karen Pinkus, *Bodily Regimes: Italian Advertising under Fascism* (Minneapolis: University of Minnesota Press, 1995).

19 Peter Bondanella, *Italian Cinema: From Neorealism to the Present* (New York: Frederick Ungar–Continuum, 1993), 10; Brunetta, *Storia del cinema italiano,* vol. 1, 104.

20 Annette Kuhn, *Cinema, Censorship and Sexuality, 1909-1925* (New York: Routledge, 1988).

21 Brunetta, *Storia del cinema italiano,* vol. 1, 58.

22 Ibid., 61-2.

23 Elaine Mancini, *Struggles of the Italian Film Industry during Fascism, 1930-1935* (Ann Arbor: UMI Press, 1985), 27.

24 Richard Abel, *French Cinema: The First Wave, 1915-1929* (Princeton: Princeton University Press, 1984), 153, 161.

25 Leprohon, *Italian Cinema,* 27.

26 Brunetta, *Storia del cinema italiano,* vol. 1, 164.

27 A. Nicholas Vardac, *Stage to Screen: Theatrical Method from Garrick to Griffith* (New York: Benjamin Blom, 1949), 218.

28 Sorlin, *Italian National Cinema,* 46.

29 Maria Wyke, *Projecting the Past: Ancient Rome, Cinema and History* (New York: Routledge, 1997), 24.

30 Ibid.

31 Angela Dalle Vacche, *The Body in the Mirror: Shapes of History in Italian Cinema* (Princeton: Princeton University Press, 1992), 28.

32 Bruno, *Streetwalking,* 30.

33 Ibid., 176.

34 Ibid., 212.

35 Sorlin, *Italian National Cinema,* 29.

36 Ibid., 40.

37 Antonio Gramsci, *Selections from the Cultural Writings,* ed. David Forgacs (Cambridge, Mass.: Harvard University Press, 1985), 190.

38 Ibid.

39 Marcia Landy, *The Folklore of Consensus: Theatricality in the Italian Cinema, 1930-1943* (Albany: State University of New York Press, 1998), xi–xii.

40 Gilles Deleuze, *Cinema 2: The Time Image* (Minneapolis: University of Minnesota Press, 1989), 7.

CHAPTER TWO: NATIONAL HISTORY AS RETROSPECTIVE ILLUSION

1 Victoria de Grazia, *The Culture of Consent: Mass Organization of Leisure in Fascist Italy* (Cambridge: Cambridge University Press, 1981).

2 Gian Piero Brunetta, "The Long March of American Cinema in Italy: From Fascism to the Cold War," in Ellwood and Kroes, eds., *Hollywood in Europe,* 139–55.

3 Elaine Mancini, *Struggles of the Italian Film Industry during Fascism, 1930-1935* (Ann Arbor: UMI Press, 1985), 26.

4 Ibid., 171.

5 Ibid., 121.

6 Walter Adamson, "The Language of Opposition in Early Twentieth-Century Italy: Rhetorical Continuities between Pre-war Florentine Avantgardism and Mussolini's Fascism," *Journal of Modern History* 64 (March 1992): 22–51, at 22–3.

7 Gianfranco Mino Gori, *Patria diva: La storia d'Italia nel film del ventennio* (Florence: Usher, 1988).

8 Marcia Landy, *The Folklore of Consensus: Theatricality in the Italian Cinema, 1930-1943* (Albany: State University of New York Press, 1998), 107–67.

9 Antonio Gramsci, *Selections from the Cultural Writings*, ed. David Forgacs (Cambridge, Mass.: Harvard University Press, 1985), 377–8.

10 Gian-Paolo Biasin, *Italian Literary Icons* (Princeton: Princeton University Press, 1985), 76–7.

11 Caroline Springer, *The Marble Wilderness: Ruins and Representations in Italian Romanticism* (Cambridge: Cambridge University Press, 1987), 1–13.

12 Peter Brooks, *The Melodramatic Imagination: Balzac, Henry James, and the Language of Excess* (New York: Columbia University Press, 1984), 56–62.

13 Friedrich Nietzsche, "The Uses and Disadvantages of History for the Present Time," *Untimely Meditations,* ed. Daniel Breazeale (Cambridge: Cambridge University Press, 1983), 57–125, at 72.

14 Gilles Deleuze, *Cinema 1: The Movement Image* (Minneapolis: University of Minnesota Press, 1986), 70.

15 James Hay, *Popular Film Culture in Fascist Italy: The Passing of the Rex* (Bloomington: Indiana University Press, 1987), 158.

16 Sue Harper, "Historical Pleasures: Gainsborough Costume Melodramas," in Christine Gledhill, ed., *Home Is Where the Heart Is: Studies in Melodrama and the Woman's Film* (London: BFI Publishing, 1987), 167–96, at 167.

17 Iain Chambers, "Maps, Music, and Memory," in David B. Clarke, ed., *The Cinematic City* (London: Routledge, 1997), 230–41, at 235.

18 Robert A. Rosenstone, ed., *Revisioning History: Film and the Construction of a New Past* (Princeton: Princeton University Press, 1995), 7.

19 Angela Dalle Vacche, *The Body in the Mirror: Shapes of History in Italian Cinema* (Princeton: Princeton University Press, 1992), 106.

20 Roberto Campari, *Il fantasma del bello: iconologia del cinema italiano* (Venice: Marsilio, 1994), 37–8.

21 Pierre Sorlin, *European Cinema/European Societies, 1939-1990* (London: Routledge, 1991), 174.

22 Antonio Gramsci, *Selections from the Prison Notebooks*, ed. and trans. Quintin Hoare and Geoffrey Nowell-Smith (New York: International Publishers, 1978), 419-20.

23 Chambers, "Maps, Music, and Memory," 237.

24 Gori, *Patria diva,* 58.

25 Dana Polan, *Power and Paranoia: History, Narrative and the American Cinema* (New York: Columbia University Press, 1986), 75.

26 Klaus Theweleit, *Male Fantasies,* vol. 1: *Women, Floods, Bodies, History*, trans. Stephen Conway (Minneapolis: University of Minnesota Press, 1987), 35.

27 Pierre Sorlin, *Italian National Cinema 1896-1996* (London: Routledge, 1996), 77.

CHAPTER THREE: THE FOLKLORE OF ROMANCE

1 Robin Pickering-Iazzi, *Politics of the Visible: Writing Women, Culture, and Fascism* (Minneapolis: University of Minnesota Press, 1997), 93.

2 Gilles Deleuze, *Cinema 2: The Time Image* (Minneapolis: University of Minnesota Press, 1989), 96.

3 Claver Salizatto and Vito Zagarrio, *La corona di ferro: un modo di produzione italiano* (Rome: Di Giacomo, 1985), 16.

4 Brian Taves, *The Romance of Adventure: The Genre of Historical Adventure Movies* (Jackson: University of Mississippi Press, 1993), 94.

5 Marcia Landy, *The Folklore of Consensus* (Albany: State University of New York Press, 1998), 107-67.

6 Pierre Sorlin, *Italian National Cinema 1896-1996* (London: Routledge, 1996), 83.

7 Ibid.

8 Millicent Marcus, *Italian Film in the Light of Neorealism* (Princeton: Princeton University Press, 1986), 26.

9 Peter Brunette, *Roberto Rossellini* (New York: Oxford University Press, 1987), 61.

10 Deleuze, *Cinema 2,* 3.

11 D. N. Rodowick, *Gilles Deleuze's Time Machine* (Durham: Duke University Press, 1997), 14.

12 Ibid., 75.

13 Gaia Servadio, *Luchino Visconti: A Biography* (New York: Franklin Watts, 1983), 133.

14 Roberto Campari, *Il fantasma del bello: iconologia del cinema italiano* (Venice: Marsilio, 1994), 58-64.

15 Angela Dalle Vacche, "Nouvelle Histoire, Italian Style," *Annali d'Italianistica* 6 (1988): 98-123, at 101.

16 Ibid.

17 Marcus, *Italian Film in the Light of Neorealism,* 184-5.

18 Antonio Gramsci, *Selections from the Prison Notebooks,* ed. and trans. Quintin Hoare and Geoffrey Nowell-Smith (New York: International Publishers, 1978), 106-14.

19 Deleuze, *Cinema 2,* 95.

20 Angela Dalle Vacche, *The Body in the Mirror: Shapes of History in Italian Cinema* (Princeton: Princeton University Press, 1992), 150.

21 Peter Bondanella, *Italian Cinema: From Neorealism to the Present* (New York: Frederick Ungar-Continuum, 1993), 99.

22 Dalle Vacche, *Body in the Mirror,* 138.

23 Ibid., 141.
24 Marcus, *Italian Film in the Light of Neorealism,* 187.
25 Bruno Wanrooji, "Dollars and Decency: Italian Catholics and Hollywood," in David E. Ellwood and Rob Kroes, eds., *Hollywood in Europe: Experiences of a Cultural Hegemony* (Amsterdam: VU University Press, 1994), 247-66, at 252.
26 Ibid.
27 Bondanella, *Italian Cinema,* 87.
28 Gian Piero Brunetta, "The Long March of American Cinema in Italy: From Fascism to the Cold War," in Ellwood and Kroes, eds., *Hollywood in Europe,* 139-55, at 146.
29 Christopher Wagstaff, "Cinema," in David Forgacs and Robert Lumley, eds., *Italian Cultural Studies: An Introduction* (Oxford: Oxford University Press, 1996), 216-33, at 228.
30 Sorlin, *Italian National Cinema,* 111.
31 Ibid., 110.
32 Bondanella, *Italian Cinema,* 90.
33 Brunette, *Roberto Rossellini,* 210.
34 Ibid., 212.
35 Peter Brooks, *The Melodramatic Imagination: Balzac, Henry James, and the Language of Excess* (New York: Columbia University Press, 1984), 2.
36 Bondanella, *Italian Cinema,* 163.
37 Deleuze, *Cinema 2,* 248.
38 Ibid., 132.

CHAPTER FOUR: COMEDY AND
THE CINEMATIC MACHINE

1 Ernesto G. Laura, *Comedy Italian Style* (Rome: National Association of Motion Pictures and Affiliated Industries, n.d.), 6.
2 Christopher Wagstaff, "Cinema," in David Forgacs and Robert Lumley, eds., *Italian Cultural Studies: An Introduction* (Oxford: Oxford University Press, 1996), 216-33, at 125.
3 Laura, *Comedy Italian Style,* 6-7.
4 Wagstaff, "Cinema," 125.
5 Ted Sennett, *Laughing in the Dark: Movie Comedy from Groucho to Woody Allen* (New York: St. Martin's Press, 1992), 63.
6 Siegfried Kracauer, *The Mass Ornament: Weimar Essays* (Cambridge, Mass.: Harvard University Press, 1995), 291.
7 André Bazin, *What Is Cinema?,* vol. 2 (Berkeley: University of California Press, 1972), 21.
8 Wagstaff, "Cinema," 227.
9 Peter Bondanella, *Robert Rossellini* (New York: Cambridge University Press, 1993), 85.
10 Peter Brunette, *Roberto Rossellini* (New York: Oxford University Press, 1987), 103-4.
11 Gilles Deleuze, *Cinema 2: The Time Image* (Minneapolis: University of Minnesota Press, 1989), 171, 172.
12 Peter Bondanella, *Italian Cinema: From Neorealism to the Present* (New York: Frederick Ungar-Continuum, 1993), 93.
13 Brunette, *Roberto Rossellini,* 103.
14 Ibid.

15 Bondanella, *Roberto Rossellini,* 93.

16 Ibid., 94.

17 James Hay, *Popular Film Culture in Fascist Italy: The Passing of the Rex* (Bloomington: Indiana University Press, 1987), 19–20.

18 Costanzo Costantini, ed. *Fellini on Fellini,* trans. Sohrab Sooroshian (London: Faber & Faber, 1994), 85.

19 Hay, *Popular Film Culture,* 64.

20 Peter Bondanella, *Italian Cinema,* 249.

21 Hay, *Popular Film Culture,* 37.

22 Deleuze, *Cinema 2,* 92.

CHAPTER FIVE: THE LANDSCAPE AND NEOREALISM, BEFORE AND AFTER

1 John Dickie, "Imagined Italies," in David Forgacs and Robert Lumley, eds., *Italian Cultural Studies: An Introduction* (Oxford: Oxford University Press, 1996), 19–34, at 22.

2 Clareece G. Godt, *The Mobile Spectacle: Variable Perspective in Manzoni's I promessi sposi* (New York: Peter Lang, 1998).

3 Peter Bondanella, *Italian Cinema: From Neorealism to the Present* (New York: Frederick Ungar–Continuum, 1993), 156.

4 Antonio Gramsci, *Selections from the Prison Notebooks,* ed. and trans. Quintin Hoare and Geoffrey Nowell-Smith (New York: International Publishers, 1978), 71.

5 Charles Musser, "The Travel Genre in 1903–1904: Moving toward Fictional Narratives," in Thomas Elsaesser with Adam Barker, eds., *Early Cinema: Space, Frame, Narrative* (London: BFI Publishing, 1990), 123–33, at 123.

6 David A. Cook, *A History of Narrative Film* (New York: W. W. Norton & Co., 1996), 138.

7 Giuliana Bruno, *Streetwalking on a Ruined Map: Cultural Theory and the City Films of Elvira Notari* (Princeton: Princeton University Press, 1993), 12.

8 Pierre Leprohon, *The Italian Cinema* (New York: Praeger Publishers, 1972), 10.

9 James Hay, *Popular Film Culture in Fascist Italy: The Passing of the Rex* (Bloomington: Indiana University Press, 1987), 116.

10 Ibid., 169.

11 Gian Piero Brunetta, *Storia del cinema italiano,* vol. 3: *Dal neorealism al miracolo economico 1945-1959* (Rome: Riuniti, 1993), 438–9.

12 Gilles Deleuze, *Cinema 1: The Movement Image* (Minneapolis: University of Minnesota Press, 1986), 3.

13 Ibid.

14 Peter Brunette, *Roberto Rossellini* (New York: Oxford University Press, 1987), 51.

15 Ibid., 44.

16 Robert Phillip Kolker, *The Altering Eye: Contemporary International Cinema* (Oxford: Oxford University Press, 1983), 17.

17 Brunette, *Roberto Rossellini,* 50–1.

18 Gilles Deleuze, *Cinema 2: The Time Image* (Minneapolis: University of Minnesota Press, 1989), 170.

19 Millicent Marcus, *Italian Film in the Light of Neorealism* (Princeton: Princeton University Press, 1986), 64.

20 Ibid., 73.

21 Pierre Sorlin, *Italian National Cinema 1896–1996* (London: Routledge, 1996), 121.

22 Mira Liehm, *Passion and Defiance: Film in Italy from 1942 to the Present* (Berkeley: University of California Press, 1984), 76.

23 Robert Phillip Kolker, *The Altering Eye: Contemporary International Cinema* (Oxford: Oxford University Press, 1983), 50.

24 Peter Bondanella, *Italian Cinema: From Neorealism to the Present* (New York: Frederick Ungar–Continuum, 1993), 237.

25 Deleuze, *Cinema 2,* 89.

26 Bondanella, *Italian Cinema,* 240.

27 Ibid., 241.

28 John Dickie, "Imagined Italies," 28.

29 Bondanella, *Italian Cinema,* 155.

CHAPTER SIX: GRAMSCI AND ITALIAN CINEMA

1 David Forgacs, *Italian Culture in the Industrial Era: Cultural Industries, Politics, and the Public* (Manchester: Manchester University Press, 1990), 117.

2 Ibid.

3 Antonio Gramsci, *Selections from the Cultural Writings*, ed. David Forgacs (Cambridge, Mass.: Harvard University Press, 1985), 421–2.

4 Gregory L. Lucente, *Crosspaths in Literary Theory and Criticism: Italy and the United States* (Stanford, Calif.: Stanford University Press, 1997), 98.

5 Antonio Gramsci, *The Southern Question*, ed. and trans. Pasquale Verdiccchio (West Lafayette, Ind.: Bordighera Inc., 1995), 20.

6 Antonio Gramsci, *The Prison Notebooks*, ed. and trans. Joseph Buttigieg (New York: Columbia University Press, 1992, 2 vols. [so far]), vol. 1, 143.

7 Ibid., 186.

8 Antonio Gramsci, *Selections from the Prison Notebooks*, ed. and trans. Quintin Hoare and Geoffrey Nowell-Smith (New York: International Publishers, 1978), 71.

9 Edward Said, *Culture and Imperialism* (New York: Knopf, 1993), 131.

10 Millicent Marcus, *Filmmaking by the Book: Italian Cinema and Literary Adaptation* (Baltimore: Johns Hopkins University Press, 1993), 49.

11 Gramsci, *Selections from the Prison Notebooks,* 260.

12 Ibid., 257–61.

13 Geoffrey Nowell-Smith, *Luchino Visconti* (London: Secker & Warburg, 1973), 101, 112; Marcus, *Filmmaking by the Book,* 52.

14 Gramsci, *Selections from the Prison Notebooks,* 210.

15 Pio Baldelli, *Luchino Visconti* (Milan: G. P. Mazzotta, 1973), 235.

16 Marcus, *Filmmaking by the Book,* 58.

17 Gilles Deleuze, *Cinema 2: The Time Image* (Minneapolis: University of Minnesota Press, 1989), 83.

18 Ibid., 94.

19 Ibid.

20 Ibid.

21 Ibid., 95.

22 Ibid., 96.

23 Nowell-Smith, *Luchino Visconti,* 51–4; see also Gaia Servadio, *Luchino Visconti: A Biography* (New York: Franklin Watts, 1983), 195.

24 Peter Bondanella, *Italian Cinema: From Neorealism to the Present* (New York: Frederick Ungar–Continuum, 1993), 100.

25 Robert Phillip Kolker, *The Altering Eye: Contemporary International Cinema* (Oxford: Oxford University Press, 1983), 80.

26 Gramsci, *Selections from the Prison Notebooks,* 93.

27 Bondanella, *Italian Cinema,* 346.

28 Ibid., 345.

29 Wallace P. Sillanpoa, "Pasolini's Gramsci," *Modern Language Notes* (1981): 120–37, at 123.

30 Gramsci, *Selections from the Prison Notebooks,* 178.

31 Gary Crowdus, "We Believe in the Power of Cinema: An Interview with Paolo and Vittorio Taviani," *Cinéaste* 3 (1983): 31–4, at 34.

32 Ibid., 31.

33 Millicent Marcus, *Italian Film in the Light of Neorealism* (Princeton: Princeton University Press, 1986), 361.

34 Crowdus, "We Believe in the Power of Cinema," 31.

35 Peter Brooks, *The Melodramatic Imagination: Balzac, Henry James, and the Language of Excess* (New York: Columbia University Press, 1984); Christine Gledhill, *Home Is Where the Heart Is: Studies in Melodrama and the Woman's Film* (London: BFI Publishing, 1987); Marcia Landy, *Imitations of Life: A Reader on Film and Television Melodrama* (Detroit: Wayne State University Press, 1991).

36 Kolker, *Altering Eye,* 119.

37 Tony Mitchell, "Towards Utopia: By Way of Research, Detachment, and Involvement," *Sight and Sound* 47(3), 171–8, at 178.

38 Gramsci, *Selections from the Prison Notebooks,* 9.

39 Kolker, *Altering Eye,* 117.

40 R. W. Witcombe, *The New Italian Cinema: Studies in Dance and Despair* (New York: Oxford University Press, 1982), 213.

41 Sam Rohdie, *The Passion of Pier Paolo Pasolini* (Bloomington: University of Indiana Press, 1995), 13.

42 Maurizio Viano, *A Certain Realism: Making Use of Pasolini's Film Theory and Practice* (Berkeley: University of California Press, 1993), 270.

43 Ibid., 70.

44 Ibid., 71.

45 Gian Piero Brunetta, *Forma e parola nel cinema italiano: il film muto, Pasolini, Antonioni* (Padua: Liviana, 1979).

46 Naomi Greene, *Pier Paolo Pasolini: Cinema as Heresy* (Princeton: Princeton University Press, 1990), 29.

47 Viano, *Certain Realism,* 79.

48 Greene, *Pier Paolo Pasolini,* 33.

49 Bondanella, *Italian Cinema,* 182.

50 Forgacs, *Italian Culture,* 10.

51 Oswald Stack, *Pasolini on Pasolini: Interviews with Oswald Stack* (Bloomington: Indiana University Press, 1970), 148.

CHAPTER SEVEN: HISTORY, GENRE, AND THE ITALIAN WESTERN

1 Pierre Sorlin, *European Cinema/European Societies, 1939–1990* (London: Routledge, 1991), 168.

2 Peter Bondanella, *Italian Cinema: From Neorealism to the Present* (New York: Frederick Ungar-Continuum, 1993), 253.

3 Christopher Frayling, *Spaghetti Westerns: Cowboys and Europeans from Karl May to Sergio Leone* (London: Routledge & Kegan Paul, 1981). See also Edward Buscombe for the treatment of Mexico in spaghetti westerns as opposed to Hollywood, e.g., in *"The Magnificent Seven," Mediating Two Worlds: Cinematic Encounters in the Americas* (London: BFI Publishing, 1993), 15-25.
4 Ibid., 157.
5 Friedrich Nietzsche, *The Gay Science,* trans. Walter Kaufmann (New York: Vintage Books, 1974), 258-9.
6 Frayling, *Spaghetti Westerns,* 29.
7 Jerre Mangione and Ben Morreale, *La Storia: Five Centuries of the Italian and American Experience* (New York: Harper Perennial, 1992), 31-67.
8 Frayling, *Spaghetti Westerns,* 64.
9 Francesco Savio, *Cinnecittà anni trenta,* vol. 2 (Rome: Bulzoni, 1979), 440.
10 Ibid., 521.
11 Brian Taves has made an initial foray into the dynamics of the adventure film in *The Romance of Adventure: The Genre of Historical Adventure Movies* (Jackson: University of Mississippi Press, 1993).
12 Jim Kitses, *Horizons West: Anthony Mann, Budd Boetticher, Sam Peckinpah - Studies of Authorship within the Western* (Bloomington: Indiana University Press, 1969); Will Wright, *Sixguns and Society: A Structural Study of the Western* (Berkeley: University of California Press, 1975); Thomas Schatz, *Hollywood Genres: Formulas, Filmmaking, and the Studio System* (New York: Random House, 1981); Lane Roth, *Film, Semiotics, Metz, and Leone's Trilogy* (New York: Garland, 1983); See also André Bazin, *What Is Cinema?*, vol. 2 (Berkeley: University of California Press, 1972).
13 George N. Fenin and William K. Everson, *The Western: From Silents to Cinerama* (New York: Bonanza Books, 1962), 10-12.
14 Kitses, *Horizons West,* 8.
15 Paul Smith, *Clint Eastwood: A Cultural Production* (Minneapolis: University of Minnesota Press, 1993), 19-26.
16 John Cawelti, *Adventure, Mystery, and Romance: Formula Stories as Art and Popular Culture* (Chicago: University of Chicago Press, 1976), 221, 225.
17 Ibid., 251.
18 Ibid.
19 Wright, *Sixguns and Society,* 97-9.
20 Mark Kermode, "Endnotes," *Sight and Sound* (October 1994): 63.
21 Antonio Gramsci, *Selections from the Cultural Writings,* ed. David Forgacs (Cambridge, Mass.: Harvard University Press, 1985), 380.
22 Angela Dalle Vacche, *The Body in the Mirror: Shapes of History in Italian Cinema* (Princeton: Princeton University Press, 1992), 6.
23 For a detailed discussion of the history of the *commedia,* see Allardyce Nicoll, *Masks, Mimes, and Miracles: Studies in the Popular Theatre* (New York: Cooper Square Publishers, Inc., 1963); for a discussion of the adaptations of the *commedia* to various cultural forms of representation from Shakespeare to modernity, see David George and Christopher J. Gossip, eds., *Studies in the Commedia dell'arte* (Cardiff: University of Wales Press, 1993); and for a specific discussion of the kinds of *lazzi,* see Mel Gordon, *Lazzi: The Comic Routines of the Commedia dell'arte* (New York: Performing Arts Journal, 1983). See also Flaminio Scola, *Scenarios of the Commedia dell'arte: Flaminio Scala's Il teatro delle favole rappresentative,* trans. Henry F. Salerno (New York: New York University Press, 1967); and Martin Green and John Swan, *The Triumph of Pierrot: The Commedia dell'arte and the Modern Imagination* (New York: Macmillan Publishing Co., 1986).

24 Gordon, *Lazzi,* 5.
25 Ibid., 9.
26 Nicoll, *Masks, Mimes, and Miracles,* 276.
27 Ibid., 258.
28 Frayling, *Spaghetti Westerns,* 60-2.
29 Nicoll, *Masks, Mimes, and Miracles,* 283.
30 Robert C. Cumbow, *Once Upon a Time in Sergio Leone* (Metuchen, N.Y.: Scarecrow Press, 1987), 98.
31 Frayling, *Spaghetti Westerns,* 55.
32 Ibid., 253.

CHAPTER EIGHT: *LA FAMIGLIA:* THE CINEMATIC FAMILY AND THE NATION

1 Chiara Saraceno, "Il circolo vizioso della famiglia contemporanea: la famiglia fa la madre, la madre fa la famiglia," *La critica sociologica* 35 (Autumn 1975): 8-18.
2 David I. Kertzer and Richard P. Saller, eds., *The Family in Italy: From Antiquity to the Present* (New Haven: Yale University Press, 1991), 4.
3 David I. Kertzer, *Family Life in Central Italy, 1880-1910: Sharecropping, Wage Labor, and Coresidence* (New Brunswick: Rutgers University Press, 1984), 2.
4 Paul Ginsborg, *A History of Contemporary Italy: Society and Politics 1943-1988* (London: Penguin Books, 1990), 2.
5 Paola Filippucci, "Anthropological Perspectives on Culture in Italy," in David Forgacs and Robert Lumley, eds., *Italian Cultural Studies:An Introduction* (Oxford: Oxford University Press, 1996), 52-71, at 55.
6 Jeff Pratt, "Catholic Culture," in Forgacs and Lumley, eds., *Italian Cultural Studies,* 129-44, at 140.
7 Ibid., 147.
8 Victoria de Grazia, *How Fascism Ruled Women: Italy, 1922-1945* (Berkeley: University of California Press, 1992), 135.
9 Étienne Balibar, "The Nation Form: History and Ideology," in Étienne Balibar and Immanuel Wallerstein, *Race, Nation, Class: Ambiguous Identities* (London: Verso, 1995), 86-106, at 101.
10 Lesley Caldwell, "Reproducers of the Nation: Women and the Family in Fascist Policy," in Davis Forgacs, ed., *Rethinking Italian Fascism* (London: Lawrence & Wishart, 1986), 110-41.
11 Mariella Graziosi, "Gender Struggle and the Social Manipulation and Ideological Use of Gender Identity in the Interwar Years," in Robin Pickering-Iazzi, ed., *Mothers of Invention: Women, Italian Fascism, and Culture* (Minneapolis: University of Minnesota Press, 1995), 26-52.
12 James Hay, *Popular Film Culture in Fascist Italy: The Passing of the Rex* (Bloomington: Indiana University Press, 1987), 126.
13 Pierre Sorlin, *Italian National Cinema 1896-1996* (London: Routledge, 1996), 110.
14 Sam Rohdie, *Antonioni* (London: BFI Publishing, 1990), 43.
15 Ibid., 48.
16 Peter Bondanella, *Italian Cinema: From Neorealism to the Present* (New York: Frederick Ungar-Continuum, 1993), 144.
17 Angelo Restivo, "The Nation, the Body, and the *Autostrada,*" in Steve Cohan and Ina Rae Hark, eds., *The Road Movie Book* (London: Routledge, 1997), 233-49.
18 Naomi Greene, *Pier Paolo Pasolini: Cinema as Heresy* (Princeton: Princeton University Press, 1990), 69.

19 Maurizio Viano, *A Certain Realism: Making Use of Pasolini's Film Theory and Practice* (Berkeley: University of California Press, 1993), 123.

20 Beverly Allen, "They're Not Children Any More: The Novelization of 'Italians' and 'Terrorism,'" in Beverly Allen and Mary Russo, eds., *Revisioning Italy: National Identity and Global Culture* (Minneapolis: University of Minnesota Press, 1997), 52-81, at 59.

21 Robert Phillip Kolker, *Bernardo Bertolucci* (New York: Oxford University Press, 1985), 167.

22 Ibid., 168.

23 Ibid., 179.

24 Bondanella, *Italian Cinema,* 408.

CHAPTER NINE: A CINEMA OF CHILDHOOD

1 Philippe Ariès, *Centuries of Childhood: A Social History of Family Life*, trans. Robert Baldick (New York: Vintage, 1962), 128.

2 Ibid., 50.

3 J. H. Plumb, "The Great Change in Children," in Arlene Skolnick, ed., *Rethinking Childhood: Perspectives on Development and Society* (Boston: Little, Brown & Co., 1976), 205-14, at 206.

4 Ibid., 208-9.

5 Ibid., 209.

6 Michel Foucault, *The History of Sexuality,* vol. I: *An Introduction* (New York: Vintage, 1980), 28.

7 Plumb, "Great Change in Children," 211.

8 Beverly Allen, "They're Not Children Any More: The Novelization of 'Italians' and 'Terrorism,'" in Beverly Allen and Mary Russo, eds., *Revisioning Italy: National Identity and Global Culture* (Minneapolis: University of Minnesota Press, 1997), 52-81, at 71.

9 Giuliana Bruno, *Streetwalking on a Ruined Map: Cultural Theory and the City Films of Elvira Notari* (Princeton: Princeton University Press, 1993), 183-4.

10 Ibid., 184.

11 Elaine Mancini, *Struggles of the Italian Film Industry during Fascism, 1930-1935* (Ann Arbor: UMI Press, 1985), 155.

12 Ibid., 116.

13 Marcia Landy, *The Folklore of Consensus* (Albany: State University of New York Press, 1998), 275-81; Jacqueline Reich, "Reading, Writing, and Rebellion: Collectivity, Specularity, and Sexuality in Italian Schoolgirl Comedies," *Mothers of Invention: Women, Italian Fascism, and Culture* (Minneapolis: University of Minnesota Press, 1995), 220-51.

14 James Hay, *Popular Film Culture in Fascist Italy: The Passing of the Rex* (Bloomington: Indiana University Press, 1987), 10.

15 Ibid., 98.

16 Reich, "Reading, Writing, and Rebellion," 227.

17 Ibid., 239.

18 Colin McArthur, "Chinese Boxes and Russian Dolls: Tracking the Elusive Cinematic City," in David B. Clarke, ed., *The Cinematic City* (London: Routledge, 1997), 19-46, at 40.

19 Mira Liehm, *Passion and Defiance: Film in Italy from 1942 to the Present* (Berkeley: University of California Press, 1984), 75.

20 Gilles Deleuze, *Cinema 1: The Movement Image* (Minneapolis: University of Minnesota Press, 1986), 208.

21 Gilles Deleuze, *Cinema 2: The Time Image* (Minneapolis: University of Minnesota Press, 1989), 3.

22 Millicent Marcus, *Italian Film in the Light of Neorealism* (Princeton: Princeton University Press, 1986), 68.

23 Ibid., 371.

24 Ibid., 366.

25 Ibid., 367.

26 Angelo Restivo, *The Cinema of Economic Miracles* (unpublished dissertation, Dept. of Critical Studies, University of Southern California, 1997), 223.

CHAPTER TEN: THE FOLKLORE OF FEMININITY AND STARDOM

1 Luisa Passerini, "Gender Relations," in David Forgacs and Robert Lumley, eds., *Italian Cultural Studies: An Introduction* (Oxford: Oxford University Press, 1996), 144–60, at 157.

2 Giuliana Bruno, *Streetwalking on a Ruined Map: Cultural Theory and the City Films of Elvira Notari* (Princeton: Princeton University Press, 1993), 279.

3 Victoria de Grazia, *How Fascism Ruled Women: Italy, 1922–1945* (Berkeley: University of California Press, 1992), 78.

4 Ibid., 60.

5 Lucia Re, "Fascist Theories of 'Woman' and the Construction of Gender," in Robin Pickering-Iazzi, ed., *Mothers of Invention: Women, Italian Fascism, and Culture* (Minneapolis: University of Minnesota Press, 1995), 76–100, at 80.

6 Ibid., 85.

7 Karen Pinkus, *Bodily Regimes: Italian Advertising under Fascism* (Minneapolis: University of Minnesota Press, 1995), 15.

8 Ibid., 154.

9 Stuart Hall, *The Hard Road to Renewal* (London: Verso, 1988), 7.

10 Christine Gledhill, ed., *Stardom: Industry of Desire* (London: Routledge, 1991), xiii.

11 Pierre Leprohon, *The Italian Cinema* (New York: Praeger Publishers, 1972), 47.

12 Ibid.

13 Walter Benjamin, *Illuminations*, ed. Hannah Arendt (New York: Schocken Books, 1976), 236–7.

14 Gian Piero Brunetta, *Storia del cinema italiano,* vol. 1: *Il cinema muto 1895–1929* (Rome: Riuniti, 1993), 81.

15 Ibid., 76–7.

16 Gian Piero Brunetta, "The Long March of American Cinema in Italy: From Fascism to the Cold War," in David E. Ellwood and Rob Kroes, eds., *Hollywood in Europe: Experiences of a Cultural Hegemony* (Amsterdam: VU University Press, 1994), 139–55.

17 Stephen Gundle, "Fame, Fashion and Style: The Italian Star System," in David Forgacs and Robert Lumley, eds., *Italian Cultural Studies: An Introduction.* Oxford: Oxford University Press, 1996, 309–27, at 315.

18 Mary Ann Doane, *Femmes Fatales: Feminism, Film Theory, Psychoanalysis* (New York: Routledge, 1991), 123.

19 Ibid., 127.

20 Benjamin, *Illuminations,* 230.

21 Doane, *Femmes Fatales,* 125.

22 Parker Tyler, *Magic and Myth of the Movies* (New York: Simon & Schuster, 1970), 82.

23 M. M. Bakhtin, *The Dialogic Imagination*, ed. Michael Holquist, trans. Caryl Emerson and Michael Holquist (Austin: University of Texas Press, 1981); John Docker, *Postmodernism and Popular Culture: A Cultural History* (Cambridge: Cambridge University Press, 1994), 168-233.

24 Christian Viviani, "Who Is without Sin?: The Maternal Melodrama in American Film, 1930-1939," *Wide Angle* 4 (1980): 4-17.

25 Mary Ann Doane, *The Desire to Desire: The Woman's Film of the 1940's* (Bloomington: Indiana University Press, 1987), 74.

26 Steven Shaviro, *The Cinematic Body* (Minneapolis: University of Minnesota Press, 1993), 56.

27 Gaylyn Studlar, *In the Realm of Pleasure: Von Sternberg, Dietrich, and the Masochistic Aesthetic* (Urbana: University of Illinois Press, 1988), 192.

28 Marcia Landy, *The Folklore of Consensus: Theatricality in the Italian Cinema, 1930-1943* (Albany: State University of New York Press, 1998), 259-69.

29 Giovanna Grignaffini, "Female Identity and the Italian Cinema of the 1950s," in Giuliana Bruno and Maria Nadotti, eds., *Off Screen: Women and Film in Italy* (London: Routledge, 1988), 111-24, at 120.

30 Ibid.

31 Ibid., 121.

32 Gillian Rose, *Feminism and Geography: The Limits of Geographical Knowledge* (Minneapolis: University of Minnesota Press, 1993), 60.

33 Millicent Marcus, *Italian Film in the Light of Neorealism* (Princeton: Princeton University Press, 1986), 50.

34 Ibid., 39.

35 Grignaffini, "Female Identity," 123.

36 Peter Brunette, *Roberto Rossellini* (New York: Oxford University Press, 1987), 90.

37 David Barth Schwartz, *Pasolini Requiem* (New York: Vintage, 1992), 406.

38 Maurizio Viano, *A Certain Realism: Making Use of Pasolini's Film Theory and Practice* (Berkeley: University of California Press, 1993), 88.

39 Ibid., 96.

40 Ibid.

41 Ibid., 90.

42 Pierre Sorlin, *Italian National Cinema 1896-1996* (London: Routledge, 1996), 110.

43 Peter Bondanella, *Italian Cinema: From Neorealism to the Present* (New York: Frederick Ungar-Continuum, 1993), 87.

44 Sorlin, *Italian National Cinema,* 97.

45 Antonio Vitti, *Giuseppe De Santis and Postwar Italian Cinema* (Toronto: University of Toronto Press, 1996), 45.

46 Costanzo Costantini, ed. *Fellini on Fellini*, trans. Sohrab Sooroshian (London: Faber & Faber, 1994), 50.

47 Marcus, *Italian Film in the Light of Neorealism,* 151-2.

48 Gundle, "Fame, Fashion and Style," 311.

49 Millicent Marcus, *Filmmaking by the Book: Italian Cinema and Literary Adaptation* (Baltimore: Johns Hopkins University Press, 1993), 83.

50 Ibid., 90.

51 Paul Ginsborg, *A History of Contemporary Italy: Society and Politics 1943-1988* (London: Penguin Books, 1990), 248.

52 David Forgacs, *Italian Culture in the Industrial Era: Cultural Industries, Politics, and the Public* (Manchester: Manchester University Press, 1990), 273.

53 Ibid., 279.

54 Bondanella, *Italian Cinema,* 210.

55 P. Adams Sitney, *Vital Crises in Italian Cinema: Iconography, Stylistics, Politics* (Austin: University of Texas Press, 1995), 135.

56 Gilles Deleuze, *Cinema 2: The Time Image* (Minneapolis: University of Minnesota Press, 1989), 205.

57 "Introduction," Bruno and Nadotti, eds., *Off Screen,* 1–17, at 7.

58 Marcus, *Italian Film in the Light of Neorealism,* 333.

59 Bondanella, *Italian Cinema,* 356.

60 Marcus, *Italian Film in the Light of Neorealism,* 337.

61 Lucy Fischer, *Shot/Countershot: Film Tradition and Women's Cinema* (Princeton: Princeton University Press, 1989), 260.

62 Ibid., 257.

63 Ibid., 256.

64 Ibid.

65 Bondanella, *Italian Cinema,* 145.

66 Fischer, *Shot/Countershot,* 260.

67 Patrizia Violi, "Language and the Female Subject," in Bruno and Nadotti, eds., *Off Screen,* 139–51, at 144.

CHAPTER ELEVEN: CONVERSION, IMPERSONATION, AND MASCULINITY

1 Karl Marx, *Capital,* vol. 1, trans. Cedar and Eden Paul (New York: Dutton, 1977), 47.

2 Jared Becker, *Nationalism and Culture: Gabriele D'Annunzio and Italy after the Risorgimento* (New York: Peter Lang, 1994), 211.

3 Ibid., 3, 207–11.

4 Antonio Gramsci, "Americanism and Fordism," in *Selections from the Prison Notebooks,* ed. and trans. Quintin Hoare and Geoffrey Nowell-Smith (New York: International Publishers, 1978), 279–322. See also *The Prison Notebooks*, ed. and trans. Joseph Buttigieg (New York: Columbia University Press, 1992, 2 vols. [so far]), vol. 2, 215–20.

5 Pierre Sorlin, *Italian National Cinema 1896–1996* (London: Routledge, 1996), 48–9.

6 Karen Pinkus, *Bodily Regimes: Italian Advertising under Fascism* (Minneapolis: University of Minnesota Press, 1995), 86.

7 Ibid., 154.

8 Klaus Theweleit, *Male Fantasies,* vol. 2: *Male Bodies, Psychoanalyzing the White Terror,* trans. Stephen Conway (Minneapolis: University of Minnesota Press, 1989), 368–9.

9 Millicent Marcus, *Italian Film in the Light of Neorealism* (Princeton: Princeton University Press, 1986), 46.

10 Peter Brunette, *Roberto Rossellini* (New York: Oxford University Press, 1987), 212.

11 Peter Bondanella, *Italian Cinema: From Neorealism to the Present* (New York: Frederick Ungar-Continuum, 1993), 158.

12 Ibid., 159; Gian Piero Brunetta, *Storia del cinema italiano*, vol. 3: *Dal neorealism al miracolo economico 1945-1959* (Rome: Riuniti, 1993), 176.

13 Bondanella, *Italian Cinema,* 159.

14 Bruno Wanrooji, "Dollars and Decency: Italian Catholics and Hollywood," in David E. Ellwood and Rob Kroes, eds., *Hollywood in Europe: Experiences of a Cultural Hegemony* (Amsterdam: VU University Press, 1994), 247-66, at 252.

15 Ibid., 257.

16 Paul Ginsborg, *A History of Contemporary Italy: Society and Politics 1943-1988* (London: Penguin Books, 1990), 212.

17 Wanrooji, "Dollars and Decency," 264.

18 Ina Rae Hark, "Animals or Romans," in Steve Cohan and Ina Rae Hark, eds., *Screening the Male: Exploring Masculinities in Hollywood Cinema* (London: Routledge, 1995), 151-2.

19 Bondanella, *Italian Cinema,* 161.

20 Ibid., 154.

21 Marcus, *Italian Film in the Light of Neorealism,* 239.

22 Peter Bondanella, *The Cinema of Federico Fellini* (Princeton: Princeton University Press, 1992), 142.

23 Ibid.

24 Charlotte Chandler, *I, Fellini* (New York: Random House, 1995), 117.

25 Ibid, 118.

26 Ibid.

27 Stephen Gundle, "Fame, Fashion and Style: The Italian Star System," in David Forgacs and Robert Lumley, eds., *Italian Cultural Studies: An Introduction.* Oxford: Oxford University Press, 1996, 309-27, at 310.

28 John Baxter, *Fellini* (London: Fourth Estate, 1993), 165.

29 Bondanella, *Cinema of Federico Fellini,* 163.

30 Robert Phillip Kolker, *Bernardo Bertolucci* (New York: Oxford University Press, 1985), 69.

31 Bondanella, *Italian Cinema,* 310.

32 T. Jefferson Kline, *Bertolucci's Dream Loom: A Psychoanalytic Study of Cinema* (Amherst: University of Massachusetts Press, 1987), 126-46.

33 Kolker, *Bernardo Bertolucci,* 218.

34 Peter Bondanella, *The Cinema of Federico Fellini* (Princeton: Princeton University Press, 1992), 308.

CHAPTER TWELVE: CINEMA ON CINEMA
AND ON TELEVISION

1 Manuela Gieri, *Contemporary Italian Filmmaking: Strategies of Subversion - Pirandello, Fellini, Scola and the Directors of the New Generation* (Toronto: University of Toronto Press, 1995), 34.

2 Ibid., 48.

3 Nina Da Vinci Nichols and Jana O'Keefe Bazzoni, *Pirandello and Film* (Lincoln: University of Nebraska Press, 1995), 86-90.

4 Jane Feuer, *The Hollywood Musical* (London: BFI Publishing, 1982), 82.

5 Ibid., 23.

6 Ibid., 3.

7 Peter Brunette, *Roberto Rossellini* (New York: Oxford University Press, 1987), 58.

8 Marguerite Waller, "Decolonizing the Screen: From *Ladri di biciclette* to *Ladri di saponette*," in Beverly Allen and Mary Russo, eds., *Revisioning Italy: National Identity and Global Culture* (Minneapolis: University of Minnesota Press, 1997), 253–75, at 259.

9 Gieri, *Contemporary Italian Filmmaking,* 123.

10 Sam Rohdie, *Antonioni* (London: BFI Publishing, 1990), 31.

11 Ibid., 39.

12 Gilles Deleuze, *Cinema 2: The Time Image* (Minneapolis: University of Minnesota Press, 1989), 205.

13 Peter Bondanella, *Italian Cinema: From Neorealism to the Present* (New York: Frederick Ungar-Continuum, 1993), 221.

14 Pier Paolo Pasolini, *Heretical Empiricism,* trans. Ben Lawton and Louise Barnett (Bloomington: Indiana University Press, 1988), 179–80.

15 Naomi Greene, *Pier Paolo Pasolini: Cinema as Heresy* (Princeton: Princeton University Press, 1990), 40.

16 Ibid., 48.

17 Maurizio Viano, *A Certain Realism: Making Use of Pasolini's Film Theory and Practice* (Berkeley: University of California Press, 1993), 217.

18 Ibid., 210.

19 Deleuze, *Cinema 2,* 175.

20 Viano, *Certain Realism,* 213.

21 Gian Piero Brunetta, *Storia del cinema italiano,* vol. 4: *Dal miracolo economico agli anni novanta 1960-1993* (Rome: Riuniti, 1993), 415.

22 Pierre Sorlin, *Italian National Cinema 1896-1996* (London: Routledge, 1996), 147.

23 Elena Dagrada, "Television and Its Critics: A Parallel History," in David Forgacs and Robert Lumley, eds., *Italian Cultural Studies: An Introduction* (Oxford: Oxford University Press, 1996), 233–48, at 233.

24 Sorlin, *Italian National Cinema,* 148.

25 Bondanella, *Italian Cinema,* 385.

26 Sorlin, *Italian National Cinema,* 144.

27 Richard Dienst, *Still Life in Real Time: Theory after Television* (Durham: Duke University Press, 1995).

28 Charlotte Chandler, *I, Fellini* (New York: Random House, 1995), 230.

29 Peter Bondanella, *The Cinema of Federico Fellini* (Princeton: Princeton University Press, 1992), 220.

30 Chandler, *I, Fellini,* 234–5.

31 Bondanella, *Cinema of Federico Fellini,* 224.

32 Gieri, *Contemporary Italian Filmmaking,* 119.

33 Ibid., 230.

34 Ibid., 250.

35 Brunetta, *Storia del cinema italiano,* vol. 4, 173.

36 Duncan Petrie, ed., *Screening Europe: Image and Identity in the Contemporary European Cinema* (London: BFI Publishing, 1992), 98.

Bibliography

Abel, Richard. *French Cinema: The First Wave, 1915–1929.* Princeton: Princeton University Press, 1984.

Abruzzese, Alberto. "Il grattacielo e lo sguardo," in Alberto Abruzzese et al., eds., *Spettacolo e metropoli: attore, messa in scena, spettatore.* Naples: Liguori, 1988, 131–7.

Adamson, Walter. "The Language of Opposition in Early Twentieth-Century Italy: Rhetorical Continuities between Pre-war Florentine Avantgardism and Mussolini's Fascism," *Journal of Modern History* 64 (March 1992): 22–51.

Albrecht, Donald. *Designing Dreams: Modern Architecture in the Movies.* New York: Harper & Row and Museum of Modern Art, 1986.

Allen, Beverly. "They're Not Children Any More: The Novelization of 'Italians' and 'Terrorism,'" in Beverly Allen and Mary Russo, eds., *Revisioning Italy: National Identity and Global Culture.* Minneapolis: University of Minnesota Press, 1997, 52–81.

Allen, Beverly, and Mary Russo, eds. *Revisioning Italy: National Identity and Global Culture.* Minneapolis: University of Minnesota Press, 1997.

Aprà, Adriano, Enrico Magrelli, Patrizia Pistagnesi, and La Biennale di Venezia. *The Cinema of the Eighties, Settore cinema e spettacolo television. Proceedings of the Meeting.* Venice: Venetian Manuscripts, 1979.

Aprà, Adriano, and Patrizia Pistagnesi. *I favolosi anni trenta: cinema italiano 1929–1944.* Milan: Electa, 1979.

Argentieri, Mino, ed. *Risate di Regime: la commedia italiana 1930–1944.* Venice: Marsilio, 1991.

Ariès, Philippe. *Centuries of Childhood: A Social History of Family Life*, trans. Robert Baldick. New York: Vintage, 1962.

Arrowsmith, William. *Antonioni,* edited with an introduction and notes by Ted Perry. New York: Oxford University Press, 1995.

Bacon, Henry. *Visconti: Explorations of Beauty and Decay.* Cambridge: Cambridge University Press, 1998.

Bakhtin, M. M. *The Dialogic Imagination*, ed. Michael Holquist, trans. Caryl Emerson and Michael Holquist. Austin: University of Texas Press, 1981.

Baldelli, Pio. *Luchino Visconti.* Milan: G. P. Mazzotta, 1973.

Balibar, Étienne, and Immanuel Wallerstein. *Race, Nation, Class: Ambiguous Identities.* London: Verso, 1995.

Baxter, John. *Fellini.* London: Fourth Estate, 1993.

Bazin, André. *What Is Cinema?*, vol. 2. Berkeley: University of California Press, 1972.

Becker, Jared. *Nationalism and Culture: Gabriele D'Annunzio and Italy after the Risorgimento.* New York: Peter Lang, 1994.

Benigno, Francesco. "The Southern Family: A Comment on Paolo Macry," *Journal of Modern Italian Studies* 2(2) (Summer 1997): 215–17.

Benjamin, Walter. *Illuminations,* ed. Hannah Arendt. New York: Schocken Books, 1976.

Biasin, Gian-Paolo. *Italian Literary Icons.* Princeton: Princeton University Press, 1985.

Blanchard, Paul. *Southern Italy: South of Rome to Calabria.* London: A & C Black, 1996.

Boarini, Vittorio, Pietro Bonfiglioli, and Giorgi Cremonini, eds. *Da Accattone a Salò: 120 scritti sul cinema di Pier Paolo Pasolini.* Bologna: Tipographia Compositori, 1982.

Bondanella, Peter. *The Cinema of Federico Fellini.* Princeton: Princeton University Press, 1992.

Italian Cinema: From Neorealism to the Present. New York: Frederick Ungar–Continuum, 1993.

Robert Rossellini. New York: Cambridge University Press, 1993.

Brizzi, Stella. *Undressing Cinema: Clothing and Identity in the Movies.* London: Routledge, 1997.

Brooks, Peter. *The Melodramatic Imagination: Balzac, Henry James, and the Language of Excess.* New York: Columbia University Press, 1984.

Broude, Norma. *The Macchiaioli: Painters of the Nineteenth Century.* New Haven: Yale University Press, 1987.

Brunetta, Gian Piero. *Cinema italiano tra le due guerre.* Milan: Mursia, 1975.

Forma e parola nel cinema italiano: il film muto, Pasolini, Antonioni. Padua: Liviana, 1979.

"The Long March of American Cinema in Italy: From Fascism to the Cold War," in David E. Ellwood and Rob Kroes, eds., *Hollywood in Europe: Experiences of a Cultural Hegemony.* Amsterdam: VU University Press, 1994, 139–55.

Storia del cinema italiano, 4 vols. (vol. 1: *Il cinema muto 1895-1929;* vol. 2: *Il cinema del regime 1929-1945;* vol. 3: *Dal neorealism al miracolo economico 1945-1959,* vol. 4: *Dal miracolo economico agli anni novanta 1960-1993*). Rome: Riuniti, 1993.

Storia del cinema italiano, 1895-1945. Rome: Riuniti, 1979.

Brunette, Peter. *The Films of Michelangelo Antonioni.* Cambridge: Cambridge University Press, 1998.

Roberto Rossellini. New York: Oxford University Press, 1987.

Bruno, Giuliana. *Streetwalking on a Ruined Map: Cultural Theory and the City Films of Elvira Notari.* Princeton: Princeton University Press, 1993.

Bruno, Giuliana, and Maria Nadotti, eds. *Off Screen: Women and Film in Italy.* London: Routledge, 1988.

Buache, Freddy. *Le cinema italien, 1945-1990.* Lausanne: L'Age D'Homme, 1992.

Buck-Morss, Susan. *The Dialectics of Seeing: Walter Benjamin and the Arcades Project.* Cambridge: MIT Press, 1997.

Buscombe, Edward. "*The Magnificent Seven,*" *Mediating Two Worlds: Cinematic Encounters in the Americas.* London: BFI Publishing, 1993, 15–25.

Buss, Robin. *Italian Films.* London: B. T. Batsford Ltd., 1989.

Butler, Jeremy G. *Star Texts: Image and Performance in Film and Television.* Detroit: Wayne State University Press, 1991.

Caldwell, Lesley. "Madri d'Italia: Film and the Fascist Concern with Motherhood," in Zygmunt G. Baranski and Shirley W. Vinall, eds., *Women and Italy: Essays in Gender, Culture, and History.* New York: St. Martin's Press, 1991, 43–64.

"Reproducers of the Nation: Women and the Family in Fascist Policy," in Davis Forgacs, ed., *Rethinking Italian Fascism.* London: Lawrence & Wishart, 1986, 110–41.

Campari, Roberto. *Il fantasma del bello: iconologia del cinema italiano.* Venice: Marsilio, 1994.

Hollywood-Cinecittà: il racconto che cambia. Milan: Feltrinelli, 1980.

Caretti, Lanfranco, and Giorgi Luti. *La letteratura Italiana: per saggi storicamente disposti, L'ottocento.* Milan: Mursia, 1985.

Casadio, Gianfranco. *Il grigio e il nero: spettacolo e propaganda nel cinema italiano negli anni trenta (1931-1943).* Ravenna: Longo, 1989.

Casadio, Gianfranco, Ernesto G. Laura, and Filippo Cristiano. *Telefoni bianchi: realtà e finzione nella società e nel cinema italiano degli anni Quaranta.* Ravenna: Longo, 1991.

Castagno, Paul. *The Early Commedia dell'arte 1530-1621: The Mannerist Context.* New York: Peter Lang, 1994.

Cawelti, John. *Adventure, Mystery, and Romance: Formula Stories as Art and Popular Culture.* Chicago: University of Chicago Press, 1976.

Chambers, Iain. "Maps, Music, and Memory," in David B. Clarke, ed., *The Cinematic City.* London: Routledge, 1997, 230-41.

Chandler, Charlotte. *I, Fellini.* New York: Random House, 1995.

Clarke, David B., ed. *The Cinematic City.* London: Routledge, 1997.

Cohan, Steve, and Ina Rae Hark, eds. *The Road Movie Book.* London: Routledge, 1997.
   eds. *Screening the Male: Exploring Masculinities in Hollywood Cinema.* London: Routledge, 1995.

Cook, David A. *A History of Narrative Film.* New York: W. W. Norton & Co., 1996.

Costantini, Costanzo, ed. *Conversations with Fellini.* San Diego: Harcourt, Brace & Co., 1995.
   ed. *Fellini on Fellini,* trans. Sohrab Sooroshian. London: Faber & Faber, 1994.

Crowdus, Gary. "We Believe in the Power of Cinema: An interview with Paolo and Vittorio Taviani," *Cinéaste* 3 (1983): 31-4.

Cumbow, Robert C. *Once Upon a Time in Sergio Leone.* Metuchen, N.Y.: Scarecrow Press, 1987.

Dagrada, Elena. "Television and Its Critics: A Parallel History," in David Forgacs and Robert Lumley, eds., *Italian Cultural Studies: An Introduction.* Oxford: Oxford University Press, 1996, 233-48.

Dalle Vacche, Angela. *The Body in the Mirror: Shapes of History in Italian Cinema.* Princeton: Princeton University Press, 1992.
   "Nouvelle Histoire, Italian Style," *Annali d'Italianistica* 6 (1988): 98-123.

De Felice, Renzo. *D'Annunzio Politico, 1918-1938.* Rome: Laterza, 1978.

de Grazia, Victoria. *The Culture of Consent: Mass Organization of Leisure in Fascist Italy.* Cambridge: Cambridge University Press, 1981.
   How Fascism Ruled Women: Italy, 1922-1945. Berkeley: University of California Press, 1992.

De Gusti, Luciano, ed. *Pier Paolo Pasolini: Il cinema in forma di poesia.* Pordenone: Edizioni cinemazero, 1979.

Deleuze, Gilles. *Cinema 1: The Movement Image.* Minneapolis: University of Minnesota Press, 1986.
   Cinema 2: The Time Image. Minneapolis: University of Minnesota Press, 1989.

Dickie, John. "Imagined Italies," in David Forgacs and Robert Lumley, eds., *Italian Cultural Studies: An Introduction.* Oxford: Oxford University Press, 1996, 19-34.

Dienst, Richard. *Still Life in Real Time: Theory after Television.* Durham: Duke University Press, 1995.

Di Scala, Spencer M. *Italy: From Revolution to Republic, 1700 to the Present.* Boulder, Colo.: Westview Press, 1998.

Doane, Mary Ann. *The Desire to Desire: The Woman's Film of the 1940's.* Bloomington: Indiana University Press, 1987.
   Femmes Fatales: Feminism, Film Theory, Psychoanalysis. New York: Routledge, 1991.

Doane, Mary Ann, Patricia Mellencamp, and Linda Williams. *Re-Vision: Essays in Feminist Criticism.* Los Angeles: American Film Institute, 1984.

Docker, John. *Postmodernism and Popular Culture: A Cultural History.* Cambridge: Cambridge University Press, 1994.

Donzelot, Jacques. *The Policing of Families,* trans. Robert Hurley. New York: Pantheon Books, 1979.

Douglass, William A. "The Southern Italian Family: A Critique," *Journal of Family History* 5(4) (Winter 1980): 338-59.

Dyer, Richard. *The Matter of Images: Essays on Representation.* London: Routledge, 1993.

    Stars. London: BFI Publishing, 1986.

Ellwood, D[avid]. W., "The 1948 Elections in Italy: A Cold War Propaganda Battle," *Historical Journal of Film, Radio, and Television* 13(1) (1993): 19-32.

Ellwood, David W., and Rob Kroes, eds. *Hollywood in Europe: Experiences of a Cultural Hegemony.* Amsterdam: VU University Press, 1994.

Elsaesser, Thomas. "Introduction," in Thomas Elsaesser with Adam Barker, eds., *Early Cinema: Space, Frame, Narrative.* London: BFI Publishing, 1990, 1-10.

Fenin, George N., and William K. Everson. *The Western: From Silents to Cinerama.* New York: Bonanza Books, 1962.

Feuer, Jane. *The Hollywood Musical.* London: BFI Publishing, 1982.

Filippuci, Paola. "Anthropological Perspectives on Culture in Italy," in David Forgacs and David Lumley, eds., *Italian Cultural Studies: An Introduction.* Oxford: Oxford University Press, 1996, 52-71.

Fischer, Lucy. *Shot/Countershot: Film Tradition and Women's Cinema.* Princeton: Princeton University Press, 1989.

Forgacs, David. "Cultural Consumption, 1940 to 1990s," in David Forgacs and David Lumley, eds., *Italian Cultural Studies: An Introduction.* Oxford: Oxford University Press, 1996, 273-91.

    Italian Culture in the Industrial Era: Cultural Industries, Politics, and the Public. Manchester: Manchester University Press, 1990.

Forgacs, David, and David Lumley, eds. *Italian Cultural Studies: An Introduction.* Oxford: Oxford University Press, 1996.

Foucault, Michel. *The History of Sexuality,* vol. I: *An Introduction.* New York: Vintage, 1980.

Frayling, Christopher. *Spaghetti Westerns: Cowboys and Europeans from Karl May to Sergio Leone.* London: Routledge & Kegan Paul, 1981.

Gatteschi, Giuseppe. *The Grandeur That Was Rome.* New York: Hastings Publishers, 1954.

Gaudreault, André. "Film Narrative, Narration: The Cinema of the Lumière Brothers," in Thomas Elsaesser with Adam Barker, eds., *Early Cinema: Space, Frame, Narrative.* London: BFI Publishing, 1990, 68-76.

George, David, and Christopher J. Gossip, eds. *Studies in the Commedia dell'arte.* Cardiff: University of Wales Press, 1993.

Gieri, Manuela. *Contemporary Italian Filmmaking: Strategies of Subversion - Pirandello, Fellini, Scola and the Directors of the New Generation.* Toronto: University of Toronto Press, 1995.

Gili, Jean A. *L'Italie de Mussolini et son cinema.* Paris: Henri Veyrier, 1985.

Ginsborg, Paul. *A History of Contemporary Italy: Society and Politics 1943-1988.* London: Penguin Books, 1990.

Gledhill, Christine. *Home Is Where the Heart Is: Studies in Melodrama and the Woman's Film.* London: BFI Publishing, 1987.

    ed. *Stardom: Industry of Desire.* London: Routledge, 1991.

Godt, Clareece G. *The Mobile Spectacle: Variable Perspective in Manzoni's I promessi sposi.* New York: Peter Lang, 1998.

Golsan, Richard J. *Fascism, Aesthetics, and Culture.* Hanover, N.H.: University Press of New England, 1992.

Gordon, Mel. *Lazzi: The Comic Routines of the Commedia dell'arte.* New York: Performing Arts Journal, 1983.

Gordon, Robert S. C. *Pasolini: Forms of Subjectivity.* Oxford: Clarendon Press, 1996.

Gori, Gianfranco Mino. *Patria diva: La storia d'Italia nel film del ventennio.* Florence: Usher, 1988.

Gramsci, Antonio. *The Prison Notebooks,* 2 vols. [so far], ed. and trans. Joseph Buttigieg. New York: Columbia University Press, 1992, 1996.

Selections from the Cultural Writings, ed. David Forgacs. Cambridge, Mass.: Harvard University Press, 1985.

Selections from the Prison Notebooks, ed. and trans. Quintin Hoare and Geoffrey Nowell-Smith. New York: International Publishers, 1978.

The Southern Question, ed. and trans. Pasquale Verdiccchio. West Lafayette, Ind.: Bordighera Inc., 1995.

Graziosi, Mariella. "Gender Struggle and the Social Manipulation and Ideological Use of Gender Identity in the Interwar Years," in Robin Pickering-Iazzi, ed., *Mothers of Invention: Women, Italian Fascism, and Culture.* Minneapolis: University of Minnesota Press, 1995, 26-52.

Green, Martin, and John Swan. *The Triumph of Pierrot: The Commedia dell'arte and the Modern Imagination.* New York: Macmillan Publishing Co., 1986.

Greene, Naomi. "Fascism in Recent Italian Films," *Film Criticism* 6(1) (Fall 1981): 31-41.

Pier Paolo Pasolini: Cinema as Heresy. Princeton: Princeton University Press, 1990.

Greenleaf, Barbara Kaye. *Children Through the Ages: A History of Childhood.* New York: McGraw-Hill, 1978.

Grignaffini, Giovanna. "Female Identity and the Italian Cinema of the 1950s," in Giuliana Bruno and Maria Nadotti, eds., *Off Screen: Women and Film in Italy.* London: Routledge, 1988, 111-24.

Gundle, Stephen. "Fame, Fashion and Style: The Italian Star System," in David Forgacs and Robert Lumley, eds., *Italian Cultural Studies: An Introduction.* Oxford: Oxford University Press, 1996, 309-27.

"Two Ideas of Stardom," in David Forgacs and Robert Lumley, eds., *Italian Cultural Studies: An Introduction.* Oxford: Oxford University Press, 1996, 347-50.

Gunning, Tom. "The Cinema of Attractions: Early Film, Its Spectator and the Avant-Garde," in Thomas Elsaesser with Adam Barker, eds., *Early Cinema: Space, Frame, Narrative.* London: BFI Publishing, 1990, 56-63.

"Non-Continuity, Continuity, Discontinuity: A Theory of Genres in Early Films," in Thomas Elsaesser with Adam Barker, eds., *Early Cinema: Space, Frame, Narrative.* London: BFI Publishing, 1990, 86-95.

"Primitive Cinema: A Frame-Up? Or, The Trick's on Us," in Thomas Elsaesser with Adam Barker, eds., *Early Cinema: Space, Frame, Narrative.* London: BFI Publishing, 1990, 95-104.

Hall, Stuart. *The Hard Road to Renewal.* London: Verso, 1988.

Hansen, Miriam. "Early Cinema – Whose Public Sphere?," in Thomas Elsaesser with Adam Barker, eds., *Early Cinema: Space, Frame, Narrative.* London: BFI Publishing, 1990, 228-47.

Harper, Sue. "Historical Pleasures: Gainsborough Costume Melodramas," in Christine Gledhill, ed., *Home Is Where the Heart Is.* London: BFI Publishing, 1987, 167-96.

Hay, James. "Invisible Cities/Visible Geographies: Toward a Cultural Geography of Italian Television in the 1990s," in Horace Newcomb, ed., *Television: The Critical View*. New York: Oxford University Press, 1994, 602-15.

Popular Film Culture in Fascist Italy: The Passing of the Rex. Bloomington: Indiana University Press, 1987.

Hughes, H. Stuart. *Prisoners of Hope: The Silver Age of the Italian Jews, 1827-1974*. Cambridge, Mass.: Harvard University Press, 1983.

The United States and Italy. Cambridge, Mass.: Harvard University Press, 1979.

Jarratt, Vernon. *The Italian Cinema*. New York: Macmillan, 1951.

Julian, Philippe. *D'Annunzio: Adventurer, Poet, Lover of Genius*. London: Pall Mall Press, 1972.

Kertzer, David I. *Family Life in Central Italy, 1880-1910: Sharecropping, Wage Labor, and Coresidence*. New Brunswick: Rutgers University Press, 1984.

Kertzer, David I., and Richard P. Saller, eds. *The Family in Italy: From Antiquity to the Present*. New Haven: Yale University Press, 1991.

Kezich, Tullio. *Fellini*. Milan: Rizzoli, 1988.

Kitses, Jim. *Horizons West: Anthony Mann, Budd Boetticher, Sam Peckinpah - Studies of Authorship within the Western*. Bloomington: Indiana University Press, 1969.

Kline, T. Jefferson. *Bertolucci's Dream Loom: A Psychoanalytic Study of Cinema*. Amherst, Mass: University of Massachusetts Press, 1987.

Kolker, Robert Phillip. *The Altering Eye: Contemporary International Cinema*. Oxford: Oxford University Press, 1983.

Bernardo Bertolucci. New York: Oxford University Press, 1985.

Kracauer, Siegfried. *The Mass Ornament: Weimar Essays*. Cambridge, Mass.: Harvard University Press, 1995.

Kuhn, Annette. *Cinema, Censorship and Sexuality, 1909-1925*. New York: Routledge, 1988.

Landy, Marcia. *Fascism in Film: The Italian Commercial Cinema, 1931-1943*. Princeton: Princeton University Press, 1986.

Film, Politics, and Gramsci. Minneapolis: University of Minnesota Press, 1995.

The Folklore of Consensus: Theatricality in the Italian Cinema, 1930-1943. Albany: State University of New York Press, 1998.

Imitations of Life: A Reader on Film and Television Melodrama. Detroit: Wayne State University Press, 1991.

Laura, Ernesto G. *Comedy Italian Style*. Rome: National Association of Motion Pictures and Affiliated Industries, n.d.

Lavery, David. "'News from Africa': Fellini-Grotesque," *Post Script: Essays in Film and the Humanities* 9(1-2) (Fall 1989/Winter 1990): 82-99.

Leprohon, Pierre. *The Italian Cinema*. New York: Praeger Publishers, 1972.

Levey, Michael. *Rococo to Revolution: Major Trends in Eighteenth-Century Painting*. New York: Frederick A. Praeger, 1969.

Levi, Giovanni, and Jean-Claude Schmitt, eds. *A History of Young People in the West*. Cambridge, Mass: Belknap Press, 1997.

Lewin, David J. *Opera through Other Eyes*. Stanford, Calif.: Stanford University Press, 1994.

Liehm, Mira. *Passion and Defiance: Film in Italy from 1942 to the Present*. Berkeley: University of California Press, 1984.

Lizzani, Carlo. *Il cinema italiano 1895-1979*. Rome: Riuniti, 1979.

Lucente, Gregory L. *Crosspaths in Literary Theory and Criticism: Italy and the United States*. Stanford, Calif.: Stanford University Press, 1997.

McArthur, Colin. "Chinese Boxes and Russian Dolls: Tracking the Elusive Cinematic City," in David B. Clarke, ed., *The Cinematic City.* London: Routledge, 1987, 19–46.

Macciocchi, Maria-Antonietta. *La donna "nera": Consenso femminile e fascismo.* Milan: Feltrinelli, 1976.

Macry, Paolo. "Rethinking a Stereotype: Territorial Differences and Family Models in the Modernization of Italy," *Journal of Modern Italian Studies* 2(2) (Summer 1997): 188-214.

Mancini, Elaine. *Struggles of the Italian Film Industry during Fascism, 1930-1935.* Ann Arbor: UMI Press, 1985.

Mangione, Jerre, and Ben Morreale. *La Storia: Five Centuries of the Italian and American Experience.* New York: Harper Perennial, 1992.

Marcus, Millicent. *Filmmaking by the Book: Italian Cinema and Literary Adaptation.* Baltimore: Johns Hopkins University Press, 1993.

   Italian Film in the Light of Neorealism. Princeton: Princeton University Press, 1986.

Martini, Andrea, ed. *La bella forma: Poggioli, i calligrafici e dintorni.* Venice: Marsilio, 1992.

Marx, Karl. *Capital,* vol. 1, trans. Cedar and Eden Paul. New York: Dutton, 1977.

Micciché, Lino. *Cinema italiano degli anni '70.* Venice: Marsilio, 1989.

   Cinema italiano: gli anni '60 e oltre. Venice: Marsilio, 1995.

   "L'ideologia e la bella forma: il gruppo 'Cinema' e il formalismo italiano," in Andrea Martini, ed., *La bella forma: Poggioli, i calligrafici e dintorni.* Venice: Marsilio, 1992, 1-28.

Micheli, Paola. *Il cinema di Blasetti, parlo così: un analisi linguistica (1929-1942).* Rome: Bulzoni Press, 1990.

Michelone, Guido. *Invito al cinema di Roberto Rossellini.* Milan: Mursia, 1996.

Mida, Massimo, and Lorenzo Quagletti. *Dai telefoni bianchi al neorealismo.* Rome-Bari: Laterza, 1980.

Mitchell, Tony. "Berlusconi, Italian Television and Recent Italian Cinema: Reviewing *The Icicle Thief.*" *Film Criticism* 21(1) (Fall 1996): 13-33.

   "Towards Utopia: By Way of Research, Detachment, and Involvement," *Sight and Sound* 47(3), 171-8.

Morgan, Philip. *Italian Fascism, 1919-1945.* New York: St. Martin's Press, 1995.

Mountjoy, Alan B. *The Mezzogiorno.* Oxford: Oxford University Press, 1973.

Murray, Edward. *Fellini: The Artist.* New York: Frederick Ungar, 1985.

Musser, Charles. "The Travel Genre in 1903-1904: Moving toward Fictional Narratives," in Thomas Elsaesser with Adam Barker, eds., *Early Cinema: Space, Frame, Narrative.* London: BFI Publishing, 1990, 123-33.

Naremore, James. *Acting in the Cinema.* Berkeley: University of California Press, 1988.

Nichols, Nina Da Vinci, and Jana O'Keefe Bazzoni. *Pirandello and Film.* Lincoln: University of Nebraska Press, 1995.

Nicoll, Allardyce. *Masks, Mimes, and Miracles: Studies in the Popular Theatre.* New York: Cooper Square Publishers, Inc., 1963.

Nietzsche, Friedrich. *The Gay Science,* trans. Walter Kaufmann. New York: Vintage Books, 1974.

   "The Uses and Disadvantages of History for the Present Time," *Untimely Meditations,* ed. Daniel Breazeale. Cambridge: Cambridge University Press, 1983, 57-125.

Nowell-Smith, Geoffrey. "The Italian Cinema Under Fascism," in David Forgacs, ed., *Rethinking Italian Fascism.* London: Lawrence & Wishart, 1986, 142-61.

   Luchino Visconti. London: Secker & Warburg, 1973.

Ojetti, Ugo. *La pittura dell'ottocento.* Milan: Bestetti & Tuminelli, 1929.

Olson, Roberta. *Romanticism and Revolution in 19th Century Italian Painting.* New York: American Federation of the Arts, 1992.

Pacifici, Sergio. *From Verismo to Experimentalism: Essays on the Modern Italian Novel.* Bloomington: University of Indiana Press, 1969.

The Modern Italian Novel from Manzoni to Svevo. Carbondale: Southern Illinois University Press, 1967.

Paglai, Morena. *Mito e precarietà: studi su Pascoli, D'Annunzio, Rosso di San Secondo, Malaparte, Diddi.* Florence: Franco Casati Press, 1989.

Pasolini, Pier Paolo. *Heretical Empiricism*, trans. Ben Lawton and Louise Barnett. Bloomington: Indiana University Press, 1988.

Lutheran Letters, trans. Stuart Hood. Manchester: Caracanet Press, 1983.

Passerini, Luisa. "Gender Relations," in David Forgacs and Robert Lumley, eds., *Italian Cultural Studies: An Introduction.* Oxford: Oxford University Press, 1996, 144-60.

Petrie, Duncan, ed. *Screening Europe: Image and Identity in the Contemporary European Cinema.* London: BFI Publishing, 1992.

Pickering-Iazzi, Robin. *Politics of the Visible: Writing Women, Culture, and Fascism.* Minneapolis: University of Minnesota Press, 1997.

ed. *Mothers of Invention: Women, Italian Fascism, and Culture.* Minneapolis: University of Minnesota Press, 1995.

Pinkus, Karen. *Bodily Regimes: Italian Advertising under Fascism.* Minneapolis: University of Minnesota Press, 1995.

Plumb, J. H. "The Great Change in Children," in Arlene Skolnick, ed., *Rethinking Childhood: Perspectives on Development and Society.* Boston: Little, Brown & Co., 1976, 205-14.

Polan, Dana. *Power and Paranoia: History, Narrative and the American Cinema.* New York: Columbia University Press, 1986.

Pratt, Jeff. "Two Images of Catholicism," in David Forgacs and Robert Lumley, eds., *Italian Cultural Studies: An Introduction.* Oxford: Oxford University Press, 1996, 178-83.

Prigozy, Ruth. "A Modern Pietà: De Sica's *Two Women* [1961] from the Novel by Alberto Moravia," in Andrew Horton and Joan Magretta, eds., *Modern European Filmmakers and the Art of Adaptation.* New York: Frederick Ungar, 1981, 78-89.

Re, Lucia. "Fascist Theories of 'Woman' and the Construction of Gender," in Robin Pickering-Iazzi, ed., *Mothers of Invention: Women, Italian Fascism, and Culture.* Minneapolis: University of Minnesota Press, 1995, 76-100.

"Gabriele D'Annunzio's Theater of Memory: Il Vittoriale degli Italiani," *Journal of Decorative and Propaganda Arts, 1875-1945* 3 (Winter 1987): 6-52.

Redi, Riccardo, ed. *Cinema italiano sotto il fascismo.* Venice: Marsilio, 1979.

Reich, Jacqueline. "Reading, Writing, and Rebellion: Collectivity, Specularity, and Sexuality in Italian Schoolgirl Comedies," in Robin Pickering-Iazzi, ed., *Mothers of Invention: Women, Italian Fascism, and Culture.* Minneapolis: University of Minnesota Press, 1995, 220-51.

Restivo, Angelo. *The Cinema of Economic Miracles.* Unpublished dissertation, Dept. of Critical Studies, University of Southern California, 1997.

"The Nation, the Body, and the *Autostrada*," in Steve Cohan and Ina Rae Hark, eds., *The Road Movie Book.* London: Routledge, 1997, 233-49.

Rifkin, Ned. *Antonioni's Visual Language.* Ann Arbor: UMI Press, 1977.

Roda, Vittorio. "Appunti sulla costruzione del personnagio dannunziano," *Annali d'Italianistica* 5 (1987): 87-111.

Rodowick, D. N. *Gilles Deleuze's Time Machine.* Durham: Duke University Press, 1997.

Rohdie, Sam. *Antonioni*. London: BFI Publishing, 1990.

The Passion of Pier Paolo Pasolini. Bloomington: University of Indiana Press, 1995.

Rose, Gillian. *Feminism and Geography: The Limits of Geographical Knowledge*. Minneapolis: University of Minnesota Press, 1993.

Rosenstone, Robert A., ed. *Revisioning History: Film and the Construction of a New Past*. Princeton: Princeton University Press, 1995.

Rosenthal, Stuart. *The Cinema of Federico Fellini*. South Brunswick: A. S. Barnes & Co., 1976.

Rossellini, Roberto. *My Method: Writings and Interviews,* ed. Adriano Aprà. New York: Marsilio, 1992.

Rossi, Giovanna. "Why Young Adults Stay at Home Longer: The Italian Case," *Journal of Family Issues* 17(6) (November 1993): 627-54.

Roth, Lane. *Film, Semiotics, Metz, and Leone's Trilogy*. New York: Garland, 1983.

Said, Edward. *Culture and Imperialism*. New York: Knopf, 1993.

Orientalism. New York: Vintage Books, 1979.

Salizatto, Claver, ed. *Prima della rivoluzione: schermi italiani 1960-1969*. Venice: Marsilio, 1989.

Salizatto, Claver, and Vito Zagarrio. *La corona di ferro: un modo di produzione italiano*. Rome: Di Giacomo, 1985.

Saraceno, Chiara. "Il circolo vizioso della famiglia contemporanea: la famiglia fa la madre, la madre fa la famiglia," *La critica sociologica* 35 (Autumn 1975): 8-18.

Savio, Francesco. *Cinecittà anni trenta,* 3 vols. Rome: Bulzoni, 1979.

Schifano, Laurence. *Le cinema Italien, 1845-1995: Crise et création*. Paris: Nathan, 1995.

Schatz, Thomas. *Hollywood Genres: Formulas, Filmmaking, and the Studio System*. New York: Random House, 1981.

Schwartz, Barth David. *Pasolini Requiem*. New York: Vintage, 1992.

Scola, Flaminio. *Scenarios of the Commedia dell'arte: Flaminio Scala's Il teatro delle favole rappresentative,* trans. Henry F. Salerno. New York: New York University Press, 1967.

Sennett, Ted. *Laughing in the Dark: Movie Comedy from Groucho to Woody Allen*. New York: St. Martin's Press, 1992.

Servadio, Gaia. *Luchino Visconti: A Biography*. New York: Franklin Watts, 1983.

Shaviro, Steven. *The Cinematic Body*. Minneapolis: University of Minnesota Press, 1993.

Sillanpoa, Wallace P. "Pasolini's Gramsci," *Modern Language Notes* (1981): 120-37.

Sitney, P. Adams. *Vital Crises in Italian Cinema: Iconography, Stylistics, Politics*. Austin: University of Texas Press, 1995.

Skolnick, Arlene. *Rethinking Childhood: Perspectives on Development and Society*. Boston: Little, Brown & Co., 1976.

Smith, Paul. *Clint Eastwood: A Cultural Production*. Minneapolis: University of Minnesota Press, 1993.

Sorlin, Pierre. *European Cinema/European Societies, 1939-1990*. London: Routledge, 1991.

"Italian Cinema's Rebirth, 1937-1943: A Paradox of Fascism," *Historical Journal of Film and Video* 14(1) (1994): 3-13.

Italian National Cinema 1896-1996. London: Routledge, 1996.

"*The Night of the Shooting Stars*: Fascism, Resistance, and the Liberation of Italy," in Rosenstone, Robert A., ed., *Revisioning History: Film and the Construction of a New Past*. Princeton: Princeton University Press, 1995, 77-154.

Springer, Caroline. *The Marble Wilderness: Ruins and Representations in Italian Romanticism.* Cambridge: Cambridge University Press, 1987.

Stack, Oswald. *Pasolini on Pasolini: Interviews with Oswald Stack.* Bloomington: Indiana University Press, 1970.

Studlar, Gaylyn. *In the Realm of Pleasure: Von Sternberg, Dietrich, and the Masochistic Aesthetic.* Urbana: University of Illinois Press, 1988.

_____. *This Mad Masquerade: Stardom and Masculinity in the Jazz Age.* New York: Columbia University Press, 1996.

Taves, Brian. *The Romance of Adventure: The Genre of Historical Adventure Movies.* Jackson: University of Mississippi Press, 1993.

Theweleit, Klaus. *Male Fantasies,* 2 vols. (vol. 1: *Women, Floods, Bodies, History;* vol. 2: *Male Bodies, Psychoanalyzing the White Terror*), trans. Stephen Conway. Minneapolis: University of Minnesota Press, 1987, 1989.

Thompson, Doug. *State Control in Fascist Italy, 1925-1943: Culture and Conformity.* Manchester: Manchester University Press, 1991.

Tonetti, Claretta Micheletti. *Bernardo Bertolucci: The Cinema of Ambiguity.* New York: Twayne Publishers, 1995.

Tyler, Parker. *Magic and Myth of the Movies.* New York: Simon & Schuster, 1970.

Vardac, A. Nicholas. *Stage to Screen: Theatrical Method from Garrick to Griffith.* New York: Benjamin Blom, 1949.

Vaughan, Dai. "Let There Be Lumière," in Thomas Elsaesser with Adam Barker, eds., *Early Cinema: Space, Frame, Narrative.* London: BFI Publishing, 1990, 63-8.

Vené, Gian Franco. *L'ideologia piccolo borghese: riformismo e tentazioni conservatrici di una non-classe nell'Italia repubblicana, 1945-1980.* Venice: Marsilio, 1980.

Verdone, Luca. *I film di Alessandro Blasetti.* Rome: Gremese, 1989.

Viano, Maurizio. *A Certain Realism: Making Use of Pasolini's Film Theory and Practice.* Berkeley: University of California Press, 1993.

Violi, Patrizia. "Language and the Female Subject," in Giuliana Bruno and Maria Nadotti, eds., *Off Screen: Women & Film in Italy.* London: Routledge, 1988, 139-51.

Vitti, Antonio. *Giuseppe De Santis and Postwar Italian Cinema.* Toronto: University of Toronto Press, 1996.

Viviani, Christian. "Who Is without Sin: The Maternal Melodrama in American Film, 1930-1939," *Wide Angle* 4 (1980): 4-17.

Wagstaff, Christopher. "Cinema," in David Forgacs and Robert Lumley, eds., *Italian Cultural Studies: An Introduction.* Oxford: Oxford University Press, 1996, 216-33.

Waller, Marguerite. "Decolonizing the Screen: From *Ladri di biciclette* to *Ladri di saponette,*" in Beverly Allen and Mary Russo, eds., *Revisioning Italy: National Identity and Global Culture.* Minneapolis: University of Minnesota Press, 1997, 253-75.

Wanrooji, Bruno. "Dollars and Decency: Italian Catholics and Hollywood," in David E. Ellwood and Rob Kroes, eds., *Hollywood in Europe: Experiences of a Cultural Hegemony.* Amsterdam: VU University Press, 1994, 247-66.

Willemen, Paul, ed. *Pier Paolo Pasolini.* London: BFI Publishing, 1977.

Witcombe, R. T. *The New Italian Cinema: Studies in Dance and Despair.* New York: Oxford University Press, 1982.

Wright, Will. *Sixguns and Society: A Structural Study of the Western.* Berkeley: University of California Press, 1975.

Wyke, Maria. *Projecting the Past: Ancient Rome, Cinema and History.* New York: Routledge, 1997.

Filmography

Note: An effort has been made to distinguish bona fide American/English release titles (in italics) from mere translated titles (in roman type), and to provide the date of release, not production.

Accattone, dir. Pier Paolo Pasolini (Cino del Duca/Arco Film, 1961)

Acciaio (Steel), dir. Walter Ruttmann (Cines, 1933)

Agnese Visconti, dir. Giovanni Pastrone (Itala-Film, 1910)

L'albero degli zoccoli (*The Tree of Wooden Clogs*), dir. Ermanno Olmi (RAI/Italnoleggio Cinematografica/GPC [Milan], 1978)

Allonsanfán, dir. Paolo and Vittorio Taviani (Una Cooperativa Cinematografica, 1974)

Amarcord, dir. Federico Fellini (FC Produzione/PECF, 1974)

Lamerica, dir. Gianni Amelio (Cecchi Gori Group, 1994)

L'assedio dell'Alcazar (*The Siege of the Alcazar*), dir. Augusto Genina (Bassoli, 1940)

Assunta Spina, dir. Gustavo Serena (Caesar, 1915)

L'avventura, dir. Michelangelo Antonioni (Cino del Duca/PCE/Lyre, 1960)

Ballerine, dir. Gustav Machaty (AFI, 1936)

Batticuore (*Heartbeat*), dir. Mario Camerini (ERA, 1939)

I bambini ci guardano (*The Children Are Watching Us,* a.k.a. *The Little Martyr*), dir. Vittorio De Sica (Scalera/Invicta, 1942)

Bell'Antonio (a.k.a. *Il bell'Antonio*) (Handsome Antonio), dir. Mauro Bolognini (Cina del Duca/Arco Film/Lyre Cinématographique, 1960)

Bellissima (The Most Beautiful)*,* dir. Luchino Visconti (Film Bellissima, 1951)

Il birichino di papà (*Papa's Little Devil*), dir. Raffaello Matarazzo (Lux, 1943)

La bocca sulla strada (The Man on the Street), dir. Vincenzo Leone (Cinecittà/Fulcro, 1941)

Una breve vacanza (*A Brief Vacation*, a.k.a. *The Holiday*), dir. Vittorio De Sica (Verona Cinematografica, 1973)

Buon giorno, Babilonia! (*Good Morning, Babylon!*), dir. Paolo and Vittorio Taviani (Italy–France–USA, Filmtre/Raiuno, 1986)

Il buono, il brutto, il cattivo (*The Good, the Bad, and the Ugly*), dir. Sergio Leone (PEA, 1966)

Cabiria, dir. Piero Fosco (pseud. Giovanni Pastrone) (Itala-Film, 1914)

La caduta degli dei (*The Damned,* a.k.a. *Götterdämmerung*), dir. Luchino Visconti (Italy–W. Germany, Praesidens/Pegaso, 1969)

La caduta di Troia (The Fall of Troy), dir. Giovanni Pastrone (Itala-Film, 1911)

Camicia nera (Black Shirt), dir. Giovacchino Forzano (LUCE, 1933)

Campo de'fiori (Field of Flowers), dir. Mario Bonnard (Cines, 1943)

Il cappello a tre punte (*The Three-Cornered Hat*), dir. Mario Camerini (Lido Film, 1935) (remade as *La bella mugnaia* [*The Miller's Beautiful Wife*], 1955)

409

Il carnevale di Venezia (*Carnival in Venice*), dir. Giuseppe Adami and Giacomo Gentilomo (Romulus/Lupa, 1940)

Caro diario (*Dear Diary*), dir. Nanni Moretti (Italy-France, Sacher Film/Banfilm/La Sept Cinema/RAI/Studio Canal Plus, 1993)

Il Casanova di Federico Fellini (a.k.a. *Fellini Casanova*), dir. Federico Fellini (PEA/TCF, 1976)

Catene (Chains), dir. Raffaello Matarazzo (Labor Film-Labor Titanus, 1949)

Cavalleria, dir. Goffredo Alessandrini (ICI, 1936)

Cavalleria rusticana, dir. Amleto Palermi (Scalera Films, 1939)

C'era una volta il West (*Once Upon a Time in the West*), dir. Sergio Leone (Rafran, 1968) (based on *Johnny Guitar*)

C'eravamo tanto amati (*We All Loved Each Other So Much*), dir. Ettore Scola (Dean Cinematografica/Delta, 1974)

La ciociara (*Two Women*), dir. Vittorio De Sica (Champion/Marceau/Cocinor/SGC, 1960)

La città delle donne (*City of Women*), dir. Federico Fellini (Opera Film/Gaumont [France], 1980)

Il colosso di Rodi (*The Colossus of Rhodes*), dir. Sergio Leone (Italy-Spain, Filmar, 1961)

Come le foglie (Like the Leaves), dir. Mario Camerini (ICI, 1934) (based on the play by Giuseppe Giacosa)

Comizi d'amore (*Love's Meetings*), dir. Pier Paolo Pasolini (Arco Film, 1964)

I compagni (*The Organizer;* lit.: The Comrades), dir. Mario Monicelli (Lux/Vides/Mediteranée/Cinema/Avala, 1963)

Condottieri, dir. Luis Trenker (ENIC, 1937)

Il conformista (*The Conformist*), dir. Bernardo Bertolucci (Italy-France-W. Germany, Mars/Marianne/Maran, 1970)

La contessa Sara (*The Countess Sara*), dir. Roberto Roberti (Bertini Film, 1919)

La corona di ferro (*The Iron Crown*), dir. Alessandro Blasetti (ENIC-Lux, 1941)

Cristo si è fermato a Eboli (*Eboli,* a.k.a. *Christ Stopped at Eboli*), dir. Francesco Rosi (Vides/RAI/Action/Gaumont, 1979)

Cronaca di un amore (*Story of a Love Affair,* a.k.a *Chronicle of a Love*), dir. Michelangelo Antonioni (Villani Films, 1950)

Darò un milione (*I'll Give a Million*) dir. Mario Camerini (Novella Film, 1935) (American remake dir. Walter Lang, 1938)

Dellamorte dellamore (*Cemetery Man*), dir. Michele Soavi (Italy-France, Audifilm/Urania Film, 1996) (based on Italian comic book series *Dylan Dog*)

Deserto rosso (*Red Desert*), dir. Michelangelo Antonioni (France-Italy, Cinematografica Federiz [Rome]/Francoriz [Paris], 1964)

1860 (*Diciotto sessanta*) dir. Alessandro Blasetti (Cines, 1934)

Divorzio all'italiana (*Divorce - Italian Style*), dir. Pietro Germi (Lux/Vides/Galatea, 1961)

Django, dir. Sergio Corbucci (Italy-Spain, BCR, 1966)

La dolce vita (a.k.a. *The Sweet Life*), dir. Federico Fellini (Riama/Pathé, 1960)

Dora Nelson, dir. Mario Soldati (Urbe, 1939)

Il dottor Antonio, dir. Enrico Guazzoni (Manderfilm, 1937)

Due soldi di speranza (*Two Cents Worth of Hope*; a.k.a *Two Pennyworth of Hope*), dir. Renato Castellani (Universal-Cines, 1952)

L'eclisse (*The Eclipse*), dir. Michelangelo Antonioni (France-Italy, Cineriz [Rome]/Interopa/Paris Film, 1962)

Ercole al centro della terra (*Hercules in the Haunted World*), dir. Mario Bava (Omnia/Sp.A. Cinematografica, 1961)

Ercole alla conquista de Atlantide (*Hercules and the Captive Women;* a.k.a. *Hercules Conquers Atlantis*), dir. Vittorio Cottafavi (Italy-France, Comptoir Français du Film/ Sp.A. Cinematografica, 1961) (U.S. release 1963)

Ercole contro i figli del sole (*Hercules against the Sons of the Sun*), dir. Osvaldo Civirani (Wonderfilm Produzione Cinematografica/Hispamer, 1964)

Ercole contro Roma (*Hercules against Rome*), dir. Piero Pierott (Romana Film, 1964)

Ercole e la regina di Lidia (*Hercules Unchained*), dir. Pietro Francisci (Italy-France, Lux/Galatea/Lux Compagnie Cinematographique de France, 1959)

Ercole, Sansone, e Ulisse (*Hercules, Samson, and Ulysses*), dir. Pietro Francisci (Lux/ Galatea, 1965)

La famiglia (*The Family*), dir. Ettore Scola (Massfilm, 1987)

Le fatiche di Ercole (*Hercules;* a.k.a. *The Labors of Hercules*), dir. Pietro Francisci (Italy-USA, Oscar-Galatea Films, 1957) (U.S. release 1959)

Fellini Satyricon (a.k.a. *Satyricon*), dir. Federico Fellini (PAA/UA/PEA, 1969)

Fellini's Roma (a.k.a. *Roma*), dir. Federico Fellini (Ultra/UA, 1972)

Figaro e la sua gran'giornata (*Figaro's Big Day*), dir. Mario Camerini (Cines, 1931)

I figli di nessuno (*Nobody's Children*), dir. Raffaello Matarazzo (Labor-Titanus, 1951)

Film d'amore e anarchia (a.k.a. *Amore e anarchia; Love and Anarchy*), dir. Lina Wertmüller (Euro International, 1972)

Fior di male (Flowers of Evil), dir. Carmine Gallone (Cines, 1915)

Il fu Mattia Pascal (*L'Homme de nulle part; The Late Mathias Pascal*), dir. Pierre Chenal (Général Productions/Ala-Colosseum, 1937) (based on a story by Luigi Pirandello)

Il fuoco (The Fire), dir. Giovanni Pastrone (Itala-Film, 1915)

Il gattopardo (*The Leopard*), dir. Luchino Visconti (France-Italy, GTCF/Titanus/SNPC/ GPC, 1963)

Gelosia (Jealousy), dir. Ferdinando Maria Poggioli (Universal-Cines, 1943) (remake dir. Pietro Germi, 1953) (based on a novel by Luigi Capuana)

Il generale Della Rovere (*General Della Rovere*), dir. Roberto Rossellini (Italy-France, Zebra/Gaumont, 1959)

Gente del Po, dir. Michelangelo Antonioni (Artisti Associati/ICET-Carpi [Milan], 1943-7)

Il giardino dei Finzi-Contini (*The Garden of the Finzi-Continis*), dir. Vittorio De Sica (Italy-W. Germany, Documento Film/CCC Filmkunst, 1970)

Ginger e Fred (*Ginger and Fred*), dir. Federico Fellini (Italy-France-Germany, PEA [Rome]/Revcom Films/Les Films Ariane/FR3 Films [Paris]/Stella Films/Anthea [Munich], 1986)

Una giornata particolare (*A Special Day*), dir. Ettore Scola (Italy-Canada, Champion/ Canafox, 1997)

Giù la testa (*Duck, You Sucker;* a.k.a. *A Fistful of Dynamite*), dir. Sergio Leone (Rafran, 1971)

Giuseppe Verdi (*The Life and Music of Giuseppe Verdi*), dir. Carmine Gallone (Grandi Film Storici, 1938)

Il grande appello (*The Last Roll-Call*), dir. Mario Camerini (Artisti Associati, 1936)

Il grido (*The Outcry;* a.k.a. *The Cry*), dir. Michelangelo Antonioni (Sp.A. Cinematografica/Robert Alexander, 1957)

Ieri, oggi, domani (*Yesterday, Today and Tomorrow*), dir. Vittorio De Sica (CCCC [Rome]/Les Films Concordia [Paris], 1963)

Inferno, dir. Francesco Bertolini and Adolfo Padovan (Saffi-Milano Film, 1911)

Intervista, dir. Federico Fellini (Aljosha/RAI Uno/Cinecittà, 1987) (U.S. release 1992)

Io speriamo che me la cavo (*Ciao, Professore!* lit.: Me Let's Hope I Make It), dir. Lina Wertmüller (Ciro Ippolito/Eurolux Produzione, 1993)

Io t'ho incontrata a Napoli (I Met You in Naples), dir. Pietro Francisci (EDI Film, 1946) (remake of *Assunta Spina*)

Kaos, dir. Paolo and Vittorio Taviani (RAI/Filmtre, 1984)

Ladri di biciclette (*The Bicycle Thief,* a.k.a. *Bicycle Thieves*), dir. Vittorio De Sica (PDS-ENIC, 1948)

Ladri di saponette (*The Icicle Thief*), dir. Maurizio Nichetti (Bambù-Reteitalia, 1989)

Il ladro di bambini (*Stolen Children*), dir. Gianni Amelio (Italy-France, Erre-Raidue, 1992)

Lo chiamavano Trinità (*They Call Me Trinity*), dir. E. B. Clucher (pseud. Enzo Barboni) (West Film, 1970)

Lorenzino de' Medici, dir. Guido Brignone (Monenti, 1935)

La macchina ammazzacattivi (*The Machine to Kill Bad People*), dir. Roberto Rossellini (Universalia/Tevere Film, 1948-52)

Maciste e la regina di Samar (*Hercules against the Moon Men*), dir. Giacomo Gentilomo (Comptoir Français du Film/Nike Cinematografica, 1964)

Il mafioso, dir. Alberto Lattuada (Antonio Cervi Prod., 1962)

Mamma Roma, dir. Pier Paolo Pasolini (Arco Film/Cineriz, 1962)

Un marito per Anna Zaccheo (*A Husband for Anna*), dir. Giuseppe De Santis (Domenico Forges Davanzati, 1953)

Matrimonio all'italiana (*Marriage Italian-Style*), dir. Vittorio De Sica (Compagnia Cinematografica Champion, 1964) (adapted by Eduardo De Filippo from his play *Filumena Marturano*)

Il mercenario (*The Mercenary*), dir. Sergio Corbucci (Italy-Spain, Sp.A. Cinematografica/Profilms 21, 1969)

Mery per sempre (Always Mary), dir. Marco Risi (Numero Uno International, 1989)

Mi manda Picone (*Where's Picone?*), dir. Nanni Loy (Medusa-AMA Film, 1984)

Mimì metallurgico ferito nell'onore (*The Seduction of Mimi;* lit.: Mimi the Metalworker, Wounded in Honor), dir. Lina Wertmüller (Euro International Film, 1972)

Il mio nome è nessuno (*My Name Is Nobody*), dir. Tonino Valerii (Italy-France-Germany, Rafran [prod. Sergio Leone], 1973)

Il miracolo (*The Miracle*), dir. Roberto Rossellini (Tania Film, 1948; U.S. release in anthology film *The Ways of Love,* 1950)

Miracolo a Milano (*Miracle in Milan*), dir. Vittorio De Sica (PDS-ENIC, 1950)

Morte a Venezia (*Death in Venice*), dir. Luchino Visconti (Alfa Cinematografica, 1971)

Napoli che non muore (*Naples That Never Dies*), dir. Amleto Palermi (Manenti Film/Sp.A. Cinematografica, 1939)

Napoli d'altri tempi (*Naples of Former Days*), dir. Amleto Palermi (Astra Films, 1938)

La nave bianca (*The White Ship*), dir. Roberto Rossellini (Scalera/Centro cinematografico del Ministero della marina, 1941)

Nel nome del padre (*In the Name of the Father*), dir. Marco Bellocchio (Vides, 1972

La notte (*The Night*), dir. Michelangelo Antonioni (France-Italy, Nepi-Film [Rome]/Silva-Film [Rome], Sofitepid [Paris], 1961)

La notte di San Lorenzo (*The Night of the Shooting Stars;* a.k.a. *The Night of San Lorenzo*), dir. Paolo and Vittorio Taviani (RAI/Ager Cinematografica, 1982)

1900 (*Novecento;* a.k.a. *Nineteen Hundred*), dir. Bernardo Bertolucci (Italy-France-Germany, PEA/Artistes Associés/Artermis, 1976) (in two parts)

Nuovo Cinema Paradiso (*Cinema Paradiso*), dir. Giuseppe Tornatore (Italy-France, Cristaldi Film/Films Ariadne, 1988)

L'oro di Napoli (*The Gold of Naples;* a.k.a *Every Day's a Holiday* [truncated]), dir. Vittorio De Sica (Gala/Ponti-De Laurentiis, 1954)

O sole mio, dir. Giacomo Gentilomo (Rinascimento Film, 1945)

Ossessione, dir. Luchino Visconti (Industria Cinematografica Italiana, 1942) (U.S. release 1975; based on Cain's *The Postman Always Rings Twice*)

8 1/2 (Otto e mezzo), dir. Federico Fellini (Cineriz, 1963)

Padre padrone (Father Master), dir. Paolo and Vittorio Taviani (RAI, 1977)

Paisà (Paisan), dir. Roberto Rossellini (Foreign Films Productions/OFI, 1946)

Palio, dir. Alessandro Blasetti (Cines, 1932)

Pasqualino Settebellezze (Seven Beauties), dir. Lina Wertmüller (Medusa, 1975)

Passaporto rosso (Red Passport), dir. Guido Brignone (Titanus, 1935)

La paura (Fear; Die Angst), dir. Roberto Rossellini (Italy–Germany, Geiselgasteig/Ariston Film/Aniene Film [Munich], 1954) (rereleased as *Non credo più all'amore,* 1955)

La peccatrice (The Sinner), dir. Amleto Palermi (Manenti, 1940)

Per qualche dollaro in più (For a Few Dollars More), dir. Sergio Leone (PEA–Gonzales Constantin, 1965) (inspired by *Sanjuro* and Carlo Goldoni's play *The Servant of Two Masters*)

Per un pugno di dollari (A Fistful of Dollars), dir. Bob Roberson (pseud. Sergio Leone) Jolly Film/Ocean Film/Constantin Film, 1964) (inspired by *Yojimbo*)

Piccolo mondo antico (Little Old-Fashioned World), dir. Mario Soldati (Ata, 1941)

Porcile (Pig Pen; a.k.a. *Pigsty),* dir. Pier Paolo Pasolini (Film dell'Orso/Idi Cinematografica/INDIEF/CAPAC [Paris], 1969)

Porzus, dir. Renzo Martinelli (CDI–Buena Vista International Italia, 1997)

Il postino (The Postman), dir. Michael Radford (Mario & Vittorio Cecchi Gori/Gaetano Daniele, 1994)

La presa di Roma (The Taking of Rome), dir. Filoteo Alberini (Alberini e Santoni, 1905)

Processo alla città (City on Trial), dir. Luigi Zampa (Film Constellazione, 1952)

Profondo rosso (Deep Red, a.k.a. *The Hatchet Murders),* dir. Dario Argento (Selda, 1975)

Profumo di donna (Scent of a Woman), dir. Dino Risi (Dean Film, 1974) (American remake 1992, dir. Martin Brest)

Quattro passi fra le nuvole (Four Steps in the Clouds; a.k.a. *A Walk in the Clouds),* dir. Alessandro Blasetti (Cines, 1942) (remade as *Era di venerdi 17 [The Virtuous Bigamist]* by Mario Soldati, 1959)

Quo Vadis?, dir. Enrico Guazzoni (Cines, 1913)

Ragazzi fuori, dir. Marco Risi (Numero Uno International/Raidue, 1990)

Rapsodia satanica (Satanic Rhapsody), dir. Nino Oxilia (Cines, 1915)

Resurrectio (Resurrection), dir. Alessandro Blasetti (Cines, 1931)

Riso amaro (Bitter Rice), dir. Giuseppe De Santis (Lux Film, 1949)

Rocco e i suoi fratelli (Rocco and His Brothers), dir. Luchino Visconti (Italy–France, Titanus/Les Films Marceau, 1960)

Roma, città aperta (Open City, a.k.a. *Rome, Open City),* dir. Roberto Rossellini (Minerva/Excelsa, 1945)

Rotaie (Rails), dir. Mario Camerini (SACIA, 1929; shot silent, sound added)

Salvatore Giuliano, dir. Francesco Rosi (Lux/Vides/Galatea, 1962) (remade as *The Sicilian,* dir. Michael Cimino, 1987)

San Miniato, dir. Paolo and Vittorio Taviani (Valentino Orsini, 1954)

Scipione l'Africano (Scipio Africanus), dir. Carmine Gallone (ENIC, 1937)

Sciuscià (Shoeshine), dir. Vittorio de Sica (Alfa Cinematografica, 1946)

Sedotta e abbandonata (Seduced and Abandoned), dir. Pietro Germi (Lux/Ultra/Vides/Lux C.C. de France, 1963)

La segretaria privata (Private Secretary), dir. Goffredo Alessandrini (Cines, 1931) (version of *Privatseketärin,* dir. Wilhelm Thiele, 1931)

Senso (*Wanton Countessa;* a.k.a. *Feeling;* English-language version, *The Wanton Countess*), dir. Luchino Visconti (Lux, 1954) (based on a novel by Camillo Boito)

La serpe (*The Serpent*), dir. Roberto Roberti (Caesar, 1920)

La serva padrona (The Head Servant), dir. Giorgio Mannini (Lirica, 1934)

La signora delle Camelie (*Lady of the Camellias*), dir. Gustavo Serena (Caesar, 1915)

La signora di tutti (*Everybody's Lady*), dir. Max Ophuls (Novella Film, 1934)

Il signor Max (*Mr. Max;* a.k.a *Max the Gentleman*), dir. Mario Camerini (CO Barbieri, 1937)

Sodoma e Gommorra (*Sodom and Gomorrah*), dir. Robert Aldrich and [2d unit] Sergio Leone (Fox-Titanus, 1963)

Sole (*Sun*), dir. Alessandro Blasetti (Augusts, 1929, silent)

Sorelle Materassi (*Materassi Sisters*), dir. Ferdinando Maria Poggioli (Cines, 1943)

Il sorpasso (*The Easy Life,* a.k.a. *The Overtaking*), dir. Dino Risi (Fair Film/Incei Film/Savero-Film, 1962)

Sotto la croce del sud (Under the Southern Cross), dir. Guido Brignone (Mediterannea Film, 1938)

Sotto . . . sotto . . . strapazatto da un anomala passione (*Sotto, sotto;* a.k.a. *Softly, Softly;* subtitle lit.: The Hardships of an Anomalous Passion), dir. Lina Wertmüller (Intercapital, 1984)

I sovversivi (The Subversives), dir. Paolo and Vittorio Taviani (Ager Film, 1967)

Spartaco (*Spartacus,* a.k.a. *Sins of Rome: Story of Spartacus*), dir. Riccardo Freda (Spartacus Consortium, 1954)

Sperduti nel buio (Lost in the Dark), dir. Nino Martoglio (Morgana Film, 1914)

Lo squadrone bianco (*The White Squadron*), dir. Augusto Genina (Roma Film, 1936)

Stanno tutti bene (*Everybody's Fine*), dir. Giuseppe Tornatore (Italy-France, Erre Produzioni/Les Films Ariane/TFI Films, 1990)

La strada (The Road), dir. Federico Fellini (Ponti-De Laurentiis, 1954)

Stromboli, terra di dio (*Stromboli;* a.k.a. *Stromboli, Land of God*), dir. Roberto Rossellini (Be-Ro/RKO [latter cut half an hour for UK/USA release], 1949)

T'amerò sempre (*I'll Always Love You*), dir. Mario Camerini (Pittaluga, 1933)

Teorema (*Theorem*), dir. Pier Paolo Pasolini (Aetos Film, 1968)

Teresa Venerdì (*Doctor Beware*), dir. Vittorio De Sica (ACI-Europa, 1941) (based on a novel by Rudolf Török)

Terra madre (*Mother Earth*), dir. Alessandro Blasetti (Cines, 1930)

La terra trema[: Episodio del mare] (The Earth Trembles[: Episode of the Sea]), dir. Luchino Visconti (Universalia, Italy, 1948)

Tormento, dir. Raffaello Matarazzo (Labor-Titanus, 1951)

La Tosca, dir. Alfredo De Antoni (Caesar Film, 1918)

La tragedia di un uomo ridicolo (*Tragedy of a Ridiculous Man*), dir. Bernardo Bertolucci (Fiction Cinematografica, 1981)

Ulisse (*Ulysses*), dir. Mario Camerini (Ponti-De Laurentis/Lux Film, 1954)

L'ultima diva (The Last Diva), dir. Gianfranco Mingozzi (Antea, 1982)

Gli ultimi giorni di Pompei (*The Last Days of Pompei*), dir. Mario Caserini (Ambrosio, 1913)

Gli ultimi giorni di Pompei (*The Last Days of Pompeii*), dir. Mario Bonnard (finished by Sergio Leone) (Cineproduzioni Associate-Procusa, 1959)

Gli ultimi giorni di Pompeii (*The Last Days of Pompeii*), dir. Luigi Maggi (Ambrosio, 1908)

Umberto D, dir. Vittorio De Sica (Dear Films, 1952)

Umberto e Margherita di Savoia a passeggio per il parco (Umberto and Margherita of Savoy Walk in the Park), dir. Filoteo Alberini (Alberini, 1896)

Gli uomini che mascalzoni . . . (*What Rascals Men Are,* a.k.a. *Men Are Such Rascals*), dir. Mario Camerini (Cines, 1932)

Uomini sul fondo (*Men of the Deep*), dir. Francesco De Robertis (Scalera, 1941)

L'uomo delle stelle (*The Star Maker*), dir. Giuseppe Tornatore (Vittorio & Rita Cecchi Gori, 1994)

Il Vangelo secondo Matteo (*The Gospel According to St. Matthew*), dir. Pier Paolo Pasolini (Arco Film/Lux Compagnie Cinematographique, 1964)

Vecchia guardia (*The Old Guard*), dir. Alessandro Blasetti (Fauno, 1934)

Viaggio in Italia (*Strangers,* a.k.a. *Journey to Italy, The Lonely Woman, Voyage in Italy, Voyage to Italy*), dir. Roberto Rossellini (Italiafilm/Junior Film/Sveva Film, 1953)

La vita è bella (*Life Is Beautiful*), dir. Roberto Benigni (Melampo Cinematografica, 1997)

Zazà, dir. Renato Castellani (Lux, 1942)

Lo zio indegno (*The Sleazy Uncle*), dir. Franco Brusatti (Ellepi Films, 1989)

NON-ITALIAN FILMS CITED

Arrivée d'un train à La Ciotat (*Train Arriving at a Station*), Louis Lumière (France, 1895)

Ben-Hur, dir. William Wyler (USA, MGM, 1959)

Boudu sauvé des eaux (*Boudu Saved from Drowning*), dir. Jean Renoir (France, Société Sirius, 1932)

Bronenosets Potemkin (*Battleship Potemkin,* a.k.a. *Potemkin*), dir. Sergei Eisenstein (USSR, Goskino, 1925 [theatrical release 1926])

Butch Cassidy and the Sundance Kid, dir. George Roy Hill (USA, 20th Century-Fox/Campanile, 1969)

Casablanca, dir. Michael Curtiz (USA, Warner Bros., 1942)

Le Diable au corps (*The Devil in the Flesh*), dir. Claude Autant-Lara (France, Transcontinental, 1947)

Flashdance, dir. Adrian Lyne (USA, Polgram, 1983)

Gilda, dir. Charles Vidor (USA, Columbia, 1946)

Gone with the Wind, dir. Victor Fleming [and uncredited George Cukor et al.] (MGM/Selznick Intl. Pictures, 1939)

La Grande Illusion (*Grand Illusion*), dir. Jean Renoir (France, RAC, 1937)

Henry: Portrait of a Serial Killer, dir. John McNaughton (USA, Maljack, 1990 [filmed 1986])

Hitlerjunge Quex (*Hitler Youth Quex*), dir. Hans Steinhoff (Germany, Ufa, 1933)

Ikiru (*To Live;* a.k.a. *Living; Doomed*), dir. Akira Kurosawa (Japan, Toho, 1952)

Mädchen in Uniform (a.k.a. *Girls in Uniform*), dir. Leontine Sagan (Germany, Deutsche Film-Gemeinschaft, 1931)

Man Who Shot Liberty Valance, The, dir. John Ford (USA, Ford Prods./Paramount, 1962)

My Darling Clementine, dir. John Ford (USA, 20th Century-Fox, 1946)

La Noire de . . . (Black Girl), dir. Ousmane Sembène (Senegal, Le Films Domirev–Les Actualités Française, 1966)

Notorious, dir. Alfred Hitchcock (USA, RKO, 1946)

Of Human Bondage, dir. Henry Hathaway (USA, MGM/Seven Arts, 1964)

Peeping Tom, dir. Michael Powell (UK, Anglo Amalgamated, 1960)

Psycho, dir. Alfred Hitchcock (USA, Shamley/Alfred Hitchcock, 1960)

Rose Tattoo, The, dir. Daniel Mann (USA, Paramount, 1955)

Sanjuro (a.k.a. *Tsubaki Sanjuro*), dir. Akira Kurosawa (Japan, Toho, 1962)

Shane, dir. George Stevens (USA, Paramount, 1953)

Sheik, The, dir. George Melford (USA, Famous Players-Lasky, 1921)

Spartacus, dir. Stanley Kubrick (USA, Universal Intl./Bryna, 1960)

Stagecoach, dir. John Ford (USA, Walter Wanger Prods./United Artists, 1939)

Stella Dallas, dir. King Vidor (USA, Goldwyn, 1937)

Sunset Boulevard, dir. Billy Wilder (USA, Paramount, 1950)

Sunshine Susie (*The Office Girl*), dir. Victor Saville (UK, Gaumont [prod. Michael Balcon], 1931)

Tom Brown's School Days (a.k.a. *Adventures at Rugby*), dir. Robert Stevenson (USA, RKO, 1940)

Vera Cruz, dir. Robert Aldrich (USA, Hecht-Lancaster, 1954)

Virginian, The, dir. Stuart Gilmore (USA, Paramount, 1946)

Wild Bunch, The, dir. Sam Peckinpah (USA, Warner Bros./Seven Arts, 1969)

Wizard of Oz, The, dir. Victor Fleming (USA, MGM, 1939)

Yoidore Tenshi (*Drunken Angel*), dir. Akira Kurosawa (Japan, Toho, 1948)

Yojimbo, dir. Akira Kurosawa (Japan, Toho, 1961)

Zéro de conduite (*Zero for Conduct*), dir. Jean Vigo (France, Gaumont/Franco/Aubert, 1933)

Index

Note: Works are listed by both title and author (e.g., director). Bold pages indicate illustrations.